D1195026

Sex Scene

*S*E*X* *S*C*E*N*E*

MEDIA AND THE SEXUAL REVOLUTION

ERIC SCHAEFER, editor

DUKE UNIVERSITY PRESS · DURHAM AND LONDON 2014

© 2014 Duke University Press
All rights reserved
Printed in the United States of America on
acid-free paper ♾
Typeset in Chaparral Pro by Tseng Information
Systems, Inc.

Library of Congress Cataloging-in-Publication Data
Sex scene : media and the sexual revolution /
Eric Schaefer, ed.
p. cm
Includes bibliographical references and index.
ISBN 978-0-8223-5642-4 (cloth : alk. paper)
ISBN 978-0-8223-5654-7 (pbk. : alk. paper)
1. Sex in mass media. 2. Sex in motion pictures.
3. Mass media—Social aspects—United States.
I. Schaefer, Eric, 1959–
P96.S452U67 2014
302.230973—dc23
2013026439

Duke University Press gratefully acknowledges the
support of Emerson College, which provided funds
toward the production of this book.

For Mom & Dad

Contents

Part IV Going All the Way

Part V Contending with the Sex Scene

Acknowledgments

We seldom consider that many of the words we now read and speak, the images or sounds that we consume and make, and the activities that we engage in—usually without a second thought—were contested, controversial, or downright illegal a half century ago. Many of the freedoms that we take for granted today were forged by pioneers in the years after World War II and into the 1970s—the period we now call the "sexual revolution."

I have been privileged to meet, to interview, or in some cases know a number of the people mentioned in this book. Some engaged in high-stakes battles to publish books or to make, distribute or exhibit films that dealt with sexually provocative, and often explicit, material. Although this resulted in wealth and fame for some, for others it came at great personal or monetary cost. And yet for every individual who made a movie or published a book or magazine, who was named in an important legal decision, or was the subject of articles in the press, there were hundreds of thousands—perhaps millions—who simply did what they felt was right and true to themselves. Female or male; straight, gay or queer; young or old; and of many races and creeds, they were the foot soldiers in the sexual revolution. This book acknowledges the challenges they faced, the sacrifices they made, the achievements they won—and the struggles that continue.

Beyond those mentioned by name in these pages and the anonymous "sexual revolutionaries" who engaged in these battles, my largest debt goes to the contributors to this collection, to the efforts they devoted to their essays, to their dedicated research, and to their patience as the collection came together over time. My thanks also goes to the staff of Duke University Press, especially to Editorial Director Ken Wissoker, who is nonpareil in the field; to Elizabeth Ault, Sara Leone, Leigh Barnwell, Courtney Berger, and Bonnie Perkel for their help; to Sonya Manes for her incisive copyediting; and to the anonymous manuscript readers for their astute suggestions. The support of my colleagues Jonathan Wacks and Daniel Tobin at Emerson College was integral to pushing this project across the finish line.

Two essays were previously published. Thanks to Duke University Press for permission to reprint "Make Love, Not War: Jane Fonda Comes Home (1968–1978)," which originally appeared as chapter 4 in Linda Williams's *Screening Sex* (2008), and to Wayne State University Press for permission to reprint Elena Gorfinkel's "Wet Dreams: Erotic Film Festivals of the Early 1970s and the Utopian Sexual Public Sphere," which first appeared in *Framework: The Journal of Cinema and Media* 47, no. 2 (fall 2006): 59–86. I am very pleased to be able to include both of these essays, which have been slightly edited for this volume.

For help with illustrations my hat is off to Ted McIlvenna and Rand McIlvenna of the Institute for the Advanced Study of Human Sexuality; Danielle Kaltz at the *Detroit News*; Andrea Pereira at UPI; Jeff Sconce and the Associated Press; Elana Levine and the American Heritage Center at the University of Wyoming; Joseph Lam Duong and Arlene Elster; Arthur Knight and the *Notre Dame Observer* and the William & Mary *Flat Hat*; and the Emerson College CARAFE Fund. Unless otherwise noted, the illustrations are from the collection of the editor.

This book is dedicated to my father and mother, Frederick and Jeanette Schaefer, who have provided me with constant love and support. They are simply the best. And as always, words cannot adequately express all that I owe to Eithne Johnson. I benefit every day from her love and encouragement, from her wit and beauty, and from the warm glow of her intelligence.

Eric Schaefer, Cambridge, Massachusetts, March 2013

Introduction * Sex Seen: 1968 and Rise of "Public" Sex

ERIC SCHAEFER

Our technological civilization, far from being disrupted by the practice of public sex, is engendering the phenomenon. As technology increasingly depersonalizes and dehumanizes our lives, it is spawning in us a need to reassert that which is most basic and vital in us, our instincts. Moreover, technology is sweeping us into an epoch when privacy is becoming quite literally impossible, on one hand because of sheer population density, and, on the other, because of rapidly advancing technical means of surveillance in a civilization whose societies obviously intend to keep all individuals under constant watch.

FRANK TRIPPETT, "What's Happening to Sexual Privacy," *Look*, October 20, 1970.

The quote above could come from an op-ed piece or a blog today, perhaps commenting on a new trend in social media, the latest scandal involving a politician "sexting" a constituent, or a fresh celebrity sex tape. It was, in fact, written in 1970 by Frank Trippett, a senior editor at *Look* magazine. He reflected, "Our times surely must become known as the Age of the Great Disrobing. Public sex pops up everywhere. Across an ever-expanding vista we behold natural rites hitherto closed off by an ancient rule of privacy. Now we witness it all—at the movies, in published stills, in the cool brave cavortings of the young at play."[1] The article, titled "What's Happening to Sexual Privacy?" was penned at the apex of the era we have come to refer to as the sexual revolution. As we have entered the twenty-first century, it has become a given that the concept of privacy has undergone a fundamental change, much of it fueled by technological advances. But has, as the headline in one Canadian paper asserted, "The Net Killed Sexual Privacy"?[2] The Trippett quote reminds us that current debates about privacy, policy, sexuality, and technology have their origins decades ago in the sexual revolution.

Sex Scene: Media and the Sexual Revolution was prompted by the curious lack of attention paid to the role that media played in the history of the sexual revolution in the United States.[3] Historians, sociologists, critics, and casual observers single out a roster of causal factors that led to that change in manners, morals, and behaviors: urbanization; women's suffrage; the automobile; penicillin; the work of Freud, Marcuse, and Kinsey among others; secularism; the Pill; sex education in schools; and coed college dorms, to name only a few. To say that the sexual revolution was overdetermined would be an understatement. Virtually all accounts of the sexual revolution mention mediated expressions of sex in print, rock-and-roll music, comics, and especially movies.[4] Most routinely cite the same handful of well-known examples: books such as *The Tropic of Cancer, Fear of Flying*, and *The Joy of Sex*; magazines such as *Playboy* and *Penthouse*; and movies that usually begin with *I am Curious (Yellow)* and *Midnight Cowboy* and end with *Last Tango in Paris* and *Deep Throat*. But these instances of public sexual expression are typically referred to only in passing, as symptoms of the experimentation or the freedom permitted by the sexual revolution. Yet for those in committed monogamous relationships, for the celibate, for those who were too young or too old to participate in it — and even for those who participated daily, in word or deed — the mass media served as the most important and visible battleground on which the sexual revolution took place. The media's artifacts linger as the primary means of accessing this unique moment in history and for developing a clearer understanding of the origins of our contemporary scene.

Defining the Sexual Revolution

Arguments about whether there was a sexual revolution or not, and if so, when it started (after World War I? during World War II? in the 1960s?), are myriad and may never be answered to everyone's full satisfaction. As David Allyn, author of *Make Love, Not War: The Sexual Revolution. An Unfettered History*, concedes, "Part of the reason that there is still so much confusion surrounding the sexual revolution of the sixties and seventies is that the term 'revolution' has two meanings: It can denote a calculated contest against the status quo (as in the 'French Revolution'); or a sudden, unexpected period of social transformation (as in the 'Industrial Revolution')."[5] Tom W. Smith summarizes,

> As commonly used, the term "sexual revolution" indicates a revolutionary uprooting of traditional sexual morality. It is associated with a plethora of attitudinal and behavioral changes: the new morality and the *Playboy* Philosophy, communes and cohabitation, free love and easy sex, wife swapping and swinging, coming out of the closet and living out of

wedlock, x-rated movies and full-frontal foldouts. It has prompted the avant garde to celebrate the overthrow of a repressive Puritanism and traditionalists to lament the triumph of libertine hedonism.[6]

If there is one thing that most people agree on today, it is that when we refer to the "Sexual Revolution" in the United States it marks a relatively discrete period in the 1960s and 1970s.

Radical changes in sexual behavior and ways of thinking about sex have often been seen at the heart of the revolution of the 1960s. And yet even at the time, research indicated that a slow, steady shift in attitudes had been taking place since roughly the start of World War II.[7] Recent reevaluation has tended to confirm this. Historian Alan Petigny notes, "Bifurcations between titillation and consummation, or between sexual suggestion and sexual license, have enabled historians to depict the sixties as a morally tumultuous decade, while viewing the 1950s as a largely conservative time with regard to sexual behavior." He goes on to point out, "Contrary to popular belief, the sexual revolution (on a behavioral level) did not start in the 1960s, it was not ignited by the introduction of the birth control pill, it was not significantly fanned by the baby boomers' coming of age, and, most important of all, the sexualization of the popular culture did not anticipate the liberalization of mass behavior."[8] Using vital statistics, notably those on "illegitimate" births, Petigny offers empirical evidence that premarital sex, as a social indicator of liberalized sexual attitudes, increased markedly during World War II and continued throughout the 1950s.

If a revolution in attitudes toward sex and sexual behavior was already well underway in the 1940s and 1950s, then what was it that occurred in the 1960s that observers of the time, as well as historians and casual commentators today, refer to as the sexual revolution? What I want to suggest in this introduction, and what the essays in this collection will make clear, is that beyond behavior and attitudes there was another key element of the sexual revolution: a rapidly and radically sexualized media accounts for what we now think of as the sexual revolution of the late 1960s and early 1970s. What constituted the sexual revolution was not only a change in manners and morals; that had already been occurring discreetly in minds and bedrooms across the nation. It was the fact that sex was no longer a private matter that took place behind closed doors. Before the 1960s sex had largely been something that was known only through personal experience. It was, for the most part, practiced in private by oneself, or between oneself and one's partner: in the marriage bed, in the back seat of a Ford, in a crib in a brothel, or through an anonymous encounter in a park. In the 1960s sex was no longer something to be concealed; it was on display in a way that was unprecedented in American history. People were not suddenly leaving their bedrooms and backseats to have sex in the streets. Nevertheless, it might have seemed that way as the mass media—film and television, recorded sound and radio, publishing—served as the vehicle that drove sex from the private realm into the public sphere.

There had been public displays of sexuality—in song, in the burlesque shows, and with the advent of mass media in spicy pulps and digest-size photo magazines such as *Wink* and *Titter* that crowded newsstands, and even in exploitation films such as *Slaves in Bondage* (1937) and *Child Bride* (1942). But these forms of popular culture trafficked in titillation; they suggested rather than showed. Changes in the public display and experience of sex became increasingly evident in the years following World War II with the popularization of publications such as *Playboy* and racy novels ranging from seedy paperbacks such as *Man-Hungry* by Mitchell Coleman (1953) to bestsellers such as Grace Metalious's *Peyton Place* (1956).

For decades the restrictive Comstock Act (1873) forbade the use of the U.S. mail for sending any obscene, lewd, and/or lascivious material, including information about birth control and abortion. Further, the "Hicklin test" (1868), borrowed from Great Britain, was used to determine whether material was, in fact, obscene, defined by its "tendency to deprave and corrupt those whose minds are open to such immoral influences." Even an "isolated passage" could be sufficient to condemn a work.[9] The Supreme Court's *Roth* decision (1957) upended the Comstock Act and threw out the Hicklin test. Although still holding that the First Amendment did not protect obscenity (something "utterly without redeeming social importance"), *Roth* averred that obscenity and sex were not synonymous. In *Roth* the court posited that obscenity could only be determined when "the average person, applying contemporary community standards, [found] the dominant theme of the material taken as a whole appeals to the prurient interest."[10]

Following *Roth*, restrictions on the printed word fell rapidly. Key court rulings freed previously banned erotic "classics," such as D. H. Lawrence's *Lady Chatterley's Lover*, John Cleland's *Fanny Hill*, and Henry Miller's *Tropic of Cancer*. Bestsellers by Jacqueline Suzanne, Harold Robbins, and others were soon read less for careful plotting and literary style than for the "hot parts." Outfits such as Midwood and Bee-Line churned out cheap paperbacks that crowded wire racks in bus stations and "adult" bookstores, pulsing with lurid cover art and titles like *Pit Stop Nympho* and *Jazzman in Nudetown*.[11] And if *Playboy* continued to reign as the leading sex magazine for sophisticates, it had to fight for space on newsstands with stacks of down-market men's magazines such as *Nugget* and *Dude*, which focused on topless photo layouts and sexy stories in contrast to *Playboy*'s literary fiction, in-depth interviews, and reviews of upscale hi-fi equipment.

The postwar motion picture industry faced a multitude of challenges: the fallout from the *Paramount* decision of 1948, declining output, steadily decreasing admissions, and the threat of television. *The Man with the Golden Arm* (1955), *Tea and Sympathy* (1956), *Blue Denim* (1959), and other Hollywood movies took on more mature themes in an effort to differentiate them from the family fare of network television, and in the process tested existing censorship and audience tolerance. As the Production Code lost its teeth, it was periodically amended to loosen restrictions on some subjects. The studios cautiously edged into franker sexual material in melodramas such as *Butterfield 8* (1960), potboilers such as *The Chapman Report* (1962), and leering comedies such as *Kiss Me, Stupid* (1964). Some theaters turned to "art cinema," movies that usually had a foreign pedigree, more adult subject matter, and glimpses of nudity, for example, . . . *And God Created Woman* (1956) and *Les Amants* (1958, *The Lovers*). Low-budget sexploitation filmmakers peddled theatrical films for "adults only" that went even further in their display of nudity, and stories of lust and sexual desire, as well as a growing list of "perversions" ranging from flagellation, to oral sex, to lesbianism. Even if one never set foot in a sexploitation theater, it was hard for urban dwellers to miss marquees that screamed with titles of the likes of *The Pink Pussy* (1964) or to avoid ads for films such as *The Promiscuous Sex* (1967; see figure I.1) in the entertainment sections of their daily newspapers. And as the ads for theatrical films flaunted suggestive titles and sexy art, an array of "dirty movies" became available to the throngs of hobbyists on 8 mm at adult bookstores or through the mail.

And everywhere there was commentary. Newspapers and magazines covered the Pill and promiscuity, rising hemlines and venereal disease rates, coed dorms and sex on campus, and singles bars and open marriage, with a mix of distanced reportage and tongue-wagging prurience. Some writers welcomed these changes and the new openness to discuss them as the shedding of repressive Puritanism and hypocrisy; others thundered about an erosion of morality that could only lead to a decline of civilization itself. A few were cognizant of the fact that the sexual

Fig. I.1 Readers of big-city newspapers were increasingly confronted with ads for suggestive sexploitation films such as *The Promiscuous Sex* (1967) from New York distributor William Mishkin.

revolution was a media revolution. *Time*'s 1964 cover story "The Second Sexual Revolution" likened America to Wilhelm Reich's "Orgone Box" (see chapter 6), stating

> the big machine works on its subjects continuously, day and night. From innumerable screens and stages, posters and pages, it flashes larger-than-life images of sex. From countless racks and shelves, it pushes books that which a few years ago were considered pornography. From myriad loudspeakers, it broadcasts the words and rhythms of pop-music erotica. And constantly, over the intellectual Muzak, comes the message that sex will save you and libido makes you free.

While claiming that the United States "seems to be undergoing a revolution of mores and an erosion of morals," *Time*'s writers acknowledged, "Publicly and dramatically, the change is evident in Spectator Sex—what may be seen and read."[12] Two years later Richard Schechner, writing on "Pornography and the New Expression" in *Atlantic Monthly*, stated, "The submerged material now available falls in to two classes: stuff that uses *words* once thought obscene; works that now show *scenes* that were once taboo."[13]

1968 and the Eruption of Public Sex

If 1967 was the "Summer of Love," then 1968 was the summer, in fact the whole year, of sex. Throughout a year in which bodies were convulsed by violence—in war, in protest, as victims of police actions, and assassination—they were also convulsed in passion. The year began when President Lyndon Johnson named the members to the Commission on Obscenity and Pornography, indicating that a sufficient change was under way to warrant investigation by a group of academics, psychologists, criminologists, religious figures, and representatives of the publishing and film industries.[14] The literary world saw publication of John Updike's *Couples*, about a group of promiscuous marrieds in a small Massachusetts town, and Gore Vidal's *Myra Breckinridge*, a gender-bending camp assault on pop culture; both were bestsellers. At the other end of the spectrum, Al Goldstein's sex tabloid-cum-consumer's guide, *Screw*, made its debut. Its raunchy combination of articles, reviews, political commentary, and pictures was emulated by other underground publications such as *San Francisco Ball, Pleasure*, and *Kiss*. Starting out as local publications, some grew to have a nationwide readership. Collector's Publications of California published a "photo illustrated marriage manual" titled *Intercourse*, which sold a half-million copies and was followed by *The Photographic Manual of Sexual Intercourse* (1969) and *The Picture Book of Sexual Love* (1969). All brought hardcore photography (although no focus on genital shots) to the masses in the guise of education.[15] Illustrated paperbacks such as Academy Press's *Sex, Censorship, and Pornography* augmented their allegedly scholarly text with hardcore photographs cribbed from Danish sex magazines.

Indeed, Denmark had become the porn capitol of the world, producing magazines such as *Color Climax*—all pictures and no text—that were soon available in the United States. The mailing of brochures pitching sexually oriented books, magazines, movies, and devices reached such a high level, along with the accompanying complaints, that on April 14, 1968, the so-called Anti-Pandering Act went into effect, giving greater recourse to the addressee through the issuance of "Prohibitionary Orders." Despite the Anti-Pandering Act, the *Technical Report of the Commission on Obscenity and Pornography* described a substantial increase in the mailing of unsolicited sexual ads through 1968 and 1969 before numbers started to drop in 1970.

On Broadway *Hair* opened in April 1968, shocking audiences with its onstage nudity. Within the year it was followed by *Oh! Calcutta!, Che!*, and other stage productions featuring nudity and simulated sex. *The*

Boys in the Band, Mart Crowley's unambiguous play about a group of gay men gathering to celebrate a birthday, opened off Broadway to a long run. Television programs such as *Rowan and Martin's Laugh-In* debuted, scandalizing some with its bawdy jokes and bikini-clad go-go dancers, while *The Dating Game* and *The Newlywed Game* laced their programs with sexual innuendo. Records and tapes provided in-home sex instruction and rock music, and radio featured suggestive lyrics such The Rolling Stones' "Let's Spend the Night Together," "Young Girl" by Gary Puckett and the Union Gap, and "Who's Making Love?" from Johnnie Taylor. Led Zeppelin made its debut in October 1968, and within the year Robert Plant was engaged in full-throttle orgasmic moaning on the song "Whole Lotta Love."

At the movies, limitations seemed to be thrown aside like so many articles of clothing. From mainstream movies, to sexploitation, to the art house and eventually the porn theater, changes in the presentation of sex were rapid and profound. In movies characters no longer got married. Now they got laid. Movies no longer had a big love scene; they now had a sex scene. Moreover, that sex scene was not avoided or elided by cutting away to crashing waves or fireworks in the night sky. It was visible, unencumbered by metaphor, uncut by the censor, often with only a carefully placed leg or sheet corner to cover unions of flesh. Whether softcore and simulated, or soon hardcore and unsimulated, 1968 marked the year in which media representations of sex were finally seen by large numbers of men and women in a public setting, the year it moved from "under the counter" to "over the top" (see figure I.2).

At the beginning of the year Vincent Canby wrote in the *New York Times* about efforts on the part of law enforcement in the Bronx and Brooklyn and in Nassau and Suffolk Counties to "slow the expansion of the sex violence film market from its 42nd Street milieu." He observed, "Not only is a picture such as *I, a Woman* finding its way into conventional theaters with increasing frequency, but there is also a growing number of theaters in respectable, middle-class neighborhoods that are screening the cruder examples of the genre on a full-time basis." Canby claimed that the number of theaters showing sexploitation on a full-time basis had more than doubled in the preceding ten months. Although Hollywood was loath to admit it, sexploitation movies were capturing a growing segment of the market and moving out of their traditional grindhouse venues, precisely what the law enforcement officials Canby wrote of were so concerned about. Sexual entertainment was no longer contained to seedy theaters in rundown, marginal urban neighborhoods. It was becoming unrestricted and reaching the masses. By end of the 1960s

Fig. I.2 The year 1968 marked a turning point for representations of sex in theatrical films. This montage still from Russ Meyer's *Vixen!*, starring Erica Gavin, attempted to convey some of the many sexual encounters the title character has through the course of the movie.

roughly 5 percent of all U.S. theaters were regularly exhibiting sexploitation films each week of the year, and another 1,500 played at least one or more exploitation films in 1968 and 1969.[16] Canby described the movies as going further in living up to their titles than ever before. He credited Radley Metzger's Audubon Films with eroding the barriers between sexploitation and conventional films and getting play in mainstream theaters.[17] In fact, on the same day that Canby's article appeared, Metzger's latest softcore opus, *Carmen, Baby* (1967), opened wide in twenty-four theaters in the greater New York City area. Meanwhile, there were in 1968 even more explicit "beaver" films spread from San Francisco to 16 mm storefront theaters in cities across the country.[18]

The increase in sex on screen, and to a lesser extent violence, led the Motion Picture Association of America (MPAA) to unveil its new ratings system. Designed to replace the anachronistic Production Code, the system went into effect on November 1. The most notorious letter in America became the X. Films were rated X "because of treatment of sex, violence, crime or profanity," and for which persons under sixteen would not be admitted under any circumstance. Writing in *Variety*, Stuart Byron concluded, "The 'X' classification is the cost 'paid' to achieve any rating plan at all. It's an open secret in the trade that not until this category was in-

Fig. I.3 While defending the X rating, MPAA chief Jack Valenti also criticized its use, as he did in an interview with KPIX-TV in San Francisco in 1969 in which he "deplore[d]" its deployment by "one picture companies." (Digital frame enlargement.)

vented and named was the cooperation of the independent distributors assured. And it's no accident that it was called 'X'—itself an intriguing letter and one which, in Britain, has already proved a selling point."[19] The head of the MPAA, Jack Valenti, protested that the X was no indication of moral or aesthetic quality while simultaneously assailing independent companies for using the X rating for economic gain. Within months the X was associated in the minds of ticket buyers with sex (see figure I.3). Many newspapers barred ads for X-rated movies, police raided theaters exhibiting them, and legislators proposed laws to penalize theaters that showed them.[20] Savvy sexploitation producers tacked additional Xs onto their films—XX and XXX—to suggest that their movies went even further than those accorded a single X.

Sexploitation movies were playing everywhere: downtown grind houses, neighborhood theaters, exclusive suburban showcases, drive-ins. Their rising profile saw a parallel uptick in censorship bills introduced in state legislatures, as well as municipal efforts to control the films through taxation, zoning ordinances, and so on. Police and zealous prosecutors busted theaters in big cities and small towns alike, confiscating prints and arresting managers, ticket sellers, and projectionists. The increased threat of prosecution prompted Dallas-based exhibitor and distributor Sam Chernoff to issue a call for the adult film industry to organize. In a letter written the same month that the ratings system went into effect, Chernoff said, "If you are an average operator, you are making more money than with studio product. Thus, what problems do you have—basically none, except for possible harassment by local authorities." Citing a double standard that saw large chains protected by the National Association of Theater Owners (NATO) and leaving independents vulnerable, Chernoff urged collective action to "put a stop to this harassment right now!"[21] In January 1969 representatives of the industry met at a hotel in Kansas City, Missouri to form an organization that would come to be known as the Adult Film Association of America (AFAA). The AFAA created a "legal kit" to help exhibitors defend themselves against prosecution, and over the next fifteen years defended the industry, fought for the rights of adults to see adult movies, and created the annual Erotic Film Awards.

It was against this backdrop that the Commission on Obscenity and Pornography began its work in 1968. Charged with evaluating and recommending definitions of obscenity and pornography, determining the volume of pornography produced and how it was distributed, the commission was also to study the effects that porn had on the public, including its relationship to antisocial behavior, and to recommend actions to regulate its flow. All of this was to be completed by January 1970.[22] When one of the original commissioners resigned, newly inaugurated President Richard Nixon replaced him with Charles H. Keating Jr., founder of Citizens for Decent Literature, later renamed Citizens for Decency through Law (CDL). Long an antipornography crusader, Keating proved to be a polarizing force, operating as a commission within the larger commission. The larger group worked diligently for months, collecting information, interviewing representatives of various constituencies, and holding hearings.

An incomplete draft of the commission's final report was leaked in August 1970. Its conclusion—that exposure to pornography failed to cause antisocial behavior in youth or adults—immediately came under attack, as did some aspects of the commission's research, such as exposing twenty-three college men to stag films and erotic material.[23] Keating filed a complaint in federal court in September to block publication of the report until a written dissent could be completed.[24] Realizing that the commission's findings could prove an embarrassment to the Nixon administration, presidential advisor John Ehrlichman assigned speechwriter Patrick Buchanan to help write the dissent to the commission's report.[25] The delay threatened to shelve the report entirely, but a compromise was finally reached with Keating that gave the dissenting faction until the end of the month to complete their rebuttal. The entire report was officially released on October 1, 1970, some nine months late.

The commission (voting 12 to 5, with one abstention) concluded that pornography "did not cause crime, delinquency, sexual deviancy or emotional disturbances." It recommended, "federal, state and local legislation prohibiting the sale, exhibition or distribution of sexual materials to consenting adults should be repealed."[26] The appended dissent, led by Keating, contended that the recommendations were based on "scanty" or "manipulated" evidence, with concurring commissioner Father Morton Hill calling the majority report "a magna carta for the pornographer." The report was issued just prior to midterm elections, and the Nixon administration immediately disavowed it. Vice President Spiro Agnew blamed the "erosion of decency" on a "political hedonism that permeates the philosophy of the radical liberals." Despite the fact that senate leaders from both parties denounced the commission's report, efforts were made to paint the Johnson administration, and Democrats in general, as smut lovers.[27] By the end of October the Senate had voted 60 to 5 to reject the commission's recommendations.

At the time the Commission on Obscenity and Pornography began its work in 1968 mediated sex was reaching a tipping point. In the parlance of the time, it had "made the scene." Or, to use Linda Williams's apt formulation, the "obscene" came "on/scene."[28] Writing in the *New York Times Magazine* in September, Richard Gilman asserted,

> That we're in a presence these days of an unprecedented and steadily increasing quantity, range and intensity of public sexual expression is an observable fact; that we're being inundated by a "wave of pornography" is the most subjective of judgments. Nudity in the films and now on the stage; the employment as theme or as incidental reference in movies, plays and books of such conditions and practices as Lesbianism and homosexuality . . . , incest, sadism and masochism, group sex, oral sex, etc.; the dropping from serious literature (and some that is far from serious) of euphemisms for the four-letter words for sexual intercourse and for the male and female genitals; all this carries greatly significant social, psychological and even metaphysical implications that spread boundlessly past the confinements of a formula or the futile grasp of an execration.

His research over several months was conducted by, as he put it, "simply keeping my eyes open." What Gilman was observing was, of course, a media revolution, and the nature of that revolution was one that would lead to a place in which "all present distinctions are broken down, where, let's say, the public and the private in sexuality retain no walls between them, what is done and what is said or shown possessing an unbroken continuity."[29]

Lost in the avalanche of commentary on the sexual revolution (not to mention the wake of assassinations, protests, riots, the escalation of the Vietnam War, a disastrous Democratic national convention in Chicago), Gilman's observation was significant—especially in light of our history since that time. It is instructive to reframe what we have called "the sexual revolution" of the late 1960s as a media revolution, one in which distinctions between the private and the public became radically destabilized. That destabilization opened the door to sexually explicit sounds and images and, over time, their gradual toleration as part of the media scene.

Privates in Public

During the 1960s the issue of privacy took on an urgency in the United States. Vance Packard, the foremost chronicler of midcentury America, produced *The Naked Society* in 1964, an account of diminishing privacy in the face of Big Government, Big Business, and Big Education. Packard wrote,

> In stable primitive societies the attitudes of the people in regard to what is proper and decent in personal relations—including respect for privacy—do not change much from century to century. In the Western world today, however, swirling forces are causing whole populations willy-nilly to change their attitudes, ideals, and behavior patterns within decades. This is nowhere more dramatic than in the United States.[30]

Concerns over privacy in the United States led to the conceptualization of privacy as a constitutional right. In the *Griswold* decision of 1965 the Supreme Court overturned Connecticut's antiquated law that prohibited contraception, even by married couples. Justice William O. Douglas wrote, "Zones of privacy are present as penumbras not only in the First Amendment but also in the Third, in the Fourth and the Fifth, and in the Ninth." "The shadowy right to privacy," as one legal scholar has written, "is thus spread through various Amendments and in each of them may have a peripheral function to play toward the rights there explicitly asserted."[31] However, even in a decade when the nation's highest courts was affirming a right of privacy, Jerry M. Rosenberg announced "the death of privacy" in 1969 with the title of his book.[32]

Political and social theorist Jeff Weintraub and others have referred to the public/private distinction as the "grand dichotomy," and in his coedited collection, *Public and Private in Thought and Practice*, Weintraub delineates four ways in which public and private are used in social and political analysis. These four frameworks developed out of Greco-Roman politics and neoclassical economics, as well as thinkers as varied as Hannah Arendt, Jürgen Habermas, Philippe Ariès, and feminist scholars who have written about the public/private divide.

For our purposes, I want to start with Weintraub's "*two* fundamental, and analytically quite distinct, kinds of imagery in terms of which 'private' can be contrasted with 'public'":

1. What is hidden or withdrawn versus what is open, revealed, or accessible.
2. What is individual, or pertains only to an individual, versus what is collective, or affects the interests of a collectivity of individuals. This individual/collective distinction can, by extension, take the form of a distinction between part and whole (of some social collectivity).[33]

More than anything, the sexual revolution of the 1960s and 1970s was a process by which that which was "hidden or withdrawn" became "open, revealed, or accessible" or, to use Weintraub's other formulation, that which "pertains only to the individual"—in this case sexual activity—suddenly "affects the interests of a collectivity of individuals." This ran the gamut from being able to see sexual activity on screen in public theaters to the growing visibility of sexual minorities, notably gays and lesbians in the wake of the Stonewall riots in the Greenwich Village neighborhood of New York City at the end of June of 1969.

The Supreme Court weighed in with two decisions during the period that attempted to delineate the boundaries between public and private regarding the newly explicit media. In the *Stanley v. Georgia* ruling of 1969, in which Robert Stanley was arrested for the possession of obscene films found during a search of his home on an unrelated warrant, Justice Thurgood Marshall wrote for an unusual unanimous majority, "If the First Amendment means anything, it means that a State has no business telling a man, sitting alone in his own home, what books he may read or what films he may watch. Our whole constitutional heritage rebels at the thought of giving government the power to control men's minds."[34] Based on *Griswold* the court held that the mere private possession of pornography was not a crime. In 1973 in *Paris Adult Theater I v. Slaton*, handed down concurrently with the *Miller* decision, the Court determined, "the States have a legitimate interest in regulating commerce in obscene materials and in regulating exhibition of obscene material in places of public accommodation, including so-called 'adult' theaters from which minors are excluded."[35] It was okay to read or watch private behavior in the privacy of one's own home, but there could be restrictions on the display of representations of sexual behavior in public places—even if those places were restricted to consenting adults.

People had become accustomed to seeing titillation used to sell everything from soap to soda, but the commodification of sex—as entertainment that could be sold and bought—was part of a broader logic of postwar consumer capitalism that demanded that everything become a product with a price. The notion that sex was turning into just another commodity was new and deeply disturbing to many. If sex, as was often claimed, was the physical affirmation of love, and if love was the most sublime of emotions, then the commodification of sex appeared to be the ultimate sellout of human ideals. The expansion of sex, in its multiplicity of forms and practices, into the public realm was greeted with alarm by conservative and religious elements in American society. In February 1970 Oklahoma-based evangelist Billy James Hargis wrote to his followers, "America is going to be destroyed by this sexual revolution bred in the pits of hell." He cited sex education and liberal colleges as culprits, but saved the bulk of his wrath for movies, television, and a record album, "which consists of the sounds of a couple engaged in sexual intercourse." Hargis solicited funds to publish his manuscript *The Sexual Revolution in the United States*, one-third of which he said would deal with "the sex revolution in motion pictures and television." "It names the motion picture companies and producers pushing pornography in movies. It gives you a VICTORY PLAN on how to organize local groups to combat this filth and rot being viewed in neighborhood theaters."[36] Keating's CDL went on tour to the hinterlands with an antiporn message, where it fell on "receptive ears."[37] Their talks were often presented to sympathetic public officials and law enforcement agencies, where CDL officials showed off a 16 mm soundproof combination of camera and stopwatch that could be used to surreptitiously gather evidence for obscenity cases.

Even in America's liberal bastions, there was a growing weariness of public privates. *New York Times* columnist Russell Baker chastised pornographers for embarrassing citizens who, he claimed, now demanded "curtailment of the rampage" of adult material on newsstands and on screens: "It is the danger of seeing those genitals named or pictured that drives Americans wild with embarrassment when they are out with the family for the evening. Ah, if only humans were hatched from hardshelled eggs, like chickens! Then we could take the wife and kids to Times Square or the drugstore and still feel clean."[38] Adult industry observer

Marv Lincoln expressed similar sentiment, concluding that the proliferation of 16 mm "loop" houses had taken their toll: "When business districts and residential sections in nearly every big city in the country became inundated with these sleazy storefront porn palaces, the foundations of a solid business began to crumble, even as the dollars came rolling in."[39] (See figure I.4.) Some cities such as Boston, responded by attempting to corral adult theaters, book stores, and strip clubs into tight districts, whereas others used zoning regulations to squeeze them out of existence.[40]

The public display of sexualized media resulted in the Supreme Court's *Miller* decision (June 1973). The Court, still declining to define obscenity, created a three-part test to determine whether a work was obscene. To be considered obscene, a work had to meet all three criteria:

1. whether "the average person, applying contemporary community standards," would find the work, taken as a whole, appeals to the prurient interest;
2. whether the work depicts or describes, in a patently offensive way, sexual conduct specifically defined by the applicable state law;
3. whether the work, taken as a whole, lacks serious literary, artistic, political, or scientific value.

The Court rejected the notion of a national standard for obscenity, instead leaving it to states and municipalities to reckon with sexually oriented material. Yet the ruling only seemed to muddy the water. In some locales, hardcore films continued to unspool, but in Georgia the state supreme court upheld an obscenity conviction of the R-rated *Carnal Knowledge* (1971).[41] It would be several years before the post-*Miller* legal landscape would begin to come into focus.

In 1973, the same year that *Miller* was handed down, a Gallup Poll determined that the sexual revolution was having a marked and measurable impact on American attitudes. A poll in 1969 had found that 73 percent of respondents objected to nudity in magazines and 81 percent objected to nudity on stage. The poll in 1973 saw those numbers drop to 55 percent and 65 percent respectively. The survey also showed that opposition to premarital sex had dropped from 68 percent to 48 percent. Among those under thirty, only 29 percent felt that premarital sex was "wrong."[42] The public's willingness to accept the exposure of private acts in the public sphere appeared to be catching up with individuals' own behavior in the bedroom.

Anthropologist and linguist Susan Gal has suggested "Public and private do not simply describe the social world in any direct way; they are

Fig. I.4 As notions of privacy began to shift in the 1960s, individuals were increasingly confronted by sexual material in public places such as Detroit's Monroe Street, shown here in 1971. (Courtesy of *The Detroit News* Archives.)

rather tools for arguments about and in that world."[43] Not only were social commentators using the distinction between public and private to make arguments about perceived costs and benefits of mediated representations of sex in the United States at the height of the sexual revolution; the Supreme Court used the distinction to make determinations about the acceptability of such representations. Thus we might argue that what made the sexual revolution "the sexual revolution" was this fairly fleeting, but highly volatile, period of destabilization of the public/private distinction. As those distinctions stabilized, and as "sex seen" became more commonplace—if not necessarily always accepted—the sexual revolution appeared to subside; or to use Gal's terms, the public/private distinction was recalibrated and recategorized. This process of recalibration has continued in the ensuing decades, exhibiting what Gal refers to as a "fractal distinction" in which the local, historically specific content of the dichotomy is "reproduced repeatedly by projecting it onto narrower contexts or broader ones."[44] We have seen such recalibrations play out in parochial disputes about the zoning of a single adult business, as well as in the expansive public debates concerning Internet privacy.

Since 1968 and the height of the sexual revolution, the diffusion of home video and home computers, of the Internet, and of mobile devices has narrowed the divide between the public and private. Despite the fact that "sleazy storefront porn palaces" seldom assault pedestrians as they navigate city sidewalks, nude imagery and private sexual acts are more public and accessible than ever before. With the click of a mouse or tap of a screen, an unlimited stream of sexual material is accessible at any time and in any place. An even more radical change has been in the impulse for individuals to display their private selves in public "space" online. This extends beyond regularly updating one's Facebook profile or posting videos of one's cat. Anyone with a digital camera or smart phone can photograph him or herself or their partners in the nude or engaged in sexual activity and post the material on the web through innumerable porn sites, video sharing services, or blogs.[45] Although names and places are seldom attached to these displays, the black bars across eyes or masks that were a staple of old stag films and "dirty pictures" have been cast off with little regard for potential embarrassment or negative consequence.

We cannot forget that the type of privacy that characterized the time before the sexual revolution facilitated a number of evils, including draconian laws, sexual ignorance, spousal and child abuse, rape, and a host of neuroses. The dismantling of sexual privacy has had many positive effects for society, including greater access to information on sex, the crumbling of the double standard of sexual behavior for men and women, and increased acceptance of gays, lesbians, and transgendered persons. Yet the impact of today's unhindered exhibitionism has yet to be measured. In 1970 Frank Trippett wrote, "One paramount need thus is dawning: the need to dwell, more or less as human beings, in a society in which privacy is out of the question. Our answer apparently is going to be to adopt a mode of life in which privacy is no longer considered necessary. So I suspect that public sex should be seen as the wave of our future just as much as it must be seen as the tide of our innocent past."[46]

Sex Scene: Media and the Sexual Revolution examines the time when "the wave of our future" was set in motion. It is organized into five broad parts. The first part deals with the way mainstream film and television approached the sexual revolution. The second part considers the intersection of mediated sex and art. Essays in the third part deal with more "marginalized" forms, and the fourth part takes into account hardcore representations in both educational and entertainment contexts. The last part details ways in which some critics and institutions reacted to sexualized media.

The essays represent a range of topics and approaches. Some operate as surveys, whereas others serve as case studies. If some of the subjects may be generally familiar to readers, the level of detail is often new or enhanced. Other essays cover material that has been only fleetingly dealt with in prior accounts of the sexual revolution if not completely overlooked. Most of the essays focus on the period from 1968 to 1973. Some reach into earlier years to provide background, and others move into the late 1970s as a backlash against the most conspicuous—and some might argue, pernicious—aspects of the sexual revolution began to be mounted by some feminists and the religious Right. Although the focus is largely on film and electronic media—the battles for literary pornography had largely been waged and won by the mid-1960s—many essays touch on publishing and the press. A number of shared themes and concerns will become apparent to the reader: the public/private divide, issues of identity and politics, individual rights and civil liberties, and the separate, but frequently overlapping, roles of the consumer and therapeutic cultures in post–World War II America.

By the early 1980s the sexual revolution appeared to be waning, done in by its excesses, a changing political climate, and the specter of AIDS. In fact, the sexual revolution was merely becoming the norm. Today's raunchy music lyrics might well make Mick Jagger blush. Theatrical films leave little to the imagination. The private lives of public figures are routinely dissected in the press or displayed in their own sex tapes. Television shows now far exceed the representation of sex in mainstream cinema of the 1960s and 1970s. Furthermore, the Internet is awash in graphic hardcore material. Although this volume focuses on a particular historical moment called the sexual revolution that occurred a half century ago, it should be clear that the sexual revolution has, in many respects, become the longest revolution.

Notes

1. Frank Trippett, "What's Happening to Sexual Privacy?" *Look*, October 20, 1970, 50.
2. Judith Timson, "The Net Killed Sexual Privacy," *Globe and Mail*, September 3, 2010, 11.
3. This is not to say that there have not been many books and articles that deal with manifestations of sexualized media and pornography during the period covered in this volume; dozens are cited in the notes and bibliography of this book. What it does say is that there have been few efforts to look at media *within the context* of the sexual revolution. One collection that does do this to some extent is *Swinging Single: Representing Sexuality in the 1960s*, edited by Hilary Radner and Moya Luckett (Minneapolis: University of Minnesota Press, 1999), and some essays in that volume make useful companions to the chapters here. There are works from the period that, though lacking historical distance, provide a unique lived perspective, though many focus strictly on filmed pornography. These books include *The Sex Industry* by George Paul Csicsery (New York: Signet, 1973); William Rotsler's *Contemporary Erotic Cinema* (New York: Ballantine Books, 1973); Carolyn See's *Blue Money: Pornography and the Pornographers. An Intimate Look at the Two Billion Dollar Fantasy Industry* (New York: David McKay Company, 1974); *Sinema: American Pornographic Films and the People Who Make Them* by Kenneth Turn and Stephen F. Zito (New York: Praeger, 1974); and *The Sex People: The Erotic Performers and Their Bold New Worlds* by Drs. Phyllis and Eberhard Kronhausen (Chicago: Playboy Press, 1975). The nine volumes of the *Technical Report of the Commission on Obscenity and Pornography* from 1971 (Washington, DC: U.S. Government Printing Office) are invaluable documents.
4. For histories or broad overviews of the sexual revolution, see David Allyn, *Make Love, Not War: The Sexual Revolution. An Unfettered History* (Boston: Little, Brown and Company, 2000); and John Heidenry, *What Wild Ecstasy: The Rise and Fall of the Sexual Revolution* (New York: Simon and Schuster, 1997). Editor Jeffrey Escoffier's *Sexual Revolution* (New York: Thunder's Mouth Press, 2003) is a wide-ranging and useful collection of essays from the period. Curiously, Mark Kurlansky's *1968: The Year That Rocked the World* (New York: Random House, 2005), a survey of all manner of events from the year, is almost completely silent on the sexual revolution.
5. Allyn, *Make Love, Not War*, 7.
6. Tom W. Smith, "The Polls—A Report, The Sexual Revolution?" *Public Opinion Quarterly* 54, no. 3 (Autumn, 1990): 416.
7. See, for instance, see Edwin O. Smigel and Rita Seiden, "The Decline and Fall of the Double Standard," *Annals of the American Academy of Political and Social Science* 376 (March 1968): 6–17.
8. Alan Petigny, "Illegitimacy, Postwar Psychology, and the Reperiodization of the Sexual Revolution," *Journal of Social History* 38, no. 1 (2004): 63.

9. Edward de Grazia and Roger K. Newman, *Banned Films: Movies, Censors and the First Amendment* (New York: R. R. Bowker, 1982), 104.

10. De Grazia and Newman, *Banned Films*, 96.

11. For an informative, illustrated look at this publishing phenomenon see Brittany A. Daley, et al., eds., *Sin-A-Rama: Sleaze Sex Paperbacks of the Sixties* (Los Angeles: Feral House, 2005).

12. "The Second Sexual Revolution," *Time*, January 24, 1964, 54.

13. Richard Schechner, "Pornography and the New Expression," *Atlantic Monthly*, January 1966, 76.

14. "Obscenity Group Set Up," *New York Times*, January 2, 1968, 30.

15. See the *Technical Report of the Commission on Obscenity and Pornography*, vol. 3, *The Marketplace: The Industry* (Washington, DC: U.S. Government Printing Office, 1971), 93, n. 66.

16. *Technical Report of the Commission on Obscenity and Pornography*, vol. 3, *The Marketplace: The Industry* (Washington, DC: U.S. Government Printing Office, 1971), 37–38.

17. Vincent Canby, "Films Exploiting Interest in Sex and Violence Find Growing Audience Here," *New York Times*, January 24, 1968, 38.

18. See Eric Schaefer, "Gauging a Revolution: 16mm Film and the Rise of the Pornographic Feature," *Cinema Journal* 41, no. 3 (spring 2002): 3–26.

19. Stuart Byron, "Code Price Equals: (S-E) 'X,'" *Variety*, October 16, 1968, 5.

20. "Stigmatized 'X,'" *Independent Film Journal*, February 4, 1970, 1, 3. See also Eric Schaefer, "Pandering to the 'Goon Trade': Framing the Sexploitation Audience through Advertising," in *Sleaze Artists: Cinema at the Margins of Taste, Style, and Politics*, ed. Jeffrey Sconce, 19–46 (Durham, NC: Duke University Press, 2007).

21. Sam Chernoff, "Letter to Fellow Exhibitors," November 1968, collection of the author.

22. "Congress Okays Anti-Pornography Commission, Academic Approach Seen," *Variety*, September 27, 1967, 5, 20.

23. "Concern on Smut Held Unfounded," *New York Times*, August 6, 1970, 22.

24. "Pornography Report May Die Or Just Fade Away," *Independent Film Journal*, September 16, 1970, 3.

25. "Senate Leaders in Both Parties Denounce Findings of Pornography Panel," *New York Times*, October 2, 1970, 70.

26. Richard Halloran, "A Federal Panel Asks Relaxation of Curbs on Smut," *New York Times*, October 1, 1970, 1.

27. James M. Naughton, "Epithets Greet Agnew in Salt Lake City," *New York Times*, October 1, 1970, 22; "Mr. Nixon's Smutscreen," *New York Times*, October 26, 1970, 36.

28. Linda Williams, "Proliferating Pornographies On/Scene: An Introduction," in *Porn Studies*, ed. Linda Williams, 1–23 (Durham, NC: Duke University Press, 2004), 3.

29. Richard Gilman, "There's a Wave of Pornography, Obscenity, Sexual Expression," *New York Times Magazine*, September 8, 1968, 36–7, 82.

30. Vance Packard, *The Naked Society* (New York: David McKay Company, 1964), 15.

31. Stefano Scoglio, *Transforming Privacy: The Transpersonal Philosophy of Rights* (Westport, CT: Praeger, 1998), 138.

32. Jerry M. Rosenberg, *The Death of Privacy* (New York: Random House, 1969).

33. Jeff Weintraub, "The Theory and Politics of the Public/Private Distinction," in *Public and Private in Thought and Practice*, ed. Jeff Weintraub and Krishan Kumar (Chicago, IL: Chicago University Press, 1997), 4–5.

34. Thomas C. Mackey, *Pornography on Trial: A Handbook with Cases, Laws, and Documents* (Santa Barbara, CA: ABC-CLIO, 2002), 65.

35. Mackey, *Pornography on Trial*, 74.

36. Billy James Hargis, solicitation letter, February 1970, attached to letter from W. Cody Wilson to Dr. Gerald Sanctuary, SIECUS, February 27, 1970, box 135 C, file: SIECUS, Commission on Obscenity and Pornography Files, Lyndon Baines Johnson Library, Austin.

37. "Anti-Pornography Film Crusaders 'Hit the Road,'" *Independent Film Journal*, November 25, 1971, 6.

38. Quoted in "Pornographers 'Flaunted' Their Wares and Embarrassed Plain Folks—Baker," *Variety*, July 4, 1974, n.p.

39. Marv Lincoln, "State of the Movie Biz," *National Ball* 118 (1973): 14.

40. See Eric Schaefer and Eithne Johnson, "Quarantined! A Case Study of Boston's Combat Zone," in *Hop on Pop: The Politics and Pleasures of Popular Culture*, ed. Henry Jenkins, Tara McPherson, and Jane Shattuc, 430–453 (Durham, NC: Duke University Press, 2002), for a study of the Boston situation.

41. Based on *Miller*, the Georgia conviction was overturned by the U.S. Supreme Court in the *Jenkins v. Georgia* decision (1974).

42. "Tolerance on Sex Is Found Growing," *New York Times*, August 2, 1973, 21.

43. Susan Gal, "A Semiotics of the Public/Private Distinction," *Differences* 13, no. 1 (2002): 79.

44. Susan Gal, "A Semiotics of the Public/Private Distinction," 81.

45. Websites come and go. Suffice to say that a Google searches for combinations of words such as "amateur nudes," "nude ex-girlfriend pictures," "naked amateur men," and "amateur sex videos" in 2012 yielded between three and fifteen million results, ranging from small free sites to expensive pay sites. The material cuts across racial and ethnic groups and across sexual orientations, and it is international. Although the majority of subjects are younger, there is no shortage of middle-aged and elderly people, and just about any fetish shy of child pornography can easily be found.

46. Trippett, "What's Happening to Sexual Privacy?," 50.

Part I: Mainstream Media and the Sexual Revolution

1 * Rate It X? Hollywood Cinema and the End of the Production Code

CHRISTIE MILLIKEN

We will oppose these intrusions into a communications art-form shielded and protected by the First Amendment. We believe the screen should be as free for filmmakers as it is for those who write books, produce television material, publish newspapers and magazines, compose music and create paintings and sculptures.

. . . I have urged film creators to remember that freedom without discipline is license, and that's wrong, too. I have, in the many meetings I have had with creative people in film, suggested that the freedom which is rightly theirs ought to be a responsible freedom and each individual film-maker must judge his work in that sensible light.

JACK VALENTI, MPAA, "Motion Picture Production Code and Ratings Program: A System of Self-Regulation," personal statement of Jack Valenti, 1968.

Commercial American movies are at last beginning to talk about sex with pertinent and refreshing candor. But although they are outspoken, most of the new movies are less revolutionary than they look. Traditional puritanical attitudes are often concealed beneath the kinky contemporary trappings, still dictating rewards and punishments for the characters. Only the language of the sermons has changed; now they are phrased in the up-to-date psychoanalytical lingo that the "permissive society" understands.

STEPHEN FARBER, "A Film That Forgets Sex Can Be Fun . . . ," *New York Times*, 1971.

Historians have described the period from the late 1960s to the end of the 1970s as one of the most tumultuous and transformative in American film history, perhaps second only to the coming of sound.[1] In addition to the myriad pressures that rocked American society at this time, the decision on the part of the Motion Picture Association of America (MPAA) to finally abandon the increasingly obsolete Production Code in 1968 in favor of a voluntary age-based rating system enabled the possibility of making more adult-themed Hollywood films that could explore, in unprecedented detail, formerly regulated topics such as sexuality and violence. Given the profound changes in sexual and cultural mores from the time of the establishment of the Production Code Administration (PCA) in 1934, this transformation was a long time coming. Although the dramatic shift in the treatment of screen sexuality was embraced by some as a sign of Hollywood's belated willingness to deal with more culturally relevant, mature subject matter, others objected to many of these new films and lamented the demise of the family audience. It is clear that the MPAA, straddling both sides of this divide, introduced the new Code and Rating Administration (CARA)[2] largely as a public relations ploy to help Hollywood's faltering box office, to refresh the organization's image, and to answer the demands of the fragmented filmgoing audience, particularly its most lucrative demographics: the increasingly well-educated adult audience, and the youth market.

This chapter examines this transitional period in film history, using the backdrop of shifts in the social, cultural, and sexual climate of the era to consider debates about sexuality and sexual representation in a number of films made at this time. My emphasis will be on those films made immediately preceding and after the implementation of the rating system through 1973–1974, when this new system was largely consolidated and Hollywood had recovered from a period of severe economic crisis and instability. I will concentrate on films that were controversial for their sexual representation, whether in the courts, through the MPAA's regulatory constraints, or through the media. Before discussing this period, however, brief background on Hollywood during the years preceding the adoption of the rating system will provide context for this transformative move from the PCA-era model of "harmless" entertainment suitable for all to one that allows for discretion and distinction on the basis of age appropriateness, a system promoted by Jack Valenti as "responsible" entertainment.[3]

Code and Law: Postwar Challenges to the PCA and the Changing Legal Status of Motion Pictures

In the postwar period the Hollywood studios were forced to forego their oligopolistic control of the film business when a Supreme Court ruling in 1948, *U.S. v. Paramount Pictures et al.*, required them to divest of their theatrical holdings. Along with the dramatic decline in film attendance that began in the late 1940s and continued into the 1960s, production costs increased significantly, fewer films were made, and more money was invested in a smaller number of films with the hopes of realizing large financial returns. Challenges to the Production Code increased significantly during the period, as the PCA-enforced morality collided with changing audience demands and industry conditions. Foreign films, notable for addressing adult themes, began to make inroads at the box office through the proliferation of art house theaters.

A foreign film became the subject of a groundbreaking legal case that changed the status of motion pictures in American society. *Il Miracolo* (*The Miracle*) was one portion of an anthology film, *L'Amore* (1948; *The Ways of Love*). Directed by Roberto Rossellini, it was the story of a peasant woman (Anna Magnani) who believes that a stranger she sleeps with is Saint Joseph, convincing herself that the baby she carries is the product of an immaculate conception. The film sparked controversy in its native Italy and was deemed blasphemous by the Catholic Church both there and in the United States. It also was condemned by the Catholic Legion of Decency, becoming the subject of localized pickets in New York City, where it opened in December 1950. Although *The Miracle* performed well at the box office, the New York State Board of Regents revoked its license in response to various pressures. When the film's distributor, Joseph Burstyn, appealed the regents' decision and the New York State Supreme Court upheld the ban, he took his case all the way to the Supreme Court and won.

Burstyn v. Wilson (1952), also known as "The Miracle decision," reversed the precedent set by the 1915 *Mutual v. Ohio* case (regarding D. W. Griffith's *Birth of a Nation*), which denied First Amendment protection to motion pictures. In the *Burstyn* case, Justice Tom Clark overturned the ban on the film, describing cinema as "a significant medium for the communication of ideas" and concluding that "the importance of motion pictures as an organ of public opinion is not lessened by the fact that they are designed to entertain as well as inform."[4] *The Miracle* decision effectively argued that films should not be subjected to censorship simply because they are produced by an industry conducted for profit (as was the press, in any case). Although the case was about a foreign film made beyond the purview of MPAA restrictions, the effect of this decision on Hollywood filmmaking was enormous. By dramatically modifying the legal status of local and state censorship boards, *Burstyn* became a "watershed moment" for future films about politically sensitive and controversial issues.

One significant outcome of the studio divestiture was that MPAA members no longer had guaranteed exhibition outlets for their products. The autonomy of theatrical exhibitors coupled with film's new First

Amendment privileges eliminated the necessary collusion among all parties required for the survival of self-regulation. The MPAA could no longer effectively police film content through the Production Code. As a consequence, independent producers and distributers—whose numbers rose dramatically as a result of industry restructuring—began to risk offering more adult fare in American motion pictures. For example, producer and director Otto Preminger released his provocative film, *The Moon Is Blue* (1953) through United Artists (UA) without obtaining a seal of approval, providing an early test of the waning relevance of the PCA. The "scandal" of *The Moon Is Blue*, adapted from a successful stage play, focused on its risqué dialogue (including the use of the previously forbidden word "virgin"). Despite its lack of a seal and its condemnation by the Legion of Decency, the film was a financial success.

Other studios and filmmakers were willing to tackle more sensational topics to draw people back into theaters and to push against the constraints of the PCA in a variety of ways. In turn, the PCA responded with increased flexibility and by revising the code several times, beginning in 1956. Some films reflect this flexibility: *From Here to Eternity* (1953), for its more liberal attitude toward adultery; *The French Line* (1954), with its revealing costumes on Jane Russell; and Preminger's *The Man With the Golden Arm* (1955) and *Tea and Sympathy* (1956), dealing, respectively, with the previously forbidden topics of drug use and homosexuality. Another controversial project, Elia Kazan's *Baby Doll* (1956), based on a notorious one-act play by Tennessee Williams, received a code seal to the surprise of many observers but was nevertheless condemned by the legion, which targeted theaters exhibiting the picture in its campaign against it.

Sex Scenes and Ratings Rumbles

Theaters became a primary target for contestation of controversial material at this time. Although the *Paramount* decision enabled theater owners to book films in a more open and competitive "free" market, they were also no longer supported by a studio oligopoly that had historically been willing and able to defend them from public pressures by lobby groups such as the Legion of Decency. The MPAA member studios had no direct financial interest in the success of newly independent theater owners and consequently adopted a policy not to intervene in local censorship issues that arose in the distribution and exhibition of challenging material. With virtually no financial or public relations support from the MPAA, many exhibitors frequently capitulated to the pressures of local activists and censorship boards. A few theater owners, however, fought back.

One such case involved a Cleveland Heights, Ohio, art theater manager, Nico Jacobellis, who defied a local police order and was arrested for exhibiting Louis Malle's film *Les Amants* (1958, *The Lovers*) in 1959. The film chronicles the unhappy marriage of a young woman and her older husband, featuring partial nudity and a long sequence in which she meets a young man, falls in love, and presumably has sex with him. The theater owner, Louis Sher, and Daniel Frankel—president of the distributor Zenith International Films—decided to challenge the obscenity ruling in a suit that took five years to make its way through the courts. *Jacobellis v. Ohio* (1964) proved to be a crucial test case both for the regulation of film content as well as state censorship in general. In the ruling, Justice William Brennan contested the use of "community standards" as a measure for labeling the film obscene, for a time redefining community not as a local jurisdiction but as "the society at large," "the public, or people in general." He argued that though obscenity might have "a varying meaning from time to time," it should not vary substantively "from town to town or county to county."[5] Interestingly, Brennan supported an age-based model to help distinguish among degrees of adult entertainment, something the MPAA would subsequently adopt. Revision of this ruling became crucial to the ways in which obscenity cases would be reconceived almost a decade later.

Another significant court case pertaining to sexual representation on screen and the issue of "obscenity" took place in 1957 with *Excelsior Pictures Corp v. New York Board of Regents*, a court decision involving a low-budget, nudist/exploitation film: *The Garden of Eden* (1954). When the case found its way to the New York State Court of Appeals, the presiding judge, Charles Desmond, ruled that the nudity depicted in the film was not obscene. *Excelsior v. Regents* was one of the crucial decisions that "effectively ended the ban on nudity in motion pictures and also contributed to breaking the New York censor board."[6] This led to the proliferation of other nudist movies and to the rise of sexploitation cinema generally, as classical exploitation films were surpassed by more daring fare, beginning with Russ Meyer's *The Immoral Mr. Teas* (1959; figure 1.1). The influence of exploitation film on mainstream Hollywood would certainly begin to show over the course of the 1960s and into the 1970s, leading one historian to label the new group of Hollywood filmmakers coming of age at this time as "the exploitation generation."[7]

By the end of the 1950s, interpretation and enforcement of the code were relaxed. The changing legal status of motion pictures with their

Fig. 1.1 The popularity of Russ Meyer's *The Immoral Mr. Teas* (1959) helped initiate a cycle of low-budget "sexploitation" films that in turn exerted an influence over Hollywood filmmaking through the 1960s and 1970s.

First Amendment protection meant that debates about obscenity on screen gradually became the primary criterion for banning a film's exhibition. The PCA was increasingly pressed to confront the murky issues around this ill-defined concept as a way of continuing to self-regulate its product in a new era of "permissiveness." The idea of classifying films based on age appropriateness gained currency by the late 1950s, since its implementation could enable the MPAA to deal with the disparate demands of audiences. That is, some sectors were seeking more adult fare, and others—such as religious and civic groups—were increasingly upset by the lax enforcement of the Production Code. Since 1936, the Legion of Decency had such a system in place with its A1 (Unobjectionable for general patronage), A2 (Unobjectionable for adults), B (Objectionable in part), and C (Condemned) categories. The United Kingdom, notoriously more conservative than the rest of Europe, also had a rating system. Yet there was division among MPAA members and within the PCA about the merits of swapping the code for a classification system. In the early 1960s the MPAA president Eric Johnston fought against the legion's lobby to get the MPAA to endorse a classificatory scheme, arguing that such a system would be undemocratic because it would supersede parental authority and decision making.[8] Various historians, however, have countered that this line of reasoning is specious and that Johnston and his supporters were far more concerned about the box-office repercussions of classification.

Clearly something had to be done to cope with the changing cultural climate that demonstrated a significant market for more adult fare. The inability of the PCA to adequately control studio product led to a situation in which, by 1966, only 59 percent of all films shown in the United States had an MPAA seal (compared to 95 percent compliance before the Paramount decree). Moreover, between 1963 and 1965, thirty-nine films by MPAA-member companies were either not submitted to the PCA or were released through subsidiaries after being denied a seal.[9] Censorial action against specific films—including local boycotts, arrests, prosecutions, confiscations, and license revocations—increased tenfold. By 1965, roughly 60 percent of the films in general release were met by some sort of local censorship action, virtually all of it targeted at the nation's exhibitors.[10]

To help broker the problems, after Eric Johnston's sudden death in 1963, the MPAA instituted a revised Production Code in September 1966 that Kevin Sandler describes as "a prototype that two years later would morph into a classification system."[11] The first "trial run" for this new system was instituted by Jack Valenti, the newly appointed president of the MPAA in 1966, in his handling of the controversial Mike Nichols film, *Who's Afraid of Virginia Woolf?* (1966). Released by Warner Bros., the film obtained a PCA exemption in order to secure an MPAA-sanctioned release when the studio agreed to label the film "Suggested for Mature Audiences" (SMA) with all advertising for the picture containing the blocked letter statement: "NO PERSONS UNDER 18 ADMITTED UNLESS ACCOMPANIED BY A PARENT." This exemption, based on the film's extensive use of profanity, left the task of enforcement to exhibitors and was viewed as a "test case" for an age-based regulatory system. Although Valenti was clear that the special code exemption offered to *Who's Afraid of Virginia Woolf?* would not set a precedent for future cases, the film's enormous box-office success certainly encouraged the accelerated production of more adult-oriented dramas in Hollywood at the time. For example, in 1967, the number of SMA-designated films rose dramatically from six to forty-four. In the twelve months preceding the adoption of the 1968 rating system in November of that year, approximately 60 percent of films released by the studios carried the SMA tag.[12] By now the picture was clear: adult-themed films made money and helped to maintain the profile of the film industry against an increasingly competitive leisure and entertainment marketplace.

Perhaps Valenti's biggest challenge after becoming MPAA president was when the British import, *Blow-Up* (1966), directed by Michelangelo Antonioni, was denied a seal of approval for release by MGM. The fight by MGM to have the film granted the SMA designation was to no avail. The problem, for the PCA, involved two scenes: one in which the main character frolics with two teenage girls and pubic hair is very briefly visible (full frontal nudity then, as now, continues to be controversial), and another in which he watches his neighbors having intercourse. Several factors made this case notable: first, MGM had a long history of vigorously supporting the code; second, Antonioni was an internationally respected Italian auteur who refused to make the two cuts requested by the PCA in order to obtain a seal. He had an ironclad agreement with MGM according him this power. Moreover, *Blow-Up* had already been released to box-office and critical success in Europe and had won the Cannes Film Festival's Grand Prix as Great Britain's official entry.

MGM ultimately got around the problem of noncompliance with the PCA by releasing the film under the banner of its wholly owned and operated non-MPAA subsidiary, Premier Pictures. After *Blow-Up* performed exceedingly well at the box office, the studio dropped the matter. But as James Monaco remarks, "The whole *Blow-Up* incident demonstrated to most observers that the Hollywood Production Code and the seal of approval had, in essence, become irrelevant."[13] From these cases, the introduction of the MPAA's age-based rating system appeared to offer a pragmatic compromise to the changing times. It provided a solution that Valenti was prepared to make in the transition from the "harmless" entertainment model of the PCA era, to the "responsible" one that Valenti would strive to standardize and maintain in the new system of boundary maintenance provided by the voluntary age-based rating system. With the newfound First Amendment freedom accorded to motion pictures, Valenti offered a contradictory message of support for creative freedom so long as this artistry conformed to CARA's model of "responsible" and "disciplined" freedom.

The Rating System and Its Vicissitudes

The rating system initially included four categories: G (suggested for "General" audiences), M (for "Mature" audiences, which changed to GP in 1970, then renamed to PG in 1972 [Parental Guidance recommended]), R ("Restricted," no one under age sixteen [later seventeen, in 1972] admitted unless accompanied by a parent or adult guardian), and X (no one under sixteen admitted [this age eventually varied across different regions]). Within a few weeks of introducing the new system on October 7, 1968, it was adopted industry-wide with the task of classifying films in advance of their release falling to the CARA. Films rated G, M, and R received an MPAA seal, while those rated X did not. The MPAA sought copyright only for the first three ratings, ultimately leaving the X rating vulnerable to widespread interpretation and appropriation. Ostensibly, Valenti felt that Hollywood and the MPAA had no use for the X rating, since it represented material that precluded an MPAA seal of approval anyway. The National Association of Theater Owners (NATO), however, had insisted on its adoption as a means of protecting its members from local prosecution. That the X classification was not copyrighted led many independent producers to freely adopt it, often as a publicity stunt and advertising gimmick, without ever submitting their films for CARA review. For filmmakers working under the purview of the Hollywood industry with mainstream aspirations, the X rating could pose an enormous threat to the widespread distribution and exhibition of films dealing with adult, controversial subject matter.

Less than a month after the new CARA system took effect, the first appeal was filed against an X rating. The claim was made by a small non-MPAA company, Sigma III, which had produced a low-budget antiwar film, *Greetings* (1968), directed by the then unknown Brian De Palma and starring a young Robert De Niro. The problematic scene was one in which several characters watch a hardcore stag reel, images of which are included in the film. Instead of merely cutting the scene down, Sigma III used the appeal process to call immediate attention to a fundamental and larger problem concerning the very structure of the new rating system, arguing that its film had been evaluated unfairly and that CARA would have given *Greetings* an R if it had been a studio picture. Jon Lewis suggests that the executives at Sigma had a point, but their argument—

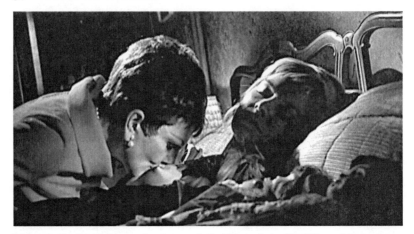

Fig. 1.2 Coral Browne nuzzles Susannah York's nipple in *The Killing of Sister George* (1968), a scene the led to an early showdown over the X rating between the MPAA and Robert Aldrich, the film's director and producer. (Digital frame enlargement.)

heard by an "all-industry committee" consisting entirely of MPAA member executives — would have been unsympathetic to such a claim.[14] In the end, the appeal was lost and Sigma III eventually released a cut R version of the film following a short release of the X. The story quickly faded from the trades.

Soon after, two other appeals were filed on behalf of *If* (1968) — a British import directed by Lindsay Anderson for a scene depicting full frontal nudity — and *The Killing of Sister George* (1968; figure 1.2) — adapted from the successful British stage play about a destructive lesbian relationship, and directed by American Robert Aldrich. From the outset, *Sister George's* subject matter automatically made it relatively groundbreaking for a Hollywood film, albeit one that was produced independently. At issue for CARA was a sexually explicit seduction scene between two women. Although Anderson made a few cuts to his film to gain an R rating for *If*, Aldrich was unable to appease CARA without significantly altering the film's content and meaning. Aldrich defended the seduction scene's inclusion in the film as a crucial and dramatic moment of betrayal that effectively ends the central couple's relationship. Despite that the story's integrity was one line of defense, in a transcribed discussion with the scene's two stars the director is quoted as saying "What gets people into the theater? This scene. . . . So it's an unavoidable must." This was arguably a way of convincing actress Susannah York to agree to a sex scene that she was quite publically and vociferously against shooting. Elsewhere, Aldrich acknowledged the scene's exploitative potential when he said: "We have to bring off the most erotic, provocative, English-language sex-scene that anyone has photographed."[15]

Aldrich lost his appeal, and subsequently sent a letter to Valenti—a portion of which was leaked and printed in *Variety*—in which he complained that the X was an unreasonable designation, one creating the false impression that *The Killing of Sister George* was "a dirty picture not fit for viewing by anyone."[16] The director went on to argue that the X rating as a descriptive classification was too broad precisely because it equated controversial content (as featured in his film) with more prurient content, ranging from softcore simulation to hardcore live action. In addition, the X designation severely undermined the film's box-office potential, since its pornographic taint spilled over into censorship of the film by national exhibitors and restricted potential advertising opportunities in many media outlets both nationally and locally.

Aldrich's letter quite rightly pointed out the problems with CARA's failure to distinguish among different categories of adult-only entertainment. The X rating, when initially outlined by Valenti, was never intended to exclusively imply "a dirty picture"; nonetheless, this was the connotation that it quickly acquired. Aldrich argued for the recognition of nonpornographic films that were clearly intended only for adult viewers and that simultaneously offered up serious dramatic fare, much like *Who's Afraid of Virginia Woolf?* In the end, Lewis surmises, Valenti refused to agree with Aldrich because the MPAA could not control the X rating[17]; nor did Valenti have any interest in having MPAA members produce X-rated pictures, especially as negative connotations accrued around the designation.

After failing in his bid to change the CARA rating, Aldrich continued to battle on behalf of *Sister George*, seeking legal assistance from the ACLU to help contend with the problem of promoting and distributing the film. Because so many newspapers refused to advertise X-rated pictures, Aldrich filed his complaint with the Federal Communications Commission (FCC), calling into question antitrust issues related to fair access to advertising. The ramifications of these restrictions were huge for independent producers and distributers who were responsible for the majority of X-rated products. Aldrich's battle also had the support of NATO, the members of which opposed advertising bans that could undermine their freedom to screen non-MPAA films.[18] Many theaters favored an AO (Adults Only) rating, which could delineate between adult-themed material and the X-rated fare that was increasingly synonymous with softcore and hardcore sexual representation. Aldrich and his legal team alleged that the newspaper syndicates, TV and radio networks, and mass-market magazines "operated in collusion with the film studios to make it difficult for independents to market their X-rated product lines."[19]

He lost the case and went on to release *Sister George* to a poor showing at the box office. Reviews of the film didn't help. Although many of the performances were praised, especially Beryl Reid as the title character, the infamous sex scene that Aldrich fought so hard to retain was singled out for attack by several critics. In the *New York Times*, Renata Adler described it as setting "a special kind of low in the treatment of sex—any kind of sex—in the movies now."[20] Stanley Kauffmann in *The New Republic* quipped:

> I suppose there may be a few remote nomads in Turkestan who haven't yet heard of the scene in *The Killing of Sister George* where Coral Browne sucks Susannah York's left nipple. I won't pretend to be blasé about it: it's a startling scene to encounter in an "aboveground" picture. But like the film's Naughty Language, it's so obvious an attempt to get the picture talked about that I resent talking about it.[21]

Since the explicitness of this so-called scandalous sex scene actually only involved the caressing and tonguing of Susannah York's nipple, it is interesting that it so unanimously placed the film's "aboveground" aspirations in question.

That the X rating didn't help *Sister George*'s performance at the box office is doubtless. On the other hand, the self-imposed X rating that UA gave to John Schlesinger's *Midnight Cowboy* (1969), released as Aldrich's legal battle was well under way, certainly didn't appear to hamper that film's enormous success at the box office. The film chronicles the journey of would-be hustler Joe Buck (Jon Voight) from Texas to New York, where he is convinced his macho cowboy persona will yield him enormous wealth from lonely upper-middle class women. His dreams are quickly dashed, and he forms an uneasy alliance with a sickly conman— Ratso Rizzo (Dustin Hoffman)—who initially hopes to profit from Buck's naïveté. Dealing with urban decay, drug use, male hustling, homosexuality, and a palpable homosocial bond in the relationship between the film's two leads, *Midnight Cowboy* ranked number seven at the box office that year, earning $11 million domestically. It also won the Best Picture Oscar for UA, Best Director for Schlesinger, Best Screenplay for former "blacklistee" Waldo Salt, and Best Actor nominations for both Hoffman and Voight.

The self-applied X rating is a curious part of the film's history that reflects, in this instance, acquiescence to the perceived "problem" of depicting homosexuality on the part of the studio rather than to CARA restrictiveness. According to Tino Balio, the film was initially accorded an R, but UA president Arthur Krim opted to self-apply the X after consulting with a Columbia University psychiatrist because he feared the adverse effects of "the homosexual frame of reference on youngsters."[22] The film's producers, Schlesinger and Jerome Hellman, agreed with the decision. Released just one month before the Stonewall Riots of June 1969, which marked a new era in the gay liberation movement, *Midnight Cowboy* is a fascinating countercultural document that draws on both the buddy film formula and a dystopian rereading of the Western genre in innovative ways. It is interesting to note that, unlike *The Killing of Sister George*, reviews at the time found little that was particularly salacious or exploitative about its treatment of homosexuality. That Joe Buck is consistently portrayed as a reluctant and unwilling partner in these inexplicit but suggestive sex scenes may be one reason. The women in *Sister George*, on the other hand, are depicted as mutually invested in their sexual pleasure. The sex seen on screen, despite that it only involves breasts, is considerably more overt.

Despite its success, *Midnight Cowboy* did not ignite an industrywide trend in X-rated filmmaking, though it certainly brought into question its industrial utility. For example, another topical film from 1969, *Bob & Carol & Ted & Alice* (figure 1.3), was cut slightly to avoid an X.[23] A satire chronicling the marital and extramarital relations between two upper middle-class couples, the film begins with Bob and Carol (Robert Culp and Natalie Wood) attending an Esalen-type self-actualization institute where they are inspired to transform their marriage and their relationships to those around them into partnerships of total honesty. The "institute" sequence is presented as a send-up of 1960s countercultural and therapeutic discourses, depicting primal scream therapy and nude massage and meditation, as well as a marathon, twenty-four-hour consciousness-raising group session (one woman, e.g., is attending in her quest for "better orgasms").

Back in Los Angeles, Bob and Carol share the "beauty" of this experience with the skeptical and more conservative Ted and Alice (Elliot Gould and Dyan Cannon). Bob has an affair, and in the spirit of their new commitment to honesty, he confesses to Carol, who is neither jealous nor angry. Instead, she tells a somewhat confused and perturbed Bob that his honest confession is "beautiful" and presses for details of the encounter as foreplay to their own sexual congress. When they later share this information with Ted and Alice, their friends react somewhat stereotypically along the lines of gender: Alice is furious with Bob for his

Fig. 1.3 Columbia's *Bob & Carol & Ted & Alice* (1969)—with Elliott Gould, Natalie Wood, Robert Culp, and Dyan Cannon—presented provocative ideas about sex but was ultimately quite demure.

matrimonial betrayal, and Ted is more shocked by Bob's confession than by the infidelity itself. Carol then has an affair that Bob is at first considerably less understanding about when he unexpectedly returns home to find his wife with her lover. He must initially fight against his own impulse to a double standard, though he soon acknowledges his shortsightedness and genially orders Carol to fetch drinks for himself and her dumbfounded paramour in a comical about face.

When Bob and Carol tell Ted and Alice about Carol's affair while the foursome is on a weekend getaway to Las Vegas, Ted confesses to his own recent extramarital affair. Partially out of shock and perhaps retaliation, Alice suggests that the foursome have an orgy. Although they eventually attempt to do so, none can follow through with it. The failed gesture ends with all four characters sitting silently alongside one another in bed: *the* suggestive and canonical image for this film in virtually all of its advertising. Whereas some critics at the time argued that the failure to depict an orgy between the two couples shows the film's refusal to offer a truly radicalized picture of sexual liberation, others observe that the failure of the foursome to follow through with such an act is perfectly in keeping with the characters themselves.[24] *Bob & Carol & Ted*

& *Alice* is a curious document of countercultural values played out by characters who strive but fail to live out the free love ideals of the sexual revolution. It positions the couples as too decidedly (and comfortably) middle class and middle aged to embrace such an ethos. In this way, *Bob & Carol* courts a limited degree of controversy—dealing with marital infidelity, the potential for group sex—at the same time that it critiques many countercultural values as naively misguided and unrealizable. Like so many countercultural films of the period, *Bob & Carol* is provocative more for its treatment of sexual themes than for its depiction of sexuality per se.

Hollywood's Desperate Measures

Despite these and other box-office successes, Hollywood was nevertheless in an economically vulnerable position at the beginning of the 1970s. The recession of 1969 produced more than $200 million in studio losses, leaving MGM, Warner Bros., and UA under new management and bringing Universal and Columbia close to liquidation.[25] Together the majors tallied $600 million in losses between 1969 and 1971. By 1970, 40 percent of Hollywood filmmakers were out of work. Of the many reasons for this predicament, in 1969 there were record high interest rates (of about 10 percent), and Hollywood began to suffer from an overproduction boom from 1966–1968. This included a large number of expensive musicals and big-budget spectacles that bombed at the box office. Hoping to repeat the enormous success of 20th Century Fox's *The Sound of Music* (1965), which grossed $135 million within two years of its release, various studios tried their hand at duplicating the formula. Fox produced *Doctor Dolittle* (1967), *Star!* (1968), and *Hello Dolly!* (1969), all of which lost money; Paramount flopped with *Paint Your Wagon* (1969); UA with *Chitty Chitty Bang Bang* (1968). Big-budget spectacles such as Fox's *The Bible* (1966) and *Tora! Tora! Tora!* (1970), Columbia's *Casino Royale* (1967), and UA's *The Battle of Britain* (1969) also failed to break even.

The repeated inability to find a winning formula with mass appeal led many studios to rethink the kind of product they were willing to produce. *Easy Rider* (1969) rather belatedly led them to consider courting the youth market, an audience that exploitation companies such as American International Pictures (AIP) had been cultivating for over a decade. Produced independently for just under $375,000 and distributed by Columbia, *Easy Rider* earned over $19 million and ranked fourth at the box office for 1969. Along with such counterculture films as *The Graduate* (1967) and *Bonnie and Clyde* (1967), the film became a symbol for "New

American Cinema," characterized as challenging the traditional Hollywood model and emphasizing, from French critics and from New Wave Cinema, the creative vision of the director/auteur with low-budget productions featuring small casts that targeted the late teen and college-age audience.[26] The "youth cult" bubble in Hollywood film production came about both as a result of economic desperation and of the rating system with its age-based reorganization of the filmgoing audience. David Cook surmises that the net effect of this situation led the major studios to "embrace exploitation as a mainstream practice" by the late 1960s, "elevating such B genres as science fiction and horror to A-film status, retrofitting 'race cinema' as 'blaxploitation,' and competing with the pornography industry for 'sexploitation' market share."[27] The "excess" of many of these genres was frequently bound up in issues surrounding sexuality and its representation.

Fox's decision to sign sexploitation pioneer and auteur Russ Meyer to a four-picture contract is an interesting consequence of this effort. Meyer built his reputation on cheaply made, independent films that yielded big box-office returns. His first feature, *The Immoral Mr. Teas* (1959), was shot in four days with a budget of $24,000 and grossed over $1 million at the box office.[28] His other films—such as *Faster Pussycat! Kill! Kill!* (1965), *Vixen!* (1968), and *Cherry, Harry & Raquel* (1970)—were all similarly reflective of his camp or trash style, demonstrating his authorial predilection for especially outrageous female characterizations, obsessive attention to large breasts, suggestive but never graphic softcore sexual situations, and bad acting, as well as cheesy scripts. Hired by Richard Zanuck, newly appointed as Fox's head of production by his father—famed studio mogul Darryl F. Zanuck—Meyer was brought on board for precisely his ability to make low-budget, highly profitable (and sensationalistic) films. The first of only two films completed before he was let go by the studio, *Beyond the Valley of the Dolls* (1970), is a curious example of Hollywood's brief flirtation with sexploitation.

Co-scripted by Meyer and film critic Roger Ebert, *Beyond* is a parody of an earlier Fox melodrama, *The Valley of the Dolls* (1967), adapted from the trashy Jacqueline Susann bestseller about the rise and fall of women in show business. *Beyond the Valley of the Dolls* has been read as a hybrid between Hollywood filmmaking practices and the more typical exploitation techniques upon which Meyer built his reputation.[29] For example, it makes some use of such exploitation staples as nondiegetic inserts, a moralizing voice-over (deployed to humorous effect toward the end of the film), and over-the-top "gore shots" of extreme violence. Nevertheless, it also conforms to Hollywood narrative conventions more than most of Meyer's earlier films.[30] The film chronicles the misadventures of a beautiful rock-girl trio who go to Los Angeles seeking fame and fortune. Once there, they get mixed up in the bizarre world of the music industry with, for example, a swinging hermaphrodite and a pop music gigolo who quite literally loses his head over the former. Ashley St. Ives (Edy Williams) is a prototypical Meyer heroine who uses men as "toys for her amusement," while a middle-aged lawyer, described by Vincent Canby in the *New York Times* as "a sort of nasty Mr. Teas," goes to bed with a member of the band without bothering to remove his black dress socks and his garters. Canby's lukewarm review of the film complained that Meyer's once "earnestly vulgar sensibility" is overwhelmed by a complete parody that the critic read as patronizing of his audience. Even worse, claimed Canby, was the fact that "[Meyer] has become downright inhibited, at least in terms of female nudity on display, but it may be that Meyer is a prude."[31]

In a second *New York Times* article, entitled "Getting Beyond Myra and the Valley of the Junk," Canby acknowledged that though it was possible, in some ways, to take Meyer seriously, the film was ultimately a brand of trash:

> Meyer has had a wonderful time showing us various ways in which lives can be collapsed; one young man gets his head chopped off; a lovely girl has her brains blown out when she commits fellatio with a revolver, a couple of others are simply shot, one full in the face. All of this is presented as middle-class camp, which is great if you want to make fun of movies. I don't, particularly. There are too many good movies one could be seeing, and too many legitimate ambiguities to be resolved, to waste time worrying whether one should laugh or cry over junk films.[32]

Canby's remarks were typical of the tepid reception given to *Beyond the Valley of the Dolls*, which still performed well at the box office. His observation about the toned-down sexuality in the studio release, which is indeed "tamer" than Meyer's independently produced films, may reflect compliance with studio or MPAA expectations. Meyer may have been more willing to exploit gore than sex on screen in *Beyond*, given the greater latitude accorded to screen violence around this time (e.g., *Bonnie and Clyde*, *The Wild Bunch* [1969], and *A Clockwork Orange* [1971]), which pushed against the boundaries of acceptability over the far more restrictive surveillance of screen sex. Meyer also admitted that his studio contract came at an opportune moment, when increasing popularity of hardcore pornography was suddenly taking over a significant audience for his own preferred softcore mode.[33] *Beyond* received an X rating (the second of two Fox releases in short succession) and, as part of a cluster of "trash" films released around this time, became embroiled in both a critical and antiporn backlash.

The other controversial film produced by Fox and released just a week before *Beyond the Valley of the Dolls* was *Myra Breckenridge*. Adapted from Gore Vidal's novel, *Myra Breckenridge* is another showbiz send-up, which chronicles the exploits of Myra (Raquel Welsh), formerly Myron (played by film critic Rex Reed), who undergoes a sex change operation in the prologue of the film. As Myra, Myron wreaks revenge on a greedy uncle, Buck Loner (John Huston), by coming to Hollywood to take over his acting school, and by her mission to attain "power over both sexes and therefore power over life itself." The film is a series of vignettes and seductions, including a scene in which Myra ostensibly dons a dildo (never shown) and sodomizes a young male ingénue before sending him onto another woman's casting couch. That casting agent is played by septuagenarian Mae West, who makes a brief appearance performing her infamous and voracious appetite for sex.

Myra Breckenridge uses the exploitation convention of nondiegetic inserts throughout, mostly old Hollywood films from the Fox archive, which often comment on the film itself in a parodic way. It even incorporates a perhaps self-referential exchange between two characters in which one asks the other for his opinion about the state of contemporary cinema and its deployment of so much "pornographic smut." *Myra Breckenridge* was universally panned. Stanley Kauffman said: "The film looks like an abandoned battlefield after a lot of studio forces tussled and nobody won," going on to quip of both films: "If this is what 20th Century-Fox needs to save itself, why bother?"[34] Vincent Canby said that though the novel was "a reasonable, dirty, witty and straightforward satire of movies, pornographic novels and earnest movie critics," the film version "satirizes nothing, except, perhaps, the desperate lengths to which today's moviemakers will go to try to be different and dirty."[35] When independent film producer Paul Monash accused Fox of pandering to the "sick fantasies of the perverted" with these two exploitation releases, a fiery debate ensued between him and Richard Zanuck in the pages of the trade press.[36]

Blaxploitation briefly became another Hollywood effort to capitalize on a target audience: the previously untapped African American demographic. As more attention began to be paid to audience research at this time, the studios quickly discovered that despite composing roughly 12–15 percent of the total population in the United States at the time, African Americans represented almost 30 percent of the audience in first-run, major city theaters.[37] The canonical films that inaugurated the cycle—*Sweet Sweetback's Baadasssss Song* (1971), *Shaft* (1971), and *Superfly* (1972)—were directed by African American men and all featured highly sexualized male leads. *Sweet Sweetback*, for example, chronicles the coming-of-age of a young boy raised in a brothel and initiated into sex as a ten-year-old by one of its employees (shown, suggestively, in the film's prologue). From performing sex acts in the whorehouse as a young adult, Sweetback (played by the film's director, Melvin Van Peebles) gradually becomes a politicized and militant pimp hustler hero: "A Baadasssss Nigger" who is "Coming to Collect Some Dues" from the white establishment, as the closing title states. When the film earned an X rating for its sexual content and racially inflammatory violence, Van Peebles responded by defiantly including the line "Rated X by an all-white jury" on all of the posters for the film. Self-financed for $500,000 and independently distributed, *Sweet Sweetback* made $10 million in its first run alone, demonstrating the enormous potential for this untapped market.

Hollywood quickly appropriated the formula and also picked up many independently produced films for distribution. *Superfly*, for instance, was produced for less than $500,000 and distributed by Warner Bros., which reportedly made $28.5 million on the deal. It features a cocaine dealer, Youngblood Priest (Ron O'Neal), who organizes one last "big deal" in order to retire from the business. Priest is portrayed heroically as a sexual stud who ventures from the bedroom of one wealthy young lover to another. Although the film never crosses into softcore simulated sex to the degree of *Sweet Sweetback* (it received an R rating), nudity is shown throughout. *Shaft*, from MGM, was toned down considerably in terms of sex seen on screen, though again John Shaft (Richard Roundtree) is portrayed as a highly sexualized detective who sleeps with a number of black and white women over the course of the narrative, all of whom are treated rather poorly. The success of the film yielded $18 million on a $2 million investment and spawned two sequels.

American International Pictures made a number of blaxploitation films featuring black heroines, most notably *Coffy* (1973) and *Foxy Brown* (1974), both directed by Jack Hill and staring Pam Grier. These films (as well as those starring Tamara Dobson as *Cleopatra Jones*) placed enormous emphasis on her highly sexualized body. Grier's persona had been established through a series of sexploitation films made at AIP and New World Pictures (former AIP producer Roger Corman's company founded in 1970) such as *The Big Doll House* (1971) and *Women in Cages* (1971), women-in-prison films that deploy lesbian subtexts. *Black Mama, White*

Mama (1973) has been read as an important transitional film in Grier's career from sexploitation to blaxploitation, continuing her "forceful woman-warrior iconicity" in a prison narrative that mimics and reverses many themes from *The Defiant Ones* (1958). Here the male buddy formula from that film is reworked with Grier as Lee, an imprisoned prostitute alongside a fellow con, Karen, a white idealistic guerilla fighter. One of several differences between the more respectable Hollywood drama and its sexploitation "remake" is the fact that Lee survives the prison escape (handcuffed to Karen) and does not sacrifice herself for her costar, who dies in the end of the film. As Mia Mask argues in her critical reappraisal of Grier's career, this marks an important break from conventions in film history (and popular literature) that portrayed the sacrifice of black characters for their white costars or counterparts.[38] Moreover, though sexploitation's female characters were frequently punished for transgressions of the patriarchal sociosexual order, *Black Mama* enables Grier's Lee to triumph.[39]

Blaxploitation films with male leads tended toward a certain sexual conservatism, notably in the "exploitation" of the nude female body, though the exploitation of the female body certainly continues into the female action films emerging later in the cycle. In Grier's first starring role, *Coffy*, for example, the eponymous character exposes her breasts on numerous occasions. When Coffy infiltrates a brothel in her vigilante quest to exact revenge on the drug dealers who disabled her addicted younger sister, the ensuing disruption instigates a prototypical "cat fight" among the prostitutes during which almost every participant is rendered topless. Coffy's success in infiltrating this underworld of sex and drug traffic depends on her promise of sexual favors as she lures and undermines the criminals, kingpins, and petty pushers responsible for the crime and despair in black communities. Although exploitation films with male protagonists certainly emphasize the sexual prowess of their leads, their sexual performances tend to be for gratification rather than bait. Moreover, the display of male nudity is hardly comparable.

On the heels of *Coffy*'s notable success, Grier also starred in *Foxy Brown* (figure 1.4). Again, Grier's breasts are bared on numerous occasions. Yet Foxy is also a model of empowered femininity, shown nurturing, protecting, and defending others around her and also enjoying and initiating sex with her boyfriend. Foxy is drawn into a criminal underworld of drugs and prostitution to seek justice for the murder of both her brother and her lover, an undercover narcotics officer. She feigns an interest in becoming a high-priced call girl in order to penetrate the

Fig. 1.4 Blaxploitation films such as *Foxy Brown* (1974), starring Pam Grier, offered an African American heroine with greater narrative, sexual, and political agency.

underworld led by a woman, Miss Katherine (Kathryn Loder). After sabotaging the sexual payoff to a corrupt judge (who has a penchant for black women), Foxy is captured and taken to a remote ranch where she is gang-raped by racist white thugs, whom she subsequently sets on fire. Critiques of both racial and patriarchal ideologies are much in evidence. *Foxy Brown* references numerous racial, social, and political issues, especially pertaining to black self-determination and social justice. Grier displays a range of hairstyles across the film, reflecting the changing image of beauty associated with African American women during this time. Toward the end of the film, she goes from long wavy hair to a striking Afro, when she solicits the aid of the "Anti-Slavery Committee" to avenge the murder of her brother and her boyfriend. This scene literally juxtaposes Foxy against a poster of Angela Davis, reinforcing a visual link between the real-life political activist and a screen incarnation of empowered black femininity. The film concludes as Foxy delivers to Miss

Katherine a pickle jar containing the penis of her lover, Steve. Although neither Foxy's castration of Steve (with a hunting knife!) nor the contents of the jar itself are explicitly shown, these acts are a not-so-subtle staging of a rape-revenge convention that literally and figuratively dramatizes Foxy's triumph over Steve (the penis) and the white patriarchal drug lords (phallus) who have violently exploited and debilitated both her loved ones and the black community more broadly. In her final confrontation with Katherine, Foxy defends herself by pulling a gun from her Afro, after the viewer has been set up to believe she is unarmed and certain to meet her death.

Interestingly, it is only the white characters in the film who objectify and strive to exploit Foxy. To all of the black men in the film, she is a crime fighter and a peer to be respected for her conviction and her strength. The combination of femininity, sexuality, and narrative agency that Pam Grier demonstrates in this cycle of films are all important precursors to the emergence of the Hollywood action heroine that will occur a decade later, first on television and then on the big screen. Grier's work in the blaxploitation cycle provides an example of the complex ways in which the formulas used by genre films were sometimes less conservative and retrograde than many critics have claimed, given the degree to which these texts may be seen to assimilate (and market) countercultural ideologies in ways that invite multiple interpretations and counterreadings.

The violence, sexuality, nudity, and coarse language in these and other blaxploitation films demonstrate the extent to which the regulation of film content had loosened over the period as Hollywood embraced exploitation tactics. To be sure, blaxploitation films courted controversy on a number of fronts, not least of which was critical reception among black intellectuals, writers and activists who, at the time, railed against the violent drug-dealing pimps and gangsters who populated the formula. For example, Marion Barry, then president of the Washington, DC, School Board, described the genre as a form of "mind genocide."[40] That said, the antidrug message of films such as *Coffy*, *Foxy Brown*, and *Cleopatra Jones* highlight the significant differences in the image of black community and female sexual and social emancipation that the female blaxploitation heroines provided. Nevertheless, as Hollywood became less dependent on exploitation formulas for short-term profit, these genres quickly disappeared from the industry repertoire, since they were ultimately too disreputable and too troublesome to conform to the MPAA's mandate of "responsible entertainment."

Obscenity, Community Standards, and Hollywood's Recovery

By the early 1970s, many films reflecting the sexual politics of the era had been produced. A case involving local censorship of an MPAA release, *Carnal Knowledge* (1971), perhaps represents a closing chapter to certain aspects of the debates about the limits of Hollywood screen sex. Adapted from an unproduced play by Jules Feiffer and directed by Mike Nichols, *Carnal Knowledge* was an adult melodrama about the sexual hypocrisy of two classmates, Jonathan (Jack Nicholson) and Sandy (Art Garfunkel), through their college days in the late 1940s to the present as they enter middle age in the dramatically changed sociosexual climate of the early 1970s. The film, rated R, does show some partial nudity, but its controversy was mostly for the frank discussion about sex conducted in the confessions and observations between the two friends. Over the course of the summer and into the fall of 1971, *Carnal Knowledge* was the subject of numerous articles on the pages of the *New York Times*. Vincent Canby praised it for being "in effect, a political and social history of this country during the last 30 years, as defined, exclusively, in the sexual triumphs, adjustments and disasters of two middle class nebbishes."[41] Stephen Farber made similar claims, arguing that it was groundbreaking for at least dealing with "the rich potential in subjects that have up to now been taboo—for instance, the way in which a thorough study of sexual failures might refer to and illuminate larger social and political failures." He argued that though the film did not go far enough, it was among the first to "try to uncover some of the relevant, disturbing secrets of American private life."[42]

In another *Times* article published a month later, Rosalyn Drexler weighed in on the debate from a feminist perspective, taking a critical stance on the marginalization and exploitation of women in the film and even reading the relationship between the two friends as "a study in latent homosexuality": "Everything that happens to Nicholson and Garfunkel becomes boasting about sex, sex, sex. It is their relationship that is the soulless center of *Carnal Knowledge*, man to drippy man: the search for each other in the vagina of a mutually shared woman."[43] The closeness between the two men, expressed primarily through their intimate discourse about sex, led many critics to remark on the buddy aspects of the film and the degree to which it plays more powerfully upon their homosocial bond than on any heterosexual coupling they achieve. As Joan Mellen contends: "It is not that these men are explicitly homosexual, but that in a culture which encourages distrust of and hostility toward women, erotic trust becomes possible only between men. *Carnal*

Knowledge acutely chronicles that sexual tension which grows up between men as an inevitable result of their treating women as the alien 'other.'"[44]

The film opens as the two young college students discuss their views about love, the ideal woman, and losing their virginity. Although this scene plays out in complete darkness—juxtaposed with the film's title sequence—the contrast between the two characters is immediately established. Jonathan is coarse, sexist, opportunistic. Sandy is naive, romantic, and decidedly less brutal. At college, Sandy begins to date Susan (Candice Bergen), whom he will later marry (then divorce). Soon after, Jonathan begins an affair with Susan, which highlights his ruthless and competitive relationship with Sandy. The explicit sex talk between the two friends thus takes on a more sinister dimension. After many scenes showing the sexual negotiations between the two couples in this triangle, kissing and petting, the first scene to visualize intercourse is carefully framed in such a way as to make us initially uncertain about whom Susan is with. A long static sequence shot frames Susan passively positioned beneath a man who is penetrating her. Her face displays a range of emotions, though she appears to be deriving little pleasure from the act. Only when her lover climaxes then collapses onto the grass beside her is he revealed to be Jonathan. One of the curious aspects of the film is that in a narrative preoccupied with sex and sexual knowledge, it ultimately depicts very little of the act.

Some twenty years later, after Sandy has left Susan and their family for a much younger woman, Jonathan unwittingly reveals the secret affair in his "Ball Busters on Parade" slide show when he presents a maliciously narrated chronology of all the women he has slept with. Jonathan's marriage to Bobbie (Ann Margaret) has ended in divorce and he now is single, bitter, middle-aged, and virtually impotent save the carefully scripted sexual scenario he controls with a prostitute, Louise (Rita Moreno), who can only arouse him by following a precisely directed description of his sexual power and potency against the fundamental weakness of women. The film ends with this encounter between prostitute and john, as Louise coaxes him into his fantasy of manhood by preparing to fellate him. With this, *Carnal Knowledge* created a fascinating and troubling picture of two men struggling to come to terms with the tumultuous changes in the sociosexual culture that evolves around them. The film courted controversy more for its antifeminist backlash, for its thematic treatment of sex, and for the frank discussion between the two men about their sexual desires and exploits than for its visualization of sexuality on screen.

In Albany, Georgia, a local ban against a movie theater exhibiting the film turned statewide. *Jenkins v. Georgia* found its way to the Supreme Court in 1974, where the Georgia ruling was summarily and unanimously reversed. At first this case against reading the film as "obscene" may have appeared to be a harbinger of complicated negotiations for MPAA-rated films in the years to come; however, its resolution actually seemed to bolster Jack Valenti's steadfast refusal to endorse X-rated and hardcore product lines. On the heals of the landmark U.S. Supreme Court ruling in *Miller v. California* the year before, which laid down the "community standards" test for determining obscenity, the courts certainly created sufficient ambiguity to plague the legal system for years to come. These and other obscenity cases all offered up reinterpretation of obscenity laws that left content regulation open to prosecutors in individual communities once again. Giving power back to local rather than national "community standards" opened up too many potential problems for almost all NATO members to risk noncompliance with the rating system. Although hardcore features—including *Deep Throat, The Devil in Miss Jones*, and *Behind the Green Door*—enjoyed a brief economic boom from 1972 to 1973, outgrossing many Hollywood films at the time, these landmark court cases gradually pushed hardcore films out of the theatrical marketplace into home video.

The outcome of this legislation bolsters Kevin Sandler's argument that by 1973, the MPAA—through CARA—and now with the full cooperation of NATO, had consolidated its new model of "responsible entertainment" (a balance of artistic freedom with restraint) that functioned in much the same way as the PCA-era's "harmless entertainment" model. He argues that CARA functioned quite similarly to the PCA insofar as both bodies aimed to control entryway and participation into the legitimate theatrical marketplace.[45] These claims are reinforced by the fact that, since 1974, studio films rated G, PG, PG-13, and R have moved through the marketplace with virtual immunity. The R rating became the tag that signified Hollywood, whereas the X became associated with American independent and foreign art fare as well as softcore and hardcore pornography.[46]

*

As Hollywood slowly showed signs of economic recovery, arguably beginning with the blockbuster success of *The Godfather* in 1972, MPAA members began to reconfigure their product, moving away from more challenging "adult" pictures into a reformulated all-ages blockbuster model.

From today's perspective, the cinematic sex scenes from this period may look simultaneously dated and new. On the one hand, the sex scenes in Bernardo Bertolucci's X-rated *Last Tango in Paris* (1972), one of the most provocative films of the period, did not lead to the anticipated transformation in motion picture content predicted by the likes of Pauline Kael.[47] On the other hand, the infantilized treatment of sexuality in so many recent teen pics and sex comedies certainly makes these older films seem refreshing in their maturity and candor. That said, the picture of sexual liberation that so many of these counterculture films seemed to offer is—more often than not—rather bleak. Although the discourse about and representation of sex and sexuality were certainly transformed in this period, many of the films still tackled these topics with a kind of skepticism and moralism that was fundamentally quite critical and wary of liberationist ideology, a point made by Farber in the epigraph at the start of this essay. Today, one is more likely to find feature films that deal with sexuality in frank and explicit ways coming from independent (including queer) cinema or from other countries (particularly France and Denmark in recent years) that appear to be invested in pushing against status quo representations. That sexuality continues to be vigorously scrutinized by CARA, whereas screen violence has continued to expand and—dare we say—flourish, is perhaps a sign of how fleeting the legacy of this cultural moment has proven to be with respect to sex scenes and sex seen in Hollywood cinema.

Notes

1. David Cook, *Lost Illusions: American Cinema in the Shadow of Watergate and Vietnam 1970–1979* (Berkeley: University of California Press, 2002), 1–7.
2. The abbreviation CARA first stood for the Code and Rating Administration but was later changed in 1977 to the Classification and Rating Administration in an effort to abolish all reference to the former Production Code, including the historical practice of vetting scripts in advance of production.
3. See, esp., chaps. 1 and 2 of Kevin S. Sandler, *The Naked Truth: Why Hollywood Doesn't Make X-Rated Movies* (New Brunswick, NJ: Rutgers University Press, 2007).
4. Cited in Jon Lewis, *Hollywood v. Hardcore: How the Struggle over Censorship Saved the Modern Film Industry* (New York: New York University Press, 2000), 102.
5. Lewis, *Hollywood v. Hardcore*, 133.
6. Eric Schaefer, *"Bold! Daring! Shocking! True!": A History of Exploitation Films, 1919–1959* (Durham, NC: Duke University Press, 1999), 300.

7. Maitland McDonough. "The Exploitation Generation. Or: How Marginal Movies Came in from the Cold," in *The Last Great American Picture Show: New Hollywood Cinema in the 1970s*, ed. Thomas Elsaesser, Alexander Horwarth, and Noel King (Amsterdam: Amsterdam University Press, 2004), 107.

8. Murray Shumach, *The Face on the Cutting Room Floor: The Story of Movie and Television Censorship* (New York: William Morrow, 1964), 258–259.

9. Sandler, *The Naked Truth*, 35.

10. Lewis, *Hollywood v. Hardcore*, 145–146.

11. Sandler, *The Naked Truth*, 35.

12. Lewis, *Hollywood v. Hardcore*, 145–146.

13. Paul Monaco, *The Sixties: 1960–1969* (Berkeley: University of California Press, 2001), 62.

14. Lewis, *Hollywood v. Hardcore*, 164.

15. Kelly Hankin, "Lesbian Locations: The Production of Lesbian Bar Space in *The Killing of Sister George*," *Cinema Journal* 41, no. 1 (fall 2001): 3–7, 5.

16. Cited in Lewis, *Hollywood v. Hardcore*, 165.

17. Lewis, *Hollywood v. Hardcore*, 165.

18. Lewis, *Hollywood v. Hardcore*, 167.

19. Lewis, *Hollywood v. Hardcore*, 167.

20. Renata Adler, "Screen: 'Sister George': Robert Aldrich Directs Film of Marcus Play," *New York Times*, December 17, 1968, 58.

21. Stanley Kauffmann, "On Films: Greetings and Groans, *The New Republic*, January 18, 1969, 34.

22. Tino Balio, *United Artists: The Company That Changed the Film Industry* (Madison: University of Wisconsin Press, 1987), 291.

23. Balio, *United Artists*, 292.

24. Roger Ebert, review of *Bob & Carol & Ted & Alice, Chicago Sun-Times*, December 22, 1969, accessed June 8, 2013, www.rogerebert.com/reviews.

25. Cook, *Lost Illusions*, 9.

26. Monaco, *The Sixties*, 188.

27. Cook, *Lost Illusions*, 4.

28. Cook, *Lost Illusions*, 92.

29. See Craig Fischer, "*Beyond the Valley of the Dolls* and the Exploitation Genre," *Velvet Light Trap* 30 (fall 1992): 18–33.

30. Fischer, "*Beyond the Valley of the Dolls* and the Exploitation Genre," 30.

31. Vincent Canby, Review of *Beyond the Valley of the Dolls, New York Times*, June 27, 1970, 19.

32. Vincent Canby, "Getting beyond Myra and the Valley of the Junk," *New York Times*, July 5, 1970, 186.

33. Fischer, "*Beyond the Valley of the Dolls* and the Exploitation Genre," 26.

34. Stanley Kauffman, "*Myra Breckenridge* and Other Disasters," *The New Republic* 392, no. 12, July 18, 1970: 22.

35. Canby, "Review of *Beyond the Valley of the Dolls*," 19.

36. Fischer, "*Beyond the Valley of the Dolls* and the Exploitation Genre," 30.

37. Ed Guerrero, *Framing Blackness: The African Image in Film* (Philadelphia: Temple University Press, 1993), 83.

38. Mia Mask, *Divas on Screen: Black Women in American Film* (Urbana: University of Illinois Press, 2009), 84.

39. Mask, *Divas on Screen*, 86.

40. Mask, *Divas on Screen*, 102.

41. Vincent Canby, "I Was Sorry to See it End," *New York Times*, July 4, 1971, D1.

42. Stephen Farber, "A Film That Forgets Sex Can Be Fun . . ." *New York Times*, August 1, 1971, D9.

43. Rosalyn Drexler, "Do Men Really Hate Women?" *New York Times*, September 5, 1971, D7.

44. Joan Mellen, *Big Bad Wolves: Masculinity in the American Film* (New York: Pantheon Books, 1977), 315.

45. Sandler, *The Naked Truth*, 43.

46. Sandler, *The Naked Truth*, 52.

47. Pauline Kael, "Introduction," in Bernardo Bertolucci and Franco Arcalli, *Bernardo Bertolucci's* Last Tango in Paris; *the screenplay, by Bernardo Bertolucci and Franco Arcalli* (New York: Delacorte Press, 1973).

2 * Make Love, Not War: Jane Fonda Comes Home (1968–1978)

LINDA WILLIAMS

In the late 1960s and early 1970s, after the demise of the Production Code, Hollywood began to devise new tropes for sexual representations that had been prohibited by the code: "going all the way." Most of these tropes involved a certain amount of simulated pelvic thrusting by male performers. At the same time, an emerging genre of hardcore pornography, under no obligation to fake sex, discovered fellatio as if it were a brand-new sexual act. Lost in the shuffle of the portrayal of these two heterosexual sex acts—genital sex and oral sex, both presented as primarily male forms of pleasure—were the different pleasures of women. In the abundance of male pelvic thrusting and ministrations toward eventually ejaculating penises, female sexual pleasure tended to be assimilated to that of the male. The possibly different rhythms and temporalities of a woman's pleasure were simply not acknowledged. It is worth asking, then, just how female pleasure came to be presented in its own right in the domain of mainstream Hollywood movies. The long answer that follows is inextricably tied to the context of resistance to the Vietnam War, emerging discourses of sexology, and the willowy body of one iconic female star (figure 2.1).

"Make Love, Not War"

"Make love, not war" was a slogan that many of my friends and I chanted at "Stop the Draft Week" demonstrations against the Oakland Induction Center in 1967 during American troop buildups for the Vietnam War. In those heady days, saying "yes" to sex felt like saying "no," not just to war but to the kind of instrumental reason that had fatefully led to one of America's now-too-familiar bellicose quagmires. Sexual revolution seemed inextricably linked in those days, as David Allyn's history of the era argues, to political revolution.[1] When we chanted "make love, not war," my draft-resisting friends and I were echoing the words of Frankfurt School theorists such as Herbert Marcuse and Norman O. Brown. These theorists argued against the Freudian premise that sexual desire

Fig. 2.1 During the late 1960s and 1970s female sexual pleasure was frequently represented in the willowy body of Jane Fonda, seen here in *Barbarella* (1968), directed by her husband at the time, Roger Vadim.

was in permanent need of sublimation if human culture and society was to persevere. Marcuse's *Eros and Civilization*, first published in 1955, envisioned a liberation that would restore "the right of sensuousness" and not simply release libido but utterly transform it.[2] Marcuse argued that the body would be "resexualized": all erotogenic zones would be "reactivated," and a "resurgence of pregenital polymorphous sexuality" would accompany a "decline of genital sexuality." The entire body would thus become "a thing to be enjoyed—an instrument of pleasure."[3] Sparked by Marcuse; turned on by music, marijuana, and psychedelics; outraged by the escalations of a war whose injustice was driven home by a draft that affected the entire population of young men, my generation really did think, at least for a moment that making love could be a political act against war.

But what was a woman's place in this loving alternative to war? Another slogan, also popular in this period, though not quite as easily chanted, was "Women Say Yes to Men Who Say No!" I never marched under this banner but as one who *had* said "yes" to a man who had said "no" by refusing induction into the army, it took me longer than it should have to realize the flaws in that slogan. Behind it stood a whole regime of patriarchy that saw a woman's pleasure as subservient to the man, who was the only real political actor in this revolutionary scenario. If I were to make love and oppose war then, as feminist cultural historian Lynne Segal notes, it "was going to have to mean something more than 'the freedom to get laid.'" It was going to have to mean, ultimately, "a radical rethinking of the whole area of sexuality and sexual politics."[4] But what *was* a politically correct form of making love? Against Freud's dictum that civilization required a certain amount of discontent, Marcuse had encouraged the decline of genital sexuality and a "pregenital polymorphous sexuality." Those were confusing words requiring a knowledge of sex that my previous education had not prepared me for. To learn what such terms might mean, my generation turned to the earlier sexology of Alfred Kinsey and the newer work of William Masters and Virginia Johnson, just emerging in the late 1960s.

Sexology and Sexual Politics

Alfred Kinsey was a zoologist whose long crusade was ultimately to dissolve the ironclad distinctions between supposedly normal and abnormal sex. Although most people (still) tend to believe that whatever they do sexually is what everyone else does, or should do, Kinsey discovered, at first just by interviewing married students in his famous "Marriage Course," that people actually did a great many different things.[5] Lecture 2 of this course, first taught at Indiana University in 1938, had already challenged Freud's orthodoxy about the vaginal orgasm. Projecting a slide of a penis entering a vagina on the wall of his lecture hall, Kinsey emphasized that the reason for the woman's pleasure was not vaginal but clitoral stimulation.[6] The married or engaged students, who were the only ones admitted into his courses, were decidedly interested in what Kinsey had to teach. And what he had to teach often derived from what he had learned from these students.[7] Through ever-widening research, conducted in the form of extended face-to-face interviews, Kinsey came to believe that there was very little sexual activity that was abnormal or perverse. In fact he eschewed these words, preferring the label "rare."

Kinsey would democratically survey every possible aspect of sexual behavior. However, he would only count that behavior *as sex* if it led to orgasm.[8] As a zoologist whose expertise was gall wasps, he valued measurability above all. Orgasms, which to him had the virtue of being countable, were his gold standard. From the very beginning, however, this meant that Kinsey's research, like that of most sexologists, was inherently androcentric. It began with men, and its tools of measurement were male centered. Although he was remarkably nonjudgmental about what behaviors might lead to orgasm—masturbation, hetero- or homosexual relations—the countable orgasm of the male was the standard. It would not be until he got to researching and writing his female volume, *Sexual Behavior in the Human Female* published in 1953, that Kinsey would discover enormous dissimilarities between male and female sexual "outlets."[9]

Most interesting for this chapter, to me, however, is the way Kinsey went about studying orgasms: he filmed them. Early in his research Kinsey had contrived to observe sexual activity live. He paid prostitutes who allowed him to watch while they performed their tricks. But prostitutes proved unsatisfying subjects precisely because they did perform "tricks" and often faked orgasm. Inevitably, Kinsey turned to film in 1948, at first to test the theory of how men ejaculated—whether in dribbles or with projecting force. Clarence Tripp and Bill Dellenback, Kinsey's trusty photographers, paid three hundred men in New York City to masturbate to ejaculation before the camera. After eventually collecting films of a thousand men masturbating, they concluded that in 73 percent ejaculate does not spurt but dribbles.[10]

Filming ejaculation soon branched out into filming the partnered sex acts of male homosexuals. By 1949 much of this filming moved into an attic room of Kinsey's home, and the research leading up to his volume on female sexual behavior began to include women.[11] The subjects of these films were certain special "friends of the research." Just as Andy Warhol would give a screen test to just about anyone who wandered into his factory, so Kinsey would film the solitary or social sex acts of just about anyone who would let him. But he especially valued the "rare" ones. One of these was a gynecologist, Dr. Alice Spears, capable of "from fifteen to twenty orgasms in twenty minutes." "Even the most casual contact could arouse a sexual response in her. Observing her both in masturbation and intercourse, we found that in intercourse her first orgasm occurred within two to five seconds after entry."[12]

In filming sex, Kinsey was only doing what Masters and Johnson would later do with married couples in their laboratory. However, his way of doing it blurred the line between objective, distanced science, and a much more involved, subjective "participant observation," since both he and his collaborators sometimes appeared in the films. The budget for this filming was cleverly disguised under the category "mammalian studies" and did, indeed, begin as a collection of how other kinds of mammals "do it"—films of porcupines had been particularly valued.[13]

For some, Kinsey's sexual proclivities, combined with his filming, utterly disqualified him as a scientist and made him complicit with criminals.[14] One recent biographer, James Jones, argues that Kinsey was a masochistic, homosexual voyeur possessed entirely by his demons. The real motivation for all his research, Jones insists, was to see if others were like him. Jones asserts that Kinsey's real interest was prurience, not science.[15] Jonathan Gathorne-Hardy, another recent biographer, disagrees. He does not deny that Kinsey had homosexual encounters, nor that he engaged in masochistic acts, nor that he liked to watch others have sex. He asserts, rather, that Kinsey was a bisexual who fluctuated on his own scale, but whose interest in diverse sexual practices is what enabled him to extract valuable histories from homosexuals and other minority sexualities in the first place.

Media scholar Thomas Waugh argues, from yet another direction, that Kinsey's problem was that he did not admit to the prurience that inevitably informed his work and that Waugh himself believes should be a fundamental principle of all "gay cultural and sexual research." Sexual science, Waugh insists, is inseparable from eroticism.[16] Waugh adds that Kinsey, in addition to being the voyeur and auditor, as well as sometime participant, in a number of these films was also their ultimate director, the grand *metteur-en-scène*.[17]

Of course, Kinsey could hardly have received funding as a proudly eroticized homosexual researcher. He is perhaps best viewed as a scientist, as a sexually interested observer, *and* as an interested participant in the sex he studied. Contra Jones and with Waugh—though with less condemnation—I believe we should no more dismiss Kinsey's science than the eroticism that fed its interest. If Kinsey was a protopornographic filmmaker, he was also interested in detailing the kinds of gestures and acts that were often faked by prostitutes or in the stag films often featuring the same "working women" of his own era.[18] However one judges Kinsey's objectivity or prurience, one only has to read the descriptions of orgasm in the female volume to recognize that behind all the graphs of respiration and blood pressure stands the kind of observation that could only have come from getting closer to the acts that literal "screening sex" afforded. Kinsey writes:

> Prostitutes who attempt to deceive (jive) their patrons, or unresponsive wives who similarly attempt to make their husbands believe that they are enjoying their coitus, fall into an error because they assume that an erotically aroused person would look happy and pleased and should smile and become increasingly alert as he or she approaches the culmination of the act. On the contrary, an individual who is really responding is as incapable of looking happy as the individual who is being tortured.[19]

He continues, "Fully 84 percent of the females in the sample who had masturbated had depended chiefly on labial and clitoral stimulation. . . . All the evidence indicates that the vaginal walls are quite insensitive in the great majority of females."[20] Kinsey concludes, contra Freud, that vaginal orgasm is a physical and physiologic impossibility that has no relation to maturity.[21]

Kinsey, however, was not in the business of fixing what was wrong with the practice of sex among heterosexual couples. Masters and Johnson, who duplicated many of Kinsey's "discoveries," concentrated on just this problem of sexual satisfaction among monogamous, heterosexual married couples. With their first book, *Human Sexual Response*, published in 1966, Masters and Johnson confirmed many aspects of Kinsey's groundbreaking work. Like Kinsey, they rhetorically stressed the similarities of male and female sexual response, while actually detailing some remarkable differences such as the fact that women could orgasm both more frequently and much longer than men.[22] Like Kinsey, also, they debunked the vaginal orgasm, asserting that "clitoral and vaginal orgasms are not separate biologic entities."[23] And like Kinsey as well, they watched and filmed sex, even placing internal electrodes to measure response. Perhaps most threatening to established hierarchies of male and female sexual response was their observation that "maximum physiologic intensity of orgasmic response" had been achieved through "self regulated mechanical or automanipulative techniques." The second-greatest intensity was achieved through "partner manipulation," and a poor third was achieved "during coition."[24] However, unlike Kinsey, they closed down Kinsey's openness to varieties of sexual "outlets," basing their study on only 694 white, middle-class heterosexual men and women.

There had been no major women's movement to absorb the lessons of Kinsey, but by the time Masters and Johnson reached print, feminists were immediately drawing inferences that may not have been consistent with the researchers' essentially masculinist and monogamous perspectives. Mary Jane Sherfey, a psychoanalyst who had studied with Kinsey as an undergraduate, was the first: "Theoretically," she asserted, "a woman could go on having orgasms indefinitely if physical exhaustion did not intervene."[25] This much Masters and Johnson would have agreed with, but she departed from the goal of their therapy when she added, "Neither men nor women, but especially not women, are biologically built for the single-spouse, monogamous marital structure."[26]

In a mood of even greater insurgency, the feminist activist Anne Koedt proclaimed, in a famous pamphlet widely circulated at radical meetings long before it was published, that if vaginal penetration is not the cause of orgasm, then women have been falsely "defined sexually in terms of what pleases men; our own biology has not been properly analyzed."[27] According to this reasoning, what was needed was thus nothing short of a redefinition of women's sexuality and a rejection of former androcentric concepts of "normal": "New techniques must be used or devised which transform this particular aspect of our current sexual exploitation."[28] Yet another feminist, Barbara Seaman, further drew out Sherfey's lesson of indefinite orgasm: "*The more a woman does, the more she can, and the more she can, the more she wants to*. Masters and Johnson claim that they have observed females experiencing six or more orgasms during intercourse and up to fifty or more during masturbation with a vibrator."[29]

No wonder the pornographer Gerard Damiano had, by 1972, been able to weave an entire film around cultural anxieties about female orgasm in his epoch-making *Deep Throat*. And no wonder that, in the early seventies after the great success of his film, Damiano proclaimed the need for "insertions and cum shots"—the only way he could imagine "real sex"—in mainstream Hollywood fare: "Look at Jane Fonda in *Klute*," he exclaimed, "hardcore sex belonged in that picture."[30] In pointing to the absence of hardcore sex in *Klute* (1971), Damiano was challenging the mainstream film industry to do what many observers of Hollywood at the time believed inevitable: the integration of hardcore sex into Hollywood films, though tellingly he could only imagine it in the formulaic way of pornography, as "insertions and cum shots." Though no such hardcore sex would materialize, it would be Jane Fonda, not Damiano's Linda Lovelace, who would pioneer the representation of female orgasm in mainstream films. In the rest of this chapter, I will trace the advent of a new kind of female carnal knowledge through Fonda's career of sexual performances, arguing that it was precisely Fonda's association with the antiwar injunction to "make love, not war," that was central to her role in the critique of phallocentric sex.

Jane Fonda, daughter of Henry,[31] is perhaps best known today for two highly mediated public roles: first as "Hanoi Jane," the antiwar activist whose opposition to the war was demonstrated in a highly publicized visit to Hanoi in July 1972[32]; second, as the guru of the home video workout, which, beginning in 1982, popularized aerobic workouts for women, utilizing the same video technology that would also bring hardcore pornography into the home. Fonda's highly disciplined, "worked out" body became an icon of do-it-yourself fitness that was every bit as big a "household word" as Linda Lovelace had been in the previous decade. It is not accidental that it was this icon who was the very first to play women characters whose orgasms mattered.

Jane Fonda's Orgasms

Jane Fonda's orgasms take on significance against the background of all the above-mentioned factors: highly sexualized antiwar activism; new discourses of sexology questioning the causes and the nature of female orgasm; feminist revision of these discourses; and the new appearance, in hardcore pornography, of explicit sex acts. In 1969 Pauline Kael reviewed the film *They Shoot Horses, Don't They?* with the observation that Fonda, who had been a "charming, witty nudie cutie in recent years," now "goes all the way" with an archetypal character, "as screen actresses rarely do once they become stars." "Jane Fonda stands a good chance of personifying American tensions and dominating our movies in the seventies."[33] Dominate she would.

Fonda had once been informed by the great stage director Joshua Logan that she would "never be a dramatic actress with that nose, too cute for drama."[34] It was this "cute" starlet who was invited to France in 1963 to make a film with Roger Vadim, whose . . . *And God Created Woman* (1956), starring Brigitte Bardot, had inaugurated a whole new era of sophisticated, if not exactly graphic, European screen sexuality. Vadim was a contemporary of the French New Wave artists, but unlike them he was unabashedly commercial. He celebrated a particularly French kind of sensual pleasure in the first film version of *Les liasons dangereuses* (1959), in a "racy" remake of Max Ophuls's *La Ronde* (1964), and in the quite remarkable and little-known *The Game Is Over* (1966, *La curée*).[35] Vadim rarely pictured graphic sex, but he was fascinated by female sensuality and did not always find it necessary, as Hollywood films of roughly the same era did, to punish female protagonists for their pursuit of sexual pleasure.[36] For a six-year period, overlapping with her career as a proto-Hollywood star in such films as *Cat Ballou* (1965), *Any Wednesday* (1966), and *Barefoot in the Park* (1967), Fonda worked in France under the tutelage of Vadim, whom she eventually married.

To his great credit, Vadim did not try to make Fonda into an American version of Bardot. What he did instead, with a screenplay authored by satirist Terry Southern, was to capitalize on her American innocence while asking her to disrobe in suggestive, but never frontally nude, ways. The credit sequence of the French-Italian coproduction, *Barbarella: Queen of the Galaxy* (1968), was emblematic: intergalactic traveler Barbarella strips off her space suit while floating weightless in space. The letters of the credits hide crucial body parts. The peeling off, or decorous shredding, of already skimpy outfits constitutes the primary visual pleasure of this film about an earthling ignorant of the "old-fashioned" sexual pleasures derived from bodily friction. Earthlings, we learn, had long ago given up such primitive "distractions." But when a hirsute, virile representative of another galaxy insists on old-fashioned friction, Barbarella is pleasantly surprised. All we see, however, is a state of extreme, presumably postcoital, satisfaction. Another sexual episode—this time with the smooth, well-built flesh of the angel Pygar (John Phillip Law)—further convinces her that old-fashioned sex has its charms. But like the first scene, this one too is elided: all we see is a postcoital Barbarella, relaxed and humming, stroking herself with a feather from Pygar's wing.

By the time Barbarella arrives at her third sexual encounter, this time with a bumbling revolutionary, Dildano, played by David Hemmings, she is eager to engage again in this supposedly retrograde activity. But Dildano is a modern man who insists that she engage in the more proper pill-induced "exaltation transference." After ingesting the transference pellets, they face one another, fully clothed, and touch only their palms, which gradually begin to smoke as their faces reveal mild pleasure. The "climax" for each appears to be a moment when their hair curls and stands up, though Dildano's hair curls more.[37] At one point the slightly bored Barbarella drops her hand, but then politely reengages.

Barbarella's plot is usually dismissed as a silly excuse to maneuver Jane Fonda into various stages of undress. This it ably does, but it is worth noting that Southern's script hinges upon Barbarella's mission to locate and eliminate a "positronic ray," possessed by the villainous Durand-Durand, which threatens the peace of the universe. It is thus to avert war that the future Hanoi Jane undertakes her mission. Our sci-fi heroine makes love, the old-fashioned way (off-screen), and averts war (on-screen) by disarming the power-mad megalomaniac Durand-Durand. But if *Barbarella* is strangely modest about the portrayal of sexual acts compared to the exhibitionist display of its heroine's body, it is especially innovative in its approach to female orgasm.

Caught in the clutches of the villain, whose peace-shattering weapon it is her mission to destroy, Barbarella is placed in a number of vaguely S/M torture devices. The most important is a futuristic version of an old-fashioned single-person steam bath from which only her head, neck—and later her upper chest—protrude. This rubber tent is attached to an organ (the musical kind) whose keys the villain plays. His plan is for Barbarella to die of pleasure from the sound vibrations caused by his playing. In "playing the organ," he thus proposes to "play" Barbarella herself—to death. What we then see is a nonexplicit extended "sex" scene in which the feminist inference drawn from Masters and Johnson is dramatized: "The more a woman does, the more she can, and the more she can, the more she wants to."[38]

As Durand-Durand begins to "play his organ," Barbarella sighs and her eyes widen as one-by-one items of her clothes are spit out at the bottom of the "Exsexive Machine." "It's sort of nice, isn't it?" she asks. "Yes," replies the sly villain, "it *is* nice . . . in the beginning." Though more of her upper body will gradually protrude from the steam-bath-like contraption, it is her face that registers the surprise of successive degrees of pleasure as the music builds. "When we reach the crescendo you will die," promises the villain. Big death—real death—is supposed to follow the excess—exsex—of the little death (*petite mort*) of orgasm. But the more frenetically the villain plays the organ as the music reaches one crescendo after another, the more it becomes apparent that Barbarella can "take" whatever pleasures it offers. In the end, it is the machine that dies. "Theoretically," as Mary Jane Sherfey put it, "a woman could go on having orgasms indefinitely."[39]

In this scene a finite, masculine concept of sexual pleasure as climax and crescendo—the quintessentially French and male concept of orgasm as a kind of finite petite mort—comes up against the lessons of Kinsey, Masters and Johnson, and feminist sexological revisions of female sexual pleasure as potentially infinite. The more the machine tries to kill her with pleasure, the more Barbarella relaxes and enjoys. Soon the tubes feeding the sound into the cubicle shrink, and the connections smoke and burn. Yet another mad male scientist's experiment has gone awry. "Wretched, wretched girl!" exclaims Durand-Durand, "What have you done to my Exsexive Machine?! You've undone it! You've undone *me!*

Fig. 2.2 Barbarella (Jane Fonda) can "take" whatever pleasure's Durand-Durand's "Exsexive Machine" has to offer. (Digital frame enlargement.)

Look! The energy cables are shrinking! You've turned them into *faggots!* You've burned out the Exsexive Machine! You've blown all its fuses!" The snickering double entendre of Terry Southern's script is evident in every word of this monologue, but the words are superfluous compared to the ever-widening eyes, open mouth, and growing beads of sweat on Barbarella's face (figure 2.2). This is one point in the film in which Fonda's face, not the game of peekaboo with her seminaked body, counts. And it is the expression on this face that presciently prefigures all of Fonda's subsequent performances of orgasm. What it reveals is Kinsey's insight that "an individual who is really responding is as incapable of looking happy as the individual who is being tortured." Such is the first (American) face of female orgasm on the American screen.

Although many have noted the campy sets and sexual innuendo of much of the film's dialogue, and though some have drawn a connection between the "Exsexive Machine" and Woody Allen's later "orgasmatron" in *Sleeper* (1973), no one has noted the sheer temporal duration of this scene or the fact that it only ends when the machine itself dies. Barbarella's pleasure endures as the machine steams up and sputters out. If the film carefully elides all views of heterosexual coitus as pelvic thrusting—more chastely, in fact, than American films of the same era—it does not elide the orgasm presumed to be the end point of sexual pleasure. Nor does it presume that this orgasm can simply be represented as a single crescendo or climax. Rather, it is suggested as something that goes on and on, beyond the capacity of the machine to control. In its own very "sixties" way, then, and in a way that will carry over, though in a much more serious mode, into Fonda's film career post-1960s, the future Hanoi Jane uses her orgasmic capacity to expose the warlike villain and his death machine as impotent and to celebrate herself as orgasmically triumphant. Make love, not war, indeed!

In the introduction to his book about Victorian pornography, first published in 1964, Steven Marcus introduced an image derived from Masters and Johnson that he considered symptomatic of the new era of twentieth-century pornography that was on the rise at the time of his writing. Noting that Masters and Johnson had "discovered" the "orgasmic capacities of women," he points out the aptness of this discovery for an era of postindustrial advanced capitalism: "It can hardly be an accident . . . that the idea of large or virtually unlimited female orgasmic capacity should act as a centrally organizing image of our time. [It] corresponds exquisitely to the needs of a society based on mass consumption. It is in effect a perfect image of mass consumption—particularly if we add to this image the further details that she is probably masturbating alone, with the aid of a mechanical-electrical instrument."[40] Fonda's Barbarella is not exactly masturbating alone, but she does have the aid of a "mechanical-electrical instrument" in the form of the Exsexive Machine. As such she seems to be an important precursor of the image of the future that so worries Marcus, perhaps as much as it worries Durand-Durand: the multiply orgasmic woman in no need of heterosexual coitus.[41]

In her autobiography, *My Life So Far*, Jane Fonda places the *Barbarella*, of 1968, as the last chapter of the first of the three acts of her life: here, the sex kitten Jane, shaped by the Pygmalion, Vadim. The second act, which begins with a chapter entitled "1968," is called "Seeking." It tells the story of her political awakening. This act would eventually be presided over by a very different Pygmalion in the form of Tom Hayden, former leader of Students for a Democratic Society. But before Hayden makes his entrance, Fonda describes witnessing some of the events of May 1968 as interpreted and explained by her sometime mentor, French actress and left-wing activist Simone Signoret. In this phase of her life, Fonda becomes pregnant, goes to an antiwar rally in Paris with Signoret, and at the latter's prodding, reads Jonathan Shell's story of the "pacification" of the village of Ben Suc in his book by that title. She learns of France's own sorry history of Vietnamese colonialism, begins to contemplate the significance of her father's legacy as an icon of American democracy in his roles as Lincoln and Tom Joad, and from there is gradually drawn into the movement of American GI war resisters.[42] Signoret, who was also a friend of Henry Fonda, is reported by Fonda to have maintained a belief that "what she loved about my father from his movie roles was waiting inside *me* to manifest itself through action."[43]

This action becomes manifest in antiwar political action as well as in the roles she takes on when she "comes home" to the United States, first to make *They Shoot Horses, Don't They?* then Alan Pakula's *Klute* (1971) and eventually the aptly named *Coming Home* (1978), directed by Hal Ashby. It would be in the latter two films that Fonda's orgasms would take on narrative relevance and no longer in the context of the "nudie-cutie" pleasure machine that was *Barbarella*. Thus whereas *Barbarella, Klute*, and *Coming Home* would all make female orgasm central to their story, it would only be the American films that would take on the challenge of how to represent orgasm in more realistic, socially embedded contexts beyond the sniggering joke of an "Exsexive Machine" but also without encroaching on the emerging territory of hardcore pornography.

How, then, did the mainstream New Hollywood cinema portray sexual acts now that the Production Code no longer necessitated the elision of all sex except the briefest of kisses? How did it portray a sex that could now be presumed to "go all the way" and that no longer need end with the cut away from, or fade out on, a kiss?[44] With the new MPAA ratings in place since 1968 there was now a category, R, that could permit the limited display of what would come to be called "simulated"—as opposed to hardcore—sex. However, that limited display had, even before the rise of the ratings system, fallen into a fairly predictable pattern of representation that I call the *Hollywood musical interlude*.[45] It is that pattern that Fonda's orgasms would disrupt, if not definitively shatter.

The Hollywood musical interlude is a formula that was forged perhaps most memorably by *The Graduate* as early as 1967. It was Hollywood's presumably "tasteful" way of suggesting carnal knowledge. This knowledge is *revealed* (we are certain the couple does have sex; no coy fade-out or narrative obfuscation typical of the Production Code years) yet simultaneously *concealed* (we are not asked to confront the visual fact of genital action). In theater history an interlude was a short humorous play between the acts of a more serious miracle or morality play. But one of the term's primary meanings is also musical: the instrumental music played between the sung parts of a song.[46] Either way, an interlude offers a break with the normal flow of drama or music. In movies before the 1960s it was conventional, in addition to the usual scoring of Romantic music throughout a film, to add interludes in the form of songs sung by performers within the narrative (for example, Dooley Wilson singing "As Time Goes By" in *Casablanca*). But in the 1960s, films began to appropriate a new model for importing a wide range of pop music into their very fabric. They moved away from "monothematic scores"—single themes that return in dramatic situations—and toward "multitheme" formats: new or old pop songs that underscore the film, often to highly edited montages.[47] The popularity of the song could thus contribute to the popularity of the film. This move to "underscore" movies and even to sell them with entire compilation scores was especially attractive to younger audiences. These lyrical montages (in some ways prefigurations of music videos) tended to stop the narrative flow of the film in order to "sell," or at least let viewers enjoy, the song.[48]

It is precisely in these lyrical montages, montages in which music amps up and narrative amps down, that a certain palatable form of carnal knowledge first found its way into mainstream American film. Indeed, the conjunction of music and sex, as opposed to the presentation of sex acts with little or no music, is enormously important in the history of cinematic sexual representation. When the sounds of sex became audible for the first time without the cover of music, and when the kind of affective control offered by musical interlude was not deployed, then a new kind of "nakedness" became available to films, even when the characters having sex were clothed. The smooch of a kiss, the smack of a slap, the slurp of fellatio or cunnilingus, the whoosh of penetration—not to mention the sighs, moans or outright cries generated by sexual connection—make the sex that is seen seem all the more proximate to the viewer-listener. Where Hollywood sound cinema was quick to provide "sound effects" for the physical blows of fight scenes, it was not equally quick to provide sound "synch points" for carnal encounters. Indeed, the trope of the musical sexual interlude seems partly designed as a new way of screening out components of sex acts that were nevertheless becoming necessary to present. We do well to recognize that *bracketing off* carnal knowledge from the rest of the film is what the music and editing of the sexual interlude does. Within this bracket, intimate sexual relations reside in a different register of time, space, and sound. Just as romantic kisses in the silent or sound film almost never occurred without soaring music, so it would prove extremely rare for post-Code Hollywood films to depict carnal knowledge without affectively controlling, and reassuring, audience response with musical accompaniment. When we do get sex without the soaring musical interlude, it usually seems more "naked," more "real," even though the acts represented remain simulated.

Something closer to this zero degree of nakedness is what we find in Jane Fonda's post-*Barbarella* American film performances of orgasm. However, it would first be through the discovery of ways of depicting nonorgasmic sex—often figured as "bad" sex displayed without music or bracketed editing, eschewing the celebratory, lyrical format of the sexual

Fig. 2.3 Bree (Jane Fonda) checks her watch while she fakes an orgasm with a client in *Klute* (1971). (Digital frame enlargement.)

interlude—that Hollywood would eventually find a new way to portray sex beyond these conventions.

"Bad" sex in Hollywood had previously been portrayed as the sex the woman did not want to have. By the early 1970s, however, it began to encompass another meaning: inauthentic or faked sex. Fonda's Oscar-winning performance in *Klute* was one of the first to complicate the sexually promiscuous figure of the femme fatale, usually a figure of villainy. In this film the woman is, in a more traditional sense and despite her sexual identity, "good."[49] Having already proved in *They Shoot Horses Don't They?* that she could act beyond the role of the ingénue, Fonda now proceeded to play Bree Daniels, a high-class call girl stalked by a mysterious killer and protected by a strong, silent cop-turned-private detective named Klute (Donald Sutherland). Bree's orgasms, both faked and real, would matter to this narrative, though only the faked, "bad," ones would be enacted. In an early scene, Bree has sex with a client. Pro that she is, she is fully in control of the orchestration of his pleasure through the semblance of her own. At the moment of her supposed orgasm she offers a patently fake show of enthusiasm while slyly glancing at her watch (figure 2.3). Analytic sessions with a female psychiatrist make this point even clearer: Bree confesses that real sexual pleasure would threaten her control over the scene.

Both Molly Haskell and Pauline Kael's reviews of *Klute* discuss this early scene of "bad" sex. Kael knowingly complains that the timing is off—realistically Bree would have looked at her watch before, not during, the faked orgasm. Haskell, for her part, notes what kind of toll such a performance exacts: "As any woman who has ever faked an orgasm knows, it's too easy to count as a great performance and too cynical not to leave behind some poison."[50] Although both critics score important points in the evaluation of the film, what is most striking is that two influential women critics of the early seventies, themselves informed by discourses of sexology and its feminist critique, now find it possible to argue about the realism of a performance of "bad" sex. They recognize it when they see it.

"Good" sex would be the new post-Code, Hollywood, answer to "bad." This may constitute a terribly impoverished range compared to the sexual performances emerging at that same time outside the Hollywood mainstream;[51] it is nevertheless fascinating to watch Fonda "progress" from the comic "exsexes" of *Barbarella* to the theatrically fake orgasms of *Klute* and finally to a more "politically correct" portrayal of simulated "good" sex in the later *Coming Home*. In *Klute*, Bree explains to her female analyst that in her affair with Klute she is fighting having real orgasms for fear of losing control. Indeed, in a scene that might seem initially to be the "good" sex antidote to the faked orgasm with the client, the two sleep on narrow adjacent mattresses in Klute's basement apartment after Bree has been frightened by a death threat. In the middle of the night Bree silently climbs onto Klute's mattress and seduces him.

The scene is striking in its stark simplicity. There is no fancy editing, no musical accompaniment, and only one ellipsis that takes us from a preliminary stage of seduction to thrusting man-on-top, woman-on-bottom missionary sex. Until we see the triumphant look of control on Bree's face as Klute expresses his (muted) pleasure, we may think that this *is* the "good" sex—at least she does not look at her watch. But the triumph is too smug, and she taunts him afterward with the knowledge that she did not come—"I never do with johns." This is her way of asserting control over a man she feels tempted to love. "Good" sex is not shown, but it is hinted at in an extended bit of "sex talk" spoken by Bree in a long monologue to her analyst, of which I excerpt a part:

> I enjoy, uh, making love with him, which is a very baffling and bewildering thing for me because I'd never felt that way before. I just wish I could let things happen and enjoy it for what it is and while it lasts and relax with it. But all the time I keep feeling the need to destroy it . . . to go back to the comfort of being numb. . . . I had more control with tricks . . . At least I knew what I was doing when I was setting things up. . . . It's so strange, the sensation that is flowing from me naturally to somebody else without it being prettied up. I mean, he's seen me horrible. He's seen me mean, whorey and it doesn't seem to matter; he seems to accept me and I guess having sex with somebody and feeling those sorts of feelings is very new to me.

Bree's words could almost be taken as Hollywood's best advice to itself on how to present sexual relations that capture a sense of a charge flowing between two bodies, without the buffer of musical interlude, without the abstraction of tight editing, and "without it being prettied up" in the usual Hollywood ways. *Klute* itself does not take that plunge beyond this verbalization, but toward the end of the decade Jane Fonda would again perform brief, "bad," nonorgasmic sex in yet another Academy Award–winning performance, in *Coming Home*. This time, however, the bad would be answered by a good that would break the pattern of most previous Hollywood portrayals of sex, while also addressing the question of whether what Anne Koedt called "certain sexual positions now defined as 'standard'" deserved to be so defined.[52]

Hal Ashby's *Coming Home* is not an antiwar film of the late 1960s. Rather, it is an antiwar film made in the late 1970s, after the Vietnam War was over, but looking back at the late 1960s. Early in the film Sally (Fonda) has perfunctory farewell sex with her Marine captain husband Bob (Bruce Dern), before he departs to Vietnam. In the dark of their bedroom, Sally lies still under Bob's body. Her eyes are open and her hands are folded on his dog tags, as he pushes tamely, passionlessly into her, emitting only a muted couple of grunts at the end. Sally does not fake orgasm; she simply holds still and passively takes what her husband gives.

An adulterous affair will be the occasion to counter this "bad" marital sex and to render shy Sally more independent. She volunteers at the hospital and develops a friendship with Luke (Jon Voight), a paraplegic Vet who channels his anger and shame about his participation in the war into antiwar activism. After Luke chains himself to the Marine base gate to protest conditions in the veterans' hospital, Sally asks to spend the night with him. In a scene almost perfectly designed to illustrate the argument of Anne Koedt's "The Myth of the Vaginal Orgasm," she achieves her first orgasm with Luke, a man paralyzed and without sensation from the waist down.

The scene begins with Luke emerging from the bathroom of his apartment in his wheelchair with only a towel draped over his crotch. Sally, still in a trench coat, helps him onto his bed and turns off the light. "Turn on the light," says Luke, "I want to see you." What follows is almost a lesson in synesthesia designed for movies. Luke informs Sally that he can't feel when she touches him (down there) but he can see. Sight, in a solution that neatly coincides with the needs of an audience screening sex, thus partly substitutes for touch in a sex scene that has a legitimate excuse to leave the light on.[53]

Fig. 2.4 Sally (Jane Fonda) and Luke (Jon Voight) negotiate new ways of touching, feeling, and looking in *Coming Home* (1978). (Digital frame enlargement.)

The first image after the light goes back on is a goldenly lit shot of the now naked couple in a tight clinch. "What can I do?" asks Sally. "Everything, I want you to do everything," answers Luke. This invitation implies a liberation from the usual temporality of a sex act that in hardcore films would progress through a certain amount of quick foreplay toward the predictable end in male orgasm and ejaculation presumed to signal the end of the female's pleasure as well. In the new, bracketed, musical interludes of post-Code Hollywood, this trajectory would be similar but the foreplay would be extended and the thrusting would be both simulated and truncated. Without this usual telos, the trajectory of the encounter is now up for grabs; we cannot assume what this sex will be. Thus when, in the next shot, we see a more distant view of Sally, her back to us astride Luke, we cannot assume that he is penetrating her (see below). At this point, the polymorphous perversity of the body in its entirety, which Herbert Marcuse had called for in *Eros and Civilization*, seems to have a chance to emerge as the couple negotiates new ways of touching, feeling, and looking (figure 2.4).

However we construe the sex that Luke and Sally have, it is emphatically not that of active, phallic thrusting. We see Luke kissing lower and lower parts of Sally's anatomy in what we may assume, but cannot confirm to be, cunnilingus. And what we hear is Sally's delighted, encouraging direction: "Oh softly!" It would seem that hard, phallic thrusting is the last thing on her mind. Were this a scene in hardcore pornography, the injunction from the penetratee to the penetrator would inevitably be "harder!" "Softer" suggests a sex of delicacy in which less movement, force, size, hardness might seem more. The following shot shows Sally's legs convulsing as they wrap around Luke's seriously scarred back. We surmise from where her feet are that his face, not visible, must now be at her genitals. A cut to her face reveals the wide eyes, and some panting convulsive movements and a series of long "ohhhs" reminiscent of Barbarella's encounter with the "Exsexive Machine." When Luke says "You're so beautiful"—again asserting that his primary pleasure is visual—Sally for a short while just goes on convulsing, raising the question of when this "sex act" might end. It does end, however, after they have embraced and held one another for a while, when Sally says, perhaps unnecessarily, "It's never happened to me before." Here, finally, is the end-of-the-decade's "good" sex that answers both Bree Daniels's hurried sex with a client in *Klute*, and Sally's passive, unresponsive sex with her husband at the beginning of *Coming Home*.

In her autobiography Jane Fonda explains that she and Jon Voight met with Vietnam veteran paraplegics and their girlfriends in preparation for their roles in the film to learn the various ways they had sex. In the process of the research, they were surprised to learn that the men were capable of occasional, unpredictable erections. She writes that until learning this, "genital penetration was not something I had considered possible between my character and Jon's."[54] Nor was she interested in portraying this somewhat rare possibility. She was more interested in finding "a dramatic way to redefine manhood beyond the traditional, goal-oriented reliance on the phallus to a new shared intimacy and pleasure my character had never experienced with her husband."[55] Hal Ashby, however, was determined to portray the sex as precisely an achievement of rare penetrative virility. Voight, for his part, agreed with Fonda that the sex scene would be more adventurous if the assumption was that his character did not have an erection and the sex was nonpenetrative.

Thus began what Fonda calls the "Battle of Penetration." Ashby had already directed Fonda's body double in the nude scenes to move as if she were being pleasurably penetrated, whereas Fonda in her own flesh refused to match those actions. The "climax" of the battle occurred in the final day of shooting the scene when she was on top of Voight and Ashby yelled at her "Ride him! Dammit! Ride him!" while Fonda, holding on to her concept of the scene, refused to play jockey. In Ashby's conception, Sally was astride Luke, who had achieved an erection. In Fonda's conception the climax of the scene was Sally's experience of oral sex. The double who acted in the long shots had been directed to "ride," whereas Fonda, in the closer shots, refused. According to Fonda, the two do not match. I would argue, rather, that they look like two phases of the couple's lovemaking, a first in which Sally is on top and could be "riding" Luke—but perhaps his thigh, not his penis—and a later phase that consists of cunnilingus and in which Fonda achieves orgasm. At this point most of Luke's body is "below," out of frame. From the evidence on the screen, I'd say Fonda won the "battle" of the depiction of this particular orgasm as resulting from nonpenetrative sex. However, one sex scene in one Hollywood film could hardly win the larger war of gender equity in screening sex. Though Sally does give evidence of a prolonged and continuous pleasure that does not have the same rhythm and telos of phallic sex, her "performance" ultimately operates to restore a semblance of masculinity to an initially emasculated veteran.[56]

Perhaps the only way to truly challenge what still remains the dominant phallic discourse of sex would have been to question the very notion of orgasm itself as the "be all and end all" of pleasure, or as the "ultimate truth" of sex for women. For in both these phrases is embedded the notion of a singular end pleasure—a climax, or as Durand-Durand would put it, a "crescendo"—that contradicts the very notion of the polymorphous and the multiple.

As feminist researcher Annie Potts demonstrates, the language of orgasm, even the more "enlightened" female-aware language of sexologists such as Masters and Johnson, tends to be organized as a teleology of excitement, plateau, and resolution in much the way it is performed by Fonda here: still privileging phallocentric models of thrusting and getting "there." Men are often portrayed as getting there too soon and women too late, if at all.[57] Potts attempts to deconstruct the binaries by showing how the privileged term of presence (getting there) is dependent on the absence of a later "falling away" from presence, of the end of orgasm.[58] Potts herself advocates a discourse of sex in which climax would not be regarded as the only source of true intimacy and a general "unfixing" of pleasure from any specific organs. This general unfixing of pleasure from any specific organ is similar to Marcuse's call for a more general reactivation of all erotogenic zones, not just the genitals.

It would be unfair to ask Fonda alone to point the way to a brave future of such deconstructed orgasm. Perhaps a simpler way to approach the problem of the figuration of orgasm(s) in this film would be to recall a somewhat simpler model for thinking about all sexual pleasure. Leo Bersani's argument that often the "pleasurable and unpleasurable tension of sexual stimulation seeks not to be released in discharge but to be increased—as in a clitoral, prolonged, way of thinking of orgasm as an excitement that prolongs itself and, in Potts's terms, reintroduces the concept of desire."[59] In other words, the hydraulic model of orgasm, which views it as mounting tension concluded by an explosion of release, can be complicated by another model of sexual excitations that seek nothing more than their own intensification and that might do so, as Sally requests, quite "softly." The "scratch" model of sexual pleasure aims at satisfaction in discharge, at hitting a specific target, or "spot." The scratch always presumes a thrusting and a targeted, focused tactility of one erogenous zone upon another. The "itch," on the other hand, is much less specifically targeted; it is ultimately whatever manages to keep desire in play. The scratch model of orgasm has obviously been the dominant, phallocentric term of much sexology and much cinema. It took an antiwar movie about a paraplegic to begin to figure the pleasure of the itch in mainstream Hollywood: anticipation, prolongation, intensification, but not necessarily hard, not necessarily discharged—to begin to challenge the dominant phallocentric model of going all the way.

Coming Home received mixed reviews but substantial recognition at Oscar time (for both Voight and Fonda as well as the screenplay). Critics were divided by the lightning rod of "Hanoi Jane" playing a docile Marine wife whose political and sexual transformation moves politically in the direction of . . . well, Jane Fonda. They were also divided about the film's focus on Sally's orgasms as well as its use of rock music from the 1960s to underscore many scenes. Vincent Canby called the film "soggy with sound"—"a nonstop collection of yesterday's song hits."[60] Pauline Kael agreed, arguing that Ashby "has filled in the dead spaces by throwing a blanket of rock songs over everything."[61] David James, writing in the early 1990s, nevertheless made an important case for the film's use of rock and roll, pointing out that though there have been many American films about the devastation of American soldiers who fought in Vietnam—and no feature-length fictional films about the devastation of the Vietnamese—this film's "unequivocal assertion" that the invasion of Vietnam was "*wrong* distinguishes it from all other films made in Hollywood."[62]

What no one seemed to notice, however, was that music was for once *not* applied to the sex scenes. Indeed, these sex scenes (orgasmic or not) were sometimes the only times in the movie when nondiegetic music did *not* accompany the action. Relative silence ruled, punctuated by the sounds of sex (the opposite of the musical sexual interlude's typical blocking out of such sounds), and that simple fact gave the sex scenes—admired or not—a more dramatically integrated status than the standard interlude. What some critics, Canby included, may really have been objecting to in the derogation of the film as a "women's picture" may not only be its politically tinged melodrama, but the postsexual revolution mutation of a love story that details a woman's sexual pleasure without that pleasure being contained in the usual ways.[63]

It is fascinating to watch American critics come to grips with an American — not European — screen sex that goes all the way. Kael, for example, undergoes an interesting change of mind in the course of her review. At first she seems to follow Canby's judgment and to trivialize the achievement-of-orgasm plot: "*Coming Home* started out to be about how the Vietnam War changed Americans, and turned into a movie about a woman married to a hawk who has her first orgasm when she goes to bed with a paraplegic."[64] In the end, however, Kael does not deride the importance of this new "women's picture" subject matter. More organically, she argues that the film does not quite deliver on the logic and motivation of its sexual subject. Contrasting the look on Sally's face when she had open-eyed sex with her husband, to the look when she also had open-eyed sex with Luke, Kael writes that the situation fairly demands that her husband discover her infidelity through the new way she would make love when they next have sex. In essence, this comment reduces to the question: Could the woman who now "really" makes love do so with a man who desperately wants to believe in the good of making war? Since the film does not depict such a scene, it, according to Kael, fails its subject.

Whether one agrees with Kael or not, the important point is that in the course of her review she begins to take the dramatic matter of the orgasm seriously, not just as something to be discussed (as in *Klute*), but as something to be represented and corporeally understood. After initially making fun of the importance of Sally's orgasm weighed against the disillusionment of Vietnam, Kael implicitly recognizes that how Fonda has sex with her two different partners represents a new cinematic codification of carnal knowledge now demanding to be respected on its own cinematic and dramatic terms. Kael's insight is to see that that first climax required yet another sex scene with Sally's husband. Without actually noting that sexual performance had now become relevant to a mainstream Hollywood film with major stars, Kael tacitly grants that a Hollywood film can use simulated sexual performance to express the complex psychology and "drives" of its characters and perhaps something more nuanced than simply "bad" or "good" sex. She also implicitly acknowledges, through her very demand for yet another sex scene, that screening sex up to and including the quality and kind of orgasm conjoins with interest in character and narrative and was now a valid expectation at the movies. Thus in 1978, three years after the American withdrawal from Vietnam, American audiences could finally understand and accept the axiom that had been the basis of my generation's activism: "Make love, not war."

*

In a documentary film by Rosanna Arquette, *Searching for Debra Winger* (2002), about the pressures of being a woman, a mother, and an actor in Hollywood, Jane Fonda provides the concluding interview. Centered on well-known female stars who had found plenty of work while young and dwindling opportunity once they hit their forties, Fonda and Vanessa Redgrave are the mature survivors whose life stories often serve as inspiration to the questioning Arquette and her cohort. Fonda freely admits that she was a bad mother who never balanced parenthood, career, and antiwar activism. But the point at which she becomes most animated, and the reason her interview concludes the documentary, is her vivid description of the eight or so times in her life when she has entered the magic "circle of light" on the movie set, when all light and energy focuses on the main actor as a kind of "eye of the hurricane." In those moments of greatest fear and tension, when one manages, perhaps just a few times in one's career, to deliver a great performance, it has all, Fonda asserts, been worth it. What is interesting, however, is that Fonda describes both the unsuccessful and the successful performances in sexual terms, first as bad sex and then as good. What if you give too much in rehearsal and "blow your wad," leaving nothing for the shoot? What, she speculates, if in the shooting you "can't get it up"? On the other hand, she eagerly describes how thrilling it is to "hit your mark" with all channels open, like a "plane taking off," "like a dance, both with the other actors and the camera and loving your co-star"; "it's this wonderful fusion . . . better than any lovemaking."[65]

It may seem surprising that Fonda sexualizes the craft and the art of acting in such extremely phallocentric terms, given her contribution to our understanding of orgasm as something more than "blowing your wad." Good feminist and antiwar activist that she is, Fonda is obviously still subject to the dominant discourses of sexuality. And if "getting it up" and "hitting the mark" are the metaphors that work, we should not demand that she also tell us how she lets go and relaxes into it. We can forgive an actor whose sexual performances were as crucial to the cinematic knowledge of sex in the 1970s and perhaps as important and influential in their own female sphere as Marlon Brando's animal sexuality was in his. It does not seem accidental that the quintessential American sexuality of both actors was forged, early in Fonda's career, later in the older

Brando's, in relation to European, and specifically French-associated, movies. Both actors brought coming—each in their own, gender-based way—"home" to our movies.

Notes

1. David Allyn, *Make Love, Not War: The Sexual Revolution. An Unfettered History* (Boston: Little, Brown and Company, 2000), 127.

2. Herbert Marcuse, *Eros and Civilization: A Philosophical Inquiry into Freud* (New York: Vintage, 1955), 174, 184.

3. Marcuse, *Eros and Civilization*, 184.

4. Lynne Segal, *Straight Sex: Rethinking the Politics of Pleasure* (Berkeley: University of California Press, 1994), 31.

5. Jonathan Gathorne-Hardy, *Sex, the Measure of All Things: A Life of Alfred C. Kinsey* (Bloomington: Indiana University Press, 1998), 121.

6. Kinsey pointed out "that the clitoris at this point is stimulated, thus providing the erotic stimulation necessary for the completion of the act on the part of the female." Gathorne-Hardy, *Sex, the Measure of All Things*, 126.

7. Kinsey discovered, as Gathorne-Hardy notes, that the "mere fact of *saying* sexual intercourse, coitus, masturbation, clitoris, orgasm, etc., in a society where even the word sex was barely mentionable, and in which 'venereal disease' had just been banned on radio, was enough to shock his audiences into electrified attention." *Sex, the Measure of All Things*, 126.

8. Gathorne-Hardy, *Sex, the Measure of All Things*, 171.

9. For example, before marriage, Kinsey calculated that the average male had experienced 1,523 orgasms whereas the average woman only 223. After marriage he calculated that most husbands achieved orgasm in almost all acts of intercourse whereas wives only 39 percent of the time. Segal, *Straight Sex*, 90. See also Kinsey, et al., *Sexual Behavior in the Human Female* (Philadelphia: W. B. Saunders, 1953).

10. Gathorne-Hardy, *Sex, the Measure of All Things*, 308; Kinsey et al., *Sexual Behavior in the Human Female*, 634.

11. Gathorne-Hardy, *Sex, the Measure of All Things*, 307.

12. Wardell Pomeroy, as quoted in Gathorne-Hardy, *Sex, the Measure of All Things*, 315. This was all the more surprising in that Spears had not had her first orgasm until she was forty and was in her sixties at the time of filming. Kinsey shot a total of seven hours of films with Spears performing with a great many different partners drawn from his entire team of male researchers, including himself. According to Gathorne-Hardy, Kinsey himself had a sexual liaison with Spears and remained friends for many years after.

13. No one knew about the human films until the 1972 publication of collaborator Wardell Pomeroy's biography of Kinsey. Had they known, Kinsey would have instantly lost his funding—as he would do soon enough after the publication

of the female volume. Kinsey's "attic films"—which meticulously recorded not only female orgasms, but male/male and female/female homosexual relations as well as scenes of sadomasochistic sex—are of obvious interest to any history of screening sex in America, and it is regrettable that the Kinsey Institute does not permit their study today. Gathorne-Hardy, *Sex, the Measure of All Things*, 333.

14. Judith Reisman, leader of a group called Restoring Social Virtue and Purity to America, has particularly targeted Kinsey as the cause of a pro-sex agenda that has, as one of her books puts it, been *"Crafting 'Gay' Children."* These claims give Kinsey an awful lot of credit—as if one man could cause a sexual revolution, let alone an epidemic of sexually transmitted diseases. Reisman's claim that Kinsey based a portion of his research upon a sexually voracious pedophile blames Kinsey for acts committed and entered in a diary long before Kinsey began research. See www.defendthefamily.com_docs/resources /6390601.pdf.

15. James H. Jones, *Alfred C. Kinsey: A Public/Private Life* (New York: W. W. Norton, 1997).

16. Thomas Waugh, *Hard to Imagine: Gay Male Eroticism in Photography and Film from Their Beginnings to Stonewall* (New York: Columbia University Press, 1996), 398.

17. Waugh, *Hard to Imagine*, 400.

18. For a discussion of stag films as an archive of sex work, see my essay, "'White Slavery' versus the Thenography of 'Sexworkers': Women in Stag Films at the Kinsey Archive," *Moving Image* 5, no. 2 (fall 2005): 106–139.

19. Kinsey et al., *Sexual Behavior in the Human Female*, 606.

20. Kinsey et al., *Sexual Behavior in the Human Female*, 580.

21. He writes, "There is no evidence that the vagina responds in orgasm as a separate organ and apart from the total body." Kinsey et al., *Sexual Behavior in the Human Female*, 582–583.

22. They write, "The female is capable of rapid return to orgasm immediately following an orgasmic experience," and "the female is capable of maintaining an orgasmic experience for a relatively long period of time," Masters and Johnson, *Human Sexual Response* (New York: Bantam, 1966), 131. Lynne Segal comments: "They in fact recorded so many physiological differences between men and women that their decision to emphasize similarities was clearly ideological." Segal, *Straight Sex*, 93.

23. Masters and Johnson, *Human Sexual Response*, 67.

24. Masters and Johnson, *Human Sexual Response*, 132.

25. Mary Jane Sherfey, "A Theory of Female Sexuality," in *Sexual Revolution*, ed. Jeffrey Escoffier, 91–99 (New York: Thunder's Mouth Press, 2003), 91.

26. Sherfey, "A Theory of Female Sexuality," 93.

27. Anne Koedt, "The Myth of the Vaginal Orgasm," in *Sexual Revolution*, ed. Jeffrey Escoffier (New York: Thunder's Mouth Press, 2003), 199. See also Mas-

ters and Johnson, *Human Sexual Response*; Sherfey, "A Theory of Female Sexuality"; and Barbara Seaman, "Is Woman Insatiable?" in *Sexual Revolution*, ed. Escoffier, 122–142.

28. Koedt, "The Myth of the Vaginal Orgasm," 101.

29. Seaman, "Is Woman Insatiable?" 133.

30. Quoted in Bruce Williamson, "Porno Chic," in *Flesh and Blood: The National Society of Film Critics on Sex, Violence and Censorship*, ed. Peter Keough (San Francisco: Mercury House, 1995), 14.

31. Recognized especially in his work with John Ford — in *Young Mr. Lincoln* (1939), in *The Grapes of Wrath* (1940), and in several Westerns.

32. She is credited with publicly exposing Nixon's potential strategy of bombing the dikes, which would have endangered hundreds of thousands of civilians. Fonda toured the country, made numerous radio speeches to American pilots informing them of the devastation they were wreaking on the country. She was called a liar and, after being photographed sitting on anti-aircraft turrets, was accused of treason. But her efforts did expose and avert the plan to bomb the dikes. Jane Fonda, *My Life So Far* (New York: Random House, 2005), 291–333.

33. Quoted in Fonda, *My Life So Far*, 216.

34. Fonda, *My Life So Far*, 128.

35. This film stars Fonda as a woman whose quasi-incestuous affair with her husband's son proves her undoing.

36. Compare, for example, Hollywood's "celebration" in 1960 of Elizabeth Taylor's sexual charms in Daniel Mann's *Butterfield 8*, which could only end with the demise of Taylor's high-class call girl.

37. We will need to remember this curling of hair. In an era as obsessed with hair as was the "sixties," curled hair on women, long hair on men, would prove a reliable indicator of predilection for pleasure.

38. Seaman, "Is Woman Insatiable?," 133.

39. Sherfey, "A Theory of Female Sexuality," 91.

40. Steven Marcus, *The Other Victorians: A Study of Sexuality and Pornography in Mid-Nineteenth Century England* (New York: New American Library, 1974), xiii–xiv.

41. According to Marcus, nineteenth-century pornography was marked by the wish-fulfilling expenditure of the scarce resource of male semen, "spent" as a utopian reversal of a social and economic economy of scarcity. Now, the multiply orgasmic woman pleasured by an electrical device is no longer a wish-fulfilling reversal of economic reality, but the somewhat scarier embodiment of that reality itself: postindustrial consumption. I have argued elsewhere that Marcus invokes a curious double standard in his utopian model of nineteenth-century (male economic) "pornotopia" and his comparatively dystopian (female economic) pornography, which implicitly represents pleasurable female self-sufficiency as depressing reality. See Williams, *Hard Core: Power, Pleasure and the "Frenzy of the Visible,"* exp. ed. (Berkeley: University of California Press, 1999), 108–110.

42. Fonda, *My Life So Far*, 176–304.

43. Fonda, *My Life So Far*, 197.

44. See my essay on the movie's kiss, "Of Kisses and Ellipses: The Long Adolescence of American Movies," *Critical Inquiry* 32, no. 2 (winter 2006): 288–340.

45. See my discussion of mainstream Hollywood's various ways of "going all the way" in chap. 2 of *Screening Sex* (Durham, NC: Duke University Press, 2008). The following three paragraphs adapt the discussion from that chapter.

46. *Webster's New World Dictionary*, 735.

47. An example would be the "Can't Buy Me Love" montage of the Beatles 1964 film *A Hard Day's Night*. See Jeff Smith, *The Sounds of Commerce: Marketing Popular Film Music* (New York: Columbia University Press, 1998). See also, Russell Lack, *Twenty Four Frames Under: A Buried History of Film Music* (London: Quartet, 1997).

48. Jeff Smith's example, in *The Sounds of Commerce*, is the playful montage to "Raindrops Keep Fallin' on My Head" in *Butch Cassidy and the Sundance Kid* (1969).

49. See Linda Ruth Williams's discussion of the film in her book *The Erotic Thriller in Contemporary Cinema* (Bloomington: Indiana University Press, 2005), 118.

50. Both Kael and Haskell praise the psychological nuances of Fonda's performance. Kael, "Pipe Dream," *New Yorker*, July 3, 1978, 40; Haskell, "Review of *Klute*," *Village Voice*, July 15, 1971, 55.

51. For example, in hardcore pornography, European art film, and the American avant-garde, not to mention Nicolas Roeg's remarkably adult "pensive" coupling in *Don't Look Now* (1973).

52. Koedt, "The Myth of the Vaginal Orgasm," 101.

53. Contrast *The Graduate*: Benjamin slams the door, the screen grows dark, and the film then shows everything but what happens in the bed between them.

54. Fonda, *My Life So Far*, 371.

55. Fonda, *My Life So Far*, 371.

56. Fonda, *My Life So Far*, 375. Ron Kovic, the paraplegic antiwar vet who had served as inspiration for the character of Luke, later told Fonda that the film had improved his sex life.

57. See Annie Potts, "The Day the Earth Stood Still," in *The Science/Fiction of Sex: Feminist Deconstruction and the Vocabularies of Heterosex* (New York: Routledge, 2002), 79–100. For example, Potts shows how many women especially value female ejaculation, which one woman calls "coming like a guy," 85.

58. Potts, *The Science/Fiction of Sex*, 90–100.

59. Leo Bersani, *The Freudian Body: Psychoanalysis and Art* (New York: Columbia University Press, 1986), 34.

60. Vincent Canby, "Coming Home," *New York Times*, February 16, 1978.

61. Pauline Kael, "Mythologizing the 60's *Coming Home*," *New Yorker*, February 20, 1978, 120.

62. David James, "Rock and Roll in Representation of the Invasion of Vietnam," *Representations* 29 (1990): 90.

63. In fact, there is just the faintest possible sound of music presented as if from an off-screen diegetic source, playing ever so "softly" under this scene. I have not been able to recognize it.
64. Kael, "Mythologizing the 60's *Coming Home*."
65. *Searching for Debra Winger* (2002).

3 ✳ The New Sexual Culture of American Television in the 1970s

ELANA LEVINE

Histories of the sexual revolution in America often address the ways that the changes in sexual mores, practices, and beliefs peaking in the 1960s and 1970s helped to shape, and were in turn shaped by, media and popular culture. Typically, such accounts are concerned with the appearance of radical or bold displays of sexuality, as in the nudity on stage in productions of *Hair* or *Oh! Calcutta!*, or the hardcore depictions of oral sex in *Deep Throat* (1972). It is not only the explicitness of such instances that makes them notable, but also their mainstream popularity. The fact that graphic advice books such as *The Joy of Sex* (1972) could be "tossed into the grocery shopping bag with the asparagus,"[1] or that porn films could play in first-run and art house theaters, has made such phenomena all the more significant to the historical record. Apart from brief mentions of a risqué talk-show guest or a suggestive commercial, however, the most popular, most mainstream medium of this era has received little to no attention as either a symptom or an instigator of the sexual revolution.

In the late 1960s and throughout the 1970s, television was a central force in the mediation of the sexual revolution. From the sexual innuendo of *Laugh-In*'s one-liners to the double entendres of *Three's Company*'s roommates, from the exposés of teenage prostitution in made-for-TV movies to the examinations of rape in daytime soap operas, sex suffused American television. In fact, I argue that television, as embodied primarily in the era's three national broadcast networks, did more than any other popular cultural form to translate the sexual revolution to mainstream America. Why, then, has it received so little attention in histories of the period, including in the rest of this book?

Television's engagement with the sexual revolution was qualitatively different from that of most other media. As an advertiser-supported, government-regulated site with a reputation for being family friendly, television of the late 1960s and 1970s would never reach the radical boldness of such cultural forms as live stage performance, sound recording, or feature film. The constraints keeping such content from reaching the airwaves were too deeply rooted in the very structure of the system. Thus it is difficult to see television's treatment of the sexual revolution as anywhere near as revolutionary as the presence of explicit sexual content elsewhere in the culture. But perhaps counting only those cultural products that seem "revolutionary" misses a key part of the sexual revolution's permeation of American culture during this period. The sexual content that came to television in the late 1960s and 1970s marked a significant shift in that medium's handling of sex. The new sexual culture of television of the 1970s not only changed television; it changed the way in which American society would represent the results of the sexual revolution up to the present day.

This chapter offers an overview of television's translation of the sexual revolution for the American mainstream, with a more specific analysis of the work of one television producer and executive, Douglas S. Cramer, as a case study of how television constructed its vision of a world altered by sexual revolution. Elsewhere, I have examined this process in great detail,[2] and it would of course be impossible for me to do justice in one chapter to the ways in which a medium with an output as vast as that of American television grappled with sexual change. I intend for the broad strokes with which I paint television's role in the first part of this chapter to achieve more detailed definition in the case study of the later part.

Before I proceed with my overview, I'd like to offer some general parameters for thinking about television's place in the new sexual culture of the 1960s and 1970s. Television's embrace of changes in sexual mores, practices, or beliefs came a bit later than did the appearance of such changes in other media and cultural sites. Despite some experimentation with sexually bolder content in the late 1960s, it would take until the middle and late 1970s for those experiments to become an established part of the images and stories television presented. In this way, it is possible to conceive of television's participation in the mediation of the sexual revolution as part of a broader commercialization of sexual change that various writers have lamented as signaling the end of the revolution's radical potential.[3]

Whether commercialization itself is detrimental is a subject for another discussion, but in the case of television embracing some of the primary changes brought about by the sexual revolution—the questioning of monogamy, the recognition of gay and lesbian sexualities, the awareness of women's sexual autonomy—commercialization via television most surely helped lead to a deradicalization. Changes such as these did find a place on American broadcast network television during this period, so television's address of the sexual revolution was not simply a matter of repression. Instead, in its treatment of such subjects, television programming found ways to make them safer, less disruptive, and less of a challenge to the dominant social institutions of patriarchy, heterosexuality, and monogamy. That said, it is also important to recognize that the coming of these markers of sexual change to TV did indicate that change of some kind would be permanent, or at least that dominant understandings of sex and gender would be altered. The incremental shifts in sensibility, awareness, and acceptance visible in television programming would help to assure a new status for such shifts that would alter American culture for years to come.

Sexual Content across the Television Schedule

Television's turn to more overt discussion and representation of sex in the late 1960s and the 1970s took place across the television schedule, at all times of day and night, and in all kinds of genres. My focus is primarily on entertainment programming, as this is the programming that commanded the largest mainstream audience and that featured much of the medium's sexual content. Such programming was the product of numerous influences. These contextual factors not only shaped that which appeared on television; they also shaped viewers' experiences of what they watched.

Like most instances of television programming, the turn to sex in the later 1960s and the 1970s was primarily motivated by the broadcast networks' drive for profits. This period marks an especially competitive moment between the "Big Three"—ABC, NBC, and CBS—in which their traditional standings were upset. During this period, ABC, the perennially third-place network, would rise to number one in the Nielsen ratings, in large part because of the network's embrace of sexually suggestive humor and other elements of television's new sexual culture. Competitive pressure led to certain innovations, as in CBS's early attempts in the 1970s to address some of the social issues of the day—the sexual revolution included—in new sitcoms such as *All in the Family*. The same could be said of ABC's efforts to counterprogram CBS with sillier, more seemingly escapist fare that referenced changing ideas about sex as, for example, in the use of nostalgia for the 1950s in *Happy Days* as a family-friendly veneer encasing double entendres and sexually suggestive humor. As is typical of American broadcast television, competitive pressure encouraged at least as much imitation as it did innovation; consequently the success of *Charlie's Angels* on ABC led that network, and the other two, to try out a number of mostly unsuccessful pilots for series that copied *Angels'* action heroine/sex symbol formula.[4] As these examples illustrate, network competition is one important context for explaining how and why the broadcast networks embraced sexual content in the late 1960s and the 1970s.

There were multiple forces guiding the kind of programming the networks offered, some of which ran counter to the networks' profit motives. Government pressure to limit representations of violence increased in the late 1960s, particularly in the wake of the assassinations of Martin Luther King Jr. and Robert F. Kennedy, as well as the confrontation between protestors and police at the Democratic National Convention in Chicago in 1968, more disturbing news from the war in Vietnam, and escalating race-based conflagrations in America's inner cities. Forty-nine members of the House of Representatives introduced resolutions calling for the Federal Communications Commission (FCC) to study the effects of TV violence on the public,[5] and Senator John Pastore convened his Communications Subcommittee in March 1969 to ask the surgeon general to take on the matter.[6] Through such initial calls for study and the subsequent hearings in which their results were presented, government regulators questioned not only the effects of TV violence, but the moral propriety of television content more generally, a turn that often included concerns about sex. Indeed, during the 1969 hearings, Pastore remarked of the broadcast networks, "I don't think there is so much competition on the showing of violence as there is on the showing of sex," a concern he threaded throughout his subcommittee's pursuit of the violence question.[7]

This sort of regulatory attention, which filtered down through Congress to the FCC; the TV industry's self-regulating organization, the National Association of Broadcasters; and the networks' own standards and practices departments, helped shape television content in particular ways. For example, some have argued that the pressure to tone down violent content led to an increase in sexual fare.[8] Elsewhere, I have argued that the suggestive, rather than explicit, treatment of sex in so much television of the 1970s is at least in part due to efforts by producers and networks to gingerly sidestep these sorts of regulatory concerns.[9] Whatever their specific impact, the regulatory debates about television content during this period had a part in shaping television's representation of the sexual revolution.

Within the broader rubrics of economic and regulatory forces were such specific pressures as those imposed by advertisers nervous about public reaction or, alternately, eager to draw attention with risqué fare. Also pertinent in this period were the pressures asserted by a number of different advocacy groups made up of citizens placing demands on broadcasters for different kinds of representations. These groups came from multiple political persuasions, with interests such as the National Gay Task Force or the National Organization for Women applying pressure from the liberal side, and organizations such as the National Federation for Decency and the Coalition for Better Television pursuing a religiously motivated conservative agenda.[10] In all of these cases, U.S. citizens and institutions sought to use television's new sexual culture as a means to an end. The changes brought by the sexual revolution and increasingly addressed on TV were controversial matters, revealing a number of different entities' investments in questions of sexual beliefs and practices.

What, then, were some of the ways in which entertainment programming addressed the sexual revolution from the late 1960s through the 1970s, in this climate of pressure and debate about television's role? Here, I will briefly outline four different strands of the networks' sex-themed content, beginning with the newest television format of the period, the made-for-TV movie. Although NBC had been airing movies made exclusively for television since 1964, telefilms became a significant part of the prime time schedule only once ABC debuted its *Movie of the Week* in 1969.[11] The ABC network sought to differentiate the movies it offered from those on NBC, which tended toward action-adventure and suspense genres.[12] Despite that some of ABC's films fell into those genres as well, the network also licensed comedies and social issue dramas. Films in each of the latter categories often dealt with subjects such as women's liberation, sexual promiscuity, and divorce. Comedies included *Playmates* (October 3, 1972), in which two divorced men secretly date each other's ex-wives; social issue dramas included films such as *Mr. and Mrs. Bo Jo Jones* (November 16, 1971), which dealt with teen pregnancy.[13] Although most of ABC's sex-themed social issue films were seen as exploitative, some achieved acclaim for their thoughtful consideration of contemporary life. Perhaps the best example of this is *That Certain Summer* (November 1, 1972), in which a gay, divorced father comes out to his fourteen-year-old son, a film widely praised for its sensitive treatment of gay male experience.

As the other two networks began to schedule made-for-TV movies to compete with ABC's successful series, high-profile, critically awarded material continued to air. But those movies and miniseries served as a respectable cover of sorts for the more exploitative fare all three networks broadcast throughout the 1970s. These films tended to follow the mode of the classical exploitation cinema of the early twentieth century in that they were largely driven by a moral panic around young people's (especially young women's) sexual endangerment.[14] In numerous telefilms featuring teenage runaways-turned-prostitutes, hitchhikers, victims of stalking and rape, and centerfold models, all three networks combined the titillating and the cautionary to address the perceived dangers of the sexual revolution. As producer Douglas S. Cramer was involved in the creation of some of these very films (e.g., *Dawn: Portrait of a Teenage Runaway, Nightmare in Badham County*), I will analyze a more specific example of these tendencies in the later part of this chapter.

Alongside the made-for-TV movies taking on the social issues of the sexual revolution in a range of ways was another new development of this period: the centering of women characters as protagonists in action-oriented series. There had been only the occasional instance of a woman in such a role before the 1970s, but during this period such characters became essential to the new sexual culture television offered. This is because these characters were not simply action heroines. Instead, they were extremely popular sex symbols, achieving their fame not only through their TV series but also through revealing pin-up posters and other star publicity. The most successful of these characters were the leads for ABC's *Charlie's Angels* (1976–1981); many attempts to clone their winning formula appeared throughout the second part of the 1970s. This trend was important to television's new sexual culture for the ways that it negotiated the women's liberation movement and debates both within the movement and between the movement and its detractors about the question of sexual difference. In asserting these women characters' status as symbols of heterosexual male fantasy, such programming made the representation of liberated women taking on conventionally masculine roles (detectives, superheroes, and the like) less threatening, even appealing, to a mass audience potentially uncomfortable with the ways the women's movement was shaking up traditional sex and gender roles. By making purportedly liberated women symbols of the new sexual openness and freedom, both women's liberation and sexual revolution could fit into patriarchal and heteronormative perspectives.

The sex symbol heroines of action-adventure shows were accompanied by a host of female sex symbol characters in more comedic contexts, as well. Here, the intimations of liberation that attended characters such as the Angels or Wonder Woman could be ignored, as the characters' status as sex objects became their primary narrative function. In series such as *Three's Company, The Dukes of Hazzard*, and *Too Close for Comfort*, the female sex symbol lived on in a more comedic vein.[15] The comedic turn in the representation of sexy young women by the late 1970s was in keeping with a trend in television's sexual content since the late 1960s—a trend of employing sexually suggestive humor to reference the sexual revolution and the changes it had brought without violating any of the medium's family-friendly parameters. As I will discuss in more detail below, sexual humor was one of the earliest and most frequent ways in which television addressed the sexual revolution. This sort of comedy appeared in sitcoms, of course, but it was also rampant in other genres, especially variety and game shows. *Match Game*, airing both on CBS daytime and in syndication, was one such show. Here, two contestants competed to match the answers offered by six celebrity panelists to a question featuring a suggestive "blank," for example, "A giant turtle tried to 'blank' a Volkswagen," or "The magician brought his 'blank' to bed with him." Although the panelists would offer a number of risqué answers, they were typically in the form of suggestive allusion or double entendre. Thus, the raciest elements of the show required the viewer's complicity; his or her understanding of the new sexual culture would make the references sexually meaningful and thereby comedic. *Match Game* was premised on this brand of humor, but much of the sexual humor across television programs and genres relied upon a similar formula.

I do not mean to suggest that television only represented the sexual revolution in exploitative, sexist, or juvenile ways. In each of the kinds of programming I have mentioned thus far, there were instances of thoughtful reflection and commentary on the changed and changing times, as well as endorsements of some of the more open sexual attitudes and practices that marked the sexual revolution. Perhaps the best example of this sort of reflection on social change appeared in daytime programming, a less culturally prominent sphere in which many of the changes of the new sexual culture could be more carefully considered. This could be the case in daytime talk shows, such as *Donahue*, in which the avowedly feminist male host addressed issues and concerns affecting women in particular, including divorce and female sexual satisfaction. Television also offered a forum for the consideration of sexual change in its daytime soap operas, in which (i.e., hetero) sexual relationships received extensive attention. In my work on this subject, I have explored in particular the ways in which the daytime soaps of the 1970s grappled with the meaning of rape and sexual violence at a time in which sexual promiscuity and antirape activism competed for public acceptance.[16] In these and other instances across the television schedule, the sexual revolution was debated and discussed, helping to make television a key site for the widespread dissemination of ideas about sexual change.

Negotiating Sexual Change: The Work of Douglas S. Cramer

To establish a more specific picture of the ways that broadcast network television of the late 1960s and the 1970s grappled with the sexual revolution, in the rest of this chapter I focus on a number of programs that spoke to such matters as premarital sex, divorce, promiscuity, rape, prostitution, and homosexuality. My focus is specific to the career of Douglas S. Cramer, who worked for Paramount as a production executive in the late 1960s, and went on to form his own production company as well as work for Aaron Spelling Productions in the 1970s.[17] As a production executive or an executive producer, Cramer had a hand in many different instances of television programming that spoke to and about sexual change, though little in his public or archived statements suggests any particular commitment to such issues. Instead, Cramer's career is marked by a savvy business sense, his ability to discover, embrace, and carry out that which can attain mass popularity. As he has claimed of the popular success of one of his series, "When *Love Boat* set sail everyone was terrified to do three stories in an hour; it would be more than an audience could accept. Nobody has ever given the audience much credit in TV, but we did and it worked."[18] The fact that so many of the shows he produced dealt with sexual themes is thus perhaps most attributable to his (and Spelling's) ability to generate and sustain program formulas that had mass appeal. In the late 1960s and the 1970s, mass appeal was often connected to the changing sexual culture; thus, many of Cramer's successes also evidence that culture. Cramer's work and influence were felt across a number of television genres, but in what follows I examine two key examples, the first being his work on comedic anthology series and the second being his work on made-for-TV movies. In both cases, Cramer's productions directly addressed the new sexual culture and in so doing helped to construct what the television version of that culture would be.

As a production executive at Paramount, Cramer supervised the creation of one of American television's first attempts at sexually suggestive humor, *Love, American Style* (1969–1974, ABC). He would borrow a similar formula for *The Love Boat* (1977–1986, ABC) later in the 1970s. Both series followed a comedic anthology story structure; they also shared a tone and a stance on sexual openness. Both series successfully walked the line between acknowledging sexual change and staying safely within television's boundaries of acceptability. Using humor and comedic situations to defuse the potential radicalness of their sexual representations, these series sought to make "love" and "sex" synonymous terms, capitalizing upon the wholesomeness of the former while trafficking in the edginess of the latter. Although they had much in common, each was a product of its specific historical moment: *Love, American Style* of the television industry's initial forays into sexual themes, and *The Love Boat* of the institutionalization of such themes, and their transformation into the naturalized, hegemonic logic of television's new sexual culture.

Love, American Style was part of ABC's attempts late in the 1960s to make itself a viable competitor in the TV industry's three-network system, an effort that led the network frequently to draw upon sexually suggestive humor as a means of distinguishing itself from its competitors. The network's first attempt at sexual humor was *Turn-On*, a variety series canceled after its February 1969 debut and widely agreed to be a colossal failure. The program was ABC's effort to clone NBC's topical, comedic hit *Laugh-In* (the producers of which also created *Turn-On*), but *Turn-On* was to even further emphasize sexual humor. This strategy of ABC's backfired when many saw the broadcast as taking that sexual humor too far. As the general manager of a Cleveland station claimed, "It may be all right to be racy, but this was plain dirty. This was a hate show. Its spirit was dirty."[19]

Failing to extend *Laugh-In*'s formula in an even more sexually explicit direction, ABC changed tactics for the season of 1969–1970, continuing to pursue sexual material as a way to reach young viewers but placing that material in other formats and taking a somewhat different tack in those formats' handling of sex. *Love, American Style* was part of this attempt, but it was paired with another, rather different ABC effort to use sex as an attention-getter. This series, *The Survivors*, was created by novelist Harold Robbins and was touted as one of his typically sexy works of fiction, but this time made for television as a serialized narrative. *The Survivors* was heralded as innovative because of its format, but also for its degree of sexual openness, particularly for television. Robbins described the series as "a story of today's morals," insisting that "if people go to bed together, they'll go to bed together on the show. We are not bowing down to TV in any way."[20] The overt sexiness promised by *The Survivors* was too risky a tactic for ABC to rely solely upon it, and so the network paired *The Survivors* with *Love, American Style* on its Monday night schedule. When *The Survivors* suffered multiple production problems and received poor ratings, ABC cancelled it midseason, suggesting that Robbins's strategy of ignoring television's typical conservatism was a misstep. *Love, American Style* was part of the same sex-centered strategy, but its approach to sexual openness proved the longest-lasting of these early attempts at sexual themes. Indeed, the *Love, American Style* formula would presage the explosion of sex-themed programming a bit later in the 1970s, particularly the comedic sort, and particularly that scheduled by ABC.

Love, American Style was not a new effort just because it dealt with sex; it was also seen as innovative because it was an anthology series, with each week's hour-long episode typically made up of two to three longer sketches with brief blackout gags interspersed throughout. Perhaps because of this unusual format, or because of ABC's investment in differentiating the series from *The Survivors* and *Turn-On*, its predebut promotion was the source of some conflict. *Love*'s producers initially planned to include a recurring motif in each story as a means of tying the show's disparate elements together. This motif was to be a bed that would be visible at some point in each sketch, even if in the background or through a window. However, when an ABC press release about the new show highlighted the fact that the program would have just "one continuing character—a large brass bed,"[21] speculation began that that bed "would hardly ever be empty, particularly in the concluding minutes of each yarn," leading to "a new low in video morality."[22] Because the controversy over *Turn-On* was so recently past, and because Robbins was so publicly touting his new show's sexual openness, ABC surely hoped that *Love* would draw some less sensational attention. Given that concerns about television's sexual and violent content were also rampant during this period (Senator Pastore referenced *Turn-On* specifically in the 1969 hearings),[23] it is no wonder that *Love*'s producers quickly sought to spin the impression of their series as morally suspect in a different direction. Thus producer Bill D'Angelo proclaimed, "People got the idea that the darned bed was the symbol of our show, ergo sex was the symbol of the show"; "the bed became something we never set out to make it. Our stories, honestly, aren't that kind of thing at all, but stories which we hope people will enjoy and laugh at."[24] Executive producer Arnold Margolin tried to make light of the controversy, claiming "Some people think we're doing 'The Erotic Life of the American Housewife.'" In contrast, he insisted, "This is a comedy show. We try to do stories which have relevance to today."[25] The producers thus sought to emphasize the comedic content of their series, asserting that comedy would be their means of achieving timeliness, even on sexual matters, and that they would thereby avoid the sexual explicitness that "the bed" had come to symbolize.

Very early in *Love, American Style*'s public life, then—even before its broadcast debut—the network and the show's producers found themselves struggling with a way to balance the program's more salacious, and thereby more attention-grabbing, potential with reassurances that the program would not go too far in its "relevant" storytelling, that it would offer a TV-friendly (and thus family-friendly) version of the sexual revolution that would not upset the advertisers, politicians, or home viewers who were uncomfortable with the recent, profound changes in sexual mores. The series ultimately managed to avert its potential public relations crisis; the bed ceased to be mentioned in network press releases, and its planned use as a motif was dropped. But *Love, American Style* also managed to balance the seemingly incompatible identities that had led to the conflicted meanings of the bed in the first place. In so doing, it set a precedent for the comedic treatment of sex across television of the 1970s.

The series made clear that its handling of sex marked it as a new kind of TV, all the while reinforcing conventional sexual morality. This is especially evident in a second-season sketch called "Love and the Only Child," which starred sitcom stars of the 1950s (and real-life married couple) Ozzie and Harriett Nelson as middle-aged parents preparing to divorce now that their only child is grown and married. Just as they are readying their move out of their house, however, their daughter Ellen comes home, announcing that she has left her husband. When her husband, played by *Leave It to Beaver*'s big brother, Tony Dow, arrives, hoping to save their marriage, the parents reveal their secret. The two had married originally because the woman was pregnant, and they stayed together for their daughter's sake. When Ellen reveals to her husband that *she* is now pregnant, not only does the younger couple reconcile but so too do Ellen's parents, more than happy to stay married for the sake of their imminent grandchild. Placing these icons of suburban domesticity and marital monogamy from the 1950s in such a sketch alone serves as commentary on the changing times (figure 3.1). The suggestion that the Ozzie and Harriett of yesteryear had premarital sex gently mocks the conservatism of the 1950s; including a *Leave It to Beaver* cast member even further marks its difference from the earlier era. When Dow's character remarks, "Gee, I didn't think that happened back in those days," in response to his in-laws' revelation, it is as if Wally Cleaver's naiveté has been transplanted into the middle of the sexual revolution, a world apart from where the character, and television itself, began. As such, the sketch manages to mark itself as contemporary, relevant, and even a bit daring, speaking so openly about pregnancy, divorce, and, most shockingly, premarital sex. Yet the story manages to contain these disruptions at the same time. After all, both couples are clearly happier with the idea of staying married than they are with the possibility of divorce, and out-of-wedlock pregnancy remains a somewhat shameful secret. As Ellen's

Fig. 3.1 The sexual revolution affects icons of television in the 1950s and marital stability Ozzie and Harriet Nelson, who play a divorcing couple dealing with the marital troubles of their adult daughter (Heather North) in *Love, American Style*'s "Love and the Only Child" (1971).

mother tells her before revealing her story, "You're a married woman now and you know everything, so I might as well tell you." Despite her own experience with premarital sex, pregnancy, and (initially) unwanted marriage, the Harriett Nelson character—and the sketch as a whole— hold up marriage not only as the romantic ideal, but also as the gateway to adulthood and the sexual knowledge that comes with it. *Love, American Style* regularly made suggestive nods at sexual change, but just as regularly managed to hold that change in check, indicating that this so-called revolution was not so revolutionary, after all.

Cramer would repeat this formula to even greater success when he produced *The Love Boat* for Aaron Spelling Productions later in the 1970s. This series compromised a bit on the anthology format from the first *Love* series; the titular cruise ship's crew as the continuing characters anchored the three anthology-style stories per episode. Much like the first *Love* series, *The Love Boat* typically relied upon the humor of sexual suggestion to make its nods to the new sexual culture while remaining safely ensconced within traditional moral codes validating heterosexual monogamy and the institution of marriage. By the late 1970s, this formula had become key to ABC's ratings success, as the network by then had risen to first place. This success, however, did not mean that the formula was an effortless mix. In fact, the efforts Cramer and his fellow producers expended in maintaining the balance between family friendliness and sexual suggestion point out how challenging it was to sustain such a combination and yet also how naturalized that very blend had become. By the time of *The Love Boat*'s reign in the late 1970s, family-friendly sexual suggestiveness had become the most widely adopted and accepted version of the new sexual culture on television.

One of the key dictums of executive producer Aaron Spelling was that the most effective comedic treatment depended upon the avoidance of "too much blatant sex." Spelling insisted that humor came from *holding off* on sex, and he thus ordered that the sex in his productions be more suggestive than overt.[26] Douglas Cramer executed Spelling's vision on *The Love Boat* in a range of ways, some of which encouraged the inclusion of sexual material and some of which qualified the kind of sexual content that would work for the series' light tone. For example, he asked of the program's hands-on producers, "Do we have enough titillating, purely sexual stories?"[27] He regularly considered each episode's three plots in relation to one another, making sure that youth and sex were prominently featured in at least one. For instance, he asked of upcoming episodes, "Do *any* of the first six hours have a *love* story for Julie [the ship's young, pretty cruise director]? *Let* the poor girl get laid—please!!"[28] Yet Cramer and his staff were also well aware that "purely sexual stories" were problematic for a series, a network, and an industry that prided themselves on offering family-friendly fare. Thus, the sexual titillation that was so central to *The Love Boat*'s appeal was necessarily couched in light-hearted humor. Indeed, humor and sex were understood to be two sides of the same coin, the former softening the potential shock of the latter. As Cramer commented on an upcoming episode, "What this beautifully emotional script needs most is FUN-HUMOR-LAUGHS-SEX!"[29] Included in the balancing of humor and sex was an old-fashioned morality in which sex, though fun, was never frivolous. Instead, it was always connected to heartfelt emotion, to the "love" of the program's title, much as was the case in *Love, American Style*. Thus, Cramer qualified his call for "purely sexual stories" as "naturally" including "heart and depth."[30]

Cramer so fully believed that *The Love Boat*'s combination of sexual openness and old-fashioned values was a "natural" fit and not an inherent contradiction that he was thrown by a letter he received from a man who identified himself as both an attorney and a father of five daughters. This viewer wrote to complain that he was "continually embarrassed" by the sexual content when he watched a recent *Love Boat* episode with his daughters and that he would keep them from watching future episodes as a result. Although Cramer at first considered ignoring the letter, he found himself bothered by this man's claims, in particular because Cramer believed that this viewer must have turned the TV off before the end of the episode, thereby missing the "*decent* resolution of the stories"—the teenagers considering sex realizing they were too young and the adults in the other two stories ending up in monogamous, loving relationships.[31] Cramer decided to send the man a letter, along with a script of the episode in question. In this correspondence, he did not deny the program's sexual content, but he did insist that "we always point out that sex carries with it a responsibility, and that sex is not love."[32] The fact that Cramer took this viewer's criticisms seriously enough to respond and that he defended the series by insisting that its version of the new sexual culture actually adhered to traditional values illustrates the precarious balance between suggestiveness and wholesomeness that had become so central to this version of TV sex, even if viewers did not always accept that balance as satisfactory.

Cramer's efforts to sustain this balance were somewhat short lived, as ABC asked *The Love Boat*'s producers for more and more sexual content as the series entered its third season, perhaps hoping to revitalize the network's ratings position once CBS began to reclaim some of its former success.[33] The ABC network was no doubt motivated in making such demands by the growing amount of sexual content across prime time, as well as the casual openness about sex permeating American culture more generally as of the late 1970s.[34] Cramer's notes on a fall 1979 script draft are telling of the pressures ABC was putting on the show's producers, as well as of the increasingly narrow ways in which sex was being represented and defined. Cramer began by commenting on a script: "Six months ago, this would have seemed an A+ show—now, I ask (as ABC will) does it have enough *hot* sizzle? Can we tune up the sexuality of the stories? . . . I've made some leering suggestions . . . and bear in mind the request for the Jacuzzi in every show!" His "leering suggestions" included eliminating the T-shirts that the characters Ben and Sally were wearing as they sat up in bed together and having the two kiss and slide down onto the bed at the end of a scene. In a later scene, he suggested that Ben and Sally be wearing bathing suits on deck "or in *hot tub*—best of all!!" He noted places where many of the characters might be dressed in swimsuits, or where couples might kiss.[35] His comments included no mention of the "heart and depth" he had sought in the past.

Concurrent with Cramer's input, *The Love Boat*'s production staff

Fig. 3.2 Sexual suggestion often led characters to the Jacuzzi or the pool on *The Love Boat*. Here guest stars Heather Thomas and Tony Danza show some skin in the "Japan Cruise" episode from show's seventh season. (Digital frame enlargement.)

met in October 1979 to devise additional changes "designed to make the show 'sexier.'" Producer Gordon Farr reiterated Cramer's note about the obligatory Jacuzzi scene in every episode, and the producers planned to include more young women in revealing attire as extras. Even the Pirate Lady statue in the Pirate's Cove lounge was scheduled for a makeover! The line producers were instructed to make sure that scenes on the Lido Deck (by the pool) and in the ship's spa emphasized the "attractive young people" (figure 3.2).[36] By the 1979–1980 season, the formula initiated by *Love, American Style* ten years earlier had seemingly outlived its usefulness. Now that sexual situations and themes, often suggested but rarely fully realized, had become standard fare across genres, networks, and time of day, *The Love Boat* had to go further than before, to embrace more of the "blatant sex" that Spelling had earlier warned against, in order to stand out. The mix of the wholesome and the risqué that had defined the decade's most successful takes on sex had become the new standard.

Cramer's contribution to television's new sexual culture was not confined to the sexual humor offered in comedic anthology series. He was also a prolific producer of made-for-TV movies, which frequently served as pilots for potential new series in the 1970s. Many of Cramer's telefilms grappled with the sexual revolution; these productions examined the darker side of sexual freedom, often by telling stories of young people endangered by their access to the new sexual culture. As I discussed above, this theme was common across many made-for-TV movies of the period, thus I am not blaming or crediting Cramer for its presence. However, the centrality of his work to the perpetuation of this theme further illustrates his role as a representative creator of the new sexual culture of television of the 1970s.

In Cramer's TV movies about sexually endangered youth, as in many such films airing in this period, both the films themselves and the promotion for them wavered between the titillating and the cautionary. Promotions for made-for-TV movies were notoriously sensational in the 1970s, in part because such programming had no chance to build an audience over time but instead needed to generate as much interest as possible for the broadcast premiere. Industry wisdom argued that sexual suggestion was key to drawing such interest. As one CBS executive explained, "You want to hint at sex but not make it too explicit"; "if you combine it with violence, you're golden."[37] This combination was certainly employed in the promotion of Cramer's *Nightmare in Badham County* (November 5, 1976, ABC). The *TV Guide* ad for this film, a story of two college-aged women who find themselves imprisoned at a southern sexual slavery operation when they have car trouble on a cross-country trip, screamed, "SLAVERY IS NOT A THING OF THE PAST!" followed by slightly smaller text that read, "The sadistic sheriff knows it. The psychotic warden knows it. But two girls, alone in a women's prison learn it the hard way."[38] The dual threats of sex and violence are used here both to draw audiences in and to offer a cautionary warning about the dangers of a postsexual revolution society, much as did the promotions for theatrical sexploitation films of the period, albeit in tamer terms.

As much as the networks willingly employed these exploitation tactics to draw audiences, they constantly struggled to justify the movies' scandalous subject matter and to protect themselves against the criticism so rampant in this period of intense regulatory scrutiny on the part of the government, advertisers, and the public. Thus, the film's producers walked a careful line between promising the networks attention-grabbing content and reassuring jittery executives of their films' appropriateness for the "family" medium, a line the networks themselves precariously straddled. In the case of *Nightmare*, ABC executive Brandon Stoddard found its "white slavery aspect" one of its most compelling features.[39] However, when another ABC executive saw rough, more sexually explicit footage meant for the version of *Nightmare* to be distributed overseas, Cramer scrambled to reassure him that the material would never be submitted for U.S. broadcast, describing it as "shoddy," "really vulgar," "tacky and tawdry," and "in no way [representing] something [he] would care to have anyone consider something [he] either approved or condoned."[40]

To meet the networks' dueling desires, producers such as Cramer tended to root their movies in real-world social problems and manipulate their stories in such a way as to fit their more licentious elements under a banner of social responsibility. These efforts are especially clear in Cramer's work on *Dawn: Portrait of a Teenage Runaway* (September 27, 1976, NBC) and its sequel, *Alexander: The Other Side of Dawn* (May 16, 1977, NBC). Cramer pitched *Dawn* to NBC as "an honest, authentic, tasteful, and yet deeply moving picture" on the "serious current problem of teen-age runaways," documenting his seriousness of purpose with newspaper clippings and reports of the scriptwriter's extensive research.[41] His juxtaposition of "honest, authentic, tasteful" with "deeply moving" suggests the contrast between attention to a serious social issue and the entertainment factor meant to appeal to audiences. Yet calling the material "deeply moving" rather than "exciting" or even "gripping" worked to legitimate even the entertainment value of the story as socially responsible art rather than a blatantly commercial exercise, differentiating the TV movie from theatrical sexploitation fare. Cramer also exhibited this effort at accountability in his work on *Alexander*, one of the few such films to deal with a male adolescent under sexual threat. Here, Cramer consulted with Newton Deiter of the Gay Media Task Force and struggled with how to communicate Alex's experiences without too explicitly representing or referencing gay male sexual activity, a turn that would have pushed the network's desire to confront the sexual revolution further than it was willing to go.[42]

In such films, the new sexual culture was primarily represented as menacing, a real danger to young people, especially to innocent young girls such as Dawn. For example, when Dawn first arrives in Los Angeles, having run away from her drunken mother and hard home life, she walks down Hollywood Boulevard. The audience is invited to share her shock at the moral decay the sexual revolution has wrought. As Dawn first leaves the bus station, a man in a suit brushes past her and she is noticeably disturbed. Next, Dawn crosses the street; a man on a motorcycle gestures for her to get on, and she hurries past him. Walking along, Dawn sees a man covered in tattoos, a midget, and an effeminate hippie-type coming out of the International Love Boutique; her eyes widen in surprise. From Dawn's point of view, we see words such as "Massage," "Nudity," "Girls," and "Pussycat" on storefront signs. In the distance, a movie marquee advertises *Deep Throat* and *The Devil in Miss Jones*. At the corner of Hollywood and Vine, a bald, middle-aged white man pulls up in a convertible and asks, "Want a ride?" Moments later, several black men talk to Dawn, trying to block her way. She then passes two young girls, one of whom is visibly pregnant. The sequence ends with Dawn crouched in an alley after being mugged. The message is unavoidable: Dawn has entered a dangerous, licentious world where men seek to exploit her sexually; her fate is to wind up pregnant, destitute, and alone.

Fig. 3.3 Teen runaway turned prostitute Dawn (Eve Plumb) confronts the dark side of the sexual revolution in *Dawn: Portrait of a Teenage Runaway* (1976). (Courtesy Douglas Cramer Collection, Box 22, Press Kit Folder, American Heritage Center, University of Wyoming.)

Dawn does indeed struggle in her new life. Once she is drawn into the world of prostitution by her pimp, Swan, she repeatedly suffers the abuses of her johns and of Swan himself. Her appearance changes from one of fresh innocence to one of hardened resignation. Her tight clothing, garish makeup, and unkempt hair signify her sexual corruption (figure 3.3). Throughout the film, the only source of hope is Dawn's sweet relationship with Alex. The two kids, both victims of the sexually loose streets, fall in love, their relationship carefully differentiated from their sexual interactions with clients. The loving, monogamous, heterosexual relationship between these two characters not only resolves the narratives of both of Cramer's teenage runaway films (*Alexander* ends with the two leaving Los Angeles together, planning to marry and start a new life), but it also heralds the triumph of more conventional sexual ideologies over those of the new sexual culture. In this way, Cramer's TV movies, as well as the others in the subgenre of sexually endangered youth, may have offered an even more conservative take on sexual change than did the sexually suggestive humor of series such as *Love, American Style* and *The Love Boat*.

Television and a Sexual Revolution?

The gradual emergence of sexual themes and references across American broadcast network television from the late 1960s through the 1970s makes television as significant a medium as any other in the cultural saturation of the sexual revolution. Because television's take on the sexual revolution was necessarily constrained by the many forces that make the medium commercially viable, its perspective on sexual change may seem less "revolutionary" than those offered in other media and cultural sites. In certain respects this is true, as television would not offer the explicitness in words or images that other media would until cable in general, and premium cable in particular, took off in the 1980s. Yet the new sexual culture of television of the 1970s played a crucial role in the dissemination of the ideas and practices of the sexual revolution across American society.

I have indicated some of the key ways in which television represented sex in the late 1960s and the 1970s. Because this content was present across the television schedule and throughout a number of genres, it is not possible to offer here a full picture of television and sex in that time. Yet it is possible to illustrate how voluable television was when it came to matters of sexual change. Most of television's discourses of sex tended to deemphasize the radical potential of the sexual revolution, finding ways to make promiscuity, gay and lesbian lifestyles, women's sexual agency, youth sexuality, and nonnormative practices more generally seem like only slight adjustments to the way sex had always been practiced and understood. But this small, partial acknowledgement of change only appeared by virtue of a constant negotiation between televisual discourses denouncing the evils of sexual looseness (as in the stories of sexually endangered youth in made-for-TV movies) and those excitedly contemplating the potential of sexual freedom (as in *Love, American Style*'s playful mocking of TV morality of the 1950s). In the new sexual culture of television of the late 1960s and 1970s, we can see the ways in which the sexual revolution moved from being an emergent culture beginning to disrupt the status quo, to one that becomes incorporated into that very status quo, losing much of its revolutionary potential in the process but nonetheless bringing small increments of change to our ways of thinking, feeling, and seeing sex.

Notes

1. Bob Greene, "Beyond the Sexual Revolution," *Newsweek*, September 29, 1975, 13.

2. Elana Levine, *Wallowing in Sex: The New Sexual Culture of 1970s American Television* (Durham, NC: Duke University Press, 2007).

3. David Allyn, *Make Love, Not War: The Sexual Revolution: An Unfettered History* (Boston: Little, Brown and Company, 2000); Dennis Altman, *The Homosexualization of America, the Americanization of the Homosexual* (New York: St. Martin's Press, 1981); Stephen Heath, *The Sexual Fix* (London: Macmillan Press, 1982).

4. Todd Gitlin, *Inside Prime Time* (New York: Pantheon Books, 1985), 69–73.

5. "Congressmen Seek Probe of TV Violence," *Television Digest*, July 8,1968, 5.

6. U.S. Senate, Committee on Commerce, Subcommittee on Communications, *Federal Communications Commission Policy Matters and Television Programming*, 91st Cong., 1st sess., Washington, DC, 1969.

7. U.S. Senate, *Federal Communications Commission Policy Matters and Television Programming*, 374.

8. Gitlin, *Inside Prime Time*, 72; Geoffrey Cowan, *See No Evil: The Backstage Battle over Sex and Violence on Television* (New York: Simon and Schuster, 1979).

9. Elana Levine, "Sex as a Weapon: Programming Sexuality in the 1970s," in *NBC: America's Network*, ed. Michele Hilmes, 234–236 (Berkeley: University of California Press, 2007), 98–99.

10. Kathryn C. Montgomery, *Target: Prime Time. Advocacy Groups and the Struggle over Entertainment Television* (Oxford: Oxford University Press, 1989).

11. Gary Edgerton, "High Concept, Small Screen," *Journal of Popular Film and Television* (fall 1991): 114–127.

12. Judith Crist, "Tailored for Television," *TV Guide*, August 30, 1969, 8–9.

13. I have not been able to view these films. Plot descriptions come from Alvin H. Marrill, *Movies Made for Television: The Telefeature and the Mini-Series, 1964–1979* (Westport, CT: Arlington House, 1980).

14. On classical exploitation cinema see Eric Schaefer, *"Bold! Daring! Shocking! True!": A History of Exploitation Films, 1919–1959* (Durham, NC: Duke University Press, 1999).

15. Levine, *Wallowing in Sex*, 162–168.

16. Levine, *Wallowing in Sex*, 208–251.

17. Cramer's television experience has spanned the advertising, network, and TV production worlds. He began his career in the late 1950s, working at New York ad agency Ogilvy and Mather, where he supervised the broadcast component of several prominent accounts. He also worked for Procter & Gamble, supervising production of some of the company's daytime soap operas. In 1962, he became director of program planning at ABC. However, in the mid-1960s, Cramer left the network business to work in television production, first for 20th Century Fox and then for Paramount. He formed the Douglas S. Cramer Company in 1971, then joined Aaron Spelling Productions in 1976. In this phase of his career, Cramer would produce not only the series and telefilms discussed in this chapter, but also such hit programs as *Dynasty* (ABC, 1981–1989) and its spin-offs, as well as producing nearly all of the miniseries based on Danielle Steele's novels. Despite Cramer's long career shepherding some of the most populist, low-prestige programming in American television, he has long held a significant place in the contemporary art world as a leading collector and patron. Carter B. Horsley, "Contemporary Art from the Douglas S. Cramer Collection," *City Review*, November 14, 2001, accessed March 15, 2008, www.thecityreview.com; Andy Meisler, "A 'Soap' Mogul with an Eye for the '90s," *New York Times*, August 29, 1993, H29.

18. John Stanley, "Producer Douglas S. Cramer: The Man Behind the Big Prime-Time Shows," *San Francisco Chronicle*, December 1, 1985, 62, accessed March 25, 2008, ProQuest, www.proquest.com/en-US/.

19. "ABC's *Turn-On* Makes like a Spec, and Web had 'Third Season' Vacancy," *Variety*, February 12, 1969, 43.

20. "Rescuing the Survivors," *Time*, August 1, 1969, accessed November 5, 2007, www.time.com.

21. George Eres, "New ABC Series Loaded with Love," *Press-Telegram*, Long Beach, CA, August 1, 1969, C9.

22. Clay Gowran, "ABC Series Gets a Racy Reputation," *Chicago Tribune*, July 31, 1969, 31.

23. U.S. Senate, *Federal Communications Commission Policy Matters and Television Programming*, 405–406.

24. Gowran, "ABC Series Gets a Racy Reputation," 31.

25. Jerry Buck, "Margolin and Parker Head Production of New Series," *Northwest Arkansas Times*, August 1, 1969, accessed November 1, 2007, Newspaperarchive.com.

26. Spelling made these comments regarding a TV movie his company was developing titled *Love on Fire Island*. Reported in a memorandum from Bob Stevens to Aaron Spelling, Douglas Cramer, Duke Vincent, Cindy Dunne, Norm Henry, and John Whelpley, September 26, 1977, box 1, file folders, ASP Development, Douglas S. Cramer Collection, American Heritage Center, University of Wyoming (hereafter, Cramer Collection, AHC).

27. Memorandum from Douglas Cramer to Gordon and Lynne Farr, June 22, 1977, box 35, *Love Boat*, Farr, Gordon and Lynne, Douglas S. Cramer Collection, AHC.

28. Handwritten comments from Cramer on memorandum from Lynne Farr to Lance Taylor, ABC, January 16, 1978, box 35, *Love Boat*, Farr, Gordon and Lynne, Cramer Collection, AHC.

29. Douglas Cramer notes on script K-54, April 10, 1979, box 36, *Love Boat*, script, K-54, Cramer Collection, AHC.

30. Memorandum from Douglas Cramer to Gordon and Lynne Farr, June 22, 1977.

31. Correspondence from Dennis P. Blackhurst to *The Love Boat*, December 4, 1979, and Marginalia by Douglas Cramer on same, box 35, *Love Boat*, Farr, Gordon and Lynne, Cramer Collection, AHC.

32. Correspondence from Douglas S. Cramer to Dennis P. Blackhurst, January 2, 1980, box 35, *Love Boat*, Farr, Gordon and Lynne, Cramer Collection, AHC.

33. The ABC network's first-place lead was beginning to erode, albeit slowly, at this point, which might have led to the network's demands for more sex on screen. Memorandum from Gordon Farr to Aaron Spelling and Douglas S. Cramer, October 15, 1979, box 35, *Love Boat*, Farr, Gordon and Lynne, Cramer Collection, AHC.

34. For more on the mainstream commercialization of sex in the late 1970s, see Allyn, *Make Love, Not War*.

35. Douglas Cramer notes in script K-64, October 10, 1979, box 36, Love Boat Script K-64, Cramer Collection, AHC.

36. Memorandum from Gordon Farr to Aaron Spelling and Douglas S. Cramer, October 15, 1979.

37. Ben Stein, "Love, Rape, Highway, Diary: Have We Sold You, Dear Viewer?" *TV Guide*, July 25, 1981, 35.

38. Display ad, *TV Guide*, October 30, 1976, A106.

39. Paraphrased in Douglas Cramer to Jo Heims, April 23, 1976, box 46, Heims, Jo, Cramer Collection, AHC.

40. Douglas Cramer to Mark Cohen, September 24, 1976, box 46, ABC correspondence, Cramer Collection, AHC.

41. Douglas Cramer to Stanley Robertson, May 5, 1975, box 21, Teenage Runaway-NBC, Cramer Collection, AHC.

42. "From Newton Deiter," box 4, Newton E. Deiter, PhD, and handwritten notes, box 9, script writer, "Alexander," Cramer Collection, AHC. For detailed analysis of the negotiations over Alex's sexuality see, Levine, "Sex as a Weapon."

Part II: Sex as Art

4 * Prurient (Dis)Interest:
The American Release and Reception of *I Am Curious (Yellow)*

KEVIN HEFFERNAN

In the documentary *Inside Deep Throat* (2005), *Deep Throat*'s director, Gerard Damiano, speaks of the early 1970s and his efforts to achieve artistic and financial success in the pornographic film industry: "I always believed that Hollywood and porn would eventually merge." Later in the film, novelist Norman Mailer laments that by the mid-1970s, pornographic cinema had almost overnight "just bec[ome] another mediocre commodity." It is easy to dismiss these hopes for a truly liberated cinema as endearing naïveté when faced with the ruthless adaptability of Hollywood on one hand and the reactionary sexual politics of much erotic cinema on the other. But between the disparate worlds of the Hollywood studios and the commercial sex film, international art cinema has often served as an area of negotiation in which models of innovation and risk taking are introduced and refined and within which the terms of "liberation" are defined and contested: distributors and exhibitors have often highlighted the salacious or forbidden spectacle in international cinema for the parochial American filmgoing public, and films seeking to push the boundaries of content have often been deliberately, at times cynically, crafted by their makers with narrative and stylistic features that diverge strongly from the norms of the classical Hollywood cinema. The late 1960s are a period that represents the high water mark of these twin trends, in which the vanishing youth audience was frantically sought by exhibitors through increasingly desperate measures, and Hollywood was in the depths of its most serious recession since the 1930s.[1]

The ultimately futile efforts of U.S. Customs and then several state and municipal censorship bureaus to halt the exhibition of the Swedish film *I am Curious (Yellow)* are often cited as examples of an outmoded way of thinking about films that would become increasingly marginalized, as the 1970s brought an unprecedented (and since unequaled) level of sexual frankness to the public exhibition of motion pictures. This purely legal and juridical view of the importance of *I am Curious (Yellow)* ignores many of the social and aesthetic changes that were taking place in the American cinema at the time of its release. For example, the film was in the unique position to be released at a time when public interest in movie censorship and classification was at an all-time high: during a two-year period the MPAA's ratings system was implemented, *I am Curious (Yellow)* was released by Grove Press, and the findings of the President's Commission on Obscenity and Pornography were published.

The success of the film at least partially grew out of its ability to straddle at least three categories of the commercial cinema (the general-release film, the exploitation film, and the art cinema) in this time of severe recession for the movie business and the temporary fluidity of these categories of movies in 1969–1970. Finally, the film's reception by critics and its hold on the popular imagination reveal much about the evolving social context in which films were received in this period. The film's qualitative change in level of sexual explicitness from that to which critics and public were accustomed—a change the film shared with several other releases including Andy Warhol's *Blue Movie* (1969)—led to a groping for new critical categories for this new viewing experience. These categories—which include appeals to spectator's notions of titillation and boredom, and to critics' notions of the filmmaker's competence—would remain to a large measure unchanged in the attempt during the following decade to understand the pornographic cinema.

Courting Controversy

In 1966, Grove Press, publishers of the highly successful New Directions paperbacks of contemporary literature and longtime crusader for First Amendment rights of publishers, acquired complete ownership of the stock of Amos Vogel's Cinema 16 film library, consisting of the distribution rights to over two hundred films. Among the films in the Cinema 16 library were many titles that had provoked censorship controversies, including several films by Luis Bunuel as well as Frederick Wiseman's heavily litigated *Titicut Follies* (1967).[2] Active in both the exhibition and distribution of nontheatrical features and shorts since 1947, Vogel and Cinema 16 had frequently courted controversy and borne the brunt of legal sanction in their commitment to expanding the freedom of the screen. In fact, it was his recognition of Grove Press president Barney Rosset as a fellow iconoclast that led Vogel to sell the library to Grove.[3] Rosset and Grove, who had successfully sued the New York City postmaster in 1959 for seizing copies of Grove's unexpurgated edition of D. H. Lawrence's *Lady Chatterley's Lover*, hoped to enter both the theatrical and nontheatrical field by distributing contemporary movies by innovative filmmakers that challenged both the censors and audiences.

A year after their acquisition of the Cinema 16 library, Rosset and Grove gained distribution rights to a film that would give them unprecedented access to the filmgoing public, controversy, and the courts all at once.

I am Curious (Yellow) was produced for $160,000 in Sweden in 1967 by the Sandrews Film and Theater company, an exhibitor-financed production house in Stockholm that had also produced *Miss Julie* (1951), Ingmar Bergman's *Sawdust and Tinsel* (1953), and Mai Zetterling's *Night Games* (1966). *Yellow* was written and directed by Vilgot Sjöman, a Bergman protégé, who had served as assistant director on *Winter Light* (1963). Sjöman's film recounts several months in the life a young Stockholm drama student, Lena, played by Lena Nyman. Her much older boyfriend, played by Börje Ahlstedt, is a philandering car salesman who keeps a number of mistresses. The story recounts Lena's quest for sexual and political enlightenment while a film crew, led by Vilgot (played by director Vilgot Sjöman) documents her interviews with political leaders; her spiritual training at an ashram in Rumskulla, where nonviolence is taught; and much private sexual behavior with Börje. Periodically, the film cuts to shots of Lena in bed with Vilgot as well as shots of Vilgot canoodling with his young female script supervisor while the film of Lena and Börje is being shot.

Based upon this and the film's other merits, Sandrews received a $100,000 advance from Grove for American theatrical distribution rights to the film that also entitled them to 30 percent of the gross receipts. Grove agreed to pay all of the expenses of advertising and legal fees, which turned out to be a fairly expensive proposition.[4] In January 1968, U.S. Customs officials in New York seized a print of the film as obscene under the Tariff Act. Arthur Click, assistant U.S. attorney, railed against the film, asserting that it "leaves nothing to the imagination, including acts of fornication." Immediately, Barney Rosset announced legal action to contest the seizure.[5] In a deliberate evocation of Grove's earlier court victories, Rosset told *Publishers Weekly* that the ensuing censorship fight "may win for the film industry the same freedom afforded literature in the *Lady Chatterley's Lover* case."[6] This contextualizing of the film's battle with the censors against the background of freedom won for the press by challenging works of literature would become a dominant theme of the film's partisans in the months to come.[7] Grove's first move was to schedule a private screening of the film for thirty critics in the hope that some of them would be willing to appear as friendly witnesses in the ensuing legal action.[8] In the hearings that followed, assistant U.S. attorney Laurence Schilling told the court that the film was obscene under the standards established in *Roth v. United States* (1957) and *Memoirs v. Massachusetts* (1966), namely, that the film's dominant theme appealed to prurient interest, that the film was patently offensive to community standards, and that taken as a whole it was utterly without social value. Schilling remarked of the film's social importance: "If this film has a message, I suggest that it is merely dross providing a vehicle for portraying deviation and hardcore pornography." In May, federal district court judge Thomas F. Murphy refused to order the release of *Yellow*, calling the film "repulsive and revolting."[9]

The next step was a jury trial to determine whether or not the film was obscene. Here Grove attorney Edward de Grazia brought forth as witnesses some of the critics who had attended their private screening, including Stanley Kauffman of the *New Republic*, John Simon of the *New Leader*, Hollis Alpert of *Saturday Review*, and Paul Zimmerman of *Newsweek*, many of whom would later defend the film in print with varying degrees of enthusiasm.[10] Each side called their witnesses to the stand: the government called the Reverend Daniel Potter of the Protestant Council of New York, and Grove called both novelist Norman Mailer, who described the film as "profoundly moral," and the film's director, Vilgot Sjöman, who described himself as a "Puritan" but also a filmmaker who avoided "romantic cliché."[11] The jury of seven men and five women took only three hours of deliberation to find the film obscene, basing its decision on the standards from *Roth* and *Memoirs*. The jury appeared to wholeheartedly agree with government attorney Schilling, who earlier had told the court that the film's scenes of explicit sex were "linked together with what can charitably be called a soap opera."[12] Grove Press appealed the decision, and in November 1968, in a 2-to-1 decision, a three-judge panel in the Second U.S. Circuit Court of Appeals overturned the federal district court jury. In the majority decision, Judge Paul R. Hays wrote, "A motion picture, like a book, is clearly entitled to the protection of the First Amendment"; "under the standards established by the Supreme Court the exhibition of the film cannot be inhibited." The court also ruled that the sex scenes in the film were part of an artistic whole unified with and related to the story and characters and not utterly without redeeming social value. Hays's decision also ruled that the state would only have a compelling interest in halting exhibition of the film if minors were not excluded from seeing it or if the distributor utilized lurid or offensive advertising (figure 4.1). As the trial progressed, Grove Press had a book made from the script of the film, illustrated with production stills,[13] "many of the sort," tittered *Time* magazine in March, "that usually come in plain brown wrappers."[14] When the film opened in New York at Grove's own downtown Evergreen Theater and the Cinema

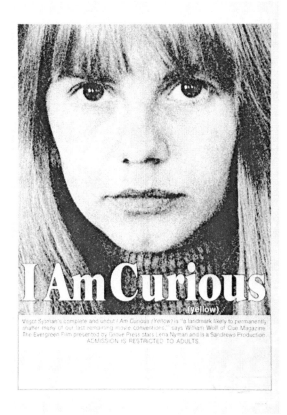

I Am Curious
(yellow)

Vilgot Sjöman's complete and uncut *I Am Curious (Yellow)* is "a landmark likely to permanently shatter many of our last remaining movie conventions," says William Wolf of Cue Magazine. The Evergreen Film presented by Grove Press stars Lena Nyman and is a Sandrews Production. ADMISSION IS RESTRICTED TO ADULTS.

Fig. 4.1 From the earliest engagements of *I Am Curious (Yellow)* in the United States, posters for the film were emblazoned with "ADMISSION IS RESTRICTED TO ADULTS."

Rendezvous, the *New York Times* ad displayed the cover of the book with the line, "Curious about 'Curious'? . . . Now See the Film!" The film's run at the two New York locations was spectacularly successful, as I will discuss below.

Yellow received attention and notoriety everywhere it was booked. It opened at the Fox Theater, a National General house, in Reno the following September and encountered no legal difficulties. In Youngstown, Ohio, however, police seized two prints of the film from the State Theater under an antipornography law signed by Youngstown mayor Anthony Flash just three and a half hours before the arrests were made.[15] The State Theater was shut down by the police, and Grove Press took the case to court.[16] In Houston, where city attorneys generally abjured obscenity prosecutions, the theater showing the film was burned down.[17]

The legal status of the film throughout the country, even after the second circuit court had ruled it not obscene in its jurisdiction, was far from sure; in fact, the decision made by the east coast circuit was not binding anywhere else in the country, and it was in the varying legal status of the film in different parts of the country that later led to the film going to the U.S. Supreme Court. When the film opened in Phoenix at the Vista Theater, Mayor Milt Graham predicted that it would be a major issue in the upcoming mayoral race. Despite (or perhaps because of) this, the film's premiere week grossed over $12,000.[18] On the other hand, in Albuquerque the film opened at the Pancho Art Theater, and the attendant obscenity charge was dropped on the grounds that the film had been ruled not obscene by a higher court, even though that higher court was in another jurisdiction.[19] By November 1969, Grove attorney de Grazia told the *New York Times* that the film had been shown in fifty-three cities; in only fifteen of these had the showing been contested. Grove Press won court cases to have the film shown in Philadelphia, Cleveland, Denver, Detroit, Virginia Beach, and Albuquerque. Cases were still pending in Youngstown, Spokane, Atlanta, and San Jose.

Since the Second Circuit Court ruling, the film had been closed down in Kansas City, Baltimore, and Boston.[20] In Kansas City, Kansas, Johnson County District Judge Herbert Walton found the film obscene under the prevailing criteria, and opined that the scenes that were not sex scenes in the film were mere "window dressing."[21] In the following appeal, a three-judge panel in U. S. District Court ruled that the state obscenity laws under which the film was banned were constitutional. The appeal then went to the Supreme Court, since the three-judge panel had the same authority as the Circuit Court of Appeals. Again, this panel had not ruled on the obscenity of the film, but rather on the constitutionality of the state's antiobscenity laws.[22] In a move that came to characterize much discourse surrounding the reception of the film, defense witness Dr. James Loutzenheiser, a psychiatrist, testified that the film is "deadly dull [and] not prurient or erotic in the least." Prosecution witness Dr. V. W. McNally of the University of Kansas Medical School asserted that the sheer obtuseness of the film insured that its social message did not come across.[23] Thus, both sides of the censorship debate began to enlist the opacity and tedium of the film to buttress their positions.

It was in Baltimore and Boston, however, that the most protracted and successful battles against the film were fought. In July 1969, the three-woman Maryland Board of Motion Picture Censors (led by Mary Avara, who would become a longtime nemesis of John Waters) voted to ban *Yellow* from Maryland theaters. Maryland state attorney general F. B. Burch supported the board, warning that passing of the film would result in an epidemic of "hardcore pornography posing as art."[24]

The following month, Baltimore Circuit Court judge Joseph Carter upheld the decision of the censor board. Carter expressed concern that the intellectuals and cultural elite who had rallied in defense of the film may not "have been aware of the attitude of the average person with respects to the problems" of the case. Further, Carter doubted that under then-current law, the courts in Maryland had the right to permit the showing of films solely because an age restriction is in place at the box office.[25] Meanwhile, de Grazia asserted that the film had been banned in ten states and shown in forty others. His desire to have the film shown everywhere reflected the need "to take steps to avoid conflicting decisions" regarding the film.[26]

The trial of the owner and the manager of Boston's Symphony Cinema I and II for knowingly exhibiting an obscene motion picture took place during the summer of 1969. In November, Suffolk Superior Court judge G. Joseph Tauro ruled *Yellow* obscene based on the *Memoirs* criteria and effectively banned the film in Boston. In the ensuing appeal to a three-judge Federal District Court panel, defense attorneys attempted to expand on the 1969 ruling in *Stanley v. Georgia*, which allowed adults to possess pornography in the privacy of their home. The federal panel asked probing questions about the relationship between private ownership and public exhibition of sexually explicit films;[27] they eventually ruled that the state's antiobscenity law was probably unconstitutional and forbid Garrett Byrne, district attorney of Suffolk County, from enforcing the ban on the film in Boston. When the state appealed, the Massachusetts Supreme Court countermanded the federal district court order. This ruling did not declare *I am Curious (Yellow)* obscene, but stayed the lower court's decision that had kept Byrne from threatening prosecution under Massachusetts state law.[28]

In early 1971, the Supreme Court finally agreed to decide if *I am Curious (Yellow)* could be barred from the United States as obscene. The U.S. District Court, it should be remembered, had already ruled against a nationwide ban of the film because of its redeeming social importance. In May 1970, Justice William O. Douglas, the High Court's most vocal opponent of censorship, declared himself ineligible to vote in the case of *Yellow* because *Evergreen* magazine, owned by Grove Press, had published excerpts from his book *Points of Rebellion*.[29] The resulting decision, *Byrne v. Karalexis*, threw out the Federal Appeals Court ruling under which the Boston law banning *Yellow* had been declared unconstitutional, remanding the case back to the federal district court.[30] Finally, in March, with Justice Douglas abstaining, the Supreme Court became involved in a legal snarl as it deadlocked 4 to 4 on the Maryland court ruling that *Yel-*

low was obscene. This split decision had the effect of affirming the lower court's ruling, but carried no weight as legal precedent. With Douglas recused from all cases involving Grove Press, it then became highly unlikely that the Supreme Court would ever decide in any meaningful way whether or not the film was obscene. The film was never challenged in court in New York, Connecticut, or Vermont, the jurisdiction of the second circuit.[31] In many ways, the lack of resolution of this case pointed toward the argument over jurisdiction that would undergird the 1973 *Miller* decision, which gave ultimate power over determining community standards to county and municipal authorities. Within a matter of days of the Court's deadlock, New York police stepped up their raids on theaters showing allegedly pornographic films, and Deputy Chief Inspector J. L. P. Keenan publicly stated that he was encouraged and emboldened by the Supreme Court's decision on *Yellow*.[32]

A Curious Hybrid

Many of the arguments surrounding the supposed redeeming social importance of *Yellow* focused on its use of documentary technique to link the film's overarching concern with sex to larger social issues. It is therefore of some interest to follow the case of another embattled Swedish import from 1969: the sex education documentary *Language of Love*. The film was imported by Unicorn Enterprises and was to be distributed by Chevron Pictures. The movie, which ran one hundred minutes, consisted of interviews with Swedish psychiatrists and gynecologists, animated footage detailing the functioning of the reproductive system, and on-camera sex performed by "non-professional volunteers."[33] In October 1969, the U.S. attorney's office sought to bar the film's entrance to the country. When Unicorn sued, a jury found the film obscene but was overruled by the Second Circuit Court of Appeals—at least partially on the basis of the citing of the precedent of *I Am Curious (Yellow)* on the part of Chevron's president, Sam Yellen[34]—the Supreme Court agreed to hear the Justice Department's appeal and rule whether the film was obscene.[35] Ephraim London represented Unicorn in the Supreme Court case, and in May 1971 the Court allowed the film to be released; it began an extended engagement at the Agee I Cinema on Seventh Avenue.[36] By this time, *Language of Love* had joined a recognizable subgenre of "white coater" adult films, which featured on-camera lectures on human sexuality by a "doctor" and which were illustrated with scenes of explicit sex. The Italian American producer and director Matteo Ottaviano, famous elsewhere as Matt Cimber, Jayne Mansfield's ex-husband, was one of the most successful practitioners of this kind of film, which included *Man and Wife* (1969) and *He and She* (1970).

At the same time, the New York Criminal Court heard the case of Andy Warhol's *Blue Movie*. Warhol's film was shot in a single three-hour session with a total cost of $3,000 and featured about twenty minutes of on-screen sex between Warhol "superstars" Viva and Louis Waldron. *Blue Movie*, also known as *Fuck*, quickly made back its cost in the first week of its run at the Garrick Theater on Bleecker Street, pulling in a $16,000 gross.[37] On July 31, the police raided the theater and seized the film, arresting the Garrick's manager, Saul Heller, even though Heller had barred patrons under the age of eighteen. A police spokesman predictably described the film as "hardcore pornography," though Warhol business manager Paul Morrissey said that the film was purposefully ambiguous as to whether the performers were actually engaging in sex and that "it is up to the viewer to decide." *Variety* reported that Warhol's legal defense of the film—which, it was finally determined, did contain actual intercourse—was his "reputation as an abstractionist artist" as well as changing conceptions of cinematic realism or "life as it is."[38] Many of the formal features of the rough-hewn film—16 mm cinematography using a single-system Auricon camera; numerous Warholian jump cuts, white frames, and exposure latitude problems; and the controversial sex scene's high-glare backlighting from a window that obliterates portions of the image—would appear ideally suited to buttress just such a defense. But, on September 24, a three-judge panel in New York Criminal Court ruled after only thirty minutes of deliberation that *Blue Movie* was hardcore pornography and that "sexual activity between male and female is portrayed graphically with no redeeming social value." Warhol and Morrissey both issued statements questioning the definition of "community standards" under *Roth* and *Memoirs*, and Warhol stated that the film was under attack largely by the "middle-aged [who] are upset . . . because they can't reconcile sex with their own blighted lives."[39]

Although hybrids such as *Yellow* and *Blue Movie* were making money and moving through the courts, the more conventional sex exploitation cinema was undergoing many changes. The New York City market was glutted with the sort of black-and-white, low-budget domestic sexploitation films that now enjoy a cult and camp following thanks to Seattle-based Something Weird Video. Booked in Manhattan for a flat fee as low as $1,500 a week, these films were being forced out of the market by the majors opting for more adventurous fare on the one hand and a steady customer runoff to the increasingly frank art films on the other. Lee Hessel, president of sexploitation distributor Cambist Films, pointed out that the New York run of *Yellow* at the Evergreen and Cinema Rendez-vous resulted in the loss of afternoon "briefcase trade" from competing theaters specializing in sexploitation films. So successful was the Grove Press release at drawing audiences to art houses to see a film for which they would never venture to a sex theater that Hessel and Cambist imitated *Yellow* with their release *The Female*, a film that had been the official 1961 Argentinian entry at Cannes under the title *Setenta veces siete*. Hessel bought the rights to the film and added several sex scenes, convinced that this film would be a sizeable crossover hit, and the movie played the sexploitation circuit for years.

The curious market niche occupied by *Yellow* is also underscored by comments made to *Variety* by Peter Kaufman of Dallas-based Jemco films about the status of the sex film in the summer of 1969. Like Hessel, Kaufman saw the days of the hyper low-budget exploitation film numbered. These films, which included some directed by cult auteurs Doris Wishman and Joseph Sarno, were produced for between $8,000 and $10,000 and required a large number of runs to amortize their costs at a flat-fee rental. The middle-range exploitation film—priced at between $25,000 and $100,000 with some eye toward production values, including color and sync sound—possessed no pretentions but in the hands of skillful filmmakers and distributors such as Russ Meyer, could reach part of a crossover market and attain box-office success, as Meyer had done in 1968 with the X-rated *Vixen*. A successful supplier of these middle-range films was Louis Sher's Sherpix, the distribution arm of Sher's Art Theater Guild (ATG) circuit. The ATG chain had been successfully showing films from abroad since the 1950s and had barred minors from its theaters for many years, both as a hedge against municipal censorship and as a means of offering a more upscale filmgoing experience to its patrons. For the season of 1969–1970, Sherpix announced several exploitation films in this price range on their release slate, including *The Stewardesses* in 3-D, which cost around $100,000 (and which would become a huge hit for them in the following year) and Richard Stockton's *Meat Rack*, a fascinating gay psychodrama produced in California for $80,000.[40]

The *Variety* article's last category, the art-sex film—with a negative cost of more than $200,000, high production values, and a story with pretensions to social value—could play in theaters that would draw both the skin flick crowd and the general audience. The *Variety* writer concluded his article with the observation that "*I Am Curious (Yellow)* stands almost by itself as an essentially art-sex pic with hardcore appeal."[41] By October 1969, the film had earned over $4 million in net rentals, which placed it fourth in *Variety*'s list of most successful foreign-language films behind Astor Picture's *La Dolce Vita* (1960; rentals of $7.5 million), Allied Artists' *A Man and a Woman* (1966; rentals of $5.6 million), and Sigma III's *Dear John* (1966; rentals of $4.2 million).[42] By November, the film had moved into third place, with domestic rentals of over $5.2 million.[43] Grove president Rosset told the *New York Times* that the film had earned over $1.2 million in its Manhattan runs at the Evergreen and Cinema Rendezvous alone. Its engagement in Washington, DC, had earned, since the winter, $573,000; Los Angeles had brought in $483,000; Philadelphia had earned $419,000; and Boston $335,000.[44]

The *Technical Report of the Commission on Obscenity and Pornography* discussed *Yellow* by name as an example of a highly successful hybrid genre combining elements of the art film, the exploitation film, and the general release motion picture. Characteristics of the hybrid film include many more play dates than exploitation films (as many as five hundred or more bookings), greater sexual content than either sexploitation or general release films, and the fact that they were usually shown in their original language with English subtitles. *I Am Curious (Yellow)* is mentioned as one of the most "outstanding" examples of the hybrid genre, and the *Technical Report* cited *Variety*'s year-end rental figures for the film as over $6.6 million.[45] Grove Press entered the motion picture market at just the time when this hybrid genre was coming into its own. One of the most successful distributors of this type of film, also mentioned in the *Technical Report*, was Radley Metzger's Audubon Films. When *Yellow* received a United Artists Theater circuit booking in November 1969, *Variety* likened the film's crossover success to "Audubon's *I, a Woman* [of 1966], which first made the break from sex to art houses."[46] Audubon, like Grove Press, eventually began to publish screenplays with profuse illustrations of the films' most titillating scenes. One of the first paperback editions put out by Audubon Books was the screenplay to Metzger's *Camille 2000* (1969).[47] Audubon was so successful with releases such as *I, a Woman* (figure 4.2) and Metzger's own *Carmen, Baby* (1967) and *Therese and Isabelle* (1968), that it successfully went public with sale of shares in 1969, and Metzger's first film after going public was the $300,000 *Lickerish Quartet*, released in the United States in 1970.[48] Like *Yellow*, *Lickerish Quartet* features a film within the film, but instead of Sjöman's Godardian pseudodocumentary approach, Metzger's film opts for a high modernist use of the figure in which the movie screened within the film mirrors and blurs the relationships between the characters we have come to know in the diegesis. Metzger would return to this trope repeatedly in his later hardcore films such as *Naked Came the Stranger* (1975) and *The Opening of Misty Beethoven* (1976), directed under his pseudonym Henry Paris.

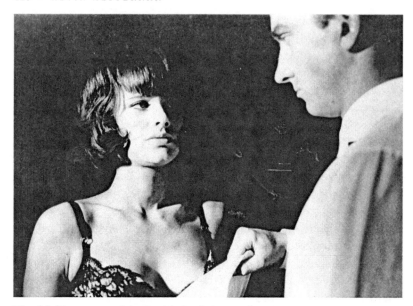

Fig. 4.2 The success of the Danish-Swedish coproduction *I, a Woman*, starring Essy Persson and released in the United States by Audubon in 1966, paved the way for so-called hybrid pictures such as *I Am Curious (Yellow)*.

It was the controversy that surrounded the original adoption of the system of age classification by the Motion Picture Association of America that made the hybrid film possible. Director Frank Perry, whose youth drama *Last Summer* (1969) was one of the first films to receive an X rating (it achieved an R with minor cuts), complained to *Variety* that the X rating was already misunderstood. Perry proposed an "art X" to distinguish it from a "porno X." It was exactly this confusion of categories that helped make *I Am Curious (Yellow)* such a sizeable hit. It is important to remember that the "X" rating by the MPAA did not at first convey the impression of pornography or even distastefulness. Where the National Catholic Office for Motion Pictures (the post–Vatican II incarnation of the Legion of Decency) had condemned Audubon's *Camille 2000*, even though it admitted that the film was "imaginative and well photographed," the same office gave the X-rated *Midnight Cowboy* its A-4 rating (morally unobjectionable for adults with some reservations), ruling that "the shock value of the film is transcended by an intense sensitivity to human values."[49] John Simon, writing on *I Am Curious (Yellow)* in the *New York Times* earlier in the year after the film's jury trial, explicitly linked the legal problems facing *Yellow* with the industry's adoption of the system of age classification, asking Juvenal's ancient question,

"Who will guard the guardians of the public?" of both the jury and the MPAA, who were, he noted, of an age advanced from that of both the protagonists and intended audience of *Yellow*.[50]

Sex, Art, and Boredom

The reception of *I Am Curious (Yellow)* by critics shows how wider social concerns with issues of art, obscenity, and motion pictures were brought to bear on this highly ambiguous film. Reviews of the film tended to touch on four major issues: First, the legal arguments about obscenity pertaining to "the work as a whole" were replayed in the reviews in terms of artistic unity, generally centered on the film-within-a-film device and issues of documentary and realism. Second, the film was discussed in relation to pornography, usually defined as the low-end sexploitation product playing in grind houses in Times Square. Third, the reviewers all engaged with the issue of the film's propensity to bore its audiences and bring a wide range of explanatory mechanisms to bear on this phenomenon. Finally, virtually every reviewer saw fit to comment on the physical appearance and/or attractiveness of protagonist Lena Nyman.

These issues played themselves out over the course of many reviews, but the reception of the film afforded its early notices in *Variety* and the *Times* show how these issues can be traced across a more or less typical bad review and good review, respectively. *Variety*'s review from November 1967 referred to the use of the "film within a film gimmick," and wrote that "despite the abundance of sex, *I Am Curious (Yellow)* is mostly boring." The reviewer asserted that the film had "political pretensions but no political viewpoint" and that it was artistically minor, though it might prove important as a case involving film censorship.[51] Vincent Canby, writing in the *Times*, praised the film's artistic unity, seeing its apparent disunities as a reflection of the provisional nature of the "truths" Lena finds over the course of the narrative. Canby found some of the sex scenes, particularly the early scene of Lena and Börje scampering around her apartment with their pants around their ankles, quite funny. Finally, he found that *Yellow* distinguished itself from exploitation films in its "full-length portrait of Lena, the troubled, liberated woman."[52] Of course, a problem in discussing the film's "unity as a whole" is the fact that *Yellow* is a film that self-consciously places itself in opposition to traditional aesthetic notions of unity; this characteristic of the film has both artistic and legal ramifications. Like the deliberate technical crudeness and countercultural sensibility of Warhol's *Blue Movie*, the aesthetic and ideological discontinuity of *Yellow* was tailor made to challenge obscenity strictures in the wake of the *Roth* ruling, which insisted that a work "taken as a whole" must possess as its dominant characteristic a morbid or prurient interest in sex or nudity. Whereas U.S. attorney Laurence Schilling had said that the nonsex scenes in *Yellow* were "soap opera," and Herbert Walton, the judge in the Boston case, had called the same scenes "window dressing," Rex Reed, in an excoriating review of the film in the *Times*, complained that all the film had to offer in addition to the sex was the "tiresome movie-within-a-movie technique."[53] Conversely, the argument of the Second District Court that the sex scenes were part of an artistic whole, unified with and related to the story and characters, was echoed in Stanley Kauffmann's review of the film in *New Republic*. Kauffmann maintained that the frankness the film displayed in its treatment of sex was mirrored in the film's frankness in its treatment of other social issues.[54]

The film mobilizes codes of the documentary film and cinema vérité inspired by Jean Rouche and Edgar Morin's *Chronicle of a Summer* (1961) to situate Lena's sexual explorations within a context of questioning the ideals of the supposedly egalitarian Swedish society in which she lives. This is done through her interviews with the Soviet poet Yevgeny Yevtushenko, Sweden's King Carl Gustav, numerous people in the street and in front of the American Embassy, and a hermit in the woods. Sjöman, himself interviewed by WNYC radio's Patricia Marx, asserted that the interviews conducted by Lena were unscripted and spontaneous. It is in the interest of naturalism and the avoidance of romantic cliché, Sjöman maintained, that he included the film's most explicit sexual scenes.[55] The importance of the film-within-the-film and documentary aspects of the film became even more critical as legal precedent in the following year, when three documentaries concerning Denmark's abolition of its obscenity laws played to packed houses in several Manhattan theaters (see chapter 8). These films — *Pornography in Denmark: A New Approach, Sexual Freedom in Denmark*, and *Wide Open Copenhagen 70* — along with the so-called white coater sex-ed movies mentioned earlier, contained sexual explicitness, including on-screen penetration and visible climax, previously unseen in publicly exhibited motion pictures. It was clearly the documentary "wraparound" consisting of travelogue and interview footage that enabled the films to play relatively free of legal harassment. A bewildered Vincent Canby, in a reaction to the films' contents quite typical of critics' and public reaction to pornographic cinema, wrote of his "shock and curiosity" giving way to "boredom," and found himself longing for the metaphoric fireworks of Hitchcock's *To Catch a Thief* (1955).[56]

The relationship between the sex scenes and the rest of the film in *Yel-*

low and its more daring successors was already the subject of arch parody and satire by early 1970. Arnold Auerbach, writing in the *Times*, related a fictional account of an interview with a cadre of writers in the employ of exhibitors to write scenes to be interspersed with the sex in foreign films. These "tweenie-writers," as Auerbach calls them, each specialize in a particular type of linking scene: one specializes in anti-American diatribes and obscurantism, another in heavy silences, still another in talk about alienation. Their boss, himself a writer, speculates that the difference between the art films and the porn playing on Eighth Avenue and Times Square is that the grind-house movies have "inferior" tweenie stuff.[57] Rex Reed made an even more explicit parallel between *Yellow* and the skin flick paraphilia on display in Broadway theaters and likened the supposedly unattractive, unimpassioned principals in Sjöman's film to "the girls in those low-budget grind-house flicks who roll around on the beds in cheap motel rooms, licking their lips a lot, but who never perspire."[58] Although a defender of the film, Penelope Gilliat was forced to tell in the *New Yorker* of arriving at the theater early and sitting through the last fifteen minutes of the film with the subtitles out of frame. Gilliat's admonition to the projectionist was apparently the first from the crowd, suggesting that the film's incomprehensible Swedish dialogue was not the reason the mostly male audience came to see the film.[59] Kauffmann, on the other hand, was at pains to demonstrate how far afield from pornography the film's portrayal of sexuality was. It was obvious, Kauffmann maintained, that in 1969 traditional notions of privacy were undergoing radical revision and reconfiguration in the culture as a whole. He remarked that *Yellow* was neither an entirely infelicitous manifestation of nor an immature response to this process. "The more intrusive a film gets in physicality," he wrote, "the less erotically effective it is likely to be with a mature viewer, who is reluctant to let his most private physical experiences be used as items of reference in a theater" (figure 4.3).[60]

Both legal and aesthetic judgments of the film engaged with *Yellow*'s ability, even its commitment, to bore the audience. In Boston, both sides in the controversy admitted that they found the film boring, whereas in Kansas City, witnesses for Grove Press asserted that the film's tedium cancelled out any prurient interest the film might otherwise arouse. Richard Corliss, writing for *National Review*, pointed out the legal strategy behind this move. Corliss likened *Yellow* to Warhol's *Blue Movie* in that the various court proceedings showed the films' distributors attempting to "hide behind the Court definition of obscenity to show sex as either ugly or boring, and thus redeemingly social."[61] Hollis Alpert,

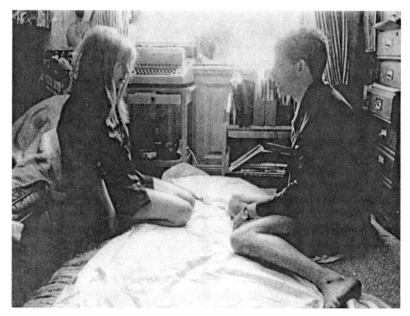

Fig. 4.3 Private physical experiences and Godardian backlighting: Lena (Lena Nyman) and Börje (Börje Ahlstedt) in *I Am Curious (Yellow)*.

in the *Saturday Review*, remarked that Sjöman, the student of Bergman, "has headed a little too far toward the camp of Godard. And that way, as many of us are beginning to be aware, lies excruciating boredom."[62] Finally, Russell Baker, in a satirical column entitled "I Am Gulled ($2.50)," wrote of a trek to see the movie with a fellow film enthusiast (both of them wear heavy disguises) and remarked that the film displays "the Swedish passion for hammering an audience into insensitivity. Minutes turned into lead." The heavy breathing of the audience soon turns to snores. When the film ends, Baker and his companion re-don their disguises, but for entirely different reasons: "Prurience you can be cheeky about, but when you have been thoroughly gulled, who wants the world to know?"[63]

Next to its ability to induce boredom, the most frequently remarked feature of the film was the physical appearance of the female lead: Lena Nyman. Rex Reed referred to the film as a "vile and disgusting Swedish meatball," and remarked of Nyman that she is "not only fat and down in the ankle [but] a real intellectual poseur too." In addition to likening the film's principals to denizens of Times Square, Reed called them "grotesque" and "repulsive."[64] Corliss, in an otherwise balanced review of the film, wrote of "the oppressively plain Lena Nyman, who looks the way

Janis Joplin will fifty years from now."[65] Even the sympathetic Canby appealed to realism in his backhanded compliment to the actress that she "somehow suggests every girl who says she will go on a diet tomorrow."[66] Richard Schickel, in *Life* magazine, asserted that Nyman's appearance was proof of the filmmakers' good intentions: "A panderer would have picked a prettier creature."[67]

The passing of time has revealed many hints that the fetishization of Lena Nyman within the film by the film's characters Vilgot and Börje were viewed with some suspicion by the real-life filmmaker Vilgot Sjöman and is intended as a critique of gender and power relations. Early in the film, Lena is asleep, and Vilgot puts various pairs of sunglasses over her eyes as he looks at photographs of ancient erotic sculpture. In an even more explicit critique of sexist notions of female beauty, Börje tells her near the end of the film to "start slimming": "I don't want those damn tits in my MG." Her near anorexic self-starvation at the retreat at Rumskulla is contrasted with her binging on sundaes when she returns to Stockholm. Some reviewers picked up on this. Alpert singled out for particular praise "the remarkably sensitive and effective performance of . . . Lena Nyman. Hardly a sexpot, she is a tubby, pendulously breasted girl of nineteen or so, who admits she is too fat."[68] Finally, the review in *Film Quarterly* explicitly linked the film's "powerful argument for the sexual equality of women" to the "refreshing [choice of] a rather plump, non-glamorous woman in the leading role of a movie."[69]

As I have attempted to show, it would be a mistake to attribute the box-office success of *I Am Curious (Yellow)* solely to its notoriety and attendant censorship controversies. There were many factors in its success, most notably the instability of critical categories and marketing segments in a rapidly changing film industry. The MPAA X rating, applied to major releases such as *Midnight Cowboy* and *Medium Cool*, attempted to forestall government intervention in the major studio's efforts to integrate more frank sexual and political content into films whose emphasis on stars, genres, and pre-sold properties clearly had much in common with studio filmmaking as it had functioned for decades. The "hybrid" character of *Yellow* enabled it to circumvent outright banning because of the characteristics it shared with the art cinema while differentiating itself from even the most adventurous studio fare.

By the time *Byrne v. Karalexis* presented its final resolution (or non-resolution) on the obscenity of *I Am Curious (Yellow)* in early 1971, the voyeuristic thrills offered by Sjöman's black-and-white film were rendered quaint by a rising tide of garish 16 mm Eastmancolor images, which brought the imagined potential of Börje's limp penis in *Yellow* to spectacular and tumescent life. Hardcore pornographic features, which had been bubbling up from behind the nondescript facades of storefront theaters for over a year, were receiving bookings in actual movie theaters.[70] In 1970, Sherpix blew up Bill Osco's *Mona: The Virgin Nymph* to 35 mm and screened it to huge grosses in its own Art Theater Guild houses. The next year, Sherpix rereleased the film accompanied with the cofeature *School Girl*, whose narrative of a young college student's sexual explorations seemed more than a little influenced by *I Am Curious (Yellow)*. *School Girl* was seized and prosecuted as obscene by the district attorney's office of Memphis, Tennessee, the same porn-obsessed prosecutors who would later convict actor Herbert Streicher (AKA Harry Reems) for acting in *Deep Throat*.

The disparate fates of exhibitors, distributors, and even actors in different jurisdictions that came to characterize films as radically different as *I Am Curious (Yellow)*, *Blue Movie*, and *Deep Throat* would lead in 1973 to the Berger Court's decision in *Miller v. California* that the "community standards" undergirding *Roth* and *Memoirs* were local rather than national. This monumental ruling succeeded in squelching high-profile national releases of sexually explicit films and relegated pornographic cinema to a small but consistent niche market for exhibitors and specialty distributors, many of whom had been showcasing conventional international films or softcore sexploitation for decades. Efforts at censorship and prosecution stymied or delayed in the case of *Yellow* could now be carried out by local prosecutors unconcerned with the legal status of the film in question elsewhere. Then, in a disguised but devastatingly effective assault on porn filmmakers, the 1976 federal tax code eliminated the deduction for motion picture investment, choking off a major source of funding for porn films and other low-budget cinema. The merging of pornographic and Hollywood cinema, for which Gerard Damiano yearned and of which the Hollywood studios were terrified, never came to pass.[71] Categories of theatrically released motion pictures and the public taste to which they catered would never again be as unstable as they were in the Hollywood recession of 1968–1969. Later films such as *Last Tango in Paris* (1972) and *Emmanuelle* (1974) achieved significant success as they straddled the categories of the sex film, the art cinema, and the major studio release, but never again would a hybrid of these forms mobilize the experiences of the counterculture and the sexual revolution and exist on the furthest edges of aesthetics and the law as they had in *I Am Curious (Yellow)*.

Notes

I would like to thank Tino Balio, Eric Schaefer, and Carolyn McCartney for their many helpful comments and suggestions on the various drafts of this essay.

1. For an excellent recounting of the rise of art theaters and the international cinema in a postwar U.S. film industry plagued by recession and declining movie output, see Barbara Wilinsky, *Sure Seaters: The Emergence of Art House Cinema* (Minneapolis: University of Minnesota Press, 2001).

2. "Grove to Fight U.S. Film Seizure," *Publishers Weekly* 193 (February 5, 1968): 46.

3. For a document-based history of Vogel and Cinema 16, see Scott MacDonald, *Cinema 16: Documents toward a History of the Film Society* (Philadelphia: Temple University Press, 2002).

4. "Grove's Rosset: All Censors Wrong, Valenti Is Encouraging Vigilantes," *Variety*, September 19, 1969, 25.

5. "Swedish Movie Is Seized by U.S. Customs for Obscenity" *New York Times*, January 19, 1968, 29.

6. "Grove to Fight U.S. Film Seizure," 46.

7. "Swedish Movie Is Seized by U.S. Customs for Obscenity," 29.

8. "Critics View Film Seized as Obscene," *New York Times*, January 25, 1968, 24.

9. "US Judge Refuses to Clear Swedish Film Seized in 1967," *New York Times*, May 4, 1968, 44.

10. "Grove Press Movie On Trial as Obscene," *New York Times*, May 21, 1968, 46.

11. "Reactions Varied on Swedish Movie," *New York Times*, May 23, 1968, 54.

12. "'I Am Curious' Found to Be Obscene Film," *New York Times*, May 24, 1968, 36.

13. "US Court Clears Swedish Sex Film," *New York Times*, November 27, 1968, 37.

14. "Dubious Yellow," *Time* 93 (March 14, 1969): 98.

15. "Curious Unopposed in Nevada Opening: Ohio Case to Court," *Variety*, September 24, 1969, 26; "Youngstown Busts 'Curious Yellow,'" *Variety*, October 1, 1969, 26.

16. "Suit to Restore 'Curious' in Ohio," *Variety*, October 1, 1969, 22.

17. "'I Am Curious' in Flames," *New York Times*, June 7, 1969, 27.

18. "'Curious' Bows in Phoenix, Becomes Issue in Political Campaign," *Variety*, October 1, 1969, 19.

19. "'Curious' Greenlight in Albuquerque Court," *Variety* October 1, 1969, 19.

20. "Passaic Court and Theater Chain Agree on Ban of 'I Am Curious,'" *New York Times*, November 24, 1969, 40.

21. "Non-Sexual Part Fake 'Redemption' of 'I Am Curious,' So Rules Judge," *Variety*, September 10, 6.

22. "Fed Judge Find Kansas Obscenity Statutes OK; No Censorship Return," *Variety*, October 15, 1969, 20.

23. "Is It Sex or Apathy in Sweden?" *Variety*, July 9, 1969, 20.

24. "MD Bans 'Curious,'" *New York Times*, July 10, 1969, 29.

25. "Curious Ban Upheld; Grove Appeals," *Variety*, August 20, 1969, 20.

26. "Court Ban Urged on 'I Am Curious,'" *New York Times*, November 11, 1970, 29.

27. "Boston's Curious Case Re 'Curious' State or Federal," *Variety*, July 30, 1969, 28. "Court to Rule on Smut Sent in Mail or Imported," *New York Times*, October 13, 1970, 29.

28. "Douglas Champions 'Curious' But Not as Obscenity Fan," *New York Times*, December 16, 1969, 58.

29. "Douglas Abstains From 3 Rulings," *New York Times*, April 28, 1970, 28.

30. "Massachusetts Obscenity Law Upheld," *New York Times*, February 24, 1971, 1.

31. "High Court Lets Stand Maryland Ban on 'Curious,'" *New York Times*, March 9, 1971, 24.

32. "3 Theaters Raided in Times Sq. Area for Obscene Films," *New York Times*, March 12, 1971, 75.

33. "US Moves to Bar Swedish Sex Film," *New York Times*, October 31, 1969, 35.

34. "US Customs Grabs Chevron's 'Language,'" *Variety*, November 5, 1969, 6.

35. "Supreme Court Actions," *New York Times*, February 23, 1971, 21.

36. "High Court Frees Film Held Obscene," *New York Times*, May 18, 1971, 47.

37. "Sex Act Film Costs 3G; Recoups Pronto," *Variety*, July 31, 1969, 1.

38. "Warhol's 'Blue Movie' Seized by DA; Trial in Manhattan Sept 24," *Variety*, September 17, 1969, 26.

39. "NY Court Finds Warhol's 'Blue Movie' Obscene," *Variety*, September 24, 1969, 24.

40. "So What Else is New? Sherpix Parlays 3-D, Homo, Satanism and Astrology," *Variety*, October 18, 1969, 22. *The Meat Rack* was shot on 16 mm and blown up to 35 mm for release. The $80,000 figure was probably considerably overstated.

41. "Sex Pic of 25: 45,000 Negative Cost Sees Bright, Not Clouded Future," *Variety*, July 16, 1969, 17.

42. "'Curious' Is Now 4th Biggest Artie Lingual," *Variety*, October 8, 1969, 3.

43. Variety Top Fifty Grossing Films, *Variety*, October 29, 1969, 11.

44. "Curious Grosses 5 Million (Green)," *New York Times*, October 20, 1969, 42.

45. *Technical Report of the Commission on Obscenity and Pornography*, vol. 3: *The Marketplace: The Industry* (Washington, DC: U.S. Government Printing Office, 1971), 48.

46. "Sex and NY Showcase Dollar," *Variety*, October 22, 1969, 5.

47. "Audubon Into Books," *Variety*, September 10, 1969, 2.

48. "Metzger, Leighton, and Sexcess Formula," *Variety*, September 3, 1969, 4.

49. "Midnight Cowboy Rated X By Code Finds Catholic Office Not So Stern," *Variety*, June 25, 1969, 7.

50. John Simon, "Getting Furious over 'Curious,'" *Variety*, January 9, 1969, 1, 17.

51. Fred., review of *I Am Curious (Yellow)*, *Variety*, November 1, 1967, 7.

52. Vincent Canby, "Screen: *I Am Curious (Yellow)* from Sweden," *New York Times*, March 11, 1969, 42.

53. Rex Reed, "I Am Curious (No)," *New York Times*, March 23, 1969, sec. 2, 3.

54. Stanley Kaufmann, "I Am Curious (Yellow)," *New Republic*, 150 (March 15, 1969): 22.

55. Patricia Marx, "Curious. Sjöman Has Some Answers," *New York Times*, May 11, 1969, D13.

56. Vincent Canby, "Have You Tried the Danish Blue?" *New York Times*, June 21, 1970, sec. 2, 1.

57. Arnold Auerbach, "How to Tweenie up Those Orgy Scenes," *New York Times*, January 11, 1970, 15.

58. Reed, "I Am Curious (No)," 1.

59. Penelope Gilliat, "The Current Cinema," *New Yorker*, April 5, 1969, 15.

60. Kaufmann, "I Am Curious (Yellow),"32.

61. Richard Corliss, "Films and Other Four-Letter Words," *National Review*, July 29, 1969, 760.

62. Hollis Alpert, "On Being Curious Twice," *Saturday Review*, March 15, 1969, 54.

63. Russell Baker, "I Am Gulled ($2.50)," *New York Times*, October 9, 1968, 46.

64. Reed, "I Am Curious (No)," 1.

65. Corliss, "Films and Other Four-Letter Words," 760.

66. *New York Times*, March 23, 1969.

67. Richard Schickel, "It Hides Nothing but the Heart," *Life*, March 21, 1969, 12.

68. Alpert, "On Being Curious Twice," 54.

69. Clyde B. Smith, "I Am Curious (Yellow)," *Film Quarterly* 22 (Summer 1969): 41.

70. For a detailed account of this process, see Schaefer, "Gauging a Revolution: 16mm Film and the Rise of the Pornographic Feature," *Cinema Journal* 41, no. 3 (spring 2002): 3–26.

71. For an account of just how terrified Jack Valenti and the MPAA were of competition from the porn filmmakers and how eagerly they relinquished the dead-on-arrival X rating to the adult movie industry, see Jon Lewis, *Hollywood v. Hardcore: How the Struggle over Censorship Saved the Modern Film Industry* (New York: New York University Press, 2000).

5 * Wet Dreams: Erotic Film Festivals of the Early 1970s and the Utopian Sexual Public Sphere

ELENA GORFINKEL

This essay presents a microhistory of the rise of erotic film festivals in New York, San Francisco, and Amsterdam in the early 1970s, mapping out the emergence of the erotic film festival as a hybrid reception sphere, a site for taste formation and erotic consumption across different modes of production such as the sexploitation film, the experimental film, the independent film, and the hardcore pornographic feature. Exemplary of a moment in which the furor over sexual explicitness in film had reached a fever pitch, erotic film festivals mobilized a discourse of sexual liberation alongside a rhetoric of aesthetic innovation, positioning themselves outside of the more mundane market of porn shops and storefront theaters selling a seedier version of sex to an older generation of "skin flick" consumers. The promotion and execution of the International Erotic Film Festival in San Francisco (which premiered in December 1970) and the New York Erotic Film Festival (which began in December 1971), and their European progenitor, the Wet Dream Film Festival in Amsterdam (November 1970), together offer a historical site for the exploration of the terms and conventions of erotic taste cultures as they were imbricated with the refinement and construction of cinephile practices in urban locales.[1]

From a contemporary vantage point, the notion of an erotic film festival, in and of itself, is not a controversial or new one.[2] Yet considering the historical moment of the early 1970s, the materialization of erotic film festivals represented a shift in the conceptualization of sexuality in film, in film culture, and in the public sphere more broadly. Although the concept of the film festival was a relatively novel one to American culture, with the earliest festivals emerging in Columbus, Ohio, and San Francisco in the 1950s, it was further institutionalized in the 1960s by the New York Film Festival, which embraced the appreciation of the cinema as an art form and built upon a vibrant cinephile culture already in play in New York City at the time.[3] In 1971 a *Variety* article made a point of the connection between the Ninth Annual New York Film Festival and the first New York Erotic Film Festival, remarking that "tired buffs" of the former could anticipate the premiere of the erotic film festival, as an alternative site of exhibition.[4] The germination of the erotic festivals had as much to do with the successes of more established sites of cineaste activity—such as the international film festival circuit, as well as film societies, and the general availability of foreign imports screened at art houses across the United States—as they did with the burgeoning sexual culture of the time. The erotic festivals in San Francisco, New York, and Amsterdam presented a utopian attitude, which anticipated that the unbinding of sexual repression in filmic representations could also loosen the cultural psyche and deregulate sexual practice within social life.

The opening out toward broader cultural and screen permissiveness and the persistent erosion of the legal definition of obscenity provided the historical backdrop that also allowed the erotic film festivals to briefly thrive, yet just as quickly expire a few years later. By self-designating as "erotic," the festivals in New York and San Francisco capitalized, perhaps unwittingly, on the public and juridical confusion of boundaries between experimental film, hardcore porn, sexploitation films, and independently made films of various stripes.[5] A series of full-page advertisements for the First Annual New York Erotic Film Festival (NYEFF) in an October 1971 issue of the *Village Voice* proclaimed, "The NYEFF has arrived, proving film is more than a four-letter word."[6] Conflating the assumption of filmic form with risqué content, the come-on alluded to the elevation of sex through the legitimizing frame of film as art, while implying a semantic reversal—in that eroticism could also elevate filmic form. A subsequent ad publicized the films to be screened, with *The Long Swift Sword of Siegfried* (1971)—a U.S./German coproduction made by sexploitation impresario David Friedman—playing in the same program with Jerry Abram's experimental film *Eyetoon* (1968) and George Csiscery's mythological-erotic paean *Andromeda* (1971). In addition, the festival announced showings of Scott Bartlett's experimental film *Lovemaking* (1971) and Constance Beeson's ode to lesbian coupling *Holding* (1971), as well as films by Warhol Factory habitué Gerard Malanga, emergent film and video artist Jud Yalkut (a documentation of a Yayoi Kusama performance, *Kusama's Self-Obliteration* [1967]), early gay porn director Arch Brown, and founder of the London Filmmaker's Co-op Steve Dwoskin.[7] The first San Francisco erotic festival also mixed its experimental and independent shorts, combining humor-oriented and animated films by local filmmakers, with films such as James Broughton's *The Golden Positions* (1971) and the sixty-minute "marriage manual" style sexploitation film *The Zodiac Couples* (1970). In U.S. theaters, it had become common for sexploitation films to play on a double or triple bill with foreign imports and broadly dubbed art house fare by the late 1960s, but the convergence of experimental films and sexploitation and hardcore shorts at these erotic festivals created unique viewing spaces that drew connections in more direct ways across differing modes of production and aesthetic styles for its audiences.

"Actualists, Not Spectators": The Wet Dream Film Festival

Much as imported European films helped liberalize U.S. screens on both sociological and legal fronts, the U.S. erotic film festivals saw a continental progenitor in the Wet Dream Festival.[8] The first international erotic film festival was created by the editors of the European underground sex paper *SUCK*, many of whom were American expatriates. Their ranks included artist and writer Jim Haynes, editor and writer William Levy, and Dutch cartoonist Willem de Ridder. With help from poet/playwright Heathcote Williams, the literary translator Susan Jansen, Australian feminist and author of *The Female Eunuch*, Germaine Greer, and New York writer Lynne Tillman, the editors spawned the organization s.e.l.f. — the Sexual Egalitarian and Libertarian Fraternity — as a means to arrange the first annual Wet Dream Festival in Amsterdam. The Wet Dream was an event devoted to the exhibition of pornographic films and to the more expansive goal of sexual freedom. Greer was invited to be a film judge along with, among others, *Screw* editor Al Goldstein, fashion model Jean Shrimpton, and *Village Voice* columnist Mike Zwerin. All festival patrons had to sign a sexual liberationist manifesto scripted by s.e.l.f., become members of the organization, and get photo identification cards to gain entry to the festival. The statement called upon the audience to subscribe to the doctrine of "sexual freedom, sexual tolerance, and sexual generosity . . . free from possessiveness."[9] It enacted a form of a Wilhelm Reich–inflected (see chapter 6) social contract, one constituted through and embedded within the act of filmgoing itself. The required membership in s.e.l.f. was also pragmatically a way to provide legal cover for the festival and prevent the potential intervention of law enforcement officers, who nonetheless attended and observed the event.[10]

Drawing together many of the readers and contributors of *SUCK* in Amsterdam, lauded as part erotic film fete and part "bacchanal," the Wet Dream Festival became ensnared in heated controversy. Greer and others were critical of the festival in retrospect, in part after a confrontation around the live sexual performance of Viennese Aktionist Otto Muehl, who appeared with a goose that he intended to maim and kill on stage. Audience members Heathcote Williams and Anthony Haden-Guest leapt on the stage and stole the goose, thus ending Muehl's performance, but not before he had defecated on stage as a final retaliatory gesture.[11]

For numerous reasons, Greer was disappointed and considered the first Wet Dream a failed experiment. For her, the Muehl incident was merely a flashpoint for deeper problems. Registering ambivalence about both the prevalence of commercial hardcore pornography and the underground films that were shown, she wrote,

> The Wet Dream Festival was not a festival of liberated sex and could not itself liberate anyone, for it is axiomatic that one can only liberate oneself. . . . Its problems were . . . felt much more keenly because felt simultaneously and together. Firstly, we were committed to showing a great number of commercial porn films, made to exploit the misery of the deprived and the perverted, at minimal cost, badly shot, worse played by the unhappy actors blackmailed by force or lack of money, dingy, murky, spotty, choppy film, sex without dialogue or soul or body. The effect of such films is a calculated turn-off, throwing the viewer back into himself, isolating us all from each other. . . . But at least the commercial porno films were aimed at sexual response, however desolate and specific. The Underground films were not even genital: either they celebrated sex in narcissistic and artistic ways or they offered a sort of commentary on decadent social mores. The hypocrisy of getting kicks out of the depiction of depraved sex while retaining the right to disapprove of it or satirize it was the worst turn-off of all.[12]

Greer's hopes for a liberationist sexual politics to spring from the festival, reflective of her larger writings affirming that women "say yes" to sexual pleasure outside of the realms of domination and violence, were not in her estimation achieved by the event. Greer's involvement, as well as her subsequent falling out with the SUCK magazine collective, also spoke, however obliquely, to the emerging discontents of the women's movement with pornographic materials. Interestingly, Greer's, Betty Dodson's, Jansen's, and Tillman's participation in the Wet Dream Festival also represented a historical moment at which women's place in the politics of sexual liberation was only beginning to be contested.[13]

The Wet Dream Festival, which continued for a second year in October 1971, was also a ground for sexual practice, as part of the sense that sex on screen should approximate the complexity and variety of sex in life. The first and second annual Wet Dream Festivals were covered in the press as much for their sex-tinged parties and libidinal postscreening events as for their films, for which reviewers doled out faint praise. For the second Wet Dream, festival organizers set up "love rooms" in the Lido Club and a seven-hour ferry trip to encourage sexual activity amongst its guests, both spaces outfitted with waterbeds, rock music, and "European dope." This led a *Rolling Stone* reviewer to remark, "There was a distinct Harold Robbins flavor to it all."[14] Robert Coover, in the *Evergreen Review*, pointed out a central contradiction between the impulse to watch sex and the impulse to do it, between filmgoing as a solitary act and filmgoing as a potentially social one, writing that "the very nature of film is counterorgiastic. Orgy is communal, and film by itself is voyeuristic, masturbatory, private."[15] Similarly, pro-sex feminist, artist, and masturbation advocate Betty Dodson recalled her experience as a judge at the second Wet Dream. She compared the films to the copious group sex in which she took part outside of the theater:

> Aside from a remarkable few, most [films] had portrayed heterosexual male fantasies with man on top fucking, no close-ups of clits, and not one woman touched her own clitoris during intercourse. There were also more blowjobs for men than oralsex [sic] for women. It was clear to me that the world needed porn that would inspire people to be better lovers that would include what women liked. While the quality of the films had been only medium to poor, I had to congratulate the festival on the aesthetic quality of the live sex—that turned out to be the real art form.[16]

The Wet Dream Festival seemed unapologetically bound to porn— in Jim Haynes's own admission, pornographic films had more prominence than erotic films at the festival, as a result of the former's abundant availability.[17] In an article covering the second annual Wet Dream, Haynes was heard quipping that the "films are incidental"; "they're just an excuse for us to be here."[18] Haynes was not, however, a stranger to cinephilia: as a consistent attendee of the Cannes, Edinburgh, and Berlin Film Festivals, he used Cannes (as well as the Frankfurt Book Fair) to promote the Wet Dream.[19] Despite the predominantly hardcore films at the festival, some of the films shown at the Wet Dream diverged from this classification, with distinctive underground and sexploitation or hardcore crossovers: Jean Genet's homoerotic classic *Un chant d'amour* (1950) and the first festival grand-prize winner, *Adultery for Fun and Profit* (1970), an early entry into the attempt to merge narrative form and explicit content in an adult film (figure 5.1).[20] In a final assessment, Greer rallied for a revisionist pornographic movement: "Confrontation is political awareness. What we discovered at the Wet Dream Festival is that we will have to generate enough energy in ourselves to create a

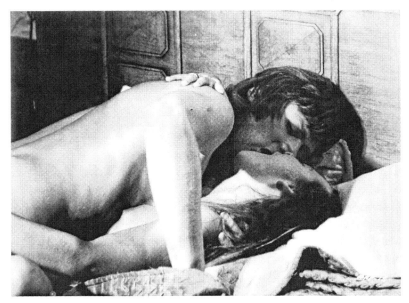

Fig. 5.1 *Adultery for Fun and Profit* (1970) was an award winner at the Wet Dream Film Festival in Amsterdam, a fact touted in advertising when the film was picked up for distribution by Sherpix.

pornography which will eradicate the traditional porn by sheer erotic power"; "we must commission films, make films, write, act co-operate for life's sake."[21]

Nonetheless, the festival's central significance remained its linking of contexts of cinematic reception to sexual practice, and the utopian sensibility which hoped—as did Greer, Dodson, and the festival organizers themselves—that film could have political and personal valence in eliminating pervasive sexual "hang-ups." The editors of SUCK still saw the Wet Dream as a success on many fronts and in relation to their stated aims,

> to establish the right to view so-called pornographic movies in an ordinary cinema situation . . . to present a complete spectrum of erotic movie-making—from sexploitation films to 8mm home movies . . . to bring together SUCK readers and contributors, so that they could come to know one another better . . . to show erotic films outside of the limitations of conventional cinema, in a physical space with a potential for erotic actualities. This happened.[22]

Proclaiming themselves "actualists, not spectators" the editors reinforced the notion that the Wet Dream was an engineered yet organic social space where the "live" sex, and its potentiality, was given pride of place as a public and political act, a space in which the workings and visceral charge of the cinematic form could help achieve these goals. In the most fitting credo of all, the Wet Dream organizers declared that "the participant is the best observer."[23]

Erotic Art, or "The Best Fuck Films": Erotic Film Festivals in the United States

The Wet Dream Festival was tumultuous and rife with ideological tensions, and ended with the collapse of the *SUCK* collective in 1972. The erotic film festivals held in the United States were similarly telling manifestations of liberationist idealism toward erotic imagery taken into the public sphere. Presenting a promotional face that professed a hip, culturally "with it" set of aims and agendas, these festivals created viewing spaces that resembled happenings and orgiastic launch pads far more than traditional film screenings. Arlene Elster and Lowell Pickett, who co-owned the Sutter Cinema, a leading "upscale" theater for 16 mm "artistically oriented" adult films, began the International Erotic Film Festival in San Francisco (see chapter 11). Both were active members in the San Francisco chapter of the Sexual Freedom League; Pickett was known to sponsor orgies at his home for the league, and Elster ran a discussion group on pornographic novels.[24] Of a younger generation than the makers of sexploitation films, Elster and Pickett were breaking the presumptions around the sexploitation and porn demographic, simultaneously with their film production company Leo Productions, their sponsorship of the festival, and their management of the Sutter Cinema. The Sutter, for instance, provided a revision of the sketchy and dilapidated porn theater ambience. The *New York Times* reported on the theater's tasteful décor, replete with rugs, erotic drawings, a tank of exotic goldfish in the lobby, and atypical amenities including free coffee and donuts during viewing hours, and discounts for seniors and couples— a demographic that Elster and Pickett were proud of attracting to their theater.[25] Elster and Pickett aspired to become the "cinematic equivalent" of Olympia Press in the 1950s, whose passel of literary finds included Burroughs, Beckett, and Nabokov, alongside second-rate erotic potboilers. One motivation for the erotic film festival, according to one reviewer, was Elster's desire to find "artistic" dirty movies; for Leo Productions, Elster and Pickett often commissioned adult films from independent directors who did not necessarily deal with sexual subjects, "in hope of getting something better than routine porno."[26]

The first annual San Francisco Erotic Film Festival in December 1970

Fig. 5.2 The Presidio Theater was outfitted as if for an old-fashioned Hollywood premiere for the First Annual San Francisco Erotic Film Festival in December 1970.

presented a group of judges known for their taste-maker status as cultural producers and intellectuals: the avant-garde filmmaker Bruce Conner; Olympia Press proprietor Maurice Girodias; and the film critic of the *Saturday Review* and the *Los Angeles Times*, Arthur Knight, who had recently penned a series of essays in *Playboy* magazine on the history of sex in cinema. The festival was remarked on as a scene fitted for Hollywood spectacle, held at the old vaudeville-era Presidio Theater (figure 5.2), and "roiling with the usual opening night freak show."[27] The theater was complete with barkers in "slightly rumpled" tuxedoes ushering the crowds along the red carpets. Opening night saw a surprise appearance by the gender-bending performance troupe the Cockettes, who were then enlivening the San Francisco club scene with their radical drag, as they belted out campy renditions of musical numbers in the theater lobby.[28] A roving film crew with 16 mm cameras had arrived, ready to film any developing action, sexual or otherwise, that might happen at the Presidio that evening.[29]

Comparably, the New York Erotic Film Festival, founded by former *Screw* magazine editor Ken Gaul and his partner Roger Sichel, promised, over the course of its two-year stint, demimonde luminaries to judge the films—pop artist Andy Warhol, film director Miloš Forman, *Happy Hooker* author Xaviera Hollander, novelist Gore Vidal, Factory superstar Holly Woodlawn, film actress Sylvia Miles, *Candy* author Terry Southern, inveterate beat William Burroughs, and Wet Dream veterans Goldstein and Dodson, among others of the literati and glitterati downtown set.[30] Of course, some never actually showed up to the events, and Warhol was reputed to have never turned in his ballots for the film prizes.[31] The first NYEFF spanned a month and was held at multiple downtown and midtown theaters: the Agee 1 and 2, the Cine Malibu, and the Cinema Village. The thrill of potentially rubbing shoulders with some of these underground, countercultural celebrities must have provided a special frisson for New York audiences, who could also ostensibly evaluate the films alongside the illustrious jury, vis-à-vis the "audience favorite" award.

Both festivals, through the deployment of underground icons as authority figures, and following the lead of the Wet Dream Festival, enacted a convergence, if not a production of, sexual tastes. Connoisseurship was linked not only with the hipness of these tastemakers but also with the edginess of an alternative space for the consumption of "artful" sexuality. Dandifying the appeal of the otherwise lurid, the promotional rhetoric of these festivals implied that viewers could partake in identifying their own erotic preferences within and amongst the various filmic techniques and genres, as well as within a sense of like-minded, liberated cosmopolitan community.[32] A New York sex weekly encouraged readers to attend the first New York festival, "for no other reason than because it is of historical significance, probably even rivalling [sic] Woodstock in its impact on the American scene."[33]

A promotional featurette that introduced the traveling film compilation The Best of the New York Erotic Film Festival (1973), which Gaul and Sichel negotiated for theatrical distribution after the first and second annual festivals, depicts the sense of this urban underground milieu. Gaul introduces the short films and provides a teaser of what the festival looked like to non–New York, nonfestival audiences, who would be seeing the films in their local theaters across the country. Sitting in an artist's studio setting surrounded by erotic sculptures and drawings, Gaul speaks in a tone leavened with sarcasm, explaining his rationale for the festival: to "get the best fuck films, invite the public, charge them three dollars, and show America the best erotica around." Gaul sardonically notes that most of the filmmakers are under thirty years old and include "men, women, those who are not sure yet, and a very attractive transsexual from Encino." Describing the prefestival press party as full of "New York beautiful people," the shot ends with a cut to shaky handheld documentary footage of the revelry. In keeping with the ambience of a happening, we see a variety of hippie and artist types drinking punch allegedly laced with "lysergic detergent," naked women dancing amidst the crowd, a man with a pet snake, a cavorting girl whose nude body is painted silver, and a naked couple in a sauna, who discuss European and American views on sexuality, profess laissez-faire attitudes toward homosexuality, and give their positive opinions of pornography. Gaul's voiceover makes a point to identify some of the people we are seeing, including Andrew Sarris, film critic for the *Village Voice*, and transgender superstar Holly Woodlawn. When asked about what it's like to judge an erotic festival, Woodlawn, shot in wobbly extreme close-up, states, "If it gets me hard, if it gets me going, it's erotic." The festival's identity, as represented in this documentary featurette, no doubt traded on the cachet of urban cultivation, youth culture, polysexuality, and ideals of sexual freedom.

The cultural pedigree of this new generation of erotica entrepreneurs facilitated the cross-fertilization of various films, audiences, and scenes allowed for at the festivals themselves. Appealing to an audience of the young and the bohemian, the directors of these respective festivals on both coasts maneuvered the cultural identities of their events and located themselves apart and distinct from both the simplicity of hardcore pornography and the obsolescence of sexploitation film and its transparently commercial pretenses. The San Francisco organizers claimed that their event was not "mere pornography," but a pursuit of the more elusive ideal of eroticism.[34] In a solicitation sent out to filmmakers by the International Erotic Film Festival, Elster and Pickett wrote,

> We feel that a festival of this sort is long overdue. Although people have been making erotic films since the inception of the cinema, the only films that have been given wide exposure have been sexploitation films. We intend this festival to provide a setting in which all types of erotic films can be seen, not just sex exploitation films. We consider an erotic film to be any film which you, the filmmaker feel is erotic.[35]

Elster and Pickett deferred to the creativity and determinative desires of independent filmmakers to constitute a new erotic cinema. They were among a new breed of 16 mm adult film merchants, who defined their theater and exhibition of independent adult films as a break with the sexploitation film trade, as well as with the shoddy crudity of others in the hardcore market.[36] In the late 1960s and early 1970s, sexploitation producers—in their focus on the soft-sell of simulated sex—were having their economic livelihood threatened by hardcore 16 mm producers such as Elster and Pickett, as well as by the developing porn feature, other larger independents, and the floundering Hollywood studios.[37] At a convention for the Adult Film Association of America in 1971, Pickett clashed with the circumspect sexploitation crowd who were resisting allowing the 16 mm filmmakers to gain membership in the three-year-old organization. Pickett, rendering the conflict in generational terms, exclaimed that "you've all been guilty of fraud for the past 10 years. You've never delivered the goods and now we are. . . . Your audiences are getting old and dying off."[38]

Sexploitation films and their producers were nonetheless represented at the San Francisco festival, most notably by the crossover film *The Zodiac Couples*; thus, Elster and Pickett's stated aims of cultural distinction belied a more capacious framing of their festival within the broader rubric of "erotica." *The Zodiac Couples* was an interesting test case of the overlaps between different cinematic genres, modes of production, and reception, as it was met with considerable audience resistance at the festival. The response registered a generational split along the axes of sexual and cinematic tastes, and pointed to the varying expectations film audiences had of adult films. One reporter noted that during the screening of *The Zodiac Couples*, the audience "amused itself (after it became obvious that jeers and catcalls were not going to stop the film) by supplying science fiction sound effects and loud laughter as the on-screen narrator ran down dialogue such as 'the Scorpio female is easily aroused, and makes a most satisfying partner. She is best mated to blah blah blah.'"[39] Arthur Knight similarly characterized the audience's reaction to the film, stating that the film "unspooled to boos and catcalls." "It was a frankly commercial, safely pornographic . . . sexploitation picture; and it compared unfavorably with the more imaginative, more experimental, more personal, and far more erotic films that preceded it."[40]

Nevertheless, the combination of sexploitation films and of experimental and independent works at both festivals represented a unique moment in the history of sexually suggestive cinema, in that they found an audience that cohered for a brief time around films designated as "erotica"; whereas previously the screening venues for such films might have been a bit more discrete, both geographically—particularly in terms of the distinction between underground film venues and grindhouse theaters—and socially, in the divergence between the presumably older, male sexploitation audience and the younger, hipper, and more sexually fluid audience for underground or avant-garde films.[41] A writer in a New York sex paper suggested that the "sophisticate" crowd was less familiar with sexploitation and hardcore fare than may have been otherwise assumed:

Being a pornographer by trade and getting to see all those Forty-Second Street flicks as a matter of course, it's easy for me to forget that, save for our readers, the world of sexploitation movies is virtually unknown. And, if the reaction that these movies received at the press party was any indication, New York's affluent elite by and large had never seen a sex movie with people fucking and sucking before that night. . . . I mean who would expect to see Sylvia Miles walk into the Cameo Art, right?[42]

This commentator drew a number of distinctions between the designated audience for sexploitation, broadly defined, and the audience that the New York festival was bringing to these films, in terms of differences in class, taste, and modes of consumption along the axes of "high" and "low" culture. In the same article, a brief interview with Gaul echoed Elster and Pickett's insistence on differentiation from sexploitation: he claimed that the films being shown were in fact erotic art, selected based on their "artistic merit," irrespective of their hardcore sexual content.[43]

Consistent with Elster and Pickett's orientation around erotica and art, the written announcement of the first festival awards by the San Francisco festival judges, Girodias, Conner, and Knight, declared,

The sexual revolution has already been achieved; what we are working on now is the erotic revolution. The purpose of this festival is to find what in films can be singled out as erotic — as opposed to merely pornographic . . . Erotic is what stimulates the intelligence and the imagination as well as the senses . . . It has more to do with the higher emotions than the lower, and as such affords an infinite challenge to the "now" filmmakers.[44]

This analysis of the difference between the erotic and the pornographic was an extension of the raging intellectual and public debates over the definitions of the truly obscene that had been happening for over a decade, especially since the 1957 *Roth v. United States* decision.[45] As early as 1959, psychotherapists Drs. Phyllis and Eberhard Kronhausen had written a book that introduced what for them was a crucial distinction between the literary tradition of "erotic realism" and the more vulgar appeals of the "hardcore" pornographic text. The Kronhausens argued that erotic realism did more than just corporeally excite the senses and arouse the passions of its reader, as did pornography. For them, what distinguished the erotic realist text from the hardcore was its humanist interest in representing "reality" to the reader, depicting a "sexual life in the wider meaning" and as a manifestation of a "basic rebellion against the social suppression of elemental drives and needs common to all mankind."[46] Like the San Francisco festival judges' assessment, the rationalization of the difference between these two modes was that the erotic appealed to the mind and not exclusively to the body of its audience.

Although the San Francisco festival took on a tone that invoked artistic elevation and the privileging of the erotic as an aesthetic form within a logic of "sexual expressionism," the New York Erotic Film Festival established a more brash environ of mercantile reception, while still partaking in the language of erotica and art, no doubt seen as a benefit for legal protection, marketing purposes, and cultural credibility. Ken Gaul, in his public spokesmanship for the New York festival, cultivated a more crassly commercial sensibility—perhaps due to his affiliation with *Screw* magazine. By the second NYEFF, Gaul was claiming that "people want to see more hard-core pornography,"[47] and that "if someone wants to pretend there is something artistic and profound about a cock up an ass, what harm is there in it?"[48]

Such distinctions between the two festivals can also be borne out by the ways in which they promoted themselves in postevent venues. In a correspondence with Victor Faccinto, one of the awarded filmmakers at both festivals, Elster and Pickett sent a form letter soliciting images from his film to be submitted to a coffee table book of collected film stills commemorating the event. This was an idea suggested by Maurice Giro-dias, and the book was to have been published by Olympia Press.[49] The New York festival correspondence underlines the distinction, with Ken Gaul requesting still photos for a glossy pictorial spread to be published in *Penthouse* magazine. In the letter, Gaul calls *Penthouse* "an outstanding international magazine," noting that the magazine's circulation of close to one million, in the United States alone, might be useful for publicity.[50] The distinction between "high" and "low" cultural modes of circulation are conspicuous and certainly mark some of the philosophical and com-mercial orientations of the two festivals and their directors—seen in the difference between the parlor status of the objet d'art of the book, and the business-minded interest in a ten-page layout in a newsstand maga-zine. Notwithstanding their differences, the San Francisco and New York festivals shared a discourse of the erotic as a distinctly new, legitimating form of cinematic curation and reception.

Sites of Reception: Critics, Audiences, and Men in Blue

Despite the language of erotica, or the means of creating cultural dis-tinction around sexual images in the public sphere, the New York Erotic Film Festival particularly was not exempt from the attentions of law en-forcement. In both installments in 1971 and 1972 the New York festival was graced with a series of police raids, in which officers confiscated a number of films, three of them festival prizewinners. Casting a diverse net, the seized films included Fred Baker's *Room Service 75* (1971), Al Di Lauro's stag film homage *Old Borrowed and Stag* (1971), gay porn filmmaker Arch Brown's *Tuesday* (1971), and John Knoop's experimental short *Norien Ten* (1971). The raids at the festival caused Dominic Sicilia to threaten to pull his film *Hot Parts* (1971), and Gaul and Sichel had to attend numerous legal proceedings to handle fines and charges.

The charges against all but one of the films were dropped, as Gaul mobilized film critics Judith Crist, Clive Barnes, and John Simon, along with the ACLU, to defend his cause. The exception was Arch Brown's *Tuesday*, which was the only gay male film at the festival. Although many of the films had hardcore sexual content, the homosexual orientation of Brown's film was perhaps the sticking point for the judge, who, according to *Screw*, claimed that "it was the worst film I've ever seen." The sex paper speculated that

> *Room Service 75* has straight hardcore sex, as well as a bestiality sequence involving two girls and a dog. But charges were dropped against the film, and against the two other flicks which only featured heterosexual acts. What is especially incongruous is that *Tuesday* is probably the most artistic and the most "socially redeeming" of the four films. It's a technically polished production and a fairly sensitive portrayal of homosexual lust. ... The message seems to be that heterosexual hardcore is becoming so widely accepted that the police and courts are willing to look the other way, but homosexual films are still an easy target for arrest.[51]

Just as in the prior decade, when *Un chant d'amour* and Jack Smith's *Flaming Creatures* (1963) met with obdurate legal responses in the United States for their representations of queer, nonnormative sexual acts, Brown's film was faced with similar police recalcitrance within the context of the film festival, which was perhaps threateningly seen as a site of "mixed-use," or at least dangerously undefined, reception. Although gay erotica was beginning to be screened in all-male adult theaters in New York, such as the Park–Miller and the 55th Street Playhouse, the combination of gay and straight fare at the festival, and implicitly the mixed gay, straight and bisexual audiences, may have attracted heightened official scrutiny.[52]

The police gave no time to hair splitting over the ostensible quality of the erotic art represented by the films of the NYEFF, even though the festival had complied with a new no-pandering law that forbade excessive, lewd advertising on theater marquees or via film stills and newspaper ads. Gaul and Sichel told *Variety* that the "police are up in arms precisely because the festival is not running at conventional hardcore sites, is spread around town and is attracting a broad audience spectrum and has been strongly promoted." The hardcore porn theater owners of New York City of course took notice while the "neophytes (we)re taking the beating" in their stead.[53] These obscenity complications likely provided more publicity for the festival. As mentioned earlier, Gaul and Sichel negotiated for distribution of a compilation program of festival highlights, allowing the afterlife of the festival to travel to film societies, universities, and art houses nationally in the following years.[54] The second annual NYEFF, reduced from one month to two weeks and limited to one theater, the Cinema Village, caused a "second annual crackdown" as theater employees were arrested for operating without a license. Gaul, undeterred, continued to send projectionists and ushers to staff the theater.[55]

The critical reception of these festivals was duly mixed, with *Variety* and the *New York Times* covering the details of the police raids, and the underground and left-of-center press often invoking the usual "I'm so bored" affectation that had become a common refrain in cultural insiders' accounts of watching the repetitive ministrations of porn. Jonas Mekas, in his review of the first NYEFF, suspected that the event was a "big capitalist swindle," suggesting that a better option would be a retrospective of stag films of the 1920s and 1930s at the Museum of Modern Art. About the festival films, he wrote:

> But boring they are, and bad they are! . . . I have figured it all out . . . An erotic movie is an arty porno movie intended to be shown at film festivals. The only change I'd consider making in this concise definition is perhaps changing the word "arty" with the word "artsy." . . . The (woman) I took forced me to walk out in the middle of the show, rightly . . . observing that she had had enough of "these male chauvinist" movies. And she didn't even belong to women's lib, at least not until this festival; she may by now.[56]

Mekas's remarks regarding changing the appellation of "arty" to "artsy," coming from one of the key architects of the New American Cinema, evinced derision for the aspirational logic of the festival, in which the festival's pretensions toward underground status were rendered flimsily transparent. Mekas's semantic quibbling mirrored the distinctions that the festival organizers were attempting to make between erotica, sexploitation, and pornography. His female companion's response, relegating the festival to the category of misogynist cultural production, again presaged the development of the feminist critique of the sexual liberationist position vis-à-vis pornography, a critique that emerged from women's involvement in the politics of the counterculture and the New Left.

Other critics were a bit more forgiving of the NYEFF. A reporter for *Newsday* gave a phenomenological account of his perceptual state after a few days at the festival, caught in the onslaught of the sexual excesses proffered on screen. Turning the reportorial lens around on himself, he wrote,

> I walk around the city with my hands in my coat pockets for fear that some post-hypnotic suggestion planted in my mind by a dirty movie will unwittingly move my hands into some act that will bring a nightstick down on my head, disgrace to my profession, and ignominy to the whole libertarian tradition by demonstrating conclusively that dirty movies should be censored because they induce criminal behavior. . . . There is nothing in moderation. There seems to be a pulsating rhythm to dirty movies—boredom followed by panic. Your brain contracts and expands involuntarily to the beat. . . . If you see enough of these movies, you'd better wear a name and address tag in your lapels so that you won't get lost when you get back out into the daylight.[57]

Attesting to a cultural logic spoken of earlier by another observer of the NYEFF, this vertiginous confessional confirms that the erotic festival format was indeed drawing in new audiences, who might have been otherwise reticent or leery of the "grind-house" theater setting.

The press roundup also included accounts of the always-compelling erotic film audience, which in this circumstance attracted attention for its "non-traditional" makeup and who could no longer be reduced to the caricature of "ancient onans."[58] These audiences were nevertheless subject to the same journalistic scrutiny as the porn audience for their behavioral quirks: "Despite the sexual razzle-dazzle on the screen, it's the audience that fascinates, because the audience—quivering or rigid, nervous or catatonically cool—continually betrays a squirmy humanity, and few of the films presented in the festival portrayed anything as authentic as what went on every night in the small theater."[59] In this, the festival was no different from its storefront theater neighbors in terms of the kinds of vocal public curiosities expressed regarding what audiences actually did in the screening space when watching adult films. Exhibiting a sociological indulgence in participant observation, this reviewer's sense of enthrallment by the temperament of the festivalgoers, as mass audience, also represents a broader cultural shift in the perception and acceptance of the adult film as a legitimate occupation of one's leisure time.

Kenneth Turan viewed the traveling collection entitled *Best of the New York Erotic Film Festival* in Washington, DC, seeing the films as a program apart from the fascinations of the young audience or post-festival parties. Turan noted that "the Cerberus hosts a younger, more sophisticated crowd, too with-it and worldly and wise to be caught with its pants down at the déclassé downtown porno shows with the tired businessmen and down and outers." Like Mekas, Turan treated the films with a cool and disinterested eye, complaining that they were not eroti-cally compelling enough, claiming that "the 11 shorts now showing to nearly capacity crowds at Cerberus 3 manage the trick of presenting the mechanics of sexual relations without evoking the feelings one expects. Undeniably arty, undeniably serious, they are no fun at all and end up about as erotic and dehumanized as computer dating" (figure 5.3). More impressed with the intensity of the downtown hardcore films, Turan claimed that the erotic fest favorites lacked "a vitality and an energy and a positive lust for sexuality which, however crude, is essential to success-ful erotic films, not to mention life itself."[60]

The first San Francisco festival was not exempt from a critique of its films, as Jerome Tarshis wrote a postmortem analysis of their short-comings and made a number of suggestions for the planning of the festival for the upcoming year. Desiring "entries of the caliber of Berg-man's *Smiles of a Summer Night* or the Japanese masterpiece *A Thousand Cranes*," Tarshis noted the absence of "feature length theatrical film from major producers" as well as a paucity of foreign films, despite a small number of international entries. Tarshis also observed a limitation that conflated underground aesthetic techniques with a symptomatic sexual discomfort:

> The films shown at the festival suggested to me that many filmmakers believe that hiding or blurring the outward appearances of the genital organs is art, while showing them clearly is porno. Undoubtedly, some of this runs parallel with the tendency toward abstraction in twentieth century painting and sculpture, but I think a lot of the abstraction was modesty—or shame—disguised as art . . . which leads me to some of the limitations of the underground film. People who dislike pornography complain that the characters have no depth and no history, and do not exist in any serious developed psychological or social context. They are

Fig. 5.3 The short film *Sport*, in which a young woman masturbates with her brother's sports equipment, was part of the traveling Best of the First Annual New York Erotic Film Festival collection.

bodies, and they perform sexual acts in an unidentified bed. The same complaint can be lodged against most of the films in this festival, although their creators might be insulted at being compared to pornographers.[61]

In a conversation Tarshis had with Bruce Conner regarding these limitations, Conner justified some of these difficulties in relationship to the sorts of skills underground or experimental filmmakers possess, such as editing and cinematography, over and above writing, script development, and choreography. Invested in the development of a cinematic art that could capaciously include experimentation with erotic form, Tarshis in his conclusion, requested,

> If I may address myself to Santa Claus, in this year's festival I should like to see less embarrassment about sex on the part of the filmmakers. An orange can indeed be a symbol, friends, but so can a cunt. . . . As for superimposed images used as substitutes for thinking about Eros, and as cheap approaches to the sublime, we had enough of that the first time around.[62]

Seeking a means of adequately and creatively transporting eroticism from its fleshy, mercurial materiality onto the film screen, Tarshis's criticisms seem an earnest mode of reception, a discursive space made possible by the institution of the erotic film festival, where the ideals of the cinephile and the sensualist could converge.

In the end, however, these festivals were as much about protecting a refashioned adult cinema, renamed "erotica," for its potentials for aesthetic innovation, as about distancing themselves from the presumed and perceived audience of a "lowbrow" pornography—heterosexual, working- and middle-class, middle-aged men. As some of the above descriptions of the erotic festivals bear out, the combination of straight- and gay-oriented films, the predominance of queer celebrity jurors such as Warhol, Woodlawn, Vidal, and so on, as well as the cultural status of the young and ambisexual audiences—dotted with not only bohemian young couples and women, but also gays, lesbians, and the transgendered—articulated a desire to create an alternative space for film consumption. This space could tap into a contemporaneous sexual openness and fluidity, linking it to an experiential marketplace of new cinematic sights and sensations.

The adult film had expanded its reach in the middle to late 1960s to the "date" and "couples" market, with the exhibition of crossover sexploitation hits by filmmakers such as Radley Metzger and Russ Meyer in "showcase" and art house theaters, and through the stateside importation of many risqué foreign features.[63] Recognizing the appeal of adult cinema for this demographic, the festivals addressed a younger, more gender diverse, and countercultural audience, full of, as one festival observer noted, "modish couples and twinkling figures of indeterminate sex."[64] Considering the post-Stonewall moment and the emergence of the gay rights movement, the erotic festivals capitalized on the shifting fields of reception around adult films at this time. Also taking into account that the first of the women's film festivals in the United States did not appear until 1972, and the first gay and lesbian film festival in San Francisco was held in 1976, the erotic festivals represented a moment before identity-based sexual politics had taken hold, and as shifts were occurring in the ways erotic consumers and their sexual identities were being constructed and addressed.[65] Although the social scientists of the Commission on Obscenity and Pornography largely reinforced the reigning preconception that the viewers of adult films were primarily men, the emerging market of couples, women, gays, and lesbians could now also tentatively enter the fray through the urbane introductions offered at the erotic film festivals.[66] Therefore, the festivals, in their facilitation of polysexual sites for film consumption, predated the emergence of gay and lesbian and women's film festivals, providing a place where sexuality, rather than identity, could be ratified and explored. Accounts of the constitution of the erotic festival audience give pause to the conventional wisdom that it was the landmark hardcore feature *Deep Throat* (1972) that opened up the possibility of adult film viewing to women and couples, and these accounts demand further nuance in the analysis of exhibition and reception of sexually oriented films in this period.[67]

But if the breakout popularity of *Deep Throat* on U.S screens in the summer of 1972 has been historically narrated as a benchmark of the changing tides of content and exhibition of adult films, it also can indicate some of the reasons for the decline and disappearance of the erotic film festivals shortly thereafter. Making their appearance during a brief period (roughly 1970–1972) between the outmoding of the softcore sexploitation feature and the attendant rise of "porno chic," the erotic festivals were soon eclipsed themselves, a significant footnote in the history of the exhibition of screen sex. Although the *Miller v. California* decision altered the legal and political climate, in trying to create roadblocks for adult films on the local level, the widespread availability and swelling fortunes of publicly exhibited hardcore seemed at this point incontrovertible.

Emblematic of the manifesto-laden spirit of the "long 1960s," a countercultural imperative inflected the presentation of the erotic film festivals in their desire to create a different space for the consumption of erotic images. With this also came an attempt to generate a "community of common interest" oriented around the development and identification of particular sexual tastes, multifarious as they were. Although brief in their institutional existence, and however ephemeral their traces remain today, what remains fascinating about the erotic film festivals for film history are the means through which they strove to present a sense of cultural refinement and sophistication around the screening of sexually explicit film, while also trafficking in the currency of utopian, sexual liberationist ideals to legitimate their events as a form of personal, political, and aesthetic enlightenment. Prior to the notorious multiblock lines to get in to see *Deep Throat*, or the "pornocopia" that would follow, the festivals and their founders had targeted a market for an optimistically novel erotic film experience, forged out of the urbane cinephile milieus of Amsterdam, San Francisco, and New York, and contingent on filmgoing as a social and collective act.

Notes

1. The International Erotic Film Festival in San Francisco was held in December 1970 and 1971, the New York Erotic Film Festival in November 1971 and 1972, and the Wet Dream Festival in Amsterdam in November 1970 and October 1971.

2. The scene for contemporary erotic film festivals is diverse; a partial list includes the Sin Cine New York Erotic Film Festival (launched in 2002); the Victoria Erotic Film and Arts Festival; the Canadian Festival of Forbidden Fruit; the O'Face Amateur Film Festival in Miami; Hot D'Or, held in Cannes, France; and the Xplicit British Film Festival. Gay and lesbian film festivals have long included programs devoted to erotic and explicitly sexual films. More recently, standalone gay erotic film festivals have emerged.

3. The first film festivals in Europe span back to the 1932 Venice Film Festival, and gained broader popularity in the postwar period with the development of festivals in Cannes (1946), Edinburgh (1947), and Berlin (1951). The first international film festival in the United States was held in Columbus, OH, in 1953, organized by the Columbus Film Council. The San Francisco International Film Festival began in 1957, sponsored by the San Francisco Film Society. Amos Vogel's Cinema 16 and other film societies also contributed to the expansion of audience tastes and preferences in its featuring of short, documentary, and experimental films.

4. "Steady on Fire: Erotic Film Fest Sets 4 Situations," *Variety*, October 20, 1971, 3, 26.

5. One account of the rising sexualization of the screen discussed the underground film alongside the sexploitation feature, noting that these two modes of production were often confused or associated with one another by an undiscriminating, "uninitiated" lay public. James Lithgow and Colin Heard, "Underground U.S.A. and the Sexploitation Market," *Films and Filming* 15, no. 11 (August 1969), 25.

6. First Annual New York Erotic Film Festival advertisement, *Village Voice*, October 21, 1971, 88.

7. First Annual New York Erotic Film Festival advertisement.

8. One can trace a long lineage of influential European films that altered U.S. film culture, from Gustav Machatý's *Ecstasy* (1933, Czechoslovakia) to Roberto Rossellini's *The Miracle* (1951, Italy) to Jean Genet's *Un chant d'amour* (1950, France) to Louis Malle's *The Lovers* (1958, France) to Vilgot Sjöman's *I Am Curious (Yellow)*, to name just a few. Evidence shows that there was also an erotic film festival in Frankfurt around this time, preceding the first NYEFF and close to the second Wet Dream, held in conjunction with the Frankfurt Book Fair. Hans Saaltink, "Amsterdam's 2nd Erotic Film Fest: 13 Jurors Promised, Three Appear," *Variety*, November 3, 1971, 25.

9. The full manifesto read: "When we are unafraid and free from possessiveness it will make little difference what kind of social organization we choose to

live under, because we will be open, kind and generous. It is sexual frustration, sexual envy, sexual fear, which permeates all our human relationships and which perverts them. The sexually liberated, the sexually tolerant and the sexually generous individuals are open tolerant and generous in all their activities. Therefore S.E.L.F. (Sexual Egalitarian and Libertarian Fraternity) wishes to encourage sexual freedom, sexual tolerance and sexual generosity." Cited in Robert Coover, "The First Annual Congress of the High Church of Hardcore," *Evergreen Review*, no. 89 (May 1971): 16.

10. Colin MacInness, a novelist reviewing the event for the British magazine the *New Society* suggested that the organizers were even more worried about the prominence of marijuana smoking at the festival, fearing that the combination of "sex *and* pot would be too much of a provocation." Colin MacInness, "Sex Marathon," *New Society* 16, no. 427 (December 5, 1970): 989; Al Goldstein, "The World's First Erotic Film Festival: A Behind the Scenes Look at Judging Porn," *Screw*, January 25, 1971, 4.

11. This unexpected conflict over Muehl's performance with the goose spurred a debate between Greer and Albie Thomas, who was one of the coordinators of the Wet Dream Festival, in the pages of the London newspaper *Friends* 22 (January 19, 1971).

12. The only exception that Greer makes is for Jean Genet's homoerotic prison classic, *Un chant d'amour*, which she rapturously praises in this essay. Germaine Greer, "The Wet Dream Film Festival," in *The Madwoman's Underclothes: Essays and Occasional Writings* (New York: Atlantic Monthly Press, 1986), 58. For another discussion of the Wet Dream Festival through Greer's perspective, see David Allyn, *Make Love, Not War: The Sexual Revolution: An Unfettered History* (Boston: Little, Brown and Company, 2000), 221–224.

13. Events such as the April 1970 protest by female employees at Rossett's Grove Press—a bastion of both free speech liberalism and a literary locus for the tenets of the sexual revolution—would foreground the ways the rhetoric of sexual liberation was coming to be seen by aggrieved and growingly militant feminists as the exploitation of women, both in deeds and in images. For an account of these events see S. E. Gontarski, *The Grove Press Reader* (New York: Grove Press, 2001), xxv–xxix. Robin Morgan, the radical feminist who coined the phrase "pornography is the theory and rape is the practice," was one of the employees and union organizers working at Grove Press and was instrumental in the takeover of the Grove offices. See Robin Morgan, *Saturday's Child: A Memoir* (New York: W. W. Norton, 2000), 276–318. See also Barbara Ehrenreich, Elizabeth Hess, and Gloria Jacobs, *Re-Making Love: The Feminization of Sex* (New York: Anchor Books, 1986). David Allyn also discusses the involvement of the feminist and antiporn advocate Andrea Dworkin in the early days of the SUCK collective and magazine (Allyn, *Make Love, Not War*, 221).

14. Robert Greenfield, "Dutch Porn Film Fest: World Ends," *Rolling Stone*, November 21, 1971, 22.

15. Coover, "The First Annual Congress of the High Church of Hardcore," 16.

16. Betty Dodson, chap. 11, "Wet Dream Film Festival: A Sexual Vacation in Amsterdam," *My Romantic Love Wars: A Sexual Memoir* (New York: self-published, 2010), 130.

17. Haynes also stated that all the films that were submitted to the festival committee were shown at the festival. Interview with Jim Haynes by the author, April 5, 2006.

18. Greenfield, "Dutch Porn Film Fest: World Ends," 22.

19. Haynes qualified that not all of the festival organizers were necessarily cinephiles. Interview with Jim Haynes by the author, April 5, 2006.

20. *Adultery for Fun and Profit* was funded by the U.S. publisher of sex pulp novels Greenleaf Classics and was brought to the festival by editor Earl Kemp. Earl Kemp, "Acres of Nubile Flesh," and "Wet Dreams in Paradiso," *eI* 15, vol. 3, no. 4 (August 2004), accessed May 2, 2006, efanzines.com/EK/eI15/index.htm.

21. Greer, "The Wet Dream Film Festival," 59.

22. Editors of *SUCK*, "The Wet Dream Film Festival Continued: Suck Cries Foul," *Screw*, March 1, 1971, 22.

23. Editors of *SUCK*, "The Wet Dream Film Festival Continued."

24. Jerome Tarshis, "Eros and the Muses," *Evergreen Review*, no. 88 (April 1971): 18.

25. William Murray, "The Porn Capital of America," *New York Times Magazine*, January 3, 1971.

26. Tarshis, "Eros and the Muses," 78. Although his films featured hardcore sex, Pickett stated that they never included "external come shots," which were "undignified" and would turn off the targeted audience of couples and younger patrons. Quoted in William Rotsler, *Contemporary Erotic Cinema* (New York: Penthouse), 211.

27. Michael Goodwin, "The Fucking Film Festival," *Interview*, no. 12 (March 1971): 29.

28. Arthur Knight, "Step Inside Folks, to an Erotic Film Festival," *Los Angeles Times*, December 13, 1970, U32.

29. Goodwin, "The Fucking Film Festival," 29.

30. It was perhaps Gaul's presence in Amsterdam for the Wet Dream Festival as the photographer for *Screw* magazine that provided the impetus for his helming the first New York Erotic Film Festival. Gaul's photographic credits appear in the article by Al Goldstein on the Wet Dream. Goldstein, "The World's First Erotic Film Festival," 5.

31. Addison Verrill, "Erotic Prizes to Films Which Attracted Cops," *Variety*, December 15, 1971, 4.

32. For an account of New York underground cinema during the 1960s as a "site for community building," see the chapter "Finding Community in the 1960s: Underground Cinema and Sexual Politics," in Janet Staiger's *Perverse Spectators: The Practice of Film Reception* (New York: NYU Press, 2000), 125–160.

33. Ed Trent, "Report on the New York Erotic Film Festival," *Naked News*, no. 1 (1971): 4.

34. The feminist movement would later take this aesthetic/ideological distinc-

tion on as its own project, particularly in Gloria Steinem's dictum: "Pornography is about dominance. Erotica is about mutuality." See Steinem, "Erotica vs. Pornography," in *Outrageous Acts and Everyday Rebellions*, 2nd ed. (New York: Owl Books, [1983] 1995).

35. International Erotic Film Festival Solicitation Letter to Victor Faccinto [n.d.], collection of the author.

36. Schaefer, "Gauging a Revolution: 16mm Film and the Rise of the Pornographic Feature," *Cinema Journal* 41, no. 3 (spring 2002): 15.

37. On Hollywood's battles over sexuality in films, hardcore and softcore, see Jon Lewis, *Hollywood v. Hardcore: How the Struggle over Censorship Saved the Modern Film Industry* (New York: New York University Press, 2000).

38. Kevin Thomas, "Current Censorship Status in Adult Film Market," *Los Angeles Times*, February 7, 1971, C22.

39. Goodwin, "The Fucking Film Festival," 29.

40. Knight, "Step Inside Folks, to an Erotic Film Festival," U32.

41. Historical research up to now has found only small connections between the world of sexually explicit adult films and suggestive sexploitation features and the works of the underground, avant-garde, and New American cinema. These were relatively distinct and ideologically divergent modes of production, generally cordoned off from each other by economic imperatives and designated audiences, as well as cultural pedigrees, even though the popular press, the lay public, and the law often bracketed these different modes together.

42. Trent, "Report on the New York Erotic Film Festival," 5.

43. Trent, "Report on the New York Erotic Film Festival."

44. Bruce Conner, Maurice Girodias, and Arthur Knight, "Statement of the Judges of the First International Erotic Film Festival" (1970), from the papers of Victor Faccinto.

45. *Roth v. United States*, 354 U.S. 476 (1957).

46. Eberhard and Phyllis Kronhausen, *Pornography and the Law: The Psychology of Erotic Realism and 'Hard Core' Pornography* (New York: Ballantine Books, 1959), 26–28.

47. David Black, "In Defense of Lobster Lust," *Boston Phoenix*, January 30, 1973, sec. 2, 3.

48. Ed McCormack, "New York Porn Film Fest," *Rolling Stone*, January 4, 1973, 18.

49. Lowell Pickett and Arlene Elster, First International Erotic Film Festival, letter to Victor Faccinto, December 28, 1970, from the papers of Victor Faccinto. The Wet Dream festival did publish a postfestival compendium: William Levy and Willem de Ridder, eds., *Wet Dreams: Films and Adventures* (Amsterdam: Joy Publications, 1973).

50. Ken Gaul, First Annual New York Erotic Film Festival, letter to Victor Faccinto, n.d., from the papers of Victor Faccinto.

51. "If This is Tuesday We Must Be in Jail," *Screw*, June 12, 1972, 15.

52. Jack Stevenson reports that by 1973 there were at least fifty urban theater venues showing exclusively gay porn, with twelve of them located in New York

City. See Jack Stevenson, "From the Bedroom to the Bijou: A Secret History of American Gay Sex Cinema," *Film Quarterly* 51, no. 1 (autumn 1997): 29.

53. Addison Verrill, "Fresh Raids, and More Expected," *Variety*, November 24, 1971, 7, 20.

54. *Best of the 2nd Annual New York Erotic Film Festival* screened at the Bijou Theater in 1973, a student-run film society at the University of Iowa in Iowa City. *Best of the 2nd Annual New York Erotic Film Festival* File, Bijou Theater Collection, Special Collections Department, University of Iowa Libraries, Iowa City.

55. "Nothing Can Daunt Erotica," *Washington Post, Times Herald*, December 13, 1972, C3.

56. Jonas Mekas, "Movie Journal," *Village Voice*, November 18, 1971, 81.

57. Joseph Gelmis, "Movies: In An Erotic Daze," *Newsday*, November 19, 1971, n.p., from the papers of Victor Faccinto.

58. Black, "In Defense of Lobster Lust," 3. This attribution of "ancient onans" was certainly a dramatic, if easy, overstatement. Studies and general understandings of adult film audiences of the period had revealed primarily middle-aged male audiences.

59. Black, "In Defense of Lobster Lust," 3.

60. Kenneth Turan, "Erotic Films: Full Range from Amusing to Dull," *Washington Post, Times Herald*, August 10, 1972, B15. The festival evidently played in some cities before being picked up for regular distribution by Saliva Films in 1973.

61. Tarshis, "Eros and the Muses," 78.

62. Tarshis, "Eros and the Muses," 78. Tarshis is referring here to Karen Johnson's prizewinning film *Orange* (1970), which showed in extreme close-up the peeling and eating of an orange, the texture and handling of the fruit rendered an allegory of sexual contact.

63. Eric Schaefer discusses this transforming demographic in the context of his history of 16 mm adult film of the late 1960s and early 1970s, in "Gauging a Revolution."

64. Black, "In Defense of Lobster Lust," 3.

65. For her recollections on women's film festivals, see B. Ruby Rich, *Chick Flicks: Theories and Memories of the Women's Film Movement* (Durham, NC: Duke University Press, 1998), 29–39.

66. Charles Winick, a researcher hired by the Commission on Obscenity and Pornography to study adult movie theater patrons, discovered that across multiple U.S. cities, the average makeup of this audience was 98 percent male, with "more females . . . observed in suburban locations than in downtown locations. All the females were with a male escort or a mixed gender group. Ninety percent of the men attended alone." President's Commission on Obscenity and Pornography, *Report of the Commission on Obscenity and Pornography* (Washington, DC: U.S. Government Printing Office, 1970), 130.

67. For an example of this common association of a broadening audience base with *Deep Throat*, see William Brigman, "Politics and the Pornography Wars," *Wide Angle* 19, no. 3 (1997): 153.

6 * Let the Sweet Juices Flow:
WR and Midnight Movie Culture

JOAN HAWKINS

*The 1960s were an amazing time, an eventful time of protest and rebellion.
. . . It was a march out of time, too—out of the constricted and rigid morality
of the 1950s. The Beats had already cracked the façade and we, the next generation, broke through it.*

SUZE ROTOLO, *A Freewheelin' Time*, 5.

*Sexual suppression forms the mass psychological basis for a certain culture,
namely, the* patriarchal authoritarian *one.*

WILHELM REICH, *The Sexual Revolution*, excerpt from Escoffier,
Sexual Revolution, 578.

At every film festival, Cynthia Gremer writes, "there is that one film that
electrifies everyone";[1] the film that catches people by surprise, makes
reputations, launches movements, and spotlights previously ignored
national cinemas. At the 1971 Cannes and Berlin Film Festivals, "that
one film" was Yugoslav director Dusan Makavejev's *WR: Mysteries of the
Organism. WR* won the Luis Buñuel Prize and received a fifteen-minute
standing ovation at Cannes. In Berlin, "audiences and critics were
floored" by the film's "sexual audacity," and *WR* received the prestigious
FIPRESCI International Critics Award.[2] The fact that the film had been
banned in its native Yugoslavia only added to its prestige as a subversive and controversial product. By the time it opened at the New York
Film Festival, on October 13, 1971, American art house and festival audiences were prepared to be impressed. Advance publicity, along with full-
page ads in the *Village Voice*, emphasized the film's potential appeal to
counterculture audiences, while simultaneously playing up its international reputation for slightly older art house patrons.[3] Cinema 5's Dan
Rugoff staged a $35,000 party at the Plaza Hotel to celebrate the film's
opening night. And Cinema II booked the film for a commercial run,
scheduled to begin October 14, 1971, the day following what everyone
assumed would be its wildly successful New York Film Festival premiere.

Although the film did not exactly bomb, it did not meet critical or popular expectations. It received mixed reviews in the *New York Times* and *Village Voice* and "was disappointing at $8,500" its opening week at Cinema II (*Variety*, October 20, 1971, 8). That same week, Louis Malle's *Murmur of the Heart*, which also began its commercial run immediately following a New York Film Festival debut, made $17,076 in box-office receipts. Despite that *WR* gained revenue during its second and third weeks at Cinema II, it remained at the low end of box-office revenues throughout its initial New York run. Even *Variety* was at a loss to explain *WR*'s performance, as it consistently made less money than the trade journal predicted it would. "A mystery this one," it wrote during week four, when *WR* once again failed to develop "legs" (*Variety*, November 10, 1971, 9). By the fifth week, *WR* had slowed to $5,900 in weekly revenues, and the word was out: if you're planning to see the film in an art house setting, you'd better see it soon. The movie that had been "that one film" at Cannes "that electrifies everyone" closed at Cinema II after only eight weeks.[4]

At the same time that *WR* had its tepid opening at Cinema II, yet another film was making its art house debut. Alexandro Jodorowsky's *El Topo* (1970), the Surreal Mexican film that J. Hoberman and Jonathan Rosenbaum describe simply as "a trip,"[5] was picked up by Allen Klein's Abkco Films. As *Variety* reported, Abkco took the film that had been "playing for months on midnight-only showings at a New York buff house, and announced that it would engage in bookings aimed solely at the 'counter-culture'" (*Variety*, October 20, 71, 7). The picture had a huge billboard sign in Times Square even before it had any bookings; it made $36,000 during its first week (*Variety*, November 3, 1971, 8).

El Topo eventually returned to the midnight circuit, where it was frequently paired with *WR*. The two films became cult classics, among the first films that "that young people and cinephiles would see over and over again at packed midnight screenings, where the odor of cannabis was stronger than the Lysol."[6] The story of *WR*'s early reception in the United States,[7] then, parallels the story of increasingly divergent trends in art cinema exhibition, divergent trends that pointed out cultural tensions that usually played out around sex, drugs, and politics.

Sex Sells? Part One

In one episode of *Mad Men*, the award-winning AMC serial drama set in an ad agency in the 1960s, a junior copywriter discusses a mildly suggestive airline ad with her boss. "Sex sells," she tells him. "Says who?" he replies. "Just so you know, people who talk that way think that monkeys can do this."[8] Fast-forward the storyline to 1971, and reset the series in a film distribution company; the exact same conversation could take place.

The cinematic marketability and market value of sex fluctuated throughout the early 1970s. I'm not speaking here of sexual themes or suggestive plot elements, but of explicit representations of and references to body parts and sexual acts. New Yorkers seemed jaded and oversated with sex. "Sex, sex, sex," Andrew Sarris wrote in his review of *WR*. "How much can you write about this subject without wearying the most lecherous reader? And how much can you show of sex on the screen before the dirtiest old men begin stifling yawns?"[9] The decline in box office revenues for porn in 1971 seemed to underscore Sarris's point. In October, *Variety* reported that "business for both homo and hetero hardcore has been on the decline in recent months." This was a national trend, and while the majority of New York adult theaters held "to admission prices set during the initial hardcore harvest . . . drastic admission reductions . . . [had] been underway for sometime in both LA and SF." And "where they go," *Variety* ominously predicted, "NY usually follows" (*Variety*, October 20, 1971, 5). The predictions turned out to be accurate. By the end of 1971, New York adult theaters had slashed their admission prices from $5 to $3, and they had eliminated the live strip tease show that had previously accompanied film screenings. In fact, it was the fall in revenues at hardcore theaters that convinced owners to experiment with midnight movies, screenings that would—they hoped—bring in the counterculture crowd.

While adult theaters were slashing admission prices, New York City's First Erotic Film Festival (November 5–December 12, 1971), a festival that coupled hardcore titles with such experimental films as James Broughton's *The Bed* (1968) and *The Golden Positions* (1970; figure 6.1), did extremely well, even with a $10 admission price. Of course, the success of the festival may have had a lot to do with the fact that it had selected downtown art theaters as venues and had highlighted "erotic" rather than "hardcore" as the festival's theme. In addition, the festival's inclusion of erotic avant-garde films, and the presence of competition judges associated with avant-garde culture of the 1960s (Andy Warhol, Gore Vidal, and Betty Dodson), may go a long way toward explaining the festival's success. As J. Hoberman and Jonathan Rosenbaum note, in the early seventies "the film avant-garde retreated from the populism" that had marked some of the best experimental films of the 1960s, "into a

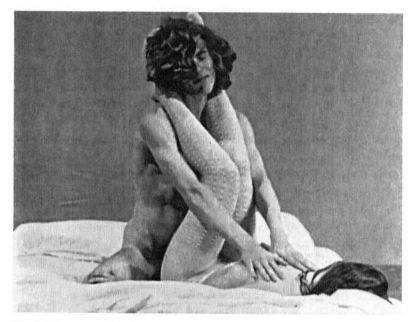

Fig. 6.1 James Broughton's *The Golden Positions* (1970) was among the films that blurred the lines between experimental films, art house movies, and sexploitation in the late 1960s and early 1970s.

rigorous involvement with issues of film form."[10] For fans of the avant-garde of the 1960s, the festival represented something of a return to a populist erotic strain of experimental cinema.

The Avant-Garde of the 1960s

The avant-garde of the 1960s played a key role in blurring the lines between experimental film, art house film, and sexploitation. And, as a result, it formed much of the impetus for the later emergence of midnight movies. As Michael O'Pray writes, both Andy Warhol and Jack Smith "reached beyond the small but highly influential avant-garde enclave to access a wider audience."[11] In part this was due to the ways in which both Warhol and Smith used popular culture in their work;[12] in part, though, it was due to the venues in which their work was shown. Warhol, Smith, Kenneth Anger, Carolee Schneemann, and James Broughton participated in the movement that has come to be known as "underground" (named for the basement theaters in which the films were often shown). The films themselves had counterculture cachet as they directly engaged

the themes of sex, drugs, and politics associated with the counterculture movement, often using rock and roll for the soundtrack. And the
underlying "story" of most of the films had to do with young adults
forging their own personal sexual and artistic identity, but this was not
the intense and serious meditation that one often sees in earlier youthful avant-garde films. Although films of Stan Brakhage and Maya Deren
(also concerned with a kind of coming-of-age in postwar America) emphasized interiority and what Juan Suárez calls "romantic notions of the
unique poetic vision," underground films frequently undermined "any
access to an inner self while emphasizing style and surface."[13] The tone
of the films was often lighthearted; sex especially was most frequently
shown in a humorous way.

Space does not permit a full discussion of underground cinema here,
but a few examples should help illustrate the complicated relationships between sex, art cinema, avant-garde cinema, and counterculture branding that characterized underground cinema and that helped
make the eventual cult status of *WR* possible. Kenneth Anger's *Scorpio
Rising* (1964) was a groundbreaking campy avant-garde film. The plot of
the film is very simple. A biker, Scorpio, reads a comic book, pets his
cat, gets dressed, and goes to a biker party. The structure of the film,
however, manages to reference themes of leather-clad bikers, Jesus, the
occult, James Dean, Marlon Brando, juvenile delinquency movies, and
Nazis. There are flashes of nudity and genitalia, the suggestion of sex and
drug use, and no dialogue. The soundtrack is composed solely of popular music from the 1950s and 1960s: Ricky Nelson, the Angels, Martha
Reeves and the Vandellas, Ray Charles, and Elvis Presley — to name a few.
The film was censored for indecency and the case went to the Supreme
Court, which ruled in Anger's favor.

Like Anger, Andy Warhol continually worked to blur the distinction
between avant-garde culture and trash culture, drawing on advertising,
camp aesthetics, Hollywood B movies, and gay pornography for inspiration. In fact, it could be convincingly argued that, more than any other
director mentioned in this section, Warhol pushed the envelope on what
could be shown — or even suggested — on-screen. *Blow Job* (1964) is a
forty-five-minute reaction take, showing the face of a man who is receiving the eponymous act. *Chelsea Girls* (1966) shows the actor Ondine
shooting heroin and brutalizing an actress. *Bike Boy* (1967) invokes biker
culture and European art cinema, as it shows a biker lathering up. *Vinyl*
(1965) is Warhol's version of *Clockwork Orange* and, like Stanley Kubrick's
later version of the same novel, shows explicit scenes of torture and sex.

More important for our purposes, however, Warhol's underground films encouraged modes of viewing that foreshadowed (or perhaps enabled) the audience mode that would soon be associated with midnight screenings. Warhol is most noted for his two lengthy films: *Sleep* (1963, over five hours) and *Empire* (1964, eight hours). As I have described elsewhere, audience members rarely sat in rapt attention for nearly six hours, watching a man sleep. Rather they were apt to come and go; to talk to the screen and to their friends; to eat, drink, smoke, and get stoned — all the behaviors later associated with midnight screenings were already present in the early underground exhibitions associated with Warhol.[14]

Like Warhol, Jack Smith is noted for his radical reconception of what might be said to be truly avant-garde. Inspired by the films of Maria Montez, star of exotic B movies such as Robert Siodmak's *Cobra Woman* (1944), Smith's *Flaming Creatures* (1963) abandons conventional narrative to depict what Constantine Verevis calls "a pantheon of gorgeous and ambiguously gendered 'creatures' in a loosely connected series of tableaux set to an inspired collage of scratchy recordings."[15] After the release of the film, reviewer and filmmaker Jonas Mekas wrote that *Flaming Creatures* had "attained for the first time in motion pictures a high level of art which is absolutely lacking in decorum; a treatment of sex which makes us aware of the restraint of all previous filmmakers."[16] Smith's film caused a national scandal. It was banned in twenty-two states and in four countries. Mekas himself brought the film to various screenings throughout the 1960s and, for his pains, was arrested.[17]

The comedic quality of Smith's film carries over into later underground films. James Broughton's *The Bed* (1970), one of the films shown at the Erotic Film Festival mentioned above, is hilarious. The film shows a bed traveling slowly downhill. Eventually it settles in a meadow and becomes the site of all manner of strange couplings. Characters — mostly nude — appear and, in the words of *WR*, "fuck freely." Broughton himself appears as a nude Pan, sitting in a tree, serenading the revelers. Carolee Schneemann's *Fuses* (1967) — discussed below — shows explicit shots of Schneemann and James Tenney making love, as observed by Schneemann's cat. Karen Johnson's *Orange* (1970) is a lengthy close-up of the peeling, sectioning, licking, and eating of a navel orange. The film is heavily indebted to Andy Warhol's *Eat* (1963), in which Robert Indiana eats a mushroom for twenty-five minutes. *Orange* won a prize at the 1970 International Erotic Film Festival. Finally, Paul Morrissey's films *Flesh for Frankenstein* (1973) and *Blood for Dracula* (1974) not only show hilarious hetero fucking, but employ actors who originally got their start making pornography.[18] Perhaps, more important, these films — designed to appeal clearly to the counterculture—were rated X and played in art houses, porn theaters, and midnight movie lineups throughout the 1970s.

Sex Sells? Part Two

On the other side of the sexual divide, the media was still conjoined by Federal Communications Commission (FCC) regulations, and at times a strange prudishness crept into even the most alternative outlets. This development also had an impact on cinema. Jonas Mekas devoted one of his October 1971 "Movie Journal" columns to condemning what he referred to as title "censorship." The *Village Voice*, home of Mekas's column, had "refused to print an advertisement with the title of Larry Rivers's 1969 film, 'Tits,'" he reported (*Village Voice*, October 14, 1971, 71). That same week, the *New York Times* did run an ad for the film, playing at the Bleeker Street Cinema. But the paper changed the title of the film to *Breasts*.

In the parlance of the times, then, the late 1960s and early 1970s were "schiz" (from schizophrenic) when it came to showing sex on-screen. As the success of the New York Erotic Film Festival demonstrates, counterculture and experimental film fans still regarded the cinematic depiction of sex as interesting and even somewhat "subversive." Amos Vogel dedicated three chapters to the topic of subversive sexuality in his book *Film as a Subversive Art* (1974), and the section in which these chapters appear is labeled "Weapons of Subversion: Forbidden Subjects of the Cinema."[19] Furthermore, the programming of the Erotic Film Festival itself played up the notion of subversive sexuality. At the same time that Larry Rivers's film *Tits* was being renamed by the mainstream press, *Lenny Bruce without Tears* (1971) was the headliner film of the Erotic Film Festival.[20] It played all four theaters to packed houses. Bruce, who had been arrested repeatedly on obscenity charges for his use of language onstage, was something of a counterculture hero; certainly his defense of words directly engaged a generation that had retooled "fuck" ("the F word") for conversational use.[21]

But at the same time that "erotica" clearly sold and that sex itself could be marketed to the counterculture, porn seemed to be temporarily in financial trouble. Interestingly enough, at the other end of the cultural spectrum, another moneymaker of the early 1960s—art house cinema—faced similarly difficult circumstances. And though porn experienced a strong revival with the release of *Deep Throat* in 1972, art house cinema never regained the financial success it enjoyed in the early 1960s.

Art House Woes

As Douglas Gomery notes, "the peak of the pure art house" came sometime in the mid-1960s.[22] Certainly throughout the seventies, independent art houses struggled to maintain their competitive edge and falling revenues were a fact of life ("houses will see more than $10,000" over the weekend "and that represents a record at the Agee I and II," as *Variety* noted earlier). At the Surf Theatre in San Francisco, where I lived, there were increasing changes in the 1970s. Free coffee was offered in the lobby (it was Farmer's Brothers, but it was brewed European style and strong) and the concessions stand began selling imported French cigarettes, as well as pastries, popcorn with "real butter," and European chocolate. An expensively priced espresso bar and café opened next door to the theater. Initially the café was there to serve the patrons' pre- and post-screening alimentary needs and was accessible only through the Surf Theater lobby. As the seventies progressed, however, the café's street door began opening more and more frequently to foot traffic, to clients who did not plan to see the films at all.

In part, this was an early counterculture form of what Naomi Klein calls "branding," a finely calculated attempt to connect product to an entire lifestyle image.[23] Branding had always been a part of art house culture, as Barbara Wilinsky demonstrates in her excellent history, but the increasing reliance on concessions and the café to generate revenue signaled a definite market change at the Surf.[24] Certainly it was one indicator of falling box office revenue.

As early as 1971, the theater also began changing its schedule in ways that ran slightly counter to the "European experience in America" brand it otherwise cultivated (the Surf always played Édith Piaf and Jacques Brel tapes in the auditorium prior to the screenings). Not only were crowd pleasing foreign titles revived more frequently (François Truffaut's *The 400 Blows* [1959], for example), but classic Hollywood titles such as *Casablanca* (1942), *To Have and Have Not* (1944), and *Duck Soup* (1933) increasingly replaced subtitled films in the calendar. In a move clearly designed to draw gay audiences away from revival houses such as the Castro, the theater began scheduling blocks of films oriented around film stars who had specific gay appeal—Greta Garbo, Marlene Dietrich, and Joan Crawford. These minifestivals frequently replaced the auteur and movement series (e.g., *Nouvelle Vague* and Antonioni retrospectives) that had been favored at the Surf throughout the 1960s.

Where San Francisco and Los Angeles go, "NY usually follows" (*Variety*, October 20, 1971, 5). And, as with the porn theater examples cited above,

New York art houses, too, experienced box office woes. In 1972 the Walter Reade chain, "one of the pioneers of the art house," sought a merger with Mayfair Atlantic Corporation. According to *Variety*, "the merger of Mayfair into the Walter Reade Organization . . . [was] 'designed to alleviate in some degree' the financial difficulties experienced of late by WRO [Walter Reade Organization] in generating or obtaining funds to meet immediate commitments" (*Variety*, October 6, 1972, 6). Bluntly put, Walter Reade sought a merger to avoid bankruptcy.

There are many reasons for the fall in art house box office revenues in the early 1970s. The rise of the New Hollywood meant that edgier American films were opening in neighborhood theaters so you no longer had to go downtown to see something provocative, and many of those films (*Easy Rider* [1969]; *Straw Dogs* [1971], to name just two) spoke to an increasingly violent American condition in ways that the foreign films did not.

The 1970s were also a time when, as Douglas Gomery notes, television was radically changing the way American audiences watched film.[25] And this was true of American art house audiences as well as the larger moviegoing public. Public Broadcasting Service stations increasingly showed films from the Janus Film Collection—subtitled and uninterrupted—in their line-ups. Series on PBS such as *An American Family* (1973) brought discussions about documentary ethics—discussions that had been common among cinephiles of the 1960s—into the mainstream press.[26] Commercial television, too, developed programs with "special audience" appeal. As early as 1963, the networks began targeting coffee house habitués with folk music programs such as *Hootenanny* (ABC). In 1965, *The Smothers Brothers Show* made its first appearance on CBS. *Rowan & Martin's Laugh-In*, whose very title announced its intended appeal to a counterculture audience, first aired on NBC in 1968 and ran until 1973. *The Prisoner* (1967–1968), an existential British serial drama, ran on CBS in 1969. Norman Lear radically changed what network television meant to the counterculture, with shows such as *All in the Family* (1971, CBS). And throughout this period, news specials about Vietnam, poverty in America, and civil rights also attracted attention. Finally, in Manhattan, cable television emerged as early as 1965; on November 8, 1972, HBO relayed its first broadcast.[27]

I have discussed television's counterculture market at length for reasons that I hope will become clear later. For our purposes now, however, the most interesting art house competition came neither from the New Hollywood nor from television, but from midnight screenings that targeted the counterculture. To begin, this was a categorically different kind of competition; midnight audiences did not necessarily patronize late night screenings in lieu of art house films; rather, they went to midnight flicks in addition to art house movies. Given the starting time for midnight flicks, frequently viewers went to both art house and midnight movies on the same night—often at the same venue. Further, since art houses themselves often sponsored midnight screenings,[28] and since films moved easily between midnight and art house runs, patrons were not necessarily choosing a specific venue or even one film over another. What they were choosing was a different mode of viewing, and the relationship that developed between art house and midnight movie screenings was a complex, symbiotic one. I use the term "competition" here simply because box office revenues for midnight films continued to rise throughout the seventies, whereas revenues for regularly scheduled art house bookings fell.

Midnight Screenings and Cult Films

The term "midnight movie" derives from several established media practices. Throughout the 1950s local television stations around the United States aired low-budget genre films as a staple feature of their late night programming. And TV played a major role in training an audience of boomers to enjoy watching what Jeffrey Sconce calls "paracinema" late at night.[29] But as Eric Schaefer points out, there was a cinematic tradition of midnight exhibitions for exploitation films long before local TV stations brought us *Creature Features*.[30] In segregated areas of the country, theaters regularly programmed "midnight rambles," midnight screenings of films—including, but not limited to, African American films—specifically targeted to a segregated black audience. However far back one traces their roots, however, theatrical midnight screenings turned up with increasing frequency during the late 1960s and early 1970s. By 1975, every American urban area that I know of had regularly established Friday and Saturday night midnight theatrical shows.

As a film category (not just a time for screening, but a label describing the kinds of films shown), midnight movies mix high art and low culture in ways similar to the paracinema catalogues that I have described elsewhere.[31] Screenings ran the gamut, including such disparate titles as Tod Browning's *Freaks* (1932), George Romero's *Night of the Living Dead* (1968), Luis Buñuel and Salvador Dali's *Un Chien Andalou* (1929), Stephen Sayadian's (Sayadian was AKA Rinse Dream) *Café Flesh* (1982), John Waters's *Pink Flamingoes* (1972), Ken Russell's *The Music Lovers* (1970), David Lynch's *Eraserhead* (1977), and, of course, the film that finally edged out all competitors, Jim Sharman's *The Rocky Horror Picture Show* (1975). In terms of cultural practice and philosophy, midnight screenings partake of an aesthetic tradition that Hoberman and Rosenbaum link to surrealism, to McMahonism, to the *Cahiers du Cinéma* (Notebooks on Cinema) and *Nouvelle Vague*, and to the film underground of the 1960s. Here, art films mingle with trash titles to "encourage a reading strategy much like the one that Fredric Jameson proposes in *Signatures of the Visible*," as I put it elsewhere. "That is, they invite us to 'read high and mass culture as objectively related and dialectically interdependent phenomena, as twin and inseparable forms of the fission of aesthetic production under capitalism.'"[32]

What happened to *WR* in the New York marketplace mirrors what happened to a number of films that showed disappointing box office receipts in their initial art house runs but that became cult hits in their subsequent midnight bookings. These were not always demanding collage films that especially reward multiple viewings, as *WR* is. Rather, they were often quirky "little" films. Philippe de Broca's charming *King of Hearts* (1966, *Le roi de coeur*), did not do well at the box office in its initial commercial art house run, but it became a midnight movie favorite in San Francisco. So, too, did Hal Ashby's quirky *Harold and Maude* (1971), a film that also suffered at the box office in its initial run. Other films— Alejandro Jodorowsky's *El Topo* (1970) and Emile de Antonio's *Millhouse* (1971), for example—premiered on the midnight circuit and then moved into art house distribution *after* attracting a following (*Variety*, October 20, 1971, 7). These films frequently returned to the midnight circuit after their art house run ended.

What distinguished midnight screenings from traditional art house exhibitions? And why would a film do well in one situation and not the other? To begin, midnight films were shown in a variety of locations. Art houses did schedule midnight films, but in many cities this was a late development, occurring only after porn theaters, bump and grind houses, revival houses, and some local neighborhood first-run theaters had begun booking midnight shows. Second, the target audience for the films was different. During normal business hours, art houses catered to an eclectic group of patrons. Émigrés in suits and dress coats rubbed elbows with counterculture college students dressed in ripped jeans. This often created a nice atmosphere, as the audience bonded around its mutual love for a frequently obscure film. The fact that outside the theater the audience had little shared common culture was beside the point.

Midnight screenings, however, took place in a countercultural setting. Most of the patrons were young. All of them seemed to come from what

Raymond Williams might call the same "cultural formation," that is, they tended to share a common politics and a common system of social values.[33] Although I rarely smelled marijuana during a regularly scheduled screening at the Surf Theatre, I frequently smelled it at midnight shows. In fact, drugs were part of the midnight movie experience and some of the most popular films—*El Topo*, for example—were "stoner" or "head" flicks," movies that seemed to reward a slightly altered mental state on the part of the audience.[34]

Midnight shows and their relatively low ticket prices encouraged multiple viewings of the same films. Films frequently had long runs, or were brought back for subsequent bookings, and there was less competition during that time slot. Before the advent of VCRs, interested cinephiles pretty much had to see movies in the theater, when they were booked. And in New York, during the 1960s and 1970s, there were a lot of films that we felt we had to see to maintain our cultural capital. Hollywood films would show up on television a year or two after the conclusion of their theatrical run, but they were usually cut to accommodate commercials. Small independent films or foreign flicks rarely showed up on commercial television, and if they did they were dubbed into English, edited for content, and interrupted by ads. As a result, most of us simply didn't have the money and time to re-view first run films or classic art house offerings as often as we wanted. It was in fact our inability to "own" our favorite films that led Grove Press to launch its published film script series in the 1960s.

Midnight screenings, on the other hand, allowed us to develop complex relationships with films over time. In the case of especially difficult films, such as *WR*, midnight screenings were invaluable; the multiple viewings allowed us to get over our initial discomfort with the movie or just to analyze it in greater detail. In some cases, midnight screenings enabled a kind of obsessive or "cult" viewing (over and over and over again) that traditionally scheduled films simply couldn't support; even if you went every night, traditionally scheduled films always reached the end of their runs. When midnight films left a venue, you always knew they'd be back (especially if they had a following).

Throughout this section I've compared art house and midnight screenings, as though they were diametrically opposed. What I want to stress, however, is the kind of symbiotic relationship that grew up between regularly scheduled art house programming and midnight fare. The fact that films opened in one arena and passed so easily into the other, the fact that midnight screenings "saved" many films that are now out on the Criterion label as "classics"—these things suggest a complex financial and cultural relationship between these two modes of exhibition, a relationship that definitely merits further study.

"Comrades, Fuck Freely!"

Despite the symbiotic relationship that grew up between midnight movies and art house fare, though, there was a tension within the intellectual elite during this time period, a fear that the counterculture was simply taking over the cultural landscape. Although it comes later in the 1970s, Sidney Lumet's *Network* (1976), written by live anthology television auteur Paddy Chayefsky, illustrates this tension nicely. Usually read as an indictment of the increasing substitution of infotainment for hard news, the film also satirizes the degree to which commercial television was willing to court the youth market during this time period (see the above-listed television programs, which were designed to have specific counterculture appeal) and to abandon previously established norms for intelligent drama. In the film, young executive Diana Christensen (Faye Dunaway) ruins the career of her older lover, Max (William Holden), when she changes programming to reflect a predominantly youth taste culture. "I want counter-culture; I want anti-establishment," she tells her programming staff. Among the shows she introduces, *The Mao Tse Tung Hour* gets the most play in the film. The *Mao* hour revolves around the Ecumenical Liberation Army (ELA), a group that stages bank robberies and abductions and films its members doing so. Christensen's idea is to use the raw ELA footage under the guise of news (so that her sources are protected and she won't be obliged to turn the film over to the FBI), write weekly backstory for the crimes, and produce a resulting drama that will tap into the nation's hunger for angry programming.

Throughout *Network*, a sharp distinction is made between people who grew up with television (the Baby Boom Generation) and those who didn't. The latter—the Maxes of the world—are presumed to have real emotions and real cultural values. The boomers, represented by Diana, are shallow, able to think only in sound bites and scripted plot lines. The fact that they are also attractive enough to turn the head of a respectable figure such as Max is part of their very danger. Certainly, the havoc they wreak on the Culture Industry in the film is palpable. Beyond its profound pessimism about television itself, *Network* neatly taps into a post-Watergate anxiety about the lasting legacy of the counterculture on the body politic and on culture.

Within the art house market, too, cultural tensions were apparent. As Raymond Durgnat notes in his book on *WR*, "Until the mid-60s, most tastes rather inclined to the traditional high culture-ish, humanist, seriousness satisfied by auteurs like Renoir, Bergman, Resnais, early Fellini, and Antonioni. By the mid-60s this older audience was vastly amplified by a younger, wider audience, or films which combined a certain 'educational IQ' with exuberant scandal, such as Ken Russell's *The Devils* and Nic Roeg's *Performance* (both 1970), and Woody Allen's *Everything You Always Wanted to Know About Sex but Were Afraid to Ask* (1972)."[35] It was this wider audience to which, Durgnat predicted, *WR* would appeal.

I don't intend to argue here that *WR* did poorly at the box office simply because it established itself as a counterculture film at a time when the counterculture was both courted and somewhat feared. As poststructuralism has taught us, binary oppositions are always problematic and certainly, in the rich cultural stew of the sexual revolution, neat cultural divisions are impossible to sustain. What I do want to argue, however, is that *WR* made its appearance in America when the nation was anxious about the direction that culture and cultural production would take. The fact that *WR* was so easily seen—and perhaps dismissed—as a counterculture film (one made for the Dianas of the world) is, however, one possible reason that it was earmarked for the midnight movie circuit early in its New York run.

WR: Mysteries of the Organism is a radical collage film and, as such, it's a deuced hard movie to summarize adequately. To begin, the "WR" of the title stands both for "Wilhelm Reich" and for "World Revolution," and it is precisely the marriage between Reich's ideas and a reinvigorated Marxism that forms the main theoretical thrust of the film. "This film is, in part, a personal response to the life and teaching of Dr. Wilhelm Reich (1897–1957)," the opening titles tell us. "All his life Reich fought against pornography in sex and politics. He believed in work-democracy, in an organic society based on liberated work and love." These titles are followed by raw 16 mm footage, showing leashed dogs outside a diner; a close-up of a "No dogs allowed" sign, prominently displayed in the diner window, completes the segment. On the soundtrack, Tuli Kupferberg—who reappears throughout the film—chants verse including the lines "Who will police our judges? And who will will our will?"

Cut to another shot, another street. A trio that Raymond Durgnat describes as "beatnik-cum-hippie" strolls by: two women, one of whom is pregnant, and a man played by Kupferberg (Durgnat, 13). They stop to unpack a box carried by one of the women. As Durgnat notes, the items they bring out and put on all "have critical intent." "US flag+steel helmet+surplus quasi uniform+machine carbine+dolls are all typical props of Street Theater protests and demos against the Vietnam War.

(Protestors burned dolls as symbols of napalmed children.) Background graffiti complement this humanitarian angle. 'Only Revolution Ends War,' 'Pill,' a row of hammer-and-sickles" (Durgnat, 14). Following this scene, we have the final segment of the film's "Overture," showing the "egg game." Here, another counterculture trio passes a whole egg yolk, hand to hand. This group, which will return throughout the Yugoslavia sequence, end by rubbing the yolk on themselves and each other, while Eastern European folkdance music comes up on the soundtrack. Over this sequence the title credits roll (Durgnat, 14–15).

After the "Overture," there is a long segment about Wilhelm Reich. Reich studied with Freud and eventually came to believe that all physical and mental illness came from repressed sexual energy. In one of his best-known works, *The Mass Psychology of Fascism* (1933), Reich argued that sexual repression fosters an authoritarian personality, one that might infect an entire society. Partly as a result of this work, Reich had to flee Germany; he came to the United States.

In the United States, Reich continued his work on what he came to call "orgone," the orgasmic energy which needs release and accumulation. He used touch alongside the talking cure in treating patients; taking an active role in repositioning patients' bodies, feeling their chests, and sometimes asking them to loosen or remove clothing. These methods caused a split between Reich and the rest of the psychoanalytic community. Reich did continue to practice, but he did so without affiliation to Anna Freud. Then, in 1947, a series of critical articles about orgone and Reich's political views appeared in the *New Republic*.[36] As a result of these articles (which claimed that Reich was treating cancer with orgone accumulator boxes), the U.S. Food and Drug Administration (FDA) began an investigation; the FDA won an injunction against the interstate sale of orgone accumulators. Reich was charged with contempt of court for violating the injunction. He was sentenced to two years and died in prison. In August 1956 and again in March 1960, several tons of his publications were burned by the FDA.

During the Reich segment of *WR*, images from what Raymond Durgnat identifies as an old Sexpol film, circa 1930, represent a copulating couple. "A prism effect, like a mosaic, shows multiple views of the lovers, from seven different angles, at different moments. . . . The array softens, *distances*, the sexuality, which becomes, not 'fleshless,' 'abstract,' but emblematic . . . philosophical" (Durgnat, 17–18). This opening gambit is followed by a long documentary section featuring interviews with Reich's daughter and son, his barber, and with some of the townspeople from Rangeley, Maine, where he settled. There are photographs of Reich

Fig. 6.2 Milena (Milena Dravic) and friends in WR: *Mysteries of the Organism* (1971).

in handcuffs and shots of the public incinerator on Gansevoort Street in New York City, where his books and papers were burned. A voiceover details Reich's professional life. Finally, we are introduced to Drs. Sharaf and Lowen, both practicing Reichian therapists. Part of a therapy session with Lowen is shown, and Sharaf explains the accumulator.[37]

The second major thread of the film is the fictional, Yugoslavian story. The heroine of this story is Milena (figure 6.2): a Communist, feminist, and practicing Reichian (she has a picture of Reich and an orgone accumulator in her apartment). Milena falls in love with a Russian ice skater visiting Yugoslavia with the Soviet Ice Capades. However, he has a hard time reciprocating her passion. When he finally does let himself go, he finishes by decapitating her with his ice skates. At the end of the film, Milena's head, retrieved by the police, is placed in a dish of water, from which it begins to speak. Intercut throughout Milena's story are a variety of fictional and documentary texts. There's footage of Jackie Curtis, transvestite "Superstar" of Andy Warhol's Factory. Like Milena, Jackie is looking for a man, and like Milena she continually meets with heartbreak. Another sequence shows a meeting of *Screw* magazine's editorial board, and publisher Al Goldstein explains *Screw*'s political credo. *Screw*'s editor-in-chief, Jim Buckley, visits sculptress Nancy Godfrey, who wishes to make a plaster cast of his erect penis. Finally, artist and sex-educator Betty Dodson also makes an appearance.

On the more political side of things, there are clips from *The Vow*, a dramatic Soviet-era propaganda film that lionizes Stalin; there's a shot of Red Square in a segment showing a hundred thousand Chinese waving their Red Books at Mao; there is what appears to be documentary footage of a man receiving electroshock therapy; and there are scenes of Tuli Kupferberg marching in his marine uniform in various locales.

Some of these segments are juxtaposed in ways that facilitate analysis. When the ice skater (whose name, interestingly enough, is Vladimir Ilyich—just like Lenin's) strikes Milena, for example, the film cuts to a close-up of Stalin from *The Vow*. One authoritarian tyrant is linked here, it would seem, with another. And, at the end of the film, when Milena's head tells us "Cosmic rays streamed through our coupled bodies," the film segues to Milena's poster of Reich, the man who believed in the healing benefits of orgone energy. For the most part, however, the film defies easy exegesis. Even Raymond Durgnat, whose book on the film probably provides the best analysis, is uncharacteristically speculative in his reading. At one point, he lists eleven different possible explanations for Vladimir's murder of Milena, each one framed as a question. "Possibility 5. Is V.I.'s brutality typical of 'Men' whose phallonarcissistic pride savages Women? Possibility 6. Is the film itself sado-sexist, as yet another lovely woman is 'punished' by Men . . . ?" (Durgnat, 49).

In a way, this resistance to exegesis makes perfect sense in a film where documentary "evidence" inevitably segues into propaganda or staged melodrama, that is, where "truth claims" and "history" are continually shown to be constructs and narratives. But it also facilitates the film's status as something of a "head flick." Precisely because there is very little linear plot development, it's fairly easy (in terms of enjoyment, anyway) to enter *WR* at any point and more or less make of it what you will.

It was precisely this elliptical quality of the film that nettled some reviewers. Writing for *The New York Times*, Vincent Canby called *WR* "an occasionally comic and brilliant collage movie that leaves me cold" (*New York Times*, October 14, 1971, 52). David Bienstock invoked his full title, Curator of Film, Whitney Museum of Art, when he wrote a scathing review for the Sunday *New York Times*. "I have never, in all my years of moviegoing, booed a film, no matter how bad, boring or insipid. . . . It is because I have a deep rooted respect and love for filmmakers that booing has never been a part of my film vocabulary, that is, until I saw Dusan Makavejev's film *WR: Mysteries of the Organism*." Bienstock was especially incensed at the way the film treated Reich's work. And booing, then became "the proper response for a film that in the name of freedom, joy and the 'avant-garde,' exploited, misinterpreted and maligned the very man's work that it professed to hold dear. Unfortunately, the deception of the film is masked so slyly and subtly that its insidiousness is not easily apparent. And it was this that outraged me." He went on to target the film's editing specifically, claiming that it obscures and often misrepresents "what is really going on" (*New York Times*, November 7, 1971, sec. 2, 9). Even the *Village Voice* gave the film mixed reviews. Amos Vogel liked *WR*; Andrew Sarris condemned it for "affect[ing] profundity" (*Village Voice*, November 11, 1971, 67).

Not every publication gave *WR* such a negative review. *Newsweek*, for example, called it a "brilliantly original swipe at all prevailing political systems" and gave it a uniformly positive write-up (*Newsweek*, November 1, 1971, 90). Still, with negative notices appearing in the *New York Times*, the *New Yorker*, and the *Village Voice*, and with so many other films to see in New York, it's understandable that art house patrons might stay away.

Sex Sells, Part Three

It's interesting that *WR*'s overt sexual content was rarely cited in reviews as the reason that critics did not like the film. For the record, there is a lot of sex in the movie. Not only does the Sexpol footage show couples copulating, but we see Milena's roommate and her soldier-boyfriend disporting rather freely throughout several early segments of the Yugoslavia story. In one scene, reminiscent of a similar sequence in *Deep Throat*, Milena comes home to find her roommate Jagoda in the middle of making love to her boyfriend (this is a small East European apartment—so she literally walks in on them). "Oh, I see we have company," she says, as she takes off her skirt, lights a cigar, and puts her feet up to read an article about Karl Marx falling in love. "He didn't even finish his tea," Jagoda giggles. "Ever ready, our military." The camera closes in on a photo of Wilhelm Reich—which is hanging over the daybed. As it pulls back out, Jagoda and Ljuba are still fucking. "The military hasn't been laid in six months," Jagoda giggles and holds up fingers to indicate the number of times they've climaxed.

Throughout the film, couples have intercourse and there are shots of full frontal nudity. The documentary footage is no less explicit. When Jim Buckley visits sculptress Nancy Godfrey to have his penis cast, the entire process is shown in detail. Godfrey strokes Buckley's penis until it's erect, covers it with plastic—stroking all the while, and then molds the plaster over the plastic sheet. Later in the sequence, we see her lovingly handle the final cast product (which is pink and somewhat translucent and a remarkably good likeness to the real thing), feeling it for rough edges, and smoothing one side of it. In another art-doc sequence, Betty Dodson discusses orgasm while sitting in front of a striking nude charcoal sketch; in the shot the nude dominates the frame. The art work at the offices of *Screw* likewise dominate the shot, and in one remarkable sequence, publisher Al Goldstein holds up a molded fake vagina, complete with pubic hairs donated, he tells us, by the female members of the magazine's staff.

There is so much sex in the film that Dan Rugoff, the film's distributor, posted warning signs in front of Cinema II. The posters read: "Some people will be offended by this film's strong language and its sexual freedom." As *Variety* noted, Rugoff followed a similar policy when he distributed Paul Morrissey's *Trash* (1970) (*Variety*, October 20, 1971, 7). In that instance, such signs had seemed to lure audiences in; in the case of *WR* — the film *Variety* called the New York Film Festival's "first more-or-less porno feature" — the signs may have scared people away (*Variety*, October 20, 1971, 6).

Certainly outside New York, the film's explicit sexual content was a problem. In December 1971, Rugoff's company, Cinema 5, took out a large ad in the *New York Times* to "berate Boston's three daily newspapers for refusing to accept ads" for *WR*, when the film opened there (*Variety*, December 29, 1971). To a certain extent, the *New York Times* ad was misleading, since it seemed to credit sophisticated New Yorkers for giving the film a warmer reception than it, in fact, received in Gotham. But the ad worked to renew a certain curiosity about the film and, to a certain extent, helped to establish a basis for the film's revival on the midnight circuit.

There are many reasons that *WR* finally achieved cult status during its revival midnight run. And the film's sexual content was certainly one of them. As any casual glance at the underground comic books of the era shows, the counterculture was heavily invested in sex, and explicit sex-coupled-with-politics was guaranteed to attract substantial midnight movie crowds. Reich, himself, was an important counterculture icon. At Cody's Books in Berkeley, there was an entire bookshelf unit (floor to ceiling) devoted to Reich's works that had been reprinted by Farrar, Strauss, and Giroux. This stood immediately next to a similar unit devoted to the works of Hegelian philosopher Herbert Marcuse. Both Reich and Marcuse were considered important theorists for the New Left. Although Reich's work wasn't quoted as frequently as Marcuse's, his influence can be felt in the dominant political slogan of the time: "Make love, not war" reads — at this remove anyway — as virtually a Reichian aphorism.

Furthermore, unlike David Bienstock and the Reich Museum, who were offended by the film's depiction of Dr. Reich, counterculture audiences liked the overall comic tone of the movie, which they read as a celebration of free love, and of Reich's spirit.[38] One of Milena's lines, "let the sweet juices flow," received an exuberant cheer from every midnight audience I experienced during this time period. The movie was *fun*. Despite a few "downer" moments—Reich's arrest and the burning of his books, the electroshock footage, and some random clips—*WR* was basically a comedy. Even Milena's decapitation was funny. The scene in which her head is removed from a bag, placed in a saucer of water, and begins to speak was reminiscent of scenes from *The Brain That Wouldn't Die* (1962), another film popular on the midnight circuit, and it always elicited a laugh. *WR* ends with the photo of Reich that recurs throughout the movie, the picture of a smiling, happy man. It was that image of Reich, the laughing sexual outlaw, that we took away from the film.

In addition, the counterculture political themes of the film were attractive to an audience still engaged in fighting the Vietnam War. The segments in which Tuli Kupferberg, dressed in military drag, parades with his faux carbine and growls, were the most obvious in this regard. But the way in which the film critiqued both Western and Eastern political systems—while still holding out the hope of a transformative and liberating, sexy Marxism—fit nicely with the political zeitgeist of the late 1960s and early 1970s. It's indicative here that Amos Vogel did not include *WR* in the sex chapters of *Film as a Subversive Art*, but rather in the section called "Left and Revolutionary Cinema." Calling it "unquestionably the most important subversive masterpiece of the 1970s," he helped cement the film's reputation as one of *the* counterculture films of the era.[39] In fact, the 1974 edition of *Film as a Subversive Art* features a famous still from *WR* on its cover (figure 6.3).

Finally, the appearance in the film of people such as Jackie Curtis and Betty Dodson, made famous by the avant-garde underground of the 1960s, also gave *WR* a certain counterculture cachet. Certainly, the film seems to have more in common with the underground and with Godard's collage movies than with anything else. While working on this chapter, I happened to resee Carolee Schneemann's *Fuses* (1964–1967), an erotic celebration of Schneemann's relationship with a man, as seen through the eyes of a cat. It's a remarkable film, not the least for being such a direct expression of female erotic pleasure and sexual desire. And the images are beautiful. After watching the film, I opened Schneemann's book *Imaging Her Erotics* and in one of those remarkably serendipitous moments, found the notes she'd written after first viewing *WR*. "What

Fig. 6.3 The iconic photo from *WR: Mysteries of the Organism* (1971) was used to illustrate the cover of Amos Vogel's 1974 book *Film as a Subversive Art*.

can it mean of range to home," she writes, "that I know everyone in the film except the Yugoslav actors." Later, she notes, "In '59 Jim and I 'discovered' the writings of Reich. Was *Function of the Orgasm* one of the arcane books I used to find in the mammoth alleys of University of Illinois Library. In mystic hunter grace for somber dusty hours wandering the aisles slowly until I felt an energy pull from the shelves." She concludes the section with notes about casting for another, previous film, *Meat Joy*. The section is worth quoting at length.

> "Casting" for *Meat Joy* (1964), by watching people in the streets, in restaurants—anywhere and went up to strangers whose physical presence was unselfconsciously sensuous, sensitive, integral when I approached these strangers to explain we would come into unpredictable exemplary celebration of flesh and physicality in motion, light sound, many or certainly several had been in Reichian therapies. And I said, Reich inspired my work, his writings had been the kick in the pants for my courage, audacity—to make vision concrete.[40]

To Conclude

What I have tried to do in this essay is, in a way, my own version of trying "to make vision concrete" by using the case study of one film to trace the intertwined cultural discourses and market histories of a specific time and cultural space. The release of *WR* in the United States engaged discourses about pornography, the function of art cinema, Wilhelm Reich, and sexual politics. It also highlighted certain market trends within the intellectual community and engaged the growing cultural tensions that existed between different generations and social formations within that market. The choice of one film to highlight a certain historical moment is always controversial. It is not the case that *WR: Mysteries of the Organism* is the only film that might be used here to get at the points I have tried to make. But I would argue that it's the best exemplary film use for such a reason in this volume. A number of art films in the 1970s engaged with Reich's theories, particularly those regarding the relationship between sexual repression and fascism: Luchino Visconti's *The Damned* (1969), Elio Petri's *Investigation of a Citizen Above Suspicion* (1970), Costas-Gavras's *Z* (1969), and Bernardo Bertolucci's *The Conformist* (1971). However, as James Roy MacBean forcefully argues, "of all the films just mentioned, Makavejev's is the only one explicitly inspired by the filmmaker's desire to come to grips with the life and work of Wilhelm Reich."[41] What makes this fact especially relevant to the volume at hand is the relevance of Reich himself. Among the many books that were burned at the public incinerator on Gansevoort Street was the volume from which the "sexual revolution" took its name, Wilhelm Reich's *The Sexual Revolution*, translated from *Die Sexualität im Kulturkampf*, by Theodore P. Wolfe, 1936.

Notes

1. Cynthia Gremer, "Yugolsav Entry Hailed at Cannes," *New York Times*, May 24, 1971, 26. Most subsequent citations to newspapers will appear in text.
2. "Essential Cinema; *WR: Mysteries of the Organism*," March 10, 2006, accessed July 28, 2012. www.fest21com/blog/newyorkfilmfestival/essential_cinema _wr_mysteries_of_the_organism.
3. Throughout the 1960s and 1970s, art theaters attracted an age-diverse crowd. For more, see Douglas Gomery, *Shared Pleasures: A History of Movie Presentation in the United States* (Madison: University of Wisconsin Press, 1992).
4. "Yugoslav Entry Hailed at Cannes," *New York Times*, May 24, 1971, 26. *Carnal Knowledge*, by contrast, was the "long-run winner with $24,000 or close in its 17th week at Cinema I," *Variety*, October, 20, 1971, 8.
5. J. Hoberman and Jonathan Rosenbaum, *Midnight Movies* (New York: Da Capo, 1983), 80.
6. "Essential Cinema; *WR: Mysteries of the Organism*."
7. Once the film garnered a reputation as a "cult classic," it enjoyed a second life, playing film festivals, art houses, and college campuses throughout the 1970s. With its DVD release by the Criterion Collection, its reputation as a "canonical" film seems to have solidified.
8. "For Those Who Think Young," *Mad Men* (Matthew Weiner, creator; AMC) first aired July 27, 2008.
9. Andrew Sarris, "Films in Focus," *Village Voice*, November 11, 1971, 67.
10. Hoberman and Rosenbaum, *Midnight Movies*, 79.
11. Michael O'Pray, *Avant-garde Film: Forms, Themes and Passions* (London: Wallflower Press, 2003), 84. See also Sally Banes, *Greenwich Village 1963: Avant-Garde Performance and the Effervescent Body* (Durham, NC: Duke University Press, 1993); and Reva Wolf, *Andy Warhol, Poetry and Gossip in the 1960s* (Chicago: University of Chicago Press, 1997).
12. For more on this, see Juan Suárez, *Bike Boys, Drag Queens and Superstars: Avant-garde, Mass Culture, and Gay Identities in the 1960s Underground Cinema* (Bloomington: Indiana University Press, 1996).
13. Suárez, *Bike Boys, Drag Queens and Superstars*, 98.
14. See Joan Hawkins, *Cutting Edge: Art-Horror and the Horrific Avant-garde* (Minneapolis: University of Minnesota Press, 2000).
15. Constantine Verevis, "Flaming Creatures," *Senses of Cinema*, accessed October 31, 2008, www.sensesofcinema.com/contents/cteq/02/21/flmaing.html.
16. Jonas Mekas, "Fifth Independent Film Award," *Film Culture* 29 (1963): 1.
17. Lest we think this is quaint and old-fashioned—in 1997 the National Endowment for the Arts gave Canyon Cinema, a renowned West Coast Distribution House that specializes in underground film from the period discussed in this essay, $15,000 to publish an updated catalog. A member of the House of Representatives contested the award, and attacked Canyon Cinema on the floor of the Congress. Pointing to pictures in the existing catalog and read-

ing descriptions of some of the films, the Representative from Michigan accused Canyon of distributing pornography. Under pressure, the NEA removed Canyon's grant and also denied funding to Women Make Movies and Frameline. I am indebted to Dominic Angerame, director of Canyon Cinema, for this information.

18. See Hawkins, *Cutting Edge*.

19. Amos Vogel, *Film as a Subversive Art* (New York: Random House, 1974), 191–258.

20. The Internet Movie Database gives a date of 1972 for this film; this was the commercial release date, but it played in festivals before that. See www.imdb.com/title/tt0151327/, accessed July 10, 2008.

21. See "Bruce Boomlet," *Time*, May 31, 1971, 73; Douglas Auchinsloss, "The Theater: The Broken Taboo Breaker," *Time*, June 7, 1971, 62; Jack Kroll, "Lenny Lives," *Newsweek*, June 7, 1971, 75+; Albert Goldman, "What Lenny Bruce Was All About," *New York Times Magazine*, June 27, 1971, 12–13.

22. Gomery, *Shared Pleasures*, 193.

23. Naomi Klein, *No Logo* (New York: Picador, 2000).

24. Wilinsky, *Sure Seaters: The Emergence of Art House Cinema* (Minneapolis: University of Minnesota Press, 2001); see chap. 5.

25. See Douglas Gomery, "Motion Picture Exhibition in 1970s America," in Cook, *Lost Illusions: American Cinema in the Shadow of Watergate and Vietnam 1970–1979* (Berkeley: University of California Press, 2002), 397–416.

26. See Craig Gilbert, "Reflections on an American Family I" and "Reflections on an American Family II," In *New Challenges for Documentary*, ed. Alan Rosenthal (Berkeley: University of California Press, 1988), 191–209 and 288–307.

27. It took HBO a while to firmly establish itself. But it is notable for our purposes that the early free weekend promotional subscription packages always included art house fare in the line-up. When the local cable station in Santa Cruz, CA, picked up HBO in 1975, for example, the free weekend of HBO included Truffaut's *La peau douce* (1964) in the line-up.

28. Sometimes theaters leased to another business concern that ran the midnight movies; sometimes the theaters themselves booked and managed the midnight flicks.

29. "Paracinema" is an elastic term that comprises old horror films, exploitation, sword and sandal epics, JD films, sex hygiene films, and art cinema. See Jeffrey Sconce, "'Trashing' the Academy: Taste, Excess and an Emerging Politics of Cinematic Style," *Screen* 36, no. 4 (winter 1995): 371–393.

30. Eric Schaefer, *"Bold! Daring! Shocking! True!": A History of Exploitation Films, 1919–1959* (Durham, NC: Duke University Press, 1999), 124–125.

31. Hawkins, *Cutting Edge*.

32. Hawkins, *Cutting Edge*, 8. The Fredric Jameson quote is taken from his *Signatures of the Visible* (New York: Routledge, 1992), 14.

33. Raymond Williams, *The Sociology of Culture* (New York: Schocken Books, 1982), 68.

34. This changed, of course, after 1973, when the Drug Enforcement Administration was created and laws against cannabis possession became much tougher.

35. Raymond Durgnat, *Mysteries of the Organism* (London: British Film Institute Publishing, 1999), 12. Hereafter, cited in the text as Durgnat.

36. See Mildred Brady, "The Strange Case of Wilhelm Reich," *New Republic* (May 26, 1947); and Mildred Brady, "The New Cult of Sex and Anarchy," *New Republic* (April 1947).

37. The accumulator is a box, large enough to accommodate a seated adult. Wood on the outside and metal on the inside, it needs to be housed in a place where the air is relatively fresh. The idea is that orgone will accumulate between the layers of the box.

38. Two Reichian therapists, Drs. Alexander Lowen and John C. Pierrakos, sought an injunction against the film, in an attempt to prevent its opening in New York. They believed they had been misled by the filmmaker and feared that their professional reputations would be harmed. *Variety*, October 20, 1971, 6.

39. Vogel, *Film as a Subversive Art*. 153.

40. Carolee Schneemann, *Imaging Her Erotics: Essays, Interviews, Projects* (Cambridge, MA: MIT Press, 2002), 102, 102–3.

41. James Roy MacBean, "Sex and Politics: Wilhelm Reich, World Politics, and Makavejev's *WR*," *Film Quarterly* 25, no. 3 (spring 1972): 2.

Part III: Media at the Margins

7 * 33 1/3 Sexual Revolutions per Minute

JACOB SMITH

In 1966, a man named Joe Davis was convicted by a federal jury of sending obscene materials through the mail. Davis was fined $1,000 and given a suspended sentence of six months in jail despite the fact that the items he had mailed contained no explicit images of bodies or sexual activity, and in some cases no discernible verbal content at all: Davis had been dealing in erotic phonograph records. In historical surveys that discuss the role of the media in the sexual revolution, little mention has been given to sexually explicit phonograph records, despite the fact that the recording industry enjoyed unprecedented prosperity and cultural influence during the decades of the sexual revolution. Beginning in the early 1950s, a lively home market existed for long-playing (LP) recordings not only of music but of poetry readings, children's entertainment, dramatizations, sound effects, and comedy performances. Adult-themed records made between the 1950s and mid-1970s provide an overlooked case study of mass-media erotica meant for home consumption before cable television or the explosion of porn on video and DVD.

Under-the-counter recordings of erotic material—referred to as either "blue discs" or "party records"—have circulated since at least the 1930s, but attained a new degree of cultural visibility in the 1950s and 1960s. Party records were often intended for a culture of male hi-fi aficionados, but the home stereo was not solely the domain of men. During the same era, records made by female comics such as Rusty Warren presented bawdy material from a female perspective and reached legions of female fans. Warren's records were intended for mixed-gender social gatherings; however, LP phonograph albums also functioned as a form of family sex education and home sex therapy for couples. In all of these cases, the LP was well suited to the frank discussion and performance of sexuality, a point that performers often made by contrasting party records with network radio and television.

The examination of party records fills a gap in the historical record of media consumption from this era, and also illustrates a variety of approaches to the vocal performance of erotic material. As such, one of the concerns of this chapter will be to examine the different ways that were found to "speak sex" for various home-listening audiences. Indeed, one of my goals is to explore how media performances work to construct the contexts of their reception. Scholars of film reception such as Robert C. Allen have argued that cinema audiences are discursively constructed by industry advertising, the design of movie theaters, and the like.[1]

In her study of audiences in Africa, Karin Barber describes the role of performance in the formation of audiences: "Performances do not just play to ready-made congregations of spectators which are out there awaiting address; they convene those congregations and by their mode of address assign them a certain position from which to receive the address. Thus performances, in the act of addressing audiences, constitute those audiences as a particular form of collectivity."[2] Following Barber, I take the performances heard on party records as one form of evidence by which we might infer details of their reception. Before I begin a discussion of specific artists and LPs, I will situate party records in a postwar debate about "obscene" phonograph records, a topic that was the source of growing concern for law enforcement officers and legislators throughout the 1940s and 1950s.

The *New York Times* reported on November 1, 1942 that a police judge in Newark, New Jersey, ordered a campaign against "dealers in indecent phonograph recordings" after four owners of radio and music shops were charged with possessing obscene records. The fact that the judge also ordered a warrant for the arrest of a record distributor alleged to have "10,000 objectionable records in stock" reveals the extent of mass production and distribution in the operation.[3] Press coverage suggests that distributors of risqué records were increasingly at risk of prosecution toward the end of the 1940s. The *Lincoln Journal* reported on October 1, 1948, that the FBI had arrested a Kansas man on a charge of "illegally transporting obscene phonograph records between states." An FBI Special Agent stated this was "the first case of its kind handled by the bureau." The man was the operator of the Kansas City Music and Sales Company, and had sold the records to "select customers on an under-the-counter basis."[4] As in other cases during the 1940s, law enforcement officials targeted music shops and record distributors who sold adult records to an exclusive clientele.[5]

Such was the case with Alexander L. Alpers, a San Francisco "record-shop operator," who was fined $200 by a district court in December 1948 for sending packages of allegedly indecent records out of state.[6] Alpers's conviction was overturned in June 1949 by the Ninth Federal Circuit

Court, which stated that the law forbidding the shipment of obscene "matters" did not apply to phonograph records.[7] That ruling was later overturned by the U.S. Supreme Court on February 7, 1950. In *United States v. Alpers*, the court held that obscene phonograph records were within the prohibition of the United States Criminal Code. In the wake of this decision, President Harry Truman updated federal law to include "obscene phonograph recordings and electrical transcriptions" in the ban on the interstate shipment of obscenity.[8] An article in the May 3, 1950, issue of *Variety* indicated that arrests continued after the new legislation: in a case called "the first of its kind" in Philadelphia, Albert L. Miller, owner of Palda Records, was indicted by the Federal Grand Jury on charges of "shipping pornographic recordings."[9] Although reports in the press suggest that the peak of law enforcement activity relating to obscene records was in the late 1940s, the pursuit of them continued. For example, the *Syracuse Herald-Journal* reported on April 2, 1958, that six music shops in Queens and a Manhattan record distributor were raided and eight men were arrested on charges of selling "obscene phonograph records": "Hundreds of records, some selling as high as $50 each, were seized."[10]

Press coverage thus indicates a thriving market for under-the-counter risqué recordings in the 1940s and 1950s. But who was buying and listening to these records? Under what social circumstances were they played? What kinds of erotic performances did they contain? How did party records fit into broader postwar discourses about gender and sexuality? How did the content of adult records change during the era of the sexual revolution? Information about these records is difficult to find, but one way we might begin to answer questions such as these is by reference to the Joe Davis court case mentioned above. One of the records that Davis sent through the mail was *Erotica: The Rhythms of Love* (Fax Records, ca. 1960). Before I describe the performances heard on this record, I would like to consider the dust jacket, which can provide some clues as to the nature of the audience for "obscene" records. The liner notes explain, "Erotica" was "the culmination of more than two years of research, utilizing today's most advanced electronic techniques and the talents of sound engineers who have pioneered a host of technical achievements." They go on to explain that a portion of the record was made "on a Magnecorder PT6AH, using an RCA 77DX microphone, and taped at 15 IPS (inches per second)," with the help of an "Ampex 300 tape recorder." Perhaps these esoteric technical facts were included in order to fend off obscenity charges by demonstrating that the record held some kind of scientific merit. Nevertheless, reference to such minutiae also suggests an address to a certain type of audience: male hi-fi audio enthusiasts.

Hi-Fi Hardcore

Many American men developed an interest in high-fidelity audio equipment after World War II, in part because of the extensive electronics training they received in the armed forces. Writers such as Keir Keightley, Pamela Robertson Wojcik, and Barbara Ehrenreich have connected the "masculinization" of hi-fi audio equipment at this time to larger trends in postwar consumer culture. As men began to question their traditional role as breadwinner, the home hi-fi stereo became a male status symbol to rival more traditional status objects that men had consumed vicariously: the family home, car, and so on. Ironically, though the hi-fi became an emblem of a new kind of male consumer spending, magazines marketed to audio enthusiasts often defined their media consumption as a "high, masculine, individualistic art," in contrast to watching television, which was glossed as a "low, feminine, mass entertainment."[11]

Similar arguments can be heard on party records made during the era of high fidelity. Consider *Stag Party Special Number 1* (Fax Records, 1959), one of a series of records released in conjunction with the men's magazine *Adam*. Comic Buzzy Greene begins his burlesque club act by announcing "You are now about to be the recipients of the last form of show business in the world today that has not been seen, or probably never will be seen on television—unless you have a very vivid imagination, and can picture Dr. Ross Dog Food or Texaco Gas sponsoring something like this, man! Huh, that'd be something wild!" Greene's comments illustrate how stag party records—like the audio tech magazines discussed by Keightley—presented hi-fi as an alternative to corporate advertising.[12] In fact, risqué records might have held a particular appeal to hi-fi enthusiasts because they so bluntly transgressed the standards of network broadcasting.

Risqué records could also provide a means of bringing frank discussions of sex and the rough language traditionally associated with men into the home. Elsewhere I have described how 78 RPM "blue discs," heard in homosocial spaces such as the tavern, often featured joking traditions associated with male organizations.[13] Similarly, some postwar LPs advertised their ability to capture the language used by men at stag parties, military barracks, burlesque clubs, and other homosocial spaces. In the words of the liner notes for Fax Records' *Wild Party Songs Num-*

ber 1: Saturday Night Riot (1960), the "bone-tickling ditties of sin, sex and seduction" found on the album were "an important manifestation of our cultural heritage": "They are the lusty songs of men under stress. . . . In army barracks, in ships at sea, at Rotarian smokers, campus dormitories, now in 'polite' society, we hear these lusty refrains." Fax advertised some of its stag party records as documenting "private club dates and 'smoker' specials," where comedians could unleash "scorching gems of heavily-spiced ribaldry" that were "too bold for large night club audiences."[14] These records were thus representations of exclusive male social spaces as much as of a certain kind of language. In fact, "Saturday Night Riot" is among several Stag Party records to feature an ambient soundtrack running between musical numbers that includes the sounds of coughing, laughter, the clinking of glasses, and conversation. These ambient sounds make one wonder if "party records" were so named because they were meant to be played at parties or because they simulated a party atmosphere for isolated, suburban men.

Recall that the liner notes to the "Wild Party Songs" record had mentioned army barracks as one of the places where one could hear such "lusty refrains." In fact, military themes are prevalent on postwar party records: from Fax's series of "Wild Service Songs" albums to blue discs that dramatized the experience of American soldiers. For example, a record from the late 1940s entitled "Lt. Rudder" features a routine that circulated amongst soldiers during the final years of World War II. The routine was described in a 1945 Associated Press article:

> Someone got weary of reading the honeyed accounts of America's returning air warriors and wrote a parody account of the homecoming of such a gay, cocky, young flier that has half the European theater of operations in stitches. The pilots, themselves, think it is wonderful, because they think the acclaim that greets their exploits is sometimes false and foolish and smacks of mock heroics.[15]

The newspaper article could only reprint what it called a "heavily censored" version of the routine, with apologies to the original anonymous author, "in whatever pub or opium den he lies dreaming." The under-the-counter recording of the routine however, was free to unleash Lt. Rudder in all his gay, cocky glory.

The "Lt. Rudder" skit articulated soldiers' ambivalent feelings about reintegrating into civilian life, where very different social rules held sway than in the homosocial context of the military. The record begins as an elaborate send-up of radio: following a fake commercial, we hear an earnest announcer declare that he is taking us to LaGuardia Airport for a special broadcast to welcome home Lt. Ronald Rudder, one of "America's leading aces" overseas. During a long buildup to the hero's arrival, we are introduced to Lt. Col. Eager Beaver, an army public relations man and liaison to Lt. Rudder. As side one of the record spins to a close, a crowd cheers and Rudder steps to the microphone. "How do you feel on being back in the United States again?" the reporter asks at the start of side two. Rudder replies in a matter-of-fact tone: "Uh, pretty damn pissed off." The army PR man anxiously interjects: "Lt. Rudder means his eyes were misty when the outlines of the States and Statue of Liberty—symbol of American faith and the fight for freedom—loomed into sight." The reporter poses a second question: "What's the first thing you're going to do in New York?" Rudder replies: "I'm going to go out and get laid." Again, Lt. Col. Beaver hastily cuts in to translate the flier's words into language fit for broadcast radio: "Uhh, he intends to say, he will fly back to his home and see his Mom and all his folks." The record continues in this manner until Rudder announces: "Well, I'm sorry fellas, but I gotta get outta here before the bars close and line up a piece of ass, ya know?" Making one last attempt to clean up Rudder's statements, Lt. Col. Beaver quickly adds, "Yes, uh, Lt. Rudder can't wait to get back to a piece of his mother's apple pie, the girl he left behind, and, and, the old Main Street where he played Indian as a small boy."

The "Lt. Rudder" record mocks the platitudes and clichés of "false and foolish" accounts of male wartime experience, accounts that are associated both with feminized domestic life and broadcasting. Unlike radio and television, bawdy phonograph records such as *Lt. Rudder* (ca. 1948) and *In Hawaii* (ca. 1948; a blue disc that dramatizes the adventures of two "lovable Marines" on leave in Honolulu), could present the rough, frank talk of soldiers, while also providing a means of virtual escape from a postwar domestic space increasingly devoted to family togetherness.[16]

We have seen that party records simulated spaces such as the burlesque club and the army barracks for a male audience. Party records were also released that represented another postwar male space: the "playboy" bachelor pad. *The Sweetest Music* (ca. 1965), an anonymous LP released circa the middle to late 1960s, begins with a monologue by a man named Phil:

> She worked on my staff at the office for several months. Cute little chick; nice shape; well dressed; but very, very naïve. Dedicated? Uh! Last bird to leave the office almost every night. You know, babes are a dime a dozen for a swinging bachelor with a decked out pad. But Sheila played hard to get. "No time for guys," she said. She was strictly the career-girl type.

Phil invites Sheila to help him celebrate his twenty-sixth birthday with "dinner and a night on the town." When she arrives at his apartment, Phil greets her with "Come on right in, doll." "Hi, handsome," Sheila answers in a breathy whisper, and then "Hey, dig that sexy purple bathrobe." Phil whistles appreciatively and says, "My, aren't we dolled-up and lookin' groovy." After toasting to his birthday ("Here's cheers to our birthday boy. May the next twenty-five swing as madly as the first"), Sheila asks, "What are all those knobs sticking out of the wall, Phil?" "Little thing I had installed a few months ago," Phil boasts, "stereo, FM, AM, the whole hi-fi bit. Music in every room in this pad, baby."

The Sweetest Music thus provides an audio representation of the playboy apartment that indicates the centrality of the hi-fi to the sexual arsenal of men such as Phil (or those who fantasized about being like him).[17] Steven Cohan has described the playboy apartment as a "theatrical backdrop" for the performance of male sexuality, a "fantasy playpen" that used modern technology for the single purpose of seduction.[18] Indeed, Cohan, Bill Osgerby, Ehrenreich, and other scholars emphasize the importance of the playboy apartment as a site of male consumerism.[19] In fact, we should note how seduction and consumerism are combined in *The Sweetest Music*, since it offers a commodified enactment of sexual seduction to be consumed via the preferred medium of the playboy apartment: the hi-fi.

The Sweetest Music dramatizes seduction with a type of erotic vocal performance that distinguishes adult LPs made during the era of the sexual revolution from their postwar predecessors. After treating Sheila to the "electronic pleasure provider" on his sensual reclining seat, and dancing to music from his hi-fi, Phil lights a Tibetan candle and orally pleases Sheila, signified by the smacking of kisses, sighs, moans, and heavy breathing. This is a type of verbal performance that Rich Cante and Angelo Restivo have called "porno-performativity."[20] Blue discs of a previous era only rarely attempted to depict the sex act with that kind of unrestrained vocalization. Instead, 78 RPM blue discs typically featured double entendres, riddles, and short burlesque sketches that suggested, but did not explicitly state, erotic ideas and situations. The extended porno-performativity heard on *The Sweetest Music* is made possible in part by the introduction of long-playing 33 1/3 RPM records, first widely produced by Columbia Records in 1948. Long-playing records provided the time to develop longer erotic narratives and to enact extended sessions of hardcore sexual action. However, during the moments of porno-performativity on *The Sweetest Music*, we are often unable to distinguish who is vocalizing, or even who is doing what to whom. We are left with only the vague outlines of a sex scene, as if the action were obscured by the pungent smoke of Phil's Tibetan candle.

A similar attempt at LP hardcore can be heard on *Erotica: The Rhythm of Love* (ca. 1960), one of the records involved in the Joe Davis obscenity trial in 1966. The recording comprises two overlapping tracks, one featuring an erratic bongo drum performance punctuated by occasional nonsensical vocal exclamations, and the other the sounds of a squeaking bed over which we hear a woman's periodic gasps and grunts. As with *The Sweetest Music*, the effect is more disconcerting than erotic. In fact, the legal discussion surrounding *Erotica* reveals considerable ambiguity about whether the record was obscene at all. In a U.S. Postal Service investigation of Fax Records in 1959, it was stated that the "exclamations, cries, moans, sighs, words and other sounds" heard on *Erotica* captured "every possible sound made by the parties or by the bed on which the act of sexual intercourse takes place" and so left "no doubt in the mind of any listener" as to what was being recorded. The post office declared the record to be obscene because it left "nothing to the imagination as to what is going on, [and] set forth the act of sexual intercourse in its most lustful aspect."[21]

Circuit judge Sterry R. Waterman, however, said that the records in the Joe Davis case failed to appeal to his prurient interest, adding "I must say that they bored me." Likewise, Supreme Court Justice Potter Stewart, in his dissenting opinion, called the title *Erotica* a "gross misnomer."[22] We might understand these comments as evidence to support Linda Williams's claim that "there can be no such thing as hardcore sound."[23] Unlike the visual depiction of male orgasm, vocalizations such as those heard on the *Erotica* LP did not count as irrefutable proof that sex had taken place. In fact, the attempt to produce indexical audio evidence of intercourse in the case of *Erotica* was deemed by some to be ridiculous. Ironically, it was when phonograph records were purporting to capture hardcore sexual action that they became less threatening to the prosecutors of obscenity. At a time when hardcore visual images in magazines and theatrical films were becoming more prevalent, and when 8 and 16 mm adult films made for home consumption were a growing concern of the U.S. Postal Service, the content of these records must have seemed comparatively less prurient and not the pressing concern that obscene records had been a decade earlier.[24] The trade in small-gauge home movies and erotic LPs shared a site of intended reception in the home, and so both of these enterprises would have been encouraged by the 1969 Supreme Court *Stanley v. Georgia* decision, which distinguished between public exhibition of pornography and home consumption. If, in the words of Justice Thurgood Marshall, the state had no business telling "a man, sitting alone in his own house, what books he may read or what films he may watch," neither did it have any business telling "a man" what records he could listen to on his hi-fi.

The sexist language in Marshall's statement is, of course, a product of its time, but also points to gendered assumptions about the consumers of adult material. I have been arguing that *The Sweetest Music* and *Erotica* were intended primarily for a home audience of men that overlapped with a culture of hi-fi audio buffs. Records such as these experimented with the LP as a means of erotic escapism and audio voyeurism for men in the 1950s and 1960s. But as Pamela Robertson Wojcik has argued, postwar phonograph culture was not the sole province of men.[25] In fact, other party records released during the early 1960s—records far more popular than *Erotica* and *The Sweetest Music*—featured a female perspective on adult material, and were made for a largely female audience.

Knockers Up

During the 1950s, female performers such as Belle Barth, Pearl Williams, and Ruth Wallis delivered bawdy material in nightclub appearances and on live recordings of their acts. In the early 1960s, the most successful female performer in this style was Rusty Warren. Born Ilene Goldman in New York in 1931, she graduated from Boston's New England Conservatory of Music in 1952 and began playing in upstate New York lounges. By the end of the decade, she had developed a risqué act and was selling records of her club performances. "At that time those records were not sold in stores," she said in a 1994 interview, "I was constantly touring in cities and towns, working in little lounges. After the show people would come up and I'd sell them an album, take a card and put them on a mailing list."[26] Her first record, *Songs for Sinners*, was released in 1959, followed by *Knockers Up!* a year later, and both *Rusty Warren Bounces Back* and *Sin-Sational!* in 1961. By the early 1960s, Warren's records were available in stores, and we might gauge her popularity by looking at the Billboard charts.[27] *Knockers Up!* debuted at no. 31 on November 7, 1960. It was still going strong at no. 26 on April 7, 1962. In fact, Warren had four LPs in the charts that week: in addition to *Knockers Up!, Bounces Back* was at no. 35, *Sin-Sational* was no. 79, and *Songs for Sinners* was no. 128. As these chart positions indicate, she was certainly selling records: an advertisement in *Parade* in December 1961 claimed that she had sold two million albums, and a 1963 newspaper ad stated that "in recordland she's a living legend—3,000,000 LP sales in little over a year."[28]

Warren was even featured in *Time* in January 1963, albeit with an unfavorable review. "She is just another dirty comedian who deprives sex of all its grace and sophistication," wrote the reviewer, "while she claims to be helping inhibited females to enjoy themselves." That statement indicates an important fact about Warren's audience: it consisted largely of women. In fact, the *Time* review focused more on her audience than her act:

> The incredible thing about Rusty Warren is the crowds she draws. She has just left Mr. Kelly's in Chicago, where Greyhound buses arrived every day from assorted plains cities full of jolly, plump, graying matrons dying to see their goddess. Car pools came in from Iowa and far Missouri. "The women are usually 40 to 50 or more, and hefty," she says. Many women regularly bring their husbands to hear her, blue-suit and brown-shoe types that have never seen a nightclub. Like Rusty, they all seem at home in a barnyard. They sit there and roar happily as Rusty expresses her desire to become the first woman to make love to an astronaut in space. The women fans wear Knockers Up buttons. They know her first LP albums by heart (more than 3,000,000 sold so far). They have made her a $5,000-a-week nightclub star, outdrawing Mort Sahl and Shelley Berman.[29]

The writer clearly had disdain for Warren's audience members because of their age and social class, but most of all because of their gender.

Warren was very aware of her appeal to women, as can be gauged by the manner in which she addressed her audience. For example, on *Knockers Up!* she begins by stating "As I look around I see a lot of married couples in the audience tonight, so if I may, I would like to talk to the wives, about what they brought with them." Furthermore, her material often pointed out male sexual inadequacies. On *Bounces Back*, she talks about men's loss of sexual vitality after marriage:

> He was young, insistent, vital, strong, passionate. Yes, he was a youthful sex maniac! And ladies, here we sit; ten, twelve, fifteen years later, with *him*. Where did he go? Where is the mad sex maniac today when we want it? Have we not had our basic training? . . . And now that we know what we know, *where the hell is he?*

At another point, Warren describes a newlywed couple in their honeymoon suite. The bashful wife emerges, wrapped in a towel. "My dear," the husband says, "we're married now, you can drop the towel." He is so struck by the sight of her naked body that he asks if he can take a picture of her, saying "I want to carry it close to my heart for the rest of my life." The wife then asks the husband to remove *his* robe, after which she asks, "May I take your picture?" The husband flexes his muscles and says, "Yes, what do you want to do with it?" Warren delivers the punch line: "Have it enlarged!" This joke was dramatized on an earlier 78 RPM blue disc called "Newlyweds": an indication of how a frank discussion of male inadequacy was always present on blue discs. Warren brought that type of bawdy humor to a more mainstream, largely female audience.

Despite that Warren deflated male pride and made female sexual desire explicit, the showcase of her act was a burlesque of female social action. At the close of her set on *Knockers Up!*, Warren adopts a serious tone and delivers this recitation: "We girls figure that we have a lot to project in this world today. . . . These men are campaigning to give the best they have. Then we, of course, must campaign to give the best that *we* have. So if I may, I would like to do a number for the young ladies to prove that we *do* have something to give. Are you girls ready?" What follows is a military march on drums and piano, with Warren shouting: "Knockers up! Come on girls, throw those shoulders back and get your knockers up!" Some women did march through the room when Warren played this song; she stated in a later interview, "Women used to march outside, around buildings and all over the place!"[30] On the follow-up LP, *Bounces Back*, Warren presented a spin-off of the successful "Knockers Up!" routine. Again, she takes on a mock serious tone, shifting from a sexual to a political register: "These men, their ancestors have given us our political freedom. There is no reason today why we should not have sexual freedom." Patriotic music swells as Warren explains, "You know girls, it's great to live in a democracy today, where freedom is everywhere. But girls, we often take this freedom for granted. . . . Proclaim your freedom! Stand at attention! Pledge allegiance, and . . ." On cue, jaunty music begins, with Warren singing "Bounce your boobies, get into the swing!" "Loosen the bra that binds you," she shouts. "Take it off if you feel like it!"

These spoofs of female empowerment can make contemporary listeners a bit uncomfortable, as they seem to both objectify and condescend to the women in her audience. It is as if the critical moments in her act needed to be defused, laughed away as the harmless expression of female silliness. Nonetheless, we shouldn't dismiss the transgressive pleasure that Warren's routines clearly provided to her female fans. In fact, Warren's conflation of "knockers" and politics simply exaggerated the prevailing national obsession with large breasts. On *Bounces Back*, Warren quipped that "you have to have big knockers to be a star" and listed Jayne Mansfield, Gina Lollobrigida, Marilyn Monroe, and

Elizabeth Taylor as evidence. The fact that Warren's "Knockers Up" and "Bounce Your Boobies" (1961) routines equate breasts with power, freedom, and social agency ("we *do* have something to give"), draws attention to prevailing standards concerning the female body and so perhaps registered as a subtle social critique.

We should note that Warren's transgressions were counterbalanced by her tendency to portray herself in a grotesque manner: she often referred to her less-than-ideal sex life and sadly inadequate "knockers." In this, Warren was similar to "unruly" female burlesque performers such as Mae West, Sophie Tucker, or Bessie Smith: performers whose transgressive power "was channeled and defused through their construction as grotesque figures."[31] Warren also disregarded standards of femininity with regard to her voice. This is not the place for an exhaustive history of female vocal etiquette, but suffice it to say that since at least the turn of the century, American women had been encouraged to consider their voices as a potential problem and urged to keep their voices low, and free from a raspy or nasal tone. We might note that the most iconic "erotic voice" of the era belonged to Marilyn Monroe, who presented a breathy whisper similar to Sheila's on *The Sweetest Music*. By contrast, Warren presents erotic material not with a demure, sensual whisper, but with a loud, full-voiced rasp (figure 7.1).

Warren's approach was influenced by earlier bawdy female comics who transgressed the cultural rules of female vocal production. Pearl Williams, for example, delivered her jokes with a harsh, raucous laugh. In an insightful essay on female comics, Michael Bronski argues that Williams and Belle Barth were part of "a distinct Jewish show-biz culture" descended from "Yiddish shtetl culture," which he argues had "long appreciated publicly assertive women." He continues, "After all, while men were expected to stay at home and study the Torah, women were in the public sphere, the marketplace, and the street. Such publicness often lent itself to outspoken candor—especially after immigration to the US."[32] The brash voices of these female comics served to project their bodily presence and assert themselves as sexual subjects. More than this, Warren conveys a remarkable sense of freedom through her gymnastic vocal ability: one minute she has the exaggerated high-pitched tone of a child, the next she delivers a salty punch line in a throaty rasp, and later she belts out a song with a chest voice that is deep and powerful. Warren said in an e-mail interview (September 7, 2006) that she "played an androgynous role, yelling, shouting, being un-ladylike," but added that she "had to be careful not to cross over into vulgarity." "I was extremely

Fig. 7.1 The "ladylike" image of Rusty Warren on her album covers, such as *Sin-Sational* from 1961, provided a contrast to the LPs' tracks, which featured her transgressive vocal performances.

careful never to veer into that zone at all. My worst words were hell, damn." Here then, is an indication of the importance of vocal inflection as a means of managing the risks involved in delivering erotic material.

Despite the fact that Warren's "un-ladylike" vocalizing added to her self-presentation as a grotesque figure, many of Warren's fans perceived her act in socially progressive terms. In fact, Warren was sometimes billed in the later years of her career as the "Mother of the Sexual Revolution," a claim that we might understand in several ways. First, Warren's records were an early example of an increasingly frank discussion of sex by women in the mass media, a trend that would become more pronounced later in the decade. Consider that David Allyn begins his history of the sexual revolution with the release of Helen Gurley Brown's book, *Sex and the Single Girl* (1962), arguing that the American public adored

Brown's "breezy style, forthright manner, and pragmatic attitude about premarital romance."[33] Barbara Ehrenreich, Gloria Jacobs, and Elizabeth Hess note that Gurley Brown's book was a bestseller at a time before "feminism" existed in "the American political vocabulary," and demonstrated that "extramarital sex did not have to mean ruin."[34] We should note Warren's presence on the entertainment scene in the years immediately before and during the release of *Sex and The Single Girl*, as well as the fact that she presented a similarly "breezy" and "forthright" message about female sexual desire and the limitations of traditional courtship and marriage.[35]

Warren stated that women in the early 1960s were "admitting that they liked sex, and that they liked men looking sexy. They were coming out of their shell of sexual inhibitions—the way they'd been trained." "That's why I was titillating them," she said; "they were trained not to talk this way, and here I was doing it!"[36] On a fan website dedicated to Warren, an essayist argues that the comedienne "used humor to deliver her message that women do have sexual appetites," and did so at a time when female sexuality was "extremely repressed." Note how the author describes what the nightclub audiences heard on Warren's records from the 1960s:

> These couples are the heads of suburban households, the mom & pop of nuclear families—or they are on the path to being such. The women sit in clothing that today seems glamorous, at least to me, but underneath their cocktail dresses, their lives are more restrictive than their foundation garments. They chafe not from underwires and rubber, but from the reality of being "Mom" even to their husbands. They dressed that night with hopes that "Daddy" would see them, once again, as a woman. They hoped the alcohol would loosen inhibitions just as they had when they were dating—and that they'd find themselves steaming up the backseat of the car, or at the very least, they'd get some action once they got home. Oh, pray that he wouldn't drink too much and the only activity she'd see would be removing his clothing as she tucked him in.[37]

The author understood Warren's records as historical documents of a time when women were waking up to the consequences of cultural double standards relating to sex and marriage, and it even situates Warren as the female answer to Hugh Hefner and *Playboy*: "Rusty exposed male hypocrisy, gender stereotypes, and the female libido to a conservative American public." These are dramatic claims, and authors such as Michel Foucault have taught us to be wary of the suggestion that sexuality has been repressed. Nevertheless, accounts of her legions of female fans, sellout performances, and chart-topping LPs indicate that Warren undoubtedly struck a nerve with a generation of women.

In fact, it is in generational terms that we might understand the claim that Warren was the "Mother of the Sexual Revolution": she was literally entertaining the *mothers* of the generation that would become sexually active in the 1960s. Consider that on her LP *More Knockers Up!* Warren tells the parents in her audience not to worry about their children. "It is now 9:15," she says, "and all your teenagers are home in front of the television set watching the Beatles. So mothers, don't even call home for the next hour because if the phone rings they won't answer it." Indeed, the boisterous female audience-members who can be heard on Warren's LPs should be placed in the history of popular culture beside the screaming female fans at performances by rock bands such as the Beatles. Ehrenreich, Jacobs, and Hess argue that the screams of female Beatles fans were a form of cathartic release from sexual repression: "Adulation of the male star was a way to express sexual yearnings that would normally be pressed into the service of popularity or simply be repressed. The star could be loved noninstrumentally, for his own sake, and with complete abandon. Publicly to advertise this hopeless love was to protest the calculated, pragmatic sexual repression of teenage life."[38] Although she had a much different relationship with her fans, Warren served a similar function for older women who were, in their own way, obliquely protesting the repression of married life. Here then, is an explanation for the dismissive portrayal of the middle-aged female audience at Warren's club appearances found in the *Time* review cited above. Beatles fans and "single girls" were carving out a cultural space for the expression of a certain female sexual agency, but this was confined to "girls." Warren's misbehaving middle-aged audiences did not fit with that emerging cultural script, and so seemed aberrant and troubling in the eyes of the article's author.

Warren's quip about the kids at home watching the Beatles on TV can be heard as another instance of a rhetoric that contrasted adult phonograph records and broadcast entertainment. In fact, Warren's *Banned in Boston?* (1963) LP contains a musical number called "Pay as You See TV," in which she imagines a future where viewers would be able to "put a dollar in the slot for the shows that you want to see." Warren suggests that the "password" for such a service would be "sex." "They say there'll be no boring commercials, a little more zest and zip," she sings, "if we could see what we want to see without any censorship." She then describes how she would be a "rising star" on this "naughty network," which would also include such programs as "lusty lurid scenes from confidential magazines" and "an hour of bawdy songs on Sing Along with Mitch." This gag points out the restrictions of broadcasting, which, as we have seen, is a recurring theme of party records of the era.

In fact, Warren's records were intended for social gatherings that were an adult alternative to television's "family circle."[39] Warren wrote in an e-mail interview of September 7, 2006, that her fans were mostly young suburban couples who were "busy building their families." "You first caught my show at your local lounge," she wrote, "took the record home and that weekend you had the neighbors over for a barbecue." In fact, Warren stressed in another interview that her records were "always a shared experience": "You never sat alone and listened with headphones like people do today," she said, "I was a 'party record' concept—you shared my records with friends at a barbecue or party."[40] The use of the home hi-fi by groups of young suburban couples for titillating entertainment represented a marked contrast to both the television family circle and the hi-fi as means of escape for male audio enthusiasts. Later in the 1960s, sexually explicit LPs were marketed to serve yet another function: home sex therapy for couples.

The Sensuous Phonograph

David Allyn has referred to the 1960s and 1970s as the "Golden Age of Sexual Science" due to the many influential books on sex published at that time. Long-playing records provided a medium for bringing the changing content of sexological literature into the home during this period, and can reveal the different ways in which listeners to such material were constructed as audiences. Before the "Golden Age" to which Allyn refers, those seeking information about sex often turned to "marriage manuals" and advice books for teenagers that provided a mixed message of "sexual conservatism and enthusiasm" and reinforced "traditional concepts of marriage and gender roles."[41] Some LPs of the 1960s presented lessons in sex education that worked in a similar manner.

The Illinois State Medical Society released a record entitled *Sex and Your Daughter* in 1965 that featured one side for parents only, and another to be heard with both parents and children present (figure 7.2). *Sex and Your Daughter* was concerned with enforcing traditional gender roles as much as with discussing sexual science. For example, parents are told on side one that their daughter's sexuality should be defined in terms of her future role as a mother. "Above all, emphasize the importance of being able to have children," the narrator states. "For the young woman approaching womanhood, it is essential that she fully understand the

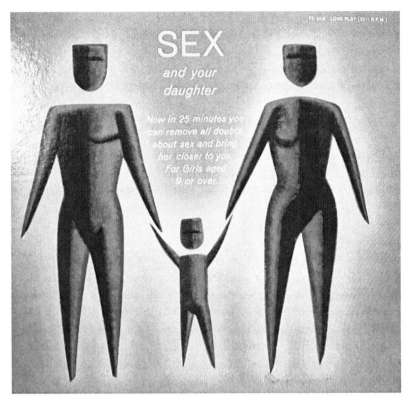

Fig. 7.2 The album *Sex and Your Daughter* (1965) included one side for parents to listen to alone, and the other to listen to with the child in a bid to combine sex education with postwar family "togetherness."

process she will experience in preparation for this sacred responsibility." The side to be played in the presence of the daughter features a dramatization in which "Dr. Sims" visits a family in order to speak to the daughter "Betty" about growing up. Dr. Sims explains to Betty that the meaning of love is best illustrated by her mother and father: "Father works hard to earn a living . . . so you can have food clothing and a home" whereas "Mother takes care of home [and] shopping." The record illustrates the "mixed message" provided by many marriage manuals: parents are encouraged to be more open with their children about the "sacred responsibility" of sex, but only in the context of the traditional family ideal.

Although the content of the Dr. Sims record was meant to train children to be future parents, the act of listening to the record was intended to fortify the family of the present. Parents were given suggestions on side one as to how to structure the listening event. The child was to be seated between the parents, with all three looking at diagrams that accompanied the LP. The sexual content of the record was thus experienced within the context of a family gathering: "During the playing of the record, do not hesitate to put your arms around her with affection," parents are told. "When the record has been played it should be a natural impulse of the child to turn to you and kiss you. The record has been worded in such a way that she will follow this natural impulse. So don't hesitate to encourage this display of affection." Parents were also told how to structure the time immediately after playing the record: "You might have a little snack with ice cream and cake. Let the conversation flow normally and naturally. This time is extremely important, so put her at ease and act normally." The record was thus intended to function as the focal point in a ritual of postwar family "togetherness" at the same time that it conveyed traditional values about sex and gender to the next generation.

The narrative of a doctor's intervention in the sexual development of a child can also be heard on Stanley Z. Daniels's *Sex for Teens (Where It's At)* (Carapan, 1969)—a record that has become a camp classic, famously sampled by alternative rock hipster Beck on his track "Where It's At" (1996). *Sex for Teens* was part of a series of sex education LPs released by Daniels. One, *Sex Explained for Children*, was nominated for a Grammy in 1972. On the LP for teens from 1969, we hear a dramatization featuring Sue, her hysterical brother Bill, and their unnamed and all-knowing therapist father. Much of the record's camp appeal stems from its strained attempts at using the slang of the counterculture. Bill is outraged that Sue is "hung up" on her phony new boyfriend—"Wow, what a loser!"—whereas Sue thinks he's groovy; Bill says he's freaky. "That guy doesn't relate to anything," Bill complains. "Man, did you see his hair? My hair's long, but it's all washed and combed." Beneath Bill's long hair resided the mind of a conservative ideologue, as demonstrated by his concerns about the welfare state: "If he doesn't find out where it's at, I'll probably have to support that slob and some dumb chick that he's knocked up and their kids, all on welfare, living off the establishment. He doesn't have what it takes to make it on his own."

In fact, despite cosmetic concessions to the counterculture and some frank discussion of contraception, the introduction of the father of Bill and Sue quickly makes the record resemble television sitcoms of the 1950s, with sage advice delivered by the basso-voiced patriarch. After hearing Bill's rants, "Dad" describes how his medical practice has taught him that the "greater freedom among young people" was linked to a high frequency of "bad relationships" where sexual pleasure was taken selfishly: "Those who give a damn and are not afraid to relate. . . . They are

the beautiful people." "You're right," Sue responds. "Dad, that's beautiful." Besides such warnings, it becomes clear that Dad's enthusiasm for
the sexual revolution is limited to the heterosexual couple. When Bill
confesses that he finds homosexuals to be "freaky," his father laments
that "unfortunately, some homosexuals may make you feel uncomfortable in their presence." He continues: "Many are social misfits because
they're often psychologically unstable. In my practice I've rarely treated
a satisfied or happy homosexual man or woman. Although one may occasionally come across some who seem to have adjusted into this type of
life and make the best of it." Later, Dad explains that with the help of
therapy, homosexuals can be converted and "attain" a heterosexual life,
where they have "more of a chance for happiness and emotional maturity." Homosexuality it seems, was not "where it's at." As was the case
with the Dr. Sims record, *Sex for Teens* illustrates how the hi-fi could
bring a patriarchal and heteronormative perspective akin to "marriage
manuals" into the home, perhaps in a context of reception similar to
that suggested on *Sex and Your Daughter.*

This style of sex literature faced competition in the mid-1960s from
sexologists who attacked the credibility of marriage manuals and offered
their therapeutic services as a more scientific alternative. William Masters's and Virginia Johnson's *Human Sexual Response* (1966) and *Human
Sexual Inadequacy* (1970) were at the forefront of an expansion in the
development of clinical programs designed to "inform, educate, and
actively assist couples to overcome sexual problems."[42] In contrast to
the mixed messages that came before, this new sex therapy was "positive and enthusiastic about sex," conveying what Irvine calls an ideal of
"hypersexuality—a 'more is better' model of performance" that helped
to make sex therapy a "viable and valuable product" in a consumer culture where sex had become increasingly commoditized.[43] Long-playing
records that offered advice on sexual technique were one commodity
outlet for the new sex therapy.

Consider an LP called *The Art of Sexual Lovemaking*, released by Helicon
Enterprises in 1967. The record's liner notes refer to its creator, Frank S.
Caprio, MD, as "a world renowned authority on sex and marriage," formerly on the staff at the Walter Reed Hospital in Washington, DC. The
record is said to provide "a frank discussion of the love relationship in
all its beauties and pleasures" as well as "the secrets of successful lovemaking": "For the first time, in the privacy of your own home, you will be
able to: listen to intimate case histories, learn numerous sex techniques,
become a better lover." *The Art of Sexual Lovemaking* presented that information in the form of a male announcer whose polished, antiseptic

delivery resembles the narrator of the social guidance films of the 1950s, and so feels awkwardly out of sync with the intimacy of the material: "Be mature in your behavior and thinking," he intones, "and keep yourself well groomed."

Two years later, Atlantic Records offered a different approach to the recorded sex manual with its release of an audio version (figures 7.3 and 7.4) of the bestselling book *The Sensuous Woman* (1969). *The Sensuous Woman* was released anonymously, with the author known only as "J," but the publisher quickly succumbed to pressure and revealed "J" to be Joan Garrity, a thirty-one-year-old former advertising copywriter. A 1970 *Chicago Tribune* review described *The Sensuous Woman* as "a steamy little sex manual," whose contents were "so sexily far out" that it had "girls gulping, guys gaping and husbands bringing it home to their wives tucked into the folds of their newspaper—after they have read it themselves."[44] Ehrenreich, Jacobs, and Hess claim that *The Sensuous Woman* offered an "iconoclastic" style that represented a "radical departure" from mainstream sexual technique in its discussion of topics such as oral sex.[45] Instead of sober moralizing about the hazards of premarital sex or homosexuality, Garrity cheerfully presented techniques such as the "butterfly flick" and the "hoover."

The book became a runaway bestseller, and was released in LP form by Atlantic Records in 1971. *The Sensuous Woman* LP features a solo monologue by "Connie Z," who recites some of the most memorable passages from the book as well as additional material that took the form of vocal enactments of sexual excitement. These added sections of pornoperformativity demonstrate how Garrity's book blurred the lines between instructional manual and pornography. In fact, the LP found some success on the latter front, judging by a *Screw* magazine review that concluded that it was "a jerk-off product disguised as an instructional guide." "The record is so good that you are guaranteed at least three erections (I had six and one intercourse)," wrote the reviewer. "The language is clear, forceful, and very straightforward. You will find yourself leaning back against a chair, and you suddenly have an uncontrollable urge to seduce the sexy voice, or almost anything you can get your hands on or around."[46] Although *The Sensuous Woman* LP was ostensibly marketed as a sex guide for women, here is evidence that the album could succeed where the *Erotica* LP had found only mixed success, and stimulate the prurient interest of men.

There was thus an underlying uncertainty about the intended addressee of *The Sensuous Woman* LP: Was it an instructional guide for women or a "jerk-off product" for men? In 1974, the *Chicago Tribune* re-

THE SENSUOUS WOMAN
RECOMMENDED FOR ADULTS ONLY

FROM THE No.1 BESTSELLER!

The way to become

The Sensuous Woman by "J"

The first *HOW-TO* record for the
female who yearns to be *ALL* woman

DELL · 7350 · 1.25

THE No.1 BESTSELLER!

The way to become

The Sensuous Woman by "J"

Fig. 7.3 and 7.4 The cover of *The Sensuous Woman* record album (1971) mimicked the austere cover of the bestselling book, first published in 1969.

viewed a new LP that had avoided that kind of confusion by presenting sexual information emphatically to a couples audience. The review argued that unlike books such as *The Sensuous Woman* and *The Joy of Sex* (1972), in which "an individual gathers new insights alone," this new LP allowed two people to "listen together and share observations."[47] The record was *The Pleasures of Love* (Life Workshop) and was largely the work of Don M. Sloan, MD.[48] Trained as a workshop fellow at the Masters and Johnson Institute in the early 1970s, Sloan went on to become the co-director of Sexual Therapy at New York Medical College, as well as the first president of the Society for Sex Therapy and Research, from 1975 to 1976. Sloan claimed in an e-mail interview that *The Pleasures of Love* was an outgrowth of his approach to therapy, which he described in the 1983 article entitled "The Dual Therapy Approach to the Treatment of Sexual Dysfunction."

Originally conceived by Masters and Johnson, the dual therapy, or St. Louis approach to sex therapy consisted of two therapists, one male and one female, working with a committed couple. Sloan stressed that sex was to be understood as a form of communication, with sexual problems best seen as a "breakdown in communication between two people": "Sex is looked upon as a means of 'speaking' . . . [one] that is as descriptive and as pointed as any communication can be despite its subtlety."[49] Thus it was the communication between the couple that became the entity for healing, and the goal of therapy was to "remove the barriers of communication" that had been set up by the couple. After an initial phase of interviews, therapy began with a series of "sensate focus exercises," in which the sense of touch was used as "a means of animal communication."[50]

Sloan's first sensate exercise involved "nongenital body touch," as the couple took turns in the roles of "doer" and "receiver." The doer was to "actively proceed through various manipulations on the nude body of the receiver," while the receiver remained passive, but was instructed to verbalize acceptance or rejection of the doer's touching.[51] The second sensate continued turn-taking bodily touch, but added the genitals. After this came the first guided coitus between the couple, with the female in the top position, followed by a second session of coitus, in which more positions were allowed. *The Pleasures of Love* LP enacts the stages of the dual therapy approach, presenting the voices of a male and female actor who describe the sensate and coitus exercises. On side one, the actors describe their bodies while looking at themselves naked in a mirror. The couple takes turns getting to know the intimate anatomy of their partner in the sensate exercises on side two, with the genitals included by side three. By side four, the two are engaging in guided sex, their verbal descriptions of the act accompanied by "wah-wah" guitar reminiscent of hardcore porn soundtracks of the time.

The LP medium was particularly well suited to communicating both an understanding of sex as a form of speaking, and a therapeutic technique in which erotic sensation was to be translated into verbal utterances. Indeed, Sloan's LP is a vivid illustration of the Western compulsion to "speak sex" that has been discussed by scholars such as Michel Foucault and Linda Williams. *The Pleasures of Love* also represents the exploration of a type of media interactivity akin to a dance instructional record, where the actions of home listeners are meant to coincide with the spoken words of prerecorded performers. Sloan's record is thus an inversion of karaoke: instead of supplying the backing tracks for a live vocal performance, listeners are invented to synchronize the movements of their bodies with a prerecorded voice. As such, *The Pleasures of Love* represents a vivid example of Angela Carter's oft-quoted assertion that pornography "has a gap left in it" so that the reader may "step inside it."[52] However, the therapeutic strategy of Sloan's record is short-circuited by the fact that the actors end up speaking *in place of* at-home listeners. Since the actors on *The Pleasures of Love* must constantly verbalize their experiences, there is never enough of a gap left for the couple at home to complete the verbal component of the exercises. In order to step inside the prerecorded therapy session, listeners had to let the LP do the talking for them.

Regardless of how well they succeeded in their therapeutic goals, the release of LPs such as *The Pleasures of Love* indicates the changing status of the home hi-fi during the late 1960s and early 1970s. By that time, home stereos were no longer primarily the domain of affluent professional men or a culture of male hobbyists. Throughout the 1960s, high-fidelity stereo components and LP records reached a growing number of households due to technological developments and the record industry's realization that LPs provided a more dependable source of income than the pop singles market.[53] The proliferation of affordable stereo sets during the late 1960s has been linked to the success of post-Beatles progressive rock bands such as Yes; Emerson, Lake and Palmer; and Pink Floyd. Sloan's gatefold double-album would not have seemed out of place beside similarly packaged rock records of this period. Progressive rock LPs—with their long, complex narratives; fantasy themes; and high production values—would have lost much of their impact if heard on the 78 or 45 RPM monophonic record players of a previous era. In fact, such studio-driven conceptual LPs were often consumed from beginning to end in a "cinematic" manner, suggesting that the stereo was an important precursor to the VCR as a form of home media consumption. I have argued that party records were often defined in opposition to radio and television broadcasting, but ultimately adult LPs such as *The Sensuous Woman* and *The Pleasures of Love* represented early experiments with home media erotica aimed at the same couples audience that would become a market for cable television services with explicit content and adult films on videocassette by the end of the 1970s.[54] It is fitting then, that one of the latest examples of an adult LP I have discovered is *Erotic Aerobics* (1982), which offered a half-baked attempt to ride the coattails of one of the earliest and bestselling videotapes of the 1980s: *Jane Fonda's Workout* (1982).

In this essay, I have suggested that sexually explicit records convened the home audience in several different configurations, and played a part in three overlapping "sexual revolutions": stag party records were used by postwar men seeking to preserve homosocial forms of talk and find escape from the spaces of suburban life; the records of sexually explicit female comics on the periphery of second-wave feminism were heard in mixed-gender social gatherings of the early 1960s; and LPs helped bring new forms of popular sexology to couples in the early 1970s. We might note a tendency in these records to increasingly frame sex as a private, therapeutic endeavor.[55] Hilary Radner has argued that the sexual revolution articulated a "new cultural arena" around the assumption that individual fulfillment rather than reproduction was the goal of sexual activity.[56] That "new cultural arena" was shaped in part by the new sexology popularized by Masters and Johnson—and heard on Dr. Sloan's LP—which, as Irvine argues, failed to address larger social relations:

> Sensate focus and the squeeze technique are potentially important therapeutic tools, but they don't touch the source of the most intractable sexual problems of heterosexuals: fear, anger, boredom, overwork and lack of time, inequality in the relationship, prior sexual assault on the woman, and differential socialization and sexual scripts. . . . In sex therapy, the "cure" is orgasm, not social change. And this is vital, because orgasms can be marketed in a profit-making system, while social change cannot.[57]

As we have seen, LPs played a role in that "profit-making system," often by marketing the vocal performance of orgasm. Although the material heard on adult-themed records became more sexually explicit during the postwar era, that material was increasingly performed in ways suggestive of intimacy. Where once risqué material was accompanied by the ambient party track heard on Fax's Stag Party records, the sounds of Rusty Warren's boisterous audience, or even Dr. Sims's enactment of family togetherness, the vocal performances on records such as *The Sweetest Music, The Sensuous Woman*, and *The Pleasures of Love* were dominated by what Michel Chion calls the "I-voice": a dry, clear voice implying subjectivity and the address to an intimate interlocutor.[58] The fact that the LP circulated such intimate performances in the public marketplace stands as a demonstration of the media's role in the destabilization and recalibration of public and private space that characterizes the era of the sexual revolution. What is certain is that sexuality could be performed and consumed in the home on LPs in ways that it could not on network radio and television during this era and in ways that reveal the interplay between the performance and consumption of erotic material. In fact, erotic records stand as a powerful example of how media performances convened and constituted audiences around discourses of sexuality at this time and, in so doing, helped to convene and constitute the sexual revolution itself.

Notes

A longer version of this essay appears in Smith, *Spoken Word: Postwar American Phonograph Cultures* (Berkeley: University of California Press, 2011).

1. Robert C. Allen, "From Exhibition to Reception: Reflections on the Audience in Film History," in *Screen Histories*, ed. Annette Kuhn and Jackie Stacey (Oxford: Clarendon Press, 1998), 17.
2. Karin Barber, "Preliminary Notes on Audiences in Africa," *Africa* 67, no. 3 (1997): 353–354.
3. "Fights Obscene Recordings," *New York Times*, November 1, 1942, 49.
4. "Obscene Records Cause of Arrest," *Lincoln Journal*, October 1, 1948, 13.
5. In earlier eras, law enforcement targeted artists such as Russell Hunting, who recorded small batches of "blue cylinders." See the CD *Actionable Offenses* (Archeophone, 2007), which contains examples of risqué recordings from this era, as well as insightful liner notes by phonograph scholar Patrick Feaster.
6. "'Indecent' Records Eligible for Mails," *Berkshire Evening Eagle*, June 2, 1949, 19.
7. "Obscene Record Ruling," *New York Times*, June 1, 1949, 42.
8. "Bill on Obscene Records Signed," *New York Times*, May 28, 1950, 46. See also "JD Seeks Censor of Dirty Disks," in *Billboard*, January 14, 1950, 12.
9. "3 Indicted in Shipment of Pornographic Disks," *Variety*, May 3, 1950, 41.
10. "N.Y. Police Seize Obscene Records," *Syracuse Herald-Journal*, April 2, 1958, 21. See also "Disker Gets Year On 'Dirty' Rap," *Billboard*, June 24, 1950, 3; "Seize Dirty Disks in Raid at Cincy," *Billboard*, April 25, 1953, 46; "Party Disk Sales Jail 5 in Philly," *Billboard*, April 27, 1959, 3.

11. Keir Keightley, "'Turn it Down!' She Shrieked: Gender, Domestic Space, and High Fidelity, 1948–1959," *Popular Music* 15, no. 2 (1996): 155–156.

12. Keightley, "'Turn it Down!' She Shrieked," 157.

13. See Jacob Smith, "Filling the Embarrassment of Silence: Erotic Performance on Recorded 'Blue Discs,'" *Film Quarterly* 58, no. 2 (winter 2004–5): 26–35.

14. This advertising copy was offered as evidence in a postal service investigation of Fax Records 1961.

15. Hal Boyle, "Pilots Parody Ovations Given Returning Heroes," *Salamanca Republican-Press*, May 19, 1945, 10.

16. See Keightley, "'Turn it Down!' She Shrieked," 150.

17. The bachelor pad typically contained gadgets such as the hi-fi stereo, which have been described as "phallic accessories that could shore up a sense of masculine power." See Bill Osgerby, *Playboys in Paradise* (Oxford: Berg, 2001), 133.

18. Steven Cohan, *Masked Men: Masculinity and Movies in the Fifties* (Bloomington: Indiana University Press, 1997), 265.

19. See Cohan, *Masked Men*, 266; and Osgerby, *Playboys in Paradise*, 134.

20. Rich Cante and Angelo Restivo, "The Voice of Pornography," in *Keyframes: Popular Cinema and Cultural Studies*, ed. Matthew Tinkcom and Amy Villarejo (New York: Routledge, 2001), 221.

21. United States Postal Service, P.O.D. docket no. 1/160, http://about.usps.com /who-we-are/judicial/admin-decisions/1960/1-160.htm, original date May 17, 1960, accessed date June 19, 2013.

22. See "Court Takes Sensible View in Latest Obscenity Cases," *Los Angeles Times*, May 31, 1966, A5.

23. Linda Williams, *Hard Core: Power, Pleasure and the "Frenzy of the Visible,"* exp. ed. (Berkeley: University of California Press, 1999), 126.

24. See Eric Schaefer, "Plain Brown Wrapper: Adult Films for the Home Market, 1930–1969," in *Looking Past the Screen: Case Studies in American Film History and Method*, ed. Jon Lewis and Eric Smoodin (Durham, NC: Duke University Press, 2007), 215–216.

25. See Pamela Robertson Wojcik, "The Girl and the Phonograph; Or the Vamp and the Machine Revisited," in *Soundtrack Available: Essays on Film and Popular Music*, ed. Pamela Robertson Wojcik and Arthur Knight (Durham, NC: Duke University Press, 2001).

26. V. Vale and Andrea Juno, *Re/Search: Incredibly Strange Music* (San Francisco: Re/Search Publications, 1994), 2:56.

27. In 1962, a writer for *Billboard* stated that though party records had been "steady sellers for years and years, it is only recently that they have turned into blockbusters." See Bob Rolontz, "After Hours, Surprise Lends Spice, Sales to Nation's Record Markets," *Billboard*, October 23, 1961, 1. See also Bob Rolontz, "Those 42d Street Record Shops: Where the Belle Tolls for Thee," *Billboard*, July 28, 1962, 8.

28. "'Knockers Up' Fans, Attention," *Times* [San Mateo, CA], March 15, 1963, 23.

29. "Barnyard Girl," *Time*, January 11, 1963, 58–59.

30. V. Vale and Andrea Juno, *Re/Search*, 2:58.

31. Robert C. Allen, *Horrible Prettiness: Burlesque and American Culture* (Chapel Hill, NC: University of North Carolina Press, 1991), 243.

32. Michael Bronski, "Funny Girls Talk Dirty," *Boston Phoenix*, August 15, 2003. Accessed June 19, 2013, www.bostonphoenix.com/boston/news_features/other _stories/documents/03090915.asp.

33. David Allyn, *Make Love, Not War: The Sexual Revolution: An Unfettered History* (Boston: Little, Brown and Company, 2000), 11.

34. Barbara Ehrenreich, Elizabeth Hess, and Gloria Jacobs, *Re-Making Love: The Feminization of Sex* (New York: Anchor Books, 1986), 57–59; Susan Douglas, *Where the Girls Are: Growing up Female with the Mass Media* (New York: Times Books, 1994); Laurie Ouellette, "Inventing the Cosmo Girl," *Media, Culture and Society* 21, no. 3 (May 1999): 359–383; Osgerby, *Playboys in Paradise*, 169.

35. Gurley Brown also released a series of LPs of her own in 1963 on Crescendo Records.

36. Vale and Juno, *Re/Search*, 58.

37. www.knockers-up.org/about.php. Accessed, circa September 2006.

38. Ehrenreich, Hess, and Jacobs, *Re-Making Love*, 97.

39. We should note that Warren's records were marketed to both men and women. One approach to promoting her to men was through offering "certificates" for a Playboy-esque "Knockers Up" club. Warren stated in an e-mail interview that her record company "thought up the 'Knockers Up Club' stuff. The guys bought the certificate, the gals marched around the backyard, and the party was on."

40. Vale and Juno, *Re/Search*, 56.

41. Janice M. Irvine, *Disorders of Desire: Sexuality and Gender in Modern American Sexology* (Philadelphia: Temple University Press, 1990), 72–73.

42. Irvine, *Disorders of Desire*, 188.

43. Irvine, *Disorders of Desire*, 189, 192.

44. Barbara Lewis, "The Sensuous Author," *Chicago Tribune*, August 9, 1970, J58.

45. Ehrenreich, Hess, and Jacobs, *Re-Making Love*, 83.

46. "Sensuous Woman LP," *Screw*, November 29, 1971, 12.

47. Linda Lee Landis, "The Sensuous Record," *Chicago Tribune*, September 8, 1974, D5.

48. See also Vern L. Bullough, *Science in the Bedroom* (New York: Basic Books, 1994), 203.

49. Don Sloan, "The Dual Therapy Approach to the Treatment of Sexual Dysfunction," in *Gynecology and Obstetrics*, ed. John J. Sciarra (Philadelphia: Harper and Row, 1983), 6:10.

50. Sloan, "The Dual Therapy Approach to the Treatment of Sexual Dysfunction," 11. Sloan's program closely resembles that devised by Masters and Johnson, who worked with couples, stressed that "the 'relationship' is considered to be the patient," and included a "sensate focus" involving "a series of massage-like exercises implemented by the couple in their hotel room." See Irvine, *Disorders of Desire*, 193–194.

51. Sloan, "The Dual Therapy Approach to the Treatment of Sexual Dysfunction," 6–7.

52. Angela Carter, *The Sadeian Woman and the Ideology of Pornography* (New York: Harper and Row, 1978), 14.

53. Roland Gelatt, *The Fabulous Phonograph, 1877–1977* (London: Cassell, 1977), 319, 327.

54. On X-rated videocassettes for couples, see Frederick Wasser, *Veni, Vidi, Video: The Hollywood Empire and the VCR* (Austin: University of Texas Press, 2001), 94.

55. See also John D'Emilio and Estelle B. Freedman on "sexual liberalism" in *Intimate Matters: A History of Sexuality in America*, 2nd ed. (Chicago: University of Chicago Press, 1997), 241.

56. Hilary Radner, "Introduction: Queering the Girl," in Radner and Moya Luckett, eds., *Swinging Single: Representing Sexuality in the 1960s* (Minneapolis: University of Minnesota Press, 1999), 4, 2.

57. Irvine, *Disorders of Desire*, 199.

58. Michel Chion, *The Voice in Cinema*, trans. Claudia Gorbman (New York: Columbia University Press, 1999), 49–51.

8 * "I'll Take Sweden": The Shifting Discourse of the "Sexy Nation" in Sexploitation Films

ERIC SCHAEFER

What is considered attractive or "sexy" changes in different times and places and between different cultures and social strata. In the United States ideals of female beauty moved from the healthy "Gibson Girl" in the early twentieth century to the waif-thin flapper in the 1920s, then to the buxom bleached blonde in the 1950s and the slender, miniskirted "hippy chick" of the 1960s. Men traded in muttonchop whiskers for a close shave and pomaded hair, only to see muttonchops return in the 1970s. An oft-recounted anecdote from the 1930s relays that sales of men's undershirts fell precipitously after Clark Gable appeared bare-chested in *It Happened One Night* (1934). From the earliest origins of the star system in the American film industry, the movies helped determine standards of beauty and sexual appeal. During the sexual revolution, the influence of the media extended beyond physical appearance to encompass a philosophy and approach to sexuality and what was "sexy"—an appeal to sexual desire or interest from a physiological, aesthetic, or intellectual standpoint. In no small measure, those ideas and attitudes were emblematized by cultures and countries outside the United States.

The strict moral code of the America's Puritan settlers later compounded by Victorian propriety had long led Americans to look beyond their borders to define what was sexy. Long before "sexy" came into widespread usage, American sexual decorum—some would say repression—was measured against what was perceived as the amorality of other peoples and nations. For many generations France to help define what was sexy in terms of behavior and style for Americans. To some, France was viewed as a threat to American morality; to others it was seen as an antidote to the puritanical attitudes citizens in the United States had toward sex. But during the period of the sexual revolution, Americans increasingly looked to northern Europe, specifically to Denmark and Sweden, to help define what was liberated and sexually appealing. The shift was even evident in the titles of movies made by Bob Hope (the master of suggestive, middlebrow yucks) as *Paris Holiday* (1958) gave way to *I'll Take Sweden* (1965). In this chapter I will consider some of the factors that converged to redefine what constituted the sexy in terms of a national point of reference, and how, in the eyes of Americans, France ceded its long-standing position as the nation-of-the-naughty to its Scandinavian neighbors. The press was filled with stories of shifting social trends and transformative policies in Denmark and Sweden; moreover, a steady stream of sexploitation movies provided a constant reminder of the seemingly progressive sexual attitudes in Scandinavia compared to the exhausted debates that pitted individual liberty against the repressive morality of the United States.

French Dressing

In 1968 the historian Crane Brinton wrote, "the firmest, most real and earthy France of legend" is the France "symbolized by, though not confined to, those two great skills and pleasures, those of the table and those of the bed." He concluded that there was no certainty that the French talked more about *amour*, nor that they practiced it more than Americans, but that the concern with love and lovemaking was a "note" of the national character that Frenchmen "often feel a kind of compulsion to display."[1] France had long been associated with louche behavior in the eyes of many Americans, whether that came in the form of palaces filled with courtesans or a culture that seemed to dwell on sexually suggestive aspects of life: Gustave Flaubert's *Madame Bovary*, Édouard Manet's *Le déjeuner sur l'herbe*, the can-can, or the writings of the infamous Marquis de Sade.

France's status as a sexy nation was cemented in the minds of Americans during World War I. As Allan Brandt notes, "The arrival of American troops at French seaports heralded a clash of sexual cultures." Tolerance of prostitution on the part of the French and their dismal record of combating venereal disease "confirmed the image of continental debauchery" for the American Expeditionary Forces and those they left behind.[2] One American officer who interviewed French prostitutes found that "Americans preferred a certain sex act above all others," which he deplored as "the twisted impulse known as 'the French way' (a euphemism from oral sex)."[3] Sexual practices picked up in France helped erode American puritanism during the Jazz Age, and doughboys returning to the states brought with them songs from the trenches such as "Mademoiselle from Armentieres" with its vaguely suggestive lyrics and a host of variations that left little to the imagination. Postwar ditties such as "Fifty Million Frenchmen Can't Be Wrong" and "How 'Ya Gonna Keep

'Em Down on the Farm (After They've Seen Paree)?" reinforced the notion of France as a naughty nation. This sentiment was manifested in language with popularization of expressions such as "French kiss" and other words prefaced with "French" (French postcards, French lessons, the French measles [a euphemism for venereal disease], and so on).

In 1950 Geoffrey Gorer observed that untraveled Englishmen and Americans "have pictured Paris in particular, and generally France as a whole as though it were a sort of erotic Elysium, with all the women as lascivious as civet cats, ready to commit fornication or adultery at the drop of a handkerchief, and where all the literature was pornographic, all the humor sexual, and all the art erotic."[4] Some years later Vance Packard speculated, "Much of France's reputation for free love, I suspect, derives from the fact that millions of young, homesick American and British males encountered some of France's less inhibited girls while on leave to Gay Paree during World War I and World War II—and embroidered their encounters when they got home."[5] Whether this reputation was promulgated by nostalgic GIs, or those who viewed France as an erotic playground from afar, the association between France and all things racy only expanded after World War II.[6] The risqué reviews of the Follies Bergère continued to be a popular tourist attraction as were the nearly nude dancers of the Crazy Horse Saloon, which opened in Paris in 1951. Maurice Girodias's Paris-based Olympia Press, the notorious publisher of "dirty books," was launched in 1953. And French films were increasingly associated with sex in the minds of Americans who frequented "art houses," notably titles such as *La Ronde* (1950) and *The Lovers* (1958). The film . . . *And God Created Woman* (1956) featured a young Brigitte Bardot, whom director Roger Vadim proclaimed to be a symbol for the "amoralist young French generation."[7] In 1958 *Newsweek* concluded that the French sex kitten "might well be taking over from Marilyn Monroe," America's reigning, homegrown sex symbol.[8]

The trend of cinematic sensuality from France continued with the advent of *La Nouvelle Vague* (the New Wave), as well as with more conventional imports such as *A Man and a Woman* (1966). Furthermore, Hollywood movies frequently chose France as a setting for tales of seduction and amour in films such as Howard Hughes's scandalous *The French Line* (1954) with Jane Russell and *Gigi* (1958), as well as *Paris—When It Sizzles* (1964) and *Made in Paris* (1966). Exploitation films also capitalized on the French connection in *Paris after Midnight* (1951), *The French Follies* (1951), and *French Peep Show* (1952). In *The Naked Venus* (1959), not only is the heroine French; she is also a nudist—a combination that indicates her innate immorality for her American mother-in-law. *The Naked Venus* and other films reliably presented French candor and joie de vivre as a stark contrast to American prudishness and repression.

By the late 1950s distributors such as William Mishkin, Audubon, and others were turning to France for films that could be imported without customs challenges; the films trimmed of extraneous plot and dolled up with inserts featuring striptease dances or additional nudity. A few of the French imports released on the American sexploitation circuit include *Nights of Shame* (1961), *Hotbed of Sin* (1961), *Vice Dolls* (1961), and *The Twilight Girls* (1961).[9] Directors Max Pecas and José Bénazéraf, who specialized in sexy potboilers, provided many, including *Sweet Ecstasy* (1962), *The Erotic Touch of Hot Skin* (1965), *Sin on the Beach* (1964), and *Sexus* (1965). Other movies made in the United States for the growing sexploitation market were set in France, such as *Indiscreet Stairway* (1966); some alluded to the location in their titles: *A French Honeymoon* (1964) and *Paris Topless* (1966).

By evoking France or Paris in their titles and their advertising, or by using the *terra erotica* of France as a setting, the movies relied on the country's permissive reputation regarding sexuality. Ads for *The Fast Set* (1961, aka *The Nude Set*) announced, "When sex takes a holiday it goes to Paris!" and introduced "the new 'French Love Kitten'—Agnes Laurent." Narration in the trailer for *The Fourth Sex* (1963) insinuated promiscuity with the words "Paris, the world capitol of love, where variety is the *necessity* of life." A trailer for *French without Dressing* (1965) claimed, "They only make females like these in la belle France. Ask any Frenchman. So round, so firm, so fully packed. So free and easy—on the eyes." For the former GIs, who made up a good portion of the sexploitation audience in the United States, such lines may have recalled memories of wartime liaisons and a time when they weren't encumbered with obligations of family and the day-to-day routine of work. Indeed, in interviews sexploitation director Russ Meyer frequently—and with a touch of wistfulness—recounted losing his virginity in a French bordello during the war.

Films made in France, as well as American sexploitation movies set in France (all of which I will refer to as "the French films"), operated out of what I term an "observational/retrospective" mode. The observational mode was rooted in a touristic gaze. A major component of the films was voyeurism from a privileged vantage point. Visiting famous Parisian landmarks or recognizable locations, or engaging in other acts of looking—in particular watching dancers, strippers, posers practice their trade, art, or avocation. In these movies, the authentically erotic in France is generally found in performative acts, which are watched by a character within the film but at a step removed by the audience viewing

Fig. 8.1 Characters often attended striptease performances in the "French" films, an expression of their "observational" mode and something highlighted in their publicity, as seen in this still from *Paris Ooh-La-La* (1963).

the film. For instance, striptease performances play a central role and are the primary erotic charge in many of the movies, such as *The Fast Set, The Fourth Sex,* and *Sin on the Beach.* This observational mode was largely retrospective in nature as it served to rekindle memories of France as a site of erotic experience for the individual who had been there. Even for those who had never set foot in France, the mode was retrospective, since it recalled images of France in the popular imagination as a setting for sexual adventure. Finally, the films are retrospective in that they maintained or promoted a status quo version of gender roles and male/female relationships—one firmly rooted in male privilege and dominance and female submissiveness. Sex in the films was usually framed as something attached to sin, which extended to feelings of guilt and shame.

Paris Ooh-La-La (1963) illustrates these points (figure 8.1). The film features American expatriate producer Dick Randall as Sam Smith, who makes a trip to Paris to see the sights and find women. As he confides to the audience in voice-over, "I've heard all the girls *vivre l'amour*, you know?" Sam's knowledge of Paris is based on stories he has heard about the city. Most of the French films have a travelogue quality to them, with postcard shots of Paris, images of boulevard life, and visits to such hot spots as the Crazy Horse Saloon and the Moulin Rouge, and notorious districts such as Pigalle. *Paris Ooh-La-La* is no exception. When Sam enters the Crazy Horse he indicates that he feels guilty, "which every self-respecting Anglo Saxon feels when he goes into an emporium of pleasure." He samples the nightlife, particularly striptease acts, and tries to sample the mademoiselles only to find that they ignore him. He watches a beauty contest, spies on some showgirls, and takes in still more shows. As the film progresses, Sam becomes increasingly despondent and disillusioned, discovering that France is not the storied sexual playground of his imagination and that observation is not as satisfying as participation. When he does find a woman who is willing to be with him, he says, "I'd always been told French girls were the most wonderful in the world. It was true." But a twist reveals that the woman, like Sam, is an American tourist. France's reputation as an erotic capital is finally shown as disappointing because it is retrospective in nature—bound to the past, to legend, more than reality—and that its appeal rests on watching rather than on participation.

Similar attitudes and tone are invested in other films with a French setting. *The Dirty Girls* (1965), Audubon's first original production directed by Radley Metzger, opens with a segment set in Paris concerning Garance, a streetwalker. As she sits in a café, the patronizing narrator intones, "Well, pretty Garance, you can be many things to many men. . . . Desire will seek you out, for every man seeks a Garance." Although the sequence is ostensibly about Garance, she is framed through the desire of several male customers in a single evening—a virgin hoping to have his first sexual experience with her, a sadist who beats her, and a married regular who has her beat him while she is dressed as a circus ringmaster. The men's encounters with Garance have a clandestine quality, cloaked in guilt. Similarly, *The Alley Cats* (1966), Metzger's second film for Audubon, centers on Leslie. She is engaged to Logan, who sees other women on the side while Leslie confronts her latent lesbian longings. When she finally acts on her desire with Irena, an aggressive social butterfly, Logan angrily tracks them down, beats Leslie in her apartment and then by a public fountain. He eventually wipes the blood off Leslie's face and walks away, commanding her to follow him. She says, "I don't know who I am." "You're my girl," Logan tells her as they depart together. *Fin*. Again, the film is retrospective in terms of the gender dynamic, as the passive Leslie denies her incipient lesbian desire and returns to her neglectful, abusive boyfriend. *Therese and Isabelle* (1968), another Metzger film set in France, is even more overtly retrospective, as Therese visits the grounds of a private school she left years earlier and reminisces about her relationship with a classmate, Isabelle. As one contemporary account concluded,

Therese "ends up as a tragic figure, frustrated and alone, contemplating her past and an impossible future."[10]

If France was relatively open and secular in its erotic expression during the 1950s and early 1960s, the legacy of Catholicism as the official state religion held on.[11] The number of times that the words "sin," "shame," and "dirty" turned up in the titles of films is evidence of this, and the country became positively Comstockian following Charles de Gaulle's consolidation of power with his reelection in 1962. De Gaulle's "rigidly puritanical" wife was said to exert tremendous influence on him, and "during his reign [until 1969], erotic movies and books were censored or banned outright."[12] From an American perspective, sex in France was looking tired and unappealing, particularly in light of new ideas and representations emerging elsewhere.

Cold Hands, Warm Hearts

As the sexual revolution commanded increasing attention in the states, France, as the sexy nation par excellence in the minds of Americans, got a run for its money from Sweden and Denmark. American impressions about the Swedes and the Danes were changing, initially fueled largely by Swedish attitudes about sex education and premarital sex. As early as 1955, *Time* magazine had published a provocative, if not entirely accurate, article on Swedish sexual mores that promoted the notion of "Swedish Sin" — a laissez-faire attitude toward sexual morality promoted by a permissive government.[13] This attention grew during the mid-1960s, the press filled with articles about the need for sex education in light of increasing venereal disease rates and out-of-wedlock births in the United States. A *Time* article in 1966 asked, "Who should teach American children about sex — parents, family doctors, clergymen or schoolteachers?"[14] What came to be known as the "Swedish welfare state" seemed to provide a model for an enlightened approach to dealing with the problems facing many industrialized Western democracies. Carl Marklund has noted that at the center of the apparent paradox between Sweden's sexual liberalism and the discipline of the modern welfare state "was the claim that breaking down traditional borders would lead to the emancipation of 'natural' forces and desires." "Sex was," he continues, "only one among many natural urges which made up part of human life, the new message went. As such it changed from something sinful (unless inside of heterosexual marriage, that is), which only promiscuous people engaged in, to becoming something natural which everyone needed in order to be happy, healthy, and satisfied members of society."[15]

In a 1966 *Look* article J. Robert Moskin wrote, "The Swedes are making sex dangerous—by American standards. They are stripping away the old taboos. Their open attitude intrigues many Americans and stimulated visions of a land where magnificent blondes enjoy their sexuality, but it also generates worry here that our young may get some Swedish ideas in their heads."[16] Classes on reproduction and sexuality had become compulsory in Swedish schools in 1956, which fascinated the American public. Indeed, when Birgitta Linnér's book *Sex and Society in Sweden* was published in 1967, it was widely reviewed, receiving favorable comment from anthropologist Margaret Mead and a *Saturday Review* write-up that called it "an important book."[17] Greater strides toward equality between the sexes were often commented on, but the aspect of Swedish society invariably noted was that a "large percentage of young people have premarital sex relations."[18] Writers, however, felt compelled to qualify this characterization. The text accompanying a 1965 *Look* photo essay on Sweden by photographer Irving Penn declared, Swedish women's "notorious sexual freedom is largely a pose."[19] An article on Scandinavian women in *Esquire* laid the characterization at the feet of Americans: "Actually the sexual mores of the Scandinavians are just about what you'd expect of a highly advanced society; they differ from ours mainly in attitude—the Scandinavians lack the hypocrisy of our Puritan heritage."[20] Oregon State University educator Lester Kirkendall concluded in his preface to the Linnér book, "American public opinion for some time now has regarded the Swedes as 'promiscuous' and, naturally, as less virtuous than ourselves."[21] Put another way, the major difference in sexual attitudes between the Swedes and Americans was, according to one member of the Swedish Royal Board of Education, "we talk about it."[22]

In addition to talking about sex, the Swedes also read about it and watched it. By the mid-1960s Sweden faced a "rash of pornographic literature," and the trend was also "apparent in commercial films, which more and more often include daringly frank scenes."[23] It was only a matter of time before enterprising distributors began to import the "frank" films for U.S. screens. Scandinavian countries had provided a handful of movies for the art and exploitation circuits from the 1930s to the 1950s that had an erotic component (*Man's Way with Women* [1934], *One Summer of Happiness* [1951], and *Summer with Monika* [1953], the latter re-edited by exploiteer Kroger Babb to become *Monika: Story of a Bad Girl*). Yet nude dips in icy waters never captured the American imagination to the degree that saucy strippers in the Paris nightclubs had. During the early 1960s, Scandinavian films appearing on the art house circuit proved to be more daring. *A Stranger Knocks* (1959), a Danish film released in the United States in 1963, featured a crucial revelation during simulated lovemaking. It churned the censorship waters—Maryland's assistant attorney general called it "pure smut"[24]—and conflict over the film contributed to the dismantling of the New York State Board of Censors. The Swedish *491* (1964), based on Lars Görling's 1962 novel, dealt with six delinquents sent to live with a naive social worker as part of an experiment. The boys destroy the social worker's home, bring a teenage prostitute in to service them, and degrade her by forcing her to have sex with a dog. Ultimately the youngest boy, crushed by his experiences, commits suicide.[25] Despite the fact that the sex acts were only suggested, *491* was barred by U.S. Customs until the courts freed the film. Although both *A Stranger Knocks* and *491* were framed as art films, they indicated that Denmark and Sweden were capable of making sexually daring movies. It was, however, a sexploitation film, *I, a Woman*, that most clearly marked the shift from France to the Scandinavian countries as the sexy terrain of choice for American filmgoers.

A Danish-Swedish coproduction *I, a Woman* (1965) was directed by Mac Ahlberg and released in the states by Audubon in 1966. Essy Persson stars as Siv Holm who, at the start of the film, waits in her apartment for the arrival of a 10 PM date while she muses about her sexual awakening through a series of flashbacks. We see Siv singing in folk-rock services in the church in her small town, where she is engaged to the uptight Sven. Carrying out her duties as a nurse, Siv meets a married middle-aged antique dealer. Sensing Siv's lack of satisfaction with Sven, he flirts with, and soon seduces, Siv. He promises to divorce his wife and marry her, but she tells him, "Perhaps you want to own me—and I don't want to be owned by anyone." Siv leaves home and moves to the city, where she has affairs with a merchant seaman and a surgeon. She turns down the sailor's offer of marriage. When the surgeon tries to tell her he is duty bound to marry another woman who is pregnant with his child, he falls apart, telling Siv he would rather marry her instead. She turns him down while doing a seductive strip in front of him. Throughout the film, Siv's lovers comment that she will never be happy with just one man. The flashbacks end with her anticipating in voice-over, "He's coming—a new man. I have the right to be happy—deliriously happy." When the new man arrives, however, he shoves into the apartment, slaps Siv around, and has rough sex with her. As he dresses to go, she asks if he must leave. The man replies that if he stays or returns, she'll want to marry him within three weeks. Siv, who has avoided commitment to any one man, laughs in his face. Despite Sven's contention that Siv will "end up a whore," she's never presented as a nymphomaniac or, as *Variety* delicately put it, "she is no prostie."[26]

I, a Woman announced its origins in its advertising ("From Sweden . . . A totally new concept in artistic motion pictures for adults!") and broke records as it played around the United States. Emancipated from downtown grind houses that typically programmed sexploitation fare, it played urban showcase cinemas and suburban theaters. It was one of the first sexploitation films to make inroads into the lucrative "date" market and to show a degree of popularity with women.[27] *I, a Woman* also points at a major difference between the Scandinavian films and the French films they would soon supplant in terms of popularity in the United States. If French films can be considered observational and retrospective, the Scandinavian films can be seen as participatory and modern—participatory in that they were more likely to present characters engaging in sex rather than watching strip shows or other erotic performances, modern in that they challenge normative moral standards that existed in the United States at the time.[28]

I, a Woman invites the audience to identify with an active, enthusiastic participant in sex: Siv. She has affairs for her own pleasure, which is the central concern of the film, rather than for economic gain such as the case with Garance in *The Dirty Girls*. Moreover, the representation of Siv's pleasure provides the primary erotic charge for the audience, whether she is tantalizing the surgeon with her languorous dance or writhing in ecstasy at the touch of her lovers. Shots of her face in reaction to erotic stimulation were the centerpiece of most of these scenes and served as key art in Audubon's advertising campaign. The film can be viewed as modern because of its presentation of a sexually liberated woman, capable and independent, confident in her sexuality, and who is ultimately unwilling to submit to the old double standard of traditional sex roles.[29] As Deane William Ferm observed in 1970, "Sweden has probably made more progress than any other country in breaking down the double standard that applies as between men and women."[30] These differences from the French model must, in some measure, account for the popularity of *I, a Woman* and its status as a crossover hit, particularly with female moviegoers, something frequently noted in stories about the film's success.

As changing attitudes toward sex in the United Stated roiled in the public discourse, the mass media continued to draw attention to the "liberal laws and attitudes on sexual matters" in Denmark and Sweden. A November 1968 *New York Times* article suggested that the two nations

Fig 8.2 Produced in Sweden, *Inga* (1968) proved to be a major hit in the United States. This was in no small measure because star Marie Liljedahl had a fresher, more innocent look than most sexploitation actresses from the period.

were "moving toward even greater freedom," citing a radical party's plans to introduce a bill in the Danish Parliament to legalize marriages between homosexuals and brothers and sisters as well as moves in the Swedish Parliament to make abortion easier to obtain. "The sexual liberty in Scandinavia," the article went on, "is championed particularly by the young who often take different views from adults."[31]

This generational divide on matters of sexuality in Denmark and Sweden had parallels to the oft-cited "generation gap" in the United States at the time.[32] The next major sexploitation import from Scandinavia focused on the rift between older and younger people. *Inga* (1968; figure 8.2) was a Danish-Swedish coproduction, bankrolled by New York exhibitor Bernard "Bingo" Brandt and directed by American sex-pic veteran Joe Sarno. Like *I, a Woman* it became a breakout sexploitation hit for Cinemation, the movie's distributor for most of the United States. *Inga* deals with the sexual coming of age of an orphaned seventeen-year-old (Marie Liljedahl). She moves to the country to live with her aunt, Greta, who uses her diminishing bank account to keep her young lover, Karl, on the hook with extravagant presents. A family friend offers Greta money to become the paramour of her brother, Einar, whose wife is in a sanitarium. Knowing of Einar's predilection for younger women, Greta tries to maneuver Inga into Einar's bed in exchange for a weekly stipend. A misunderstanding causes the plan to backfire, and Inga decides to lose her virginity to Karl. They leave the town together on the boat that Greta bought him. Again, this film can be seen as participatory because the audience is invited to identify with Inga and her awakening sexuality, most notably in a scene in which she masturbates alone in her bedroom. It can be considered modern because Inga loses her virginity on her own terms, not those of her aunt, who attempts to steer her toward an older man for her own economic gain.

Inga, much like *I, a Woman*, was aligned with the sexual ethos ascribed to Denmark and Sweden in their espousal of individual autonomy, equality, and healthy experimentation, and in their rejection of guilt feelings and traditional notions of sin associated with premarital sex. Sex in these films conforms to what anthropologist Don Kulick identifies as "good sex in Sweden":

> Sex, Swedish authorities and politicians tell us, is good. The catch is that for sex to be good, it has to be good sex. That is, it has to be socially approved, mutually satisfying sexual relations between two (and only two) consenting adults or young adults who are more or less sociological equals. It must not involve money or overt domination, even as roleplaying. It should occur only in the context of an established social relationship. This relationship does not have to be a particularly deep one, and sex on the first date is acceptable, with the proviso that the date has to have happened and there has to have been conversation.[33]

By the standards of Sweden (as well as the developing mores of the sexual revolution in the United States at the time), *Inga* represented "good sex" on every count—especially in Inga's rejection of her aunt's machinations to pair her with an older man in exchange for material gain. Moreover, the behaviors in the film aligned closely with the attitudes that were becoming accepted norms of sexual behavior in the United States, notably, the notion of "permissiveness with affection" identified by sociologist Ira L. Reiss in a large-scale postwar study.[34]

When Inga and Karl finally have their sexual encounter, it is shown as gentle and seemingly natural, and the Scandinavian films often framed sex in this fashion. Regarding the presentation of sex in the Swedish films of the time, Kulick suggests that they "most commonly represented sex by lingering on clean, fresh, svelte women who without hesitation or guilt had intercourse with their clean, fresh, svelte boyfriends."[35] Film scholar Tytti Soila has written,

> In the Scandinavian world, nature is perceived as a fundamentally positive phenomenon—something that provides strength and competence for survival and which is a source of renewal and recreation. The naked human body is perceived as part of nature, and is assigned the same value of nature itself. In addition to this—and despite the hostile views of many nonconformist movements—sexuality is considered natural and thereby principally positive."[36]

It is worth noting that the actors in the Scandinavian films also possessed a more "natural look," which was gaining popularity at the time, when compared with their French counterparts. A *Life* magazine spread on Swedish fashion in 1968 managed to include two dominant discourses on the Swedes into a single sentence: "A new style of *uninhibited* and imaginative dressing has been added to their *natural* attractions and is thrusting their country into the bigtime fashion scene."[37] Marie Liljedahl, *Inga's* main attraction, possessed an innocence and freshness that was unusual for the majority of sexploitation starlets, and most of the other Scandinavian actresses who would join her embodied this more "natural" style. With straight hair, little makeup, and simple clothing, they provided contrast to the French reputation for excess, be it in haute couture, voluptuous figures, strong perfume, or heavy cosmetics.

The "natural look" was being embraced in the United States by the counterculture as yet another rejection of the establishment and the status quo. This included long hair, minimal makeup, and a general lack of artifice. It was quickly taken up by Madison Avenue as a new marketing tool in its arsenal and used for shilling everything from shampoo to the latest fashions. The advertisements for sexploitation films were not immune either. *Siv, Anne & Sven* (1972), another Sarno made-in-Sweden effort, explicitly tied Swedish sexuality to nature. Text blocks on U.S.-release posters quoted "Edmund Edro," who claimed, "Make no mistake, what goes on on the screen is strictly 'no holds barred,' but this overpowering emphasis on the possibilities of pleasure with more than two people is dramatically balanced with a story set against the breathtaking beauty of the Swedish countryside." Canned stories in the pressbook for *One Swedish Summer* (1968), about a young man's sexual awakening in the countryside, described the "beautiful archipelago surroundings, a natural habitat for the color camera." Adopting "the natural look"—emphasizing the ties between Scandinavian culture and the natural landscape, as well as Scandinavians' more "natural" approach to sexuality, which was unencumbered by restrictive social strictures—made the Scandinavian films more youthful and more modern in their outlook.

Sexual freedom; a greater sense of gender equality; an apparently cooler, more rational approach to sexual matters—these elements combined with a more youthful and natural look to made Denmark and Sweden appear both more enlightened and more sexy than France, which was increasingly mired in social and political turmoil. A 1968 article in *Candid Press*, a weekly tabloid out of Chicago, made the link between sexy movies and Sweden's progressivism. After ticking off a long list of dubious "firsts" ("Sweden was the first country to every make a movie for public consumption that showed bare female breasts . . . to ever show the actual birth of a child in startling filmed closeups . . . to ever show a man actually touching a female's breast," etc.), the author tied permissive films to the policies of the Swedish welfare state, including compulsory sex education, sympathetic attitudes toward unwed motherhood, and the widespread availability of birth control. "While American films were worried about showing an extra inch of breast, the Swedes were talking about showing a woman's vagina on screen. The whole Swedish attitude towards movie sex is a world apart from that of our own country." The article made special note of a new film, referred to as *I am Inquisitive*, because it showed "the actual act of sexual intercourse." However, a member of the Swedish Film Censorship Board interviewed for the article said, "I know that when Swedish people walk out of the theater after seeing this movie, they will be talking about everything but the sex act."[38]

As detailed in chapter 4, that film, *I Am Curious (Yellow)*, became a phenomenon when it hit U.S. theaters in 1969—and not because audiences were talking about its political content. One writer described the scene in front of New York City theaters not as lines,

> but hordes of the curious clogging 57th Street . . . in all kinds of weather; front-page debates appearing on Sunday in the entertainment section of the *New York Times*; a run-away flood of irate Letters to the Editor drowning columns and columns of the same distinguished newspaper; tourists from out of town tapping native sons in restaurants and whispering low, "Say, buddy, where can I see that dirty movie? You know, the curious yellow thing."[39]

Scandinavian sex films constituted enough of a trend to generate two satiric articles in the *Times*. In one, a boy asks, "Where do movies come from, Daddy?" The nonplussed father, alluding to adult films, says, "From

Scandinavia, mostly." He explains, "The Scandinavians are a very diligent people. They used to be diligent at furniture-making and stainless steel and stuff like that. But they were always getting splinters, or cutting themselves, so they changed products." The other piece features three imaginary upcoming sex films, including *Hjolga, a Woman, Part IV*, "at once a bitingly satiric attack on those ostensibly serious filmmakers who hypocritically turn out prurient movies merely for financial gain and, with its daringly explicit scenes of nude driving instruction, a ringing cry for Scandinavian highway safety."[40] That these spoofs even appeared in the *Times* meant its readers were sufficiently aware of the status of Denmark and Sweden as exporters of sex films to appreciate the lampoon.

Filmmakers in Scandinavia were cognizant of their new status as exporters as well. In 1970 Frederic Fleischer wrote, "*Export or die* is the guideline of the Swedish film industry. Everyone concerned realizes that the domestic market alone is much too small to keep Swedish producers in business and to enable creative talent to flourish." Fleischer claimed that "Swedish sex was known to appeal to foreign audiences," and "Now they realized that they could win a more secure distribution footing abroad by exposing their nation's advanced attitudes in an artistic context." He quoted a producer from one of the three major Swedish companies who said his firm's films sold well abroad, "because they are controversial and because Swedish directors are interested in subjects that attract foreign attention, particularly sex."[41] Per Olov Qvist and Tytti Soila have noted that smaller independent companies, such as Swedish Film Production Investments, were able to take advantage of this growing interest.[42]

An Unfettered Sexual Utopia

If there had been a steady increase in American attention to Scandinavian sex ways, it exploded in mid-1969, when Denmark abolished laws restricting the sale of pornography. After initially freeing the sale of pornographic literature in 1967, Parliament lifted the remaining restrictions on the sale of photographic and filmed porn to those sixteen and older.[43] Much as the Swedish system of sex education had fascinated and frightened readers in the states, the Danish experiment with pornography had a mesmerizing effect—particularly in light of the growing availability of sexually explicit material in bookstores and in theaters in the United States as well as in anticipation of the findings of the Commission on Obscenity and Pornography. Press accounts indicated that the Danes greeted the open availability of porn with a yawn and that the largest market for their newly found freedoms came from tourists. In October, Sex 69, a pornographic trade show in Copenhagen's Sports Arena, opened to "lines that stretched around the block"[44] and drew some 350 reporters from around the world. Statistics showed that the curious who attended were not the proverbial dirty old men: 75 percent of males were under the age of forty; 85 percent of the women who attended were between eighteen and forty.[45]

Coverage of Sex 69 further solidified the notion that the Danes and their attitudes represented both progressivism and youthfulness. An extensive piece in the *New York Times Magazine* in early 1970 tied the sex fair to social and political progressivism.[46] The foreword to a book on the Danish porn fairs reflected on the sexual openness and equality represented by the Danes:

> We can opt for the kind of situation which obtains in the contemporary United States in which monogamy is still the legal norm but in which divorce is a usual event, and where the establishment with devoted hypocrisy attempts to defend the citadel of rectitude; or we can choose the way of Scandinavia which is an attempt to accept the fundamental sexual nature of man and woman, and to build sexual relationships which are free from inhibition and fear.[47]

Within months, American publishers were offering accounts of the Danish experiment, such as Banner Books' *A Report on Denmark's Legalized Pornography* and Academy Press's two-volume *Decision in Denmark: The Legalizing of Pornography*. For those not wishing to wade through pages of interviews with clerics and psychologists or reprints of Danish penal codes, the publishers cut to the heart of the matter by reprinting pages of black-and-white and color photos of hardcore action from Danish sex magazines. A book on the sex fair concluded, "Pornography is becoming one of Denmark's most prosperous industries. If it had shares on the stock market, their value would have already multiplied by five, and dividends would keep pouring on the astonished stockholder. The outlets for this industry are considerable, particularly abroad, and the main efforts are directed at countries with a strong currency."[48] In 1970 one Danish official remarked, "Without foreign tourists and illegal exports, this trade would probably fade away."[49]

American publishers were joined by opportunistic filmmakers from the United States, eager to capitalize on the change in the Danish laws by making documentaries for the American market.[50] Alex de Renzy, who made short films for his pioneering San Francisco porn theater, the Screening Room, traveled to Copenhagen for Sex 69 to shoot *Pornogra-*

phy in Denmark: A New Approach (1970).[51] Los Angeles–based producer-distributor John Lamb made the trip to produce *Sexual Freedom in Denmark* (1970); Signature Films' *Wide Open Copenhagen 70* (a.k.a. *Pornography: Copenhagen 1970*) was also in the mix. The films were often confused by ticket buyers, but that, according to *New York Times* critic Vincent Canby, "should be to the detriment of no one, except perhaps to the movies' distributors, and to those moviegoers who measure their entertainment in terms of the number of feet exposed to the mechanics of lust." "In outline and in content," he determined, "the documentaries are almost indistinguishable." All featured shots of Danish landmarks, man-on-the-street interviews, "then interviews with producers, directors and actors of porno films, visits to porno clubs, interviews with psychologists, sociologists and 'sexologists' . . . followed by, or preceded by, an extended sequence showing a porno film being made."[52] *Sexual Freedom in Denmark* also included sequences on anatomy, venereal disease, childbirth, and the mechanics of coitus—sequences that Lamb's Art Films International frequently loaned to medical schools and colleges. Each film featured hardcore material within its documentary frame, prompting critic Stanley Kauffmann to deem their theatrical exhibition "too pressing to ignore."[53]

Kauffmann, normally the most aloof of reviewers, found the films shocking "because I could walk in off the New York street and see them." He continued, "In other countries, other customs; shock is a matter of place and time, and in New York, this month, those pictures shocked me, by their availability. . . . These films are sheerly sexual functions; they extol porno as physically and morally desirable, and they praise Copenhagen as the Rome of a new church."[54] Kauffmann had plenty of company with whom to share his anxiety—even those considered among the most secular and sophisticated—because the films that concerned him were among the first theatrical features to include hardcore material on U.S. screens.[55] Even *Variety*'s jaded chronicler of the sex scene, Addison Verrill, concluded that *Pornography in Denmark* "in a mere 75 minutes exploded the last of the screen conventions honored in recent permissive years."[56]

In keeping with the other Scandinavian films, the porn documentaries were predicated on the precepts of participation and modern notions about sexuality rather than on the shame and regressive attitudes of most sexploitation movies up to that time—including the French films. In an on-the-street interview in *Sexual Freedom in Denmark* (figure 8.3), reporter Ole Lassen asks a young woman named Karen her opinion of premarital sex. She responds, "Yeah, all my girlfriends think it's okay.

Fig. 8.3 Sex was continually framed as a participatory activity in the "Scandinavian" films. Here, Ole Lassen interviews several participants in a porn movie shoot in *Sexual Freedom in Denmark* (1970).

Everybody in school is having sex before marriage." Dorritt Frantzen, a model and Miss Denmark in the Miss International beauty pageant, expresses her opinion that premarital sex at thirteen or fourteen is the norm while averring that she did not have her first "affair" until she was eighteen. Lassen talks to a photographer, Freddy, shooting a porn film; he agrees with the statement that sexual freedom is good: "My personal opinion is that it can't be free enough." The models participating in the shoot all express a blasé attitude about their work and sex in general. Even the instructional scenes showing sexual positions in *Sexual Freedom in Denmark* are designed to encourage participation through imitation of positions, explaining the kinds of sensation and pleasure that each one affords.

Similarly, in *Pornography in Denmark*, people questioned outside the Sex 69 fair express their enthusiasm for the show and the increased liberties in Denmark. During an interview with Toni, a young woman who does porn shoots with her boyfriend, the narrator intones, "Toni takes pride in her work. . . . Toni is more interested in having a warm emotional relationship with the people she works with, and in making a good movie." Later scenes of Tanya, a dancer, and Ilsa, a performer in a live sex show, are more concerned with the development of their performances as creative expression rather than the mere acts for the audience to observe for pay. The film concludes by urging the viewers to ask themselves "to question the validity of the legal sanctions against such material in this country." It asks, "Is there sufficient justification for censorship of adult entertainment? Do you feel that the suppression of pornography in the United States constitutes an infringement on the inalienable rights of adults? Should legislation against pornography be restricted in the United States?"[57] *Pornography in Denmark* guided viewers toward affirmative responses to the latter questions by positing Denmark as an exemplar. Writing about the Scandinavian documentaries in the *New York Times* in early 1971, Foster Hirsch recognized their role in reminding "Americans of the Scandinavians' sexual health and happiness."[58]

Reviewers were not so naive as to believe the films were made for altruistic purposes, but many accorded them more latitude than they did the typical sexploitation fare. After suggesting that *Sexual Freedom in Denmark* often oversimplified its case, John Mahoney concluded, "So long as ignorance allows for an audience seeking titillation, there is no reason why that curiosity should not be satisfied by an intelligent presentation. . . . [It] is one of the few films on the circuit which is genuinely erotic without the necessity of making its audience feel dirty."[59] *Daily Variety* determined, "Although its market motives may be suspect, it is nevertheless a frequently interesting document, slickly produced, edited and photographed, and not less intelligently scripted than an average TV news special."[60] Even if the documentaries were made to pull in a quick buck, reviewers reluctantly admitted they could initiate a dialogue about the sexual attitudes in Denmark and how they differed from prevailing norms in the United States. The movies certainly invited their viewers to consider their own relationships to those norms.

Of course relatively few Scandinavian sex films were documentaries. Most were narratives such as *I, a Woman* and *Inga*. Some featured typical sexploitation scenarios, but even when they did they often had a more positive spin than their French or American counterparts. Rather than focusing on degradation and exploitation, the prostitute protagonist of *Dagmar's Hot Pants* (1971) sees sex as a means to an end. "To some girls it's a way of life. To me it's been a temporary, high-paying job," she tells a friend. The end of the film finds her marrying her boyfriend, whom she has been putting through medical school in Stockholm with her earnings. *Anita* (1973) deals with a nymphomaniac who samples all the men in her small Swedish village, scandalizes her family, and then moves to the big city. A student named Erik runs into her—literally—as she emerges from a tent at a construction site with one of her pickups and resolves to help her overcome her condition. He determines that poor self-esteem, difficult family relations, and an inability to have orgasms have led to her life of promiscuity. Unlike many other films that deal with nymphomania (e.g., *Nympho—A Woman's Urge* [1965], *Alley Tramp*

Fig. 8.4 Birte Tove played the title role in *Christa* (1971, a.k.a. *Swedish Fly Girls*), the embodiment of modern, enlightened sexual attitudes of Denmark and Sweden.

[1968]) that end ambiguously or tragically, *Anita* concludes with the troubled girl cured and in a mutually satisfying relationship with Erik.

Christa (1970; figure 8.4) stands as a prime example of a movie that extolled the virtues of the Scandinavian lifestyle and political system as the vanguard of sexual freedom. Most commonly—and incongruously—known by the title *Swedish Fly Girls*, the film follows Christa, a Danish flight attendant. The story involves her search for the right man to be her husband and a father to her toddler, Rolf, who lives with her parents. Torben, her former lover and the child's father, wanted her to have an abortion and still hopes to win Christa over, although she wants nothing to do with him. Christa is characterized as a young woman who is both principled and pragmatic, as someone simultaneously free-spirited but also rooted in the real world. Lyrics of the Manfred Mann songs on the soundtrack describe her as "free as the early morning sun." She takes on a veritable United Nations of lovers—Italian, American, French, Australian. She engages in "now" behaviors: smoking pot, visiting a porn shop, weaving at her loom in the nude, and living in a commune with several other young men and women who share a bathroom and are comfortable with casual nudity. At the same time Christa admits to being "straight" because she works for a big corporation and her lovers are essentially auditioning for the role of husband and provider. She eventually decides to marry the Australian, Derek, but is confronted by Torben with information detailing her string of affairs. He says he'll take her to court to have her declared an unfit mother. On a drive in the country, Torben and Christa talk of reconciliation. But realizing that a reunion is futile, Torben lets Christa out of the car and speeds into a wall, killing himself. The film concludes by cutting between Torben's funeral and Christa, Derek, and Rolf on a beach, with a final shot of the setting sun dissolving into images of a galaxy in space.

The symbolism in *Christa* is obvious, yet sincere: Christa represents the modern Scandinavian welfare state, combining the best elements of socialism and capitalism, modernity and tradition, individual liberty and personal responsibility—all wrapped in a progressive approach to sex. Although Christa auditions a series of men as a potential husband and a father for her child, the sex she has is "good sex" and the film was, as Howard Thompson wrote in the *New York Times*, "a determinedly civilized and confident tribute to [Denmark] as an unfettered sexual Utopia."[61] *Christa* received limited play in the United States under its original title with a mod ad campaign, but as *Swedish Fly Girls* it became a drive-in staple and perpetuated the image of the Scandinavian countries' modern and socially enlightened sexual attitudes. Other films, whether made in Scandinavia (*Without a Stitch*, 1970), or in the United States (*Danish and Blue*, 1970), conveyed similar sentiments.

Regardless of plot specifics it was, above all else, the provenance of the Scandinavian films that helped sell them and secured their success. If having "France," "French," or "Paris" in the title of a film or specifying its Gallic roots had once pointed to its provocative quality, by the late 1960s sexploitation titles announced their Nordic origins or subject matter, at times alluding to their "newer" or "freer" take on morality: *One Swedish Summer* (1968), *Scandal in Denmark* (1969), *Swedish and Underage* (1969), *My Swedish Cousins* (1970), *Sexual Practices in Sweden* (1970), *Maid in Sweden* (1971), *A Touch of Sweden* (1971), *Sexual Customs in Scandinavia* (1972), *1001 Danish Delights* (1972), *Swedish Wife Exchange Club* (1972), and *Swedish Swingers* (1974) are just several examples.[62] If a film's Scandinavian roots or setting were not immediately apparent in the title, advertising tags provided the necessary information. Ads for *Without a Stitch* (1969) stressed "This is the first film to enter the U.S. from Denmark since its liberalization of permissiveness!" *Threesome* (1970) claimed to be "the first film made in Denmark since that country abolished all censorship." London's *Cinema* magazine, quoted in *Threesome*'s ad, called it, "bold and interesting" saying it "smacks of Bergman in intensity . . . high powered lesbian drama . . . certainly the best film yet in the fast moving new vogue of Scandinavian-American co-productions."[63] *Yes* (1968, a.k.a. *To Ingrid, My Love, Lisa*) was "From Sweden, A Cannon Production"; *Relations* (1970) was "the love story from Denmark." Distributors were happy to double up the title and tag line as with *Love, Swedish Style* (1972) in which ads said of the heroine, "She comes fully equipped . . . from Sweden!" Other movies recalled earlier Scandinavian hits: *2—I, a Woman, Part II* (1968), *The Seduction of Inga* (1971), and *Ann and Eve* (1970), whose tag suggested that "Just when you thought you'd seen it all" . . . "the love animals of *Inga* and *I, a Woman, Part II* trade secrets."

By 1970 the Scandinavian origins of a film were a significant enough selling point to warrant slapping an "imported" label on domestic product. *Sexual Practices in Sweden* (1970)—a typical, dry marriage manual film showing foreplay and various sexual positions—might just as well have been called *Sexual Practices in Hoboken* were it not for the hokey "Swedish" accent of the on-screen narrator.[64] Advertising for *Ride Hard, Ride Wild* (1970) simply stated "From Denmark," as though its status as a Scandinavian import were enough to tell potential ticket buyers all they needed to know about the film. In reality it was from Los Angeles, shot by R. Lee Frost for Phoenix International Films.[65] And films from other countries were offered up as Scandinavian imports. For instance the West German movie *Teenager Report: Die Ganz Jungen Mädchen* was released in the United States as *Swedish Lessons in Love* around 1973, sold with the tagline, "They teach love all the way. The way Swedish schoolgirls are taught."

The words "Danish" and "Swedish" soon came to signal the hardest material available in the U.S. market in the late 1960s into the 1970s. Sex magazines were peppered with ads hawking the latest offerings from Scandinavia. For instance, a random 1971 issue of the sex tabloid *Screw* offered Swedish "Invisible Mini-films" that arrived via air mail letters and supposedly evaded customs, "50 different action films" from Sweden, an "original Danish Mag without customs problems," "shocking sex scenes, Swedish style," and new color catalogues from the "sex-countries of Sweden and Denmark," among others.[66] The Copenhagen-based Color Climax Corporation exported its eponymous magazine to the United States and Europe, and soon became associated with pornographic material that stretched the boundaries of sexual freedom, even for its staunchest defenders: bestiality and child pornography.[67]

Toward a More Rational View of Sex

By the early 1970s the association between Scandinavian countries and sexual liberty was cemented. A few examples: American pornographic films continued to evoke Denmark and Sweden in their titles such as *The Danish Connection*, a 1974 hardcore film featuring John Holmes, and *Swedish Sorority Girls* (1978). In the early 1970s entrepreneur Noel Bloom and his father created a line of cross-marketed 8 mm movies and magazines titled *Swedish Erotica*, even though the films were made in the United States with American performers. The company eventually developed into an early powerful video porn enterprise: Caballero Home Video.[68] In Martin Scorsese's *Taxi Driver* (1976), the unstable Travis (Robert DeNiro) takes the object of his obsession (Cybill Shepherd) to a "dirty movie," *Swedish Marriage Manual*, much to her disgust.[69] In the late 1980s Old Milwaukee Beer began featuring "The Swedish Bikini Team," a group of sexy swimsuit-clad blondes in a series of ads. The list could go on. Elisabet Björklund has observed that the characterization of "Swedish Sin"—originally seen as derogatory within the country—was transformed, and today "the connection between Sweden and sex has also become part of the self-affirming national discourse."[70]

The general shift away from France and the embrace of the Scandinavian films as a source of interest and inspiration for Americans can be seen as symptomatic of a general easing of social and moral constraints on sexuality in the United States. It would be misleading to suggest that American audiences received any kind of accurate depiction about sexual life and liberty in Denmark and Sweden from the films made in, or about, those countries during the sexual revolution—any more than they had been given a faithful account of France's sex ways in earlier films and popular culture. However, Americans did come away with an impression about those cultures, one that during the sexual revolution was appealing as the more hidebound aspects of American sexual attitudes and behavior began to flake away. They presented a new and engaging ideal.

Writing about "Swedish sin," Carl Marklund remarks on the predominant, often male, sexual fantasy "of a somehow 'free' love which is made possible only because of the 'natural' naivety of the predominantly 'female' native, such as the one enjoyed by European sailors, missionaries and artists philandering about the Southern Seas." He suggests that the fantasy of "the Swedish sin" flipped the equation because its "reason" was the Swedish female's liberating a male outsider "from the burden of his own traditionally conceived sin." Here we can locate the appeal of the Scandinavian films for American audiences. As Marklund speculates,

What is exotic and possibly titillating in this message is that rationality replaces naivety as the sexually coded core of the image. This is also where "Swedish sin" becomes the most quintessential sin, the sin which is so sinful that it even rejects its own sinfulness as it unceremoniously and straightforwardly—rationally, even—denies the possibility of sin altogether. There are just natural needs and the right to enjoy their fulfillment.[71]

For Americans negotiating the sexual revolution and a new, highly sexualized media in the 1960s and 1970s, the Scandinavian films offered sex a mantle of rationality, modernity, and naturalness. A new ideal of what constituted the "sexy" had begun to put some distance between Americans and their Puritan legacy of shame and sinfulness associated with one of the most fundamental of human acts.

Notes

1. Crane Brinton, *The Americans and the French* (Cambridge: Harvard University Press, 1968), 35, 37.
2. Allan M. Brandt, *No Magic Bullet: A Social History of Venereal Disease in the United States Since 1880* (New York: Oxford University Press, 1987), 101.
3. James R. Petersen, *The Century of Sex: Playboy's History of the Sexual Revolution, 1900–1999* (New York: Grove Press, 1999), 66.
4. Geoffrey Gorer, "The Erotic Myth of America," *Partisan Review*, July/August 1950, 589.
5. Vance Packard, *The Sexual Wilderness* (New York: David McKay, 1968), 71.
6. Although Americans looked to Europe as the source of sexual sophistication in the postwar years, some on the Continent saw American "sex-mindedness" as a threat, especially in light of the Kinsey reports and Cold War anxieties. As Miriam G. Reumann documents, "Liberals and conservatives alike noted time and again that negative international opinion regarding the United States harmed the nation, and many saw American sexual behavior as a particularly sensitive topic." "In the charged context of the cold war," she writes, "as the United States sought ideological alliances abroad, its image as a 'sex-mad' nation could harm key diplomatic and military relationships." See Miriam G. Reumann, *American Sexual Character: Sex, Gender, and National Identity in the Kinsey Report* (Berkeley: University of California Press, 2005), 44, 45.
7. Genet (Janet Flanner), "Letter from Paris," *New Yorker*, October 11, 1958, 191.
8. "Peck's Bad Girl," *Newsweek*, January 6, 1958, 68.
9. Note: Because the French films distributed in the U.S. often underwent considerable change, the dates listed here, along with the titles, are for their American release, not their original French release.
10. Review of *Therese and Isabelle, Candid Press*, April 27, 1969, 22.

11. A law was enacted in 1905 officially separating the state and the church in France.
12. "After De Gaulle—Sex Sells," *Newsweek*, September 29, 1969, 61.
13. Joe David Brown, "Sin and Sweden," *Time*, April 25, 1955, 29. For an extended analysis of the article and the role that it played in shaping Sweden's image abroad, see Frederick Hale, "*Time* for Sex in Sweden: Enhancing the Myth of the 'Swedish Sin' During the 1950s," *Scandinavian Studies* 75, no. 3 (2003): 351–374.
14. "Sex in the Classroom," *Time*, July 1, 1966, 83. In an article published the following year in *Saturday Review*, authors William Simon and John H. Gagnon summarized the questions as "What should be taught? How and when should it be taught? Who should do the teaching?" ("The Pedagogy of Sex," November 18, 1967, 76).
15. Carl Marklund, "Hot Love and Cold People: Sexual Liberalism as Political Escapism in Radical Sweden," Nordeuropa Forum, January 2009, accessed May 15. 2011. edoc.hu-berlin.de/nordeuropaforum/2009-1/marklund-carl -83/XML/.
16. J. Robert Moskin, "Sweden's New Battle over Sex," *Look*, November 15, 1966, 37.
17. Margaret Mead, "What We Can Learn from Sex Education in Sweden," *Redbook*, October 1968, 34; George Krupp, "Swedish Design for Living," *Saturday Review*, July 29, 1967, 26.
18. Eleanor Adams, "Sex Education: The Swedish System," *Scholastic Teacher*, April 21, 1967, 17.
19. "Sweden's Pagan Beauty," *Look*, February 9, 1965, 57.
20. Richard Joseph, "Nothing Rotten in the States of Denmark, Norway, Sweden and Finland—Especially the Girls," *Esquire*, May 1965, 86.
21. Lester A. Kirkendall, Preface in Birgitta Linnér, *Sex and Society in Sweden* (New York: Pantheon, 1967), vi. At least some measure of this "superior" attitude might be traced to the popular Swedish-born actress Ingrid Bergman's affair with director Roberto Rossellini that scandalized Hollywood and the nation in 1950.
22. Moskin, "Sweden's New Battle over Sex," 42. For an in-depth account of sex education and the Swedish welfare state, particularly in relation to media, see Elisabet Björklund, "The Most Delicate Subject: A History of Sex Education Films in Sweden," PhD diss., Lund University.
23. Linnér, *Sex and Society in Sweden*, 3.
24. "Calls Danish Film 'Pure Smut,'" *Variety*, July 14, 1965, 17.
25. The film *491* was directed by Vilgot Sjöman, who would go on to make *I Am Curious (Yellow)*. Lena Nyman, who starred in *I Am Curious*, played the prostitute in *491*.
26. Kell, review of *I, a Woman, Variety*, September 29, 1965, 6.
27. *I, a Woman* advertisement, *Boxoffice*, January 23, 1967, NC-3; "Far out (Long Island) Sex," *Variety*, June 14, 1967, 13; Vincent Canby, "*I, a Woman* a Hit De-

spite Its Origin," *New York Times*, August 10, 1967, 44; Richard Corliss, "Radley Metzger, Aristocrat of the Erotic: An Interview by Richard Corliss," *Film Comment* (January 1973): 23.

28. In establishing the difference between those films made or set in France and those made or set in Scandinavia, I do not want to give the impression that every movie hewed tightly to this standard. There were certainly exceptions to the rule, but they are rather rare.

29. See Linnér, *Sex and Society in Sweden*, 9–12.

30. Deane William Ferm, "The Latest Scoop on Swedish Sex," *Christian Century*, January 14, 1970, 46.

31. John M. Lee, "Danes and Swedes Are Moving toward Greater Sex Freedom," *New York Times*, November 6, 1968, 44. "Men's magazines" were especially eager to explore the sexual freedom of Denmark and Sweden. *Playboy* featured a "Girls of Scandinavia" pictorial in its June 1968 issue; *Sir!* included an article titled "A Sociological Experiment in Denmark" (March 1970); *Swank* asked, "Is Sweden Really the Sex-Utopia?" (November 1970); and so on.

32. See, for instance, the *Life* magazine cover story by Richard Lorber and Ernest Fladell, "The Generation Gap," *Life*, May 17, 1968, 81–92.

33. Don Kulick, "Four Hundred Thousand Swedish Perverts," GLQ: *A Journal of Lesbian and Gay Studies* 11, no. 2 (2005): 208.

34. "Permissiveness with affection" held that premarital sex was acceptable within a committed relationship. Ira L. Reiss, *Premarital Sexual Standards in America* (Glencoe, IL: Free Press, 1960), 83–84.

35. Kulick, "Four Hundred Thousand Swedish Perverts," 209.

36. Tytti Soila, "Sweden," in Tytti Soila, Astrid Söderbergh Widding, and Gunnar Iversen, eds., *Nordic National Cinemas* (New York: Routledge, 1998), 186–187.

37. My emphasis. "Sweden's Smashing Fashions," *Life*, September 27, 1968, 89.

38. Jerry Victor, "Those Hot New Swedish Films!" *Candid Press*, January 7, 1968, 16.

39. Natalie Gittelson, "Sweden II: The Love Image," *Harper's Bazaar*, June 1969, 22.

40. "Where Do Movies Come From, Dad?" Arnold M. Auerbach, *New York Times*, June 7, 1970, sec. 2, 2; Thomas Meehan, "If You're Still Curious . . . ," *New York Times Magazine*, June 29, 1969, 12.

41. First quotation: emphasis in the original. Frederic Fleischer, "Export or Die: Sweden Feeds the World's Appetite for Swedish Films," *Film Comment* (summer 1970): 36–37.

42. Swedish Film Production Investments produced *One Swedish Summer* (a.k.a. *As the Naked Wind from the Sea*, 1968), *The Language of Love* (1969), and *Swedish and Underage* (1969), among others, many of which received play on the American sexploitation circuit. See Per Olov Qvist and Tytti Soila, "*Eva—Den Utstötta; Swedish and Underage*," in *The Cinema of Scandinavia*, ed. Tytti Soila (London: Wallflower Press, 2005), 152.

43. The Danish government stopped enforcing restrictions on the sale of porn

some months prior to July 1, 1969. "Pornography: What Is Permitted Is Boring," *Time*, June 6, 1969, 47.

44. John M. Lee, "Pornography Trade Show Is Opened in Demark," *New York Times*, October 22, 1969, 5.

45. "Who Buys Smut? Report from the Free World," *Screw*, November 24, 1969, 10.

46. Tom Buckely, "Oh! Copenhagen!," *New York Times Magazine*, February 8, 1970, 33+. Buckley noted that the Swedes stereotyped the Danes as "a rosy-cheeked machine for eating and love-making, devoid of subtlety, mysticism and passion," whereas the Danes viewed Swedes as "icebound, aloof and morbid."

47. Jean-Claude Lauret, *The Danish Sex Fairs*, trans. Arlette Ryvers (New York: Pent-R Books, 1971), 10.

48. Lauret, *The Danish Sex Fairs*, 66.

49. "When Pornography Curbs Are Lifted," *U.S. News and World Report*, October 19, 1970, 68.

50. Even before the American documentaries were released, the Italian-made "mondo" film *Sweden: Heaven and Hell* (1969) hit theaters. Trailers for U.S. release promised "things you just don't see at home": "In America, you don't see beautiful girls bouncing boldly out of the sauna, into the snow," as it depicted seminude blondes bounding for snow banks. "In America, you don't see public pornography shops where erotic books are displayed for both sexes—with government approval." In typical exploitation "See! See! See!" prose, it went on: "See the floating sex lab, a moon-lit cruise where 15-year-old girls learn the practical side of sex," and so on.

51. The film was picked up for national distribution by Sherpix, a company that had released some of Andy Warhol's Factory films such as *Lonesome Cowboys* (1968) and sexploitation items such as *The Stewardesses* (1969). Sherpix distributed the movie as *Censorship in Denmark* and succeeded in booking it "simultaneously in three classy cinemas in New York (the Fifty-fifth Street Playhouse, Lido East, and the Eleventh Street Theater) rather than in the dingy sexploitation-type houses where such movies are customarily shown." See Dorothy Allen, review of *Censorship in Denmark: A New Approach, Cinema X and Theater Annual*, 1971, 39.

52. Vincent Canby, "Have You Tried the Danish Blue?" *New York Times*, June 21, 1970, sec. 2, 1, 29.

53. Stanley Kauffmann, "Public Privates," *New Republic*, July 11, 1970, 22.

54. Stanley Kauffmann, "Public Privates," 22.

55. The others were the "white coaters" or "marriage manual films"—such as *Man and Wife* (1969), *He and She* (1970), and *Swedish Marriage Manual* (1969)—although they were often relatively discreet. *Pornography in Denmark* included "money shots," explaining they were an expected convention in Danish porn.

56. Addison Verrill, "Fear U.S. Sexplicit Films Made Tame, Biz Hurt Via 'Pornography in Denmark,'" *Variety*, April 22, 1970, 28.

57. *Pornography in Denmark* and *Sexual Freedom in Denmark* are both obtainable on DVD. *Wide Open Copenhagen 70* may be lost.

58. Foster Hirsch, "He's Happy in His 'Blue' Heaven," *New York Times*, January 24, 1971, 13.

59. John Mahoney, "'Sex Freedom' In Denmark Has Everything to Be Seen," *Hollywood Reporter*, April 1, 1970, 8.

60. Rick., review of *Sexual Freedom in Denmark*, *Daily Variety*, n.d., n.p., contained in *Sexual Freedom in Denmark* press packet, collection of the author.

61. Howard Thompson, "Seeking Mr. Right," *New York Times*, August 21, 1971, 17.

62. As is typical with exploitation films, these movies were often released under multiple titles. This list, which is by no means exhaustive, is based on the films themselves, reviews, and existing posters or other advertising material.

63. Ad for *Threesome* in Hugh Fordin, ed., *Film-TV Daily 1970 Yearbook of Motion Pictures and Television* (New York: Wid's Films and Film Folk, 1970), 43.

64. Although the film was supposedly made by the Svenska Institut of Sexual Response, it appears to have been the brainchild of New York distributor William Mishkin and was almost certainly made exclusively for the U.S. market.

65. Frost and producer Armand Atamian made two other ultra-low-budget quickies passed off as Danish productions around the same time: *The Captives* (1970) and *Slaves in Cages* (1971). Although posters exist for both these obscurities, it is not entirely clear if they are distinct movies or if they are actually one and the same film.

66. *Screw*, March 1, 1971, various pages.

67. *Color Climax* featured photo spreads of a Danish woman, Bodil Joensen (spellings vary), engaged in sex with animals. Joensen was featured in a short documentary, *A Summer Day* (1970), engaging in sex acts with a boar, a dog, and a stallion. The film won the Grand Prize at the Wet Dream Film Festival in Amsterdam in 1970. She also appeared in *Animal Lover* (ca. 1971), which received some play in the United States and featured similar acts. For information see Jack Stevenson, "Dead Famous: The Life and Movies of Erotic Cinema's Most Exploited Figure," in *Fleshpot: Cinema's Sexual Myth Makers & Taboo Breakers*, ed. Jack Stevenson (Manchester, England: Critical Vision, 2000, 177–189). Color Climax's "Lolita" series (ca. 1971–1979) was one of the few instances of "kiddie porn" manufactured by a large-scale producer.

68. See Frederick Wasser, *Veni, Vidi, Video: The Hollywood Empire and the VCR* (Austin: University of Texas Press, 2001), 107.

69. Although the marquee of the theater displays the title *Swedish Marriage Manual* (AKA *The Language of Love*), the scenes intercut as Travis and Betsy watch are from *Sexual Freedom in Denmark*.

70. Elisabet Björklund, "'This is a dirty movie'—*Taxi Driver* and 'Swedish Sin,'" *Journal of Scandinavian Cinema* 1, no. 2 (2011): 172.

71. Marklund, "Hot Love and Cold People."

9 * **Altered Sex:** Satan, Acid, and the Erotic Threshold

JEFFREY SCONCE

A mining expedition in the South American jungle: Edward MacKensie, jealous of his business partner's lover and wanting to keep the expedition's riches for himself, engineers an "accident" that kills the partner and his lover. Twenty years later, MacKensie is a rich and successful man, married with a teenage daughter. Despite (or perhaps because) of his wealth and success, MacKensie finds himself bored with life, in particular, his sex life. He pays the office boy and secretary to have sex in front of him, and then cruelly mocks them when they do not perform to his expectations. He searches for hookers who might better understand his peculiar "tastes," which center on sadistic forms of torture and humiliation, and longs for the Victorian era for the fabled abandon of its sexual underground. "Now there was an era," he laments to himself, "when a woman like Mrs. Berkeley would earn a thousand pounds for inventing a whipping horse on which a pretty girl could be postured in a thousand different lascivious ways for the lash."[1] After another humiliating failure with a prostitute, MacKensie meets the mysterious Carlos Sathanas, a worldly, rich sophisticate. Their conversation quickly turns to "unusual pleasures." "To put it bluntly," he tells MacKensie, "for all this talk about the new sexual freedom, I for one fail to perceive it except in the huge dissemination of titallitory books and magazines and movies, which are nothing more or less than pure psychic masturbation. They depict fantasies that are not in existence, but perhaps were in another century."[2] Sathanas confides that he is the founder and sole proprietor of "the Satan Club," an organization devoted to fulfilling the most bizarre sexual desires of its secret, exclusive membership. MacKensie joins eagerly and soon finds himself participating in a series of increasingly exotic sexual scenarios.

Three weeks into his membership, MacKensie anticipates what promises to be the most provocative show yet, the one that will make him an official member of the Satan Club for life. Encouraged to partake of a very special mixture of Spanish fly—an hallucinatory blend discovered by Sathanas himself—a blindfolded MacKensie is escorted into a basement and strapped into a strange device called "the chair of Tantalus," guaranteed by Sathanas to enhance his sexual arousal to unprecedented heights. With the blindfold now removed, a curtain parts to reveal two nude women intertwined on a couch. Aroused to point of physical pain, MacKensie looks down to see there is a collar device attached to his penis making orgasm impossible: the chair of Tantalus! But his horror and despair are only beginning. As the effects of the Spanish fly begin to wane, he recognizes the two women on the couch as his wife and her recently hired personal masseuse. They mock him with contemptuous laughter as their sexual escapades become more intense. Worse yet, his teenage daughter now enters the tableau on all fours, eagerly mounted by the family dog! The agony of arousal and humiliation is overwhelming, and MacKensie begs for release. Calm and collected, Sathanas appears on stage to explain. He is in fact the business partner MacKensie left for dead twenty years ago in the jungle. Having been told of MacKensie's murderous past and philandering ways, his family now hates him — utterly. All money and property have been transferred to the wife, who plans to divorce him and run away with the masseuse. His daughter no longer has any interest in men, only her beloved German Shepherd. His former partner's revenge is complete. The show is over. Later, as the lights go up, MacKensie is alone but still strapped into the chair of Tantalus. He realizes the night's spectacle has unfolded in the basement of his very own Long Island home—of which he is now dispossessed. Destroyed by material and erotic greed, he stares "unseeingly at that stage where all his life had collapsed about him."

As a book trading in sexual fantasy, the very "psychic masturbation" so deplored in the text by Sathanas, *The Satan Club* is rather relentless in its emphasis on frustration, failure, and damnation. As one would expect from a "dirty book," MacKensie's saga links a number of extended and graphically rendered sexual interludes clearly crafted for the reader's arousal. Yet the overall structure of the book, despite its "immoral" status as pornography, is strangely, even prudishly *moral* in its actual execution. We must assume until the very last page that Sathanas is in fact Satan himself, tempting MacKensie's desire for ever more perverted sexual scenarios in order to take possession of his soul. In any case, MacKensie's lust does lead to his "damnation," broke and humiliated in Long Island if not actually burning in hell. Sexually adrift through most of the novel, MacKensie learns a powerful lesson about fantasy and desire, a lesson, in turn, that one would think might prove unsettling to the man who would seek out and buy a copy of *The Satan Club* for his own arousal. What exactly is the pleasure to be had in following the inexorable downward spiral of a man seeking to realize his own sexual fantasies? Moreover, what is gained by situating this prurient yet prudish narrative within the "satanic" conventions of temptation, trickery, and damnation?

The Satan Club serves as a reminder that of all the various avenues of morality policed by religion, none absorbs more mental and social energy than sexuality. Innumerable historians of religion, culture, and sexuality have discussed how civilization emerged (at least in part) from the social regulation of unfettered sexual expression, leading in the West to the eventual ascendance of property relations, heteronormative monogamy, and reproductive futurism—as well as all of this social order's attending "discontents."[3] Playing on these repressions, Lucifer's role within modernity has focused most intently on tempting the chaste to overthrow their superego masters, profane their faith, and reclaim forbidden desires and practices, forsaking the stabilizing institution of monogamous reproductive marriage for the entropic energies of "unbridled" lust. In modern fiction, this template is at least as old as J. K. Huysmans's scandalous account of fin de siècle Satanism, La Bas (1891). Huysmans's narrator, Durtal, a bored author interested in learning more about satanic sects said to be proliferating within the Catholic Church, infiltrates a Black Mass presided over by one Paris's most respected priests. Like any good decadent, he assumes the rite will at least be diverting. Attending with his lover—the wife of a rival author—his bemusement turns to horror as the priest "wipes himself" with the Eucharist, women writhe in ecstasy on the floor, and the choirboys "give themselves" to the men. Escaping this "monstrous pandemonium of prostitutes and maniacs," Durtal flees with his mistress (a possible succubus) to a seedy hotel, where he is then seduced (seemingly against his will) in a bed "strewn with fragments of hosts."[4] Satan makes no definitive appearance in La Bas—like much nineteenth-century fiction, Huysmans's realism emphasizes the plausible horrors of clerical contamination over the gothic pyrotechnics of supernatural intervention—but the novel's interlinking of power, profanity, sexual transgression, and shame remains central to the genre even today.[5]

Published in 1970, The Satan Club stands at the threshold of the most recent wave of popular interest in Satanism, one that traces its beginnings to the social transformations of the 1960s, especially the baby boomer alignment of sexual, spiritual, and psychedelic politics attending the so-called hippie counterculture. By the end of the 1960s, "Satanism" assumed an increasingly public identity, traceable in large part to the efforts of Anton Szandor LaVey. Although neither a hippie nor a baby

Fig. 9.1 This widely circulated AP photo from 1967 captures the "perversity" of Anton LaVey's "Church of Satan." Here LaVey baptizes his three-year-old daughter Zeena, while a priestess (Isabel Bolotov) serves as a "living alter." (Courtesy the Associated Press.)

boomer, this former carnie and crime-scene photographer exploited the countercultural currents of San Francisco when he founded the Church of Satan in 1966 (see figure 9.1). Fluent in the art of self-promotion, LaVey garnered international press in founding the church, including pieces in such journalistic mainstays as *Time, Life, Look,* and *McCall's.* LaVey also appeared as a guest on *The Tonight Show* with Johnny Carson and as the devil himself in Roman Polanski's *Rosemary's Baby* (1968), a film that ushered in a decade-long wave of satanic fictions. *The Exorcist* (1973), *The Omen* (1976), and their various sequels further mined this vein, as did a made-for-TV movie asking the question: *Look What's Happened to Rosemary's Baby?* (1976). By the mid-1970s, Satan had become such big business that Alan Ladd Jr., then president of Fox's film division, noted that "almost every movie company has five or six Devil movies in the works," a sentiment echoed by Ned Tanen of MCA: "Devil movies" have "eclipsed the western in popularity all over the world."[6] The reason, for Tanen, was clear, a logic still invoked to explain any and all trends in moviemaking: "Devil movies play equally well in Japan, Ecuador, and Wisconsin," he observed.[7] A more "pop" Satan also became a staple of the Christian-publishing industry in this period, most notoriously in the widely read screeds of Hal Lindsey, including *The Late Great Planet Earth* (1970) and *Satan Is Alive and Well on Planet Earth* (1972). Long before the "Left Behind" series transformed the Book of Revelation into an epic soap opera, Lindsey scoured the headlines for signs of the antichrist's arrival and the onset of the apocalypse. Flirtations between rock music and Satanism are well know in this period, from Led Zeppelin guitarist Jimmy Page's purchase of Aleister "the Beast" Crowley's Boleskin House to the coded imagery of the Rolling Stones' album, *Goats Head Soup*. The devil was such a ubiquitous presence in the American popular culture of the 1970s that minister C. S. Lovett even penned a diet book in 1977 under the alarming title: *Help Lord—the Devil Wants Me Fat!* "When You're Watching TV, the commercial break is one of the devil's favorite moments," warns Lovett. He then suggests a script for warding off Satan's "food attacks": "I know you're trying to dominate me with food, Satan. So, in the name of Jesus Go . . . get off my back!"[8]

Beneath this sheen of Hollywood "black horror," devil rock, and mass-market Satanism, however, lurked another circle of hellish cultural production. Shadowing "mainstream" Satanism was a cycle of sexploitation films, pornographic magazines, and adult paperbacks that—like *The Satan Club*—centered not so much on the gravitas of demon possession, the antichrist, and the apocalypse, but on a more licentious engagement of sexual tourism and erotic experimentation. As the dark overlord of a larger interest in occult sexuality, Satan presided over a ludic proliferation of transgressive temptation and "forbidden" pleasures in adult media of the 1960s and 1970s. Explicit paperbacks of the era promoted Satanism as a nonstop orgy in such titles as *Infernal Affair* (1967), *Devil Sex* (1969), *Sex Slaves of the Black Mass* (1971), and *Satan, Demons, and Dildoes* (1974), to name only a few. At the grind house, sexploitation movie titles also foregrounded the lure of satanic spectacle with such offerings as *The Lucifers* (1971), *Satanic Sexual Awareness* (1972), *Sons of Satan* (1973), *The Horny Devils* (1971, aka *Hotter Than Hell*), and the perhaps inevitable *Exorcist* knock-off: *Sexorcism Girl* (1975). In the increasingly targeted market for print pornography, magazines such as *Sexual Witchcraft* and *Bitchcraft* specialized in provocative images of occultists staging sexualized rituals ("Nudity in Witchcraft! The True Inside Story," proclaims one banner headline). Even the infamous Ed Wood Jr. threw his hat into the occult-sex ring by appearing (most painfully) in the 1971 cheapie, *Necromania*.[9]

Already a central figure in the West's psychic economy of sexual prohibition (at least in its religious iterations), the devil's historical relation to God, religion, and faith made "occult sex" a fundamentally perverse genre, even when tales such as *The Satan Club* ultimately sided with "real-world" explanations over the supernatural. As the Christian embodiment of evil temptation, Satan promised access to any and all sensual pleasures—an invitation to lustful exploration that resonated within the postwar era's ongoing disarticulation of sex, marriage, and reproduction. And yet, as a product of the *authority* of religious morality, this eroticized occult could not, by definition, escape the very moral order it sought to evade, undermine, or destroy. Satan (or a surrogate such as Sathanas) is both a saboteur of morality and its most *damning* enforcer, the ambassador of temptation and the executioner of guilt. Drawing his prey from their moral orbit by appealing to their most base and selfish of desires, Satan—in his supernatural, dialectic relation to God—ultimately reasserts the very repression that a bored MacKensie foolishly believes might be overcome. Such is the essence of "taboo" pleasure—a desire to violate convention and custom that ultimately reaffirms the authority of the law on which the taboo depends. This dynamic made satanic sexploitation a doubly perverse genre—"perverse" in its appetites and its effects. Although such fare offered the lure of ever-more "exotic" sexual adventures, for both protagonist and audience, the horned ambassador of such indulgence demanded nothing less than the sexual adventurer's eternal soul!

The "Black Pope"

As the author of *The Satanic Bible* and self-appointed spokesman of modern Satanism, LaVey frequently spoke to the press as the authority on Satanism's history and future—a heritage LaVey often cast in terms of sexual indulgence. "The Satanic Age started in 1966," LaVey explained. "That's when God was proclaimed dead, the Sexual Freedom League came into prominence, and the hippies developed as a free sex culture."[10] Within the sweeping social transformations of the postwar era, LaVey's brand of Satanism contributed to a significant rewriting of the devil, one that cast Satan more as a dandy or libertine than the Lord of Darkness. This "urbane" Satan was largely a function of growing secularization and new strategies for organizing erotic and social life within the so-called sexual revolution. Hoping to compete with the growing popularity of Hugh Hefner's *Playboy*, Stanley Publications introduced *Satan* magazine in 1957, billing it as "Devilish Entertainment for Men." The magazine only survived for six issues, leading historian Bethan Benwell to speculate, "There were limits to how far the 'playboy ethic' could be pushed.

Perhaps . . . the magazine's title and allusions flaunted the libertine ideal a little too brazenly."[11] Certainly, not everyone saw this new sexual "ethic" as progress—satanic or otherwise. "Increasing divorce and desertion and the growth of prenuptial and extramarital sex relations are signs of sex addiction somewhat similar to drug addiction," accused Pitirim Sorokin in his book *The American Sex Revolution* (1956). It was a claim that has resonated with moral reformers to this very day.[12] Responding to Sorokin, Edwin M. Schur commented in 1964 that many sociologists of the era believed "there really may not have been any startling change in sexual behavior in the very recent years."[13] Schur located perceptions of a sexual revolution more in an ongoing redefinition of the socioeconomic relationship between the individual and the family, pushing this "revolution" back even further in time by citing Walter Lipmann's observation in 1929 that once "chaperonage became impossible and the fear of pregnancy was all but eliminated, the entire conventional sex ethic was shattered."[14] Whether sexual practices were actually changing across the 1950s and 1960s was less important than the widely held *perception* that more people were having more sex in more "liberated" scenarios. This sense that individual desire, expressed in sexuality and selfishness had eclipsed familial and social responsibility and would remain a core moral debate of the twentieth century, creating the conditions not only for LaVey's Satanism, but also the Moynihan Report, Thomas Wolfe's "The Me Decade," and Christopher Lasch's *The Culture of Narcissism*.

Promoting the Church of Satan in 1966, LaVey frequently invoked the libertine connotations already attached to such satanic sophistication, even as he attempted to distance his new religion from mere hedonism. Sex might lure converts to the church, but LaVey's ambitions for his "religion" were more about philosophical empowerment than licentious abandon. In truth, LaVey's Satanism had little to do with Satan. Although he was never reticent to appear in the trappings of Christianity's satanic dramaturgy—donning capes, horns, and pentagrams for the camera—LaVey took great pains to divorce his version of Satanism from any actual biblical entity, his devil having more in common with Zarathustra and Ayn Rand than Lucifer the fallen angel. Although aspiring to provide a new philosophy of the mind, LaVey's background in carnie ballyhoo made him more than willing to hustle some flesh in publicizing the church. An early promotional event involved LaVey booking a San Francisco nightclub to stage an eroticized witches' Sabbath, a theatrical piece concluding with then stripper and soon-to-be Manson murderer Susan Atkins emerging nude from a coffin.[15] Ever the showman, LaVey sparked another round of national press by performing a satanic wedding ceremony in 1967, complete with a nude red-head serving as the altar. "The altar shouldn't be a cold unyielding slab of sterile stone," reasoned LaVey, but "a symbol of enthusiastic lust and indulgence."[16] He also cultivated a public relationship with sex symbol Jayne Mansfield, leading to the rumors of her conversion to Satanism, amplified in the wake of her untimely and gruesome death in a car accident in the summer of 1967. Yet despite the salacious aspects of the early church ("Phase One . . . the nudie stuff," LaVey would later call it), LaVey also made several attempts to deemphasize the sexual abandon seemingly promised by the "religion," no doubt to defend against the many "sex criminals" who apparently contacted him just prior to their release from prison in hopes of joining the congregation. Many potential converts, he reported, were disappointed to discover there were no "orgies" in the ceremonies; indeed, LaVey appears to have had only contempt for the type of orgiastic ritual imagined by Huysmans and, according to LaVey, allegedly still practiced in the "amateur" Satanist congregations of Los Angeles (presided over, according to LaVey, by "dirty old men"). The church made no judgment about the morality of any sexual pursuit, advocating "the practice of any type of sexual activity which satisfy man's individual needs, be it promiscuous heterosexuality, strict faithfulness to a wife or lover, homo-sexuality, or even fetishism," in short, "telling each man or woman to do what comes naturally and not to worry about it."[17] Those looking to affirm their sexual appetites, whatever they might be, were welcome at the church; those actually looking to have sex were not. "There are some beautiful women that belong to the Church," claimed LaVey, "but they don't have to come here to get laid. They could go down to any San Francisco bar and get picked up."[18]

Building on fantasies of libertine conquest and masculine sophistication, LaVey was savvy enough to recognize that one growth market would be sexual empowerment for women. Toward that end, he published *The Compleat Witch* in 1971, a manual teaching women how to seduce or otherwise manipulate men through witchcraft. Writing at the high-water mark of second-wave feminism, LaVey's advice is strangely prescient of Camille Paglia and other postfeminist provocateurs. "Any bitter and disgruntled female can rally against men, burning up her creative and manipulative energy in the process," he writes. "She will find the energies she expends in her quixotic cause would be put to more rewarding use, were she to profit by her womanliness by manipulating the men she holds in contempt, while enjoying the ones she finds stimulating."[19] No doubt such advice was appealing to women hoping to find a strategy for sexual success, and male readers fantasizing that they themselves might become the prey of such "sexual witchcraft." LaVey's practical advice for the aspiring witch included such tactics as positive visualization ("Extra Sensory Projection"), "indecent exposure" (showing as much flesh as legally possible—a "power" denied to men, notes LaVey), and not "scrubbing away your natural odors of seduction" (including keeping a swatch of dried menstrual blood in an amulet). As this is a book about *witchcraft*, LaVey includes some thoughts on the art of "divination," but even here his comments are more in line with the art of the con than the art of the occult. A woman willing to follow LaVey's sartorial and psychic program was promised an enhanced sense of personal power over the weak-minded male of the species, the book combining a rather conservative view of feminine seduction with a sexual will to power. Here LaVey put an occult spin on Helen Gurley Brown's *Sex and the Single Girl*, another book notorious for allegedly empowering women by cultivating their essentialized wiles. Indeed, Dodd and Mead's print campaign for *The Compleat Witch* dubbed it a study of "hex and the single girl," suggesting the publisher saw the book more as a "relationship" title than a primer in black magic.[20]

LaVey may have had his own detailed ideas about the philosophy of his religion and great ambitions for the future of Satanism, but he ultimately had little control over how the satanic 1960s and 1970s would play in the popular imagination; indeed, much of LaVey's time as Satanism's "official" spokesman appears to have been consumed in distancing his church from the atrocities of Satan-linked killers such as Charles Manson, "Nightstalker" Richard Ramirez, and dozens of cat-killing teenage boys in the Midwest—not to mention the general religious competition offered by the Process, the Raelians, the People's Temple, and California's other proliferating sects, cults, and "kooks."[21] Satan may have just been a convenient symbol for LaVey, but Lucifer's very real presence in the lives of those hoping to either invoke or avoid him made it difficult for LaVey's more "magical" form of Randian Objectivism to gain traction. Moreover, by building his church's public facade, not on rock or sand but on images of a devilish libido and fantasies of a guilt-free eroticism, LaVey's brand of Satanism could not help but be linked to the era's larger transformations in sexuality, especially among those already intrigued or repulsed by the highly visible growth of various "countercultures" of the 1960s. As a "hot" new scenario promising unlimited sexual action and erotic power, LaVey's bid to resurrect self-interested materialism became more naughty than Nietzschean, emerging as a prominent subgenre in the era's developing and increasingly brazen pornography industry.

Comfortable Deviance

As with so much sexploitation in the late 1960s and early 1970s, the era's satanic and otherwise "occult" sex stories—*The Satan Club* and others—motivated their graphic erotic content through a premise that promised copious sexual spectacle at the "deviant" margins of society—participating in what Eric Schaefer has called exploitation's "expansion of the acceptable sphere of desire." Schaefer argues that as sexploitation moved from the purportedly "educational" nudie/nature films of the early 1960s to more explicit content at the threshold of hardcore's arrival in the early 1970s, the industry increasingly incorporated themes of shock, adventure, and curiosity into its product and advertising, promising patrons "they would see and understand more about various 'forbidden' sexual practices."[22] This convention was also prominent in publishing. In the wake of a number of challenges to censorship restrictions in the late 1950s and early 1960s, new publishing houses emerged to offer multiple softcore titles on a monthly basis, opening the era of the adult bookstore.[23] The industry's move toward "kinkies," "roughies," and "weirdies"—both on film and in print—grew in part from the need to differentiate product in an increasingly crowded field of sexploitation releases. This move toward the erotic margins and the "forbidden" also speaks to transformations in a larger sexual imaginary. Even if sexual practices changed little in the 1950s and 1960s, qualitatively or quantitatively, the promise of expanding sexual horizons proliferated within the realm of cultural fantasy and its attending industries. Some people somewhere else *seemed* to be having more sex—be they international playboys, single girls at the office, shaggy bohemians living in the Village, or satanic witches living in San Francisco; all of them appeared to be united in the project of reclaiming a more vibrant sexuality unfettered by prevailing social institutions.

This symbolic expansion of the perceived sexual field actually began in the mid-1950s and early 1960s, not just in *Playboy* and its imitators, but also in a series of "nightstand" paperbacks detailing new sexual opportunities thought to be flourishing in the nation's growing suburbs. In this case, the "deviant" margins of society, not unlike the Communists, flourished even within the nation's revered social institutions of home and middle-class marriage.[24] Most often, these novels focused on rapacious young wives left home alone all day by their ambitious "rat-racing" husbands, making the women easy prey for various rogue males wandering the suburban landscape. Others depicted the ritual of "wife-swapping" as a trend quickly sweeping a sexually jaded country-club set. The titles alone provide a tidy index of the sexual restlessness simmering within the era's domestic containment: *Suburban Sin Club* (1959), *Discontented Wives* (1961), *The Friendship Club* (1963), *The Bored Young Wives* (1964), *Commuting Wife* (1964), *The Wife Traders* (1965), *Weekday Widows* (1966), *Suburban Sin* (1968). Such fiction presented a novel change in pornographic strategy. Although the smut industry had traditionally located sexual spectacle among "professionals" (strippers, models, nudists) and within conventionally eroticized locations (burlesque stages, nature or nudist camps), these novels suggested that available sexual partners might be waiting just beyond the front door of the American split-level. As Schaefer argues, sexploitation's development in the 1960s crafted a mise-en-scène in which "seemingly mundane settings" came to be "eroticized in some way: photographer's studios, motel rooms, suburban homes, college campuses, hippie pads."[25] The eroticization of these locations, each metonymic of a certain community, allowed for a fluidity between these spaces and helped create the impression of a growing "sexual underground" flourishing beneath the surfaces of "normal" American life.

As the ultimate "underground," satanic sexploitation presented perhaps the most aggressive hybridization of these two trends, combining an emphasis on subterranean sexuality with a fascination for increasingly "adventurous," thus taboo, forms of sexual behavior. If "commuter widows" and "swap clubs" suggested the placid suburbs were in fact laboratories for adultery and open marriages, occult sex suggested that even more "deviant" and "far out" sexual practices lurked in the community for those willing to dig deeper. In this respect, occult sexploitation cast its erotic spectacle as the most secret, "shocking," and "forbidden" of all—a sexuality that was, in its pure hedonism, libertine experimentalism, and profane transgression, as far removed as possible from the procreative functions of the married monogamy that had so long served as the symbolic center of American sexuality. Serving as a gateway to "far out" fornication, Satanism quickly became aligned with the more visible promotion of "free love" within the "hippie" subculture, another space of danger and desire prominent in the middle-class imagination. Although Satanism and hippiedom had little use for one another in the real world (LaVey's church was for the elite professional, not the unwashed "Deadhead" living in the Haight), they nevertheless appeared to many as overlapping communities, geographically (with San Francisco as the epicenter of both movements) and ideologically (as two prongs in a shared assault on traditional values). For sexploitation merchants, meanwhile, associating occultism with the hippie ethos further expanded the promise and justification for presenting shocking, forbidden, and otherwise unusual sexual content. Each "subculture" brought a unique element to this mix. Whereas satanic sexploitation promised an erotic "R&D" in which the greater the experimental "perversion," the greater the pleasure, the hippie face of sexploitation frequently centered on the attractions of a more promiscuous generation—one willing to engage in sex without all the "hang-ups" that come with Western morality. For those who have only participated in "traditional sex," notes the author of *Psychedelia Sexualis*, "it will take a great effort not to be shocked by what he reads upon these pages. Remember though that innovations are always shocking. We have long hailed the great scientists and composers and so forth of history," he continues, "but in the most important area of our lives, sex, we have paid very little heed to the heroes and heroines."[26]

The "adults only" novel *Commune Cult* exemplifies this meshing of sexual, occult, and psychedelic Otherness, a deviance that, like the suburban swapping that preceded it, could hide in plain sight in society. The book follows the exploits of a seventeen-year-old runaway as she seeks admittance to an occult organization that "liked their sex and liked their drugs—and had almost perfect license to combine them."[27] As with LaVey's *Satanic Bible*, followers of this commune's mysterious "Dr. Janus" consult "The Book of Shadows," a text imagined by *Commune Cult*'s anonymous author as an index of spiritual promiscuity in the Age of Aquarius, containing "old Zen Buddhist Rites," "American Indian Rites," "a little from the Bible," a section from "the Book of Chairman Mao," and "recipes for everything from LSD brownies to Hashish Hash."[28] Like so many adult paperbacks of the era (and the emerging hardcore cinema), *Commune Cult* stages this young initiate's quest as a series of increasingly "exotic" sexual unions, proceeding from "straight sex" with a recruiter in Greenwich Village, to sex with a warlock sporting a "flayed penis," to sex on acid, to equine bestiality, to a final hallucinatory consummation with Dr. Janus, complete with a ceremonial circle, incense, and, for good satanic measure, a goat tied to a stake. Significantly, this quest for some form of transcendent sex takes place, not in a distant land or secret location, but in the everyday world of American life. For most of the novel, the heroine's sexual instruction proceeds under the supervision of an occultist couple who have "the standard white frame house with a mortgage, two sons of grammar school age, a cat and a couple of dogs—hardly a hint of anything unusual."[29] In the end, the police rescue the young woman from the cult, but she vows to escape her parents and return for more sexual exploration as soon as possible. "They have a lovely world!" she concludes.[30]

Consciously removing themselves from the terrain of middle-class values (if not necessarily middle-class privilege), Satanists and hippies presented a more complicated terrain for sexploitation patrons in negotiating the desires and dangers attending the countercultural promise of absolute sexual liberation. The hippie call for "free love," for example, involved promoting a sexual liberty believed to exist beyond the founding economies of money and morality underpinning the Capitalist institution of marriage—"free" in practice and "free" in cost. For men and women married in the postwar years or earlier who were witnessing the emergence of a more openly sexual generation, removing sex from these larger institutions was no doubt both alluring and frightening.[31] Satanists, meanwhile, promoted a more philosophical, thus more terrifying, form of moral freedom, a creed best encapsulated in Aleister Crowley's pronouncement: "Do what thou wilt shall be the whole of the law."[32] Absolute freedom—be it posed as existential epiphany or simply a chance to tryst with the milkman—carries with it the threat of destroying all that came before it, irrevocably shattering the symbolic (or at least marital) order that had anchored life within "the Establishment." Assuming most consumers of psychedelic and satanic sexploitation were not hippies or Satanists (who, presumably, were too busy having sex and worshipping Satan), the industry's mining of these more transgressive fronts in the sexual revolution required a complex set of conventions to motivate, display, and then ultimately constrain these amoral fantasies of complete sexual liberation. A central challenge for sexploitation and pornography of the era, one addressed in most punitive form in *The Satan Club*, was how to stage these seemingly new, tantalizing, and "forbidden" sexual spectacles without completely dismantling the hierarchies of heteronormative, middle-class, and middle-aged power that had incubated the "sexual revolution" in the first place. How could a desire to see sexual experimentalism be acknowledged—maybe even celebrated in a certain pluralistic spirit—without wholly dissolving the moral agency, social legitimacy, and personal responsibility of the spectator?

In this respect, *Commune Cult's* decidedly unrepentant heroine—de Sade's Juliette as acid freak—is something of an anomaly. In a society that typically frowns (at least putatively) on nonheteronormative, nonmonogamous sexuality, such absolute dedication to sexual, social, spiritual, and pharmaceutical experimentation most often ended in disaster, drawing the forbidden spectacle back to a comforting moral center. By the 1960s mandatory retribution for deviant behavior on screen, once policed in Hollywood by the Production Code and on the exploitation circuit by the "square-up," had become increasingly weak. Yet even with the much-heralded death of the PCA—or more generally, a basic sense of "decency" in American society—the reassertion of a "moral center" remained a fixture even in the most explicit wings of the sexploitation industry. Given the slow death of censorship, the persistence of such moral reaffirmation speaks to the structural need in these fictions to accommodate the sexual tourist spying on these "deviant" fringes of society. MacKensie's fate in *The Satan Club*, for example, is secured from the very first page: he is a murderer. The brutally sadistic sexual scenarios that follow, many of them involving incest and rape, thus appear to issue from his immoral character and not the reader's own prurient interest. Indeed Sathanas, as Satan's surrogate, somewhat ironically becomes the agent of moral justice, the seemingly supernatural tempter transformed, in a stunning last-minute reversal, into the victim who warrants the enacting of extreme justice and retribution. Rather than remain simply an index of sadistic perversions, the novel becomes, in a perfunctory yet crucial final turn, the document of murderous deviance justly punished. MacKensie's "tastes" and transgressions remain comfortably distant from those of the reader. The reader, in turn, can also see what MacKensie cannot: his impending doom.

One reason MacKensie walks blindly into his own personal theater of sexual damnation is that he is high on some form of hallucinogenic "Spanish fly," not acid, but acidlike. The drug famously made its screen debut in William Castle's *The Tingler* in 1959. Given its association with hallucinations and subjective distortion (in the black-and-white *Tingler*, acid allows Vincent Price—and the viewer—to briefly see in color), the drug became a prominent narrative and stylistic device in films, exploitative and otherwise, but appearing especially frequently in satanic smut, psychedelic sexploitation, and their various hybrids. Beyond the famous acid titles such as *The Trip* (1967) and *Psych-Out* (1968), LSD also figures in lesser-known films of the era such as Sam Katzman's *The Love-Ins* (1967), Herschel Gordon Lewis's *Something Weird* (1967), and even Otto Preminger's recently resurgent oddity of 1968, *Skidoo* (featuring the spectacle of Jackie Gleason on acid). By the late 1960s, "Hippie-acid sex" had itself become a prominent subgenre of sexploitation in such titles as *Alice in Acidland* (1969), *Mantis in Lace* (1968), and *The Acid-Eaters* (1968). In many respects, Satan and LSD serve a similar structural function in sexploitation narratives. Both are agents—one occult and one chemical—for dissolving self and responsibility in order to motivate a "sex beyond sex," accelerants for promiscuity and perversity that bid their respective (and often mutual) followers to engage in ever more esoteric and otherwise "altered" sexual practices. "I want more than this," says one acid-tripping young informant for *Psychedelia Sexualis* after a night of group sex, "Isn't there something real wild I can do?" Sure, responds her friend, "take more acid and chase it with an aphrodisiac."[33] Much as acid was thought to "expand the mind," then, it also figured within the world of sexploitation as a means to expand the sensual array and thus achieve some form of sexual innovation or even cosmic eroticism. If alcohol, the traditional lubricant of scandalous intercourse, merely lowered inhibitions to conventional sex, acid inspired one to reimagine the sexual universe in its entirety—as did Satan's orgiastic call for a sex that destroyed all previous boundaries and identities.

This expansion of the mind and the erotic was not without risk. If the sexual and drug undergrounds, by definition, threatened to implode the normative social landscape above, then the revolutionary free-doms promised by satanic psychedelia—cult sex on acid—ultimately demanded some form of confrontation with an absolute moral hori-zon, a line at which these freedoms, perhaps laudable in moderation, simply went too far.[34] Most often, satanic psychedelia's wanton pursuit of altered consciousness, occult power, and expanded sensuality resulted in the erotic, spiritual, or psychotropic adventurer going too "far out" and "losing control," leading either to repentance, self-destruction, or violent retribution. Staged to deliver provocative spectacle, such titles ultimately equated unchecked experimentation with a dangerous disso-lution of self, thereby reaffirming the necessity and imperatives of the spectator's social order. Consider, for example, the familiar convention of the acid "freak-out," most often staged as a threshold event (and in film, a stylistic set-piece) at which this ever-escalating quest for indi-vidual "freedom" (sexual and otherwise) breaks down into asocial ter-ror. Anthony Yewker's paperback *Acid Party* (1969) is typical: a group of LSD revelers engage in trippy sex—only to have one of the group freak-out and commit murder. As so often happens in this genre, no one can remember who the guilty party is—including the murderer! Distrust stalks the survivors (though there are still ample opportunities for sex) until the guilty party is revealed and arrested.[35] There is in this familiar sequence, one might argue, a reversal of Freud's general theory of sexu-ality. Acid returns one to a type of polymorphic perversity, an unstrained and multisensual eroticism that negates both subject and object and so threatens a full retreat into pre-Oedipal psychosis. As so many antidrug films of the era emphasized, LSD mimics the symptoms of a psychotic fit. Acid promised a temporary encounter with the oceanic, but in that surrender to the "oneness" of the universe, it ultimately destroyed the

Fig. 9.2 In her acid-induced frenzy, exotic dancer Lila (Susan Stewart) alternately imagines one of her victims to be a cantaloupe and a piñata as she hacks away at him with a garden hoe in *Mantis in Lace* (1968).

crucial foundations of ego necessary for sex and society to continue. A "community" bound together by acid alone cannot cohere—a point made most forcibly in the 1970 gorefest, *I Drink Your Blood*. Here Satan-worshipping hippies unwittingly infected with rabies make things worse by dropping acid, which quickly proves the accelerant for a night of gruesome attacks and mutilations. To drop acid is to court social alienation unto death (with or without rabies)—thus the genre's emphasis not only on acid's psychotic dissolution of the subject, but also on the later repression, the "blacking out" that further erased the subject from the terrain of social responsibility.

No film presented the "freak-out/blackout" hazard in more elemental form than *Mantis in Lace* (1968; figure 9.2), in which a stripper named Lila lures men back to her apartment, drops acid, and then murders them while in a state of hallucinatory freak-out. In its brutally repetitive structure (strip, seduce, hallucinate, kill, repeat), *Mantis in Lace* rather elegantly condenses the hazards to be found in searching for so-called far out fornication for both the acidhead and the acid voyeur. In a perverse travesty of Laura Mulvey's canonical work on the male gaze, the film stages (and ultimately punishes) all members of the central triangle of scopophilic relay central to Mulvey's thesis: male patron of sexploitation goes to theater to see male patrons on-screen in a strip club looking at strippers; stripper takes man home, drops acid, and then kills him.[36] Lila "the mantis" is arrested. Sexploitation patron returns home rethinking his desire to engage in actual contact with countercultural sexuality. In the end, sociosexual curiosity is indulged, but with the lesson that one should respect certain psychological, sociological, and pharmacological boundaries. There but for a tab of acid go I, one might say.

Tragically, those most likely to freak out and even die from LSD, often by imagining they could fly, were the young, innocent, naive, and stupid. Here appeals to the "generation gap" provided yet another means of insulating sexploitation viewers from the implications of their own spectatorship. Characters such as Dr. Janus appeared frequently in sexploitation of the 1960s—charismatic yet ultimately *suspect* older men who serve as spiritual, sexual, or pharmaceutical guides for their younger and more naive followers. Harvard professor turned LSD advocate Timothy Leary provided the most obvious template for this convention (Janus's commune was, we are told rather legalistically, "like the Timothy Leary group, but with no connection to Leary at all. . . . But wild. And groovy."). Figures such as LaVey and, later, Manson also helped inform the image of the predatory middle-aged Svengali exploiting the innocence of youth, preaching equality and collectivism while in fact solidifying their own fascistic psychosexual power.[37] Such "cult leaders" provided the audience, and in particular middle-aged men, with a unique surrogate in the text—a figure who cultivates titillating access to teenage hippie chicks and yet, in the end, absorbs the spectator's or reader's punishment for indulging in transgenerational sexual exploitation.

As the title suggests, Janus's "Commune Cult" is both a commune and a cult, mixing images of hippie collectivity with messianic authority, implying the two modes of political organization were one in the same, or at least codependent. So widespread was this convention that it became a popular thesis for explaining the countercultural unrest of the 1960s in its entirety, going well beyond the narrow purviews of adult fiction and sexploitation. For example, in Sam Katzman's thinly veiled rendering of the Leary story, *The Love-Ins* (1967), an English professor resigns his post and ends up crashing with a group of hippie-students in Haight-Ashbury. An advocate of free love and LSD, the professor's platitudinous philosophy of peace and harmony makes him a magnet for a new cult, called, conveniently enough, "the Cult." In the end, the professor's call for peace and love becomes little more than an opportunity for more power, fame, and sex with coeds. Anticipating the "important" social commentary of its exploitation cousin, *Wild in the Streets* (1968), *The Love-Ins* ends with the professor martyred by an assassin's bullet, suggesting that his "scam" will continue when a new figurehead emerges. The psychedelic Svengali even became a stock device on television, appearing in perhaps its most allegorical form on NBC's *Star Trek*. In "The Way to Eden," a brilliant scientist preaching a return to pretechnological utopia stops at nothing to take his idealistic young followers to the fabled plant of "Eden." They succeed by hijacking the Enterprise, but in the end discover that the nectar in the planet's otherwise luscious fruit and beautiful vegetation is in fact . . . acid! (not LSD, but actual acid). The fatal discovery is made by a young man named Adam. "His name was Adam," notes Spock for anyone still too stupid to understand the rather ham-handed lesson by the episode's forty-eighth minute.

Locating the perceived "problems" of hippiedom in the vanity, avarice, and "mind-games" of older men provided a convenient way of negotiating countercultural challenges to the older moral order. Peace and love are desirable *in theory*—as is, perhaps, a more enlightened approach to sexuality—but in practice, youthful idealism is an easy target for exploitation by older, wiser, and sleazier men. The "cult" leader, be he satanic or pharmaceutical, demonstrated just how easy the younger generation was to manipulate, or more to the point, seduce—no doubt an appealing fantasy to those "too old" or "too square" to actually dare contact with hippies and "free love." Particularly inventive in negotiating these issues was Troy Conway's adult paperback *The Big Freak-Out* (figure 9.3), one of a series of sexual adventures featuring undercover agent Rod "the Coxeman" Damon. Here a composite of Leary and LaVey known as "The Big Head" presides over a young congregation at the "Church of the Sacred Acid," a "religion" dedicated (like the "Commune Cult") to LSD and "LOVE, LOVE, LOVE." Suspecting the Big Head is behind a plan to take over the U.S. government by spiking the Potomac with LSD, Damon "the Coxeman" is sent to infiltrate the sect. Following the Leary paradigm, both men are professors, and each takes full advantage of the era's sexual and chemical revolutions.

Conway pits the two men against one another as contrasting models of mature masculine professionalism, competency, and potency. The Big Head, we learn, studied "experimental psychology" at Penn and then served in Korea, but was mysteriously discharged (probably under less than "honorable" circumstances). In the early 1960s, the Big Head "was on the faculty of no fewer than six different universities" in five years, "each of lower academic standing than its predecessor." This descent into

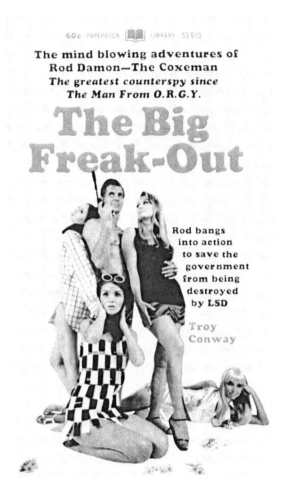

The mind blowing adventures of
Rod Damon—The Coxeman
*The greatest counterspy since
The Man From O.R.G.Y.*

The Big Freak-Out

Rod bangs
into action
to save the
government
from being
destroyed
by LSD

Troy
Conway

Fig. 9.3 Troy Conway's *The Big Freak-Out*: A "mind-blowing" smut paperback trading on James Bond and LSD.

academic oblivion complementing four divorces over the same period, suggests that the Big Head's professional and matrimonial difficulties stemmed from the same cause—sex with students. He is, then, a military, professional, and marital failure—lacking in just about every conventional measure of masculine success. Damon, on the other hand, is a respected sociologist, successful in landing large government grants to research the sexual practices of various subcultures—research that naturally requires him to act as a participant-observer. So accomplished is Damon that the government routinely employs him as a counterspy to infiltrate diverse communities, or as the cover of *The Big Freak-Out* promises: "Rod bangs into action to save the government from being destroyed by LSD." To underscore this contrast in masculine models, the

Big Head, despite his endless talk of "LOVE, LOVE, LOVE," is completely impotent. Damon, on the other hand, boasts a most peculiar form of priapism, one that makes him eternally erect and yet also endlessly orgasmic.

Like *The Man from U.N.C.L.E.* (and its sexploitation echo: *The Man from O.R.G.Y.*), *The Big Freak-Out* operates in the realm of parody and farce. Still, Conway's archly drawn portraits of the impotent Acid-King and the sturdy Coxeman elucidate the complex modes of identification at work within this genre. Building on the already prominent image of the middle-aged wolf among young hippie sheep, the tale promotes a sexual-political economy that demonizes the ambition of one professor while lionizing the prowess of another. The Big Head, in short, is a fraud and a failure—unsuccessful in any endeavor until acid and age gave him an advantage and power over youth (even if, alas, his impotence prevents him from practicing what he preaches). Damon, on the other hand, enjoys the power and prestige of a post-Kinsey sex researcher, succeeding professionally and contributing to a more enlightened sexuality by turning his priapism into a valuable research tool—literally: he "bangs" hippies in the interest of science and in the service of nation, giving him (and the reader) unproblematic access to "free love" while the Big Head's fraudulent scams deflect and absorb the sleazier implications of sexualizing the generation gap.

Before Damon embarks on his mission, his government sponsor issues him several tabs of "LSP," said to be a close chemical cousin of LSD. This "new" hallucinogen offers the additional benefits of making the "trips" shorter in duration, more cognitively lucid, and more intense sexually—qualities that Damon can better integrate into his professional mission of pleasure (he is given the pills so that he might better "fit in" and then ply his hallucinating sexual conquests for information). The drug LSP is obviously a fabrication, and seemingly an unnecessary one. Why the substitution? No doubt the author, like so many others in the psychedelic age, wanted to exploit the potentially positive qualities of LSD while excluding its more negative pharmaceutical and ideological impact. Thus, LSD as a real drug championed by the scummy Big Head is potentially dangerous (leading not only to individual "freak-outs," but the "Big Freak-out" of the title that threatens the government). The imaginary LSP, on the other hand, delivers the same "benefits" but under tighter and thus more desirable control. As the exemplar of appropriate masculine power and sexuality, the Coxeman simply cannot afford to cross the freak-out threshold and all that it implies—sexually, politically, ideologically.

Submit to Me

If the freak-out served as acid fiction's primary device for exploring the tantalizing yet terrifying boundary between personal freedom and social disintegration—a vanishing point where the quest for individual liberty and self-enlightenment crossed over into anarchistic psychosis— occult sexploitation took a somewhat different, though no less damning, approach to staging and then constraining sexual experimentation. As LaVey so often reminded the public, Satanism was a religion of *power* and *will*, witchcraft a practice of *spells* and *curses*. Accordingly, occult sexploitation most typically involved perverse scenarios of *sexual domination*, either in mind or body (or both), of unwitting subjects placed under occult control. As a pornographic plot device, such control has advantages. Once under this invisible influence, otherwise "straight" subjects could be compelled into group sex, fetishism, bestiality, and homosexuality. Most often, invoking the supernatural for sexual thrills ended in the sexual explorer's final and ultimate subjugation to an occult overload. Unlike the acid freak-out, however, which typically played as a serious danger (due to the reality of "bad trips" acknowledged even among LSD enthusiasts), occult enslavement could be handled as either a terrifying threat (more often in horror proper) or as a type of playful parable.[38] Doris Wishman's *Indecent Desires* (1968), for example, employs a type of sexual "voodoo" for laughs—a young woman unwittingly put under the control of a creep who finds some type of magical Barbie doll in a trash can. In *The Acid-Eaters* (1968), the eponymous cast arrives at their cultish alter—a gigantic cube of LSD in the desert—only to find themselves trapped in hell and menaced by Satan (or at least a man in a rented devil costume brandishing a pitchfork—with sugar cubes on its prongs, no less). In *Wanda the Sadistic Hypnotist* (1969; figure 9.4), finally, Wanda uses her occult powers of hypnotism to compel those around her to perform various forms of sexual theater, transforming an Avon lady into a burlesque stripper and a lesbian into a heteronymphomaniac. Hypnotism—as a "drug-free" form of altered consciousness (with its own tradition of occult and sexual associations going back to its founder, Franz Mesmer)—provided another popular way of staging illicit eroticism, "latent" sexual desires given expression by the power of the hypnotist's external will.[39] For good measure, *Wanda* ends with an elaborate LSD orgy and the strangely reflexive turn in which Wanda herself ensnares a movie patron attending a screening of . . . *Wanda the Sadistic Hypnotist*. Having been lured into a life of depravity, these characters are in various ways threatened with some form of enslavement—

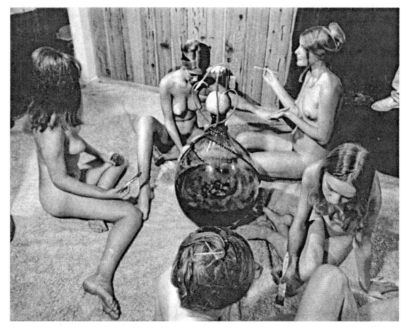

Fig. 9.4 *Wanda the Sadistic Hypnotist* (1969) was one of many "adult" films in the late 1960s and early 1970s to use varying combinations of acid and "witchcraft" as a logic for staging exoticized erotic displays.

humorous, perhaps, but enslavement nonetheless. Indeed, it is difficult to imagine a more pronounced master/slave relationship than Satan and his minions, the *occultist* and his or her *cult*. The Black Mass, in particular, is replete with sadomasochistic props and icons, especially as imagined by the many filmmakers who have consistently staged this ritual as unfolding in a kind of S/M dungeon.[40]

Whether played straight or for laughs, both the acid freak-out and occult enslavement speak to a changing historical relationship between self, sexuality, and responsibility, a triangular relationship thought by many in the 1960s and 1970s to be in a state of crisis. As emblems of a *counter* culture, acid and Satan each promised rewards for removing oneself from Established society, either by expanding consciousness or increasing one's personal potential for domination. In that "trip" elsewhere, however, both agents also threatened a final horizon, a threshold that if crossed might forever remove one from the human community. Linked as strategies for first motivating exotic spectacle but then ultimately constraining a wholly open play of fantasy, LSD and Satan differed greatly in the ultimate implications of their danger. Often exploited by cultist elders, responsible adults who should know better, the "acid casualty" stumbles in the perhaps noble quest to see beyond, to transcend the mundane materiality of the world. Some psychedelic enthusiasts even claimed that the drug allowed them to see the face of God. The acid freak-out, however, ultimately disintegrated this explorer's will and ego, removing him or her from the social world by "blowing the mind"—permanently. The cautionary lesson here is not unlike the myth of Icarus, a warning to take care in exploring higher sensual and metaphysical knowledge lest one crash back down to earth. Occult enslavement, on the other hand, presents a more fearsome punishment for a more wicked transgression. Self-absorbed, self-interested, and self-indulgent, the Satanists willingly sell their souls, not for transcendental enlightenment, but for the most base and selfish of pleasures and powers. Worse yet, they do so of their own *free will*. "I would do anything for a good piece of ass," says a randy housewife in *The Lucifers*, "even sell my soul to the Devil." Her wish, of course, comes true immediately.

No doubt moral conservatives could cite such low humor as evidence of just how toothless Satan has become in the era of secularization, little more than a prankster at a cocktail party symbolizing a universal desire to get laid. The humor here, however, might also serve as a clue as to just how profoundly serious "occult enslavement" actually is. Behind this rather ridiculous "joke," so widely circulated in Western culture, is perhaps nothing less than the essence of religion itself. Even in its most comic renderings, occult sexploitation presents a quite literal and direct call to return to the demonic mysteries that preceded the ethical foundations of the Western subject, to return once again to a Dionysian realm that violates the lines between the human, the animal, and the divine (a call echoed in the frequent obsession with bestiality on the part of satanic sexploitation, a perversion dating back to the days when the Greek gods would have sex with anyone or anything!). Having made a bargain for the woman in search of "a piece of ass," the Satan of *The Lucifers* next offers a night of sex to an impotent man. "Render up your eternal soul to me. Is it a deal?" asks the devil. "Yeah. What the fuck. Why not?" responds the man. Again, the exchange is funny because it must be: the stakes of occult sex, if confronted directly, are simply too high to risk, even acknowledge. Christianity is a zero-sum game. Accepting Satan's offer, or even requesting an audience with him, can only lead to disaster. If he actually appears at your invocation, grants your wish, you are now in league with Satan, complicit in his power; if he does not, there remains the lingering anxiety that even the request, though unanswered, may itself have led to eternal damnation. This is a damnation before *the eyes of God*—whose all-powerful gaze penetrates every atom of Creation—a gaze, moreover, that extends beyond the characters in a film or book to the reader himself. Curled up on your couch with a paperback, locked in your car at the drive-in, or slumping down in the last row of a grimy grind house, there is no escaping His omnipotent vision, the universal eye of the numinous. Here Satan stands apart from the usual menagerie of movie "monsters": the vampires, Frankensteins, werewolves, zombies, aliens, and psychotics that have become the staples of popular horror (and at times, pornography as well). Those creatures emerged either from now quaint European folklore or a fearful topicality that eventually wanes in its sensationalist impact. Lucifer, on the other hand, is underwritten by faith and a belief in things unseen, both sublime and terrible. To "accept" him, to invoke him in achieving worldly power (even if only to get laid for a night), is to accept the entire mythology that produced him in the first place, and by so doing, knowingly relegating oneself to inevitable damnation. Satanic sex thus offers the promise of absolute liberation in return for absolute subjugation, ripping up an internalized social and moral contract and replacing it with one signed in blood, ultimately reaffirming the Law of man, God, and the unconscious. That temptation and unlawful pleasure remain so alluring necessitates the comedy, a disavowal of one's complete subservience to both the explicit codes of "normality" and the internal guilt of religious inculcation. Put simply, only a masochist would join "the Satan Club"— a metaphysical masochist hoping to invoke the pain and humiliation of absolute, eternal abjection. Behind the humor, there lurks within occult sexploitation a haunting suspicion that satanic sex is indeed the most "far out" of all the sexual undergrounds—so *underground*, in fact, that it leads all the way down to hell.

Notes

I would like to thank David Gurney for his research assistance.

1. A. DeGranamour, *The Satan Club* (New York: Bee-line Books, 1970), 73.
2. DeGranamour, *The Satan Club*, 152.
3. See Sigmund Freud, *Civilization and Its Discontents*, trans. Jean Riviere (New York: J. Cape & H. Smith, Standard Edition 1930).
4. J. K. Huysmans, *La-Bas*, trans. Keene Wallace (New York: Dover Publications, 1972), 248–251.
5. A lapsed Catholic and vocal atheist, Huysman returned to the church most devoutly shortly after writing *La Bas*.

6. Quoted in Earl C. Gottschalk Jr., "It's Finally True: Movies Are Going Straight to the Devil," *Wall Street Journal*, October 25, 1976, 1+.

7. Quoted in Gottschalk, "It's Finally True," 19.

8. C. S. Lovett, *Help Lord–The Devil Wants Me Fat!* (Baldwin Park, CA: Personal Christianity, 1977), 50–54.

9. Earlier in his career, Wood had also written the script, such that it was, for the occult-burlesque film *Orgy of the Dead* (1965), in which dead strippers seal their fate in either heaven or hell by appeasing the TV psychic Criswell with their erotic dancing.

10. LaVey quoted in Lyons, *The Second Coming: Satanism in America* (New York: Award Books, 1970), 7.

11. See Bethan Benwell, *Masculinity and Men's Lifestyle Magazines* (London: Blackwell, 2003), 78.

12. Pitirim A. Sorokin, *The American Sex Revolution* (Boston: Portor Sargent, 1956), 14.

13. Edwin M. Schur, "Social Science and the Sexual Revolution," in *The Family and the Sexual Revolution*, ed. Edwin M. Schur (Bloomington: Indiana University Press, 1964), 3.

14. Schur, "Social Science and the Sexual Revolution," 5. Schur refers here to Walter Lippman's *A Preface to Morals* (New York: Macmillan, 1929).

15. For her account of this performance, see Susan Atkins, *Child of Satan, Child of God* (Plainfield, NJ: Logos International, 1977), 55–56.

16. "Priest of Satan Performs S.F. Marriage," *Los Angeles Times*, February 2, 1967, 3.

17. Lyons, *The Second Coming: Satanism in America*, 190.

18. Lyons, *The Second Coming: Satanism in America*, 187.

19. Anton Szandor LaVey, *The Compleat Witch* (Los Angeles: Feral House, 1989), vii. The book was later retitled *The Satanic Witch*.

20. In a wonderful historical accident, the print ad for LaVey's book (subtitled, in a nod to de Sade, *What to Do When Virtue Fails*) appeared in the *New York Times* adjacent to an ad for an etiquette book by the editors of *Seventeen* magazine ("Wherever she goes she will be "in the know" proclaims their ad), demonstrating, if nothing else, that there has never been a shortage of books telling young women how to behave, be it in the pursuit of "virtue" or "vice." See ad art and copy, *New York Times*, February 7, 1971, 33.

21. John M. Crewdson, "How California Has Become Home for a Plethora of Cults," *New York Times*, November 30, 1978, A18.

22. Schaefer, "Pandering to the 'Goon Trade,': Framing the Sexploitation Audience through Advertising," in *Sleaze Artists: Cinema at the Margins of Taste, Style, and Politics*, ed. Jeffrey Sconce, 19–46 (Durham, NC: Duke University Press, 2007), 29.

23. For an overview of this era, see Brittany A. Daley, Hedi El Kholti, Earl Kemp, Miriam Linna, and Adam Parfrey, *Sin-A-Rama: Sleaze Sex Paperbacks of the Sixties* (Los Angeles: Feral House, 2005).

24. Elaine Tyler May discusses the links posited between Communists and secret

sexuality in her chapter "Explosive Issues: Sex, Women, and the Bomb," in *Homeward Bound: American Families in the Cold War Era* (New York, Basic Books, 1988), 80–99.

25. Schaefer, "Pandering to the 'Goon Trade,'" 29.

26. Jonathan H. Giles, *Psychedelia Sexualis: Sexual Turn-ons — 1970s Style* (Libertyville, IL: Oligarch Publishing, 1969), 13.

27. Anonymous, *Commune Cult* (n.p., n.d.), 12.

28. *Commune Cult*, 35–36.

29. *Commune Cult*, 34.

30. *Commune Cult*, 60. A very similar "induction" plot can be found in *Sexual Satanic Awareness* (1972), a hardcore feature directed by Ray Dennis Steckler. Although best known for his "camp" titles such as *Wild Guitar* (1962) and *The Incredibly Strange Creatures Who Stopped Living and Became Mixed-Up Zombies!!?* (1964), Steckler went on to direct and star in a series of occult sexploitation pictures, including *Sinthia: The Devil's Doll* (1970), *Sacrilege* (1971), and *Sexorcist Devil* (1974).

31. Hollywood had begun exploring these ambivalences in a number of high-profile sex farces of the early 1960s. *Boys' Night Out* (1962) is particularly emblematic.

32. In using this phrase, Crowley built on the eighteenth-century British tradition of "Hellfire Clubs," which in turn took their inspiration from François Rabelais's Abby of Thélème in *Gargantua*.

33. Sexuality, asserts the study's author (purportedly a young sociologist who submitted this material as a dissertation "far too hot for his college"), depends on a dynamic of habit and individual personality. "This is why new things are constantly being thought up . . . by the psychedelics all over the country. Individual personalities have individual imaginations and they come up with individual variations and sexual themes." See Giles, *Psychedelia Sexualis*, 54–55.

34. Even LaVey referred to Satanism as "hedonism with control." See Brian Vachon, "Witches are Rising," *Look*, August 24, 1971, 40.

35. Anthony Yewker, *Acid Party* (N.p.: Bell House Classics, 1969).

36. See Laura Mulvey, "Visual Pleasure and Narrative Cinema," *Screen* 16, no. 3 (autumn 1975): 6–18.

37. For a more detailed discussion of Manson's place in sexual discourse of the early 1970s, see Sconce, "XXX: Love and Kisses from Charlie," in *Swinging Single: Representing Sexuality in the 1960s*, ed. Hilary Radner and Moya Luckett (Minneapolis: University of Minnesota Press, 1999), 207–226.

38. Most notorious was the death by defenestration of Art Linkletter's daughter, Diane, on October 6, 1969, an event memorialized by John Waters and Divine in their early short subject, *The Diane Linkletter Story* (1969).

39. Such a scheme also provides the central plot of *The Love Cult* (1966).

40. Consciously or not, pornographers of the era exploited the occult's general foundations in the psychic mechanisms of sadomasochism, making the black

leather bustier—accessorized with whips and chains—the costume of choice in photo spreads of sexual witchcraft, a form of feminine magic that most often seems to have centered on disciplining men kept under restraint. Playing on this fantasy, LaVey opens *The Compleat Witch* with a *Cosmo*-like "Test of the Thirteen Factors," asking potential witches such diagnostic questions as "Is black your favorite color? Have you ever been considered 'cheap?' Do you often wear undergarments that are black in color or of a flashy nature?" LaVey, *The Compleat Witch*, 1–2.

Part IV: Going All the Way

10 * The "Sexarama": Or Sex Education as an Environmental Multimedia Experience

EITHNE JOHNSON

One important class of experiential products will be based on simulated environments that offer the customer a taste of adventure, danger, and sexual titillation or other pleasure without risk to his real life or reputation.
ALVIN TOFFLER, *Future Shock*, 228.

In the 1960s, much was made of the potential for combining audiovisual technologies in order to stimulate the senses within what were referred to as environmental forms of exhibition. While the space program was concerned with sensory exposure under extreme conditions, IBM, Bell Labs, Disney, and other corporations were invested in the commercial potential of sensory effects. Indeed, the potential for media, in the widest sense, to transform humanity was hotly debated, much as society was reimagined in terms relevant to the ascendant discourses of communications and cybernetics. Marshall McLuhan famously theorized that every medium represented an "extension of man"; by shifting attention away from content, it was possible to hypothesize that audiovisual technologies could have specific effects on the human sensorium in relation to their environmental forms—that is, the ways in which they were installed or exhibited.[1] Of course the movie theater already offered its audiences a particular environmental experience. Considering the spatial models that preceded it, Anne Friedberg observes that the cinema emerged from the "panorama and the diorama," which were "building-machines . . . designed to *transport*—rather than to *confine*."[2] The cinema's theatrical environment offered its patrons a metaphoric journey simulating the escape from confinement. But in the 1960s, some saw the traditional movie theater as stultifying. As Gene Youngblood put it, the "popular media" had "dulled" people's senses because "commercial entertainment" was merely "a system of temporarily gratifying, without really fulfilling, the experiential needs of an aesthetically impoverished culture."[3] Drawing on cybernetic-communications theories, as did McLuhan and Toffler, Youngblood anticipated a new media synthesis that would provide aesthetically richer sensory experiences. At the same time, new "building machines" were equipped to project simultaneous or multiply timed films and slide shows onto large-scale screens, panoramic screens, or both, which were designed to surround the participants and seemingly transport them into exciting new spaces, identified as "simulated" or "immersive" environments.

As Toffler noted in *Future Shock*, immersive installations, commonly called "multimedia," combined media technologies that were "devoted to the creation or staging of specialized psychological experiences."[4] In 1966, one of the most recognizable artists in the United States was identified with producing "multimedia" events: "A touring unit, created by Pop Artist Andy Warhol and equipped with movie projectors and musicians has been playing Los Angeles before moving on to San Francisco."[5] Warhol was already notorious for making sexually oriented films such as *Blow Job* (1964), in his "Factory" studio in Manhattan, and now he was creating sensory-rich environments at off-site locations. Toffler also described "fun palaces" as immersive spaces where "the patron steps inside a work of kinetic art."[6] Industry-sponsored attractions at Disneyland and the Expo 1967 in Montreal invited visitors into exhibits combining sound and image, promising sensory excitement as well as product promotion. In the fields of business and education, the term "multimedia" typically referred to presentations that used film, slide shows, or a combination of both and that temporarily transformed offices and classrooms into potentially eventful spaces.

Given this historical context, it is not surprising that environmental exhibition techniques promising immersive experiences would strike some as the future for sex education. Multimedia installations organized to excite the senses would be articulated as a means to enhance participants' knowledge of sexuality and to explore their sexual potential. Here I'll examine how this theory was put into practice by the National Sex Forum (NSF) in what it officially called the SAR, an acronym that refers both to "Sexual Attitude Reassessment" and "Sexual Attitude Restructuring."[7] Originally known as the National Drug and Sex Forum, the idea for the NSF as a provider of sex education and "innovative training materials" started at the Institute for Sex Research in Bloomington, Indiana, and it "began officially in October 1968, as part of the Glide Urban Center," a foundation based in San Francisco.[8] Through the work of its founders, Ted McIlvenna and Laird Sutton, and associates, Marguerite Rubenstein, Loretta Haroian, and Phyllis Lyon, the NSF created its multimedia SAR method of sex education, amassed an archive, launched a media distribution division (Multi Media Resource Center [MMRC]), and became a producer of what it identified as erotic films.[9] In 1976, the NSF was converted into the Institute for the Advanced Study of Human Sexuality (IASHS).

Publications by both the Glide Foundation and the NSF not only make a compelling case for sex education, but also provide empirical evidence that the NSF's associates and supporters were engaged in the productive "prurience" that Thomas Waugh finds in Alfred Kinsey's practice of sexual science manifested in his desire to collect sexually explicit materials and to film sex acts.[10] The NSF's immersive multimedia SAR method of sexual consciousness-raising continues to be included in the IASHS curriculum, though its peak circulation on college campuses has long passed. Nevertheless, it was an important precursor to the feminist-identified "antipornography" and "pro-sex" presentations that proliferated in its wake, both in its deployment of sights and sounds that were identified as dangerous or titillating, particularly for women, and in the popularization of assumptions from behavioral psychotherapy about how exposure to pornographic or erotic stimulation could be channeled to change people's beliefs and behaviors.[11]

Sensory Stimulation Techniques for Entertainment, Therapy, and Education

Environmental multimedia forms of entertainment typically promised to saturate or bombard the participants' senses to presumably pleasurable ends. In 1966 *Life* magazine offered ironic commentary on this new "madness" at nightclubs: "To enjoy the latest thing in discothèques, you had better wear ear plugs, dark glasses and shin guards. Otherwise, you may be deafened, blinded and bruised in an electronic earthquake that engulfs you completely in an experience called 'total recreation.'"[12] Although Toffler warned against the shock effects of sensory stress (i.e., "information overload") brought on by increased exposure to communications media as well as to the reflexivity of cybernetic systems, he nevertheless predicted that the expanding "experience industries" would aim for beneficial effects on the human sensorium through targeted approaches to "psychic gratification."[13] Within the context of this popularization of immersive multimedia as well as the proliferation of new portable media technologies, self-identified sex researchers, sex therapists, and sex educators eagerly explored the premise that sensations could be manipulated and refined for improved psychological health, sensual pleasure, and satisfactory orgasmic performance.[14] In the class-room, exposure to sexually explicit materials was intended to produce health professionals who would be more aware of the range of human physical traits and sexual behaviors.

In *Future Shock*, Toffler described a novel example of an immersive multimedia entertainment that cocooned patrons in a luxuriously out-fitted sensory environment: the "Cerebrum" was "an 'electronic studio of participation' where, for an hourly fee, guests . . . strip off their clothing, don semi-transparent robes, and sprawl comfortably on richly padded white platforms"; each guest was given "a stereophonic headset [and] a see-through mask." While projected slides and light shows stimulate the eyes, "folk and rock music, interspersed with snatches of television commercials, street noises and lecture by or about Marshall McLuhan fill the ears."[15] Whether or not the Cerebrum rocked anyone's psyche, Toffler linked it with what he considered the new gratification-oriented economy. Referring to the productive flow of ideas between the counter-culture or avant-garde and corporate capitalism, he drew comparisons between Club Med, which started as a members-only nonprofit holiday club and became a hugely profitable brand-name resort, and the Esalen Institute, which gained recognition for popularizing the "human poten-tial movement." At its Big Sur, California, location, Esalen originated the "encounter group," encouraged meditation and bodywork, and inspired the growth of psychotherapies as well as the concept of the therapeu-tic spa.[16] Up the coast in San Francisco, the NSF attracted people who shared Esalen's commitment to exploring human potential through eclectic methodologies as well as the presumed health benefits of soak-ing in hot water. Returning to Toffler's argument, all-inclusive vacation clubs and self-actualization organizations can both be seen as symptom-atic of the "psychologization" that accompanies an "economy geared to the provision of psychic gratification."[17] Also referring to Esalen's influ-ence, Janice Irvine states that the NSF's institutional discourse aimed to give all people "permission to recognize and feel their own sexuality."[18] This perspective was too radical to some of those who had brought the NSF into existence, and, according to its website, its financial survival in the early 1970s hinged on removing its affiliation with its churches.[19] But even after the NSF modified the word "sex" in its name and became the Institute for the Advanced Study of Human Sexuality, it quickly ac-quired new naughty nicknames—"Hot Tub University" and "Fuck U."[20] This hints at the tricky relationship between psychic gratification and physical gratification that exists at the foundation of behavioral psycho-therapy and its techniques for sensory experiences—that is, their potential to be identified by others as pornographic education and a rationale for openly recreational sex.

In his critical history of psychology, Morton Hunt argues that the discipline "was not originally an applied science, and its training centers produced not 'health care providers' but researchers and theorists. . . . By the 1970s, however, psychology was growing not as a pure science but as several forms of applied science, of which health care was by far and away the largest."[21] The practice of behavioral psychotherapy "increased geometrically" after South African researcher Joseph Wolpe relocated to the United States, and his "method of 'reciprocal inhibition' or 'desensitization'" was incorporated into both training and treatment programs.[22] Compared to environmental multimedia entertainments designed to bombard the senses, Wolpe's method of behavioral therapy took a more controlled approach to sensory manipulation: a "structured" experience directed by the therapist. Although William Masters and Virginia Johnson did not credit behavioral psychotherapy, their "structured" program for treating sexual dysfunction in married couples was implicitly indebted to that applied model of desensitization (Hunt, 576).[23] Hunt states that desensitization therapy follows these steps, derived from laboratory experiments with animals: (1) "induce a pleasant trancelike state," (2) "link its agreeable feelings by associative training with the fear-inducing stimulus," and (3) "thereby overcome the fear" (Hunt, 573). Wolpe's influential treatment technique was organized around exposure to a feared object through a "series of scenes" that required participation by therapist and patient (Hunt, 573, 575).

For example, to treat a woman suffering from "frigidity," whose "anxiety was triggered by situations involving the sight or touch of a penis, which she found revolting," Wolpe directed her through a structured desensitization in which the woman, her husband, her hand, and his penis all became objects that she could learn to control within her imagination (Hunt, 574–575). Like a slide show, this narrative was sequential: it began with a scene in which the woman saw a "nude male statue in a park thirty feet away"; then "a series of scenes in which she imagined herself [in] the bedroom, seeing her husband's penis from a distance of fifteen feet"; then gradually moving closer, until she could touch it without anxiety, until "by about the 20th session she reported that she was enjoying sexual relations with her husband and having orgasm about half the time" (Hunt, 575). Wolpe's frightened patient was reportedly desensitized—her fear mitigated—through imagined exposure to sexually explicit scenes that sequentially intensified her relationship to the specific object both in treatment and through private practice with her husband at home. As a result, she experienced what other therapy practitioners would term a "resensitization," becoming positively excited by seeing the previously "revolting" penis.

This notion was not new, but it was articulated through a contemporary scientific discourse that could be traced to the postwar significance of the concepts of feedback and reflexivity as articulated by theorists of cybernetics and communications. Looking farther back into the interest of Western culture in the "eroticization of the senses," Paula Findlen finds an intriguing example in the literary pornography of Pietro Aretino's *Ragionamenti* (1534–1536): the heroine, Nanna, encounters an "erotic panopticon" through which she "is initiated into the pleasures of sex by observing different images of couplings decorating the walls of the monastery and by watching others through various peepholes." Suddenly sensitized after spying on these displays, Nanna becomes "susceptible to every sight, sound, and smell she encounters." Organized around imagining sequentially intensified sexual encounters, behavioral psychotherapy's structured treatment design promised to deliver its own "eroticization of the senses." Wolpe's method also resulted in a female subject who could, as Findlen describes the successful outcome of Nanna's sex education, be a "manipulator of the pornographic gaze."[24] Although Wolpe apparently relied on his patients' imaginations to provide the sexual imagery, some enterprising sex researchers, therapists, and educators would soon incorporate sexually explicit media into their treatment and training programs. Going beyond individual therapy sessions and imagined sex acts, they would draw on the popularity of environmental entertainment and would include college students as participants.

In their teacher's guide for his textbook *Becoming a Sexual Person*, Robert Francoeur and Linda Hendrixson credit Indiana University professor Edward Tyler as the first educator to apply behavioral psychotherapy techniques to sex education through a multimedia installation in 1968: "Knowing the resistance of the medical students, Tyler knew he would have to desensitize, break down anxiety, and overcome inhibitions. Tyler decided on sensory overload with several hour-long sessions of explicit films, often shown simultaneously, each followed by intense but relaxed small group discussions with trained leaders."[25] For films, Tyler had an archive within reach at the Kinsey Institute. As to Tyler's inspiration for multiscreen projections, he would probably have been aware of this technique from the national coverage of multimedia events by Warhol and others. Tyler may also have heard about movie marathons, which offered audiences longer-than-normal viewing experiences.[26] Like corporate environmental entertainments, movie marathons, "midnight movies," and "underground" screenings were perceived as exciting sensory experiences. Unlike corporate-sponsored entertainments, the rules governing audience behavior could be looser during these alternative screenings. Underground programs were also notorious for showing films that were more sexually explicit.[27] As described in Tyler's classroom, this technique of combining the structure of behavioral psychotherapy's treatment—desensitization followed by resensitization—with the technique of multiply projected sexually explicit films running for longer-than-normal times resulted in a new method of sex education that subjected its participants to a unique experience in sensory bombardment.

Given the increase in college enrollments as well as the expansion of youth cultures, Toffler predicted that education, "already exploding in size, will become one of the key experience industries as it begins to employ experiential techniques to convey both knowledge and values to students."[28] Tyler's method of multimedia sex education for medical students spread from Indiana University to other institutions, with medical and health science classrooms typically serving as the environments for what were also known as "saturation" sessions or workshops. Journalist Phil Tracy explained in 1970 that this type of sex education was intended to allow individuals to have "meaningful exposure to a realistic objectification of the range of behavior into which their own experiences and those of other humans fall."[29] As the inherently dramatic narrative of desensitization and resensitization became culturally significant, the supposed effects—positive or negative, as defined in binary terms—of exposure to sexually explicit media would serve as justifications for governmental and institutional funding. Before long, however, desensitization would also be used to mean a detrimental numbing effect and objectification would be narrowly defined to refer to an act of representational violence, typically by men against women, especially in relation to pornography after it became more widely available in a variety of settings. Specifically, in arguments against sexually explicit imagery in pornography (as well as advertising), desensitization and its process of objectification would no longer be understood by some as a necessary step in the education or refinement of the senses, serving to make them more receptive to stimulation as well as more perceptive about the means of stimulation. But back in the late 1960s, those were the prosocial objectives of the NSF when creating the multimedia Sexarama and its roadshow workshops, designed especially to teach the "flower generation" about sex.[30]

Environmental Multimedia Sex Education

In a 1970 interview, Ted McIlvenna explained the NSF's institutional mission: "While Masters and Johnson are doing some individual counseling, nobody has set up a full-time realistic sex education program."[31] According to the coauthors of the NSF's *SARGuide*, "McIlvenna and his staff began experimenting with a methodology that would help professionals grasp a broader view of human sexuality. The answer seemed to lie in the use of sexually explicit films and slides."[32] The *SARGuide* claimed that the SAR workshop was "one of the most revolutionary methods ever designed for educating adults about what people do sexually and how they feel about it."[33] At the time, a multimedia method may have seemed more realistic to the NSF associates because, as Francoeur explained in 1977, the "technique recognizes the dependence of today's youth on the visual image, and the need for sex-positive comfortable educators who are not embarrassed by any aspect of human sexual behavior."[34] Although one approach to a sensory-stimulating environment was to cocoon each participant in a private mediated experience, as with the Cerebrum, the NSF's SAR was organized around sensory bombardment of a group of participants; in this way, it was more like a cross between a multimedia event and a movie marathon at which everyone is exposed to the same stimuli.

In addition to focusing on collective consciousness-raising, the NSF's associates would make their mark in the discipline of sexology by taking a countercultural position in relation to Masters and Johnson, who dominated sex research at the time with their focus on "structured" private therapy sessions. Furthermore, in contrast to Masters and Johnson's concentration on heterosexuality, the NSF associates would promote Kinsey's spectrum theory of sexuality. According to Irvine, when it started at the Glide Urban Center the NSF was "originally committed to work in the gay community."[35] It soon expanded its scope by focusing on what it claimed as healthful aspects of sexuality rather than on sexual dysfunction: the NSF's "founders coined what could be the slogan for humanistic sexology as a whole: 'We believe it is time to say "yes" to sex.'"[36] They were skeptical about what advice doctors could offer, due to traditional curricula for medical training programs. As McIlvenna said in 1970: "Physicians are practically as ignorant about what people actually do in bed as is the general public."[37] Therefore, from the NSF's perspective, the SAR was a "logical progression in the history of the field of sex education."[38] Resisting the warnings of Masters and Johnson against using media "crutches" and their narrow definition of heterosexuality, the NSF discourse championed the idea that exposure to sexually explicit media could liberate audiences from ignorance about what naked humans look like and how they perform sex acts.[39] It also attempted to promote potential pleasures that might arise while seeing and hearing sexual material in an environment that was designed to be both comfortable, as in recreation rooms, and immersive, as in total sensory entertainments.

According to the Glide Foundation's report for the President's Commission on Obscenity and Pornography, the NSF gathered an "interdisciplinary group of 20 professionals" to study a variety of "materials and procedures" in the process of developing the SAR.[40] The NSF encouraged academic health professionals and community activists to share ideas about sexually explicit materials, a partnering that might have been more culturally resonant in San Francisco, where bookstores and movie theaters were also bringing pornographic materials to the public. The report stated that during the investigation process, "it was immediately evident that the persons attending our first experimental training sessions were far more interested in graphic sexual materials than in the traditional sex education materials."[41] They were, apparently, an audience primed for such excitement. The commitment of this eclectic group to its task points to the interdisciplinary character of sexology in the late 1960s. As Irvine explains, the discipline soon began to split between the scientific sexologists, exemplified by Masters and Johnson, and the humanistic sexologists, such as those affiliated with the NSF.[42]

According to Irvine, the difference between humanistic and scientific sexologists is also evident in their media productions: in contrast to scientific sexology's modernist preference for "dense, complex textbooks, replete with charts, graphs, and anatomical drawings," humanistic sexologists are open to representations "that tend to be visually aesthetic rather than anatomically accurate." Moreover, "when humanistic sexologists want to impart information, they attempt to embed it in an experiential exercise, since they believe that people will more readily grasp and integrate it."[43] Determined to expose themselves to a wide range of sexual materials in the service of creating their own experiential exercise, the NSF's group poured over thousands of photographs and "looked at more than 5,000 films" as well as many art books and "slides of erotic art objects." Some material would likely have been considered obscene in other contexts. Attentive to aural sensations, they listened to tapes of "music, poetry, lectures, [and] sounds of people engaging in sexual relations"; and they tested "small group discussions with persons reacting to the shared experience of looking at erotic materials"[44]

In short, they educated themselves as self-selected volunteers in their own desensitization-resensitization sessions, becoming self-proclaimed experts—perhaps even fans—of sexually explicit media. Through their seemingly exhaustive and perhaps stimulating research, the group arrived at what they called "a unique environmental approach . . . using a variety of multimedia methods involving multiple projection, light, sound, and tactile environments which facilitate both information-giving and feeling-response" (Glide Foundation, 355).

Having selected the materials, the NSF then developed a "specially designed Awareness Room" at its headquarters with an operator's "control booth" facilitating "use of 26 pieces of equipment at the same time" (ibid., 357). This unique building-machine was designed to stimulate the senses through the technique of saturation/bombardment. For *Commonweal* in 1970, Tracy observed that this "specially-designed 'awareness room,' . . . contains soft rugs, large pillows and . . . waterbed. The walls are sculptured and have a projection-surface quality. At any one time several things are going on at once."[45] Explaining the SAR to the readers of the adult magazine, *Oui*, Edward Brecher credited McIlvenna with understanding "that effective sex education required much more than merely increasing a student's store of knowledge. Sexual feelings, attitudes, and bodily responses must also be affected."[46] Whether understood as a psychological process of attitude "reassessment" or a "restructuring" of one's preconceived notions, the SAR's form borrowed from behavioral psychotherapy's method of the structured treatment program. Instead of deploying imaginary scenes in a controlled sequence exclusive to therapist and patient, the SAR immersed groups of people in what resembled a total recreational environment that could be rationalized in terms of humanistic sexology's emphasis on experiential learning.

Indeed, the NSF's Sexarama offered audiences the opportunity to be exposed to sexually explicit materials in a socially "clean" environment, without having to set foot in a "dirty" bookstore or theater specializing in pornographic movies. According to the Glide Foundation's report, the NSF also "design[ed] training events to fit the participants" who could not come to San Francisco for the full SAR workshop in the Awareness Room.[47] To make off-site exhibition possible, the NSF created its own Multi Media Resource Center to distribute SAR workshops as well as other media productions by artists, therapists, and its own production team, headed by its cofounder Laird Sutton as media director. Because it could be packaged in different components, a SAR workshop could last from several hours up to "two to six days," depending on the site and the exhibitor's intent.[48] Sketching a general description of these events,

Irvine writes, "The SAR format is a marathon. Participants gather in a room for twelve or more hours . . . and watch explicit sex films. They usually sit on the floor on large, fluffy pillows, in the stereotypic marathon fashion, and are surrounded by screens. Often several films run simultaneously."[49] Pushing the boundaries of what could be exhibited in art house movie theaters (though not in private shows, such as stag parties or exclusive events at Warhol's Factory) the Sexarama included films on "heterosexual intercourse, male and female masturbation, lesbian and gay male sex, and occasionally 'paraphilia' (bestiality or sadomasochism) . . . also short humorous films."[50] Taking a pragmatic view of the SAR's use of commercial pornography at the time, the NSF's Maggi Rubenstein observed,

> It *is* the way that people get information, a lot of people can't afford to go to counseling or come to workshops and may instead go to watch a film, or may go to a theater. At least they see, well it may be exaggerated, as all films are, larger than life and more gorgeous than life, but it does show what people do, sexually. So it does have benefit.[51]

Because the NSF's institutional intent was to deploy the "visual impact of movies and television" to saturate participants' senses, the SAR was part of what they took to be the logical progression in sex education from print media to a multimediated environment. Perhaps more important, the SAR was designed to teach its audiences how to distinguish between erotic and pornographic audiovisual materials.

Desensitizing with Pornography, Resensitizing with Erotica and the Need for New Sex Films

Masters and Johnson's first book, *Human Sexual Response*, published in 1966, revealed that they had filmed their research participants, reportedly focusing on physiological evidence of responsiveness.[52] Although the pair denied anyone, including other scientists, access to their films, *Newsweek* quoted a popular joke in response to the book: "'Have you read [it]?' 'No, I'm going to see the movie.'"[53] Filmmakers seized the opportunity to capitalize on public curiosity by making and releasing sex documentaries, including the new "marriage manual films," which were narrated by fake doctors.[54] Some theaters not only showed these movies, but also the more sexually explicit "beaver" films, which brought female genitalia to the big screen.[55] Aware of the new pornographic films, the NSF also wanted, as associate Teresa Welborn put it, "to do visually what Masters and Johnson had done in their research."[56] Not only did

Fig. 10.1 Ted McIlvenna (bottom, center) interviewed in the SAR room at the NSF for the film *Sexual Liberty Now!* (1971). Note the overhead, slide, and film projectors in the booth at the top. (Digital frame enlargement.)

NHF feel the need to produce their own films (figure 10.1), which they identified as erotic and educational, but they divided their multimedia SAR into two sessions to correspond with the therapeutic techniques of desensitization and resensitization. According to Brecher's description of the SAR, desensitization involved bombarding the participants with "three or more films projected simultaneously on as many screens." "The films are snippets from hardcore commercial porno films portraying in explicit detail all of the sexual ways in which mouths, cocks, cunts, tits, and asses can interact."[57] The "resensitization films shown at the next session are mostly Laird Sutton's best products," he noted. "They are equally explicit, but the emphasis is on the couple making love together."[58] In the NSF's discourse, the SAR's educational environment would serve positive prosocial purposes and would not incite dangerous antisocial behaviors, as was assumed about obscene materials and as they had been legally defined.

The theory behind this two-part programming for multimedia sex education was that the "commercial fuck films" would "take the *threat* out of sex" for the participants when they were projected in the first session.[59] Following from the method of behavioral psychotherapy, the exposure to a feared object would reduce fear of it. In the second session, as the NSF's Phyllis Lyon explained, their films showed "sex in the context of involvement, love, joy, and happiness."[60] Brecher suspected that the NSF "associates built [their] films into a crash program of sex education" because they were less appealing to audiences than commercial porn films.[61] Regardless of which films participants preferred, the SAR's division of sexually explicit media into the desensitization or re-sensitization sequences may have educated some to distinguish between the commercial porn films and the films made by or distributed by the NSF and to identify these productions as "erotic," rendering them more socially acceptable. To meet—or to encourage—demand for materials deemed appropriate for sex education and therapy, the NSF's MMRC distributed its own films as well as slide shows, photo series, and SAR packages, all of which were marketed as erotic rather than pornographic.

In the 1960s, as the marketplace for sexually explicit materials expanded, the effort to distinguish erotica from pornography became significant. As Lynda Nead argues, the discursive maneuver to differentiate erotic art from commercial pornography was tied to the humanistic belief in "the liberatory and therapeutic effects of erotic art and of sexual behavior freed from the conventions of bourgeois authoritarianism and repression."[62] The NSF was committed to a similar notion of sexual liberation. According to Irvine, though both scientific and humanistic sexologists shared a disciplinary concern for "erotophobia"—"an irrational fear of the erotic"—the latter openly appreciated erotic art and expounded on the concept of erotology, that is, "the practical study of lovemaking."[63] By linking erotic art with the experience of sexual pleasure, humanistic sexologists, psychologists, and therapists actively campaigned for what Michel Foucault would describe as humanism's impossible "dream of a complete and flourishing sexuality."[64] Through the new circuit of erotic film festivals, the NSF's own films would reach a mostly self-selected audience and some acclaim. In 1974, Sutton described their film *Fullness* in an interview for the adult magazine *Oui*: "One of the films I recently completed had sodomy in it—anal intercourse—as an alternative to sex during pregnancy. An incredible film. The woman was eight months pregnant. It just took first place at the Baltimore Erotic Film Festival."[65]

By linking "eros"—love—with some sexually explicit products, such as those that were accepted into film festivals and classrooms, humanistic sexologists offered audiences a way to distinguish the erotic from the pornographic and soon the distinction would be made that women, in particular, preferred the former over the latter. In fact, the NSF's institutional discourse helped link erotica with the feminist movement, and Betty Dodson, Joani Blank, and Lonnie Barbach, who participated in the interdisciplinary research for the SAR, would each contribute to the growth of feminist-influenced sex products. The NSF associate Lyon was also cofounder of the influential lesbian organization, Daughters of Bilitis.[66] In a 1975 survey of sex education films for the adult magazine *Gallery*, Don Carson quoted Lyon stating that the NSF wanted its films to show "sex in the context" of loving relationships. Carson noted, the NSF's films were intended to challenge the "all-male bias of commercial porn": "The problem was that most of the films on the market were not only made *for* men, but they were made *by* men, too, Ms. Lyon says."[67] The NSF was committed to producing films that Lyon claimed debunked the "myths" of male and female sexual performance featured in commercial porn films: specifically, "the man who can go on forever in bed" and the "woman who gets incredibly excited when somebody merely touches her genitals." According to Carson, the "trouble with commercial sex films was not their explicitness, or lack of it, but what the [NSF] directors saw as a tendency to 'mythologize' sex and divorce it from 'relationship.'"[68] Brecher quoted McIlvenna's description of such films: "The porn cameras . . . focused in tight on tits, cocks, cunts, asses, and tongues. . . . Human beings and their relationships were largely ignored." Having seen the NSF's films as part of the Sexarama, Brecher wrote, "Sutton's films are as physiologically explicit as the commercial fuck films, but there is a major added ingredient. While the participants are balling, they are also making love."[69]

The NSF's claim for differentiating its films from commercial pornography was staked on the articulation of a kind of documentary style, which was in keeping with the didacticism associated with erotic art. If the commercial pornographic cinema provided, as Gertrude Koch puts it, the "night school for sex education," then the NSF's own productions were intended as the day school for sex education.[70] As McIlvenna told Tracy, their intent was to "show what people do, not what they ought to do."[71] In the 1960s, revolutionary claims were made for the new documentary film movements—direct cinema and cinema vérité. Whereas scientific sexologists assumed that universal truths about the "human sexual response" would be revealed through an aggregate of modernist data collected via recording technologies, including film, the NSF's discourse adhered to the humanistic assumption that individual erotic truths would be revealed by filming apparently ordinary people engaged in their preferred sexual activities. In 1997, NSF associate Rubenstein described their filmmaking practice: "Regular people, not actors, were hired, who don't work in the sex field, the sex industry, but are just people sharing their sexual patterns on film for education, not to be shown in theaters."[72]

The claim to a representative ordinariness echoed the enthusiasm within documentary practice at the time for what Brian Winston identifies as the direct documentary's focus on "the private life of ordinary people in ordinary circumstances."[73] In interviews, Sutton identified the NSF's films as "sexual *cinema vérité*," whereas McIlvenna referred to them as "pattern films," following from the Kinsey practice of creating data-rich representations of people's sex habits through extensive interviews.[74] As Carson described the NSF directing style, "It's not unusual, Sutton says, for the participants in one of his films to forget all about him and his one-, sometimes two-member crew. 'That's easy to do, because, once I start shooting, I don't interrupt the people in any way or tell them what to do.'"[75] Similar to what Masters and Johnson reported about making films in the laboratory, Sutton assumed his camera could be ignored by the sexual performers, thereby simply recording reality, as if the process were no more intrusive as a "fly on the wall."[76] Although edited and sometimes narrated, the films had an authenticity rooted in the fact that the NSF's performers hailed from a Bay Area milieu in which humanistic sexology crossed paths with sexual countercultures variously invested in the sexual revolution as well as feminist and gay liberation movements.[77] The films had ordinary titles, privileging first names. About *Rich and Judy* (1971), the NSF's MMRC catalogue from the early 1980s suggested using "this film to introduce and portray heterosexual intercourse within a very loving relationship."[78] *Visions of Rasberry* (1979) offered "an interweaving of sensual/sexual fantasies of Rasberry by her husband Laird Sutton. . . . There are fleeting scenes of explicit sexual activity, both heterosexual and bisexual" (Multi Media Resource Center, 12). About *Johnnie and Bonnie* (1981), "The country is the setting for this black couple taking a horseback ride, having an outdoor picnic and having sex in the sunshine" (Multi Media Resource Center, 18). Performers tended to conform to the natural body appearance of the period, identified with hippies and normalized in *The Joy of Sex*: long hair and beards for men; long hair, hairy armpits, and bushy pubes for women.[79]

The NSF also made films about self-loving, specifically female masturbation, which was considered crucial both to the representation of female sexual pleasure and to the competent practice of female sexuality. More to the point, the NSF sought to represent female sexuality differently from the commercial porn films; as Lyon explained, "Natu-

Fig. 10.2 The first film released by the NSF, Constance Beeson's *Unfolding* (1969), attempted to represent female sexuality through a more humanist-feminist techniques that could be called "erotic" when compared with commercial pornography. (Digital frame enlargement.)

rally, our first film was made by a woman, specifically about female sexuality."[80] The catalogue copy for that first film, *Unfolding* (1969) by Constance Beeson, gives an idea of the NSF's association of humanist-feminist ideas about sex with filmic techniques that could be defined as erotic rather than pornographic (figure 10.2): "*Unfolding* is a series of dream-like episodes, double and triple images blending ocean, hills, poetry and ethereal feelings. While various persons take part in the film fantasy, two couples are focused on illustrating sexual pleasure and orgasm" (Multi Media Resource Center, 26). Beeson's imagery had a lot in common with other experimental art films of the period, notably Carolee Schneemann's *Fuses* (1964–1967).[81] However, the NSF's own productions privileged their documentary style, and this was true for the films on female masturbation: *Susan* (1971), *Margo* (1972), and *Shirley* (1972) each featured a woman masturbating to orgasm. Describing Margo as a "heavyset woman in her thirties," Carson quoted her perspective on participating:

> At first, when I started really getting into masturbating, I thought, Well, if I'm ever going to come, I'm going to have to black out the fact that I'm

making a film. Laird had said to do that, but then somehow my whole head got turned around, and I realized what a far-out, radical, and wonderful thing it was to be making a film that would turn other women on to their bodies and their sexuality.[82]

In *Susan* the performer looks at the camera and smiles after her final act of masturbation, enthusiastically waving her vibrator at the camera. Whether or not she received off-screen direction, which would certainly violate the cinema vérité ideal, the scene conveys her personal celebration of sexual agency. Such a self-conscious moment was in keeping with the NSF's institutional intent to say yes to sex.[83] Over the years, the NSF's Multi Media Resource Center produced, distributed, and exhibited a variety of explicit media productions by women.[84]

Speaking for a *Gallery* audience familiar with porn films by 1975, Carson attempted to distinguish between the commercial product and the NSF's films that he said were "probably as gamey . . . as the weekly bill at your local inner-city movie complex. But, in actuality, the movies it describes are probably 'cleaner' than most *Gallery* readers would care for."[85] Carson was skeptical about the NSF's claim to an erotic documentary style. Already familiar with *Deep Throat* and its theatrical depiction of fellatio, he opined, "Take the way Sutton zoomed up and pointed his camera at the woman in *Sun Brushed* as she performed fellatio. There was something downright school-marmish about the maneuver, as if Sutton—high-minded as hell—had rapped his ruler and said, 'Class, repeat after me: See Jane suck. Jane likes to suck. You can suck, too.'" Carson summed up his view of the NSF's documentary style with reference to *Possibilities* (1973), which featured a quadriplegic man and his lover: it was "another UPI-style visual report on a sexual pattern."[86] Given that the NSF catalogue copy promised sexually explicit imagery, Carson asked, "What makes these films different from what they appear to be— kinky and far-out porno?"; he answered his question by noting that the "the difference is intent" as stated by the NSF. Moreover, he noted that "a contract clause . . . stipulates that the films are to be knowingly sold or rented only to church and social agencies, colleges, and professionals engaged in therapy, counseling, and education."[87] The NSF's institutional discourse prohibited the exhibition of its films as popular—or, to extend Carson's point, "dirty"—entertainment. Instead, it permitted the inclusion of experimental art films in its distribution catalogue, and the circulation of its own films as both erotic art and instructional media. Of course, like the porn entrepreneurs who pushed the boundaries of censorship, the NSF could have claimed that its films were not sex pictures (entertainment), but pictures about sex (education), and a few of them were even award winners at erotic film festivals. But by the late 1970s, exhibiting sexually explicit materials in public spaces would again seem to be a riskier activity in the face of new social forces, including the rise of the Christian Right and morality campaigns; the emergence of feminist antipornography groups; and increased public awareness of sexual harassment, incest, and rape; as well as renewed concern over sexual promiscuity and sexually transmitted diseases, especially AIDS.

The SAR Experience, Then and Now, Public and Private

The new image-exchange and duplication technologies are a formidable obstacle to effective sexual censorship. Home videotape recorders, Polaroid cameras, and 8 mm. film cartridges render censorship nearly powerless.

GENE YOUNGBLOOD, *Expanded Cinema*, 114.

Like prior building machines, the Awareness Room of the NSF and IASHS was structured to simulate the experience of being metaphorically transported somewhere sensational (figure 10.3). Through this sexually explicit audiovisual journey, the captive, and perhaps captivated, audience was simultaneously supposed to learn about forms of human sexuality and to appreciate erotic sensory stimulation. Echoing the names of those precursors, the diorama and the panorama—from the Greek word "horama," for a sight, a view, or a vision—the SAR's nicknames, Sexarama and Fuck-o-rama, suggest that people expected it to deliver a sexual spectacle.[88] At the time, the country's best-known sexologists, Masters and Johnson, were promoting the popular bias against viewing sexually explicit materials; indeed, they theorized that men with erectile performance issues suffered from a debilitating self-consciousness they termed the "spectator" problem, the cure for which was to emphasize tactile over visual stimulation.[89] This was a challenge for those who believed in the therapeutic and educational potential of a visual sexual aesthetics, and the NSF met it by dividing its SAR into two distinct sections sanctioned by behavioral therapy: the commercial fuck films for desensitization and its own films for resensitization. In doing so, the NSF reinforced the bourgeois humanistic cultural judgment that was then deployed around the provocative problem of distinguishing between pornography and erotica. To borrow from Nead's argument about the role of discernment in the identification of erotic art, the NSF's SAR offered sensationally spectacular transportation to the "frontier of legitimate culture" without, however, sacrificing their ability to make

Fig. 10.3 The SAR room circa 1977. Multiple images projected on the walls and comfortable pillows were an integral part of the SAR experience. (Courtesy IASHS.)

intellectual judgments.[90] The NSF's institutional discourse articulated a distinction between erotic art and commercial pornography in relation to an educated preference for authentic sexual "patterns" instead of pornographic "myths," for lovemaking as opposed to balling, for didactic rather than fictional films. Thus, the NSF's claim to the liberatory, therapeutic, indeed resensitizing, value of its own films rested on the premise that they could be identified as erotic art, not pornography.

Indeed, they were training their audiences to perceive the NSF films that way. Regarding the experience of watching pornographic films in public spaces, Koch ventures an important aside: "It is possible that the social environments in which the films are seen determine their effect more than the film's form and content. That is, the organization of the audience's sexuality defines the mode of the product's appropriation."[91] In its ideal environment, or perhaps in any installation with prolonged exposure, the NSF's multimedia SAR was designed to organize "the audience's sexuality." Along with sounds to stimulate erotic listening, the SAR was expected to encourage an eroticized experience of looking, what Koch describes as a pleasurable and touristic "lust to see."[92] But as Brecher observed, the NSF films "proved a disappointment. You couldn't just show them cold to an uptight audience; they made many of the viewers even more uptight—and the ones that needed enlightenment most were the ones most likely to walk out."[93] In other words, the commercial porn films may have served to warm up the audiences for the NSF's didactic films and that suggests a specious correlation between the categorization of porn versus erotica and their presumably different sensitizing effects. If audiences reported feeling favorably inclined—resensitized—to sexually explicit materials after experiencing the SAR, it could well have been a function of the order of the two-step exposure program. Another way to test their theory would have been to program their films in the first session and the commercial films in the second session, then compare reactions to the original program. According to Irvine, the ultimate reaction to the SAR would involve the participants' removal of their clothes in the full expression of humanistic sexology's commitment to experiential learning, to getting in touch with their feelings, and saying yes to sex, right there on the shag carpet.[94] At the IASHS, the SAR continues to be a requirement in the graduate studies curriculum: "#311 SAR 4 Units. An intensive 7-day educational and experiential program for sex educators, therapists, counselors. Each year's SAR focuses on new methodologies in the sex field and new applications of the SAR process. An integral part of SAR is the opportunity for interaction with professionals from throughout the world who attend."[95] Although the SAR's historic moment as a new media experience has long passed, it is important to consider its possible impacts on its audiences as well as its influence on subsequent educators. Much as movie theaters drew protests as well as audiences during the period in which porn films went mainstream, college campuses also became contested spaces for environmental multimedia exhibitions claiming to educate audiences about sex and gender, to teach them to see and to decode images correctly.

After the SAR was created, people affiliated with the NSF attempted to measure audiences' responses in order to bolster their claims about the purported benefits of sensory saturation in service to sex education. For the 1970 Commission on Obscenity and Pornography, the Glide Foundation reported their results of the "effects of erotic stimuli" on a sample of SAR participants: "It is difficult to make evaluations of individual categories of a training program specifically designed to be experienced as a whole. In terms of ranking, the multimedia approach was first, with 92.8 percent saying that it 'helped' or 'greatly helped.'"[96] This awkward remark hints at skepticism on the part of humanistic sexology about scientific methods for quantitatively measuring experience. Nevertheless, the authors clearly recognized the political value of such data, stating that "close to 90 percent of the 329 persons found that historic and current sex action films, which are graphic depictions of sexual activity, helped or greatly helped in the [NSF's] training courses."[97] Of course, this sample was likely composed of self-selected people, perhaps favorably inclined toward sexually explicit materials, or at least willing to subject themselves to such exposure.

For a 1975 report published by the Sex Information and Education Council of the United States, Derek Burleson echoed the Glide report's conclusions, stating that the SAR provided a "rich laboratory for investigating the effectiveness of explicit audiovisual media in helping both professionals and the general adult public to deal with sexual attitudes on a personal-affective level."[98] In 1977 the NSF assessed the impact of the SAR and published its results in its *SARGuide*: "30,000 persons have taken the SAR process courses either through the National Sex Forum or through other groups using the process. Roughly half of these persons have been counselors, doctors, social workers or others in the 'helping' professions."[99] Apparently, the other half of the thirty thousand was not so easily categorized, perhaps because, as Carson noted, the SAR was "originally geared for professionals only but later opened to the public," which implied that people outside the field of sex education and therapy may have attended.[100] Whether or not evaluations were collected for all thirty thousand, the *SARGuide* enthusiastically stated that "statistics indicate that 96 percent find the SAR very helpful both personally and professionally."[101]

How people responded may have depended on whether they attended the NSF's SAR in the Awareness Room or a roadshow SAR. After attending one in Minneapolis, Robert Miller described his experience in 1970: "The windows were blacked out and the doors were locked. Slides of erotic art and pornography were being projected one after another—sometimes three at a time—on a screen while the taped voice of an evangelistic preacher came on strong extolling the rewards of free sexuality."[102] The environmental aspect of the roadshow SAR would vary by location. The packages of audiovisual materials would include slides, films, or both, and they would have to be projected and amplified, proficiently or not, in church basements, college classrooms, therapy offices, community centers, and other spaces lacking the technical, theatrical, and tactile specifications of the original Awareness Room. College students certainly made up a portion of the overall audience for the NSF's packaged SAR, and it would appear that medical, social service, and health students were most common. Considering survey data for SARs held in Minnesota and California medical schools, Brecher reported in 1974 that the results indicated "overwhelmingly favorable responses" immediately after the SAR; apparently, survey data from a year later continued to be positive.[103] In their 2007 essay published by the IASHS's *Electronic Journal of Human Sexuality*, Butler, Hartzell, and Sherwood-Puzzello reported that a "Midwestern" university's undergraduate human sexuality survey course included a SAR component, which they described as follows: "The purpose of the contemporary SAR programs is to provide an opportunity for attendees to assess their own cultural influences, deconstruct their own assumptions about human sexuality, and become desensitized to unfamiliar sexual practices and sexological issues."[104] The researchers' focus group study of the "perceived benefits" to students serving as "peer-facilitators" for this course included this participant's quote about the SAR component: "When I discuss some of the issues with the students I notice on a real general level along with them I'm sort of breaking my own discomfort zone on whatever issues we're tackling with them."[105]

Other evidence suggests that people reacted inconsistently and even negatively to the SAR and its perceived discomforts. In 1982 Francoeur and Linda Hendrixson published their *Instructor's Resource Manual* for other professors to adapt his "Becoming a Sexual Person" course to their curricula. About his "Sex Saturday" SAR, Francoeur and Hendrixson stated that "the students are much more relaxed and communicative in class" after experiencing it. Taking a longer view, they concluded that it "generally takes several months for students to sort out their feelings about the SAR." They also described what happened as a result of an off-site event, when Francoeur held "a two day SAR for the nursing students at Northwestern Louisiana State University," where the "homosexual films . . . brought very strong negative reactions from the students." Although "some students protested the immorality of the experience to the university president," Francoeur and Hendrixson reported that the students' responses changed over time: "When a final evaluation of the program was done, every student reported a positive final evaluation of the SAR."[106] Such positive assessments could be used to support the humanistic perspective on the liberatory potential of multimedia when applied to experiential education, but it also indicated that participants might have to be monitored over a period of time.

The surveys by the Glide Foundation and the NSF as well as the college course evaluations obviously shaped participants' responses into data for quantitative analysis without necessarily representing their felt experience, which was so important to humanistic sexologists. According to Irvine, the NSF's multimedia method put a premium on feelings: as "in earlier encounter groups, participants in SARs are encouraged not to intellectualize by analyzing the film, but instead to find out which aspects of sexual behavior give them a 'visceral clutch.'"[107] How individuals experienced the SAR and what they felt during and after may have depended on one's willingness to be emotionally expressive in public. Written descriptions provide some evidence of people's spontaneous responses. Calling the SAR "an illusion-shattering experience," Brecher wrote, "people usually experience a whole range of reactions to the films—from delight to anger to disgust," and "freak-outs occasionally occur during or immediately following a SAR. They generally take the form of temper tantrums, hysterical outbursts, anxiety attacks, or depression."[108] For *Commonweal*, Miller remarked: "some people are all wound up in some kind of other-world ecstasy. Their excitement grates on the rest of us, and, as I look at them I see they are the same people who become unplugged in any milieu which places a premium on feeling."[109] Although Miller was bored by the SAR, he seems to have shared Toffler's concern that groups of excited people could fall victim to "social irrationality."[110] Indeed, Miller not only criticized the multimedia Sexarama for excluding specifically "moral" limitations, but also waxed negatively on the consequences of desensitization, as he understood it: "The great American vulgate will not be satisfied for long with mere voyeurism. . . . Desensitization will demand that they proceed toward more participatory approaches to the subject—or turn away from it altogether—until they reach satiation, which is really what it is all about, the goal of any sexual encounter."[111]

Similarly, Toffler expressed concern about the use of sensory manipulation techniques for "political or religious brainwashing." Rather than look to organized religion or political parties, he wrote disparagingly about rock concerts: "The glazed stares and numb, expressionless faces of youthful dancers . . . where light shows, split-screen movies, high decibel screams . . . and writhing, painted bodies create a sensory environment characterized by high input and extreme unpredictability and novelty." In addition to characterizing attendees of these multimedia events as blindly numb, he ominously linked them with "hippie cultists," guilty of "drug abuse," as well as "group experimentation" in "sensory deprivation and bombardment."[112] Miller's and Toffler's comments expressed concern about controlling people, especially youth, in group settings, echoing long-standing fears of mob behavior in public spaces. In particular, Miller's comment recalled the government's case against hardcore pornography: that it posed "a clear and present danger" to society. As early as 1977, Francoeur's Saturday SAR for his students was targeted by "Rev. Morton Hill, president of Morality in Media, Inc."; the *Instructor's Resource Manual* quoted from the Hill's text: "Demand investigation as to whether state or federal laws are being violated . . . Unless this is done every college in America will follow the example of Fairleigh Dickinson University . . . Academic freedom does not justify use of obscene material."[113] Such calls to political action—in particular to policing expressions of sexuality in public—would be issued from both religious groups as well as feminist organizations, and both would gain student followers on many college campuses.

Whether its student audiences were bored or excited, disgusted or enchanted, or experienced all those feelings at once, the NSF's multimedia experiment tapped into the youth culture's expectations both for radically new sensory experiences and for frankly sexual films. In this way, the NSF's discourse linked humanistic sexology with technological innovation. Because the discourses around media technologies emphasized experimentation, new aesthetic practices—experimental, underground, and direct documentary or cinema vérité—could be embraced as a form of expression to resist and to challenge commercial visual cultures. Although the SAR was not widely adapted across college curricula, the impetus to educate people, especially college students, about sexually explicit imagery would be claimed by antipornography advocates on the one hand, and "pro-sex" experts on the other.[114] Not surprisingly, both would consider it necessary to expose their audiences to sexually explicit media. Although these events fell short of the total sensory experience of the multimedia SAR, these new sex education sessions implicitly relied on the behavioral psychotherapy technique of bombarding their audiences with sensory stimulation in order to teach them to identify and to prefer some sexually explicit materials—or none—over others.[115] It was as if the two factions split the two-step SAR, and each one claimed one part of the process—either the desensitization with pornography or the resensitization with erotica—to bolster their own arguments.

In contrast to the goals of Tyler, Francoeur, and the NSF's associates, antiporn educators reoriented the saturation method of the multimedia workshop to frighten audiences with sexually explicit imagery. Like Miller and other critics, they redefined desensitization to mean a numbing effect, and the antiporn show warned audiences away from what it widely identified as pornographic imagery—ranging from porn films to mainstream advertising—deemed to "objectify" and "dismember" women's bodies. In addition to screening select films, such as *Killing Us Softly: Advertising's Image of Women* (1979) and its sequels and *Not a Love Story* (1981), the antiporn educators created slide shows and video compilations. The fairly rapid disappearance of porn films in mainstream theaters, before it became more socially acceptable for women to see them, further minimized the degree to which female college students in particular could readily compare them with what was identified as pornographic in these antiporn presentations. Furthermore, the process of sensory bombardment can result in emotional responses that may discourage or delay intellectual engagement. Although the antiporn critics promulgate Laura Mulvey's theory of the "male gaze," pro-sex educators claim a pornographic gaze for women. Willing to engage with porn and recognize the emergence of more sexual products by women and for women, the pro-sex educators, such as Susie Bright and Annie Sprinkle (PhD, IASHS), lobbied for the eroticization of the senses through their own resensitization process, encouraging audiences, especially women, to appreciate examples of sexually explicit materials from a variety of sources, including work by women porn directors. The pro-sex program was articulated to undermine the twin assumptions supported by both the antiporn educators and feminist theorists, who did not challenge what dominant sexologists presumed: that women are less capable of being turned on by visual stimuli and are generally represented as objects to men for their visual stimulation. Like the NSF's Sexarama, the pro-sex shows emphasize saying yes to sex of various kinds and to addressing female sexual pleasure, in particular. No matter their goals, both the antiporn and the pro-sex educators have offered their audiences a spectacular collective and public experience that can be traced back to the 1960s, the sexual revolution, and the rise of the Sexarama.

In conclusion, the discourse of the NSF and its multimedia SAR attempted to refute the long-standing argument against pornography: that its potential to stimulate the senses is dangerous, leading, as the law has often put it, to the incitement of sexual experimentation for the sole purpose of physical gratification. Indeed, the humanistic sexologists affiliated with the NSF argued for the benefits of sensory stimulation, without assuming, as did Masters and Johnson, that such exposure was a detrimental substitute or replacement for actual sexual activities, potentially leading to what the country's most famous sexologists considered an unhealthy "dependency" on audiovisual media.[116] If the NSF's environmental multimedia approach seems quaint now, that is because not only have technologies changed, but also the home—with its array of consumer media devices—has become the most acceptable environment for experiencing sexually explicit materials.[117] In fact, the IASHS's media division turned to video early on as a new means of exhibition.[118] The MMRC catalogue from the early 1980s advertised the SAR Video Systems I: "a self-help program for personal sexual enrichment and education . . . including four hours of 1/2" video programming—the best of the educational films produced by the National Sex Forum," priced at $995. After the MMRC became Multi-Focus, Inc., the catalogue from the mid-1990s also offered the SAR Video Package—"for use by individuals and couples in the home setting as well as for classes or workshops, and doctors with patients"—at the new price of $795, with the old films from the 1970s and 1980s. The SAR video packages only included the second, resensitization, session from the multimedia SAR. Meanwhile, some IASHS graduates produced sex instruction videos for home viewing.[119]

Even though the NSF/IASHS was instrumental in expanding the range of sexually explicit media products, its emphasis on collectively experienced sex education and its commitment to sexual heterogeneity were not advanced by the makers of sex instruction videos. Generally such productions, now on DVD, favor heterosexual couples and the treatment of sexual dissatisfaction or dysfunction. Meanwhile, commercial porn does a bang-up business delivering all manner of specialty sex acts across consumer media platforms to the millions of private screens now owned by the flower generation and their descendants.

Note

This essay is a revision of a chapter from my PhD dissertation, "Sex Scenes and Naked Apes: Sexual-Technological Experimentation and the Sexual Revolution," University of Texas at Austin, 1999.

1. Marshall McLuhan, *Understanding Media: The Extensions of Man* (McGraw Hill: New York, 1964).
2. Anne Friedberg, *Window Shopping: Cinema and the Postmodern* (Berkeley: University of California Press), 1993, 20; italics in original.
3. Gene Youngblood, *Expanded Cinema* (New York: E. P. Dutton, 1970), 42.
4. Alvin Toffler, *Future Shock* (New York: Bantam, 1970), 220, 227. Youngblood preferred the term "intermedia."
5. "Wild New Flashy Bedlam of the Discothèque," *Life*, May 27, 1966, 72.
6. Toffler, *Future Shock*, 177.
7. Formerly the NSF, the Institute for the Advanced Study of Human Sexuality (IASHS) spells out SAR as "Sexual Attitude Restructuring": see IASHS, www.iashs.edu/history.html. Search under History of the Institute. No date.

Accessed November 30, 2010. In her study of the contribution by NSF or IASHS to the field of sexology, sociologist Janice Irvine refers to "Sexual Attitude Re-Assessment." See *Disorders of Desire: Sexuality and Gender in Modern American Sexology* (Philadelphia: Temple University Press, 1990), 106.

8. IASHS, no date. Accessed November 30, 2010.

9. According to the IASHS, "Ted McIlvenna & Laird Sutton, two Methodist ministers who chose sexuality as their ministry, invented the Sexual Attitude Restructuring (SAR), the sexual pattern film, and the doctoral program in human sexuality." Given that sources credit them as well as several associates for creating specific NSF projects, I prefer to refer to the NSF founders and associates collectively, except for individual quotes and materials identified with a specific person's name. See www.iashs.edu/history.html.History of the Institute. No date. Accessed November 30, 2010. Thanks to Ted McIlvenna for granting me an interview when I visited the IASHS in 1996.

10. Thomas Waugh, *Hard to Imagine: Gay Male Eroticism in Photography and Film from Their Beginnings to Stonewall* (New York: Columbia University Press, 1996).

11. For an analysis of the antiporn and pro-sex presentations, see my essay "Appearing Live on Your Campus! Porn-Education Roadshows," *Jump Cut* 41 (1997): 27–35.

12. "Wild New Flashy Bedlam of the Discothèque," *Life*, May 27, 1966, 72.

13. Toffler, *Future Shock*, 200, 227.

14. Often such materials addressed female pleasure and how to achieve it, starting with specular self-examination and masturbation. See Eithne Johnson, "Loving Yourself: The Specular Scene in Sexual Self-Help for Women," in *Collecting Visible Evidence*, ed. Jane M. Gaines and Michael Renov (Minneapolis: University of Minnesota Press, 1999), 216–240.

15. Toffler, *Future Shock*, 229. In *Expanded Cinema*, Youngblood also refers to the Cerebrum.

16. Walter Truett Anderson, *The Upstart Spring: Esalen and the American Awakening* (Reading, MA: Addison-Wesley, 1983).

17. Toffler, *Future Shock*, 220, 227. For Esalen's role in developing alternative therapies and influence on humanistic sexology, see Irvine, *Disorders of Desire*.

18. Irvine, *Disorders of Desire*, 117.

19. IASHS, History of the Institute. No date. Accessed November 30, 2010.

20. Irvine, *Disorders of Desire*, 117, 128. She notes that some women reported feeling pressured into having sex in that environment.

21. Morton M. Hunt, *The Story of Psychology* (New York: Anchor, 1993), 560.

22. Hunt, *The Story of Psychology*, 573. Hereafter, cited in the text as Hunt. For more on Wolpe's research, see Joseph Wolpe, *The Practice of Behavior Therapy* (New York: Pergamon, 1973); and Joseph Wolpe and Arnold A. Lazarus, *Behavior Therapy Technique: A Guide to the Treatment of Neuroses* (New York: Pergamon Press, 1966).

23. See also Irvine, *Disorders of Desire*, 192.

24. Paula Findlen, "Humanism, Politics and Pornography in Renaissance Italy," in *The Invention of Pornography: Obscenity and the Origins of Modernity, 1500–1800*, ed. Lynn Hunt, 48–108 (New York: Zone Books, 1996, 74).

25. Robert T. Francoeur and Linda Hendrixson, *Instructor's Resource Manual to Accompany Becoming a Sexual Person* by Robert T. Francoeur (New York: Wiley and Sons, 1982), 268.

26. For more on midnight and underground movies, see J. P. Telotte, "Beyond All Reason: The Nature of the Cult," *The Cult Film Experience: Beyond All Reason*, ed. J. P. Telotte (Austin: University of Texas Press, 1991), 5–17.

27. Underground cinema also provided a public venue for homosexuality on-screen and off. See Juan A. Suárez, *Bike Boys, Drag Queens, and Superstars: Avant-garde, Mass Culture, and Gay Identities in the 1960s Underground Cinema* (Bloomington: Indiana University Press, 1996).

28. Toffler, *Future Shock*, 234.

29. Phil Tracy, "The National Sex and Drug Forum," *Commonweal*, November 28, 1970, 195.

30. Robert T. Francoeur "Sex Films," *Society* 14, no. 5 (July/August 1977): 33–37.

31. Tracy, "The National Sex and Drug Forum," 195.

32. Toni Ayres, Phyllis Lyons, Ted McIlvenna, et al., *SARGuide for Better Sex Life: A Self-Help Program for Personal Sexual Enrichment/Education Designed by the National Sex Forum*, 2nd rev. ed. (San Francisco: National Sex Forum, 1977), 13.

33. Ayres, Lyons, McIlvenna, et al., *SARGuide for Better Sex Life*, 13.

34. Francoeur, "Sex Films," 33.

35. Irvine, *Disorders of Desire*, 117.

36. Irvine, *Disorders of Desire*, 106.

37. Tracy, "The National Sex and Drug Forum," 195.

38. Ayres, Lyons, McIlvenna, et al., *SARGuide for Better Sex Life*, 14.

39. Virginia Johnson, quoted in Sally Quinn, "Sex Counselors: They're No Laughing Matter," *Boston Globe*, April 6, 1978, 19.

40. Glide Foundation, "Effects of Erotic Stimuli Used in National Sex Forum Training Courses in Human Sexuality" in *Technical Report of the Commission on Obscenity and Pornography* (Washington, DC: U.S. Government Printing Office, 1971), 5:356–357. The NSF's 1977 *SARGuide* reported that eighteen people participated.

41. Glide Foundation, "Effects of Erotic Stimuli Used in National Sex Forum Training Courses in Human Sexuality," 356.

42. The NSF's associates broke with their academic affiliates on the way to establishing the IASHS as an independent graduate program. IASHS, History of the Institute. No date. Accessed November 30, 2010.

43. Irvine, *Disorders of Desire*, 115.

44. Glide Foundation, "Effects of Erotic Stimuli Used in National Sex Forum Training Courses in Human Sexuality," 357.

45. Tracy, "The National Sex and Drug Forum," 194.
46. Edward M. Brecher, "The Lush New Body of Knowledge," *Oui*, September 1974, 50.
47. Glide Foundation, "Effects of Erotic Stimuli," 347.
48. Francoeur "Sex Films," 34; Brecher, "The Lush New Body of Knowledge," 50.
49. Irvine, *Disorders of Desire*, 128.
50. Irvine, *Disorders of Desire*, 128.
51. Elizabeth Sullivan, "God Mother of SexEd: Maggi Rubenstein, 'I Was There,'" foundsf.org/index.php?title=Godmother_of_SexEd:_Maggi_Rubenstein. Search under I Was There. Archived interview, dated 1997. Accessed January 27, 2011.
52. Based on interviews, Thomas Maier dramatically describes a rare screening of one of their films, which may have shown Virginia Johnson as the anonymous performing body, at a seminar for ob-gyn faculty at Washington University; see Maier's *Masters of Sex: The Life and Times of William Masters and Virginia Johnson, the Couple Who Taught America How to Love* (New York: Basic Books, 2009), 134–140.
53. "Response to 'Response,'" *Newsweek*, May 23, 1966, 94.
54. Eithne Johnson, "Sex and 'the Naked Ape': The Marriage Manual Film Shows How Humans Do It," paper presented at the Society for Cinema Studies Conference, San Diego, April 1998.
55. See Eithne Johnson, "The 'Coloscopic' Film and the 'Beaver' Film: Scientific and Pornographic Scenes of Female Sexual Responsiveness," in *Swinging Single: Representing Sexuality in the 1960s*, ed. Hilary Radner and Moya Luckett (Minneapolis: University of Minnesota Press, 1999), 301–324.
56. Don Carson, "See Jane Screw: New Dimensions in Sexual Education Training Films," *Gallery*, February 1975, 112.
57. Brecher, "The Lush New Body of Knowledge," 120.
58. Brecher, "The Lush New Body of Knowledge," 120.
59. Brecher, "The Lush New Body of Knowledge," 120; italics in original.
60. Carson, "See Jane Screw," 112.
61. Brecher, "The Lush New Body of Knowledge," 50.
62. Lynda Nead, "'Above the Pulp Line': The Cultural Significance of Erotic Art," in *Dirty Looks: Women, Pornography, Power*, ed. Pamela Church Gibson and Roma Gibson (London: British Film Institute, 1993), 151.
63. Irvine, *Disorders of Desire*, 9, 188.
64. Michel Foucault, *The History of Sexuality*, vol. 1, trans. Robert Hurley (New York: Vintage, 1980), 71.
65. Robert Weider, "Expanding the Body of Knowledge: A Mini Interview with Laird Sutton, Candid Cameraman of Sex Documentaries," *Oui*, September 1974, 123.
66. See Lonnie Barbach, *For Yourself: The Fulfillment of Female Sexuality* (New York: Anchor, 1975); and Betty Dodson's *Liberating Masturbation: A Meditation on Self Love* (New York: Bodysex Designs, 1974) and *Sex for One: The Joy of*

Self Loving (New York: Crown, 1987). Joani Blank founded Down There Press as well as Good Vibrations, the store for sex products. Daughters of Bilitis was established in 1955.

67. Carson, "See Jane Screw," 112–113; italics in original.

68. Carson, "See Jane Screw," 112–113.

69. Brecher, "The Lush New Body of Knowledge," 50.

70. Gertrude Koch, "On Pornographic Cinema: The Body's Shadow Realm," trans. Jan-Christopher Horak. *Jump Cut* 35 (1990): 17–29, 22.

71. Tracy, "The National Sex and Drug Forum," 195.

72. Sullivan, foundsf.org/index.php?title=Godmother_of_SexEd:_Maggi_Rubenstein. I Was There. Archived interview, dated 1997. Accessed January 27, 2011.Robert Eberwein compares Sutton's film *Free*, featuring an African American couple, with the commercial marriage manual film, *Black Is Beautiful* (a.k.a. *Africanus Sexualis*, 1970). See Eberwein, *Sex Ed: Film, Video, and the Framework of Desire* (New Brunswick, NJ: Rutgers University Press, 1999), 190.

73. Brian Winston, *Claiming the Real: The Griersonian Documentary and Its Legitimations* (London: British Film Institute, 1995), 155.

74. That the NSF's film style was identified both as documentarist and sexological suggests that the production process was based on the notion that people's sexual responsiveness had to be accurately represented, but not in the abstract, modernist style of scientific sexology. Previously affiliated with the Kinsey Institute, Wardell Pomeroy brought his method of sex history-taking to the NSF. See, for example, the NSF video, *Pomeroy Takes a Sex History* (1972). Of course, this process could be understood to direct—or perhaps inscribe—"patterns" onto the performers.

75. Carson, "See Jane Screw," 113.

76. According to Brian Winston, new portable film technologies made it possible for documentary filmmakers to elaborate fresh claims on reality: "It is the experimental method and the place of the camera as scientific instrument that provides the context in which the filmmaker/observer, a veritable fly on the wall, emerges." See *Claiming the Real*, 149.

77. People who might have been recognized for playing themselves included the NSF's Margo Rila (*Margo*), affiliated with the San Francisco Sex Information Hotline, and Salli Rasberry (*Visions of Rasberry* and *Self-Loving* [1976]), who was listed in the production credits for some NSF films.

78. Multi Media Resource Center, Catalog, n.d. (possibly 1982), 16.

79. Alex Comfort, ed., *The Joy of Sex: A Cordon Bleu Guide to Love Making* (New York: Fireside Books, 1972).

80. Carson, "See Jane Screw," 113.

81. The NSF's Multi Media Resource Center distributed films directed by Constance Beeson, James Broughton, Anne Severson, and Honey Lee Cottrell that could be categorized as "sexperimental" films. Richard Dyer identifies three films produced by the NSF as "affirmation politics documentaries." See

Dyer, *Now You See It: Studies in Lesbian and Gay Film* (London: Routledge, 1990), 231–235.

82. Carson, "See Jane Screw," 113. Margo Rila was a coauthor of the *SARGuide* and is currently listed as faculty on the IASHS website, www.iashs.edu/faculty.html. Search under Faculty. No date. Accessed November 30, 2010.

83. In this respect, the NSF's film style might be compared to the exhibitionism of the later amateur porn, which, as David James points out, privileges the performers' experiences, in comparison to the professional porn movie, which subordinates the performers' experience to the production process. See James, "Hardcore: Cultural Resistance in the Postmodern," *Film Quarterly* 42, no. 2 (winter 1988–1989): 31–39.

84. Women artists whose early work was distributed by the NSF include Honey Lee Cottrell, Tee Corinne, and Pat Califia. Along with Susie Bright, Annie Sprinkle, and others, they would continue to articulate distinctions between pornography and erotica in their subsequent projects, challenging assumptions about lesbian identities, female sexualities, and whether or not women experience visual pleasures.

85. Carson, "See Jane Screw," 111.

86. Carson, "See Jane Screw," 113 (first quote), 112–113 (second quote). The NSF produced and distributed several films under the category "disability."

87. Carson, "See Jane Screw," 111.

88. Irvine refers to Sexarama and "Fuckarama"; see *Disorders of Desire*, 128. Rubenstein identifies the "fuck-o-rama" as the first section of the SAR, featuring commercial pornography; see foundsf.org/index.php?title=Godmother_of_SexEd:_Maggi_Rubenstein. I Was There. Archived interview, dated 1997. Accessed January 27, 2011.

89. Masters and Johnson, *Human Sexual Inadequacy* (Boston: Little, Brown, 1970).

90. Nead, "'Above the Pulp Line,'" 147.

91. Koch, "On Pornographic Cinema," 20.

92. Koch, "On Pornographic Cinema," 21. Jan-Christopher Horak provides this translation for the German term, *Schaulust*.

93. Brecher, "The Lush New Body of Knowledge," 50.

94. Irvine refers to survey data from "eleven SARs in 1978" showing that "body contact" and "nudity" were rare when sexologists outside of the NSF modified them for their own use. See *Disorders of Desire*, 129. When I visited the Awareness Room in 1996, it was a shadow of its former tactile glory: the waterbed was gone; the beanbag chairs were shabby, and the shag carpet worn and dated.

95. IASHS, www.iashs.edu/index.html. Search under Courses. No date.

96. Glide Foundation, "Effects of Erotic Stimuli Used in National Sex Forum Training Courses in Human Sexuality," 357.

97. Glide Foundation, "Effects of Erotic Stimuli Used in National Sex Forum Training Courses in Human Sexuality," 368.

98. Derek Burleson, "Explicit Media – Sources and Suggestions," *SIECUS Report* 3, no. 6 (July 1975): 4.

99. Ayres, et al., *SARGuide for Better Sex Life*, 13.

100. Carson, "See Jane Screw," 112.

101. Ayres, et al., *SARGuide for Better Sex Life*, 13.

102. Robert B. Miller, "Sex, Sex and Sexxzzzzzz," *Commonweal*, November 28, 1970, 193.

103. Brecher, "The Lush New Body of Knowledge."

104. Scott M. Butler, Rose M. Hartzell, and Catherine Sherwood-Puzzello, "Perceived Benefits of Human Sexuality Peer Facilitators," *Electronic Journal of Human Sexuality* 10 (May 26, 2007), accessed March 15, 2010, www.ejhs.org /volume10/peer.htm.

105. Butler, Hartzell, and Sherwood-Puzzello, "Perceived Benefits of Human Sexuality Peer Facilitators."

106. Francoeur and Hendrixson, *Instructor's Resource Manual*, 271.

107. Irvine, *Disorders of Desire*, 128–129.

108. Brecher, "The Lush New Body of Knowledge," 120–121.

109. Miller, "Sex, Sex and Sexxzzzzzz," 194–195.

110. Toffler, *Future Shock*, 351.

111. Miller, "Sex, Sex and Sexxzzzzzz," 197.

112. Toffler, *Future Shock*, 349 (first quote), 348 (second quote).

113. Francoeur and Hendrixson, *Instructor's Resource Manual*, 269.

114. Andrew Ross, *No Respect: Intellectuals and Popular Culture* (New York: Routledge, 1989), 171–208.

115. Eithne Johnson, "Appearing Live on Your Campus! Porn-Education Roadshows."

116. "Sex Counselors: They're No Laughing Matter," *Boston Globe*, April 6, 1978. 19.

117. See Jane Juffer, *At Home with Pornography: Women, Sex and Everyday Life* (New York: New York University Press, 1998).

118. Eberwein mentions the SAR as a method for training to become a sex counselor. See *Sex Ed*, 209–210, 233.

119. These graduates include Michael Perry, *Sex: A Lifelong Pleasure* series (1991), Betty Dodson, *Selfloving* (1991), and Judy Seifer, *Videos for Lovers* series (1996).

11 ∗ San Francisco and the Politics of Hard Core

JOSEPH LAM DUONG

Between the late 1960s and early 1970s, hard core film and the burgeoning hard core film industry moved from the illicit to the licit. Like never before, celluloid of visually explicit sex was projected through the darkened spaces of movie theaters rather than in homes, fraternal organizations, or bars. Hard core transformed from loops and short featurettes to feature-length narratives, becoming within a few years a mass cultural phenomena. A reporter for the *New York Times* coined the term "porno chic" to describe the long ticket lines, packed movie houses, and publicity generated by hard core features such as *Deep Throat* (1972). By the mid-1970s, the porno chic phenomena had spread to cities throughout the United States.[1]

Beyond the popular interest and cultural cachet these films created, they grossed millions of dollars for a small circle of producers, distributors, and theater owners. Much historical evidence illustrates how economic gain motivated people's participation in the industry, especially the segment that took root in Northern California. No one articulated this more succinctly than the Mitchell brothers, the San Francisco-based pornographers who produced *Behind the Green Door* (1972) and *Resurrection of Eve* (1973). In an interview conducted for a 1974 book entitled *Sinema*, Artie Mitchell explained, "Our early motivation was almost a hundred per cent, you know, in it for the money"; Jim Mitchell added, "There was never any other motivation, it's always a hustle, this was a hustle, a way to make some bucks. It was an opportunity to make money and we latched onto it, you know. I mean. I wouldn't want to take it so seriously and think it was anything else than that." The Mitchells' desire to turn a profit and their warning to not read into their actions fits nicely with the story we tell ourselves about hard core.[2]

Reducing the motivations of industry participants to a monetary pursuit, however, has concealed the oppositional politics that was an integral part of the sex film industry. What happens to our conception of hard core when porn stars such as Mary Rexroth, the daughter of poet Kenneth Rexroth, categorically expressed their motivations in terms other than economic? "Anybody who says she's doing it for the bread is hedging a bit." Mary Rexroth explained, "There's a definite sense in a subtly political kind of way, of 'us-against-them' in the industry."[3]

This chapter suggests that the adversarial politics that Mary Rexroth conveyed was a defining characteristic for a small but important number of individuals taking part in the sex film industry of the 1970s. Using Rexroth's quote as a touchstone, it details how Arlene Elster, a young college graduate, developed a political consciousness through her involvement in the Sexual Freedom Movement. The chapter discussion then follows Elster as she applied the movement's ideas, as well as her middle-class values, to the production and exhibition of sexually explicit film. In 1968, Elster began making X-rated loops with her boyfriend, Lowell Pickett. Two years later, the pair founded Sutter Cinema, a theater that screened tasteful erotic films geared toward young couples (figure 11.1). Elster held the belief that erotic films—done with art and sensitivity, and projected in a welcoming environment—could be a catalyst for sexual liberation and a way to make money. Eventually, police harassment and a dearth of high quality films convinced Elster to abandon Sutter Cinema around 1975. Elster's story is, nevertheless, significant because she challenged the perceived wisdom of who could make, display, and watch pornographic films. More importantly, Elster is the vital link that connects the overt politics of an idealistic sexual community to the hard core film industry. Elster's story illustrates, for a brief moment in time, what hard core could have looked like when it incorporated the political aspirations of the sexual revolution. This chapter also sketches out the problematic story of the Mitchell brothers, whose self-serving characters make the general claim of political activism within the industry tenuous. Unlike Elster, the Mitchells employed a political rhetoric after entering the pornographic film industry, rather than bringing one with them. Dozens of arrests and a fortune in legal fees awoke them to the political consequences of projecting sexually explicit films. The Mitchells adopted the language of the counterculture, among many discourses, to defend their business interests. They derided civil authorities in the newspapers and used the charges brought against them to test obscenity law. In this coercive atmosphere, even their films seemed to purposely transgress racial and sexual taboos as a rude finger to the establishment. Profit initially motivated the Mitchells' actions in the pornographic film industry, but they found themselves engaged in activities with political ramifications.

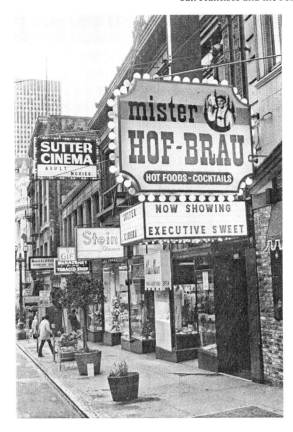

Fig. 11.1 San Francisco's Sutter Cinema at 369 Sutter Street near Stockton, circa 1971. Compared to other adult theaters, the Sutter eschewed a gaudy front and glaring ads in favor of a more understated approach.

Counterinstitutions

The narrative of the youth movements of the 1960s and their aftermath goes like this: idealistic middle-class youths protested the unjust policies, racial customs, and government institutions shaped by their parents. As the 1960s drew to a close with the end of the Vietnam War nowhere in sight, a failing economy, and burn out setting in among radicals, disillusioned protesters gave up public life. Corporate capitalism's ability to appropriate the movement and a new form of possessive individualism worked in tandem to quell dissent while assuring young people that their problems could be solved in the private sphere. Youths, who only a few years earlier had marched in the streets, now joined the counterculture, forgoing political activism in exchange for "sex, drugs, and rock 'n' roll."[4]

To describe the period through a narrative of decline creates false distinctions between the youth movements of the 1960s and the counterculture. This splitting has privileged the political activism of civil rights organizations such as the Congress of Racial Equality (CORE) over the apolitical hedonism of counterculture groups such as Jefferson Poland's Sexual Freedom League (SFL). An examination of the SFL's records, however, indicates that the two groups shared much in common politically. In the summer of 1963, Poland took part in CORE's voter registration drive in Plaquemine, Louisiana. When Poland founded the SFL, "a political action group for sex issues," a few months later, he brought CORE's tactics—leafleting, picketing, and civil disobedience—with him. Moreover, SFL members established a "counterinstitution" that carried out a great deal of institutional labor, such as drawing up bylaws, recording minutes, forming committees, and collecting dues. SFL's counterinstitution fostered political activism in a similar fashion to the organizational structure that had made CORE's work possible. By focusing on the overlaps in political tactics, as well as the institutional characteristics, it becomes clear that the SFL, usually portrayed as pleasure seeking, acted in ways universally recognized as political.[5]

Constructed from a civil rights blueprint, Poland's SFL brought the fight for sexual liberation to the San Francisco Bay Area. The SFL, along with Poland's Psychedelic Venus Church (PVC), would mold Arlene Elster's thinking about the relationship between sex and politics. Elster became an active SFL member and attended service at Poland's church, while her hard core movie theater, Sutter Cinema, established close ties with both organizations. Together the three counterinstitutions would politically work toward the common goal of sexual freedom, promoting "sex without sexism," interracial relationships, mutual orgasms, bisexuality, and other related ideas.

Sexual Freedom League and Psychedelic Venus Church

Jefferson Poland's political agenda consisted of two desires: to remove the state from all sexual matters between consenting adults and to show Americans how to live a sexually liberated life. Many newspapers articles and letters attest to how Poland employed the SFL to make his utopian vision a reality. *Newsweek*, for instance, published an article in 1965 about SFL's "nude swim-in," a demonstration against the bathing suit requirements at San Francisco's public beaches. Poland wrote a letter to the California Penal Code Revision Commission demanding the abolishment of statues that punished unwedded parents. The SFL's leader even went so far as to legally change his surname to "Fuck" in order to raise awareness about the movement, as well as to incite the authorities. The Alameda County Clerk revoked Poland's voter registration over the episode. The SFL, in turn, picketed the county courthouse. Through a variety of means, Poland used the SFL as a vehicle to make sex a political issue. Arlene Elster would imitate Poland's model but first she had to find herself sexually.[6]

The league was best known within the San Francisco Bay Area for its orgies. Poland and other leaders of the SFL wanted to create a "sexually free situation" in which members could have sex with "no restrictions . . . no coercion, no force." Elster, who began attending the SFL orgies in the mid-1960s, described them this way: "There was always lots of good food to eat. People that wanted to had sex. People that didn't want to, didn't, it was quite open. It was mostly heterosexual sex, although, there was some same sex with women. I don't recall ever seeing any same sex with men—at those parties." Besides the opportunities for sex at these parties, the celebrations also served as a way for members such as Elster to demonstrate, before the community, the degree of their sexual liberation. Participation in an orgy, watching a sex film, or other liberated activities was as a marker of how one had left, in the language of the time, her "hang-ups" at the door.[7]

In the late-1960s, because of infighting over the league's mission, Poland splintered from the SFL to establish the PVC, a "nature/earth" church that explored the spiritual dimensions of sexuality. The fellowship smoked a marijuana Eucharist, prayed over naked bodies, and encouraged bisexuality. At one service, members read William Blake and then listened to a sermon on Taoism. "It was wilder. It was a smaller bunch of people. And it was wilder," Elster said. "It was clearly devoted to, more to, a little more ritual, a little more of the psychedelic infusion and sex. Because there was this idea that sex was a positive, healthy thing to do." Members of the PVC believed that spirituality and psychedelic drugs could help people reach deeper sexual truths about themselves. The self-realizing goals of the church, however, did not mean that members should abandon politics. On a sunny Memorial Day in 1968, a naked Poland led an antiwar "pray-in" in Golden Gate Park. When police arrested Poland, he directed his lawyer to use his case to test the city's public nudity laws. Again, Poland showed individuals like Elster a way to experience pleasure and fight for sexual rights.[8]

The league and church papers reveal that another one of Poland's goals was to connect other counterinstitutions—homophile organizations, the underground press, co-ops, and communes—by putting together a phone and address directory. Unsurprisingly, Arlene Elster's name could be found in this directory. Along with listing people such as

Allen Ginsberg, the PVC directory named Elster an "Honorary Sexton" and her theater, founded in 1970, as a "SISTER GROUP." A PVC newsletter reported, "San Francisco's newest erotic theater, Sutter Cinema at 369 near Stockton, managed by PVC Rev. Arlene Elster, offers reduced rates to Psychedelic Venus Church members. Singles $3, couples $5, when you flash your blue-on-white card. Fucking and sucking on the screen, plus art."[9]

Arlene Elster forged her sexual politics within these circles. Poland's counterinstitutions taught a handful of young people to believe (maybe naively, but always idealistically) in sexual freedom. "I was good friends with Jeff Poland," Elster recalled forty years later. "He was quite, I thought he was, brilliant with his thinking and ways." Members of the SFL and PVC fused sex, spirituality, psychedelic drugs, and politics to search for and help others explore their sexuality. Ultimately, their beliefs could be boiled down to the idea that "sex was a positive, healthy thing to do." Elster and individuals like her would go to great lengths to spread this idea.[10]

Sexual Freedom at 369 Sutter Street

Arlene Elster's movie theater, located in downtown San Francisco at the suggestive address of 369 Sutter Street, opened its doors in the early spring of 1970. As it was situated near Union Square, where Sutter Street runs into Stockton Street, finding parking must have been difficult in the congested streets of downtown. Young moviegoers traveling by car probably parked a few blocks away. Continuing their journey on foot, they approached the building, opened the front door, and ascended a narrow flight of stairs lit by chandeliers with faux candles to reach the cashier waiting on the second floor. One can imagine some moviegoers with sweaty palms or maybe a devilish smile as they handed over the $3 admission charge to the young black woman with the large Afro sitting behind the register. Once inside the theater's lobby, which used to be a famous Chinese cabaret, they could help themselves to complimentary coffee and pastries.[11]

While waiting for their erotic film shows to begin, some customers may have spent a few minutes conversing with the cashier or Elster, who was always at the theater. Others may have been drawn to the brightly colored tropical fish swimming in the large saltwater aquarium in the lobby. The faint ticking sound of the projectors must have mixed with the recording of moans playing on the theater's stereos, causing a rhythmic staccato of anticipation or just plain nervousness. Taking their eyes off of Elster, the cashier, the fish, or their date, Sutter Cinema's customers might have noticed the abstract paintings of sex organs that hung from the golden walls of the lobby.[12]

As the showtime drew near, the moviegoers walked from the lobby to their seats, their feet sinking into the sumptuous carpet that had just been installed. Everything about Elster's place was nicer than the seedier grind house adult theaters around town; customers, especially young people, could experience that difference anytime between 8 AM and 12 AM, seven days a week. Elster's theater affected a progressive middle-class aesthetic, reinforced through its inviting decor, understated advertisements, and the politics behind the type of films it screened. "We are trying to create as dignified an image as we can. We feel that there is nothing wrong with watching sex films. We don't feel there should be any shame attached to it. But we also realize that we're in the minority with this opinion," Elster said. "We want to be totally honest, but we don't want to push anything on anyone."[13]

Young people found themselves making their way to San Francisco, or as Joan Didion describes, "Slouching towards Bethlehem," an evocative phrase taken from Yeats's poem "The Second Coming." Like the Pied Piper in urban form, San Francisco attracted young people with its hypnotic melody. The charisma of the city enticed America's youth with its promise of personal discovery. Recalling the dark tone underlying the Pied Piper's music, Didion writes of San Francisco's pull on her: "All that seemed clear was that at some point we had aborted ourselves and butchered the job, and because nothing else seemed so relevant I decided to go to San Francisco. San Francisco was where the social hemorrhaging was showing up. San Francisco was where the missing children were gathering and calling themselves 'Hippies.'"[14]

In her essay, Didion draws a distinction between the apolitical messages "the missing children" mimicked to the press and what the "imaginatively anarchic" activists had known; she described what the press had missed: "We were seeing something important. We were seeing the desperate attempt of a handful of pathetically unequipped children to create a community in a social vacuum. Once we had seen these children, we could no longer overlook the vacuum, no longer pretend that the society's atomization could be reversed." Didion's prose gives the reader a time and space in which to situate Elster and her actions. Elster became one of these missing, "unequipped children" who tried to create her own "community in a social vacuum." Contrary to Didion's reading, though, Elster's actions showed that for a short time a few of these "Hippies" successfully created a community shaped by counterinstitutions such as Sutter Cinema. Along with its sister organizations, Sutter Cinema worked to free Americans from sexual repression. People such as Poland and Elster did so by piecing together the shards left after the center did not hold.[15]

The hypnotic melody, charisma, and chaos emanating from San Francisco worked no differently on Elster than it had on Didion. Elster was born into an upper-middle-class Jewish family that settled in Port Arthur, Texas. Her father, a medical doctor, owned a successful diagnostic clinic while her mother kept house. Elster had a good relationship with her parents until high school. Elster's mother disapproved of her friends, especially Janis Joplin. The girls were mischievous, maybe a little rebellious—each lost her virginity before turning sixteen—but for the most part they were just bored teenagers from a small town. After graduating in 1959, Elster enrolled at the University of Texas, where she purposely avoided controversial issues such as racial integration; instead, she majored in laboratory science and joined a Jewish sorority. Elster dated a member of the Jewish fraternity she had met at a Greek function. Toward the end of college, the young couple married and relocated to Houston. Predictably, their marriage ended in divorce only a few months later. "I did not have a direction in life and I could see the writing on the wall if I stayed there. It just was, I did not want to become trapped in that life, that I saw," remembered Elster. Unhappy with her parents and the choices she made, Elster drove to San Francisco because it looked like a beautiful place that was far away from Texas.[16]

In November 1964, the twenty-three-year-old Elster arrived in San Francisco, where she rented an apartment in the Marina and found lab work at Irwin Memorial Blood Bank. She made the city her home in the next three years, even agreeing to marry again. Elster's post-Texas life had seemed ideal, but she felt a gnawing "curiosity" that left her restless. This curiosity led her to volunteer at the Haight-Ashbury Free Clinic, a counterinstitution that offered free health services to the hippies pouring into the city. "I thought I might be missing something. I thought I wasn't, well, free enough. Like the hippies were into the free thing, and I had my nose stuck in a laboratory all the time." Soon after, Elster began an affair with Lowell Pickett, the clinic's executive director, drawn to the belief that he lived the kind of life that Elster wanted for herself. Pickett belonged to counterculture organizations like the SFL. His bohemian friends made music and avant-garde art. Most important for this story, Pickett was a pornographer who supplied the local movie houses with stag and beaver films.[17]

Elster's affair with Lowell Pickett changed her life in a dramatic fashion. Even though she had figuratively run away from home, Elster tried in vain to live the middle-class life that her parents would approve of: she held a decent-paying job as a medical technologist, volunteered, and had a stable relationship. "I had been engaged to a man—a straight man—and I was seeing Lowell on the side, and the other guy didn't know about it. We were scheduled to be married. . . . Five days before the wedding, my mother was there and I called it off," Elster remembered. "I can't do this. Once again, I can't, I can't go that, that way." Her decision to move in with Pickett ended what she called her "straight arrow life." Pickett introduced her to nude beaches and took her to wild Art Institute parties. *Playboy* claimed she even modeled in "early 'beavers.'" Elster joined the SFL, but still considered her commitment to the Sexual Freedom Movement half-hearted because, as she put it, "I was always concerned about my welfare—how was I going to live. . . . Something about me couldn't simply drop out." Elster's fears were assuaged when she saw that the porn business was both profitable and "pretty innocent." In 1968, Elster quit her job at the blood bank to shoot films for Pickett's Leo Productions, a company that produced and distributed pornographic film. "I began rebuilding myself and finding my identity through my work," Elster told an audience in Davis, California.[18]

In 1969, Elster and Pickett submitted a $39,750 documentary film proposal to the SFL. The proposal illustrated how Elster combined her business savvy and sexual politics. Elster wrote that her goal for the documentary was "to make a significant film for sexual liberalization, proving ourselves to be a significant filming company, and receiving a profit" (a sentiment that foreshadowed Sutter Cinema's business philosophy). Arguing against a nonprofit venture, Elster thought that the SFL would garner the most exposure if the film had a wide distribution and played in a large number of art houses. The SFL needed to understand that theater owners and distributors would not show or distribute a nonprofit film. This collaborative documentary had to work "within the profit-geared structure." The couple argued that the SFL must use the market to disseminate its message of sexual freedom, working within the system to subvert it. Elster and Pickett ended the proposal with this reassurance: "We want to show the SFL in the best possible light. Doing anything that would put down, make the SFL look bad, or exploit it would work against the entire goal of the film for both parties."[19]

As Elster branched out from making film to screening it, she knew that the public would question the depth of her political commitments. Profiting from an SFL documentary in the name of sexual liberalization differed from making money off a pornographic film. Elster understood this suspicion, but pointed out that young people wanted a more open discussion about sex and saw sex films as one way to initiate this discussion. Elster thought that the distribution and exhibition of sex films were a social imperative. Acknowledging the negative conception most had about pornographic film, she said, "I can't help that. I feel that the times now not only allow but require films like ours." Furthermore, Elster made plain that economic concerns would not take precedence over her sexual politics: "Running this theater means nothing to me unless what plays in it pleases me."[20]

Elster politically distanced herself from the earlier generation of pornographers and movie theater owners by showing that she was cognizant of the problems surrounding the sex film industry. To accusations of exploitation she replied, "We're against exploitation, just using sex to make money like, 'We're going to show you P going into the C,' the way the average stag film house does. There's something wrong with that." Elster believed that the marketplace was inundated with pornographic films without plot because the industry only saw porn as a masturbatory aide for dirty old men. Trying to correct the situation, Elster promised to screen "erotic realism"—narrative hard core films that depicted real sexual fantasies. Mary Rexroth's *Intersection* (1971; figure 11.2), which debuted at Sutter Cinema, portrayed the story of a woman who tries "to come to grips with her earlier transition from puberty into sexual maturity." The sexual coming-of-age film allowed Rexroth to act out her own erotic fantasies—she sleeps with multiple partners of both sexes in different locations throughout San Francisco, including her childhood home—and met Elster's requirements that films she screened have "plot or story line" and be a "turn-on." Elster placed a premium on narrative and eroticism because sex was more than a penis going into a vagina. Sex, as *Intersection* suggests, could be psychologically complicated, inextricably linked to fantasy, and tied to important liminal stages. Elster believed that the multidimensional nature of sex required erotic films that appealed to all the senses, not just the lower ones.[21]

By emphasizing how her films differed from those of her competitors, Elster hoped to fill the seats of her theater with young middle-class couples, instead of the unattached men who currently patronized the industry. Her business decision to target this demographic combined the countercultural belief that sexual revolution started with young people and the historical reality that individuals from the middle class played a significant role in past sex liberation movements. Elster designed Sutter Cinema's advertisements with a middlebrow sensibility. One ad featured

Fig. 11.2 Mary Rexroth, who considered her appearance in sex films to be "subtly political," starred in *Intersection* (1971), the story of a woman's transition to sexual maturity.

a line drawing of naked women touching herself next to a quote from James Joyce's *Ulysses*. Elster's business card featured a similar art design but of a Victorian couple about to make love on a gilded bed. Elster cultivated this romantic aura (figure 11.3) to bring in open-minded middle-class youths who were interested in broadening their ideas about sex and sexuality.[22]

In interview after interview, Elster maintained the conviction that erotic films served as sexual pedagogy. She told the *Los Angeles Free Press*, "People learn how to make love better by watching other people make love." To another newspaper reporter Elster was more explicit: "People can learn some things from watching these films. For instance, you might never think to fuck someone in the ass unless you saw it first." Elster undoubtedly channeled her own experiences in the Sexual Freedom Movement when she made these statements. She had learned to be comfortable with her body and open to different sexual activities by going to nude beaches, attending SFL parties, and watching good erotica. Now, she wished the same for others and planned to teach them through film.[23]

The idea of a woman's right to an orgasm specifically motivated Elster

391-6656

369 SUTTER
AT STOCKTON

DAILY
8 A.M. TO MIDNITE

FRIDAY
& SATURDAY
MIDNITE SHOW

NO MINORS

SUTTER
CINEMA

Bring your loved one
We'd like to turn you on

Arlene
Proprietress

Fig. 11.3 Ads for the Sutter Cinema cultivated a romantic aura as they attempted to draw couples to the theater. Note that Arlene Elster "signed" this invitation in her role as the Sutter's "proprietress."

to keep Sutter Cinema open. She wanted to see erotic film where women experienced pleasure; she wanted to project erotic film that women like her could identify with.

> The average stag movie is totally male orientated, made of, by and for males. We want to stress the basic equality of the situation, or the equality that we feel should be there. In most of our films the woman is not just a sexual object, but an equal participant with as much right to be pleased as the man.

According to Elster, erotic film needed to be made of, by, and for men *and* women. Female orgasms needed to be portrayed on screen at an equal rate to male orgasms. "In fact, one of my main complaints is that I don't see women having orgasms in the films." Elster said, "You can see men coming all over the place, but I want to identify with the chick, and I can't tell if she made it or not most of the time."[24]

Elster never defined herself as a "feminist"; instead she saw herself as a sexually liberal female entrepreneur who wanted to elevate pornographic film to a higher level of respectability. In December 1970, Sutter Cinema and Leo Productions sponsored a five-day erotic film festival to meet this end. A prize committee, which included Bruce Conner, the experimental filmmaker, judged submissions that ranged from an "extreme close-up" of a woman eating an orange to a Leo Productions film of a model masturbating on an American flag. Although the films were quite different, they succinctly captured Elster's hard core politics: *Orange* spotlighted her idea that sexual arousal did not require "P going into the C," and the American flag/masturbation film spoke, however crudely, to the role that hard core played in expressing dissent from mainstream society. Elster hosted the erotic film festival to legitimize pornographic film and to help her theater's bottom line—after all, if people thought of porn as "art" then it would become normal to not only watch, but also to screen explicit sex.[25]

In 1971, prosecutors convicted Elster of obscenity; even so, she continued to use Sutter Cinema as a space to facilitate activism while she appealed the court's decision. (The appeal went all the way to the Supreme Court.) Elster hosted an SFL benefit in support of Assembly Bill 437, sex reform legislation introduced by Assemblyman Willie Brown. The bill sought to remove California's antiquated laws that made sex acts such as sodomy and oral copulation illegal. On the night of the benefit, Elster indicated her position on the laws by screening two gay male sex films and *Cozy Cool* (1971), starring Mary Rexroth, an erotic crime parody in which "even guys are said to be involved in relationships that are based on their covert sexual happenings." The benefit raised $759 that paid for ads supporting the bill and travel expenses to a rally at the state capital. Heather Fields, Elster's co-coordinator for the event, explained the reason for the benefit: "We must get away from the Puritanical, hypocritical attitudes that anything that is non-procreative is morally and legally wrong. Procreative sexual practices lead to child-bearing and population pollution. Besides, these laws can be used against you politically."[26]

Elster practiced her hard core politics, or, in the words of Mary Rexroth, cultivated her "us-versus-them" attitude, by joining the Sexual Freedom Movement, producing erotic films, and founding Sutter Cinema. Elster viewed her participation in the pornographic film industry as an opportunity to spread sexual freedom and earn a living. Sutter Cinema played films that Elster wanted to see, films in which woman possessed sexual desires and "made it" just like men. In spite of the time Elster invested in Sutter Cinema, police harassment (officers arrested Elster fourteen times) and the negative direction of the films made Elster rethink her commitment to screening hard core. "The films were going actually downhill. And they were just scuzzy. You just saw graphic depictions of sex without art or skill, without sensitivity. That didn't interest me," Elster said. "I could see my future. I could see, well I could stay in this and make a lot of money, but it just didn't interest me. And so I chose to get out of it." Between 1975 and 1976, Elster sublet Sutter Cinema and moved to Sonoma County. She and her lesbian partner opened a whole-sale plant nursery that they would run for two decades.[27]

The state forced many idealistic young people such as Elster to quit the industry, which left it in the hands of few brash pornographers who possessed the will, along with the financial resources, to fight the state. "The young turks don't give a damn," Jim Mitchell said in regard to the police harassment. "They'll keep on making movies. They don't know any better. After all, we're only in it to have a good time and make money." The Mitchell brothers did not have Elster's wide-eyed faith in the revo-lutionary potential of erotic film. They did, however, share her desire to produce and exhibit quality pornographic films, but only because they wanted the best product on the market. Economic gain motivated the Mitchells, and when their actions caused political consequences, they adopted a rhetoric that merged a diverse set of ideological beliefs — sexual freedom, civil liberties, and libertarianism — to justify porno-graphic film.[28]

The Mitchell Brothers

Around the time Arlene Elster thought about leaving the industry, the Rancho-Westdale branch of the American Civil Liberties Union (ACLU) made an unambiguous statement about what the Mitchell brothers and their hard core films represented for the defense of civil liberties. The Rancho-Westdale ACLU rented out the Mitchells' Four Star Theater for their annual summer fundraiser in 1974. A double bill played that day. The Mitchell brother's *Behind the Green Door* (1972; figure 11.4) — an abduction and rape fantasy that climaxes with a montage of differ-ent men ejaculating on Marilyn Chambers's face — and *Resurrection of Eve* (1973) — a film about a white woman who finds sexual fulfillment after leaving her cheating boyfriend for a black man — projected onto the screen of the Four Star Theater.[29]

As the synopsis above suggests, the Mitchells' films are rife with scenes that degraded woman and perpetuated racial stereotypes. How could the Rancho-Westdale ACLU support such films and, by extension, the pornographers who produced them? Shelia Wells's "Pussy Power," an article published in the underground press, helps explain why groups on the Left could celebrate the Mitchells' films. Wells argues that the state,

Fig. 11.4 Although the Mitchell Brothers claimed they entered porn production with films such as *Behind the Green Door* (1971) "for the money," they came to articulate a hardcore politics that incorporated the First Amendment, libertarianism, and sexual freedom.

embodied in President Nixon and "the pigs," has taught women to be afraid of the very things it fears most: "dope, long hair, black penises and . . . porny." Wells concludes that Americans should embrace these things, especially "pornography of all kinds" because it "breaks down the power of the controllers." The Rancho-Westdale ACLU held a fundraiser at the Mitchells' theater because the brothers screened films that integrated the very things—hippies, black male sexuality, and pornography—that the counterculture identified as threatening to the state. The brothers' subsequent persecution by civic authorities turned them into symbols of the state's encroachment on Americans' civil liberties. In this case, the Mitchells became political actors despite themselves; the Rancho-Westdale ACLU had seized upon their situation to make a statement about how the First Amendment protected an adult's right to make and watch hard core films. Eventually, the Mitchells would become political actors in their own right. An atmosphere of police harassment and legal prosecution would transform the pair from self-serving pornographers into self-serving pornographers with a shrewd political consciousness.[30]

California law enforcement treated pornographers and porn stars like pimps and prostitutes. From Buena Park to San Jose, police used anti-prostitution legislation to move against porn theaters. The Red Light Abatement Act of 1913 designated any building used for "illegal gambling, lewdness, assignation, or prostitution" as a "nuisance," ordering it shut down for one year. Undercover officers sat in porn theaters trying to catch patrons soliciting sex or masturbating to demonstrate that the theaters violated the Red Light Abatement Act. (In 1975, the Mitchell's Four Star Theater would be closed down under this law.) Meanwhile, Los Angeles police charged pornographers with pandering, or acting as a go-between in illicit sex. Los Angeles cops, in other words, considered it pimping when pornographers hired two actors to have sex. "You cannot make a hard-core film without violating the prostitution laws," warned Vice Captain Jack Wilson in 1975. "When you pay actors to engage in sex or oral copulation, you've violated laws. You've solicited individuals to engage in prostitution by asking them to engage in sex for money." One porn star claimed that the policing tactics in Southern California were so effective that the majority of hard core films from the era of 1970s and 1980s had to be made in Northern California.[31]

San Francisco Supervisor Diane Feinstein's antipornography stance guaranteed that state pressure would be applied to proprietors of sexually oriented businesses operating within the city. Feinstein, for example, issued an emergency moratorium on any new sex-related businesses. She then passed a zoning ordinance that provided for façade control and banned these businesses from operating within one thousand feet of each other. In the interim, Feinstein lobbied state legislators to push through a bill that gave communities the ability to circumvent unfavorable obscenity rulings. San Francisco police, the foot soldiers of Feinstein's "anti-smut campaign," conducted raids on pornographic theaters, seizing films and harassing theater owners. "I am not worried about it. I don't give a shit, really," Jim Mitchell said in response to the city's efforts against porn theaters. "You know, if they could close them down, they think it would be so great for the country. Like, if all the students would go home, everything would be great all over. Nixon would be happy." Between 1968 and 1973, police arrested the Mitchells forty different times.[32]

In light of the circumstances, the Mitchell brothers kept themselves abreast of the latest obscenity defense strategies, as well as social-science research on pornography. Jim Mitchell described the brothers' proactive legal strategy, "We try to keep an offense attack at all times, instead of just hiding and let them come in and give you a lot of shit." Michael Kennedy, the Mitchells' lawyer, commissioned a research corporation to conduct a statewide survey on "The Public Display of Pornographic Material." When given the choice to ban, place no restrictions on, or limit the advertising of pornographic material, over 60 percent of survey respondents chose the latter. Even more telling, only 2.4 percent of respondents went on to list "Sex, Pornography" as a serious problem facing the country. Essentially, Kennedy proved that according to "contemporary community standards," a key legal phrase used to determine obscenity, a majority of the public did not consider pornography worth the court's attention.[33]

Reading the survey together with government documents such as *The Report of the Commission on Obscenity and Pornography* (1970), the Mitchell brothers knew the antipornography forces were wrong when they claimed that watching pornographic films led to sexual perversion and violent crime. The commission's results found no scientific link between antisocial behavior and watching pornographic material. Much to the Mitchells' self-satisfaction, the commission took an additional step, recommending that the federal government lift all restrictions on the adult consumption of pornographic materials. "I'm not as interested in trying to defend the movies to anyone," Artie Mitchell said. "I'm more interested in the fact that people have the freedom to see any film they want to see—especially since it seems so easy to prove that they're not going out and hurting anyone else after they've seen them. It's just the straight fascist trip again—wanting everyone to be like them, you know?"[34]

Jim Mitchell, adding to Artie's libertarian rhetoric, marshaled the language of the Constitution, along with sexual freedom, to criticize their political opponents. "We don't think the judge should tell people what to see," Jim Mitchell said. "We think we have the right, under the First Amendment, to make the movies and distribute them, and we're willing to go to jail on that." Jim, sounding very similar to Jefferson Poland and Arlene Elster, gave notice that he would use his cases to test obscenity laws, "We think this is the way to change the law—court by court, case by case. Our movies aren't obscene. Sex is the first big lie we all get told and taught. Judges feel guilty about sex. We don't." The Mitchells came to articulate a hard core politics that incorporated the First Amendment, libertarianism, and sexual freedom. They used it to echo familiar counterculture grievances such as their generation's sexual mis-education, and the ways in which civic authorities attacked the new sexual ethos reified in pornographic films.[35]

If any doubt existed as to the character of the Mitchell brothers' "us-against-them" politics, all the authorities had to do was visit their theaters. The Mitchells flashed this message before the start of each film:

> To our customers: You are advised that there are presently plainclothes vice cops in the audience of our theater. They prefer watching movies to protecting our persons. They are here to harass us and spy on you. We have a constitutional right to screen films and you have a constitutional right to view them. Simply ignore the vice cops and they will go away. The Management.[36]

As this message clearly indicates, police spent a great deal of time undermining the Mitchells' business. The Mitchells responded to the state's harassment by perfecting a politics of agitation, going so far as to place Diane Feinstein's unlisted phone number on their marquee. Their very public feud became symbolic of the state's flowering cultural war against young people who challenged authority figures on moral, political, and sexual grounds. Even their problematic films, placed within a historical context, can be viewed as critiques of a state bent on curtailing Americans' individual freedoms.

Conclusion

In an industry where participants' motives are usually reduced to monetary gain, the stories of Elster and the Mitchells underline the fact that oppositional politics was a key component of the pornographic film industry in the 1970s. San Francisco counterculture transformed an unlikely young woman into a pornographer and adult movie theater owner. Elster's participation in hard core wedded a concern for her economic well-being with her belief in consensual sex without guilt, shame, or sexism. Leo Productions and Sutter Cinema allowed Elster to simultaneously earn a living and advance the Sexual Freedom Movement by projecting high quality erotic films aimed at idealistic middle-class youths in a pleasing atmosphere. The Mitchells, on the other hand, were more than willing to screen "P going into the C," if it attracted paying customers. State pressure caused the brothers to become politicized. They formulated, out of necessity, a political language that brought together libertarianism, sexual freedom, and the Constitution. The Mitchells employed this rhetoric to call attention to the hypocrisy of those controlling the levers of power.

These stories outline the general contours of hard core's political history, but more research is needed to fill in the missing pages. Investigating the relationship between politics and the following areas would bear fruit: gay male porn, race, and feminism. Preliminary evidence suggests that the gay rights movement and hard core were deeply connected. Harold Call, president of Mattachine Society, one of the first homophile organizations in the United States, advocated for gay rights while he shot pornographic films, sold gay erotica, and operated a private screening room. The links between politics, race, and porn are also tantalizing. The McKnights, two black theater owners who exclusively screened interracial porn, said to a reporter, "It helps knock down these myths about the black man." Meanwhile, porn stars such as Annie Sprinkle and Candida Royale thought of themselves as feminists. They even described their activities in hard core as feminist acts. Exploring these relationships will detail the different kinds of politics the hard core film industry engendered.[37]

While a complete political history of hard core has yet to be written, the history we do have reshapes our understanding of America in the 1970s. Tom Wolfe described the 1970s as the "Me Decade" to capture how Vietnam, Watergate, and a stagnant economy caused Americans to turn their backs on public life to embark on self-absorbed journeys of personal liberation. The stories of Elster and the Mitchells fail to map onto this narrative in one critical way: they did not abandon public life. Elster continued to engage in conventional forms of political activism, while she sought sexual freedom. It was mainly police harassment, not a loss of faith that caused Elster to eventually leave the public realm. The Mitchells, following the decade's economic mantra, wanted the freedom to turn a profit, but state pressure forced them to take part in public life. Perhaps the Me Decade is better defined by a guise of individualistic pursuits that masked an active, yet complicated relationship between Americans and the public sphere.[38]

Notes

1. Ralph Blumenthal, "Porno Chic," *New York Times*, January 21, 1973, E28; Seth King, "Pornographic Shows Spread in Midwest," *New York Times*, March 11, 1973, 48.
2. Kenneth Turan and Stephen F. Zito, *Sinema: American Pornographic Films and the People Who Make Them* (New York: Praeger, 1974), 170–171.
3. "The Porno Girls," *Playboy*, October 1971, 148.
4. Bruce Schulman, *The Seventies: The Great Shift in American Culture, Society, and Politics* (New York: De Capo Press, 2002); Roszak, *The Making of the Counter*

Culture (Berkeley: University of California Press, 1995); Christopher Lasch, *The Culture of Narcissism: American Life in a Culture of Diminishing Expectations* (New York: Norton, 1979), 18–19.

5. Sexual Freedom League Records, *1964–1983*, ctn. 1–9, the Bancroft Library, University of California, Berkeley (hereafter, SFL Records); Jefferson Poland and Sam Sloan, *Sex Marchers* (Los Angeles: Elysium Press, 1968), 12–16.

6. "Sexual Freedom?" *Newsweek*, September 5, 1965, 20; John Miller to Jefferson Poland, August 13, 1970, ctn. 1, folder 5, SFL Records; for more on SFL see David Allyn, *Make Love, Not War: The Sexual Revolution: An Unfettered History* (Boston: Little, Brown and Company, 2000), 41–53.

7. Richard Ogar, "Inside the SFL," *San Francisco BALL*, no. 4 (1970): n.p.; Poland and Sloan, *Sex Marchers*, 12; Poland and Valerie Alison, *The Records of the Sexual Freedom League* (New York: The Olympia Press, 1971), 181; Arlene Elster, interview with the author, February 25, 2011.

8. Chas Clifton, *Her Hidden Children: The Rise of Wicca and Paganism in America* (Lanham, MD: AltaMira Press, 2006), 148–152; PVC, liturgy, 1970, ctn. 3, folder 32, SFL Records; Elster, interview with the author, February 25, 2011; Jefferson Poland to Chief Art Kleps, June 7, 1968, ctn. 1, folder 23, SFL Records; Jefferson Poland to Sal Balistreri, October 7, 1968, ctn. 1, folder 23, SFL Records.

9. SFL, directory, ctn. 1, folder 10, SFL Records; PVC, members directory, March 1971, Arlene Elster Papers, Gay Lesbian Bisexual Transgender Historical Society (GLBTHS), San Francisco, California (hereafter, Elster Papers); PVC, membership directory, April 1972, Elster Papers; PVC, newsletter, 1970, ctn. 3, folder 32, SFL Records.

10. Elster, interview with the author, February 25, 2011.

11. Arlene Elster shared photos of Sutter Cinema with me which provide the basis for my description of the theater; William Murray, "The Porn Capital of America," *New York Times Magazine*, January 3, 1971, 23; Ted Mahar, "Dignified Image Sought for Erotic Films," *Sunday Oregonian*, November 15, 1970, 20.

12. Kenneth Turan, "Sex Films in San Francisco Reach Plateau of Legitimacy," *Los Angeles Times*, October 30, 1970; Kenneth Turan, "San Francisco's Erotic Film Palaces Have Classical Look," *Washington Post*, October 25, 1970, n.p.; Tracy Johnston, "Arlene Elster: Sutter Cinema's Lady Erotographer," *Night Times*, February 9–22, 1972, 3.

13. Turan, "San Francisco's Erotic Film Palaces Have Classical Look," n.p.; for an example of Sutter Cinema's advertisements, see *Berkeley Barb*, December 25–31, 1970, 15; and Mahar, "Dignified Image Sought for Erotic Films," 20.

14. Joan Didion, *Slouching toward Bethlehem* (New York: Noonday Press, [1968] 1996), 85.

15. Didion, *Slouching toward Bethlehem*, 122–123.

16. Elster, interview with the author, February 25, 2011.

17. Elster, interview with the author, February 25, 2011; Fred Struckey, "The Day They Raided Sutter Cinema—Again," *San Francisco* (November 1971): 60–61;

Phil Pukas, "Arlene-of-the-Sutter Raps on SF's Sexy Filmfest, Or . . . . High Art of the Wet Dream," *Berkeley Barb*, November 13–19, 1970, 7–8.

18. Elster, interview with the author, February 25, 2011; John Bowers, "The Porn Is Green," *Playboy*, July 1971, 180; Mahar, "Dignified Image Sought for Erotic Films," 20; Tony Perry, "Celluloid Marriage Manual: Porn Dispells [sic] Sex Mystique," the *Davis Enterprise*, August 14, 1972, 20.

19. Arlene Elster and Lowell Pickett to SFL, December 12, 1969, ctn. 1, folder 22, SFL Records.

20. Murray, "The Porn Capital of America," 20.

21. Pukas, "Arlene-of-the-Sutter Raps on SF's Sexy Filmfest," 7; Muriel Dobbin, "Explicit Sex Films Divide San Francisco," *Sun* [Baltimore], December 3, 1970, A16; Sutter Cinema, press release, n.d., Elster Papers; Maitland Zane, "New Star of S.F.'s Porny Films," *San Francisco Chronicle*, January 20, 1971, n.p.; Zephyr catalogue, Elster Papers.

22. Jefferson Poland, "Sutter Cinema's Soulful Screwing: Erotic Flicks for Erotic Heads," *Berkeley Barb*, July 24–30, 1970, 19; Sutter Cinema ad, *Berkeley Barb*, July 17–23, 1970, 7; Elster showed me her business card.

23. Clay Geerdes, "Pornography Rides Again: Theater Owner Convicted of Obscenity," *Los Angles Free Press*, February 26, 1971, n.p.; Johnston, "Arlene Elster — Sutter Cinema's Lady Erotographer," 3.

24. Mahar, "Dignified Image Sought For Erotic Films," 20; Elster's quote about female orgasms can be found in Pukas, "Arlene-of-the-Sutter Raps on SF's Sexy Filmfest," 13.

25. Arthur Knight, "'Step Inside, Folks, to an Erotic Film Festival,'" *Los Angeles Times*, December 13, 1970, U32; Jerome Tarshis, "Eros and Muses," *Evergreen Review* no. 88 (April 1971): 18.

26. Stanley Smegma, "Sutter Super Fuck," *San Francisco BALL*, no. 3 (1970): 24; Mother Boats, "Fuckfilm for Freedom," *Berkeley Barb*, July 16–22, 1971, 6; Frank Rila to Arlene Elster, report, Elster Papers.

27. Geerdes, "Pornography Rides Again," n.p.; "Porno 'Conspiracy' Bust," *Berkeley Barb*, October 8–14, 1971, 4; Arlene Elster, telephone interview with Eric Schaefer, June 9, 2003.

28. "Smut Maker Call Business Viable," *New York Times*, July 1, 1973, 78.

29. "X-Rated Movie Party Scheduled by ACLU," *Los Angeles Times*, August 4, 1974, WS7.

30. Shelia Wells, "Pussy Power," *Berkeley Barb*, February 13–20, 1970, n.p.

31. California Penal Code, section 11225; Myrna Oliver, "Court Orders Judge's Theater to Close: Patrons' Lewd Conduct Blamed on Lessee, Owner Exonerated," *Los Angeles Times*, December 3, 1975, 32; Gregg Kilday, "The Movies and Pornography: Part II, Financial Versus Artistic Motivation," *Los Angeles Times*, July 12, 1973, E1, 14; Nina Hartley, telephone interview with the author, May 18, 2006.

32. Dianne Feinstein to Laura Lederer, August 3, 1977, box 2, Women Against Violence in Pornography and the Media Records, GLBTHS; Richard Ogar, "The

Making of a Movie: How the O'Farrell Does It," *San Francisco BALL*, no. 6, 1970, 17; "Film Pornography Flourishes Despite Court Ruling," *New York Times*, November 4, 1973, 22.

33. Ogar, "The Making of a Movie," 17; Field Research Corporation, "Fieldscope Report: Statewide Survey of Public Opinion About the Public Display of Pornographic Materials," May 1971, Elster Papers.

34. Field Research Corp., "Statewide Survey of Public Opinion"; *Technical Report of the Commission on Obscenity and Pornography* (Washington, DC: U.S. Government Printing Office, 1970); Ogar, "The Making of a Movie," 17.

35. Robert Berkvist, ". . . And What About the Peeps?" *New York Times*, December 9, 1973, 44.

36. Oliver, "Court Orders Judge's Theater to Close," 32.

37. *Harold L. Call Papers*, One National Gay and Lesbian Archives; Dobbin, "Explicit Sex Films Divide San Francisco," A16. On Annie Sprinkle, see Linda Williams, "A Provoking Agent: The Pornography and Performance Art of Annie Sprinkle," *Social Text* no. 37 (winter, 1993): 117–133. See also Kim Masters, "Some Might Call It Art . . . : But Annie Sprinkle's Act Is An Open Question," February 8, 1992, *The Washington Post*, G1; Hunter Drohojowska, "Annie Sprinkle Brings 'Porn Modernist' to California Theater," April 30, 1992, *Los Angeles Times*, 8.

38. Tom Wolfe, "The 'Me' Decade and the Third Great Awakening," *New York Magazine*, August 23, 1976, http://nymag.com, search under [The "Me" Decade].

12 ✴ Beefcake to Hardcore: Gay Pornography and the Sexual Revolution

JEFFREY ESCOFFIER

The cultural constraints under which we operate include not only visible political structures but also the fantasmatic processes by which we eroticize the real. . . . The economy of our sexual desires is a cultural achievement.

LEO BERSANI, *Homos*, 64.

Hardcore pornography emerged as a significant current of popular culture in the 1970s. The first porn movie ever reviewed by *Variety* was Wakefield Poole's *Boys in the Sand* (1971), a sexually explicit gay film shot on Fire Island with a budget of $4,000. Moviegoers, celebrities, and critics—gay and straight—flocked to see *Boys in the Sand* when it opened in mainstream movie theaters in New York, Los Angeles, and San Francisco. Within a year, *Deep Throat*, a heterosexual hardcore feature, also opened to rave reviews and a huge box office—exceeding that of many mainstream Hollywood features. It was quickly followed by *The Devil in Miss Jones* and *Behind the Green Door*. *Variety* reported that between June 1972 and June 1973, these three movies earned more—on a per-screen basis and in terms of gross revenues—than all but a handful of mainstream Hollywood releases. Thus was launched the era of "porn chic."[1]

Pornography was an integral part of the discourse that emerged during the sexual revolution of the 1960s and 1970s. Porn, however, played a more significant role in the life of gay men than among heterosexual men, not only because homosexuality has been a stigmatized form of behavior but because historically there were so few homoerotic representations of any kind. Gay men become sexually active adults without any socialization in the social and sexual codes of the gay male subculture. Pornography contributes to the education of desire.[2] "For gay male culture," observes Thomas Yingling, "porn has historically served as a means to self-ratification through self-gratification."[3] This tendency was especially true during the late 1960s and early 1970s. But for young gay men of the last few generations, porn has provided knowledge of the body and of sexual narratives, and examples of gay sexuality and of sexuality within a masculine framework. Of course, it also has provided an extremely "thin" discourse, premised on an almost utopian lack of obstacles, encumbrances, and inhibitions. Moreover, in spite of its liberatory promise, it has conveyed stereotypes and other kinds of social misinformation. Porn emerged as part of a heterogeneous social framework that encompassed "many institutional structures, economics, modes of address and audiences"[4]—including magazines, mail-order businesses and postal inspectors, movie theaters, public sex, vice squads, and the closet. During the sexual revolution and since that time, porn has played a vital function in gay male life.

The transition from softcore pornography to hardcore represented a dramatic break in the production of pornographic films—both in how sex was portrayed on film and in the way the production of porn was organized, who performed in it, and what other kinds of activities were associated with it. It required new filmmaking conventions and new rhetorical devices.[5] As a rule, in softcore pornography the performers are actors, the sex simulated, and production is more akin to traditional movie production; in hardcore porn the performers are sex workers and the production of hardcore scenes focuses on embodied sexual functions—on genitalia, erections, and orgasms. To be credible the sexual encounters represented in hardcore require *real* erections and *real* orgasms—and those *reality effects* anchor the fantasy world that porn offers to its audience. Porn films serve as passports to worlds of sexual fantasy—enacted by real people with real bodies and, in the case of men, real erections and orgasms. The everyday obstacles to untrammeled sex are removed.[6] Fantasies are made more real because they are caught in motion and on film.[7]

For gay men, the Supreme Court's dismantling of the regulatory discourse set up and maintained since 1873 by the Comstock Act allowed for sexually explicit representations of homosexuality to move from *private spaces* inside the homes of gay men into *public spaces* on the screens and inside movie theaters. The transition from "beefcake," or softcore images, to sexually explicit hardcore porn films in the late 1960s was a change not only from one medium to another—from primarily still photography and drawings to a cinematic medium, from a *static image* to an *action image*—but a shift that entailed a modification in the representation of homosexual desire from a focus on men as the *objects of desire* to men as the *active agents of homosexual desire*.

Obscenity and Democracy

The sexual revolution of the 1960s and 1970s would never have taken place were it not for the battles fought over obscenity and pornography during the late 1950s by pornographers, stand-up comics, literary writers, and publishers.[8] Even though Samuel Roth, the plaintiff in the Supreme Court's *Roth v. United States* decision (1957), lost the case, Justice William Brennan's opinion altered the legal landscape. Over the next ten years, the Court decided several major obscenity cases, generally finding for greater freedoms of sexually oriented material.[9] Two of the cases reviewed by the Court dealt with issues that directly affected homosexuals. At the time, homosexual conduct was illegal in every state of the union, and no doubt many Americans considered the topic of homosexuality itself to be "obscene" or "pornographic." In 1954 the Los Angeles postmaster seized copies of ONE, a homophile civil rights publication, and banned it from the mail on the grounds that it was "obscene, lewd, lascivious and filthy." Lower courts upheld the postmaster's ban, but in 1958 the Supreme Court, citing *Roth*, reversed the lower courts' findings without issuing a written opinion.[10] The second case actually involved pornography. The U.S. Postal Service seized *MANual*, *Trim*, and *Grecian Guild Pictorial*, three "beefcake" magazines that carried photographs and illustrations of men scantily dressed in posing straps and bathing suits, all published by MANual Enterprises. The postmaster believed the magazines explicitly appealed to the prurient interests of homosexuals. MANual Enterprises sued the Postal Service. By 1962 the case had made its way to the Supreme Court, where the justices once again reversed the lower courts. The *MANual* decision contributed a new wrinkle — "patently offensive" — to the *Roth* test for obscenity:

> These magazines cannot be deemed so offensive on their faces to affront current community standards of decency — a quality that we shall hereafter refer to as "patently offensive" or "indecency." Lacking that quality, the magazines cannot be deemed legally "obscene" and we need not consider the question of the proper "audience" by which their "prurient interest" appeal should be judged.[11]

Although homosexual readers might find the pictures arousing, the Court concluded that as "dismally unpleasant, uncouth, and tawdry" as the images were, they "lacked patent offensiveness" and were thus not obscene.[12] In the wake of *Roth* and these other decisions, publishers and booksellers had increased reason to believe they could win their pleas against local censorship convictions; they were proven right.

At the end of this process, there was virtually no constraint on print publications. However, the issue was less clear cut with regard to sexually explicit films. By the early 1970s, controversies no longer tended to focus on erotic nudity, four-letter words, or frank dialogue so much as on explicit content that often involved actual sex acts, often perverse ones. The ultimate irony of the *Roth* decision, and the later *Miller v. California* (1973) in which the Supreme Court sought to establish a stricter test for obscenity, is that if some so-called prurient work (like the hardcore film *The Devil in Miss Jones*) could be shown to have some socially redeeming value (as the Supreme Court found in the prurient novel *Fanny Hill*) or some "serious literary, artistic, political or scientific value" (as Justice Burger stipulated in *Miller*) then that prurient work would have some constitutional protection. Thus many hardcore theatrical releases in the 1970s adopted some sort of high concept, psychological angle, or plot as an alibi against prosecution for obscenity. Eventually even the need for that stratagem evaporated.[13]

Beefcake

In September 1960, only a few years after the *Roth* decision, Newton Arvin—an eminent professor of literature at Smith College, a political activist, and a literary scholar who'd written a National Book Award-winning book on Herman Melville and another on Nathaniel Hawthorne—was arrested in his home in Northampton, Massachusetts, for possessing a collection of "beefcake" magazines illustrated with semi-nude pictures of men. Among the magazines seized were *Grecian Guild Pictorial* (figure 12.1), *Gym*, and *Physique Artistry*. Arvin's name had surfaced as the result of a recent postal investigation, and federal authorities had notified the local vice squad. Ned Spofford and Joel Dorius, two colleagues of Arvin, were arrested at the same time. Local newspapers referred to the men as a "sex ring," and the *Boston Herald* published a story under the headline "Suspect's Diary Studied for Clues to Smut Traffic." The careers of all three men were destroyed in one way or another by the arrests. Arvin, who was forced into retirement and spent a year hospitalized for depression after a suicide attempt, died in 1963. Spofford and Dorius, both untenured faculty members at Smith, were fired.[14] Their convictions were overturned in 1963 after the Supreme Court ruled in *MANual Enterprises, Inc. v. Day, Postmaster General* (370 U.S. 478 [1962]) that beefcake magazines could not be considered obscene.[15]

Gay life in the years before the Stonewall riots of 1969 was centered among small groups of friends and in bars; casual sex often occurred in

Fig. 12.1 Physique magazines featuring "beefcake" photos of male models, such as *Trim* or the *Grecian Guild Pictorial* seen here, were one of the few expressions of a gay male community prior to the Stonewall riots and the beginnings of gay liberation.

public rest rooms, parks, and piers. Homosexuality was still considered a loathsome perversion by a majority of the population. Psychiatrists categorized it as a mental illness; every state in the union criminalized sex between men, and most states criminalized sex between women.[16] Pornographic materials—whether written or visual—were difficult to obtain, expensive, and even dangerous to possess. Homoerotic images— that is, photographs of nude men or drawings of erotic scenes—were available only through private networks or to "select mail-order customers." Such material was considered obscene and could not be sent through the mail, though in fact pornography has been distributed via the postal system since the Civil War.[17] In such a context, gay male erotic culture emerged very slowly into the public light.[18]

Starting out as an underground phenomenon during the 1950s, small magazines with photographs of almost nude men were sold on newsstands in larger cities: New York, Chicago, Los Angeles, and so on. These "physique magazines" and the mail-order businesses based upon them became central to development of the gay erotic imagination.[19] Photographs of nearly nude men were frequently published in health and bodybuilding magazines to serve as models of physical health and bodily development, not as objects of desire. The homosexually oriented physique magazines, however, aimed deliberately at an audience with a sexual interest. These magazines were not merely one aspect of a wider gay male culture, but as Valentine Hooven argues in his history of beefcake magazines, "they virtually *were* gay [male] culture."[20]

In 1948, the United States Postal Service launched one of its periodic campaigns to clean up the mail-order advertisements in the men's magazines—clamping down on sales of suggestive cartoons, recordings of risqué night club acts, and novelty items, as well as images of nude women and men. The Postal Service warned the magazine publishers that if they did not exclude such advertising, they would not be able to use the mail. Although the photographs were technically not illegal, many magazines quickly banned all physique ads.[21] Bob Mizer, an amateur photographer living in Los Angeles, had frequently advertised in men's magazines and suggested to other photographers that they pool their mailing lists and issue their catalogues jointly. In 1950, while Mizer was experimenting with grouping the catalogue pages together, it occurred to him to create a magazine; he called it *Physique Pictorial*. The publication featured photographs of young men wearing only posing straps, bathing suits, or loin cloths and almost no editorial content—except for long and deceptively chatty captions that frequently functioned as "editorials."[22]

By the mid-1950s there were more than a dozen small-scale (five by eight inch) beefcake magazines—including *Apollo, Physique Pictorial, Male Nudist Review, Fizeek Art Quarterly, Grecian Guild Pictorial, Art and Physique, Trim, Tomorrow's Man, Male Pix, Vim, Adonis,* and *Young Adonis*—all publishing photographs and illustrations of attractive, almost nude young men, often posed in sexually suggestive situations. In their back pages, photographs of tanned and oiled bodybuilders were available by mail order.[23] Most publishers of beefcake were extremely cautious about identifying their readers as gay men, and by the 1960s nearly every major publisher or photographic studio had suffered legal persecution or harassment from the police—Bruce of Los Angeles and others had even gone to jail for periods of time, whereas *Playboy* had been publishing "cheesecake" images at least since the 1950s. If the Supreme Court's decision in *MANual* in 1962 helped to alleviate some of the legal repression, it did not completely stop harassment of beefcake photographers; as late as the mid-1960s Mizer, who regularly referred the models represented by his studio (the Athletic Model Guild) to other photographers, was convicted of running a male prostitution business.

Despite the challenges, the beefcake magazines created a loose counterdiscourse to the homophobic discourses in American society at that time.[24] Christopher Nealon has argued that through their pictures, comments and stories, the magazines suggested some sort of gay male solidarity, "an imagined community" that countered the pathological model of gender "inversion" ("a woman's soul in a male body") and that appealed to classical "Greek bodily and political ideals."[25] According to Thomas Waugh the total circulation of beefcake magazines during the late 1960s was over 750,000, probably the largest audience of gay male readers and consumers ever assembled up to that point in time.[26] That far exceeded the circulation of the more "political" homophile publications such as *One* or the *Mattachine Review*. "A minuscule magazine featuring a bunch of guys with their clothes off but not completely naked may not seem like much of a revolution in the history of sex," Hooven has argued, "but to the men who bought them, they were something new and daring. It took courage to purchase one of those little magazines in 1955."[27] That such was the case is illustrated by the experience of Arvin, Spofford, and Dorius. "The consumption of erotica was without question political," Waugh writes, "however furtive, however unconscious, however masturbatory, using pictures was an act of belonging to a community," and he notes that in the period before Stonewall, consuming erotic images was for gay men the "most important political activity of the postwar decades."[28]

Sex in the Cinema

A combination of industrial and social factors created a growing market for softcore sex films during the 1960s. The growth in the number of theaters showing sexploitation movies, with their predominately male audiences, also provided new opportunities for all-male sexual encounters.[29] Theaters showing porn had become a public space that facilitated sexual arousal because it provided its male audiences with an erotic mise-en-scène.[30] The male audience watched pornographic films in a state of arousal, and the movies elicited images and fantasies that not only involved women but—in contrast to most heterosexual men's private sex lives—male performers who engaged in various sex acts with female performers with varying degrees of prowess, endowment, and sexual skill. Thus heterosexual male spectators found themselves in a state characterized by prolonged desire and an ambiguous relation to the objects of desire and fantasized events on the screen.[31] Although female prostitutes also worked in theaters showing softcore and hardcore heterosexual movies, such a charged context increased the likelihood that the men in the audience, whatever sort of film was being screened, might have sexual encounters with one another.[32] It was part of a pattern found over and over again in public restrooms, jails, prisons, military facilities, and other same-sex environments.[33] In such a situation even a "straight" man in the audience may engage in mutual masturbation with another man or allow a man to suck his penis.[34] The porn theater, part of the cinematic apparatus itself, had become a complex form of sociosexual space, an erotic signifying system and a stage for fantasy scenarios.[35]

The cinematic and architectural complex of the softcore porn theater had created a unique space in which various kinds of sexual exchanges could take place, cinematic representation of sex (softcore and later hardcore) on the screen and real sexual activity in the audience.[36] Brendan Gill described the space and the activities that went on in the the-aters:

> For the homosexual, it is the accepted thing that the theatre is there to be cruised in; this is one of the advantages he has purchased with his expensive ticket of admission. Far from sitting slumped motionless in one's chair, one moves about at will, sizing up the possibilities. Often there will be found standing at the back of the theatre two or three young men, any of whom, for a fee, will accompany one to seats well down front and there practice upon one the same arts that are being practiced upon others on the screen. One is thus enabled to enjoy two very different sorts of sexual pleasures simultaneously.[37]

In the late 1960s, the live action in the audience often surpassed the erotic appeal of the relatively innocuous beefcake shorts and rather lugubrious softcore narrative features.

Starting in the late 1960s, the writer Samuel Delany went regularly to the porn theaters in the Times Square area. He cruised in them and frequently had sex with the men who attended them, despite the fact that the vast majority of the theaters showed straight porn and that most of the men there were also straight. Nevertheless, patrons, in large part because of the sexual activity that went on in the theaters, also developed a sense of community. In *Times Square Red, Times Square Blue*, Delany suggests that the encounters that took place in porn theaters encouraged the development of social relationships crossing lines of class, race, and sexual orientation and conveyed a sense of community.[38] The independent feature *Porn Theatre* (2003) by French director Jacques Nolot offered homage to the porn theater and the sexual diversity and solidarity that often emerged among its patrons from the 1960s through the early 1980s.

Only a few exploitation movies and nudie-cuties dealt with male homosexuality or gender deviance.[39] In fact, most porn filmmakers refused to make gay films, and the older generation of gay physique photographers—especially some of those who had made short 8 or 16 mm movies for their mail-order customers, such as Mizer, Dick Fontaine, and Pat Rocco—were initially cautious about showing their work theatrically. Instead, homosexual themes were most commonly explored in avant-garde or experimental films by filmmakers such as Kenneth Anger, Jack Smith, and Andy Warhol, and these films were more likely to have theatrical showings in "art" venues.[40] Anger's short film *Fireworks* (1947) was one of the earliest films to touch on a homosexual topic. Inspired by the Zoot Suit riots in Los Angeles in 1943, it portrayed a young man who, awaking from an erotic dream, goes out into the night in search of sexual adventure. The film is permeated with surrealistic sexual symbolism—statues under sheets representing erections and a Roman candle spewing white sparks from a sailor's crotch. Pervaded by homoeroticism, erotic images of male physiques, and violence, Anger's *Scorpio Rising* (1963) paid homage to the macho rites of a motorcycle gang, juxtaposing and intercutting images of fascism and delinquency, of community and rebellion, of motorcycle gangs and a Nazi rally, and of ritual and violence, bringing together the sacred and the profane. The references to Nazism seem to point to the famed brutality of the Los Angeles Police Department—which terrorized Latinos and African Americans, as well as lesbians and gay men for so many years.[41]

Made for a mere $300, Jack Smith's *Flaming Creatures* (1963) was another experimental film that touched on homosexual subject matter. The film is an abstract montage of the human body and its parts: penises (limp and erect), nipples, feet, and lips, a campy and bizarre tale of orgies, vampires, and transvestites. It created a sensation when it played in New York in 1963 and 1964. Intentionally shocking as were so many of the experimental films of the era, it was considered the most offensive of them all, generating a huge public outcry. When it was showed at the Gramercy Arts Theatre the following March, along with *Un chant d'amour* (1950), Jean Genet's portrayal of homoeroticism in prison, the police raided the theater, confiscated the print, and arrested the program's director for obscenity. Proclaiming the film as a milestone in the sexual revolution, critic and avant-garde film advocate Jonas Mekas wrote: "*Flaming Creatures* [was] . . . a manifesto of the New Sexual Freedom

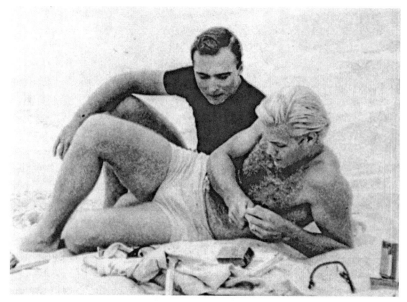

Fig. 12.2 Experimental and avant-garde films—such as Andy Warhol's *My Hustler* (1965), featuring Paul America (foreground)—dealt with homosexual desire, though most did so in a largely nonexplicit fashion. (Frame enlargement.)

riders." In later years, the film inspired directors as different as Federico Fellini and John Waters.[42]

Warhol had directed or produced a number of the films that had touched on homosexual themes or subtexts, involved male nudity, or featured beefcake stars (Joe Dallesandro). Two of his early experimental films were included in the Park Theater film festival. Warhol shot *Blow Job* in the same year that Smith made *Flaming Creatures*. The title alone creates "pornographic" expectations. The entire course of the thirty-minute film focuses on the face of a handsome young man, a man who is getting his cock sucked. We never see who is giving the man the blow job. We don't know whether it is a man or a woman, whether a homosexual or heterosexual blow job—we can't even be sure that it is a "real" blow job, though it seems to be. It is a pure reaction shot. We see only the man's face, but we see him gaze into space, look down, drift off into an erotic reverie. We see him wince—with pain or pleasure? we don't know—then we see him relax; now and then he seems about to have an orgasm. Finally after a moment of apparent ecstasy, he lights a cigarette. We assume that he's had an orgasm.[43]

In 1966, after the success of his film *Chelsea Girls* in mainstream theaters, Warhol was contacted by the manager of the Hudson Theater on

West Forty-fourth Street, just off Times Square, for something that he would be able to show there. Warhol's collaborator, Paul Morrissey, suggested *My Hustler* (1965, figure 12.2). "They want to show something," Morrissey urged Warhol, "and the title will make them think it's a sex film like all the girl films being shown there." *My Hustler* opened there in July 1967 and grossed $18,000 in its first week. The movie has a loose narrative, and unlike *Blow Job* it had sound. Set at Fire Island Pines, the film opens with a panoramic view of a beach. Far out toward the surf is someone, a speck on the sand until we move in closer, sitting in a beach chair. The camera zooms in on a handsome young man, a hustler named Paul America. On the sound track, we hear the voices of a man (Ed Hood) and two other people, another man and a woman arguing about the hustler whom they are both attracted to and whom they want to take for their own use. It is a movie about "sex" or at least as much about sex as movies of that period allowed—that is, no explicit sex—and more definitely about homosexual desire between men. The gossip magazine *Confidential* reported:

> *My Hustler* has touched off the trend toward full homosexual realism in the movies. The reason according to the film critics, is that it is the first full length film to take a look at the lavender side of life without pointing a finger in disgust or disdain, but concentrating instead on the way life really is in the limp-wristed world.[44]

Considering that it has no sexually explicit scenes, *My Hustler* had done surprisingly well in the Times Square arena.

The first theatrical screening of a complete program of gay softcore "erotic" films took place at the Park Theater (e.g., figure 12.3) in Los Angeles in June 1968, predating the Stonewall riots that sparked the gay liberation movement by a year—and was not explicitly labeled as "gay."[45] Billed as "A Most Unusual Film Festival," it drew upon both experimental filmmakers and the local physique photographers and filmmakers such as Bob Mizer and Pat Rocco, for the first time showing their 8 mm short films theatrically. The program listed in the *Los Angeles Free Press* announced *Flaming Creatures, My Hustler,* and an Anger trilogy—all experimental films that alluded to sexual or homosexual themes in symbolic or coded ways. Other films billed for the series included gay softcore titles such as Rocco's *Love Is Blue, Nudist Boy Surfers, Boys Out to Ball,* and "Warhol's *B-J* (call theatre for title!)."[46] The narrative structure for gay softcore films had not yet evolved into a strict formula. The short films of Mizer and Rocco were quite different in that regard. Many of Mizer's films involved disrobing, wrestling, or fights; Rocco's tended to be love

Fig. 12.3 The Park Theater in Los Angeles began showing programs of softcore gay films in 1968. The back of a four-page flier from November/December 1968 promoted films made by Pat Rocco.

stories—with disrobing, kissing, and walking nude. None showed erections or penetration. Within the year, audiences in Los Angeles and other cities had grown tired of the sentimental and softcore short films made by the beefcake photographers.[47]

The first gay softcore feature film produced after the Park's film festival was Tom DeSimone's *The Collection*, released in 1970. Eschewing the sentimental style of Rocco's movies or the boisterous boyishness of Mizer's wrestling films, it told the story of a gay man who kidnaps young men and keeps them locked in cages for his sexual pleasure. Although there was nudity and simulated sex, there were no erections. However, the Los Angeles theater that showed it was raided by the police because of its S/M-styled subject matter.[48] The most ambitious gay softcore feature produced in this period was *Song of the Loon*, a romance between a white man and Indian set in the wilderness of the American West. Made for $70,000 it was released in 1970, just as hardcore movies started playing in San Francisco.

Gay softcore films had barely moved beyond frontal nudity and kissing. Very rapidly, by late 1970, interest in softcore movies had begun to wane. Theater managers and exhibitors were clamoring for more explicit sexual action on the screens. None of the experimental art films had explicitly adopted homo-*erotic* narratives, and the softcore features of DeSimone and other directors had merely sought to apply Hollywood formulas—especially sentimental or melodramatic ones—to homosexual content.

Going Hardcore, Representing Sex

By the middle of 1969 producers wanted "heavy, hard stuff."[49] The defining characteristic of hardcore porn is "insertion"—oral, vaginal, or anal—and penetration was the last frontier, signaling the shift from sexploitation into hardcore.[50] Once the transition to hardcore action took place, the production of sexually explicit pornographic films underwent a dramatic change. Whereas in the production of softcore cinema, many standard cinematic conventions of genre, performance, and narrative held sway, virtually everything changed in hardcore production. Feature-length sexploitation resembled Hollywood films to some extent, with some female nudity thrown in. The move to hardcore required the development of new moviemaking techniques, but ones that had not yet developed or established the narrative conventions, iconographic formulas, or rhetorical strategies of a full-fledged genre.[51]

Hardcore emerged very quickly as a commercial imperative. Distributors and exhibiters clamored for movies showing explicit sexual acts to bring audiences back into their theaters. San Francisco was the first city where hardcore films were extensively played—by 1969 the city had twenty-five theaters offering hardcore movies.[52] New York soon followed, and estimates at the time placed the number of theaters nationally showing sex films between one and four hundred in cities from Indianapolis to Dallas, Houston, and New York.[53]

In 1969, when the owner of a company that made softcore movies told his staff about the decision to move into hardcore porn, he asked anyone uncomfortable with his decision to leave immediately. For those who chose to remain, he explained that he would stand by them and get them the best lawyers, but that if asked he would deny any knowledge of their activities. "And of course," one director noted, "we all knew that we'd have to go even further underground, because everything was getting busted."[54] At the time, hardcore producers not only operated outside the law; many conducted fly-by-night operations. "Stories are written on matchbook covers, and dialogue is made up by performers more noted for looks than talent," said an interviewee.[55] Having to perform "real" sex also changed who was willing to be cast in pornographic movies. Said one director of softcore films, "When you get into hardcore you are dealing with a different class of people. You can't get actors or actresses anymore, but pimps and whores."[56] In California it was illegal to pay performers to have sex. "You cannot make a hardcore film without violating the prostitution laws," Captain Jack Wilson of the LAPD told Kenneth Turan and Stephen Zito. "When you pay actors to engage in sex or oral copulation, you've violated the laws."[57] Sex films were no longer merely products made on the margins of the Hollywood film industry; they were both outside the law and outside the film industry.

The shift to hardcore necessitated creating a new production framework and conventions of performance that facilitated the enactment of real sexual activity, that is, with erections and orgasms. The director's role changed from directing actors in simulated sex scenes, with dialogue and some degree of character development,[58] to directing and choreographing the performers through a series of sex acts that required encouraging and monitoring erections as well as eliciting and photographing successful "cum shots." Producers had to establish the social and physical conditions for sexual performances: a bounded space where sexual performances will be filmed, a supply of sexual partners (via casting) who expect to perform sexual acts before a camera with other performers, and some sort of production crew—at the very least, a director and a cinematographer had to articulate the mise-en-scène. And certain aspects of sexual performance—including erections, orgasms, or ejaculations—became central to the production process. The "cum shot," known also as "the money shot," emerged as the sign of the sex scene's narrative conclusion. Ultimately, it was up to the producer/director to establish the overarching visual and fantasy vocabulary of the movie—the erotic gestalt (the mise-en-scène) of the hardcore movie. In real-life sexual activities, personal "scripts" are usually improvised, to some degree, from the participants' personal fantasies, social roles, cultural codes, and symbols, in addition to the socially available interactional strategies and are used to orchestrate a sexual encounter.[59] That mise-en-scène in hardcore organized the sexual performances and set the stage in order to create a credible *fantasy world* on film. Despite the many challenges, the switch from simple nudity to hardcore action took place almost seamlessly.[60]

For gay men, the transition from softcore beefcake to hardcore was extremely important. The primary focus of beefcake publications had been on men as objects of desire, not as agents of desire. Although there was an extensive underground business in sexually explicit drawings of men having sex with one another, the beefcake magazines were never able to publically show men having sex.[61] Over time, the magazines eventually began to show men interacting with one another—though not sexually. In images that were often coy and suggestive, the illustrations that were published in the magazines did imply (especially in the drawings and illustrations) that the men portrayed might have some potentially "erotic" interest in one another. In place of the "worship" of ideal bodies sponsored by beefcake publications, hardcore films offered images, roles, and "scripts" that could serve as models and legitimate active sex. Only with the advent of gay hardcore movies showing in public theaters were gay audiences able to see gay men as active agents of homosexual desire.

In 1969 and 1970, the challenge of making gay porn movies was, as it was for straight films, discovering the most effective way to represent sexual action. Straight hardcore sex fit easily into the existing narrative formulas; dealing with erections and getting cum shots were the new challenges. But gay hardcore sex posed unique obstacles to filmmakers: erections, anal penetration, and ejaculations (whose?) were seen as essential. Yet no standard sequence of sexual action had emerged. Who sucked or fucked whom, in what order, remained an open question. Initially the approach was purely quantitative: "Generally, I keep my actors to about six people," one director explained, "and that gives me three sex scenes and six cum-shots."[62]

Thus, determining the narrative significance of different sexual acts and recognizing the importance of shooting penetration shots, erections, and orgasms was of primary importance. For instance, fucking "doggie style" was impersonal; in some narrative contexts, face-to-face anal intercourse missionary position was considered more intimate. Riding a man's cock "cowboy style" was sometimes physically easier for maintaining an erection. Most of the conventions that we've come to expect in gay pornographic films—such as the sequence of sex acts from kissing to fellatio to anal sex, the close-up of penetration shots, and of performers' cum shots—were not yet in place. On top of everything else, production values were quite crude; locations, hair, clothing, the dialogue, and sound track resembled more closely a home movie than a professional theatrical feature.

One early gay hardcore film, *Desires of the Devil*, aptly illustrates the transitional phase of the new film genre.[63] Probably made sometime during 1971, it was directed by Sebastian Figg, a former actor who had appeared in softcore films (*Escape to Passion*, 1970) and who directed *The Specimen*, a straight hardcore feature, released a year later.[64] The movie has five scenes, but there is only one cum shot in the entire film. For example, in the first sex scene Jim Cassidy, the film's star, meets a man at a theater and is invited home for a drink. Eventually they go into the bedroom and undress. They embrace naked on the bed and the man sucks Cassidy's penis, but the camera does not focus on the fellatio. They shift position and the man lies on his back as Cassidy inserts his penis, but we never see the penis penetrating the man's ass. They fuck for a few minutes, separate, embrace, and fall asleep. The fucking looks faked; neither man has an orgasm. Cassidy wakes up and sneaks out after taking some cash from the man's wallet.

After Cassidy leaves the first man's apartment, he meets another man on the street and goes back to that man's apartment. They undress and quickly move from the man sucking Cassidy's cock, to "sixty-nine," to Cassidy fucking the man. There is no penetration in this scene either, but it is more convincing and it looks as though there was real fucking. The man comes while he's being fucked, though again Cassidy doesn't himself reach an orgasm. The last three scenes have very little sexual action—only oral sex—no anal penetration and no orgasms. It's not clear why neither penetration nor the money shot were portrayed. Virtually none of the formulas used in later porn were in evidence. It is possible that the film was originally conceived as a softcore feature film and incorporated some explicit sex while in production during the period's hasty transition to hardcore. Perhaps the film's director and producer assumed that the story, the nudity, and the quasi-hardcore and simulated sex put it satisfactorily into the hardcore category. It may also reflect the fact that the conventions surrounding penetration, erections, and the cum shots were not yet firmly established.

Once the transition to hardcore had taken place, theater managers set out to find hardcore material for their gay audiences, and a number started to produce hardcore films to show in their own theaters. Amateur filmmakers produced many of the early gay pornographic movies, and to some degree many of the films made in this period represented an expression of the filmmaker's own newly "liberated" homosexuality; this was especially true for many of the performers. Eventually after the gay movement gained momentum, numerous small companies were formed to explicitly produce gay male pornographic films and the gay porn "industry" began to take shape in San Francisco, Los Angeles, and New York.

Pornographic Realism and Sexual Emancipation

On a hot June night in 1969, police raided a bar in Greenwich Village. For once, instead of meekly lining up to file into a paddy wagon, the bar's patrons and the crowd that gathered outside fought the police, setting off five days of rioting. Drag queens, street hustlers, lesbians, and gay men—many politicized by the movement against the war in Vietnam—rioted and taunted the police, throwing bottles and rocks at them. The riots crystallized a broad grassroots mobilization across the country. The raided bar, known as the Stonewall Inn, became the central symbol of a gay and lesbian political movement that dramatically changed the public image of homosexuals. Ironically, in the same month, theaters in San Francisco screened the first hardcore pornographic films.[65]

A year later Broadway director and choreographer Wakefield Poole, his boyfriend, and two other friends decided to go the Park-Miller Theatre to see an all-male porn film. It turned out to be a disappointing evening and for Poole a somewhat jarring experience, not only because they had all begun to feel a new sense of self-respect and appreciation after the Stonewall riots but unlike the theaters that screened straight porn, the lights at the Park–Miller, which showed gay porn, were bright enough that the theater's customers could actually read. Indeed one patron, Poole reported, was reading the *New York Times*. There was no sex going on anywhere in the audience, which routinely took place in the theaters showing straight porn, in part because at the Park-Miller the police repeatedly walked in and looked over the audience. A film called *Highway Hustler* was the main feature. It portrayed a young hitchhiker who is picked up and taken to motel where he was fucked while being held at knifepoint. Poole's companions reacted to the dreary unerotic plot by laughing or falling asleep. He and his friends had failed to find the film either arousing or romantic. Afterward, they wondered aloud whether it was possible to make a sexy porn film that wasn't degrading.

After his experience at the Park-Miller, Poole decided to make a "quality" porn movie. During a summer stay on Fire Island, he shot three sexually explicit scenes. Poole called his movie *Boys in the Sand*. The title evokes both the idyllic sexual playground that Fire Island had become and implicitly repudiates Mart Crowley's vision of campy and guilt-ridden gay men in his play *Boys in the Band*. It thus rejected gay male effeminacy as an erotically legitimate expression of gay male sexuality.

In *Boys in the Sand* each scene evokes some mythical or magical element: in the first scene, a beautiful man rises from the sea like Botticelli's Venus (figure 12.4). It is a scene deeply indebted to Poole's dance ex-

Fig. 12.4 Casey Donovan rises out of the sea in the first segment of Wakefield Poole's *Boys in the Sand* (1971), one of the first gay hardcore features and one that had crossover appeal with straight audiences. (Digital frame enlargement.)

perience with the Ballets Russes; its Debussy soundtrack evokes Vaslav Nijinsky's famous ballet *Afternoon of a Faun*. (The ballet itself provoked a huge furor at the premier in 1912, when the faun—danced by Nijinsky himself—relieved his sexual frustration by lying on a nymph's scarf and rubbing against it seemingly to the point of orgasm.) In the second scene, a man responds to an ad in a gay newspaper for a magic pill to create a beautiful man. He tosses the pill into the pool and, like a genie from a magic lantern, a beautiful man emerges for a passionate sexual encounter. And in the third, a torrid sexual encounter is created in the imagination of two gay men as they openly cruise one another—one black, the other white—like the mythical homoerotic male couple of American literature: Melville's Ishmael and Queequeg in *Moby Dick*, or Mark Twain's Huck Finn and Jim.[66] In one fell swoop, Poole invoked the cultural archetypes underlying the American homoerotic imagination of the 1960s.

Boys in the Sand offered a new erotic template for the gay male erotic imagination. The tortured sublimated violence in the films of Kenneth Anger; the passive exhibitionism of Bob Mizer's physique photography; the flamboyant ode to androgyny in Jack Smith's *Flaming Creatures*; the blank eroticism of Andy Warhol's *Blow Job*, or *My Hustler*; or the primitive homoerotic idolatry of Joe Dallesandro in Paul Morrissey's *Flesh*

(1968) and *Trash* (1972)—all these were suddenly surpassed in Poole's three scenes.

By the end of 1972, four other feature-length gay hardcore movies were released in theaters in Los Angeles, San Francisco, and New York. Most of these films also played in New York at the Fifty-fifth Street Playhouse, where many of Warhol's sexually themed movies had played. Poole's *Boys in the Sand* opened there in December 1971 and was an immediate critical and financial success. It was followed by J. Brian's *Seven in a Barn* (1971), which was made in the Bay Area. In the following year, Fred Halsted's gritty sadomasochistic feature, *LA Plays Itself* (1972), opened; then Jack Deveau's *Left-Handed* (1972), an urban tale of hustlers and betrayal set in New York City; and finally Jerry Douglas's *The Back Row* (1973), an almost documentarylike portrait of New York's raunchy post-gay-liberation sexual scene. Casey Donovan, who starred in two of these movies—*Boys in the Sand* and *The Back Row*—went on to become the first nationally recognized gay porn star. These five films launched the new wave of postliberation, gay, hardcore pornographic cinema.[67]

Two of the hardcore movies were made in New York during 1971–1972: *Left-Handed* (1972) and *The Back Row* (1973). Jack Deveau and his lover Robert Alvarez began making *Left-Handed* even before Poole's film had premiered. Encouraged by the actor Sal Mineo, Deveau and Alvarez were actively involved in both the city's avant-garde cultural scene and in the new gay sexual scene that had emerged in the 1960s. Deveau was an industrial designer, and Alvarez had worked for a number of years as a film editor on documentaries for National Educational Television (NET) as well as a few "underground" films.[68] *Left-Handed* showed a cross-section of gay male life in Manhattan in the early seventies. The film told the story of an antique dealer, his hustler boyfriend, and their pot dealer—a typical story of the 1960s and early seventies. In the story it recounts a gay man (the hustler) seducing a straight man (the pot dealer), the gay man eventually topping the straight man. The straight man becomes emotionally involved and begins to explore homosexuality, even participating in a gay orgy. At that point, the gay man loses interest in the sexually curious "straight" man.

In February 1972, within months of the premier of *Boys in the Sand*, Jerry Douglas, a young playwright and off-Broadway director known for directing nude plays (a somewhat unique theatrical specialty of the 1960s), was approached by a producer of TV commercials to make a gay hardcore film. The producer asked Douglas to hire *Boy*'s star, Casey Donovan, who was another old friend and had appeared in an off-Broadway play that Douglas had directed.[69] *The Back Row*, the movie that

Douglas wrote and made, was a sexually explicit takeoff of *Midnight Cowboy*, the X-rated movie that recently won an Academy Award for Best Picture. Like *Midnight Cowboy*, *The Back Row*'s hero was a naive young cowboy just off the bus from the West who takes a walk on the wild side of New York's gay sexual subculture. Following in the footsteps of *Boys in the Sand*, it too packed theaters.

The two films made in California, one in San Francisco and one in Los Angeles, defined two major strands of gay pornographic filmmaking. One was J. Brian's *Seven in a Barn*, made in 1971. It is shot almost entirely in a single setting, a straw-filled barn in which seven suntanned All-American young men, many of them blond, sit in circle playing strip poker. The sexual action—ranging from a circle jerk, a round of oral and anal sex, a series of three-ways, some light bondage, and a dildo—established many of the conventions that gay pornography has continued to follow. "Brian's films," wrote Ted Underwood several years later, were "characterized, first and foremost, by the breathtaking golden boys. . . . All seem to be fresh, young, healthy, versatile, creatively kinky and apparently insatiable."[70] Brian originated a style of gay porn and a type of casting that eventually dominated the gay porn industry in the late 1970s and 1980s—the All-American young man in search of sexual fulfillment, suntanned and often blond. The films were often set outdoors, in idyllic surroundings that were increasingly exemplified as California. Throughout the 1970s numerous small companies—Jaguar, Brentwood, Colt, Falcon, and Catalina—set up shop in Los Angeles and San Francisco to make short films as well as feature length movies set within the California fantasy.[71]

If J. Brian initiated the mythical California of golden boys and muscular outdoorsmen, in *LA Plays Itself* (1972), Fred Halsted propelled gay porn into a darker, noir-like Los Angeles. Clearly influenced by the films of Kenneth Anger, Halsted had no connection to either the physique photographers or the early local porn production companies. Nevertheless, Halsted established elements of a homoerotic film genre and style that later gay adult filmmakers drew upon. *LA Plays Itself* opens with the camera moving quickly in the countryside outside Los Angeles. Zooming to wildflowers, rocks and insects, it comes to rest on an idyllic sexual encounter in the Malibu Mountains: two young men kiss, suck each others' cocks, and casually fuck. The second scene opens on a gritty street in a rundown neighborhood of Los Angeles. Fred Halsted himself drives through seedy side streets in Hollywood—lined with young men hustling, porn theaters, and shabby storefronts. On the sound track, a young man with a Texas drawl is reading a porno story. As we cruise the streets of Los Angeles, we overhear a conversation between two young men, one just arrived, the other coyly offering to show him around and warning the newcomer to avoid certain kinds of men. In the third scene, we look down at a young man standing at the foot of a long stairway. Halsted stands at the top, pale, shirtless, wearing only jeans and boots. For a moment, we are suddenly prowling with Halsted again among half-naked men standing in the shadows in Griffith Park. Then just as suddenly, we are back on the stairway again; Halsted pushes the young man into a bedroom and throws him on the bed. He ties up the young man, whips him, and finally puts his fist up the young man's ass.

Halsted had started working on the script for *LA Plays Itself* in 1969 and finished it shortly before its premiere in the spring of 1972. It was essentially the first installment of a trilogy of films summarizing what he called his "philosophy of sex." The second work of the trilogy, *The Sex Garage*, was shot over the course of six hours in December 1971. Then, after prolonged work on the script, he started shooting *Sextool*, the third installment, during the summer of 1974. Shot in high-contrast black and white, *Sex Garage*—unlike *LA Plays Itself*, which was shot in color—opens with a young woman giving a blow job to a garage mechanic, then a macho biker replaces her, but he seems more interested in fucking his motorcycle. He literally fucks the motorcycle's exhaust pipe. *Sex Garage* was confiscated by the NYPD purportedly for the latter scene.[72]

Halsted's films were booked as porn, but local critics reviewed them as contributions to experimental art film genres. There is also no clear sense of homosexual identity in Halsted's films. "I consider myself a pervert first and a homosexual second," he said.[73] Nor did he acknowledge the purely recreational aspect of sex. According to Halsted, sex violates the male characters' sense of self-possession in order to create an encounter with the sacred: "Coming is not the point. The point is revelation—the why."[74] Halsted's philosophy shared much with that of pornographer and philosopher Georges Bataille. Like the philosopher, Halsted believed that the erotic is transgressive and sacramental, that it is inherently violent, and that it involves acts of violation. Human beings, according to Bataille, are closed off from one another and cannot communicate because the bodies of others are closed off to them. In the erotic encounter those physical barriers are breached, if only briefly, through the other's bodily orifices. Although Halsted made only a handful of films, director Joe Gage—in *Kansas City Trucking Company* (1976), *El Paso Wrecking Company* (1977), and *L.A. Tool & Die* (1979)—developed more thoroughly the ultramasculine style that Halsted initiated.

After *Boys in the Sand*, Fred Halsted's *LA Plays Itself* was the most successful gay porn movie of the time. Similarly, it was one of the first *porn* movies, not just gay porn movies, reviewed in mainstream newspapers. Both movies helped to define "porn chic" as a significant cultural moment in the early 1970s, and each was an example of an artistically serious hardcore film. Moreover, both films preceded *Deep Throat* as a pornographic film that played to general moviegoing audiences, though neither one was the first gay hardcore film playing in theaters. These films created the public perception that gay pornographic films represented a new more serious kind of commercial pornography compared to the softcore shorts or the Hollywood-style potboilers showing in theaters.

Pornography, Perversity, and History

Hardcore pornographic films are historical documents of sex and of the scripts, fantasies, bodies, and styles of sex.[75] They succeed in the market because they articulate or propose wish-fulfilling fantasies that resonate with their audience. Commercial success, however, also fed the perverse dynamic—the constant push to identify new varieties of polymorphous sexual possibilities—and at the same time generated strategies of symbolic containment. Thus the transition from softcore porn to hardcore was also in part a shift from more euphemistic, somewhat idealized, versions of sexual desire and conduct to ones that were more realistic and perhaps more perverse, though not, of course, without the compensating idealizations of breasts, penises, and body types.

Gay porn films reinforced its gay viewers' identity as gay men. That identification was enunciated through the pornography's dominant semantic and syntactical conventions: the "standard" narrative sequence (kissing, undressing, oral sex, rimming, anal intercourse) of sexual acts, a convincingly energetic performance, and, most important, the erections and visible orgasms that authenticate (and narratively end the erotic scene) the embodied forms of homosexual desire. Operating within the *realism* of porn and its "reality effects," the real erections and the real orgasms putatively "prove" to a gay male spectator that these "sexually desirable, masculine, and energetic performers" are really gay—thus affirming the gay male identity. Even when an individual movie deviated from these generic expectations, either through failure to provide a credible performance or by offering new or creative sexual variations, the film affirmed gay identity.

Ironically, the generic conventions that consolidated and reinforced the identity effects coexisted with representations of "straight" men engaging in homosexual acts. In this way gay porn reinforces the incongruity between male homosexual desire—traditionally stigmatized and abject—and the heterosexual dominance of the masculine regime of desire. It serves to situate homosexual *desire* within masculine territory irrespective of heterosexual or gay identities.[76] Thus, the widespread employment of straight performers in gay pornography intensifies the contradiction between *gay male identity* and *homosexual desire without identity*, which conferred legitimacy on homosexual *behavior* independent of gay identity.[77]

Gay hardcore pornography also helped to legitimate a reconfiguration of gay masculinity.[78] As gay men rejected the traditional idea that male homosexual desire implied the desire to be female, they turned to a traditionally masculine or working-class style of acting out sexually. Camp as an effeminized gay sensibility was out. The new style of gay men was macho and sexually provocative, and that style included denim pants, black combat boots, a tight T-shirt (if it was warm), covered by a plaid flannel shirt (if it was cooler). The rugged look of the Marlboro man was the iconic masculine model for the 1970s.[79]

Anal intercourse became the central act of gay male pornography. Rather than a strict dichotomy between the "trade"/masculine role and "queer"/effeminate role, or top and bottom (terms and a distinction not in use during the early 1970s), versatility represented the politically fashionable style of fucking. It promulgated a fantasy of sexual surrender to the intense pleasure of discharged sexual tension, and ultimately to the psychic shattering of the self through anal intercourse.[80] Pornographic film relies upon the real erections and the real orgasms (the reality effects of porn production) of sexual performers and is at the same time a fictional representation of sexual fantasies. The realism is central, if not always absolutely necessary, to the rhetorical effectiveness of porn cinema. "Ultimately, what viewers want to see is guys *having* sex, not actors *pretending* to have sex," one reviewer wrote.[81]

Freud classified all forms of nonreproductive sexual behavior—kissing, oral sex, homosexuality, and various fetishes—as perverse sexual desires. Moreover, he argued that perverse desires were incompatible with a stable social order; instead, he believed that perverse sexual desires must be transformed, through repression and sublimation, into forms of energy more compatible with "civilized society."[82]

Pornography normalizes perversity. The men who regularly went out to the adult theaters saw thousands of hours of porn films and videos.

In his memoir about his experience in New York's porn theaters, Samuel Delany has described the audience's changing response to the sex portrayed in hardcore movies. The movies, he suggested, "improved our vision of sex . . . making it friendlier, more relaxed, and more playful."

> For the first year or two the theaters operated, the entire working-class audience would break out laughing at everything save male-superior fucking. (I mean, that's *what* sex is, isn't it?) At the fellatio, at the cunnilingus even more, and at the final kiss, among the groans and chuckles you'd always hear a couple of "*Yuccchs*" and "*Uhgggs*." By the seventies' end, though, only a few chuckles sounded out now—at the cunnilingus passages. And in the first year or two of the eighties, even those had stopped. . . . Indeed, I think, under pressure of those films, many guys simply found themselves changing what turned them on. And if one part or another didn't happen to be your thing, you still saw it enough times to realize that maybe *you* were the strange one.[83]

Starting in the 1970s, the proliferation of pornography opened up social space for the emergence of the "perverse dynamic."[84] Under the banner of sexual intercourse outside of the heteronormative marriage, pornography harnessed voyeurism and exhibitionism to portray sex with multiple partners, group sex, fellatio and cunnilingus, anal intercourse, lesbianism, male homosexuality, all kinds of sexual fetishisms, sex toys, BDSM, and other sexual practices. Porn and its reality effects both harness those perverse desires and generates them. The production of pornography operates along the "continuum of perversions which underlies human sexuality," contributing to the historical dynamic of a polymorphic sexual economy that allows for selection of many different kinds of objects of desire.[85]

The shift to hardcore triggered the drive to seek out ever more unusual sexual fantasy content material, which would later become the central dynamic of the porn industry. And the sexual fantasies supplied, whether viewed as cultural expressions or commercial products, grow out of a complex dynamic between the familiar and the new, the normal and the taboo, the ordinary and the perverse. In this pursuit, the industry has turned to fantasies that represent ever more "perverse" sexual combinations in order to sustain erotic excitement among its jaded fans. Thus the sexual revolution and its discourses of sexual liberation both emancipated those who were stigmatized for their sexuality, and facilitated the social discipline of the newly emancipated identities.[86] Pornography played, and continues to play, an ambiguous role in this process.

Notes

I am indebted to my friends Jerry Douglas, Rod Barry, Wash West and Michael Stabile who have worked in the porn industry for their advice, suggestions and information; to Lee Jones for his amazing knowledge of pornographic film history; to John Gagnon and Alain Giami, for valuable discussions about the sexual revolution; to Christopher Mitchell for reading several drafts carefully and offering historical clarifications and above all to Eric Schaefer for his patience, steadfastness and many sage and practical editorial suggestions.

1. Jon Lewis, *Hollywood v. Hardcore: How the Struggle over Censorship Saved the Modern Film Industry* (New York: New York University Press, 2000), 192–195.

2. See the chapter "Coming to Terms, Gay Pornography," in Richard Dyer, *Only Entertainment* (London: Routledge, 1992).

3. Thomas Yingling, "How the Eye Is Caste: Robert Mapplethorpe and the Limits of Controversy," *Discourse* 12, no. 2 (spring/summer 1989): 3–286.

4. Earl Jackson, *Strategies of Deviance: Studies in Gay Male Representation* (Bloomington: Indiana University Press, 1995), 129–132.

5. For an exploration of the significance of the shift in the representation of sex by hardcore films, see Linda Williams, *Hard Core: Power, Pleasure and the "Frenzy of the Visible." Exp. ed.* (Berkeley: University of California Press, 1999); and her *Screening Sex* (Durham, NC: Duke University Press, 2008).

6. Jeffrey Escoffier, "Scripting the Sex: Fantasy, Narrative and Sexual Scripts in Pornographic Films," in *The Sexual Self: The Construction of Sexual Scripts*, ed. Michael Kimmel (Nashville: Vanderbilt University Press, 2007), 61–79.

7. Christian Metz, *The Imaginary Signifier: Psychoanalysis and Cinema* (Bloomington: Indiana University Press, 1982), 42–57.

8. Jeffrey Escoffier, "Pornography, Perversity and the Sexual Revolution," paper presented at the seminar on the Sexual Revolution, Amsterdam, April 8–9, 2011, sponsored by University of Amsterdam and the Institut National de la Santé et de la Recherche Médicale, Paris.

9. Joseph W. Slade, *Pornography in America: A Reference Handbook* (Santa Barbara, CA: ABC-CLIO, 2000), 209–215.

10. John D'Emilio, *Sexual Politics, Sexual Communities: The Making of a Homosexual Minority in the United States, 1940–1970* (Chicago: University of Chicago Press, 1983), 115.

11. Slade, *Pornography in America*, 212–213.

12. Thomas Waugh, *Hard to Imagine: Gay Male Eroticism in Photography and Film from Their Beginnings to Stonewall* (New York: Columbia University Press, 1996), 413–417. Also see Christopher Nealon's chapter on the broader political and cultural significance of beefcake magazines, "The Secret Public of Physique Culture," in his book *Foundlings: Lesbian and Gay Historical Emotion before Stonewall* (Durham, NC: Duke University Press, 2001), 99–140.

13. Laurence O'Toole, *Pornocopia: Porn, Sex, Technology and Desire* (London: Serpent's Tail, 1999), 7–10.

14. Barry Werth, *The Scarlet Professor, Newton Arvin: A Literary Life Shattered by Scandal* (New York: Anchor Books, 2001).

15. Slade, *Pornography in America*, 212–213; Werth, epilogue in *The Scarlet Professor*.

16. On the criminalization of homosexuality after World War II, see Allan Berube, *Coming out under Fire: The History of Gay Men and Women in World War Two* (New York: Free Press, 1990), 228–279.

17. Helen Lefkowitz Horowitz, *Rereading Sex: Battles over Sexual Knowledge and Suppression in Nineteenth-Century America* (New York: Alfred A. Knopf, 2002), 299–318.

18. For the history of the physique magazines, see F. Valentine Hooven III, *Beefcake: The Muscle Magazines of America, 1950–1970* (Cologne: Taschen, 1995); for an excellent account of the commercial and legal aspects of physique magazines from 1945 to 1963, see Waugh, *Hard to Imagine*, 215–283; and on the availability of illegal images, see 284–365.

19. Hooven, *Beefcake*; Waugh, *Hard to Imagine*, 215–252; Nealon, *Foundlings*, 99–140.

20. Hooven, *Beefcake*, 74.

21. See Waugh, *Hard to Imagine*, 215–283; and Hooven, *Beefcake*.

22. Nealon, *Foundlings*, 99–140; Dian Hanson, *Bob's World: The Life and Boys of AMG's Bob Mizer* (Cologne: Taschen, 2009).

23. Waugh, *Hard to Imagine*, 215–227; Hooven, *Beefcake*, 27–32.

24. Nealon, *Foundlings*, 1–23.

25. Nealon, *Foundlings*, 99–140.

26. Waugh, *Hard to Imagine*, 215–219.

27. Hooven, *Beefcake*, 52.

28. Waugh, *Hard to Imagine*, 217–219.

29. On sexual activity in porn theaters and arcades, see Samuel Delany, *Times Square Red, Times Square Blue* (New York: New York University Press, 1999); Brendan Gill, "Blue Notes," *Film Comment*, January–February 1973, 10–11; C. A. Sundholm, "The Pornographic Arcade: Ethnographic Notes on Moral in Immoral Places," *Urban Life and Culture* 2, no. 1 (1973): 85–104; Jose B. Capino, "Homologies of Space: Text and Spectatorship in All Male Adult Theater," *Cinema Journal* 45, no. 1 (autumn 2005): 50–65; and Amy Herzog, "In the Flesh: Space and Embodiment in the Pornographic Peep Show Arcade," *Velvet Light Trap* 62 (fall 2008): 29–43.

30. On desire and sexual identification, male spectatorship, and pornographic film, see Williams, *Hard Core*, 80–83; Elizabeth Cowie, "Pornography and Fantasy: Psychoanalytic Perspectives," in Lynn Segal and Mary McIntosh, eds. *Sex Exposed: Sexuality the Pornography Debate* (New Brunswick, NJ: Rutgers University Press, 1993), 133; and Thomas Waugh, "Homosociality in the Classical American Stag Film: Off-screen, On-screen" in *Porn Studies*, ed. Linda Williams (Durham, NC: Duke University Press, 2004), 127–141.

31. Linda Williams, "Film Bodies: Gender, Genre and Excess," in Grant, ed. *Film Genre Reader III* (Austin: University of Texas Press, 2003), 154.

32. Laurence Senelick, "Private Parts in Public Places," *Inventing Times Square: Commerce and Culture at the Crossroads of the World*, ed. William R. Taylor (Baltimore: Johns Hopkins University Press, 1991), 329–353; Delany, *Times Square Red, Times Square Blue* (New York: New York University Press, 1999).

33. William Leap, ed., *Public Sex, Gay Space* (New York: Columbia University Press, 1999); Laud Humphries, *Tearoom Trade: Impersonal Sex in Public Place* (New York: Aldine De Gruyter, 1975).

34. See Delany, *Times Square Red, Times Square Blue*; Richard Cante and Angelo Restivo, "The Cultural-Aesthetic Specificities of All-Male Moving Image Pornography," in Williams, *Porn Studies*, 142–166.

35. For a discussion of the theater as an integral component of the cinematic apparatus, see Jean-Louis Baudry's classic articles: "Ideological Effects of the Basic Cinematographic Apparatus," and "The Apparatus: Metapsychological Approaches to the Impression of Reality in Cinema," in Philip Rosen, ed., *Narrative, Apparatus, Ideology: A Film Theory Reader* (New York: Columbia University Press, 1986), 286–298 and 299–318.

36. Capino, "Homologies of Space," 58–64.

37. Gill, "Blue Notes," 10–11.

38. Delany, *Times Square Red, Times Square Blue*, xiii–xx.

39. Eric Schaefer, *"Bold! Daring! Shocking! True!: A History of Exploitation Films, 1919–1959* (Durham, NC: Duke University Press, 1999), 210–214.

40. See Juan A. Suárez, *Bike Boys, Drag Queens and Superstars: Avant-garde, Mass Culture, and Gay Identities in the 1960s Underground Cinema* (Bloomington: Indiana University Press, 1996).

41. Alice Hutchison, *Kenneth Anger: A Demonic Visionary* (London: Black Dog Publishing, 2004).

42. Steven Watson, *Factory Made: Warhol and the Sixties* (New York: Pantheon, 2003), 72; Sally Banes, *Greenwich Village 1963: Avant-Garde Performance and the Effervescent Body* (Durham, NC: Duke University Press, 1993), 172.

43. Stephen Koch, *Stargazer: The Life, World and Films of Andy Warhol*, rev. and updated (New York: Marion Boyers, 2002); Wayne Koestenbaum, *Andy Warhol* (London: Phoenix, 2003).

44. Watson, *Factory Made: Warhol and the Sixties* (New York: Pantheon, 2003), 336–337.

45. Jeffrey Escoffier, *Bigger than Life: The History of Gay Porn Cinema from Beefcake to Hardcore* (Philadelphia: Running Press, 2009), 47 88.

46. Escoffier, *Bigger than Life*, 47–48.

47. Escoffier, *Bigger than Life*, 57–58.

48. Jerry Douglas, "Interview with Tom De Simone," *Manshots*, June 1993, 12.

49. Paul Alcuin Siebenand, "The Beginnings of Gay Cinema in Los Angeles: The Industry and the Audience," PhD diss., University of Southern California, 1975, 50.

50. Legs McNeil and Jennifer Osborne, *The Other Hollywood: The Uncensored Oral History of the Porn Film Industry* (New York: Reagan Books, 2005).

51. Thomas Schatz, *Hollywood Genres: Formulas, Filmmaking and the Studio System* (New York: Random House, 1981), 14–41.

52. Kenneth Turan and Stephen F. Zito, *Sinema: American Pornographic Films and the People Who Make Them* (New York: Praeger, 1974), 77–80.

53. Turan and Zito, *Sinema*, 77–80.

54. Douglas, "Interview with Tom De Simone," 12.

55. Turan and Zito, *Sinema*, 128.

56. Siebenand, "The Beginnings of Gay Cinema in Los Angeles," 85.

57. Turan and Zito, *Sinema*, 128.

58. Whereas some sexploitation films included synch-sound dialogue, others featured awkwardly post-dubbed "dialogue"; still others were essentially silent with narration.

59. Escoffier, "Scripting the Sex."

60. Siebenand, "The Beginnings of Gay Cinema in Los Angeles," 27.

61. See Thomas Waugh, ed., *Out/Lines: Underground Gay Graphics from before Stonewall* (Vancouver: Arsenal Pulp Press, 2002).

62. Siebenand, "The Beginnings of Gay Cinema in Los Angeles," 92.

63. Schatz, *Hollywood Genres*, 37–38.

64. Sebastian Figg, accessed March 27, 2008, www.imdb.com/name/nm0276544/.

65. David Carter, *Stonewall: The Riots that Sparked the Gay Revolution*, new ed. (New York: St. Martin's Griffin, 2010).

66. *Boys in the Sand* (2002). See also Wakefield Poole, *Dirty Poole: The Autobiography of a Gay Porn Pioneer* (Los Angeles: Alyson Books, 2000), 145–164.

67. Escoffier, *Bigger than Life*, 47–116.

68. Jerry Douglas, "The Legacy of Jack Deveau," *Stallion*, April 1983, 22–25, 46–47.

69. Douglas was the author of *Rondelay* (1969), a musical version of Arthur Schnitzler's *La Ronde*; *Score* (1970), and under the pseudonym, A. J. Kronengold, *Tubstrip* (1973), which was set in a gay bathhouse.

70. Ted Underwood "Raw Country," *Stallion's* HOT 50: *All-Time Best Male Films and Videos 1970–1985*, special issue no. 4 (1985): 46.

71. Escoffier, *Bigger than Life*.

72. Siebenand, *The Beginnings of Gay Cinema in Los Angeles*, 231. For accounts of Fred Halsted's life and work, see chap. 6 in Patrick Moore's *Beyond Shame: Reclaiming the Abandoned History of Radical Gay Sexuality* (Boston: Beacon Press, 2004); and William E. Jones, *Halsted Plays Himself* (Los Angeles: Semiotext[e] Books, 2011).

73. Siebenand, *The Beginnings of Gay Cinema in Los Angeles*, 222.

74. Siebenand, *The Beginnings of Gay Cinema in Los Angeles*, 211.

75. For example, the documentary film by director Joseph Lovett, *Gay Sex in the Seventies* (2006) uses clips from porn films by Jack Deveau and Peter Romeo to illustrate the gay sexual mores of the 1970s. See also Jeffrey Escoffier, "Video Pornography as an Archive of the History of Sexuality," forthcoming.

76. Brian Pronger, *The Arena of Masculinity: Sports, Homosexuality, and the Meaning of Sex* (New York: St. Martin's Press, 1990).

77. Henning Bech, *When Men Meet: Homosexuality and Modernity* (Chicago: University of Chicago Press, 1997); Jeffrey Escoffier, "Gay-for-Pay: Straight Men and the Making of Gay Pornography," *Qualitative Sociology* 26, no. 4 (winter 2003): 531–555.

78. See Michael Bronski, *Culture Clash: The Making of Gay Sensibility* (Boston: Alyson Books, 1984), 166–174. Dyer, *Only Entertainment*, 121–134; Jackson, *Strategies of Deviance*, 126–172; Waugh, *Hard to Imagine*, 402–416; and Pronger, *The Arena of Masculinity: Sports, Homosexuality, and the Meaning of Sex* (New York: St. Martin's Press, 1990), 125–150.

79. Edmund White, *States of Desire: Travels in Gay America* (New York: Plume, 1980), 45–46.

80. See Leo Bersani's *Baudelaire and Freud* (Berkeley: University of California Press, 1977) and *The Freudian Body: Psychoanalysis and Art* (New York: Columbia University Press, 1986).

81. A. Foxxe, "Home Bodies," *Unzipped*, August 31, 1999, 40.

82. Sigmund Freud, "'Civilized' Sexual Morality and Modern Nervousness," in Jeffrey Escoffier, ed. *Sexual Revolution* (New York: Thunder's Mouth Press, 2003), 557–577.

83. Delany, *Times Square Red, Times Square Blue*, 78.

84. Jonathan Dollimore, *Sexual Dissidence: Augustine to Wilde, Freud to Foucault* (Oxford: Clarendon Press, 1991), 219–230; Michel Foucault, *The History of Sexuality*, vol. 1: *An Introduction*, trans. Robert Hurley (New York: Vintage, 1980), 36–50; Williams, *Hard Core: Power, Pleasure and the "Frenzy of the Visible,"* exp. ed. (Berkeley: University of California Press, 1999), 272–273.

85. Williams, *Hard Core*, 272–273; Escoffier, "Pornography, Perversity and Sexual Revolution." See for example, Escoffier "Imagining the She/Male: Pornography and the Transsexualization of the Heterosexual Male," *Studies in Gender and Sexuality* 12, no. 4 (2011): 268–281."

86. Michel Foucault, "'Omnes et Singulatim': Toward a Critique of Political Reason," in *Power, Essential Works of Foucault, 1954–1984*, vol. 3, ed. James D. Faubion (New York: New Press, 2000), 298–325.

Part V: Contending with the Sex Scene

13 ∗ Publicizing Sex through Consumer and Privacy Rights: How the American Civil Liberties Union Liberated Media in the 1960s

LEIGH ANN WHEELER

On February 8, 1961, J. P. McGlynn, a diesel instructor with the Union Pacific Railroad, fretted over the latest achievements of the local Citizen's Committee for Decent Literature. The group had convinced several newsstands in Omaha, Nebraska, to stop selling *Playboy*, McGlynn's favorite magazine and one he enjoyed reading with his two teenage sons. Suspecting that Hugh Hefner, the magazine's editor, and Pat Malin, executive director of the American Civil Liberties Union (ACLU) would share his frustration, McGlynn implored them to defend his "freedom to read." McGlynn's letter points to a budding relationship between the ACLU, *Playboy* magazine, and *Playboy* readers, one that also signaled important developments in popular conceptions of the First Amendment. It represented a growing sense among many citizens that civil liberties included not just an individual right to speak but also rights as individual consumers to read, see, and hear.[1]

This chapter explores ACLU contributions to the sexual revolution by examining the roots of two rights that many now take for granted. The first was a reinterpretation of the First Amendment to protect, not just the rights of speakers—producers of speech—but the rights of consumers of speech as well. Political theorists had long linked a particular type of consumption, citizens' access to information, with democracy, but they did so by treating citizens in the aggregate as a tool for achieving and sustaining democracy.[2] What the ACLU did, increasingly in partnership with commercial producers and other interest groups, was fundamentally different and designed to empower citizens to claim access to information and images as an individual right.

The second right that contributed to the sexual revolution is the right to sexual privacy, beginning with the right to use birth control and later extending to the right of adults to engage in consensual sexual relations. Ironically, both opponents and proponents of "sexual freedom" demanded privacy, but the sexual revolution of the 1960s emerged through increasingly visible sex—in the media, public behavior, and the various stages of dress and undress that passed for fashion or political protest. Practically every facet of public life exhibited transformations in displays of sexuality. The media contributed to the shift by using daring sexual material to make quick and easy profits (figure 13.1). Medical, legal, and demographic changes also played a role as the development of the birth control pill, concerns about overpopulation, and the expanding rights revolution helped to bring sexual expression and conduct into the public realm even as laws against their public presence withered under an emerging right to privacy.

By exploring how sex became more public even as privacy rights trumped sex laws, this chapter corroborates historian Beth Bailey's observation that the sexual revolution grew out of "tensions between public and private."[3] It does this by considering an unexamined source and shaper of the sexual revolution: the ACLU. Ultimately, it argues that the ACLU advanced the cause of sexual liberation by empowering media consumers. More specifically, the ACLU established the consumer's First Amendment rights to sexual material even as it battled, with mixed success, more conservative groups and individuals who invoked privacy rights to limit particular aspects of the sexual revolution.

The ACLU, Consumer Rights, and the First Amendment

The notion of media-related consumer rights was not entirely new when the ACLU began to transform it into a constitutional claim. The idea of consumer rights to media had been deployed by radio and motion picture reformers since at least the 1920s but as collective rather than individual rights.[4] Leaders in the ACLU began to fashion an individualized version of media-related consumer rights by the middle of the 1940s in response to widespread concerns about corporate consolidation. American Civil Liberties Union board member and attorney Morris Ernst warned that media monopolies such as the Motion Picture Producers and Distributors of America (MPPDA) and the National Association of Broadcasters (NAB) reduced the availability of diverse views to consumers by restricting the access of certain speakers. "While we [in the ACLU] are fighting a particular effort to suppress the freedom of thought or expression of a particular man," Ernst lamented, "the curse of bigness" assures that "fewer and fewer people" dominate "the pipelines of thought—the newspapers, the radio and the movies."[5] Some of his colleagues worried that tackling the problem of media consolidation would divert their energies into economic battles that were only tangentially related to civil liberties. The majority redirected Ernst's critique toward more conventional

Fig. 13.1 By the late 1960s it was easy for consumers to purchase sexually oriented material in bookstores across the United States. Here, police detectives examine film in a New York City shop in 1970. (Courtesy UPI.)

civil libertarian goals by refocusing on the individual First Amendment rights of media consumers.[6]

In 1945, ACLU leaders publicized their new, consumer-oriented approach to the First Amendment in a formal resolution. "Freedom of speech, press and assembly," they declared, "imply freedom to hear, read and see without interference by public authorities" or by "private agencies." Affiliates of the ACLU quickly adopted the new language and perspective, agreeing that the real victims of censorship had always been not the publisher but the consumer.[7]

This new consumer-oriented policy helped the ACLU inspire wider public interest in its work. Since the organization's earliest days, leaders complained that, beyond those who stood to profit—producers, exhibitors, and publishers—few people protested the closing of a burlesque theater, censorship of a motion picture, banning of a nudist magazine, or seizure of a racy novel. But by shifting attention from *producers* to *consumers* the ACLU's new approach promised to persuade more people to take censorship personally. As ACLU member and censored author James Farrell urged ACLU president and founder, Roger Baldwin, we need to "popularize the idea that censorship is not [only] an invasion of the rights of the author; it is also an invasion of the rights of the reader. If this idea is popularized in the minds of liberal readers it would then be possible to stir them" to write letters and conduct protests on their own. Hoping for this very outcome, Baldwin issued a press release and a new ACLU pamphlet "Are you FREE to READ—SEE—HEAR?" which pledged the ACLU to support the rights of audience members. He was delighted to receive an enthusiastic response from ACLU watchers and members, one of whom wrote simply, "I am glad to see the A.C.L.U. on the side of the consumer-listener."[8]

This consumer-rights approach to the First Amendment also sharpened the ACLU's criticism of private business practices that prevented "the public from seeing, hearing or reading." It implicated commercial vendors who deferred to pressure groups or exercised their own discretion in declining to stock particular material. In defense of consumer rights, the ACLU denounced the local theater exhibitor who rejected Howard Hughes's *The Outlaw* (1943), the druggist who refused to stock *Esquire,* and the community bookseller who removed Edmund Wilson's *Memoirs of Hecate County* from the shelf. In line with this new approach, ACLU leaders now supported the federal government's antitrust suit against Paramount Pictures, arguing that producer ownership of theaters violated "the fundamental rights of motion picture audiences" who should be able to "see all films freely and on an equitable basis." On these same grounds, ACLU leaders considered initiating a lawsuit against the MPPDA for restricting the movies available to consumers through its Motion Picture Production Code.[9] Ironically, the new policy also crystallized a shared interest between the ACLU and the MPPDA. Although the two organizations would continue to tangle over the MPPDA's own internal censorship apparatus, leaders of both organizations agreed on the usefulness of casting censorship more broadly as a violation of consumer rights.

Ernst's proposals were timely. They easily gained traction in the burgeoning postwar consumer economy that emerged alongside Cold War–inspired concerns about media monopolies, pressure group censorship, and freedom of speech. But for Ernst, media consumers were a tool for opening up the marketplace to more speakers, more producers of speech. For the ACLU, by contrast, simply enhancing media consumers' rights to what had already been produced became the whole point. So whereas Ernst wanted to challenge media monopolies and create alternative new media outlets with broad public access, the majority of his ACLU colleagues considered such activity a distraction from their core civil liberties concerns. By defending the individual rights of media consumers "to see, read and hear"—whether those rights were threatened by private agencies or state censorship—the ACLU channeled Ernst's broad communitarian arguments for an open marketplace of ideas into a narrower theory of individual consumer rights.[10]

The "Right to Read"

By the 1950s, the ACLU faced new censorship threats. Racy books, magazines, and pinups proliferated in the consumer-driven, postwar era, arousing the ire of "decency" groups and inspiring a series of congressional hearings on obscenity, pornography, and juvenile delinquency. Sponsored by Congressman Ezekiel C. Gathings in 1952, Senator Estes Kefauver in 1954, and Congresswoman Kathryn E. Granahan in 1959, friendly witnesses cast pornography as a covert tool for subverting the superior morality of the United States in its Cold War against Communism.[11] Leaders of the ACLU too spoke in a Cold War idiom, urging legislators to recognize freedom of speech and consumer rights rather than morality and Christianity as the distinguishing features between "our way of life" and Communism. "It is not only the freedom of the publisher that is at stake," the ACLU's executive director explained. "It is also the freedom of 160,000,000 Americans whose Constitution guarantees them that no governmental official may tell them what they may or may not read." But ACLU testimony could not compete with findings that Americans spent $1 billion annually on mail-order pornography and that millions of postal patrons received unwanted "lewd and obscene material." These reports inspired the creation of the Comics Code, gave rise to new obscenity laws, and provoked even more activism by pressure groups.[12]

In response, ACLU leaders mobilized a consumer-rights-based campaign against pressure groups guilty of divesting "citizens of their right to read." The national office issued press releases and pamphlets, challenged commission findings, lobbied against censorship bills, prevailed upon media code authorities, and condemned pressure groups as agents of censorship, all in the name of consumers' rights. One ACLU radio announcement directly asked listeners, "Are you being deprived of the chance to read, see, or hear things in the press, films, radio, theater, books and magazines?" The national office also advised its affiliates — most of which responded enthusiastically — to protect "the public's right to see, read and hear" by monitoring local exhibitors and booksellers who might be try to censor their own offerings. Local media outlets enjoy a "special relationship to the public," the ACLU argued, so they must take responsibility for maintaining the "public's freedom to see, read and hear everything."[13]

The ACLU confronted resistance to its position on pressure group censorship from within and beyond its own ranks, but it also enjoyed the support of powerful allies in its defense of the consumer's right to read, see, and hear. In 1951, *Redbook* published "What Censorship Keeps You From Knowing." Later condensed for *Reader's Digest*, this prominent article refocused concerns about censorship on the consumer and encouraged readers to join the ACLU. The concept of a "right to read" took hold as librarians, teachers, publishers, lawyers, and judges used it to defend themselves against censorship inspired by the Red Scare. Librarians too fought for the "freedom to read" when local officials and citizens demanded that they withdraw "un-American" materials from circulation. In 1953, the American Library Association (ALA) issued a widely publicized manifesto "On Freedom to Read," which condemned "private groups and public authorities" who banned books or otherwise aimed to restrict their availability to the public. In a simple statement that delighted ACLU leaders, the ALA declared that "the freedom to read is guaranteed by the Constitution." The American Book Publishers Council (ABPC) signed the ALA statement, initiated the formation of Right-to-Read Committees around the country, and joined with the ALA to form the Commission on the Freedom to Read, made up of prestigious university professors. That same year, Judge Curtis Bok, a prominent Pennsylvania judge, delivered a radio address entitled "The Freedom to Read," and the American Bar Association pronounced "the freedom to read" a "corollary of the constitutional guarantee of freedom of the press." In 1955, Paul Blanshard—a trade union activist, journalist, and attorney who worked closely with the ACLU—published *The Right to Read: The Battle Against Censorship*. One year later, the ACLU and its affiliates helped Columbia Pictures advertise its new film *Storm Center*, featuring Bette Davis as an embattled librarian who defended "the freedom to read!" And in 1957, an ACLU board member published *The Freedom to Read: Perspective and Program*. American Civil Liberties Union leaders communicated regularly with freedom-to-read groups and celebrated the extensive alliance they formed for "readers' rights" and against censorship.[14]

In a sweeping call to arms in 1957, the ACLU offered to assist not only producers but also buyers who have "the will to explore legal avenues for the maintenance of their freedom." The plea showed up in magazines and newspapers with national circulations and in the ACLU's own widely circulated pamphlets with a cover letter by Morris Ernst titled "Your *Freedom to Read* is in Danger." Leaders from the ACLU did not just offer assistance; they begged for an opportunity to provide it. For purposes of standing, or the right to bring a lawsuit, they needed a complainant who could demonstrate that s/he had been deleteriously affected in a way that legal action could resolve. Such lawsuits against pressure groups and other private entities were very difficult to execute, so ACLU leaders concentrated on educational work, urging consumers to defend their rights to read, see, and hear; exhorting producers and distributors to hold the line against pressure groups; and prevailing upon pressure groups themselves to eschew activities the ACLU considered censorious.[15]

A growing number of individuals—empowered by the concept of a right to read, see, and hear, and acting only in their capacity as consumers—began to demand access to and influence over the media. Many contacted the ACLU to report on and seek advice regarding pressure groups that tried to censor movies and books in their communities. They also created thousands of Right-to-Read Committees that mobilized consumer influence to counter the pressure wielded by groups such as the National Organization for Decent Literature (NODL). In addition, groups associated with more liberal causes mobilized and used the discourse of consumerism to demand that the media portray African Americans and women more positively, for example, and drug use and alcohol abuse more negatively.[16]

In the 1960s, consumers gained a powerful legal tool for defending their rights under the First Amendment, when two ACLU attorneys in Chicago established the media consumer's standing to sue. The notion that consumers' rights to hear, see, and read might bear legal weight and establish standing was new but timely; the notion of a "right to read, hear and see" now saturated American culture.[17]

It all began with a wave of lawsuits inspired by the 1961 publication of *Tropic of Cancer*, the blockbuster "sex-capade" by Henry Miller. The book itself was not new, having appeared originally in a 1934 French edition released by Obelisk Press. In it, Miller narrated a relentless litany of sexual encounters, many described in intimate, graphic, and shameless detail. Attempts to import the book or publish it in the United States attracted support from the ACLU's Northern California branch in the 1950s, but the novel failed in federal court. Founder of Grove Press, Barney Rosset—whose own youth was inspired by a smuggled copy of *Tropic*—was determined to publish the book in the United States. He began to lay the legal groundwork and introduce American readers to Henry Miller and, in 1959, his magazine, *Evergreen Review*, published Miller's passionate "Defense of the Freedom to Read," a piece designed to rally American readers to support his work by lamenting their victimization by censorship. Three years later, when Rosset released *Tropic of Cancer*, police confiscated the book, decency groups attacked it, librarians banned it, booksellers returned it, consumers demanded it, and Rosset prepared to defend it. But he was not financially ready for the more than sixty lawsuits that took *Tropic* into court all over the country. Attorneys of the ACLU were, and they represented *Tropic* itself, book dealers who sold it, the press that published it, librarians who offered it to the public and, even more significantly, prospective readers—would-be consumers who for the first time claimed the right to sue under the First Amendment.[18]

The idea behind a reader's right to sue for access to banned material dovetailed nicely with the maturing right-to-read movement. Joining long-standing efforts by the ACLU and ALA, Rosset and Miller crafted a high-profile right-to-read defense of *Tropic of Cancer* even as the editorials "Who Is to Censor What We See, Hear, Read?," "Your Right to Read, to Know," and the like appeared regularly in the press. By 1962, in cooperation with the ACLU and the ABPC, the National Council of Teachers of English (NCTE) issued its own statements against censorship by pressure groups, entitled "The Right to Read" and "The Students' Right to

Read." That year, the ABPC's regular newsletter "Censorship Bulletin" became "Freedom-to-Read Bulletin." At the same time, a group of citizens formed Audience Unlimited to fight against censorship on behalf of consumers, and an ABPC leader published "Freedom to Read" in the Public Affairs Pamphlet series. The emerging homosexual press also made use of the new motto, announcing its efforts to "guarantee your FREEDOM TO READ" and running articles on "Freedom to Read and the Law."[19]

As efforts to mobilize consumers on behalf of their right to read peaked, Rosset became one of the first publishers to organize an independent right-to-read crusade on behalf of a commercial publication. Chicago provided rich soil for his campaign, not only because it was Rosset's hometown, but also because its police force was so widely reviled for its brutality and excess that citizens readily mobilized against it. As one ACLU attorney remembered, police seizures of *Tropic of Cancer* were a "gift horse" for galvanizing public opinion against censorship. Taking full advantage of local sentiment against the police and national attention to the right to read, Rosset recruited prominent literary figures to sign the "Statement in Support of Freedom to Read" and used it to arouse the community further. Letters to the editor echoed Rosset's language as ordinary Chicagoans declared their right to read *Tropic of Cancer*. Elite Chicagoans also picked up the language. As a top official at Bell & Howell wrote, "I haven't read [*Tropic of Cancer*] but I'll be darned if I want a policeman telling me I can't."[20] So even as decency groups advocated censorship in the press, in the courts, and behind the scenes in precinct offices, bookstores, and newsstands, others—including Rosset, the ABPC, the ALA, the NCTE, and the ACLU—readied the cultural environment for dramatic legal change on behalf of the consumer's right to read.

The creative thinking of Joel Sprayregen and Burton Joseph, both general counsel for the ACLU's Illinois Division, took the idea of consumers' rights under the First Amendment to the next level—establishing prospective readers' standing to sue for access to banned material. Sprayregen, a "feisty young lawyer" fresh out of Yale Law School, and Joseph, a working-class graduate of DePaul University Law School, actually shared many things including a Jewish heritage; frustration with the reluctance of booksellers, publishers, and distributors to challenge censorship; and an eagerness to take on the Chicago police. Together, they worked to establish the "new and unique principle that a private citizen, as a potential reader, has the right to challenge police censorship in the courts." The task of establishing standing was "formidable," Sprayregen acknowledged, given that the First Amendment referred only to producers not consumers of speech, but he and Joseph assumed the job with gusto and optimism.[21]

The two firebrands found willing plaintiffs among their Northwestern University acquaintances. They included Franklyn Haiman, Sprayregen's communications professor and director of the Northern Illinois ACLU; Isabel Condit, Joseph's friend and neighbor and the wife of another professor; and Joseph Ronsley, an ACLU member and graduate student in English literature. The plaintiffs' job was to canvass booksellers and confirm that they could not purchase *Tropic of Cancer* in Lake County, Illinois. They would then bring suit on behalf of themselves and all residents in their communities against suburban police chiefs who confiscated *Tropic of Cancer*, ordered dealers not to sell it, or otherwise violated the public's right to read it.[22]

In *Haiman v. Morris*, Sprayregen argued before Samuel B. Epstein, chief judge of the Superior Court of Cook County, Illinois, that a prospective consumer must have standing to sue to protect the "constitutional right to read." "We frankly concede," his brief began, that "we know of no prior English or American decision presenting the precise question of the standing of citizens to sue against illegal official conduct which has deprived them of the right to read books of their choice." Even so, he argued, the ideas behind a prospective consumer's standing were deeply rooted in American history and democratic theory. The First Amendment was not designed primarily to protect a publisher's right to earn a profit, but the American public's right to enjoy a free exchange of ideas. "It must surely follow," Sprayregen continued, "that American citizens have standing to sue against unlawful official interference with that access." Judge Epstein agreed and granted Haiman and Condit status to sue as consumers and prospective readers. That alone represented a significant victory. Epstein's final ruling brought yet another. Epstein came down firmly on the side of the consumer in an influential opinion that declared the "freedom to read" a "corollary to the freedom of speech and press." One without the other would be "useless," he asserted. To protect "the inherent constitutional rights and privileges of the reading public," the police must cease and desist from interfering with the "free distribution and sale" of *Tropic of Cancer*.[23]

All but forgotten now, Epstein's decision received a great deal of attention in its day. It was covered extensively in the national press and widely declared a landmark case in First Amendment jurisprudence. Sprayregen called it "the first English or American case in which the right of *readers* to sue to challenge censorship has been upheld." Meanwhile, Rosset worked to draw greater attention to the opinion's unique consumer-orientation by recruiting two hundred prominent authors and publishers to endorse the opinion in a "Statement in Support of Freedom to Read" published on the front cover of his *Evergreen Review*.[24]

In the meantime, *Ronsley v. Stanczak* proceeded to the Circuit Court of Lake County, Illinois, where Joseph too argued for the consumer's standing to sue public officials who demanded that bookstores remove *Tropic of Cancer* from their shelves. The "social value" of the First Amendment was not to protect "the right of the publisher to earn a profit," he argued, but the public's "free access to ideas and publications." Like Epstein two months earlier, Judge Bernard M. Decker reaffirmed Ronsley's standing to sue as a "prospective purchaser" and also proclaimed "the public's right to read and have access to books of their choice." Declaring that "the constitutional safeguards are designed not only to protect authors and publishers but the reading public as well," Decker issued an injunction against police interference with *Tropic*.[25]

The ACLU's consumer approach to freedom of speech carried the day. It circumvented the reluctance of commercial producers and distributors to sue and brought public pressure to bear on the judiciary in new ways. It also inspired members of the public, as consumers, to take censorship personally. After the success of *Haiman* and *Ronsley*, ACLU attorneys and others brought successful consumer-initiated suits against public officials in other cities, including South Bend, Indiana; Los Angeles; and Montgomery County, Maryland. And when ACLU affiliates represented booksellers, distributors or publishers, they now couched their role as "defending the right of a free people to choose their own reading matter." The Supreme Court ended the three-year *Tropic* case craze in 1964, when it issued a per curiam ruling to reverse Florida's holding that *Tropic of Cancer* was obscene. The words would come later in Justice William J. Brennan's memorable observation that "it would be a barren marketplace of ideas that had only sellers and no buyers." Meanwhile, John F. Kennedy fortified the relationship between consumerism and civil liberties, when he issued what amounted to a Consumer Bill of Rights, complete with presidential support for the right "to be informed" and "to choose."[26] Thus, by the middle of the 1960s, the ACLU's concept of consumer rights had moved to the center of the Supreme Court's First Amendment jurisprudence and received a presidential seal of approval.

Consumer rights also presented the ACLU with exciting new ideas for membership recruitment. Leaders of the ACLU Illinois affiliate, for example, targeted buyers of *Playboy*, a Chicago-based magazine with national circulation that confronted frequent censorship threats (figure 13.2). Because "*Playboy* readers," the local affiliate's development di-

Fig. 13.2 The ACLU's Illinois affiliate attempted to recruit readers of the Chicago-based *Playboy* magazine for membership by appealing to their sophistication while linking both freedom and the First Amendment with consumption.

rector explained, "are 'naturals' for the ACLU," they requested and obtained, without charge, names and addresses from *Playboy*'s subscriber list. "Sophisticated people like yourself," one recruitment letter began, "are not afraid to read whatever magazine or book you want to," including one that features "a picture of a divine figure with smasheroo legs." Another acknowledged that "most men who like to gaze at pictures of beautiful women in a magazine . . . couldn't care less about such stuffy business as civil liberties. After all, what has *that* got to do with a divine figure and elegant legs?" But the letter assured readers that "there are many people—you know the kind—who would do away with pictures of beautiful women" and censor books, movies, and magazines, "though you have a right to read these—a right guaranteed by the Bill of rights of the Constitution of the United States." In a final pitch for membership, the letter pointed out that "a reader who enjoys reading what you enjoy reading about . . . should care enough to join the ACLU," the only organization that defends "the rights of readers, writers, and publishers."[27] Through this recruitment strategy, the ACLU's Illinois affiliate strengthened the growing tendency among civil libertarians to identify freedom and the First Amendment with consumption, adding a new dimension to that equation by treating consumers of cheesecake as especially laudable citizens whose rights to read represented the vanguard of First Amendment jurisprudence.

By the middle of the 1960s, the much-touted marketplace of ideas had taken on a character that would have been unrecognizable to the framers of the First Amendment two centuries earlier. Thanks in part to the deliberate efforts of civil libertarians riding the wave of postwar cultural and political trends, the public arena was increasingly conceived of less as a forum for the exchange of ideas and information among citizens of a polity than as a marketplace of buyers and sellers, consumers, and producers. No longer a community with aggregate needs, the marketplace now hosted individuals with singular claims to speak, to publish, and also to access all that was spoken and published. But even as ACLU attorneys fashioned this new understanding of individual consumer rights under the First Amendment, opponents employed this notion in ways that undermined the ACLU's goal to open up and diversify the marketplace of ideas by maximizing consumer access to the products of American media.[28]

Consumption and Privacy

Consumerism could cut many ways, and ACLU leaders soon confronted consumer-driven legislation designed to restrict and even homogenize the media marketplace. In 1963 and again in 1967, Congress held hearings on a series of bills that would allow postal patrons to identify material as "obscene," "obnoxious" or "Communist propaganda" and demand to be removed from the sender's mailing list. Supporters of the bill argued that mass mailings violated the privacy and sanctity of the home by bringing into it unsolicited advertisements from "an outfit called EROS," "a homosexual group called the Mattachine Society," and "a full-sized vibrating rubber finger for women." In testimony replete with barbs directed at the ACLU, Charles Keating—founder of Citizens for Decent Literature (CDL)—assured legislators that Soviet leaders did not permit the circulation of such pornography, because they considered it "inimical to creativity and to a healthy, strong nation" (figure 13.3). For Keating, a nation's values and priorities, not differences between a command economy and a consumer-driven one, explained the relative absence of pornography from Soviet public life. Carol Trauth,

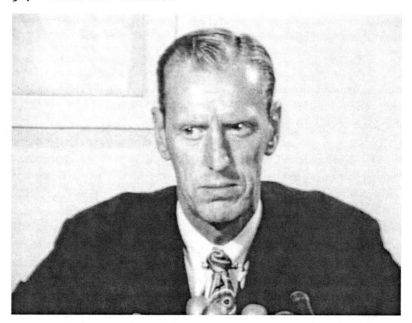

Fig. 13.3 Charles Keating, founder of Citizens for Decent Literature and seen here in news footage in the film *Sexual Liberty Now!* (1971), supported consumer-driven legislation to restrict sexually oriented material. (Digital frame enlargement.)

a young woman associated with Keating's CDL, criticized *Playboy* and other magazines for treating women as consumer objects, "as a plaything for men—a toy to be used and discarded."

Throughout the hearings, friendly witnesses insisted that preserving the sanctity and privacy of the home required postal legislation that would allow potential recipients to reject particular types of material. Indeed, many postal patrons received mail directly into their homes in the 1960s; through a slot in the front door, mass mailings crossed physical boundaries between public and private. A graphic ad for "Strippers School Book," "Men Only!," "Scanty Panties," or "Vibra Finger" might drop through the mail slot and hit the entryway floor, awaiting the homecoming of curious teens. Whereas earlier postal censorship involved public officials, these hearings showcased consumers who argued that without the postal bill they could not maintain their privacy by controlling what material entered their homes.[29]

Testifying for the ACLU, Herbert Monte Levy argued against the bill. Mass mailings did not jeopardize domestic privacy, he insisted. Without any new laws at all, consumers could tear up unsolicited circulars and throw them away. Junk mail could be annoying, Levy admitted, though he had not been "fortunate enough . . . to get some of the salacious mail" others had described. After an extended debate over whether or not mass mailers targeted children and whether sexual immorality was more prevalent among Russians or Americans, the discussion turned again to privacy. Edward Roybal, a congressman from California, acknowledged "the right of the individual to solicit, to use the mails," but "on the other hand, there is also the right of privacy." Without missing a beat, Levy replied, "I would say that the right of privacy is not a constitutional right. The right of freedom of speech and press is."[30] Thus, just two years before the ACLU would argue confidently and passionately in *Griswold v. Connecticut* (1965) that a constitutional right to privacy protected the right of individuals to use birth control, its legal director denied the existence of such a right when opposing postal bills that empowered consumers to refuse particular types of mail.

Four years later, constitutional rights to privacy were no longer in question, but the debate over postal legislation raged on as each side took different positions on the relative importance of privacy vis-à-vis freedom of speech. Postal officials demanded a law that would address the 200,000 complaints about unsolicited sexual mailings received in 1966 alone. Some were undoubtedly responses to the three million brochures for *Eros* recently mailed out by Ralph Ginzburg, who personally received at least ten thousand angry letters from recipients of his mailing. The postal service's general counsel testified that when sexual displays are "thrust upon us . . . our privacy is invaded." Legislation allowing postal patrons to demand removal from certain mailing lists might thwart constitutionally protected speech, he admitted, but the patron must retain the "right to secure the privacy of his home." The ACLU's Washington, DC, director, Lawrence Speiser, argued for the absolute primacy of the First Amendment, contending that privacy, though one of "the most precious rights of men . . . must yield when it comes in conflict with the paramount right of freedom of speech." Allowing mail recipients to refuse mail from any concern they deemed responsible for having sent, in the past, erotic or sexually arousing material would invite abuse. Individuals would reject mail from "any company that includes a shapely female in its mail advertisements," Speiser predicted, including creditors, the Internal Revenue Service, retail outlets, publishers, churches, charities, or political organizations. "The effect," he warned, would be "the sexual sterilization of American business and industry." Women's bodies figured prominently in Speiser's testimony as he concluded that if enacted, this law would result in "a 20th Century Mother-Hubbard-gowning" of American culture.[31]

In the end, consumers who demanded privacy won. Congress passed a number of laws enabling postal patrons to stop items from mailers who had, in the past, sent "erotically arousing or sexually provocative" material. By 1969, ACLU leaders realized that they were, for the foreseeable future, fighting a losing war on this matter. Given the "temper of the times," the presidential administration of Richard Nixon, and "the kind of Supreme Court which will be sitting two years from now," they expected the postal laws to stick. And they did. In 1970, the Supreme Court declared that "a mailer's right to communicate" must "stop at the mailbox of an unreceptive addressee" in order to "protect minors and the privacy of homes."[32] Here, the ACLU's arguments for freedom of speech failed, succumbing to the powerful case made by legislators and witnesses who effectively appropriated two of the ACLU's cherished civil liberties: consumer rights and privacy.

The ACLU and the Movies

Consumer rights also shaped the ACLU's ongoing battle with the motion picture industry. American Civil Liberty Union leaders had long objected to the Motion Picture Production Code of the MPPDA, renamed the Motion Picture Association of America (MPAA) after World War II, as a restraint on trade, a form of private censorship, and a mechanism for pressure group blackmail.[33] The ACLU continued to attack both the code and the handful of local movie censorship boards that hung on in several states and cities around the country, filing amicus briefs that highlighted consumer rights. In *Times Film Corp. v. Chicago* (1961), Sprayregen decried the censor's ability to determine "what is appropriate for the public to hear and to see," and in *Jacobellis v. Ohio* (1964), ACLU legal director Melvin Wulf accused film censors of violating "the right of members of the adult public to exercise their freedom of choice." Parents as consumers, not public officials, should supervise children's movie selections, they argued. A Supreme Court victory for the ACLU and its allies in *Jacobellis* left local censorship statutes in tatters. But the majority opinion approved of "laws aimed specifically at preventing distribution of objectionable material to children, rather than at totally prohibiting its dissemination," thereby inspiring an explosion of grassroots demands for state-mandated classification systems to categorize movies by age group. A deluge of movie classification laws followed.[34]

The ACLU joined movie industry representatives in condemning state-sponsored movie classification as censorship. Such systems would hold theater owners accountable for barring juveniles from movies rated for adults and also impinge on adults' rights to attend movies of their choosing. "A mother with a babe in arms," one flier protested, "couldn't go into a theatre playing an 'adults only' motion picture." Together with motion picture interests, the ACLU insisted that state classification laws violated the rights of parents by usurping "the parent's judgment as to what is good or not good for the children."[35]

The trend toward classifying movies had deep roots, but it also grew from new sources. Pressure groups had long compiled lists of approved and condemned movies, denoting those recommended for family viewing and inspiring the MPAA to sponsor its own lists.[36] State-mandated movie classification grew out of this past but was also a reaction to more recent developments, including the postwar era's increased attention to consumers and individual consumer choice. More specifically, the emerging field of market research and the ability of many industries to meet consumer demand with limited product runs allowed producers of consumer goods to cater to a segmented market even as they helped to create it. Recognizing the emerging, independent buying power of teenagers, postwar businesses offered fashions, music, food, and magazines such as *Seventeen* that further distinguished them as a unique age group with particular consumer needs. Meanwhile, television bypassed parents and advertised directly to children, using Tony the Tiger to sell cereal, promises of adventure to peddle space helmets, and dreams of glamour and domesticity to promote Barbie and the Easy-Bake Oven. Market segmentation also fueled and followed the tumultuous cultural and political climate that saw the rise of "identity politics" as individuals asserted group identities based on race, age, and gender. Thus, the Black Power movement emerged alongside Clairol hair treatments for Afros; the women's movement saw its ideals of independence echoed in Virginia Slims' "You've Come a Long Way Baby" commercials; and as the Gray Panthers fought against "ageism," *Modern Maturity* advertised products to ease the pains and celebrate the freedom of the golden years. In the increasingly segmented cultural and political milieu of the 1960s and 1970s, motion pictures joined other commercial enterprises to direct products at particular and often identity-based groups of buyers.[37]

Leaders from the MPAA worked closely with the ACLU as they developed a new movie rating system. Their general counsel, Barbara Scott, met several times with the ACLU's board of directors to seek advice, answer questions, and address civil liberties concerns. Scott assured the board that the system would be voluntary but admitted that because the MPAA dominated the industry, participation would feel mandatory. Board member Harriet Pilpel objected to "a small body making judgments for the entire film industry," a practice likely to "stifle diversity of opinion" and inhibit the creative work of artists. Scott replied that producers and artists actually approved of the new system because, by providing a range of rating options, it would free them from the restrictions of the code and allow them to produce "films on a more mature level." Other committee members worried that the rating system would violate the rights of parents by preventing them from taking their children to X-rated movies. The ACLU board finally voted unanimously to oppose the MPAA's rating system and publicized the decision in a passionate defense of consumer rights. When the industry determines who may and who may not see a particular film, the ACLU declared, "the public has lost its right of choice." Accordingly, "those who value highly the First Amendment guarantee of free expression should oppose the rating system."[38]

The MPAA unveiled its comprehensive movie rating system in 1968 over loud objections from the ACLU. It defended the new system as one that would allow moviegoers to make informed selections and parents to provide intelligent guidance to their children. Unspoken was the usefulness of the rating system for defending the movies against pressure groups, obscenity law, state-mandated classification, and renegade movie producers who released films without the MPAA seal of approval. Indeed, the timely passage of the rating system helped the movie industry weather two important events at the federal level. The Supreme Court, in *Ginsberg v. New York* (1968), upheld a New York statute that created an audience-specific definition of obscenity, "variable obscenity," outlawing the sale to minors of material considered sexually harmful to them alone. Just a few months later, the U.S. Senate held hearings to explore the possibility of creating a "Committee on Film Classification" to make recommendations regarding the creation of a federal film classification system. American Civil Liberty Union leaders actively opposed both of these developments, but it was the MPAA's rating system that protected movies against a federal ratings system and censorship laws inspired by *Ginsberg*.[39]

The MPAA's new rating system struck many people as momentous. "Social historians may someday write," opined Vincent Canby for the *New York Times*, "that on Nov. 1, 1968, for better or worse, the American movie industry inaugurated its voluntary film classification system, designed to bar children under 16 from seeing movies that the industry's code people deem to be too vulgar, violent, or sexy." The rating system met with widespread approval from Catholic bishops, theater owners, and parents who praised the rating system as a major advance in private industry's responsiveness to consumer demands. The ACLU stood practically alone in sturdy opposition.[40] Consumerism, albeit essential to the ACLU's campaign to erode restrictions on sexual expression, had proven slippery ground on which to stake a civil liberties agenda.

Conclusion

By some measures, the ACLU failed in its efforts to diversify and expand material available to consumers. The postal law passed, as did others like it, many still in effect today. Despite the ACLU's consistent opposition, the MPAA rating system survives through the Classification and Rating Administration (CARA). Although it is less effective at keeping adolescents from attending movies rated R, PG-13, or NC-17 than many might wish, it nevertheless influences the movie choices made by millions of people and functions to keep movies awarded an X out of mainstream theaters and inaccessible to many.[41] In these particular battles, the ACLU lost, trumped by consumer and privacy-based arguments that undermined its broader agenda of expanding and diversifying the media market.

But despite the apocalyptic predictions of many ACLU leaders, no return to Victorianism ensued. Indeed, *Playboy* reader J. P. McGlynn would have been pleased at the outcome. The ACLU may have lost its battle to free mass marketers from postal laws and save movies from rating systems, but there can be little doubt that it won the war. By establishing in law, jurisprudence, and the broader culture a consumerist approach to the First Amendment, the ACLU raised public concerns about censorship and heightened the sense of violation experienced by consumers denied access to particular media. Individual consumer demands, now interpreted as an exercise of First Amendment rights, would drive media culture even as pressure groups and collective efforts to reshape media content were recast as censorship.[42]

The ACLU piloted these transformations, advancing the cause of sexual liberation by bringing to sexual expression the gloss and respectability of constitutional rights and the crowd-pleasing allure of the buyer's choice even as it battled more conservative groups on the territory of privacy and consumer rights. Moreover, the postal laws and rating system that withstood the ACLU's assault in the 1960s would matter little in a world of free-flowing video and Internet pornography, material protected not only by the producer's but also by the consumer's right to free speech and privacy. Even as the ACLU helped make it possible for sexuality to enter the public realm in new ways, it reinforced the notion that privacy rights apply to sexual behavior and that such rights protect consumer access not only to sexual literature and images but also to sexual conduct and the means to control its reproductive consequences. As a result, sex would become ever more public even as privacy rights were trumped by sex laws, ultimately fulfilling ACLU leaders' broader agenda of making sexual expression of all kinds more accessible.

Notes

1. Quote from J. P. McGlynn to Hugh Hefner with note to Pat Malin, February 8, 1961, American Civil Liberties Union Microfilm Collection (hereafter, ACLU-MF), reel 59. This essay joins earlier calls "to discover how consumption became a cultural ideal, a hegemonic 'way of seeing' in twentieth-century America." See Richard Wightman Fox and T. J. Jackson Lears, eds. *The Culture of Consumption: Critical Essays in American History, 1880–1980* (New York: Pantheon Books, 1983), x–xi.

2. Legal scholars have lamented the mostly unmarked slippage from the rights of speakers to the rights of listeners. Geoffrey L. Thomas, "The Listener's Right to Hear in Broadcasting," *Stanford Law Review* 22, no. 4 (April 1970): 863–902. "Case Note: The First Amendment and the Right to Hear: *Urofsky v. Allen,*" *Yale Law Journal* 108, no. 3 (December 1998): 669–676; John M. Steel, "Comments: Freedom to Hear. A Political Justification of the First Amendment," *Washington Law Review* 46 (1971): 323–334.

3. Bailey, "Sexual Revolution(s)," in *The Sixties: From Memory to History*, ed. David Farber (Chapel Hill: University of North Carolina Press, 1994), 235.

4. See Friedman, *Prurient Interests: Gender, Democracy, and Obscenity in New York City, 1909–1945* (New York: Columbia University Press, 2000), 101–3, 136–138, 155; Leigh Ann Wheeler, *Against Obscenity: Reform and the Politics of Womanhood in America, 1873–1935* (Baltimore: Johns Hopkins University Press, 2004), 37–38, 45, 54–55, 66; "Statement of Policy Concerning the Ownership of Radio Stations by Newspapers," March 11, 1942, ACLU-MF, reel 220; Amy Toro, "Standing up for Listeners' Rights: A History of Public Participation at the Federal Communications Commission," PhD diss., University of California, Berkeley, 2000, 10, 46–49, 74–75, 81–82, 149–161; Morris Ernst, *The First Freedom* (New York: Macmillan Co., 1946), 179; Richard McChesney, *Telecommunications, Mass Media & Democracy: The Battle for the Control of America's Broadcasting Industry, 1928–1935* (New York: Oxford University Press, 1995), 236; and Paul Starr, *The Creation of the Media: Political Origins of Modern Communications* (New York: Basic Books, 2004), 327–384.

5. Quote from Ernst, "Memorandum by Morris Ernst Prepared at the Request of the Board of Directors at the Special Meeting Held Thursday Oct. 9, 1941," ACLU-MF, reel 192.

6. Baldwin to Ernst, December 11, 1944, ACLU-MF, reel 228. Ernst, "Memorandum on the Problems of Freedom and Diversity in Communications," December 1944; Baldwin to board of directors, January 4, 1945; ACLU Board of Di-

rectors Minutes, January 8, 1945; Baldwin to the National Committee and Affiliated Committees, January 17, 1945, all in ACLU-MF, reel 227.

7. Quotes from Baldwin to Mr. C. E. Boyer, May 19, 1945; and "Are you FREE to READ—SEE—HEAR?" n.d., both in ACLU-MF, reel 232. See also Chicago Division, ACLU, "Statement on Censorship of Indecent and Obscene Literature," February 28, 1949, ACLU-MF, reel 261.

8. First quote from Jim Farrell to Baldwin, March 26, 1947; see also E. A. Ross to Baldwin, January 25, 1945; and Alexander Meiklejohn to Baldwin, January 30, 1945, all in ACLU-MF, reel 227. J. B. Milgram to ACLU, November 24, 1947, ACLU-MF, reel 242. Second quote from Herbert Babb to ACLU, August 2, 1946, ACLU-MF. See also Raymond L. Wise, "Minority Report of Special Committee to Consider Certain Aspects of Free Speech," December 26, 1946; Harry Eckstein et al. to ACLU board of directors, May 23, 1946, both in ACLU-MF, reel 234. Milner, "Memorandum of Telephone Conversation with Morris Ernst," November 30, 1944; Baldwin to Ernst, December 11, 1944, ACLU-MF reel 228. Ernst, "Memorandum on the Problems of Freedom and Diversity in Communications," December 1944; ACLU board of directors minutes, January 8, 1945; Holmes to Baldwin, January 11, 1945; Baldwin to Holmes, January 12, 1945; Baldwin to members of the ACLU National Committee and Affiliated Committees, January 17, 1945, all in ACLU-MF, reel 227. Ernst to Holmes, April 2, 1942, ACLU-MF, reel 203. "Are you FREE to READ—SEE—HEAR?" n.d.; Baldwin to Mr. C. E. Boyer, May 19, 1945; ACLU news release, June 7, 1945, both in ACLU-MF, reel 232. Archer Winston, "Movie Talk: Meeting on Movie Censorship Discusses the Problems," *New York Post*, May 7, 1945, n.p., ACLU-MF, reel 228. Baldwin to John C. Flinn, August 17, 1942, ACLU-MF, reel 220. Farrell to Baldwin, March 26, 1947, ACLU-MF, reel 242. Arthur Jenner to ACLU, December 5, 1950, ACLU-MF, reel 41. Rice to Rev. William Howard Melish, April 14, 1948, ACLU-MF, reel 40. Mrs. E. L. Wilson to Malin, February 5, 1953, ACLU-MF, reel 46. On motion picture exhibitors' resistance to censorship, see Laura Wittern-Keller, *Freedom of the Screen: Legal Challenges to State Film Censorship, 1915–1981* (Lexington: University Press of Kentucky, 2008). The ACLU struggled to persuade exhibitors, booksellers, and publishers to take cases to court. See Hazel Rice to Screen Writers' Guild executive secretary, December 4, 1941, ACLU-MF, reel 192. Ernst to Forster, March 2, 1944; Frederic Melcher, February 16, 1944, both in ACLU-MF, reel 220. Andrew Heiskell to Rice, Holmes, and Baldwin, November 26, 1946, ACLU-MF, reel 234.

9. First quote from "Memorandum on the Limits of Boycott: Adopted by the Board of Directors," March 8, 1948, ACLU-MF, reel 252. ACLU news release, December 7, 1942, ACLU reel 203. Forster to Luther Knight Macnair, November 25, 1953, ACLU-MF, reel 47. Baldwin to William Goldman, December 8, 1947. Hays to Harold W. Seidenberg, December 1, 1947, ACLU-MF, reel 242. Second and third quotes from ACLU press release, June 7, 1945 (second quote); Hays to Fitelson and Mayers, June 25, 1945 (third quote), both in ACLU reel 232. Pilpel to Forster, January 23, 1945; "After Censorship?" *Motion Picture*

Herald, May 19, 1945, n.p.; "Memorandum on Motion Picture Censorship," February 19, 1945, n.p.; Quincy Howe to Norman Thomas, February 21, 1945; DeBra to Baldwin, March 9, 1945; "Memorandum on the Meeting on Motion Picture Censorship," March 6, 1945; ACLU board of directors minutes, March 19, 1945; Henry Eckstein, "Memorandum of conversation (April 5, 1945) with Mr. Arthur Mayer on Mr. Morris Ernst's memo re: Movie Censorship," April 6, 1945, all in ACLU reel 232. Baldwin and Harold Sherman amicus briefs in *U.S. v. Paramount Pictures*, October 1, 1945, and September 29, 1945, ACLU-MF reel 234. Ernst to Levy, April 14, 1949; Levy to Forster, April 21, 1949; Baldwin to Sidney Schreiber, April 29, 1949; "Memorandum of Conference Between Sidney Schreiber, Phillip O'Brien and . . . for the Motion Picture Association, and Herbert M. Levy and Clifford Forster for the American Civil Liberties Union, March 29, 1949"; Levy to Mr. R. F. Windron, June 20, 1950, all in ACLU-MF reel 270. Reitman to Barry Marks, July 17, 1952, ACLU-MF, reel 44. "Statement on Codes Which Restrict Freedom of Expression," January 28, 1953, ACLU-MF, reel 46.

10. Quote from "Memorandum and Outline on the Study of Freedom in Communication," July 28, 1945, ACLU-MF, reel 227. See also "Resolution to be Submitted at the Close of the Conference," November 14, 1945; Rice, "Memorandum," May 25, 1945, both in ACLU-MF, reel 232. Harry Eckstein et al., to the board of directors, May 23, 1946, ACLU-MF, reel 234. Ernst, untitled memo, May 2, 1945; "To the Members of the Board of Directors," May 16, 1945; ACLU Board of Directors Minutes, n.d., 1945; "Memo from Morris Ernst in Response to Objections Raised to His Proposal," June 8, 1945; Hays to Baldwin, June 29, 1945, all in ACLU-MF, reel 227. Richard W. McChesney, *Telecommunications, Mass Media and Democracy: The Battle for the Control of America's Broadcasting Industry, 1928–1935* (New York: Oxford University Press, 1995), 236.

11. Paul Boyer, *Purity in Print: Book Censorship in America from the Gilded Age to the Computer Age* (Madison: University of Wisconsin Press, 2002), 288–289; Whitney Strub, "Perversion for Profit: The Politics of Obscenity and Pornography in the Postwar United States," PhD diss., University of California, Los Angeles, 2006, 20–22; Richard Kielbowicz, "Origins of the Junk-Mail Controversy: A Media Battle over Advertising and Postal Policy," *Journal of Policy History* 5, no. 2 (1993): 248–272.

12. First three quotes from "Testimony of Patrick Murphy Malin . . . Before Gathings Select Committee on Current Pornographic Materials, December 5, 1952, ACLU-MF, reel 243. See also "Testimony of Herbert Monte Levy, Staff Counsel of the American Civil Liberties Union, Before the Gathings Select Committee," December 5, 1952, SC-ACLU, box 1, Charles E. Young Research Library, University of California, Los Angeles, American Civil Liberties Union of Southern California Records; Joughin to Edward H. Meyerding, June 21, 1954, ACLU-MF, reel 47. ACLU press release, May 9, 1955, ACLU-MF, reel 49. "Testimony of Ernest Angell, Chairman of the Board of Directors of the American Civil Liberties Union," July 31, 1959, ACLU-MF, reel 55. Spencer Coxe to Reitman, July

13, 1959 (fourth quote); Reitman to Dan Lacy, August 5, 1959, both in ACLU-MF, reel 252. Fifth quote from Boyer, *Purity in Print*, 288. See also 287 and Amy Nyberg, *Seal of Approval: The History of the Comics Code* (Jackson: University Press of Mississippi, 1998).

13. First quote from Rice to Joseph Meyers, February 25, 1953, Austin, University of Texas, Harry Ransom Center-Elmer Rice Collection (hereafter, HRC-ERC), box 85. ACLU press release, April 26, 1951 (second quote); Reitman to Leon Goldstein, May 3, 1951 ("Spot Announcement" enclosed) (third quote), both in ACLU-MF, reel 43. See also "Statement of Brig. General David Sarnoff," April 30, 1951; ACLU, Colorado Chapter, "Censors without Portfolio: Keep Right to Choose for Ourselves," *Denver Post*, April 23, 1953; "Speech for Miss Lillian Gish at Censorship Meeting," 1951, all in ACLU-MF, reel 43. All other quotes from Forster to Gentlemen, November 26, 1952, and Forster to all affiliates, November 26, 1952, ACLU-MF, reel 47. See also ACLU press release, November 12, 1952, ACLU-MF, reel 45; ACLU press release, February 21, 1953, ACLU-MF, reel 47. Rice to Theodore N. Lewis, September 15, 1948, ACLU-MF, reel 49. Forster to members of the Censorship Committee, March 12, 1948, ACLU-MF, reel 252. National Council on Freedom from Censorship Minutes, April 2, 1948, HRC-ERC, box 84. Rice to Dear——, May 10, 1948; minutes, Discussion on Freedom of Expression, May 21, 1948; NCFC, "Proposal for more effective organization of the forces opposing censorship," June 4, 1948, all in ACLU-MF, reel 40. Levy to editor, *Goshem Indiana News*, February 27, 1950, ACLU-MF, reel 270. Rice to Malin, March 24, 1950, ACLU-MF, reel 269. "Pressure Group Censorship: The Policy of the American Civil Liberties Union," November 1951, SC-ACLU, box 2. Forster, "Memorandum on the projected 'National Council for Freedom of Expression,'" May 1949, Princeton Mudd Library–American Civil Liberties Union Collection (hereafter, PML-ACLU), box 77. "By-Laws of National Council for Freedom of Expression," n.d.; Rice to Malin, February 13, 1950, ACLU-MF, reel 269. Malin to Arthur Summerfield, September 30, 1959, ACLU-MF, reel 252. Reitman to Charles F. Murphy, January 3, 1955; Spencer Coxe to H. J. Maxwell, June 15, 1955; Coxe to Philip Lopresti, September 15, 1955, all in ACLU-MF, reel 49. Malin to Mrs. Guy Percy Trulock, October 10, 1956; Douty, "Spot Check of Bookstores for Censorship Pressures," August 1, 1957; Marvin Mirsky, "Report on Spot Check on Chicago Bookstores for Censorship Pressures, June 1957," all in ACLU-MF, reel 52. Rice to publishers, February 25, 1953, HRC-ERC, box 85. Benjamin Roth, "Statement for Immediate Release," January 2, 1954, ACLU-MF, reel 48. Joughin to Ken Douty, June 17, 1955, and July 8, 1955; Tom Murray to Bill Sanborn, December 17, 1956, all in ACLU-MF, reel 51. Morris H. Rubin to Forster, December 22, 1953, ACLU-MF, reel 46. Malin to Douty, June 6, 1957, ACLU-MF, reel 53. Martha Thomas to Joughin and Reitman, July 19 and 25, 1958, ACLU-MF, reel 54.

14. First four quotes from "Texts of Librarians' Manifesto and Resolution on Book Curbs," *New York Times*, June 26, 1953, and "Working Paper, ALA/ABPC Conference on the Freedom to Read, Westchester Country Club, Rye, New

York, 2–3 May 1953," April 23, 1953; sixth and seventh quotes from "Recent Developments in the Censorship Field," September 2, 1953, ACLU-MF, reel 45; fifth quote from "Council's Statement on Censorship," *Censorship Bulletin* 1, no. 2 (March 1956), ACLU-MF, reel 50; eighth quote from "Storm Center" advertisement. See also "Story of the Story of 'Storm Center'"; Reitman to Jonas Rosenfield Jr. et al., May 25, 1956, June 28, 1956; Reitman to Affiliates, July 2, 1956; Reitman to Daniel Taradash, July 9, 1956; and ACLU, Greater Philadelphia Branch, July 24, 1956, all in ACLU-MF, reel 51. Ninth quote from Reitman to Sanray Smith, May 27, 1957, ACLU-MF, reel 53. See also Tom Murray to Ohio Civil Liberties Union, December 17, 1955, ACLU-MF, reel 51; "The American Civil Liberties Union notes the 10th anniversary of the American Book Publishers Council . . . ," n.d.; Frank K. Kelly, "President and Press, Librarians and Lawyers, Courts and Citizens Beat Censors on Many Fronts in 1953," *American Book Publishers Council Bulletin*, January 3, 1954, ACLU-MF, reel 47; "Can Minnesota Escape Censorship," *Minneapolis Star*, January 17, 1957; "Statement of the [Freedom-to-Read Citizens'] Committee," n.d., both in ACLU-MF, reel 57; Bob Sykes, "Right to Read," [The New Jersey Committee for the Right to Read,] n.d., ACLU-MF, reel 63; Donald G. Paterson (MN ACLU) to Stewart H. Benedict, March 6, 1958, ACLU-MF, reel 54; "Radio Book Festival," *New York Times*, March 29, 1953; Louise S. Robins, *Censorship and the American Library: The American Library Association's Response to Threats to Intellectual Freedom, 1939–1969* (Westport, CT: Greenwood Press, 1996), 22–25; Dennis Thomison, *A History of the American Library Association, 1876–1972* (Chicago: American Library Association, 1978), 184–191; "Bar Favors Books and Bricker," *Life*, September 7, 1953, 40; Paul Blanshard, *The Right to Read: The Battle against Censorship* (Boston: Beacon Press, 1955); Walter Gellhorn, Richard McKeon, and Robert K. Merton, *The Freedom to Read: Perspective and Program* (New Providence, NJ: R. R. Bowker Co., 1957); Collie Small, "What Censorship Keeps You from Knowing," *Redbook*, July 1951, 22–24, 81–85 Small, "Too Many Self-Appointed Censors," *Reader's Digest*, September 1951, 109–112. Leaders from the ACLU attended ALA meetings to discuss censorship issues as early as 1940. Thomison, *A History of the American Library Association, 1876–1972* (Chicago: American Library Association, 1978), 144. Many scholars simply assume that the right to read is identical to the right to speak. See, for example, Jack B. Payne, "The Changing Right to Read: American Society, the Courts, and the Problem of Literary 'Decency,'" MA thesis, University of Wyoming, 1951.

15. Quote from ACLU press release, May 2, 1957. See also Reitman to *Times-Journal* Editor, June 7, 1957; "ACLU Censorship Panel Meeting," October 24, 1956, Princeton, NJ, PML-ACLU, box 80. Morris Ernst, "Your *Freedom to Read* is in Danger," n.d., ACLU-MF, reel 53. See also Malin to Monsignor Thomas Fitzgerald, May 5, 1958, ACLU-MF, reel 54. See also Reitman to Malin, May 2, 1958, ACLU-MF, reel 54. Reitman to H. David Leventhal; Reitman to Paul Obler, September 11, 1957, September 9, 1957, all in ACLU-MF, reel 53.

16. See William Peters, "What You Can't See on TV," *Redbook*, July 1957, ACLU-

MF, reel 51. Arnold Grossman, "A Disturbing Report on Why More and More Librarians Are Taking Books out of Circulation," *Redbook*, April 1960, ACLU-MF, reel 56. The Editors, "How to Deal with Obscene Books," *Redbook*, November 1957, ACLU-MF, reel 52. Frank J. Fogarty to *The Bergen Evening Record*, October 28, 1955, ACLU-MF, reel 50. Leslie M. Zatz to Malin, January 1, 1957; Mrs. Burton D. Wechsler to Ruth Smith, January 27, 1957; Smith to Wechsler, January 30, 1957, all in ACLU-MF, reel 52. Paul Obler to Sirs, September 9, 1957; H. David Leventhal to ACLU, October 11, 1957; Reitman to Lee Swartzbereg, December 11, 1957, all in ACLU-MF, reel 53. Steven S. Schwarzschild to Louis Joughin, April 2, 1957; Stewart H. Benedict to ACLU, February 18, 1958; Malin to Fitzgerald, March 11, 1958, all in ACLU-MF, reel 54. Esther Rubinstein, May 9, 1959, ACLU-MF, reel 55. Clarke Shabino telegram to ACLU, March 22, 1963, Los Angeles, University of California, Charles E. Young Research Library, American Civil Liberties Union of Southern California Collection (hereafter, SCA-ACLU), box 65. Morris Lowenthal to "Those Interested in Protecting the 'Freedom to Read,'" April 9, 1965, San Francisco, California Historical Society, North Baker Research Library, American Civil Liberties Union of Northern California Archives (hereafter, NCA-ACLU), box 35. LeRoy Charles Merritt to Samuel Rapport, March 17, 1958, NCA-ACLU, box 25. L. R. Boston to editor of *drum: sex in perspective* (July 1965), 33. Frustrated consumers also formed "Right-to-Read Committees." See "Right to Read" (with Reitman to Leanne Golden, September 16, 1964), ACLU-MF, reel 64. "Freedom to Read," *Playboy*, December 1967, 89; Kathryn C. Kathryn Montgomery, *Target: Prime Time. Advocacy Groups and the Struggle over Entertainment Television* (Oxford: Oxford University Press, 1989); Steven D. Classen, *Watching Jim Crow: The Struggles over Mississippi TV, 1955–1969* (Durham, NC: Duke University Press, 2004).

17. See Toro, "Standing Up for Listeners' Rights," 161–169, 172–173, 175, 178, 180, 220–223. See also Levy to Alfred A. Albert, July 12, 1954, ACLU-MF, reel 47. "Note: Standing to Protest and Appeal the Issuance of Broadcasting Licenses: A Constricted Concept Redefined," *Yale Law Journal* 68, no. 4 (1959): 783–796; Louis L. Jaffe, "Standing to Secure Judicial Review: Public Actions," *Harvard Law Review* 74, no. 7 (May 1961): 1265–1314. Relevant case law includes *Martin v. City of Struthers* 319 U.S. 141 (May 3, 1943); and *Associated Industries v. Ickes*, 134 F.2d 694 (February 8, 1943).

18. Henry Miller, "Defense of the Freedom to Read," *Evergreen Review* (summer 1959), quoted at length in Jay Martin, "'The King of Smut': Henry Miller's Tragical History," *Antioch Review* 35, no. 4 (1977): 342–367. Forster to Ernest Besig, September 15, 1952; Levy to Forster, November 13, 1953, both in ACLU-MF, reel 47. *Two Obscene Books v. United States of America*, 92 F. Supp. 934 (October 23, 1953). Miller to Rosset, summer 1960, quoted in Brian McCord, "An American Avant-Garde: Grove Press, 1951–1986" (PhD diss., Syracuse University, 2002), 88–89, 90–92, 95–96. Phyllis Bellows to Ernst, March 7 and 23, 1961; Ernst to Bellows, March 9, 1961, Austin, University of Texas, Harry Ransom Center, Morris Ernst Collection (hereafter, HRC-MEC), box 530. Louisa

Thomas, "The Most Dangerous Man in Publishing," *Newsweek*, December 6, 2008; Al Katz, "The *Tropic of Cancer* Trials: The Problem of Relevant Moral and Artistic Controversy," *Midway* [Chicago], January 1, 1969, 99–125. Charles Rembar, *The End of Obscenity: The Trials of Lady Chatterley, Tropic of Cancer, and Fanny Hill by the Lawyer Who Defended Them* (New York: Harper and Row, 1968), 168–169. Examples of local *Tropic* cases that involved the ACLU include *Dorothy Upham v. Robert W. Dill*, 195 F. Supp. 5 (June 27, 1961); *Attorney General v. The Book Named "Tropic of Cancer,"* 345 Mass. 11 (May 16, 1952); *Yudkin v. State*, 229 Md. 223 (July 5, 1962); *California v. Bradley Smith*, Calif. Sup. Ct. (February 1962); *William J. McCauley v. Tropic of Cancer*, 20 Wisc. 2d 134 (May 20, 1963); *Grove Press, Inc. v. Gerstein*, 378 U.S. 577 (June 22, 1961); and *Jacob Zeitlin v. Roger Arnebergh*, 59 Cal. 2d 901 (July 2, 1963).

19. "Who Is to Censor What We See, Hear, Read?" *Kalamazoo Michigan Gazette*, January 25, 1961; "Your Right to Read, to Know," unidentified Alabama newspaper, December 28, 1962, both in ACLU-MF, reel 59. "Big Brother Will Read for You," *Portland Reporter*, February 27, 1963, ACLU-MF, reel 61. "'The Right to Read,' The NCTE Speaks out on Censorship!," *Modern Language Journal* 47, no. 2 (February 1963): 70–71. Peter Jennison, "Freedom to Read," Public Affairs Pamphlet, no. 344, 1963; "Freedom-to-Read Bulletin," vol. 5, no. 1 (March 1962), ACLU-MF, reel 60. "Audience Unlimited News," May–June 1966, ACLU-MF, reel 64. Final quotes from *Dorian Book Quarterly*, January–February–March 1964. See also advertisement cited in Martin Meeker, "Behind the Mask of Respectability: Reconsidering the Mattachine Society and Male Homophile Practice, 1950s and 1960s," *Journal of the History of Sexuality* 10, no. 1 (January 2001), 78–116, esp. 101.

20. First quote from author interview with Joel Sprayregen, January 21, 2010; second quote from Charles W. Gray to Elmer Gertz, both quoted in Gertz to Henry Miller, February 16, 1962, in Elmer Gertz and Felice Flanery Lewis, eds., *Henry Miller: Years of Trial and Triumph, 1962–1964* (Carbondale: Southern Illinois University Press, 1978), 41. See also McCord, "American Avant-Garde," 102–105; "Statement in Support of Freedom to Read," *Evergreen Review* 6, no. 25 (July–August 1962), reprinted in *The Outlaw Bible of American Literature*, ed. Alan Kaufman, Barney Rossett, and Neil Ortenberg, *The Outlaw Bible of American Literature* (New York: Thunder's Mouth Press, 2004), 630–631; Rosset to Rice, April 5, 1962, HRC-ERC, box 86; and Rosa Eberly, *Citizen Critics: Literary Public Spheres* (Urbana: University of Illinois Press, 2000), 70, 90–92.

21. First and last quotes from author interview with Sprayregen, January 26, 2010; second quote from Sprayregen to Spencer Coxe, December 7, 1961, both in ACLU-MF, reel 58. See also Sprayregen to Louis L. Jaffe, October 26, 1961, University of Chicago Library, American Civil Liberties Union Illinois Division Records (hereafter, UCL-ACLU), box 32. Sprayregen credited the following two influential law review articles with his ideas: Jaffe, "Standing to Secure"; and his "Notes: Government Exclusion of Foreign Political Propaganda," *Harvard Law Review* 68, no. 8 (June 1955): 1393–1409. On ACLU frustration with

booksellers' reluctance to sue for the right to sell *Tropic of Cancer*, see Gordon Young to ACLU, October 30, 1961; R. Vance Fitzgerald to Reitman, December 12, 1961; Reitman to Fitzgerald, December 18, 1961, all in ACLU-MF, reel 58. Reitman to Mr. E. R. Hutchison, October 9, 1964, ACLU-MF, reel 62. ACLU Censorship Committee Report, n.d., PML-ACLU, box 83.

22. Sprayregen, interview with author, January 26, 2010; Joseph Ronsley, interview with author, January 26, 2010. *Haiman v. Morris*, 61 S 19718, Sup. Ct. of Cook County Ill. (1962); *Wilson v. Haiman*, Ill. Sup. Ct. (October 1961), both in Osmond K. Fraenkel and Ann Fagan Ginger, eds., "Civil Liberties Docket," VII, 4 (July 1962), http://dpg.lib.berkeley.edu/webdb/meiklejohn/meikcase?sortno=0704&caseno=&title=wilson+v.+haiman&desc=&sortno=0704 (retrieved June 30, 2013); "Notes: Government Exclusion of Foreign Political Propaganda." Gertz and Lewis, *Henry Miller*, xx; Eberly, *Citizen Critics*, 65–66. "Illegal Seizures of Books Charged," *New York Times*, October 17, 1961. "Verified Complaint for a Temporary and Permanent Injunction," *Haiman v. Morris*, October 13, 1961, Princeton, NJ, Princeton University, Mudd Library, American Civil Liberties Union National Capital Area ACLU Affiliate Collection (hereafter, PML-ACLU-DC), box 14. "Amended Verified Complaint for a Permanent Injunction," *Haiman v. Morris*, January 25, 1962, Chicago, Northwestern University Archives, Franklyn Haiman Papers (hereafter, NUA-FHP), box 23. ACLU Illinois Division News Release, October 16, 1961; Alexander Polikoff and Burton Joseph, "Memorandum in Opposition to Defendants' Motion to Strike Complaint and Dismiss Action," both in *Ronsley v. Stanczak*, n.d., Washington, DC, Library of Congress, Elmer Gertz Papers (hereafter, LOC-EGP), box 258.

23. Sprayregen quotes from "Brief and Argument for Plaintiffs-Appellees," *Haiman v. Morris* (September 1952), NUA-FHP, box 11; Epstein quotes from *Haiman v. Morris* (February, 21, 1962), NUA-FHP, box 23. See also Gertz to Henry Miller, February 22, 1962, reprinted in Gertz and Lewis, *Henry Miller*, 52–54. Grove Press's lead attorney, Gertz, did not initially approve of the ACLU's focus on the right to read. See Elmer Gertz, *A Handful of Clients* (River Grove, IL: Follett Publication Co., 1965), 231, 256–257; "Tropic of Cancer Wins," *New York Times*, February 22, 1962; Stephen Wise Tulin to Milton Stanzler, December 27, 1961, ACLU-MF, reel 60; Hoke Norris, "'Cancer' in Chicago," *Evergreen Review* (July–August 1962): 41–66; "Freedom to Read Is Upheld," *Chicago Daily News*, February 23, 1962; Sprayregen to Haiman et al., July 9, 1964, NUA-FHP, box 23, folder 11; and *Chicago Daily Law Bulletin*, February 22, 1962, 1.

24. Quote from Sprayregen to president, West Publishing Company, March 13, 1962, UCL-ACLU, box 32. See also Gertz and Lewis, *Henry Miller*, 28–29, 51–52; Gertz, *A Handful of Clients*, 280–281, 301; Eberly, *Citizen Critics*, 91, 102–103n12; "Suppression of 'Tropic of Cancer' Spreads as ACLU Continues to Fight," February 5, 1962, ACLU-MF, reel 60; Jean Shanberg to Larry Speiser, October 24, 1961, PML-ACLU-DC, box 14; Gertz to Henry Miller, February 1 and 15, 1962; Rosset to Rice, April 5, 1962, HRC-ERC, box 86; "Statement

in Support of the Freedom to Read," in Kaufman, Rossett, and Ortenberg, *The Outlaw Bible of American Literature*, 630–631; and Stanley L. Lind, "Judge Epstein Rules 'Tropic' Is Not Obscene," *Chicago Daily Law Bulletin* 108 (February 22, 1962), 1, 8:

25. The defendants filed a motion to dismiss the case, arguing that Ronsley lacked standing to sue in part because he stood to suffer no damage to his property. First three quotes from Alexander Polikoff and Burton Joseph, "Memorandum in Opposition to Defendants' Motion to Strike Complaint and Dismiss Action," in *Ronsley v. Stanczak*, n.d.; final three quotes from Judge Bernard M. Decker, "Memorandum of Opinion," *Ronsley v. Stanczak* (April 6, 1962). See also Gertz to Sprayregen, April 9, 1962; Gertz to Polikoff and Joseph, April 9, 1962; and "Motion to Strike Complaint and Dismiss Action," in *Ronsley v. Stanczak* (February 15, 1962), all in LOC-EGP, box 258. See also "Uphold Citizen's Right to Challenge Censorship by Public Official," n.d., ACLU-MF, reel 60; and Brief for the Plaintiffs-Appellees, *Haiman v. Morris* (September Term 1962), NUA-FHP, box 23.

26. First quote from "Freedom through Dissent," ACLU 42nd annual report, July 1, 1961, June 30, 1962 (New York: Oceana Publishers, 1962), 5–7; second quote from Brennan's concurrence in *Lamont v. Postmaster General*, 381 U.S. 301 (May 24, 1965). The ACLU filed amicus briefs in *Lamont* and *Martin v. City of Struthers*, the two key Supreme Court cases that wrote consumer rights into the First Amendment. See *Martin v. City of Struthers*, 319 U.S. 141 (May 3, 1943). Many legal scholars at the time were unaware of the lower court rulings that laid the groundwork for Lamont. See, for example, Michael Klein, "Towards an Extension of the First Amendment: A Right of Acquisition," *University of Miami Law Review* 20 (1965): 141. Shortly after the Supreme Court decided *Grove Press*, the Supreme Court of Illinois–to which Morris appealed after his defeat before Judge Epstein—quietly reversed its holding that *Tropic of Cancer* was obscene. See Sprayregen to Haiman et al., July 9, 1964, NUA-FHP, box 23. Third quote from "Text of Kennedy's Message to Congress on Protections for Consumers," *New York Times*, March 16, 1962. See also *Jacobellis v. Ohio*, 378 U.S. 184 (June 22, 1964); *Grove Press v. Gerstein*, 378 U.S. 577 (June 22, 1964); Lizbeth Cohen, *Consumers' Republic: The Politics of Mass Consumption in Postwar America* (New York: Vintage Books, 2003), 345; and "Kennedy Submits a Broad Program to Aid Consumer," *New York Times*, March 16, 1962.

27. First two quotes from Sandra Silverman to Richard F. Morton, July 19, 1966, UCL-ACLU, box 6. See also Silverman to Shel Silverstein, May 4, 1966; Silverman to Anson Mount, May 4, 1966, both in UCL-ACLU, box 6. All other quotes from undated drafts and Theodore Berland to Dear Friend, July 15 and 19, 1966, August 3 and 10, 1966; Theodore Berland to "You know," August 10, 1966, all in UCL-ACLU, box 6.

28. In 1978, consumers assembled the Right to Read Defense Committee and won a suit against local public schools in Chelsea, MA, which forced school officials to restore a volume that had been removed from the library due to sexual con-

tent. *Right to Read Committee v. School Committee of Chelsea*, 454 F. Supp. 703 (July 5, 1978). In the 1980s, efforts to place limits on corporate donations to electoral campaigns floundered under courts' assertion of a consumer's right to hear what corporations wanted to say. See Charles N. Eberhardt, "Note: Integrating the Right of Association with the *Bellotti* Right to Hear," *Cornell Law Review* 72 (November 1986): 159. In the Supreme Court's more recent opinion on campaign finance and the First Amendment, the consumer's right to hear is assumed. See *Citizen United v. Federal Elections Commission*, 130 S. Ct. 876 (January 21, 2010).

29. Quotes from "Hearings before the Committee on Post Office and Civil Service, House of Representatives, Eighty-Eighth Congress" on H.R. 142, H.R. 319, and Similar Bills, June 25–27, and July 10 and 24, 1963, 7–8, 11, 17, 20, 27, 34, 35, 48, 56, 64, 75–81, 85, 106, 110, 114–115. See also Strub, "Perversion for Profit," and Schaefer, "Plain Brown Wrapper: Adult Films for the Home Market, 1930–1969," in *Looking Past the Screen: Case Studies in American Film History and Method*, ed. Jon Lewis and Smoodin (Durham, NC: Duke University Press, 2007, 201–226).

30. Quotes from "Hearings before the Committee on Post Office and Civil Service, House of Representatives, Eighty-Eighth Congress" on H.R. 142, H.R. 319, and similar bills, June 25–27, and July 10 and 24, 1963, 66–93.

31. First two quotes from "Statement of Timothy J. May, General Counsel, United States Post Office Department Before United States Senate Special Subcommittee on Juvenile Delinquency," February 17, 1967, quotes from 7 and 9; third quote from "Statement of Lawrence Speiser," April 13, 1967; all other quotes from "Testimony of Lawrence Speiser," October 30, 1967, all in ACLU-MF, reel 65. See also Speiser to Pemberton, Reitman, and Marvin Karpatkin, March 1, 1967; Karpatkin to Pemberton et al., March 27, 1967, ACLU-MF, reel 65. Speiser rallied *Playboy* editors to the cause by characterizing the bill as a threat to the magazine, claiming that it was aimed at "non-obscene mail matter." See "Postal Pandering," *Playboy* (January 1968), 61–62, 66. On Ginzburg see Boyer, *Purity in Print: Book Censorship in America from the Gilded Age to the Computer Age* (Madison: University of Wisconsin Press, 2002), 300–305.

32. First quote from 39 USCS section 3008; 39 USCS section 4009 (1964 ed., Supp. IV); and Title III of the Postal Revenue and Federal Salary Act of 1967, 39 USCS section 4009; second and third quotes from "Summary of May 28, 1969 Meeting of National Organization on Legislative Proposals to Curb Mailing of Obscene Materials," June 30, 1969, PML-ACLU, box 194; fourth, fifth, and sixth quotes from *Rowan v. U.S. Post Office*, 397 U.S. 728 (May 4, 1970). See also Kielbowicz, "Origins of the Junk-Mail Controversy: A Media Battle over Advertising and Postal Policy," *Journal of Policy History* 5, no. 2 (1993): 248–272.

33. Rice to Eric Johnston, June 11, 1953; Forster to DeBra, September 21, 1953; Forster to Kenneth Clark, December 3, 1953; Forster to Johnston, December 30, 1953; Forster to DeBra, December 30, 1953, all in ACLU-MF, reel 46. Forster to Schreiber, January 21, 1954, ACLU-MF, reel 48. Patrick Malin to Johnston,

December 5, 1955, ACLU-MF, reel 50. Malin to Johnston, November 23, 1956, ACLU-MF, reel 51. ACLU press release, December 5, 1955, ACLU-MF, reel 50. Reitman to Manning Clagett, September 14, 1956; Claggett to Reitman, September 20, 1956, both in ACLU-MF, reel 51. Schreiber to Reitman, May 26, 1959, ACLU-MF, reel 56. "Production Code Revised," December 12, 1956; "New Motion Picture Association of America Code," February 7, 1957; Louis Joughin to Reitman, March 6, 1957; Malin to Johnston, April 18, 1957, all in ACLU-MF, reel 52.

34. First quote from *Times Film v. Chicago*, Brief of American Civil Liberties Union, Illinois Division, as Amicus Curiae, October 10, 1960. See also Watts to Charles Davis, January 27, 1961, ACLU-MF, reel 60. Second quote from *Jacobellis v. Ohio*, Brief of American and Ohio Civil Liberties Unions as Amici Curiae, October Term, 1962. See also Berkman to unknown, November 3, 1962; Wulf to Berkman, February 18, 1963; de Grazia to Leroy Charles Merritt, March 16, 1965, all in ACLU-MF, reel 63. Third quote from *Jacobellis v. Ohio*, 378 U.S. 184 (June 22, 1964). By 1965, movie censorship boards could still be found in Maryland, New York, Virginia, Kansas, and several cities, including Chicago, Detroit, Fort Worth, and Providence, RI. See ACLU office to censorship committee, "Memorandum prepared by Barbara Scott," n.d., SC-ACLU, box 115; *Times Film Corp. v. City of Chicago*, 365 U.S. 43 (January 23, 1961); Tim Clagett to Reitman, February 3, 1961, ACLU-MF, reel 59. Reitman to Clagett, February 28, 1961, ACLU-MF, reel 60. Barbara Scott to Reitman, March 6, 1963; Reitman to Ernest Mazey, March 8, 1963; "Summary of Present Status of Film Censorship and Classification," March 18, 1963, all in ACLU-MF, reel 61. Richard S. Randall, *Censorship of the Movies: The Social and Political Control of a Mass Medium* (Madison: University of Wisconsin Press, 1968), 177. Pressure group action increased at least sevenfold between 1962 and 1965. The decisive blow to state movie censorship came in *Freedman v. Maryland*, 380 U.S. 51 (1965).

35. First quote from "Kit for Use against Censorship Legislation," Council of Motion Picture Organizations, Inc., January 13, 1960, ACLU-MF, reel 56. "'COMPO' Formed to Combat Attacks on Filmdom," *New York Times*, October 29, 1950, 101, ACLU-MF, reel 56. "Statement to: The State of New York Joint Legislative Committee . . . The Judiciary Committee of the New York Assembly, The Public Education Committee of the New York Senate," the Council of Motion Picture Organizations, Inc., January 21, 1960, ACLU-MF, reel 57; second quote from the [ACLU] office to the board of directors, February 28, 1963, ACLU-MF, reel 61.

36. Wheeler, *Against Obscenity*, 54–58, 82–85.

37. Wheeler, *Against Obscenity*, 54–58, 82–85; Gary Cross, *Kids' Stuff: Toys and the Changing World of American Childhood* (Cambridge, MA: Harvard University Press, 1997), 147–187; Cohen, *Consumers' Republic: The Politics of Mass Consumption in Postwar America* (New York: Vintage Books, 2003), 292–344.

38. Pilpel and Scott quotes from "Minutes, Communications Media Committee,"

October 29, 1968; the Office to Communications Media Committee, December 11, 1968; and "Minutes, Communications Media Committee," December 18, 1968, all in ACLU-MF, reel 65. Paul N. Halvonik, "Notice to the Legal Committee, ACLUNC and Legal Coordinators," May 19, 1971, NCA-ACLU, box 13. Final two quotes from "ACLU Policy Statement on Voluntary Motion Picture Classification," March 10, 1969, all in ACLU-MF, reel 65. See also Reitman to Pilpel, March 10, 1969; "ACLU Policy Statement on Voluntary Motion Picture Classification," March 10, 1969; Reitman to Wolper, July 8, 1969; Wolper to ACLU, April 14, 1969, June 10, 1969; Reitman to Wolper, July 8, 1969, all in ACLU-MF, reel 65. See also Peter Bart, "Hollywood's Morality Code Undergoing First Major Revisions in 35 Years," *New York Times*, April 7, 1965. MPAA to Rev. Roderick J. Wagner, September 22, 1965, ACLU-MF, reel 63. "Hollywood Is Preparing a Broad Film Classification System," *New York Times*, September 21, 1968; "As Nation's Standards Change, So Do Movies," *New York Times*, October 8, 1968; "Ratings to Bar Some Films to Children," *New York Times*, October 8, 1968. Paul N. Halvonik, "Notice to the Legal Committee, ACLUNC and Legal Coordinators," May 19, 1971, NCA-ACLU, box 13.

39. Quote from *Ginsberg v. New York*, 390 U.S. 629 (April 22, 1968). See also Reitman to Pemberton, January 15, 1965, HRC-ERC, box 88. "Statement of Lawrence Speiser . . . before the Committee on Commerce, United States Senate," June 11, 1968, ACLU-MF, reel 65. "Plan to Classify Movies Debated," *New York Times*, June 12, 1968; Bosley Crowther, "Towards a New Order," *New York Times*, April 4, 1965. Leonard J. Leff and Jerold L. Simmons, *The Dame in the Kimono: Hollywood, Censorship, and the Production Code* (Lexington: University Press of Kentucky, 2001); Richard A. Brisbin Jr., "Censorship, Ratings, and Rights: Political Order and Sexual Portrayals in American Movies," *Studies in American Political Development* 16 (spring 2002): 1–27; Jon Lewis, *Hollywood v. Hard Core: How the Struggle over Censorship Saved the Modern Film Industry* (New York: New York University Press, 2000); Justin Wyatt, "The Stigma of X: Adult Cinema and the Institution of the MPAA Rating System," in *Controlling Hollywood: Censorship and Regulation in the Studio Era*, ed. Matthew Bernstein (New Brunswick, NJ: Rutgers University Press, 1999), 238–263.

40. Quotes from Vincent Canby, "For Better or Worse, Film Industry Begins Ratings," *New York Times*, November 1, 1968. The *New York Times* predicted that the rating system would encourage the production of more films with adult themes. Canby, "Bishops Applaud Eased Film Code," *New York Times*, September 28, 1966; Canby, "New Production Code for Films Endorsed by Theater Owners," *New York Times*, October 1, 1966; "Catholics Criticize a Film Code Ruling," *New York Times*, November 17, 1966. Motion Picture Association of America press release, September 20, 1966, ACLU-MF, reel 65. "Mature Audiences Only," *New York Times*, October 7, 1966. Reitman to Scott, September 14, 1966; Scott to Reitman, September 16, 1966; Reitman to Scott, October 3, 1966, all in ACLU-MF, reel 65.

41. In 2008, the law prevented a mailer from continuing to send material to a

patron who complained that it was "erotically arousing or sexually provocative." 39 USC section 3008. On the current rating system, see the MPAA website, retrieved July 1, 2011. www.mpaa.org/ratings.

42. Indeed, by the end of the first decade of the twenty-first century, lead ACLU staff attorney Chris Hansen averred that consumers' rights under the First Amendment are so well established today that the ACLU will readily bring a lawsuits on behalf of consumers, but rarely needs to do so, because censorship itself has become so rare. Chris Hansen, interview with the author, November 24, 2009. For examples of ACLU cases argued in part on behalf of consumers, see *Ashcroft v. Free Speech Coalition*, 535 U.S. 234 (April 16, 2002); and *Ashcroft v. ACLU*, Brief for the Respondents, 542 U.S. 656 (June 29, 2004). Authors of law review articles express frustration at courts' unwillingness to distinguish between producers' and consumers' rights under the First Amendment. See, for example, Dana R. Wagner, "The First Amendment and the Right to Hear: *Urofsky v. Allen*," *Yale Law Journal* 108, no. 3 (December 1998): 669–676; and Geoffrey L. Thomas, "The Listener's Right to Hear in Broadcasting," *Stanford Law Review* 22, no. 4 (April 1970): 863–902.

14 * Critics and the Sex Scene

RAYMOND J. HABERSKI JR.

New Yorker film critic Pauline Kael declared that the night of October 14, 1972, "should become a landmark in movie history comparable to . . . the night *Le Sacre du Printemps* was first performed." She wrote this after attending the American premier of *Last Tango in Paris* (see figure 14.1), Bernardo Bertolucci's erotic melodrama. So moved by the film's daring sexuality, the audience for the closing night of the tenth New York Film Festival gave the director a standing ovation. But Kael also observed that later in the lobby, the moviegoers, as individuals, were quiet. Perhaps she mused, this was because they were in a state of shock—they had just witnessed the "most powerfully erotic movie ever made," a film that "altered the face of the art form."[1]

Pauline Kael was no pushover. Her praise for any film was hard won; her dedication to a film with sex as its theme was almost unprecedented. By the early 1970s, though, critics had reason to hope that movies might absorb aspects of the sexual revolution and provide mass and authentic, erotic experiences. *Last Tango in Paris* seemed to promise the dawning of a new era of sexualized films for critics such as Kael. And yet, for a combination of reasons—financial, artistic, and legal—the sex scene fell flat on the big screen for most American film critics.

The summer before Bertolucci released his film, New York audiences had also lined up to see the soon-to-be-classic X-rated phenomenon *Deep Throat*. Audience reaction to a wave of sex films was not fickle, but voracious, and thus both emboldened and confounded critics. On one side was the hope that authentic erotic films could become popular, confirmation of critic Susan Sontag's hope in her essay "The Pornographic Imagination." On the other side was the crass commercial exploitation of cinematic sex, as Ellen Willis complained in the highbrow *New York Review of Books*: "As an ideology the fuck-it-and-suck-it phase of the sexual revolution may be passé," but, "as a mentality it is nonetheless big business."[2]

The paradox of this particular moment rode on the back of two trends in American movie culture: the rising significance of film critics and

Fig. 14.1 Film critic Pauline Kael dubbed *Last Tango in Paris* (1972) "the most powerfully erotic movie ever made" after attending its American premiere.

the avalanche of sex films. The publicity campaign for *Tango* confirmed the convergence of these trends by reprinting Kael's review as an ad in the *Times*. The use of the review illustrated how important it was for a well-known critic to establish the legitimacy (because she in fact could establish the legitimacy) of a highly sexualized film. The assumption of course was that readers seeing the ad would understand the importance of the film through the critic's declaration; here was a sex film of real artistic consequence. Thus *Last Tango* presented an auspicious juncture: filmic liberation coupled with sexual liberation. Yet, cinematic sex placed critics in a profound bind—few, if any, knew how to approach the most hyped movement in film history since the introduction of sound.

Many American critics writing in the late 1960s saw the sex scene as part of a larger, radical revolution that had begun to sweep through movie culture with the advent of the French New Wave and the elevation of their profession to intellectual respectability. Movies had matured as an art, and audiences all over the world had come to embrace cinema as vital, as well as popular, cultural expression. Expectations among critics and moviegoers were very high when the sexual revolution came to the big screen. Thus when critics viewed sex films, they did so in terms similar to those they used to champion art films and condemn Hollywood's tired genre pictures. Yet, most American film critics wrote for publications that had given almost no attention to sex films until the mid-1960s. Moreover, even though audiences had grown more accustomed to sex in the arts, critics still needed to maintain a kind of distance from or coolness toward such films in order to maintain the edge they had over the popular tastes. It was not surprising, therefore, to hear critics rail against sex films for being devoid of intellectual substance. At the same time, however, many of them nearly rejoiced that these films reflected popular expectations of a sexually liberated era. Thus it was possible at once to dismiss most sex movies as commercial trash and accept that some sex films someday might be worth real thought.[3]

In her essay from 1967, "The Pornographic Imagination," Sontag provided insight into the desire for real thought about real sex. Her vision coupled the image of the heroic artist with the liberated audience joined together in a revolutionary project of transgressing boundaries. The artist would offend public norms so that the audience could acknowledge and participate in what amounted to a radical cultural crime. She called this the "poetry of transgression." "He who transgresses not only breaks a rule. He goes somewhere that the others are not; and he knows something the others don't know."[4]

Critics had the task of mediating this cultural crime for audiences. Moviegoers made easy accomplices; they became rebels by simply seeing sex movies. But they also wanted confirmation from critics that this cultural rebellion was for real. For their part, critics risked ruining the moment by talking too much. Sex films were not going to remake filmmaking by introducing new techniques or even new narrative structures. The important thing was the sex—nudity, naked bodies, erotic scenes, lovemaking in the raw—this was the stuff that audiences finally had a chance to see. Moreover, critics had to be careful not to sound anachronistic when writing about the easy exploitation of cinematic sex. No critic wanted to suffer the same kind of fate as Bosley Crowther—the powerful *New York Times* critic who was rhetorically crucified by his colleagues and moviegoers for panning *Bonnie and Clyde* (1967) because he found it excessively violent. Crowther's tragic mistake had been to misunderstand the rise of New Hollywood and the visceral connection it had with audiences. Like violent movies, sex films projected a new intellectual freedom and a stylized social revolution.

What did moviegoers want from their experience? Movies have always created the illusion that audiences could become what they saw on the screen. People could smoke like movie stars and be heroes like

Hollywood cowboys. Now fans could cross-copulate with the stars of sex films. Critics had to be careful not to ruin this illusion. But they also had to be careful not to be willing accomplices and advertisers for huckster producers looking to make some easy money.

Oh, *Fuck*

Sex had been an important part of the history of filmmaking from the beginning—"The Kiss" might be the first "sex scene." Yet, film history had also been burdened by censorship and industry codes. Scenes that went beyond much more than a passionate kiss were simply cut. Thus developing in the shadow of the legit film history was a rather diverse body of sex films, known alternatively as "blue movies" or "stag films." During the postwar period, that world—though rarely acknowledged by mainstream society—began to emerge. The sexploitation films of the 1950s and 1960s established a kind of industry standard for the carnal experiences audiences craved. A few foreign films had also tantalized the sexual appetites of moviegoers, though such pics rarely delivered on what they advertised. And Hollywood movies occasionally suggested strong sexual content, but for the most part regimes of censorship effectively prevented any substantial glimpses of naked bodies.

By the mid-1960s, magazines that catered to these movies and their audiences began to appear. In 1965, Marv Lincoln of the Golden State News became a pioneer of the business, publishing *Wildest Films* which was followed by *Torrid Film Reviews, Daring Films and Books*, and *Fiery Films*. Orbit Publications and Classic Publications joined the fray in 1968 providing screen shots of such classics as the "Nazi" sexploitation picture, *Love Camp 7*—a film that enticed viewers with the tag, "All the youthful beauty of Europe enslaved for the pleasure of the 3rd Reich." Within five years, this genre of magazine offered constant publicity for the explosion of films that, as another line for the poster of *Love Camp 7* declared, went beyond "X." Movie culture had clearly matured.[5]

In the 1950s and early 1960s, the web of control that knitted together Hollywood production codes, conservative morals, and civil servant censors unraveled in a series of legal challenges. Film critics cheered the demise of censorship and the rise of a free screen; after all the one thing that almost all could agree upon was their general disdain of censors. For example, Bosley Crowther wrote a number of pieces for the Sunday "Arts" section throughout the 1950s and 1960s defending the ability to see more adult pictures. Of course to Crowther that did not mean hardcore or even softcore pornography, only films with themes and subjects that were more mature. In one notable piece he asked:

> What do we expect the medium of motion pictures to convey? Do we allow that motion pictures should be free to contemplate life as it is, which means aspects of it that may be seamy, such as infidelity, prostitution and treachery, as well as aspects of fine and noble nature, such as devotion, courage and self-sacrifice? Or do we expect motion pictures to be only about the good and cheerful things—about absent-minded professors, Swiss families and Dalmatian dogs?

A few months after making these remarks, Crowther defended Ingmar Bergman's film *The Virgin Spring* and its depiction of a rape in his Sunday column against action taken by New York's censors. Crowther thundered, "What amounts to a valid and artistically brilliant scene has been denied to New York viewers of this picture on the stupid pretext that it is 'obscene.'"[6]

Somewhat unwittingly, Crowther had identified a transition that defined the sexual awakening of cinema. In the past, the depiction of sexual acts had been almost completely eliminated from the American screen. By 1966, such nonsense was fading fast as the use of sex as action as well as subtext became more commonplace. Rather than merely showing naked bodies or intimating sexual relations, movies appeared that showed the real thing. However, the ability to see the most private of acts portrayed in the most public of places presented a new problem for critics.

It took the ironic mind of Andy Warhol to reveal where movie culture was headed. In 1969, he released *Fuck* (retitled, *Blue Movie*). He made a blunt statement—two people fucking—and as result provided with excruciating clarity the implications of the emerging sex scene. No one knew how to deal with this sexual turn. New York City officials reacted as they had in the past by attempting to confiscate, prosecute, and ban the film. When *Fuck* went before a panel of city judges, it was a film critic, the precise and prescient Parker Tyler, who had to explain that the film showed "attitudes of the cool world toward sex . . . an indifference to emotions, everything in a cool way." What were the judges preventing, then, if the film failed to do anything? Was it obscene or pornographic if it wasn't titillating? And what were critics left to discuss? Was it good or bad; art or entertainment; banal or significant?[7]

So, here it was: the scene censors and moral guardians had most feared—two people having real sex on a movie screen. But this wasn't a stag film; this was film by a major American artist. Moreover, this was reality, not a depiction of reality or a simulation of the real thing. Parker Tyler noted at the time: "This film is not meant *to represent*; it is meant *to be*. And therein, like it or leave it, lies its great, really cool distinction." *Fuck* was different than any sex film yet created, and at the same time so commonplace as to suggest a future no one in 1969 could possible have understood. After all, fucking happens, and now it had happened in an art film. How would one critique it? Tyler suggested you couldn't. "*Fuck* is not a sexploitation film. . . . In those, everything is calculated, however gauchely, to provide an illusion of erotic pleasure or lust, whether by innuendo of supposed actual copulation. *Fuck* is definitely not as exciting as possible to the emotions. Which is the one sole reason why it is so exciting to the intelligence." In this way, Warhol established a dichotomy for movie culture as he had for the art world. One could either accept cinematic sex or reject it; there would be no unifying theory, no "mise-en-sex."[8]

Warhol's artistic achievement had been to reduce the desires moviegoers had harbored for years to single sexual acts—a blow job, fucking— and then parody the emotions one felt. One might want to think deeply about a Warhol movie but doing so risked realizing that you had failed to enjoy the sex. One could approach a Warhol film just hoping for a turn-on only come away feeling cool, not hot. In short, his films were antiaesthetic statements. What you wanted to find wasn't there. Yet, by creating this anti blue movie, Warhol also revealed something about exploitation pictures that had both preceded Warhol and capitalized on the fame of sex in the underground. Writing in *Films and Filming*, critic Colin Heard wondered if the time wasn't "ripe for a similar reassessment of *Whip's Women, The Animal, The Taming*, and so on. If artistic justifications can be read into one particular case, there's no reason why this method of criticism can't be applied wholesale."[9]

Did *Curious* Kill Criticism?

Heard touched upon a concern that persisted among critics throughout this period, that criticism would be either so expansive that any film, no matter how exploitative, could be found redeemable or that criticism would simply become irrelevant. Many mainstream critics never paid attention to sexploitation, but that didn't mean they didn't care about sex. What critics hoped for was a test case, a film that used sex in a way that was smart and significant. In the same year *Fuck* hit screens, so did

I am Curious (Yellow), a Swedish film that attracted critical and popular attention.

Critics wrote about this film with verve and commitment. Never had a film with a reputation built on sex elicited this much ink, and it was the film that became the first touchstone for a critical debate over the cinematic sexual revolution.[10] Two critics in the *New York Times* dwelled on the meaning of this phenomenon. In parallel columns Vincent Canby and Rex Reed took shots at each other and the film. For Canby, the film was a "wise, serious, sometimes deadpannedly funny movie about the politics of life—and of moviemaking." He explained that even though the movie was *not* his favorite kind because it did not appeal to him "on all levels," he felt compelled to defend it."[11] Canby argued that using sex in this movie to sell it was no different from song in *The Sound of Music*, concluding that the moral opponents of *Curious* had to be "right-wing moviegoer[s]" who had deluded themselves by buying the sugarcoated world of Old Hollywood. *Curious* was not a landmark film, but it did mark another stage in "a revolution in movie mores of really stunning rapidity and effect." And he observed that the sex scenes were real enough to make one wonder what it was like for the actors to perform them, and to imagine—without much trouble—that in the future these new conventions would most likely be broken.[12]

Reed was his reactionary self. He considered the film part of a "trash explosion" and a movie that was at the "bottom of the garbage dump." "This genuinely vile and disgusting Swedish meatball is pseudo-pornography at its ugliest and least titillating, and pseudo-sociology at its lowest point of technical ineptitude." What most "distressed" Reed was the popular reaction to *Curious*—the movie was a hit. He strongly suggested that the people lined up to see it were a bunch imbeciles being duped by a pretentious filmmaker and a dishonest marketing campaign. "All this pretentious, revolting, cheapjack Grove Press sideshow proves . . . is that there are as many stupid and provincial no-talents trying the make a fast buck in Sweden as there are in every other part of the world. They're just more devious about it in Sweden; they call it art there."[13]

Philip Hartung in *Commonweal* dismissed *Curious*, saying it lacked little if any social or aesthetic significance. As a statement about the decline of film censorship, he conceded that it was undoubtedly an important document—but for a critic that was a thin line to peddle. Hollis Alpert in the *Saturday Review* saw the film for a second time months after he had watched it as part of his obligation to testify in the legal case against it. Upon viewing it again, Alpert said he saw less and enjoyed more. He liked the film's politics and the way it used sex to say something about contemporary social issues. In the *New Yorker* Penelope Gilliat wrote that upon her second viewing, she stumbled into a telling scene: she arrived for the last five minutes of the previous show and "noticed that there were no subtitles." The projectionist fixed the problem, but it didn't matter much to the audience "who had been sitting through the length of this Swedish-language film and losing the redeeming social worth in its hours of puerile street interviews without missing redemption one bit." While the public cheered the fall of censorship, it had little time for the heroic work of the critic who survived its collapse.

Stanley Kauffmann, the erudite critic for the *New Republic*, captured this dilemma in brief: "The film seems to me an utterly serious work. But that's not much of an aesthetic recommendation." Indeed, critics could discuss the heroic accomplishment of depicting sex on the screen and report on the audience's euphoria, but so what? Such observations couldn't pass as criticism. Kauffman explained that what interested him the most about "this quite honest and quite mediocre picture [was] its possible effect on concepts of privacy." He reasoned that "all of human behavior ought ideally to be available to the serious artist. On the other hand, human beings do need areas of privacy for themselves." As a critic of the theater as well as the cinema, Kauffmann had seen eroticism, nudity, and sex in as many performative forms as was legally possible in 1969.[14]

This was certainly the fear of Andrew Sarris, the most severe formalist among American film critics. Sarris had created a reputation based on his interpretation of the auteur theory and deployed an encyclopedic knowledge of (mostly) Hollywood movies with a razor-sharp analysis of their directors. Like almost all other critics, Sarris was happy to bid farewell to censorship, but he too had objections to "sexual intercourse and nudity on screen." He had no moral or social objections; rather, in a series of articles published in the *Village Voice, Sight and Sound*, and the *New York Times*, he argued that the closer films came to showing real sex, the less ably they would approach drama. "Pornography by its very nature," he wrote, "is more concerned with certifying its own criminality than with establishing an erotically viable point of view." So, in this sense Warhol's film *Fuck* should have the final statement on the sex act—we've seen it, let's move on. Instead, Sarris feared that *Curious* and films to follow would "destroy the fictional facade of cinema" by focusing exclusively on sex acts, as if that kind of realism made enough of an artistic point. Exhibitionism was not art but rather a kind of "nihilism of nudity." "Apart from the rhetorical reflex of defending the artists against society on every possible occasion, it is difficult," he argued, "to become concerned, much less inspired, by the issued involved in *Blue Movie, I am Curious (Yellow)*, and all the other cheerlessly carnal exercises in film-making."[15]

In an astute observation made in the *Times*, Sarris thought that part of the problem with sex films had little to do with the films themselves—most made few pretensions to be anything but skin flicks. What annoyed critics like himself was the media storm that accompanied the wave of sex films. In "30 or 40 years no one will mourn the coming of skin," and like the coming of sound in 1929, the coming of skin in 1969 would not, despite reports to the contrary, bring the end of Western civilization. In another *Voice* essay he concluded: "It is a mistake to over-dramatize the situation. The saga of the screen's liberation is singularly lacking in heart-warming heroics." There had not been and most likely would not be the kind of history-defining moment that some revolutions provide. The sexual revolution was a big letdown for the cinema. "Doity movies," as Sarris called exploitation films of the late 1950s and 1960s, had a filmic style that created the only kind of theatrical atmosphere required—"steamy temptation, degraded and disreputable . . . proceedings." Elevating sex films to either revolutionary proportions or, even worse, artistic pretensions destroyed the only suitable context for them.[16]

Confession

Underlying Sarris's view was a relatively simple proposition: these films were titillating though not provocative. If they did provoke anything it was a singular emotional reaction to watching sex on the screen. Thus it was unnecessary to give this genre much thought. Rather, at least a few critics took this opportunity simply to confess they liked to watch. Among mainstream critics who provided this sort of approach were two who would eventually share reviewing duties at *Time* magazine: Richard Schickel and Richard Corliss. In 1970, Schickel was the better established of the two, writing for *Life* and, in a memorable essay, *Harpers*. Corliss wrote a number of genuinely insightful and humorous pieces revealing his interest in sexploitation films for the *Voice*. The common link between the critics was humor. Schickel attended a film festival on Russ Meyer at the most ivy-covered of the Ivy League schools: Yale. In his essay entitled "Porn and Man at Yale," Schickel noted the unavoidable box-office success of Meyer and the effect such success had on opening American theaters to the "skin trade." Thus while he acknowledged that such films usually existed "beneath the critic's lofty gaze," they were popular and therefore "attention should be paid."[17]

In a review of Meyer's *Cherry, Harry & Racquel* (1970), Corliss suggested,

> a distinction has to be made between the movie masturbator of the early and middle '60s (my heyday) and the patron of today's theatrical stag films. I and my kind were romantics. . . . The films of the era nurtured those lewd but laconic tendencies. . . . We aficionados realized that sex films had to be romantic in temperament and fictional narratives in form.

Success came, so to speak, when the viewer (almost exclusively male) forgot he was in a theater with a hundred other men. Although Radley Metzger imported films that did the job, Metzger and Meyer both used stylistic devices that ultimately placed viewers at a distance. To Corliss, the best year was 1965 when *Sexus, Erotic Touch of Hot Skin*, and Metzger's own *The Dirty Girls* (figure 14.2) appeared and played the grind house circuit for the next few years. "A genuine scene of romance pervaded that otherwise syphilitic film genre—an odor, with mixed associations, that has been replaced by the smell of fuckers' sweat." In the end, though, he found that "the love of a good woman" trumped anything he had discovered in a blue movie house.[18]

The same could not be said for Brendan Gill. Gill was a drama critic for the *New Yorker*, and his interest in "blue movies" was fairly well known to his coworkers. In an especially revealing piece for *Film Comment*, he lamented that his defense of porn had not endeared him to colleagues who dismissed the whole genre with "aggressive indifference." Thus it must have been somewhat cathartic for him to have an opportunity to put his passion in print: "I go to as many blue movies as I can find time for and it amounts to a blessing that two of the most important theatres housing hard-core porn in New York City—the Hudson/Avon for heterosexual blue movies, and the Park–Miller, for homosexual ones—are within a couple of hundred yards from my office." Gill made his remarks with a kind of nostalgic reflection for this unprecedented period of permissiveness. His essay "Blue Notes" was a swansong of sorts to films and experiences that he believed would soon be gone.[19]

Gill did not offer criticism so much as confession. "Many otherwise sophisticated men are embarrassed to be seen entering or leaving a blue movie house." Not Gill. Upon leaving such a theater, he said,

> my own tendency is to saunter. Since I have the reputation of being an exceptionally fast walker, my own pace under the marquee must be a way of

Fig. 14.2 By the late 1960s critics such as Richard Corliss were waxing nostalgic for films from a few years earlier that featured a "genuine scene of romance"—for example, *The Dirty Girls* (1965)—in contrast to more explicit films.

affirming that attendance at blue movies is not to my mind a clandestine activity. Grubby, yes, it may be that, but I have long since made my peace with grubbiness. There are a number of things in my life that I cherish and that lack elegance.

Gill's experience in hardcore exceeded that of Schickel and Corliss, but like them he too mourned the passing of an era. "The present license to depict anything one pleases on the screen has led to a falling off in the ingenuity of the plots of blue movies—never a strong point in the best of circumstances—therefore to a lessening of sympathetic interest on the part of the spectator." The combination of technical progress and increasing popular interest had sapped the blue movie experience of its peculiar charm. The turn to massive close-ups and constant action dehumanized the "plot" for Gill, and depersonalized the enjoyment of watching.[20]

Taking Measure

The much more common experience for American men was to encounter the cinematic sex scene through stills in the magazines. By far the most popular venue for presenting sex in movies was *Playboy*, the wildly popular mass-marketed publication. *Playboy* inaugurated a popular series called "The History of Sex in the Cinema" written by two well-respected film critics: Arthur Knight and Hollis Alpert. Both men had written for *Saturday Review*, perhaps the single most popular magazine in American history, and neither had any connection to the underground world of skin flicks and blue movies. Their original project for *Playboy* was a series of essays, accompanied by hundreds of stills, documenting sex in movies. The series ran from 1965 through 1969, and in twenty separate essays encompassed an admirable array of topics, from nudity in the silent era to stag films and homosexuality in the postwar period. The success of Knight and Alpert's "The History of Sex in the Cinema" led to an annual review of *Sex in Cinema* in *Playboy*. Knight ended up producing a television series by the same name for *Playboy* in the mid-1980s. *Playboy*'s exposure of cinematic sex helped to hasten the transition in movie culture from a world of censorship to an era of relative sexual freedom by illustrating how often sex was part of mainstream, as well as underground, cinema. But by cataloguing stills, and offering relatively little real criticism of the films themselves, the magazine also continued its tradition of divorcing sex from any genuine thought. After all, the point was to titillate not provoke.

Magazines outside the mainstream took that aesthetic to its logical end. Al Goldstein and his New York City–based magazine *Screw* were among the most often consulted sources for softcore and hardcore films. Goldstein rated, or measured, each film by his perfectly crass "Peter Meter." Each film was scored by how well it aroused the reviewer; the better the score the "harder" the "Peter" measured on the "Meter." This system avoided any criteria that might make the review needlessly ambiguous, an especially appropriate gesture to an audience that typically went to theaters with one thing in mind.

Reviews in dozens of skin slicks that appeared in the early 1970s had enough respect for their readers to tell them whether or not a movie was worth the relatively high ticket price. These readers sought arousal and required little more than confirmation one way or another. A rather extreme illustration of this single-mindedness appeared in a *Naked News* review of the film *Hot Circuit*. The reviewer recounted that the day he saw it, a man in the first row of the theater had begun to make terrible noises about an hour into the film. Patrons in the surrounding seats scurried away from the disturbance as ushers in the theater began hustling around the man. It turned out that the guy was suffering a heat attack, and "all the others could think about was getting new seats and getting away from this nuisance who's distracting them from the sweet porn up on that screen."[21]

Warren Beatty could only have dreamed that his magnetism had such an effect on moviegoers. Unlike critics for the mainstream press, writers for these magazines didn't need to sell any particular idea regarding the films they reviewed. Their most immediate obligation was to the sex; their long-term engagement with it now helps us understand these films as a genre. We read about films that attempted to integrate underground-filmmaking styles (with little success); about the hope that the *Story of O* might be made into a movie; about how when porn stars looked like they enjoyed their job, the audience seemed to enjoy the movie; and about the steady improvement of production quality as sex films matured from the days of nudie-cuties and blue movies, to the early 1970s, when porn producers made sizeable sums of money by attracting some critical attention. As one writer in *Naked News* put it: "With the imagination thus freed to explore eroticism in film, we can expect nearly anything in the way of non-sexual film elements, such as story, pacing, tone, meaning, though so far there has been a lamentable lack of exciting material." The appearance of *Deep Throat, The Devil in Miss Jones*, and *Behind the Green Door* in the early 1970s seemed to signal a change, prompting the question: Could sex films retain their credibility and add a measure of respectability as entertainment?[22]

Contending with Porno Chic

To Al Goldstein and his compatriots, talk about sex films in the early 1970s must have sounded like a lot of blathering. Many of the articles, essays, and pieces in the mainstream press contained the requisite exclamation regarding just how much sex one might see in new films. Yet the overall tone of these many pieces suggested that their authors felt compelled to react to a trend like one reacts to a dramatic change in the weather—we might be surprised by the severity of a blizzard, but talking about it pretty much states (and restates) the obvious. The year 1973 was the peak of this scene.

By January 1973, *Deep Throat* had been pulling in money for more than six months and breaking box-office records for a hardcore feature (figure 14.3). Moreover, its success opened the turnstiles for *The Devil in Miss Jones* and *Behind the Green Door* to reap financial windfalls. In light of such hits, the term "porno chic" had officially entered into the American lexicon through Ralph Blumenthal's essay by that title in the *New York Times Magazine*. As one of the reporters who had provided extensive

Fig. 14.3 Film critics and the press expended large amounts of ink on *Deep Throat* and its legal woes at the World Theater in New York City and in the process helped popularize the notion of "porno chic." (Courtesy UPI.)

coverage of the New York City trial involving *Deep Throat*, Blumenthal seemed uniquely qualified to explain the significance of popular porn. At almost the same time, America's two biggest political weeklies, *Time* and *Newsweek*, both ran sensational stories on *Last Tango in Paris* (it opened in the United States on February 1, 1973), thus securing at least for a moment the landmark status of the film that Pauline Kael had first declared in October 1972.

The media created the idea of porno chic; critics did not. The attention that critics had paid to sex films was a combination of legitimate interest in the implications of sex for the cinema and journalistic obligation to speak about something because it was popular. For example, Vincent Canby, who became Bosley Crowther's successor at the *New York Times*, explained in a Sunday column that he "undertook . . . an urban field trip to study examples of the four main categories [of porn]." Canby concluded that the genre would never produce anything of worth. The *Voice*'s fashion writer Blair Sobol felt duty bound to see *Deep Throat* because "it was part of my higher education." She went to the World Theater with a male friend of hers, felt quite conspicuous as the only woman in the theater, and left a bit nauseated. The *New York Post*'s longtime movie critic Archer Winsten saw *Deep Throat* because "public curiosity, not to say demand, [had] forced the issue." He found it boring. Shana Alexander wrote in *Newsweek* that Truman Capote had encouraged her to see that moment's most notorious sex film, but came to the realization that "after only a few moments at 'Throat,' one's lifelong opposition to any form of sexual censorship becomes difficult to defend." But Bernardo Bertolucci's *Last Tango in Paris* promised to redeem the sex scene.[23]

Charles Champlin declared: "If *Deep Throat* is the cost of the new freedom, *Last Tango* is the reward." The *Los Angeles Times* film critic expressed a hope that many of his fellow critics shared, that *Last Tango* would bring a seriousness to cinematic sex and, therefore, provide critics a way to combine popular fascination with critical discourse. Even if one was not willing to fall in behind Kael's rather overblown rhetoric, few critics passed by the opportunity to wax profound about *Tango*.

It is easy to understand the excitement surrounding *Last Tango*. Marlon Brando, the most iconic American actor of the time, played a role that required him to use his legendary hypermasculinity to ravage a young French actress in scenes that were notable for both their nudity and graphic expression of physical sex. Although Brando is never naked and his costar, Maria Schneider, often is, Brando's character Paul has that sort of "nakedness of the soul" that makes critics swoon. Thus, it was not surprising that this potent combination of star power and almost insanely high expectations would produce, in a historical sense, a burnout of porno chic. As David Thomson more recently noted, the hype surrounding the film made it the most fashionable film either "to laud to the skies or snidely put down." In short, this was the moment of truth for the sex scene.[24]

At the end of her infamous review, Kael explained that she had "tried to describe the impact of a film that [had] made the strongest impression on me in almost twenty years of reviewing. This is a movie people will be arguing about, I think, for as long as there are movies." Among Kael's strongest assets as a critic (and I think she had many) was her attentiveness to audience reactions. She was at her best when explaining why we respond strongly to movies. Thus when she sat with the kind of audience that attended the New York Film Festival and registered their shock, it was almost inevitable that she would read audience members' passion and complexity into the film itself. In other words, though she might have exaggerated the significance of the film for cinema, she was right about how deeply the audience—including her fellow critics—wanted it to be *the* film that revolutionized movie sex.[25]

In *Last Tango*, many critics (but especially Kael) had found the work of art that transgressed a boundary of the mind, not merely of the law. Champlin summed this up nicely: "It would be hard to think of another movie that needs to be defended quite so urgently from both its enemies and its friends." Isn't this often what happens with the best art? Indeed, taken in its parts, *Last Tango* was a culmination of sex films to that point: it had narrative eroticism to get one interested, salacious nudity and sex to get one hot, and a cool undertone to keep one thinking. Was it a singular statement on film sex?[26]

No. Instead, the film became the biggest target for critics of all stripes, so much so that a good number of critics ended up ruminating over what was being written about the film rather than the film itself. James Wall, a critic for *Christian Century*, both summed up this situation and contributed to it. "As a film, *Last Tango in Paris* is not 'available' at the moment for clear analysis. It is rather a social phenomenon, elevated to superstar status by a rash of media attention." He believed that what made "it difficult to deal with *Tango* as either art or social statement [was] the awareness that the significance of this creation may in some way be related to the dollars involved." And so, the movie sells because of the sex in it, or the sex advertised as in it, thus making it nearly impossible and perhaps impractical to discuss the film apart from the circus of which it was a part.[27]

Two weeks before *Last Tango* opened in American theaters, *Time* told its readers they could expect "frontal nudity, four-letter words, masturbation even sodomy" but that all of it was handled by acclaimed Italian director Bernardo Bertolucci, albeit with "a voyeur's eye, a moralist's savagery, and an artist's finesse." Here then was a cultural event of which audiences needed to be a part. Just in case anyone missed the progression in sex films recently, *Time* explained that *Last Tango* was part of a new tradition that included *I am Curious (Yellow)*, *Midnight Cowboy*, and *A Clockwork Orange*. "Going beyond all of these, *Tango* proclaims the liberation of serious films from restraints on sex as unequivocally as the 1967 *Bonnie and Clyde* proclaimed liberation from restraints on violence." So don't be square, the essay seemed to say; this was a movie missed at great peril to one's ability to posture at cocktail parties.[28]

With such publicity, it was no wonder that scuffles literally broke out among New Yorkers over tickets for *Last Tango*. Critic David Denby noted

Fig. 14.4 Critics noted that whereas Marlon Brando may have bared his soul in *Last Tango in Paris*, it was Maria Schneider who bared her flesh. This provocative image of Schneider frequently accompanied reviews and stories about *Last Tango*.

that *Time* also had a fight on its hands. "Within two weeks the magazine had received over three thousand letters, almost all of them negative and many of them furious, as well as hundreds of subscription cancellations. It was the largest outburst of reader antagonism since the 'Is God Dead?' issue a few years ago." So what did Denby think of the actual movie—not merely its hype? Like Kael, the vulgar, physical, erotic power of the movie knocked him over. "If people can discard all the nonsense they've heard about the movie, it could provide one of the strongest moviegoing experiences in recent years."[29]

The hype about *Last Tango* led many to believe the sex would be extraordinary. It wasn't. Critics howled at the unequal naked time between the actors (figure 14.4). David Brudnoy wrote in *National Review, Last Tango* "is not . . . an utterly honest film as its devotees insist; it bares Brando's backside but no more, while exploiting Schneider's exquisite body as in pre-'liberation' days, and it is at times revoltingly arty, movie-ish, hence inherently fake." Thomas Meehan in *Saturday Review* wrote that for him it was a "sexual turn-off. . . . I can think of practically nothing that is more of a drag to watch on a movie screen than scenes of heavily breathing couples pretending to have sexual intercourse." Meehan didn't reveal whether couples actually having sex did anything more for him. For Robert Hatch in the *Nation*, Schneider's body was everything he had hoped it would be, but felt "the erotic scenes [ran] away with the story, the way tabasco runs away with a sauce." Moira Walsh writing for the relatively staid *America* brokered, "If this a breakthrough, I'll eat my mid-Victorian bonnet." Stanley Kauffmann concurred: "A lot has been written about the 'breakthrough' in *Tango*, about how porno films have paved the way. Don't believe it. In explicit detail *Tango* does nothing that has not been done in the past 'program' films, and it is physically fake where porno is not."[30]

In the age of *Deep Throat*, sex on the screen had become unremarkable. Thus that left one final area open to discussion: the philosophical aspects of sex scenes. Critics debated Bertolucci's and Brando's existential relationship to the film's sexuality. In *New York*, Judith Crist offered a frustratingly mixed review: she charged that it was both "all machismo filled with such detestation of and contempt for women that its universality is limited" and that the sex was so powerful it "causes us to explore ourselves." In *Film Quarterly*, Joan Mellen said much the same thing, though in decidedly more rigorous terms. "What is interesting about *Last Tango* is not its simulation of forbidden sex (sodomy and masturbation), but its tracing of the boundaries of free choice in controlling one's relationships and forging one's separate identity. . . . It is . . . the use of sex as a catalyst to explore our mythological capacity to forever begin anew and live life in defiance of what we have been."[31]

Yet, if the catalyst was the film's sex, the meaning of that sex came completely out of Brando's character. Reviewers who remarked about the blatant misogyny of the film decried Maria Schneider's character. E. Ann Kaplan tore into Bertolucci on this point:

> For all his claims to be on the side of woman's liberation, Bertolucci cannot have it both ways. . . . As it is, the relationship is presented in a sexist way. It is not enough to argue that the entire sexual relationship is intended to symbolize Paul/Brando's hatred of bourgeois society; or that there are in fact girls like Jeanne who deserve all they get by putting themselves in the situation in the first place. Men's hatred of bourgeois society does not justify taking out this hostility on women.

In short, Jeanne was as useless as any of Russ Meyer's overdone vixens.[32]

What had *Last Tango* done? Despite all the hope, hype, and discussion that attended porno chic, *Last Tango* marked the end of an era. *Variety* critic Addison Verrill explained why. Verrill was not one to pontificate about the transcendental quality of really good sex scenes; he was much more likely to explain what worked and what didn't and why. And throughout his columns in 1973, he recorded the fading of cinema's sexual revolution in legal, commercial, and intellectual terms. In the legal realm, the U.S. Supreme Court handed down a series of decisions in the summer of 1973 that caused a fundamental shift in authority over who could define and prosecute obscene material. No longer would a national standard prevail and thereby protect sex films; from then on, communities would be able to determine local thresholds for the public display of sex. Verrill reported that the Court's decisions had an immediate effect on the porn industry, forcing companies to rethink how their production, distribution, and advertising could avoid endless legal entanglements.

However, Verrill's reviews of sex films told an additional story. Unlike many of his colleagues, Verrill consistently reviewed hardcore offerings. He did so within the typical condensed and concise *Variety* style. Thus, in his reviews for 1973, one can also see a steady decline in the commercial quality of cinematic sex. Porn, both hetero and gay, had hit a wall. Although the production quality of porn films had improved and the number of films had increased, Verrill seemed to suggest that at least for the moment the industry had run out of ideas. Thus, he might praise a film such as *High Rise* for its "technical slickness," but find that such quality "overwhelm[ed] the sexpo content." "Performers tend to get lost in the visuals," he explained, "and disappoint the more avid hardcore buff since it lacks some of the 'essential' climactic moments now de rigueur in porno features." Likewise, in his review of *It Happened in Hollywood* (edited by a young Wes Craven), he suggested that the picture failed because it capitalized on "the recent trend of porno-comedy features . . . some of them funny, some very flat, but all working against the kind of sustained sexual passages with 'communicating' characters so necessary for real erotic involvement." Even movies he liked, such as *The Devil in Miss Jones*, posed problems. He called it the first porno that approached an "art form," containing a performance by Georgina Spelvin that was comparable to Marlon Brando's in *Last Tango* for its "nakedness." "Pic poses one problem," he thought. "Booking a film of this technical quality into a standard sex house is tantamount to throwing it on the trash heap of most current hardcore fare. On the other hand, more prestigious houses may shy away because of the explicit nature of the material." The film contained "some of the most frenzied and erotic sex sequences in porno memory."[33]

Verrill was especially disappointed with the direction of gay porn.

Very few critics in the mainstream press ever bothered to review such films. For gay male porn the standard seemed to be *Boys in the Sand* (1971). According to Verrill, few films matched the "elegant eroticism" of that one and the promise of its star, Casey Donovan. And very few films were worth the relatively high $5 admission.[34]

Verrill's overall dissatisfaction turned to ironic nostalgia when he reviewed the porn industry's first musical: *The Newcomers*. It was not much of a stretch for him to imagine that the release of this film had symbolic significance as he wrote: "It bows at what could be the end of the porno pic era, and its one 'redeeming value' for hardcore buffs is its cast." The film was a catchall of New York's porn industry set to music. Verrill noted that this "mass casting . . . combined with knowledge of the recent Supreme Court decisions, gives pic an instant nostalgia flavor. It almost plays as a swan song, and the only thing the script leaves out is a booming narrator at the finale saying: 'As porn sinks in the West, we bid fond adieu to Georgina Spelvin, Harry Reams, Tina Russell, Marc Stevens, etc.'" Indeed, many of his colleagues had already said good-bye to their short-lived attraction to porn.[35]

In January 1974, Verrill wrote a piece for *Variety* on a trend among journalists to distance themselves from porn. He reported: "The chic is thoroughly tarnished now, and some media outlets, apparently embarrassed by their excess, have begun to act like adolescents caught playing 'doctor' behind the garage." He gave a brief but telling overview of press coverage of porn, noting that the paper most sympathetic to it was the *New York Post*. But the new executive editor, Paul Sann, had established a policy that would severely limit coverage by critics and writers. Gone would be interviews with porn actresses that were usually accompanied by photos of the subjects. *Post* film critic Archer Winsten had given a decent amount of coverage to porn movies, but his columns expressed a fatigue with the scene. The *Post* was far from obsessed with the industry, but it had been the only New York daily to give porn enough attention that the paper attracted publicists. Of course the *New York Times* had given the legal case involving *Deep Throat* an enormous amount of coverage, which included the entire cultural staff attending a matinee of the movie. However, *Times* critic Vincent Canby probably spoke for many of his colleagues when he suggested in a Sunday opinion piece that perhaps the attention given to *Deep Throat* and to porn in general had been "warping the minds" of his fellow critics.[36]

Porno chic has had a lasting and determinate effect on critical discussion of sex films. Canby's suggestion has lingered as a warning—discussing sex films only provides free advertising for porn, and besides a journalist just might lose his integrity from all that watching and talking. Moreover, the attitude projected by critics such as Schickel, Corliss, Sarris, and Gill suggested that the only way to think about sex films was to reject serious thought at all. It was as if the act of taking intercourse as a legitimate means of expression undermined whatever cinematic enjoyment the audience was suppose to receive. Linda Williams responded to this point in a strong essay on cinema and sex acts in 2001. She acknowledged that in the early 1970s "porno chic" had indeed "devolved into 'porno gonzo,'" but contended that such a development did not, in theory, rule out the possibility of "emotionally complex erotic performances." The larger problem, Williams argued, was that "the popular mainstream still turns away from—or looks elliptically at—the physical and emotional details of sex."[37]

A few recent films—including Lars Von Trier's *The Idiots* (1998), Patrice Chereau's *Intimacy* (2001), and Catherine Breillat's *Fat Girl* (2001)—gave Williams an opportunity to extend a debate she had reawakened in the early 1990s regarding the audience's relationship to porn. In this essay, she engaged with admirable directness the role film critics play in mediating audience taste for sex scenes. "In the U.S. we have grown so used to the separation of pornography from art that we tend to assume—sometimes rather hypocritically—that any arousal response is antithetical to art and emotional complex art antithetical to arousal." Although we might quibble over Williams's definition of "arousal" (after all *The Unbearable Lightness of Being* had to arouse a few moviegoers), her point seems especially relevant when she discussed the reaction of *Los Angeles Times* critic Kenneth Turan to *Romance*.[38] Turan is no prude, but his objection to the film echoed a familiar line—sex and thought cannot be a turn-on and therefore can only be pretentious. Turan argued: "Distant sex, no matter how explicit, and bogus posturing turn out to be a deadly cinematic combination." The voice-over during the sex scenes—too much talk—ruined the moment for Turan. Williams countered:

> It is as if, for Turan, the French tradition of philosophy in the bedroom spoils the 'pure' pleasure of the sex. But it is precisely the firewall between philosophy, politics, and emotion, on the one hand, and 'pure' pornography on the other, that this new European cinema is breaking down, forging new ways of presenting and visually experiencing cinematic sex acts.[39]

The conflict between Turan and Williams is a product of the sex scene of the early 1970s. It is the legacy of porno chic that pretentious talk about truly awful films created a context that continues to stifle even the ability to imagine a different cinematic world. There is no doubt that critics should be free to denounce those films that are artistically pathetic. When art exploits emotion for the sake of profit or grotesque shock, fire away. However, as Williams points out:

> What kind of moving-image art do we condemn ourselves to if sex must be so compartmentalized? I would argue that the even greater pretension may be the very idea that sex is mindless. If it seems pretentious to Turan to mix ambivalent emotions and philosophical thought with sex, it is also simplistic to assume that sex is monopathic and without thought.[40]

It's not the sex warping the minds of critics and audiences; it's the lack of thought about the sex. Should we welcome every sex film as a triumph, as was seemingly the case during the sexual revolution? Of course not, but we shouldn't approach any other cinematic innovation with such blanket euphoria either. When taking a long look back at Pauline Kael's reaction to *Last Tango* and, perhaps as important, her observations of the audience's reaction, we might conclude now that just maybe she had witnessed an authentic and intellectually honest experience.

Notes

1. Review of *Last Tango in Paris*, reprinted in Pauline Kael, *For Keeps: Thirty Years at the Movies* (New York: Plume, 1994), 450.
2. Ellen Willis, "Hard to Swallow," *New York Review of Books*, January 25, 1973, 22.
3. For more on the emergence of a new postcensor movie culture, see Raymond J. Haberski Jr., *Freedom to Offend: How New York Remade Movie Culture* (Lexington: University Press of Kentucky, 2007), especially chaps. 6 and 8.
4. See the essay "The Pornographic Imagination," in Susan Sontag's *Styles of Radical Will* (New York: Viking, [1969] 1994), 45.
5. Schaefer, *"Bold! Daring! Shocking! True!": A History of Exploitation Films, 1919–1959* (Durham, NC: Duke University Press, 1999), esp. chaps. 4 and 9; Tom Brinkmann, *Bad Mags: The Strangest, Most Unusual, and Sleaziest Periodicals Ever Published!* Vol. 1 (London: Headpress, 2008), 107.
6. Bosley Crowther, "Not for the Children," *New York Times*, April 4, 1961, sec. 2, 1; Crowther, "Around in Circles," *New York Times*, August 13, 1961, sec. 2, 1.
7. Morris Kaplan, "Professor Defends Warhol 'Blue Movie' As 'Not Stimulating,'" *New York Times*, September 17, 1969, 55.
8. Parker Tyler, *Sex, Psyche, Etcetera in the Film* (New York: Horizon Press, 1969), 16, 17.
9. Janet Staiger, *Perverse Spectators: The Practice of Film Reception* (New York: NYU Press, 2000), 144; James Lithgow and Colin Heard, "Underground U.S.A. and the Sexploitation Market," *Films and Filming* 15, no. 11 (August 1969): 25.
10. For more details on *I Am Curious (Yellow)* and its legal travails, see chapter 4.

11. Vincent Canby, "'I Am Curious (Yes),'" *New York Times*, March 23, 1969, D1, 16.

12. Canby, "'I Am Curious (Yes).'"

13. Rex Reed, "'I Am Curious (No),'" *New York Times*, March 23, 1969, D1, 16.

14. Stanley Kauffmann, "I am Curious (Yellow)," *New Republic*, March 15, 1969, 22, 32.

15. Andrew Sarris, "The Nihilism of Nudity—II," *Village Voice*, March 27, 1969, 51; Sarris, "A View from New York," *Sight and Sound* 38 (autumn 1969): 203.

16. Sarris, "A View from New York," 203; Andrew Sarris, "If Rhett Loved Scarlett Today . . . ," *New York Times*, December 14, 1969, D23+; "The Ethos of Doity Movies," *Village Voice*, October 7, 1971, 76.

17. Richard Schickel, "Porn and Man at Yale," *Harper's*, July 1970, 34.

18. Richard Corliss, "Film: Cherry & Harry & Racquel," *Village Voice*, June 11, 1970, 56, 59; "Confessions of an Ex-Pornologist," *Village Voice*, June 3, 1971, 62, 64, 70.

19. Brendan Gill, "Blue Notes," *Film Comment*, January–February, 1973, 7.

20. Gill, "Blue Notes," 8, 11.

21. "Hot Circuit," *Naked News* 1, no. 10 (1971): 10–11.

22. "The Long Swift Sword of Siegfried," *Naked News* 1, no. 14 (n.d.): 12.

23. Vincent Canby, "The Blue Movie Blues," *New York Times*, May 10, 1970, 89+; Blair Sobol, "The Only Girl in the World: Seeing 'Deep Throat,'" *Village Voice*, September 14, 1972, 75; Archer Winsten, *New York Post*, November 27, 1972, in "Deep Throat" Clippings File, Billy Rose Theater Collection, New York Public Library, Lincoln Center, New York; Shana Alexander, "At the Sexual Delicatessen," *Newsweek*, February 5, 1973, 43.

24. Charles Champlin, *Los Angeles Times*, March 11, 1973, n.p.; David Thomson, *Last Tango in Paris* (London: British Film Institute Publishing, 1998), 21.

25. Kael, *For Keeps*, 456, 450.

26. Charles Champlin, "Last Tango in Paris," in Peter Rainer ed., *Love and Hisses: The National Society of Film Critics Sound off on the Hottest Movie Controversies* (San Francisco: Mercury House, 1992), 62.

27. James M. Wall, "Tango Partners: Money and Media," *Christian Century*, February 24, 1973, 251.

28. "Self-Portrait of an Angel and Monster," *Time*, January 22, 1973, accessed www.time.com.

29. David Denby, "Media Orgy," *Atlantic*, April 1973, 120, 122, 123.

30. David Brudnoy, "Love Is . . . ," *National Review*, May 25, 1973, 586; Thomas Meehan, "Last Tango: No Masterpiece," *Saturday Review*, April 1973, 68; Robert Hatch, *The Nation*, February 12, 1973, 222; Moira Walsh, "Last Tango in Paris," *Commonweal*, February 24, 1973, 172; Stanley Kauffmann, "Last Tango in Paris," *New Republic*, March 3, 1973, 20.

31. Judith Crist, "Last Tango in Paris," in Rainer, *Love and Hisses*, 67; Joan Mellen, "Sexual Politics and 'Last Tango in Paris,'" *Film Quarterly* 26 (spring 1973): 15.

32. E. Ann Kaplan, "Last Tango in Paris," *Jump Cut*, 4 (1974), accessed at www.ejumpcut.org/archive/onlinessays/JC04folder/LastTangol.html.

33. Addison Verrill, *Variety*, January 17, 1973, reprinted in *Variety Film Reviews 1973* (hereafter, VFR); Verrill, *Variety*, January 31, 1973, and February 21, 1973, reprinted in VFR.

34. Verrill, *Variety*, February 21, 1973, and March 7, 1973, reprinted in VFR.

35. Verrill, *Variety*, July 18, 1973, reprinted in VFR.

36. Verrill, *Variety*, January, 30, 1974, reprinted in VFR. Vincent Canby, "Have You Met Miss Jones–and Mr. Oscar?" *New York Times*, April 8, 1973, sec. 2.1.7.

37. Linda Williams, "Cinema and the Sex Act," *Cineaste* 27 (winter 2001): 20.

38. Williams, "Cinema and the Sex Act," 22.

39. Williams, "Cinema and the Sex Act," 22.

40. Williams, "Cinema and the Sex Act," 22.

15 ∗ Porn Goes to College: American Universities, Their Students, and Pornography, 1968–1973

ARTHUR KNIGHT AND KEVIN M. FLANAGAN

On February 7, 1969, on the campus of the University of Notre Dame in South Bend, Indiana—an all-male (until 1972) Catholic university in a fairly conservative, moderately sized rust belt city—students and police clashed for the first, and possibly only, time in the school's history. As the conflict came to its climax, a photographer caught a shot of a non-uniformed officer macing a student (figure 15.1). The image is a familiar one from the era, but what had caused the clash was not the students protesting the Vietnam War or occupying the administration building. Rather, they had been attempting to screen—albeit in defiance of strict instructions from the county prosecutor and university administrators not to do so—two "obscene" experimental art films that showed genitalia and sexual acts: Jack Smith's *Flaming Creatures* (1963) and Andrew Noren's *Kodak Ghost Poems* (1968).

Four and a half years later, on September 29, 1973, at the College of William & Mary in Williamsburg, Virginia—a coed but barely integrated state university in a fairly conservative small, tourist town—eight hundred students, along with a few townsfolk, spread themselves around the college's new basketball arena. They were assembled to hear sexploitation pioneer Russ Meyer, critic Judith Crist, Citizens for Decent Literature (CDL) spokesman Robert K. Dornan, Virginia-based evangelist Pat Robertson, hardcore impresario Gerard Damiano, and—presumably in the name of inclusiveness—*Mission: Impossible*'s African American co-star, Greg Morris, debate issues of obscenity and the law. Both before and after the debate, attendees were invited to screen Meyer's softcore *Vixen!* (1968) and Damiano's decidedly hardcore *The Devil in Miss Jones* (1973) at the twin cinema near campus. Although the debate got heated and the shows were packed, there were no riots or arrests—the screenings took place under the watchful eyes of a sheriff and a judge dispatched by the Commonwealth's attorney.

In *Hollywood v. Hard Core*, Jon Lewis notes that in August 1973, the New School for Social Research in New York promoted "the first porn movie course ever offered at an American university." Lewis says it was

Fig. 15.1 A South Bend, Indiana, undercover police officer maces a University of Notre Dame student protester, February 7, 1969. This photo first appeared in a special edition of the *Notre Dame Observer* the following day and was reprinted at the head of a special section in the University yearbook for 1968–1969. (Courtesy the *Notre Dame Observer*.)

"less a course than a lecture series"—with no films but publishers from Grove Press and *Screw* magazine and a CDL spokesman as guests, it was a version of the William & Mary panel strung out over a series of weeks—nonetheless *Variety* covered it under the headline "Pornography Joins the Curriculum." For Lewis, "the academy's confirmation of the cultural significance of porn affirmed the fact that by late summer of 1973 hardcore was no longer so significant anymore."[1]

Given the difference between the Notre Dame experimental film riot of 1969 and the peaceful William & Mary porn double bill of 1973, there is something compelling about Lewis's argument. Certainly, using the macroscopic lens of industrial-cultural history that Lewis deploys, his conclusion makes sense. Still, there was an audience of eight hundred people for a *debate*, an audience most campus events with even a hint of scholarly flavor only dream of. And there was that sheriff and judge. From the perspective of *Variety* in New York, the New School's lecture series might appear as "a kind of curio, even a gag," but the news hadn't yet traveled to small-town Virginia.[2] Put differently, cultural significance develops unevenly, and the specific locales of differing iterations of "the academy" may play an important role in those processes. In this essay, we pursue a microhistorical analysis to try to understand how and why these events happened at Notre Dame and William & Mary and, more broadly, to start to understand the role that college campuses and students may have played in bringing attention to film pornography outside America's big cities.

Before continuing, we should note several things about our relation to these events as subject for scholarly analysis. First, we are implicated in our study: both of us are or have been directly affiliated with William & Mary (W&M) and indirectly with Notre Dame (ND).[3] Second, our discovery of these events was coincidental: we came upon the W&M event as part of ongoing research on film exhibition and moviegoing in Williamsburg across the twentieth century; we "discovered" the events at ND when Kevin told his father about the W&M event, and Mr. Flanagan recalled a story from his freshman yearbook. Third, we were surprised to discover—and initially quite skeptical—that such events had taken place at ND and W&M. The ND riot and the W&M panel and screenings did not match our sense of the present-day character of these two universities and their adjoining communities or our understanding of how they had developed those characters over the last several decades. We were not alone in our surprise. Colleagues at both institutions were flabbergasted by reports of our initial findings.

This third point perhaps implies our last point of relation: we believe that there are quite direct, but also obscured, connections between the events of the late 1960s and early 1970s and present-day events at ND and W&M, and beyond. The events we examine here, which catalyzed around films labeled obscene or pornographic, were about struggles over public representations of and discussions about sex and sexuality. As we've researched these events from roughly forty years ago, we've seen surprisingly similar struggles unfold around us—albeit with motion picture pornography now more frequently as an unspoken background rather than the foreground—as though these earlier events had never happened. All attempts to narrate, analyze, and understand the past are inevitably shaped by the time in which they are undertaken, but for our project the desire to understand the past's complex place in the present has become explicit.

Film was the catalyst for the events at ND and W&M for several reasons. American cinephilia was reaching its apex in this period, a phenomenon generally seen as situated in cities. But university film series and clubs played a vital role in cultivating young, educated, intellectual audiences who read critics such as Andrew Sarris and Pauline Kael, patronized the first film festivals in the United States, and supported institutions such as Dan Talbot's New Yorker repertory cinema. As many critics and historians have noted, an important element of the rise of post–World War II cinephilia was an appreciation of the serious and "mature" themes exemplified by European art films. Ultimately, this demand was accommodated in mainstream American movie culture via the adoption in November 1968 of the MPAA rating system, which stratified the audience by age (younger and older than seventeen) and level of maturity. Consequently, the ratings system both gave rise to films aimed at the "mature" audience and made that audience—coinciding precisely with the majority of college-age students—emphatically visible. This new, doubled visibility dovetailed with rising concerns that the mature, college-aged audience was changing in fundamental ways, particularly in its approaches to sex and sexuality. Film did not cause these changes. But as a popular medium with a half-hidden history of "blue" representations, as a commercial interest in representing current trends that seemed to be tending toward the explicit, as a mediated quality that could present events unfolding in time but shield its viewers from live flesh, *and* as a site of consumption at once dark and private and brazenly public and social, cinema could powerfully focus attention on such changes and distill the attendant anxieties.

The tensions around this knot of issues is nicely symbolized by reports that during the Notre Dame riot Kathy Cecil, a junior at ND's all-women's sister school, St. Mary's, attempted to rescue *Flaming Creatures* and *Kodak Ghost Poems* from the police by hiding the reels under her dress.[4] Judith Crist, one of the participants in the W&M events, recalled for us her first opportunity to see a stag film around 1960, when she was covering the hearings by the Senate Subcommittee on Juvenile Delinquency. A piece of evidence—she thinks it was called "Breaking in Blondie"—was about to be screened for the reporters pool, but as the film began her fellow journalists, all men, demanded she leave the room. "It's not that they didn't want me to see the film," she asserts. "They didn't want me to see them seeing the film."[5] In South Bend a bit less than a decade after Crist's screening room ejection, the landscape of *seeing* was both the same and different. Apparently Kathy Cecil's fellow male students didn't mind being seen looking, but as importantly, Cecil was willing to be seen looking—and to go to considerable lengths to be permitted to do so. For the ND administration and for the county prosecutor, such empowered looking was untenable. At the later W&M events, mixed looking was still policeable, if not as spectacularly so.

This chapter has three parts. The first describes an array of discourses, public events, and episodes that focus on the intersection of colleges and college students with obscene film and pornography. During the Vietnam years, college and university campuses were becoming more visible to the American public as a home to the "counterculture." The most violent clashes between the mainstream of American society and the counterculture—the Kent and Jackson State killings of May 1970—happened in the middle of our period. In light of such events, controversies over pornography on college campuses may appear trivial, but such controversies existed on a continuum that emphasized the increasing symbolic visibility of colleges and their students. The second and third parts of this chapter examine more closely the ND and W&M events. Our aim is to provide detail about how pornography began to make its way "on/scene," to use Linda Williams's term, in areas of the country outside the metropoles.[6] Our cases also provide new information about the unevenly gendered spaces for the public consumption of porn. *Deep Throat* and the rise of "porn chic" in 1972 have often been noted as a watershed, when women began to attend hardcore porn films and when women and men first began to encounter hardcore together. Although these generalizations have some basis, our research suggests that in lived experience, especially in small towns, the picture was more complex. Outside of cities, the quasi-public/quasi-private, apparently noncommercial, pedagogical, and "protected" space of the college campus was the primary location of the mixed, public look at porn.

"Porn and Man [and Woman] at Yale," and Beyond

We've admitted being surprised at discovering the ND and W&M events, but should we have been? Yes and no.[7]

Our first assumption was that if such attention to pornographic film had occurred at these two universities, similar attention must have been commonplace. As far as we have been able to determine, beside the New School lectures, that was not the case. So our surprise was warranted. Perhaps. The qualification is necessary because colleges and universities provide a challengingly dispersed field of research. We describe at the end of this section the efforts we've made to cover the field, but we may as well put the cliché here rather than at our conclusion: more research is needed. College or university faculty members and students may wish to explore their own school's and town's historical relationship to porn.

Nevertheless, if our surprise about these two *specific* events was warranted, at a more general level it was probably not. There are connections of long standing between colleges and ideas about and images of sex. For instance, the coed seems to have percolated in the American (male) sexual imaginary's stock of desiring, and possibly lascivious, female characters since at least the late 1920s, when precode Hollywood made films such as *The Bare Co-Ed* (1928) and *Confessions of a Co-Ed* (1931). The fraternity house provides one of the storied, elusive, semiopenly secret locations for the all-male enjoyment of stag films: Judith Crist recalled her brother telling her about such events during his college days in the late 1940s and early 1950s; Tom Waugh reports seeing a stag film with his dorm mates in 1968; also, in the late 1960s, researchers for the Commission on Obscenity and Pornography noted that "college fraternities in the [Denver] area frequently scheduled stag parties" and that, along with "an Air Force officer, an advertising agency executive, an automobile salesman, [and] a lifeguard, . . . several college athletes . . . could 'get' Class A [i.e., hardcore] films."[8] Finally, the Kinsey Institute at Indiana University became a site for the academic study of human sexuality and also for the collection of pornography in 1947.[9]

Beyond these broad associations of colleges and pornography, we have found three more specific instances that we believe began circulating in the late 1960s and early 1970s. The first is proximity of purveyors of pornography, especially movie theaters, *near* university campuses. Such instances sometimes appear in the historical record via legal action and reform efforts. For example, one of the Supreme Court's late rulings of the 1960s against prior restraint was in the case of *Lee Art Theatre vs. Virginia* (1968). The Lee Art Theatre went through many incarnations as a cinema, but by the late 1960s it showed porn. It was also adjacent to Virginia Commonwealth University (VCU) in Richmond, which was growing and consolidating at the time.[10] The Court's short ruling makes no mention of VCU or its students, but it is hard to imagine that the proximity of the "mature" audience offered by VCU wasn't both an inducement to the Lee's owners and to the prosecutors. Similarly, a sociological study of antiobscenity activists around 1970 finds that reformers at both study sites, "Midville" and "Southtown," focused their attention on locations next to college campuses. The reformers' worries over obscenity were spurred in large measure by this location, and those concerns had two somewhat contradictory flavors: first, concern for students' moral well-being and, second, anxiety that universities and the college-age audiences would serve as a sort of Trojan horse of liberality or libertinism.[11] Another study from the same period, albeit one done in San Francisco and using a self-selecting survey method, found evidence that would have alarmed the Midville and Southtown reformers: 53 percent of adult movie theater patrons had college or graduate degrees, and another 29 percent had at least some college education. By comparison, 17 percent of adult bookstore patrons had college degrees, with 14 percent more having some college and none having graduate degrees.[12] In a different survey, adult film exhibitors reported that their "customers [were] almost invariably males in their late twenties to fifties, and that young people typically are not customers except in theaters near a college."[13]

Proximity of porn purveyors to colleges garnered attention by itself, but additional attention was drawn by the gender makeup of audiences for college-town porn cinemas. In Waterloo, Iowa, home of the University of Northern Iowa, one journalist writing in 1970 estimated that women were 40 percent of the audience at the Mini Cinema 16.[14] At about the same time, in Amherst, Massachusetts, only 13 percent of the audience for the "adult theater" were women. When put into context, however, this comparatively small number is in fact quite large. Studies of similar theaters in New York City, Los Angeles, Chicago, Atlanta, Kansas City, Missouri, and Springfield, Massachusetts, showed the proportion of women in the audience was no greater than 5 percent (in the suburbs of New York) and in most other locations was 1 or 2 percent.[15] The women of the Amherst-area colleges may not have gone to the adult theater as often as those at the University of Northern Iowa, but they went in much greater numbers than women outside college towns.

A second class of association between colleges and porn is students as porn actors and makers. Performer Mary Rexroth seems to have been a student when she began her career in San Francisco.[16] Researchers for the Commission on Obscenity and Pornography interviewed another Mary (no last name attributed), also in San Francisco, the daughter of a small-town dentist, who "was an anthropology major at U.C. Berkeley until she dropped out in June 1969." They also spoke to a San Francisco theater owner who claimed, "Most of the girls come from well-off middle-class families. They have gone to college, if not graduated. Their appearance in sex films is a way to show off their new-found sexual freedom."[17] The college connection was not just in front of the camera. Rexroth claimed that many of the filmmakers she encountered were students who wanted "to play around with the camera and not have to spend eight years loading magazines at a television station."[18] Leo Productions, a pioneer in 16 mm porn production, drew heavily on San Francisco State University's filmmaking program, and Jim Mitchell (of the Mitchell Brothers, makers of *Behind the Green Door* [1972]) moved into his career directly from San Francisco State.[19] Beyond college connections to porn audiences, performers, or makers, Eric Schaefer argues that because of campus film societies, the increasingly common 16 mm *format* of porn in the late sixties was seen as associated "with college students [and] implicitly linked with . . . radical change."[20] Richard Schickel, writing in 1970, claimed "most colleges these days [are] full of film freaks."[21] Some of those "freaks" wanted to be filmmakers and some, at least in San Francisco, became pornographers. By the early seventies, the Midville and Southtown reformers, the country prosecutor in South Bend, and the Commonwealth's attorney in Williamsburg didn't need to know these specific connections to follow the more general associative logic of cultural infection (the "natural curiosity" of students, as one Midville reformer put it) and grow very alarmed.[22]

The final class of association between colleges and porn brings us still closer to the Notre Dame and Williamsburg events—that is, formal college community scrutiny of pornography or, more often, of its putative social effects. Although the ND and W&M events appear to have been unique in their size and ambition to mix debate, critical reflection, and the display of sexually explicit films, there were smaller events at many colleges around the country. Judith Crist said she spoke on the "hot topic" of film obscenity and censorship at quite a few universities at the time—"Texas, Montana, similar Midwestern places"—though she recalled generally being the only speaker on the bill and that films weren't shown.[23] In 1971, Reverend Morton A. Hill, founder of Morality in Media, lectured on "Erotic Literature and Pornography" at the SUNY Buffalo School of Library and Information Science, and in the same year, William B. Lockhart, University of Minnesota law professor and chair of the Commission on Obscenity and Pornography, lead a discussion on obscenity at Mankato State College in Mankato, Minnesota.

But critics, reformers, and professors weren't the only campus guests to address issues of porn. In this period pornographic filmmakers and performers also started getting invited to campuses: in February 1970— its first academic year admitting women—Yale held an eight-film Russ Meyer retrospective. Richard Schickel, covering the event for *Harper's*, noted that "many [Yale men] brought dates," that "a couple of girls from the Women's Liberation movement" protested, and that, in coming to Yale, Meyer had crossed "age and class [and regional] barriers and . . . been greeted as a conquering hero."[24] Other Meyer retrospectives were held over the following year at the University of Illinois, University of California, Northwestern, Georgia State, and Princeton.[25] Although details are scant and dates uncertain, Linda Lovelace's autobiographies and interviews with various other porn stars also sometimes mention in passing appearances before college audiences in this period.[26]

By 1969–1971, then, before "porno chic" and congruent with more well-publicized and spectacular events—for instance, erotic film festivals in expected places such as San Francisco and New York—it seems porn had gone to college. And college students—including, apparently, more and more women—had gone to porn. Still, the evidence we've presented for this is somewhat scattered and fugitive. In the absence of centralized collections of college and university newspapers, we've turned to the American alternative press—collected on microfilm in the "Underground Newspaper Collection"—to provide further background for our claims about the connections between colleges and pornography.[27] A significant proportion of the alternative press, especially outside of large cities, was explicitly "alternative" to official university newspapers. For instance, the Austin *Rag* self-consciously positioned itself in opposition to the University of Texas's *Daily Texan* and was staffed largely by students at UT; the Newark, Delaware, *Heterodoxical Voice* was at odds with the University of Delaware; and the Grinnell, Iowa, *Pterodactyl* was an alternative voice for Grinnell College students. The underground press was heterogeneous, but it divided roughly between papers that focused on a specific issue (e.g., labor, anarchism, vegetarianism) and those that focused on cultural politics.

This latter form, still recognizable in much of the remaining U.S. alternative press, was the form most often associated with colleges and universities. It was, quite literally, born out of the rising tensions in the United States around normative (or nonnormative) sex and sexuality, especially as represented in public. Sex and sexuality were topics that featured in many first issues of college alternate papers, that made the headlines frequently in these papers, that provided for eye-catching visuals (predominantly, but not exclusively, depicting female nudity), and that sometimes led to the papers themselves being declared obscene or pornographic.[28]

Film was an important substrand of this alternative press discourse on sex. It first appeared in the mid-1960s as a slightly embarrassed camp attention to nudie-cuties, which then overlapped attention to experimental and European art films, which, in turn, overlapped attention to the rise of hardcore porn features and related fare. The alternative press was consistently pro-sex and pro free expression, but from the mid-1960s to the Supreme Court's *Miller v. California* decision in 1973 its writers, photo editors, layout artists, and advertising people struggled to balance a celebration of sexuality that used direct, pictorial representation with critiques of commodification and female objectification. By the time of *Deep Throat*, this balance of celebration and critique was becoming more apparently difficult. The Alternative Features Service (AFS), which syndicated news to underground papers, reported at the start of

1973 that "sex papers"—formerly alternative papers that had turned to sexual content to sustain circulation—were "driv[ing] the alternative papers off the streets, [making] the chances for papers concerned with the evils of sexism and other social issues to have a meaningful impact on the public consciousness appear dim."[29] Whether the AFS diagnosis of the causes of the waning underground press was accurate or not, many papers, including many affiliated with colleges, had closed by 1973. But such developments were uneven: the *Ghent Press*, a short-lived paper from the Norfolk, Virginia, neighborhood that houses Old Dominion University (ODU), themed one of its first issues in September 1973 with the question, "What is Smut?" The issue mixed free speech and positions against commodification of sex but was anchored by a condemnation of the local "Porno Raid," which shut down—and ensured ODU students as well as students at the nearby, historically black Norfolk State University couldn't see—*The Devil in Miss Jones*.[30]

"This is Insane, I Can't Believe It"

The "Pornography and Censorship Conference" at Notre Dame precipitated a perfect storm of American anxieties of the late 1960s in which pornography and obscenity came to stand for a host of other concerns about the autonomy of young people, the culture and politics of youth, the proper political organization of the United States, and even the behavior of the United States as a world superpower.[31] These concerns were hardly particular to ND or South Bend, Indiana, but what was unique was the conflicting ideas that existed about ND's status as America's best-known Catholic university. These conflicts provided the catalyst for the deployment of "mace at Notre Dame."[32]

The impulse behind the conference held on February 1969 at Notre Dame originated in February 1968, when the Notre Dame Center for Continuing Education sponsored a one-day "seminar on the problem of obscenity, particularly its availability to young persons" and the "national and local implications" of that availability.[33] No students were involved in organizing the seminar, and they went unmentioned in the outreach materials that promised "the affair will bring together attorneys, postal officials, law enforcement officers, publishers, legislators, doctors and interested citizens."[34] Local members of the antipornography CDL played a key role in organizing the event, which may account for the swerving in its publicity materials between the rhetoric of "intelligent inquiry" and nationalist nostalgia: "Not so long ago, many of the books and periodicals currently available on our newsstands were held to be obscene by the courts. They could be secured only at great expense and with great secrecy. . . . Today, our motion pictures and plays also reflect changes in public attitudes and in the laws governing obscenity."[35] No one involved in the production, distribution, or sale of (or admitted consumption of) these materials was included among seminar participants.

The event in 1969 differed dramatically from the organization and spirit of the 1968 seminar. The "Pornography and Censorship Conference" was organized and sponsored by the Student Union Academic Commission, and it was ambitious in scope: It was to begin on a Wednesday evening with Allen Ginsberg reading and end the following Monday with an open community discussion. In between would be an art exhibit (works by Claes Oldenberg and Ed Ruscha among others); a performance by New York's avant-garde Theatre of the Ridiculous of *Lady Godiva*; a poetry reading by Gerard Malanga; a performance by the Fugs; presentations by judges, lawyers, and national representatives of the CDL; and films by "Andy Warhol, Jean Genet, Andrew Noren, Kuchar Brothers, Jack Smith, and others." "Delegate cards," which entitled the holder to attend all events, were available to students ($2), faculty and staff ($3), and the general public ($5). Single tickets were also available for many of the events, though the delegate cards were, it seems, designed to give the organizers some control of the audience for especially sensitive or controversial exhibitions: "Due to limited capacity, only delegates [would] be admitted to films and several other conference events."[36]

By all accounts the opening Ginsberg event succeeded, with an "overflow crowd" and Ginsberg, in an ND sweatshirt, reading, chanting, and saying to the crowd, "I didn't come prepared for the Pornography and Censorship Conference. The occasion is scary, then, for all of us."[37] The *South Bend Tribune* kept an eye on the proceedings, observing that "only about a dozen persons left during the 90 minutes he recited, and those were all men. . . . The audience included many young women and several conservatively dressed middle-aged women, who, according to their facial expressions, enjoyed the poetry a la Ginsberg."[38] The next day, some rough patches developed: concerns were raised that the art show and *Flaming Creatures* (figure 15.2) might be in violation of Saint Joseph County criminal statutes. Since the county prosecutor had recently been active in two cases against local bookstores, since members of CDL were both part of the conference and had expressed skepticism about it, and since ND student opinion about the merits of the conference seemed divided (the school paper had editorialized that it was "inappropriate"),

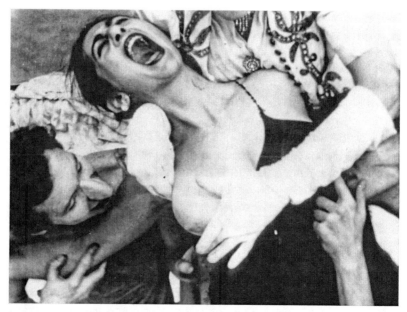

Fig. 15.2 A scheduled showing of Jack Smith's *Flaming Creatures* (1963) seen here, among other films, at the "Pornography and Censorship Conference" at Notre Dame University degenerated into a boisterous student protest and police action on the campus in February 1969. (Frame enlargement.)

the organizers proceeded with caution.[39] Conference organizers opened the art show after a sit-in of about 350 students demanded entry, but they cancelled *Flaming Creatures* midscreening, which apparently had been mislabeled and wasn't to have been shown, but they promised the other films would run the next day.[40] That evening, *Lady Godiva*, complete with female nudity, took the stage.[41]

The threats of legal action were reiterated on Friday. About six hundred students and a few faculty met to discuss a student-initiated petition against the showing of the films and decide how to proceed. The *South Bend Tribune* reported that a vote was held with 244 — "probably most . . . [being] members of the Students for a Democratic Society, a radical group" — in favor of showing at least Andrew Noren's *Kodak Ghost Poems* and 128 opposed.[42] Between two hundred and three hundred students, along with Noren, then took over a lecture hall and prepared to show *Kodak Ghost Poems* and, possibly, some of the other films, including *Flaming Creatures*. Apparently alerted by members of the CDL, about thirty sheriff's deputies, many in plain clothes, arrived on campus. Six made their way to the auditorium and, without identifying themselves or showing a warrant (which they did have), attempted to confiscate the films. Students surrounded the projectors and passively resisted, but the officers discovered Kathy Cecil attempting to smuggle the films out of the room under her dress, knocked her down, took the films, and left with the students in pursuit. Outside the students pelted the deputies with snowballs and attempted to block access to their cars. The deputies responded with mace, spraying about fifteen students, and took refuge in the Faculty Club, finally escaping out the back. In the aftermath, the Student Union Academic Commission voted 240–120 to cancel the remaining conference events.[43]

A bit more than a week after this "fracas," the president of Notre Dame, Father Theodore Hesburgh, issued a new "tough policy" on how the university would handle "disruptive demonstrators": The dean of students would determine whether a protest impeded the normal university operations. If it did, protesters would be given fifteen minutes to stop. If they persisted, students would be suspended and nonstudents would be turned over to civil authorities as trespassers.[44] Although the policy with its focus on disruption and disorder was clearly precipitated by the conference events, it was also a response to a larger set of issues. These ranged from a nonviolent-but-much-noticed ND protest against Dow Chemical and CIA campus recruiting in the fall of 1968, to the blossoming of protests on many other campuses that year; from the local crackdown on "obscenity," to nationally shifting sexual mores; and from a desire within ND to ensure academic freedom, to a pushback against that effort both by the Catholic Church magisterium and by anxious Americans, not always Catholic, who saw increasing appeal in the church's hierarchy, clear rules, and moral code.

A week after Hesburgh announced his policy, President Nixon sent him a letter, released simultaneously to the press, lauding him and using the occasion to initiate investigations into how the federal government might intervene in university protests.[45] Hesburgh, who had been trying to renegotiate ND's relation to the church and who was a spokesman for Catholic educators seeking more autonomy, hardly welcomed this idea.[46] But the fact that the academic freedom he championed had been used to show "obscene" films, which had in turn led to a riot, required damage control. Notre Dame would continue to assert its autonomy, its liberality, and its scholarly bona fides, but it wouldn't again be put in the position of having its students seen shamelessly looking at shameless displays of cinematic sex.

Deep Throat and Circle K

Nearly five years after the ND conference, the W&M conference "Pornography and the Law" came about for many of the same reasons—most pointedly as a student challenge to perceived paternalism, both inside and outside the university. The cultural, political, and legal landscape were different, however, as were the specific local circumstances. In 1969, U.S. involvement in Vietnam was escalating, and Richard Nixon was just starting his presidency. By 1973, U.S. combat forces were out of Vietnam, and Nixon was embroiled in the Watergate scandal. In 1969, Notre Dame was a rising school—private and with a national reputation—at the geographic margins of a small, declining industrial city. In 1972–1973, W&M was a state-run school attempting to capitalize on its history as the second oldest college in the United States and its location next to the pioneering living history museum, Colonial Williamsburg. It sat squarely in the middle of a small town that was rapidly expanding as a tourist and retirement destination.

Although W&M students had participated in the political activism of the late 1960s, they had been a comparatively muted presence on the campus and in the town. There had been no equivalent to the ND sit-in in opposition to the CIA and certainly no rioting. Multiple factors contributed to the relative quiet, but important among them were a deeply conservative college president, the ongoing work to integrate the college (as well as the town and its schools), and, perhaps paramount for focusing student energy, the struggle to modernize the college's parietal rules. Instead of a sit-in opposing the CIA, in October 1969 W&M students had held a "dorm-in" to protest visitation restrictions—limits that were finally eliminated at the start of the school year starting in 1972, just as ND was matriculating its first women.[47] In this context, the newly visible pornographic feature films of the early seventies—understood to circulate nationally and globally but consumed locally—provided focus at W&M for expression and debate.

If Notre Dame sat somewhat aloof and off at the edge of South Bend—a circumstance perhaps emphasized by the paucity of off-campus advertising, including ads for movie theaters, in the school's newspaper—William & Mary sat right in the center of Williamsburg. Consequently, the college's students had easy access to the town's two commercial movie theaters, the Williamsburg Theatre and the Blane Twin Cinemas, both within walking distance of the campus, and the college's students were often on the minds of the theaters' managers. The Williamsburg

Theatre, immediately adjacent to the college, had been in the increasingly tourist-dominated center of town since 1933, when it replaced another cinema that had stood at the same site from the early 1920s. The Blane opened in 1969 in a developing area of town meant for locals and, to a lesser degree, students, as opposed to tourists; a couple years earlier, the Chamber of Commerce had feared this area was falling prey to "'honky tonk' blight," and the Blane along with other businesses were perhaps intended to counter this trend.[48] Williamsburg resident and theater employee Clay Riley recalls that the two theaters illegally colluded to split product and, in theory, share the market, but that Williamsburg was most receptive to general audience fare and attracted tourists, families, and older residents, as well as students.[49] This situation left the Blane searching for its niche and product it could call its own, which over time yielded a grab bag of blaxploitation, spaghetti westerns, contentious art films, horror, and, eventually, pornography. After trying to sell itself as a family-oriented theater, first with all-ages films and later with Saturday matinees for children, Paul Blane, the theater's owner and manager, grew willing to risk controversy to draw an audience. In 1969, he screened *I am Curious (Yellow)* and moved from there to screening softcore sex films such as *Is There Sex After Death?* (1971) and *The Erotic Adventures of Zorro* (1972).[50]

Starting on September 20, 1972, the Blane began showing Gerard Damiano's soon-to-be porn classic *Deep Throat*. In context, this move over the line from soft to hardcore both was and wasn't a programming shift. The film ran two weeks without obvious local controversy.[51] Further, our local informants—admittedly a small, all-male sample—recall the Blane's regular *Deep Throat* showings (and most of its softcore, as well as other porn they saw in the region) as all-male affairs, suggesting that perhaps this move "on/scene" was incremental and comparatively modest—no apparent couples audience for Williamsburg.[52]

Deep Throat was enough of a success that Blane revived it in March 1973. Before the run began, a letter written to the *Daily Press*, a regional newspaper, revealed a citizen's complaints that the Blane "pointedly aimed ['a fairly steady diet of X-rated and provocative films'] at possible lucrative trade from curious young people" and, further, that "lax [ID] screening policies permit school kids of a tender age to see this trash."[53] (One of our interviewees confirmed that it was quite easy to buy a ticket for one film at the Blane Twin and sneak into the other; he had used this strategy to see *I am Curious [Yellow]* with his girlfriend.[54]) The local Commonwealth's attorney subsequently asked Blane to close the film,

Fig. 15.3 The marquee of the Blane Twin Cinema and the headline from page one of the William & Mary *Flat Hat*, March 20, 1973. (Courtesy William & Mary *Flat Hat*.)

arguing that based on precedents elsewhere local courts would likely find it obscene. Blane acquiesced and announced his decision to his audience with a spectacular marquee (figure 15.3).[55]

"We Apologize 'Throat' Has Been Cut"

Enter Cornell Christianson, a William & Mary junior and president of the College's Student Assembly. More than three-quarters of W&M students were Virginians in the early seventies, but Christianson was from New Jersey, and he considered it imperative, as well as in keeping with his liberal political views, that W&M and Williamsburg be open to a variety of perspectives—perhaps especially controversial ones. The national attention recently lavished upon *Deep Throat* had apparently captured the imaginations of enough of the student body to make its cancellation a disappointment. Christianson saw an opportunity. In an attempt to allow curious students to see the film while avoiding the Commonwealth's attorney and public criticism, Christianson collaborated with

Blane to arrange for a screening for students only, with proceeds benefiting the campus's Circle K charity and its efforts to buy a new activity bus. The showings sold out, attracting an audience of 805 people and raising $402.50 as well as some controversy over how such affiliations might sully the reputations of Circle K (which accepted the money), the college, or the college's new president.[56]

Pornography in Williamsburg might have ended there, but the summer of 1973 yielded the U.S. Supreme Court's *Miller v. California* ruling. *Miller* formalized President Nixon's and Congress's rejection of the 1971 recommendations of the President's Commission on Obscenity and Pornography that porn be decriminalized. Further, by confirming the place of local community standards for judging obscenity, *Miller* complicated the developing national market for hardcore film pornography, proved the Williamsburg Commonwealth's attorney's right, threatened a significant revenue source for the Blane Twin, and reminded students that though W&M now gave them the liberty to visit one another's rooms, there were still those who did not want students to look at certain things and certainly did not want them to be seen looking.[57]

Prompted by the *Deep Throat* cancellation, *Miller v. California*, and by Richmond and Norfolk-area prosecutions related to *The Devil in Miss Jones* over the summer of 1973, Christianson collaborated with students from the William & Mary Law School and with Blane to conceive an event that would examine the legal ramifications of publicly exhibiting sexually explicit materials while highlighting the spectacular aspects of the topic. Across the early fall, local and regional newspapers trumpeted names of possible guests: Barry Goldwater, Hubert Humphrey, Allen Ginsberg, Hugh Hefner, Bishop Fulton J. Sheen, Linda Lovelace.[58]

Supported with Student Association and Student Bar Association funds, the conference took place on Saturday, September 29, 1973. Constitutional scholar and chairman of the President's Commission on Obscenity and Pornography, William B. Lockhart opened with an address detailing the history of the censorship cases that were precedents for *Miller*. Four panels on various implications of the ruling followed. A panel of writers, publishers, attorneys, and law professors discussed the decision's effects on the publishing industry. Next a panel focused on the ruling as it pertained to the film industry. Here Ira Goldberg, a professor of Constitutional Law at Rutgers University, seemed to capture the sense of a number of panelists when he said,

> I can't help having the feeling as I've been listening today that this symposium was organized by Franz Kafka. There's a certain illusion about

it all. We're talking about a decision by the Supreme Court that no one seems to understand, which does something about obscenity which no one can define, which is to be suppressed to protect us from a danger which no one can define either. I find it all very puzzling.[59]

The third panel dealt with issues pertaining to the decision's effects on the local community. The talks culminated with the main celebrity panel of Russ Meyer, Judith Crist, Robert K. Dornan, Pat Robertson, Gerard Damiano, and Greg Morris. It featured panelists yelling at each other (Dornan started this pattern early in the day and kept it up), an attorney attempting to serve papers on Damiano (he'd already been served), and discussion that ran considerably past the scheduled end time.

Held in the college's cavernous new basketball arena, the first panels drew little more than one hundred people at most, but there were at least eight hundred for the celebrity panel. Although the conference proceedings were transcribed, it is difficult to determine who was in attendance. The invited participants were a more diverse lot than had been at Notre Dame in 1969, where the participants, except some of the performers in *Lady Godiva*, were all men and all white. Among the twenty-seven W&M panelists, there were four women and two African Americans. In their discourse, the panelists seem to indicate that significant numbers of women were also in the audience, but no photographs of the crowd at the event exist to confirm this. In the Q&A sessions that ended each panel, the majority of questioners seem to be men. However, two questioners who capped the evening were women—one a law school student, the other the wife of a law school student—who battled with Dornan and Robertson over their paternalism and issues of freedom of speech.[60] According to the follow-up reporting on the conference, these women— who were anti-*Miller* if not pro-porn and who seemed fully aware of how issues of "local standards" had been used for racially repressive purposes in Virginia and elsewhere—represented the clear majority of the feeling of the audiences throughout the day.[61]

After the panels were screenings at the Blane of Damiano's *The Devil in Miss Jones*—with the sheriff and judge sent by the Commonwealth's attorney to watch the watchers—and Russ Meyer's *Vixen!* (1968), neither of which had ever shown in town. The screenings were only open to those who had registered for the conference and were reportedly enthusiastically attended by about seven or eight hundred people, many of whom, apparently, had paid the dollar registration, skipped the panels, and attended only the films. The effect of the screenings, which the Commonwealth's attorney had been so concerned about, was in the blasé, if also somewhat disappointed, words of the W&M student paper's editors "less than a state of shock."[62]

The conference had attempted to address attitudes on censorship and obscenity in American society by way of the *Miller* ruling, with constant emphasis on screen hardcore. Richard Williamson, a panel participant and law professor at William & Mary, recalls that the conference was successful insofar as it promoted a "juicy" discussion of a hot-topic legal issue.[63] Despite the surveillance of *The Devil in Miss Jones* no police were called in, so in contrast to the ND event in 1969, the conference apparently took a step toward legitimizing a taboo topic—the representation and discussion of sex in public, a topic many of the panelists and questioners linked to sex education—both positioning it in an academic context and seeking communitywide involvement. However, the press after the conference seemed to view the event as something of an "anti-climax," though it's hard not to see that as partly the fault of the giant venue and, judging from the comments of several panelists, a torrentially rainy day.[64] Besides losing money, it didn't reveal any new positions or ideas but rather clarified clearly divided ground. And the functional effect of the clarification was this: No more public pornography in Williamsburg or at W&M. William & Mary students could visit one another freely in their dorms, but they couldn't use public representations of sex and sexuality to imagine and discuss what might happen if they did.

Two weeks after the conference, the Blane again courted controversy by playing *Last Tango in Paris*. But there was none. It never showed hardcore films again. About six months later Paul Blane sold his theater to the Martin Cinema chain, which promised it would show nothing stronger than R-rated films. "Williamsburg has seen its last x-rated movie," the local paper announced with confidence.[65] The theater continued to run as a chain cinema until 2001, when it closed and was turned into an Evangelical Christian church.

*

Maybe, then, Jon Lewis is right that "the academy's confirmation of the cultural significance of porn affirmed the fact that by 1973 hardcore was no longer so significant."[66] But the testiness of the exchanges at the W&M event—even if they didn't involve mace—together with the number of people who came out to take part in Williamsburg that fall at least hint that the case was not yet closed. For a variety of people on different sides of the issue of the public consumption of porn, the stakes were still high. By 1973 at the W&M conference, speaking for the CDL Robert Dornan ceded the territory of the home consumption of pornography, but collective, public consumption—instances in which the "mature audience" could be seen looking—remained of paramount concern.[67] Over the coming years, Dornan's position prevailed: porn has moved off the public stage. But it has also proliferated, leading Linda Williams to write of the "paradox" of "on/scenity": pornography that is known and available to the public, but at the same time not *in* public.[68]

Indeed, because the moments of explicit cinematic sexual representations truly *on-scene*—public, collective—were so brief at Notre Dame and William & Mary, we may still be living in some ways with the consequences of the spectacular repression of the ND conference and the perceived "anti-climax" of the W&M conference, as well as the apparent absence of similar events at other college campuses (figure 15.4). As we researched and wrote this chapter, events that seemed distant suddenly began to echo, increasingly loudly, in the present. A little digging revealed controversies around motion picture pornography at places such as Yale, Carnegie Mellon, and the University of California San Diego. What was controversial in all these instances was no longer motion picture porn per se, since that is available to most anyone in the United States with access to a DVD player or the Internet. Rather, what was controversial is that college students were being public with their motion picture pornography, both as consumers (at Carnegie Melon) and producers (Yale, though perhaps mythically, and UCSD). Like the students at ND in 1969 and at W&M in 1973, they were willing to be—insistent, even, on being—seen seeing.

And as we worked, the echoes grew louder and closer. At Notre Dame and William & Mary in the last decade, students wishing to display in public and reflect on feminist and queer sexualities encountered significant resistance—most pointedly focused on film. At Notre Dame, in response to criticisms by the church hierarchy and dis-ease by administrators, a "Queer Film Festival" (2004, 2005) became "Gay and Lesbian Film: Filmmakers, Narratives and Spectatorship" (2006) and the elusively named "Qlassics" (2007) before ceasing altogether. None of the films shown at these events (e.g., *Hedwig and the Angry Inch* [2001]) would qualify as pornography or "obscene" in a legal sense, but they still qualified as things Notre Dame students shouldn't be seen (publicly) seeing.[69] At William & Mary, students for four years (2006–2009) sponsored campus visits by the Sex Workers Art Show (SWAS), which was predominantly a set of live performances. Student organizers told us that the only part of the show that was not permitted on campus in any form was a segment of the show that would have shown old stag films, presumably because—unlike the live show, which uses words and simu-

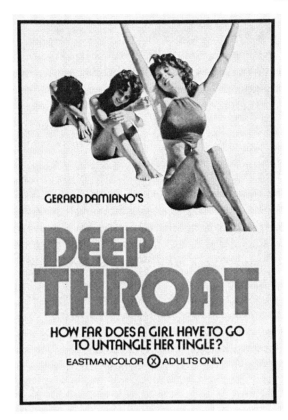

Fig. 15.4 Although there is no evidence that after its final screenings at the Blane Cinemas, *Deep Throat* (or other films widely recognized as pornography) played publicly in Williamsburg, the concerns it raised about the appropriateness of open, public discussions about sex and sexuality continued to resonate at the College of William & Mary for years to come.

lations and not much nudity—they photographically represented penetrative sex.[70] In each successive year, SWAS saw increasing controversy. In 2008, four members of the college's governing Board of Visitors were called before the State Assembly, and the College's president—a constitutional scholar who refused to prohibit the show—found that his contract would not be renewed; this event materialized fears expressed *in 1973* that the then-President might pay with his job for allowing porn on campus.[71]

It is certainly wishful thinking to believe that the peaceful completion of the Notre Dame conference in 1969 or the "success" of the William & Mary conference in 1973 would have led to some utopian state of affairs vis-à-vis public discussions of sex and sexuality.[72] What might have constituted such a success? It's hard to say, but we have an anecdote that is, perhaps, illuminating: probably at the same time as the postcancellation Circle-K benefit showing of *Deep Throat* at the Blane Cinemas, a late show of the film was also offered for the many members of William & Mary's sororities. The showing was not formally advertised but rather promoted by word of mouth. David Essex, a W&M alumni who told us about this show (Paul Blane confirmed that it took place), was one of small group of four or five men who got the word and decided to see if they could crash—wearing trench coats and Groucho glasses. According to Essex, the sorority women had come out en masse, packing the theater, and they welcomed him and his friends with bemusement. However, once the show started, he says, things got uncomfortable for the men—not because the women made them feel unwelcome—in fact, they no longer seemed to notice Essex and his friends. Rather, what was discomfiting was the atmosphere of intensity that developed as the women watched and commented on *Deep Throat*, sometimes with banter—"It'll never taste the same" yelled out during the film's infamous Coca Cola sex scene—but more often with a sort of collective groan that Essex very much understood did not signify pleasure. On top of that, he and his friends quickly realized that in this context they were no longer certain how they felt about the pleasures and desires the film was soliciting from them.[73] For these women and these few men in Williamsburg in 1973, pornography wasn't just between men anymore, and they were given a brief sense of how a differently configured, differently gendered world of pleasure and desire might look: not, apparently, much like *Deep Throat*. Such an understanding—however initial, rudimentary, and underexplored—could only begin because the obscene was brought on/scene in unprecedented ways for the sorority women of William & Mary. And, at least in Williamsburg, Virginia, in 1973—though we think Williamsburg was not wholly exceptional—that could only happen, briefly and provisionally, because porn could go to college.

Notes

1. Jon Lewis, *Hollywood v. Hardcore: How the Struggle over Censorship Saved the Modern Film Industry* (New York: New York University Press, 2000), 269. "Pornography Joins the Curriculum," *Variety*, August 8, 1973, 3, cited in Lewis.

2. Lewis, *Hollywood v. Hardcore*, 269.

3. Arthur Knight has been a faculty member at W&M, 1993 to the present, and Kevin M. Flanagan was an undergraduate there, 2002 to 2006. Knight's father-in-law taught at ND from 1968 until 2005, and he has friends on the current faculty; Flanagan's father is an ND alumnus, class of 1973. We should note that because Knight is a faculty member at a Virginia state-supported school, state law requires that he not use any state-owned equipment—e.g., his office computer—to view pornographic or obscene material. Scholars at Virginia state schools may use their office computers to view what may be pornographic material *for research purposes*, as long as they first get permission from the des-

ignated authority—in Knight's case, the College's dean of Faculty of Arts and Sciences. Knight obtained such permission, for which he thanks former Dean Carl Strikwerda.

4. "Film Is Confiscated in Nieuwland Hall; Ensuing Struggle Results in Injuries," *Notre Dame Observer*, February 8, 1969 (special ed.), 1.

5. Phone interview with Judith Crist, January 26, 2006. For a written account of this story see Crist, "The Critical Years," May 1997. Accessed October 11, 2011, /gos.sbc.edu/c/crist.html. Crist told us that after missing the opportunity with "Breaking in Blondie," she waited nearly a decade and saw her first "blue movie" as part of two of Alex de Renzy's "documentaries," *Pornography in Denmark* (1970) and *A History of the Blue Movie* (1970), and that *Deep Throat* was the first pornographic narrative feature she saw.

6. Linda Williams, *Hard Core: Power, Pleasure and the "Frenzy of the Visible,"* exp. ed. (Berkeley: University of California Press, 1999), 282.

7. Our section subtitle is borrowed from Richard Schickel, "Porn and Man at Yale," *Harper's*, July 1970, 34–38. Schickel's title is a revision of William F. Buckley Jr.'s conservative critique of his alma mater, *God and Man at Yale: The Superstitions of "Academic Freedom"* (Chicago: Henry Regnery Company, 1951).

8. Crist interview. Waugh, "Homosociality in the Classical American Stag Film: Off-Screen, On-Screen," *Porn Studies*, ed. Linda Williams (Durham, NC: Duke University Press, 2004)," 132–133. Morris E. Massey, "A Marketing Analysis of Sex-Oriented Materials in Denver, August 1969: A Pilot Study" in *Technical Report of the Commission on Obscenity and Pornography*, vol. 4: *The Marketplace: Empirical Studies* (Washington, DC: U.S. Government Printing Office, 1971), 64. Other commission researchers found that significant numbers of adult bookstores were located "near a university or college," especially in the south and north central regions. See John J. Sampson, "Commercial Traffic in Sexually Oriented Materials in the United States (1969–1970)," in *Technical Report of the Commission on Obscenity and Pornography*, vol. 3: *The Marketplace: The Industry* (Washington, DC: U.S. Government Printing Office, 1971), 110–111.

9. From 1957 to 1964, Masters and Johnson also had their research center—less well known to the public than Kinsey's—at Washington University in St. Louis.

10. For "Richmond's First Adult Theatre," which details the Lee Art Theatre's life in that role, no date, accessed February 20, 2006, as well as other articles on its history of in its various incarnations, see www.library.vcu.edu/jbc/spec coll/lee.html. See also "Movie Morlocks: The Lee-Art Theatre? An Introduction to Continental Adult Cinema," May 31, 2008. Accessed October 11, 2011, moviemorlocks.com/2008/05/31/the-lee-art-theatre-an-introduction-to -continental-adult-cinema.

11. Louis Zurcher Jr. and R. George Kirkpatrick, *Citizens for Decency: Antipornography Crusades as Status Defense* (Austin: University of Texas Press, 1976), 51, 53, 55–73. "Southtown" was probably Austin; "Midville" may be Ann Arbor or East Lansing, MI. *Citizens for Decency* began as part of the research for the

Commission on Obscenity and Pornography; see Zurcher and Kirkpatrick, "Collective Dynamics of Ad Hoc Antipornography Organizations," in *Technical Report of the Commission on Obscenity and Pornography*, vol. 5: *Societal Control Mechanisms*, 83–142.

12. Harold Nawy, "The San Francisco Erotic Marketplace," in *Technical Report of the Commission on Obscenity and Pornography*, 4: 200–203.

13. Sampson, "Commercial Traffic in Sexually Oriented Materials in the United States," in *Technical Report of the Commission on Obscenity and Pornography*, 3:37.

14. "How Skin Flicks Hit Bible-Belt Waterloo, Iowa," *Newsweek*, December 21, 1970, 26.

15. Charles Winick, "Some Observations on Characteristics of Patrons of Adult Theaters and Bookstores," in *Technical Report of the Commission on Obscenity and Pornography*, 4:234.

16. Kenneth Turan and Stephen F. Zito, *Sinema: American Pornographic Films and the People Who Make Them* (New York: Praeger, 1974), 102.

17. Nawy, "The San Francisco Erotic Marketplace," 180–181.

18. Mary Rexroth quoted in Turan and Zito, *Sinema*, 102.

19. Schaefer, "Gauging a Revolution: 16mm Film and the Rise of the Pornographic Feature," *Cinema Journal* 41, no. 3 (spring 2002): 3–26, 14. Turan and Zito, *Sinema*, 168. See also McNeil and Osborne, *The Other Hollywood: The Uncensored Oral History of the Porn Film Industry* (New York: Reagan Books, 2005), 81, 84.

20. Schaefer, "Gauging a Revolution," 14.

21. Schickel, "Porn and Man at Yale," 35.

22. Zurcher and Kirkpatrick, *Citizens for Decency*, 51; the authors use free indirect discourse, so this exact phrase may be theirs rather than belonging to Midville reformer "Mrs. Roberts."

23. Crist interview.

24. Schickel, "Porn and Man at Yale," 35–38. See also *Independent Film Journal*, April 1, 1970, 18. According to Schickel's report, this retrospective also had some scholarly component, though more in an auteurist—and for Schickel, funny—vein. Roger Ebert delivered opening remarks, and there was a discussion of "Art and Pornography" and a "concluding seminar."

25. "Flesh King has Fourth Festival," *Hollywood Reporter*, September 21, 1971, 8, quoted in David K. Frasier, *Russ Meyer: The Life and Films. A Biography and a Comprehensive, Illustrated and Annotated Filmography and Bibliography* (Jefferson, NC: McFarland Classics, 1990), 46; see also similar citations in Fraiser, 44–50. Meyer's presence on so many campuses was likely due to the promotional muscle of 20th Century-Fox, which produced his first Hollywood feature: *Beyond the Valley of the Dolls* (1970).

26. See Linda Lovelace and Mike McGrady, *Out of Bondage* (Secaucus, NJ: Lyle Stuart, 1986), 12–13, 20, 190, 203, and various interviews in McNeil and Osborne, *The Other Hollywood*.

27. "Underground Newspaper Collection" (Bell & Howell Micro Photo Division, 1970–1985), 476 reels.

28. See, for example, Jeff Shero, "*Playboy*'s Tinseled Seductress," *Austin Rag* 1, no. 1 (n.d.): 4, and "Sexual Freedom League is Dead," *Austin Rag*, 1, no. 2 (August 17, 1966): 1. For a few examples of nudity featured in marketing the underground press, see *Austin Rag*, 2, no. 12 (January 29, 1968): 14; *Pterodacty* [Grinnell, IA], February 3, 1968, 1; *Washington Free Press*, July 16–30, 1970, n.p. Examples of nudity used prominently in ads in the underground press are so numerous as to make sampling unnecessary.

29. R. E. Maxon, "Sex Papers Subvert the Undergrounds," "AFS Packet #78," January 19, 1973. On this phenomenon, see also "Alternative Media," *Austin Rag*, October 9, 1972, 5. For examples of differing reactions to *Deep Throat* in the alternative, college-related press, see Ed Naha, "Movie Review: *Deep Throat*," *Free Aquarian* [Passaic, NJ], January 1973, 73; Valentina, "*Deep Throat*," *All You Can Eat* [New Brunswick, NJ], March 1973, 20; and "The Daily Texan and *Deep Throat*," *Austin Rag*, June 17, 1974.

30. *Ghent Press*, September 1973.

31. "'This is Insane, I Can't Believe It'" (editorial), *Notre Dame Observer*, February 8, 1969 (special issue), 3; the quotation is attributed to Notre Dame English professor Peter Michelson.

32. Photo caption, *Notre Dame Observer*, February 8, 1969 (special edition), 1.

33. Richard W. Conklin, "For Release A.M. Papers, Sunday, Feb. 4th [1968]," University of Notre Dame Department of Public Information press release; "A Seminar on the Problem of Obscenity" program brochure, n.d., both in the University of Notre Dame Archives.

34. "Study Obscenity Problem," *South Bend Tribune*, January 14, 1968, 26.

35. "A Seminar on the Problem of Obscenity" program brochure, back cover.

36. "Pornography and Censorship Conference" advertisement, *Notre Dame Observer*, January 10, 1969, 7.

37. "At Pornography Kick-off: Overflow Crowd Hears Ginsberg Chant, Recite," *Notre Dame Observer*, February 6, 1969, 2.

38. William Stoner, "Ginsberg Lauded at Recital at N.D.," *South Bend Tribune*, February 6, 1969, 38.

39. "Inappropriate," *Notre Dame Observer*, February 7, 1969, 6.

40. "Art Show, Film Cancellation Brings Legal Issues," *Notre Dame Observer*, February 7, 1969, 2. Patricia Koval, "Hesburgh Cancels Pornography Films: N.D. Conference Plans Upset by Abrupt Halt in Showing," *South Bend Tribune*, February 7, 1969, 17.

41. Michael Patrick O'Connor, "Lady Godiva Comes in a Quaker Oats Box," *Notre Dame Observer*, February 7, 1969, 7. See also "Hesburgh Cancels Pornography Films" in the same issue.

42. Patricia Koval, "Calm after Fracas over Film: End of Pornography Conference," February 8, 1969, 1, 3. On the petition, see "Student Petition Blasts Conference Films," *Notre Dame Observer*, February 7, 1969, 4.

43. "Police Raid Screening of Film: Pornography-Censorship Conference Cancelled," *Notre Dame Observer*, February 8, 1969 (special edition), 1; the entirety of this issue is dedicated to the events of Friday, February 7. See also "Calm after Fracas over Film."

44. Patricia Koval, "N.D. Adopts Tough Policy: Statements on Protests Issued by Hesburgh," *South Bend Tribune*, February 17, 1969, 1, 2. See also John Leo, "Notre Dame Gives Warning: Hesburgh Threatens Ousters," *New York Times*, February 18, 1969, 1, 25; in this article, "students forced their way into a campus building to show stag movies."

45. Nan Robertson, "Nixon Letter Hails Notre Dame for Tough Stand on Disruption," *New York Times*, February 25, 1969, 29. See also Patricia Koval, "Polled Students Support N.D. Policy," *South Bend Tribune*, February 18, 1969, 15; and "Excerpts from Hesburgh's Letters to Agnew and Notre Dame Students," *New York Times*, February 28, 1969, 18.

46. "Notre Dame President Sees Threat of Outside Control," *South Bend Tribune*, February 20, 1969, 25. For more on Hesburgh in this era, see also Thomas J. Fleming, "Hesburgh of Notre Dame—(1) 'He's Destroying This University' (2) 'He's Bringing It into the Mainstream of American Life,'" *New York Times Magazine*, May 11, 1969, 56–57, 59–65.

47. For a full account of the W&M "dorm-in" see Susan H. Godson et al., *The College of William & Mary: A History*, vol. 2 (Williamsburg, VA: King and Queen Press, 1993), 825–842.

48. James S. Kelly, President, Williamsburg Chamber of Commerce, letter to members, June 8, 1967. Thanks to Will Molineux for bringing our attention to and sharing his copy of this with us.

49. Interview with Clay Riley, January 13, 2006.

50. Programming shifts of this nature this have been oft noted in relation to urban centers (e.g., the Times Square cinemas of New York), but the Blane makes clear this not just an urban phenomenon. See Cook, *Lost Illusions: American Cinema in the Shadow of Watergate and Vietnam 1970–1979* (Berkeley: University of California Press, 2002).

51. The Blane cannily programmed only other adult fare—e.g., *Cabaret*—in its second theater when *Deep Throat* ran, though it did have, late in the run, one kiddie matinee of *Lassie, Come Home*.

52. Interviews with Riley; Robert Jeffrey, January 10, 2006; David Essex, January 16, 2006; and Richard Williamson, January 9, 2006.

53. Name Withheld By Request, "Filthy Flicks and Laxity of Screening" [letter to the editor], *Daily Press*, March 13, 1973, 4. In this period the *Daily Press* carried a steady stream of letters debating whether to censor pornography in print and, especially, on screen. In seeming response, the paper had started to enforce a policy against explicit advertisements for film; thus the Blane did not advertise *Deep Throat* in the *Daily Press* for this second run.

54. Jeffrey interview.

55. An image of the marquee is preserved thanks to the *Flat Hat*, March 20,

1973, 1. By referencing the famous marquee of the New Mature World Theater in New York (see chapter 14, figure 3) when it had been forced to stop showing the film in 1972, Blane was tying his theater to a brewing national phenomenon.

56. *Flat Hat*, March 20, 1973, 3. See also Cornell Christianson and Jerry Hendricks, letter to the editor, *Flat Hat*, March 20, 1973, 6. Circle K International is the college affiliate of the Kiwanis Clubs.

57. Lewis, *Hollywood v. Hardcore*, 259–266 provides a useful overview of the Miller decision and its effects on the American film industry.

58. "William & Mary Blush," "Conference Set on Pornography," "Senators, Miss Lovelace Asked to Confab at W&M," undated and unsourced (though the first is credited to the Associated Press) news clippings provided by Cornell Christianson.

59. "3:30 PM Panel: Effect of Decision on the Film Industry," 7 1/2. The entire transcript for the conference proceedings is held at the University Archive in the Special Collections of the Earl Gregg Swem Library at the College of William & Mary.

60. "8 PM — Main Panel: The Effect of the Miller Decision on American Society," n.p. These two women named themselves, as did most of the questioners that evening. The three panels earlier in the day had not followed this practice.

61. Jack V. Priest, "Attitudes Were Not Changed at Pornography Conference" and Janet McMahon, "Conference Largely Soap Box Preaching," *Virginia Gazette*, October 5, 1973, 10; "Two-Faced Pornography" (editorial), *Flat Hat*, October 5, 1973, 8.

62. "Two-Faced Pornography" and "Campus Sleeps Soundly . . ." (editorial), *Flat Hat*, October 5, 1973, 8; interview with "Anonymous," September 20, 2006. Anonymous, a graduate of William & Mary from the mid-1970s, still lives in Williamsburg; he was happy to share his memories of the William & Mary event's film screenings (he did not attend the panels) but preferred not to have his name associated with this event in the historical record. *The Devil in Miss Jones* was also screened the morning before the conference panels began; a number of the conference panelists refer to having seen the film at that screening, but it is not clear if anyone else was invited to that showing.

63. Williamson interview.

64. Priest, "Attitudes Were Not Changed at Pornography Conference," 10.

65. "Blane Cinemas Changes Hands," *Virginia Gazette*, April 5, 1974, 5. Not long after selling the cinema, Paul Blane left Williamsburg. He told us that to this day his wife holds that they had to leave because the scandals around the cinema had made continuing to live in the community impossible; he disagrees. Phone interview with Paul Blane, August 8, 2007.

66. Lewis, *Hollywood v. Hardcore*, 269.

67. "8 PM — Main Panel," 15–22.

68. Linda Williams, "Porn Studies: Proliferating Pornographies On/Scene," in *Porn Studies*, ed. Linda Williams (Durham, NC: Duke University Press, 2004), 3–4.

69. Marcela Berrios, "'Qlassics' Stirs Quiet Controversy: Former Queer Film Festival Undergoes Second Name Change in Two Years to Avoid Conflict," *Notre Dame Observer*, February 12, 2007, accessed April 21, 2008, from the *Observer's* online archives at http://www.ndsmcobserver.com/archives. Coverage of this controversy was substantial and ranged from the campus paper to regional presses, the Catholic press, and national outlets such as the *New York Times*; much of it can be found online. After this iteration, the festival ceased.

70. Conversation with Constance Sisk and Sean Barker, April 2006.

71. It is important to emphasize that the nonrenewal of Gene Nichol as William & Mary's president—which lead to his voluntary resignation—came about for a complex set of reasons, of which SWAS was just one, and perhaps a minor one. Extensive coverage of the SWAS controversies and the controversies surrounding President Nichol can be found in a variety of sources, including the *Flat Hat* at flathatnews.com and the *Daily Press* at www.dailypress.com.

72. In *Sex and the University: Celebrity, Controversy, and a Student Journalism Revolution* (New Brunswick, NJ: Rutgers University Press, 2010), Daniel Reimold argues that the rise in the past decade of student-penned sex advice columns in college newspapers constitutes an ongoing and robust public discussion of sex and sexuality on campuses (and sometimes beyond). The William & Mary *Flat Hat* introduced such a column in 2003; the Notre Dame *Observer* does not run a regular column.

73. Essex interview.

Bibliography

Allen, Robert C. "From Exhibition to Reception: Reflections on the Audience in Film History." In *Screen Histories*, edited by Annette Kuhn and Jackie Stacey, 13–21. Oxford: Clarendon Press, 1998.

———. *Horrible Prettiness: Burlesque and American Culture*. Chapel Hill: University of North Carolina Press, 1991.

Allyn, David. *Make Love, Not War: The Sexual Revolution. An Unfettered History*. Boston: Little, Brown and Company, 2000.

Altman, Dennis. *The Homosexualization of America, the Americanization of the Homosexual*. New York: St. Martin's Press, 1981.

Anderson, Walter Truett. *The Upstart Spring: Esalen and the American Awakening*. Reading, MA: Addison-Wesley, 1983.

Anonymous. *Commune Cult*. N.p.: N.d.

Atkins, Susan. *Child of Satan, Child of God*. Plainfield, NJ: Logos International, 1977.

Ayres, Toni, Phyllis Lyon, Ted McIlvenna, et al. *SARGuide for Better Sex Life: A Self-Help Program for Personal Sexual Enrichment/Education Designed by The National Sex Forum*. 2nd rev. ed. San Francisco: National Sex Forum, 1977.

Bailey, Beth. "Sexual Revolution(s)." In *The Sixties: From Memory to History*, edited by David Farber, 235–262. Chapel Hill: University of North Carolina Press, 1994.

Balio, Tino. *United Artists: The Company That Changed the Film Industry*. Madison: University of Wisconsin Press, 1987.

Banes, Sally. *Greenwich Village 1963: Avant-Garde Performance and the Effervescent Body*. Durham, NC: Duke University Press, 1993.

Barbach, Lonnie. *For Yourself: The Fulfillment of Female Sexuality*. New York: Anchor, 1975.

Barber, Karin. "Preliminary Notes on Audiences in Africa." *Africa* 67, no. 3 (1997): 347–362.

Bech, Henning. *When Men Meet: Homosexuality and Modernity*. Chicago: University of Chicago Press, 1997.

Benwell, Bethan. *Masculinity and Men's Lifestyle Magazines*. London: Blackwell, 2003.

Bersani, Leo. *Baudelaire and Freud*. Berkeley: University of California Press, 1977.

———. *The Freudian Body: Psychoanalysis and Art*. New York: Columbia University Press, 1986.

———. *Homos*. Cambridge, MA: Harvard University Press, 1996.

Bertolucci, Bernardo and Franco Arcalli. *Bernardo Bertolucci's* Last Tango in Paris; *the screenplay, by Bernardo Bertolucci and Franco Arcalli*. New York: Delacorte Press, 1973.

Berube, Allan. *Coming out under Fire: The History of Gay Men and Women in World War Two*. New York: Free Press, 1990.

Björklund, Elisabet. "The Most Delicate Subject: A History of Sex Education Films in Sweden." PhD diss., Lund University.

———. "'This is a dirty movie': *Taxi Driver* and 'Swedish Sin.'" *Journal of Scandinavian Cinema* 1, no. 2 (2011): 163–176.

Blanshard, Paul. *The Right to Read: The Battle against Censorship*. Boston: Beacon Press, 1955.

Boyer, Paul S. *Purity in Print: Book Censorship in America from the Gilded Age to the Computer Age*. Madison: University of Wisconsin Press, 2002.

Brandt, Allan M. *No Magic Bullet: A Social History of Venereal Disease in the United States Since 1880*. New York: Oxford University Press, 1987.

Brigman, William E. "Politics and the Pornography Wars." *Wide Angle* 19, no. 3 (1997): 149–170.

Brinkmann, Tom. *Bad Mags: The Strangest, Most Unusual, and Sleaziest Periodicals Ever Published!* Vol. 1. London: Headpress, 2008.

Brinton, Crane. *The Americans and the French*. Cambridge: Harvard University Press, 1968.

Brisbin, Richard A., Jr. "Censorship, Ratings, and Rights: Political Order and Sexual Portrayals in American Movies." *Studies in American Political Development* 16 (spring 2002): 1–27.

Bronski, Michael. *Culture Clash: The Making of Gay Sensibility*. Boston: Alyson Books, 1984.

Brown, Helen Gurley. *Sex and the Single Girl*. New York: B. Geis Associates, 1962.

Bullough, Vern L. *Science in the Bedroom*. New York: Basic Books, 1994.

Burleson, Derek. "Explicit Media – Sources and Suggestions," SIECUS *Report* 3, no. 6 (July 1975): 4–5.

Butler, Scott M., Rose M. Hartzell, and Catherine Sherwood-Puzzello. "Perceived Benefits of Human Sexuality Peer Facilitators." *Electronic Journal of Human Sexuality* 10 (May 26, 2007). Accessed March 15, 2010, www.ejhs.org/volume 10/peer.htm.

Cante, Rich, and Angelo Restivo. "The Voice of Pornography." In *Keyframes: Popular Cinema and Cultural Studies*, edited by Matthew Tinkcom and Amy Villarejo, 207–227. New York: Routledge, 2001.

Capino, Jose B. "Homologies of Space: Text and Spectatorship in All Male Adult Theaters." *Cinema Journal* 45, no. 1 (autumn, 2005): 50–65.

Carter, Angela. *The Sadeian Woman and the Ideology of Pornography*. New York: Harper and Row, 1978.

Carter, David. *Stonewall: The Riots That Sparked the Gay Revolution*. New ed. New York: St. Martin's Press, 2010.

"Case Note: The First Amendment and the Right to Hear: *Urofsky v. Allen*." *Yale Law Journal* 108, no. 3 (December 1998): 669–676.

Chion, Michel. *The Voice in Cinema*. Translated by Claudia Gorbman. New York: Columbia University Press, 1999.

Classen, Steven D. *Watching Jim Crow: The Struggles over Mississippi TV, 1955–1969*. Durham, NC: Duke University Press, 2004.

Clifton, Chas. *Her Hidden Children: The Rise of Wicca and Paganism in America*. Lanham, MD: AltaMira Press, 2006.

Cohan, Steven. *Masked Men: Masculinity and Movies in the Fifties*. Bloomington: Indiana University Press, 1997.

Cohen, Lizbeth. *Consumers' Republic: The Politics of Mass Consumption in Postwar America*. New York: Vintage Books, 2003.

Comfort, Alex, ed. *The Joy of Sex: A Cordon Bleu Guide to Love Making*. New York: Fireside Books, 1972.

Cook, David. *Lost Illusions: American Cinema in the Shadow of Watergate and Vietnam 1970–1979*. Berkeley: University of California Press, 2002.

Coover, Robert. "The First Annual Congress of the High Church of Hardcore." *Evergreen Review*, no. 89 (May 1971): 16, 84.

Corliss, Richard. "Radley Metzger, Aristocrat of the Erotic: An Interview by Richard Corliss." *Film Comment* (January 1973): 18–29.

Cowan, Geoffrey. *See No Evil: The Backstage Battle over Sex and Violence on Television*. New York: Simon and Schuster, 1979.

Cross, Gary. *Kids' Stuff: Toys and the Changing World of American Childhood*. Cambridge, MA: Harvard University Press, 1997.

Csicsery, George Paul. *The Sex Industry*. New York: Signet, 1973.

Daley, Brittany A., Hedi El Kholti, Earl Kemp, Miriam Linna, and Adam Parfrey, eds. *Sin-A-Rama: Sleaze Sex Paperbacks of the Sixties*. Los Angeles: Feral House, 2005.

DeGranamour, A. *The Satan Club*. New York: Bee-line Books, 1970.

D'Emilio, John. *Sexual Politics, Sexual Communities: The Making of a Homosexual Minority in the United States, 1940–1970*. Chicago: University of Chicago Press, 1983.

D'Emilio, John, and Estelle B. Freedman. *Intimate Matters: A History of Sexuality in America*. 2nd ed. Chicago: University of Chicago Press, 1997.

De Grazia, Edward, and Roger K. Newman. *Banned Films: Movies, Censors and the First Amendment*. New York: R. R. Bowker, 1982.

Delany, Samuel. *Times Square Red, Times Square Blue*. New York: New York University Press, 1999.

Didion, Joan. *Slouching toward Bethlehem*. New York: Noonday Press, [1968] 1996.

Dodson, Betty. *Liberating Masturbation: A Meditation on Self Love*. New York: Bodysex Designs, 1974.

———. *My Romantic Love Wars: A Sexual Memoir*. New York: self-published, 2010.

———. *Sex for One: The Joy of Self Loving*. New York: Crown, 1987.

Dollimore, Jonathan. *Sexual Dissidence: Augustine to Wilde, Freud to Foucault*. Oxford: Clarendon Press, 1991.

Douglas, Susan J. *Where the Girls Are: Growing up Female with the Mass Media*. New York: Times Books, 1994.

Durgnat, Raymond. *Mysteries of the Organism*. London: British Film Institute Publishing, 1999.

Dyer, Richard. *Now You See It: Studies in Lesbian and Gay Film*. London: Routledge, 1990.

———. *Only Entertainment*. London: Routledge, 1992.

Eberhardt, Charles N. "Note: Integrating the Right of Association with the *Bellotti* Right to Hear." *Cornell Law Review* 72 (November 1986): 159.

Eberly, Rosa. *Citizen Critics: Literary Public Spheres*. Urbana: University of Illinois Press, 2000.

Eberwein, Robert. *Sex Ed: Film, Video, and the Framework of Desire*. New Brunswick, NJ: Rutgers University Press, 1999.

Edgerton, Gary. "High Concept, Small Screen." *Journal of Popular Film and Television* 19, no. 3 (fall 1991): 114–27.

Ehrenreich, Barbara, Elizabeth Hess, and Gloria Jacobs. *Re-Making Love: The Feminization of Sex*. New York: Anchor Books, 1986.

Ernst, Morris. *The First Freedom*. New York: Macmillan Co., 1946.

Escoffier, Jeffrey. *Bigger than Life: The History of Gay Porn Cinema from Beefcake to Hardcore*. Philadelphia: Running Press, 2009.

———. "Gay-for-Pay: Straight Men and the Making of Gay Pornography." *Qualitative Sociology* 26, no. 4 (winter 2003): 531–555.

———. "Imagining the She/Male: Pornography and the Transsexualization of the Heterosexual Male." *Studies in Gender and Sexuality* 12, no. 4 (2011): 268–281.

———. "Scripting the Sex: Fantasy, Narrative and Sexual Scripts in Pornographic Films." In *The Sexual Self: The Construction of Sexual Scripts*, edited by Michael Kimmel, 61–79. Nashville: Vanderbilt University Press, 2007.

———, ed. *Sexual Revolution*. New York: Thunder's Mouth Press, 2003.

Field Research Corporation. "Fieldscope Report: Statewide Survey of Public Opinion About the Public Display of Pornographic Materials." N.p.: May 1971.

Findlen, Paula. "Humanism, Politics and Pornography in Renaissance Italy." In *The Invention of Pornography: Obscenity and the Origins of Modernity, 1500–1800*, edited by Lynn Hunt, 48–108. New York: Zone Books, 1996.

Fischer, Craig. "*Beyond the Valley of the Dolls* and the Exploitation Genre." *Velvet Light Trap* 30 (fall 1992): 18–33.

Fleischer, Frederic. "Export or Die: Sweden Feeds the World's Appetite for Swedish Films." *Film Comment* (summer 1970): 36–37.

Fonda, Jane. *My Life So Far*. New York: Random House, 2005.

Fordin, Hugh, ed. *Film-TV Daily 1970 Yearbook of Motion Pictures and Television*. New York: Wid's Films and Film Folk, 1970.

Foucault, Michel. *The History of Sexuality*. Vol. 1: *An Introduction*. Translated by Robert Hurley. New York: Vintage, 1980.

―――. "'Omnes et Singulatim': Toward a Critique of Political Reason." In *Power, Essential Works of Foucault, 1954–1984*. Vol. 3. Edited by James D. Faubion, 298–325. New York: New Press, 2000.

Fox, Richard Wightman, and T. J. Jackson Lears, eds. *The Culture of Consumption: Critical Essays in American History, 1880–1980*. New York: Pantheon Books, 1983.

Fraenkel, Osmond K. and Ann Fagan Ginger, eds. "Civil Liberties Docket," VII, 4 (July 1962).

Francoeur Robert T. "Sex Films." *Society* 14, no. 5 (July/August 1977): 33–37.

Francoeur Robert T., and Linda Hendrixson. *Instructor's Resource Manual* to Accompany *Becoming a Sexual Person* by Robert T. Francoeur. New York: Wiley and Sons, 1982.

Frasier, David K. *Russ Meyer: The Life and Films. A Biography and a Comprehensive, Illustrated and Annotated Filmography and Bibliography*. Jefferson, NC: McFarland Classics, 1990.

"Freedom through Dissent." ACLU 42nd annual report, July 1, 1961, June 30, 1962. New York: Oceana Publishers, 1962.

Freud, Sigmund. *Civilization and Its Discontents*. Translated by Jean Riviere. New York: J. Cape & H. Smith, 1930.

Friedberg, Anne. *Window Shopping: Cinema and the Postmodern*. Berkeley: University of California Press, 1993.

Friedman, Andrea. *Prurient Interests: Gender, Democracy, and Obscenity in New York City, 1909–1945*. New York: Columbia University Press, 2000.

Gal, Susan. "A Semiotics of the Public/Private Distinction." *Differences* 13, no. 1 (2002): 77–95.

Gathorne-Hardy, Jonathan. *Sex, the Measure of All Things: A Life of Alfred C. Kinsey*. Bloomington: Indiana University Press: 1998.

Gelatt, Roland. *The Fabulous Phonograph, 1877–1977*. London: Cassell, 1977.

Gellhorn, Walter, Richard McKeon, and Robert K. Merton. *The Freedom to Read: Perspective and Program*. New Providence, NJ: R. R. Bowker, 1957.

Gertz, Elmer. *A Handful of Clients*. River Grove, IL: Follett Publication, 1965.

Gertz, Elmer, and Felice Flanery Lewis, eds. *Henry Miller: Years of Trial and Triumph, 1962–1964*. Carbondale: Southern Illinois University Press, 1978.

Gilbert, Craig. "Reflections on an American Family I" and "Reflections on an American Family II." In *New Challenges for Documentary*, edited by Alan Rosenthal, 191–209; 288–307. Berkeley: University of California Press, 1988.

Giles, Jonathan H. *Psychedelia Sexualis: Sexual Turn-ons — 1970s Style*. Libertyville, IL: Oligarch Publishing, 1969.

Gill, Brendan. "Blue Notes." *Film Comment* (January–February, 1973): 7–11.

Gitlin, Todd. *Inside Prime Time*. New York: Pantheon Books, 1985.

Godson, Susan H. et al., *The College of William & Mary: A History*, vol. 2. Williamsburg, VA: King and Queen Press, 1993.

Gomery, Douglas. *Shared Pleasures: A History of Movie Presentation in the United States*. Madison: University of Wisconsin Press, 1992.

Gontarski, S. E. *The Grove Press Reader, 1951–2001*, ed. New York: Grove Press, 2001.

Gorer, Geoffrey. "The Erotic Myth of America." *Partisan Review* (July/August 1950): 589–594.

Grant, Barry Keith, ed. *Film Genre Reader III*. Austin: University of Texas Press, 2003.

Greer, Germaine. *The Madwoman's Underclothes: Essays and Occasional Writings*. New York: Atlantic Monthly Press, 1986.

Guerrero, Ed. *Framing Blackness: The African Image in Film*. Philadelphia: Temple University Press, 1993.

Haberski, Raymond J., Jr. *Freedom to Offend: How New York Remade Movie Culture*. Lexington: University Press of Kentucky, 2007.

Hale, Frederick. "*Time* for Sex in Sweden: Enhancing the Myth of the 'Swedish Sin' During the 1950s." *Scandinavian Studies* 75, no. 3 (2003): 351–374.

Hankin, Kelly. "Lesbian Locations: The Production of Lesbian Bar Space in *The Killing of Sister George*." *Cinema Journal* 41, no. 1 (fall 2001): 3–7.

Hanson, Dian. *Bob's World: The Life and Boys of AMG's Bob Mizer*. Cologne: Taschen, 2009.

Hawkins, Joan. *Cutting Edge: Art-Horror and the Horrific Avant-garde*. Minneapolis: University of Minnesota Press, 2000.

Heath, Stephen. *The Sexual Fix*. London: Macmillan Press, 1982.

Heidenry, John. *What Wild Ecstasy: The Rise and Fall of the Sexual Revolution*. New York: Simon and Schuster, 1997.

Herzog, Amy. "In the Flesh: Space and Embodiment in the Pornographic Peep Show Arcade." *Velvet Light Trap* 62 (fall 2008): 29–43.

Hoberman, J., and Jonathan Rosenbaum. *Midnight Movies*. New York: Da Capo, 1983.

Hooven, F. Valentine, III. *Beefcake: The Muscle Magazines of America, 1950–1970*. Cologne: Taschen, 1995.

Horowitz, Helen Lefkowitz. *Rereading Sex: Battles over Sexual Knowledge and Suppression in Nineteenth-Century America*. New York: Alfred A. Knopf, 2002.

Humphries, Laud. *Tearoom Trade: Impersonal Sex in Public Places*. New York: Aldine De Gruyter, 1975.

Hunt, Morton M. *The Story of Psychology*. New York: Anchor, 1993.

Hutchison, Alice L. *Kenneth Anger: A Demonic Visionary*. London: Black Dog Publishing, 2004.

Huysmans, J. K. *La-Bas*. Translated by Keene Wallace. New York: Dover Publications, 1972.

Irvine, Janice M. *Disorders of Desire: Sexuality and Gender in Modern American Sexology*. Philadelphia: Temple University Press, 1990.

J. *The Sensuous Woman*. New York: Lyle Stuart, Inc., 1969.

Jackson, Earl. *Strategies of Deviance: Studies in Gay Male Representation*. Bloomington: Indiana University Press, 1995.

Jaffe, Louis L. "Standing to Secure Judicial Review: Public Actions." *Harvard Law Review* 74, no. 7 (May 1961): 1265–1314.

James, David. "Hardcore: Cultural Resistance in the Postmodern." *Film Quarterly* 42, no. 2 (winter 1988–1989): 31–39.

———. "Rock and Roll in Representation of the Invasion of Vietnam." *Representations* 29 (1990): 78–98.

Jameson, Fredric. *Signatures of the Visible*. New York: Routledge, 1992.

Johnson, Eithne. "Appearing Live on Your Campus! Porn-Education Roadshows." *Jump Cut* 41 (1997): 27–35.

———. "The 'Coloscopic' Film and the 'Beaver' Film: Scientific and Pornographic Scenes of Female Sexual Responsiveness." In *Swinging Single: Representing Sexuality in the 1960s*, edited by Hilary Radner and Moya Luckett, 301–324. Minneapolis: University of Minnesota Press, 1999.

———. "Loving Yourself: The Specular Scene in Sexual Self-Help for Women." In *Collecting Visible Evidence*, edited by Jane M. Gaines and Michael Renov, 216–240. Minneapolis: University of Minnesota Press, 1999.

———. "Sex Scenes and Naked Apes: Sexual-Technological Experimentation and the Sexual Revolution." PhD diss., University of Texas at Austin, 1999.

Jones, James H. *Alfred C. Kinsey: A Public/Private Life*. New York: W. W. Norton, 1997.

Jones, William E. *Halsted Plays Himself*. Los Angeles: Semiotext(e) Books, 2011.

Juffer, Jane. *At Home with Pornography: Women, Sex and Everyday Life*. New York: New York University Press, 1998.

Kael, Pauline. *For Keeps: Thirty Years at the Movies*. New York: Plume, 1994.

Kaufman, Alan, Barney Rossett, and Neil Ortenberg, eds. *The Outlaw Bible of American Literature*. New York: Thunder's Mouth Press, 2004.

Keightley, Keir. "'Turn it Down!' She Shrieked: Gender, Domestic Space, and High Fidelity, 1948–1959." *Popular Music* 15, no. 2 (1996): 149–177.

Kielbowicz, Richard. "Origins of the Junk-Mail Controversy: A Media Battle over Advertising and Postal Policy." *Journal of Policy History* 5, no. 2 (1993): 248–272.

Kinsey, Alfred C., Wardell B. Pomeroy, Clyde E. Martin, and Paul H. Gebhard. *Sexual Behavior in the Human Female*. Philadelphia: W. B. Saunders, 1953.

Klein, Naomi. *No Logo*. New York: Picador, 2000.

Koch, Gertrude. "On Pornographic Cinema: The Body's Shadow Realm." Translated by Jan-Christopher Horak. *Jump Cut* 35 (1990): 17–29.

Koch, Stephen. *Stargazer: The Life, World and Films of Andy Warhol*. Revised and updated. New York: Marion Boyers, 2002.

Koedt, Anne. "The Myth of the Vaginal Orgasm." In *Sexual Revolution*, edited by Jeffrey Escoffier, 100–110. New York: Thunder's Mouth Press, 2003.

Koestenbaum, Wayne. *Andy Warhol*. London: Phoenix, 2003.

Kronhausen, Eberhard, and Phyllis. *Pornography and the Law: The Psychology of Erotic Realism and 'Hard Core' Pornography*. New York: Ballantine Books, 1959.

———. *The Sex People: The Erotic Performers and Their Bold New Worlds*. Chicago: Playboy Press, 1975.

Kulick, Don. "Four Hundred Thousand Swedish Perverts." GLQ: *A Journal of Lesbian and Gay Studies* 11, no. 2 (2005): 205–235.

Kurlansky, Mark. *1968: The Year That Rocked the World*. New York: Random House, 2005.

Lack, Russell. *Twenty Four Frames Under: A Buried History of Film Music*. London: Quartet, 1997.

Lasch, Christopher. *The Culture of Narcissism: American Life in a Culture of Diminishing Expectations*. New York: Norton, 1979.

Lauret, Jean-Claude. *The Danish Sex Fairs*. Translated by Arlette Ryvers. New York: Pent-R Books, 1971.

LaVey, Anton Szandor. *The Compleat Witch; or What to Do When Virtue Fails*. New York: Dodd Mead, 1971.

———. *The Satanic Witch*. Los Angeles: Feral House, 1989.

Leap, William, ed. *Public Sex, Gay Space*. New York: Columbia University Press, 1999.

Leff, Leonard J., and Jerold L. Simmons. *The Dame in the Kimono: Hollywood, Censorship, and the Production Code*. Lexington: University Press of Kentucky, 2001.

Levine, Elana. "Sex as a Weapon: Programming Sexuality in the 1970s." In NBC: *America's Network*, edited by Michele Hilmes, 234–236. Berkeley: University of California Press, 2007.

———. *Wallowing in Sex: The New Sexual Culture of 1970s American Television*. Durham, NC: Duke University Press, 2007.

Levy, William, and Willem de Ridder, eds. *Wet Dreams: Films and Adventures*. Amsterdam: Joy Publications, 1973.

Lewis, Jon. *Hollywood v. Hardcore: How the Struggle over Censorship Saved the Modern Film Industry*. New York: New York University Press, 2000.

Linnér, Birgitta. *Sex and Society in Sweden*. New York: Pantheon, 1967.

Lippman, Walter. *A Preface to Morals*. New York: Macmillan, 1929.

Lithgow, James and Colin Heard. "Underground U.S.A. and the Sexploitation Market." *Films and Filming* 15, no. 11 (August 1969): 18–29.

Lovelace, Linda, and Mike McGrady. *Out of Bondage*. Secaucus, NJ: Lyle Stuart, 1986.

Lovett, C. S. *Help Lord–The Devil Wants Me Fat!* Baldwin Park, CA: Personal Christianity, 1977.

Lyons, Arthur. *The Second Coming: Satanism in America*. New York: Award Books, 1970.

MacBean, James Roy. "Sex and Politics: Wilhelm Reich, World Politics, and Makavejev's WR." *Film Quarterly* 25, no. 3 (spring 1972): 2–13.

MacDonald, Scott. *Cinema 16: Documents toward a History of the Film Society.* Philadelphia: Temple University Press, 2002.

Mackey, Thomas C. *Pornography on Trial: A Handbook with Cases, Laws, and Documents.* Santa Barbara, CA: ABC-CLIO, 2002.

Maier, Thomas. *Masters of Sex: The Life and Times of William Masters and Virginia Johnson, the Couple Who Taught America How to Love.* New York: Basic Books, 2009.

Marcus, Steven. *The Other Victorians: A Study of Sexuality and Pornography in Mid-Nineteenth Century England.* New York: New American Library, 1974.

Marcuse, Herbert. *Eros and Civilization: A Philosophical Inquiry into Freud.* New York: Vintage, 1955.

Marklund, Carl. "Hot Love and Cold People: Sexual Liberalism as Political Escapism in Radical Sweden." *Nordeuropa Forum,* January 2009. Accessed May 15, 2011. edoc.hu-berlin.de/nordeuropaforum/2009-1/marklund-carl-83 /XML/.

Marrill, Alvin H. *Movies Made for Television: The Telefeature and the Mini-Series, 1964–1979.* Westport, CT: Arlington House, 1980.

Martin, Jay. "'The King of Smut': Henry Miller's Tragical History." *Antioch Review* 35, no. 4 (1977): 342–367.

Mask, Mia. *Divas on Screen: Black Women in American Film.* Urbana: University of Illinois Press, 2009.

Masters, William, and Virginia Johnson. *Human Sexual Inadequacy.* Boston: Little, Brown, 1970.

———. *Human Sexual Response.* New York: Bantam, 1966.

May, Elaine Tyler. *Homeward Bound: American Families in the Cold War Era.* New York, Basic Books, 1988.

McChesney, Richard. *Telecommunications, Mass Media and Democracy: The Battle for the Control of America's Broadcasting Industry, 1928–1935.* New York: Oxford University Press, 1995.

McCord, Brian. "An American Avant-Garde: Grove Press, 1951–1986." Ph.D. diss., Syracuse University, 2002.

McDonough, Maitland. "The Exploitation Generation. Or: How Marginal Movies Came in from the Cold." In *The Last Great American Picture Show: New Hollywood Cinema in the 1970s,* edited by Thomas Elsaesser, Alexander Horwarth, and Noel King, 107–130. Amsterdam: Amsterdam University Press, 2004.

McLuhan, Marshall. *Understanding Media: The Extensions of Man.* McGraw Hill: New York, 1964.

McNeil, Legs, and Jennifer Osborne. *The Other Hollywood: The Uncensored Oral History of the Porn Film Industry.* New York: Reagan Books, 2005.

Meeker, Martin. "Behind the Mask of Respectability: Reconsidering the Mattachine Society and Male Homophile Practice, 1950s and 1960s." *Journal of the History of Sexuality* 10, no. 1 (January 2001), 78–116,

Mellen, Joan. *Big Bad Wolves: Masculinity in the American Film.* New York: Pantheon Books, 1977.

———. "Sexual Politics and 'Last Tango in Paris.'" *Film Quarterly* 26 (spring 1973): 9–19.

Metz, Christian. *The Imaginary Signifier: Psychoanalysis and Cinema*. Bloomington: Indiana University Press, 1982.

Morgan, Robin. *Saturday's Child: A Memoir*. New York: W. W. Norton, 2000.

Monaco, Paul. *The Sixties: 1960–1969*. Berkeley: University of California Press, 2003.

Montgomery, Kathryn C. *Target: Prime Time. Advocacy Groups and the Struggle over Entertainment Television*. Oxford: Oxford University Press, 1989.

Moore, Patrick. *Beyond Shame: Reclaiming the Abandoned History of Radical Gay Sexuality*. Boston: Beacon Press, 2004.

Mulvey, Laura. "Visual Pleasure and Narrative Cinema." *Screen* 16, no. 3 (autumn 1975): 6–18.

Nead, Lynda. "'Above the Pulp Line': The Cultural Significance of Erotic Art." In *Dirty Looks: Women, Pornography, Power*, edited by Pamela Church Gibson and Roma Gibson, 144–155. London: British Film Institute, 1993.

Nealon, Christopher. *Foundlings: Lesbian and Gay Historical Emotion Before Stonewall*. Durham, NC: Duke University Press, 2001.

Norris, Hoke. "'Cancer' in Chicago." *Evergreen Review* (July–August 1962): 41–66.

"Note: Standing to Protest and Appeal the Issuance of Broadcasting Licenses: A Constricted Concept Redefined." *Yale Law Journal* 68, no. 4 (1959): 783–796.

"Notes: Government Exclusion of Foreign Political Propaganda." *Harvard Law Review* 68, no. 8 (June 1955): 1393–1409.

Nyberg, Amy. *Seal of Approval: The History of the Comics Code*. Jackson: University Press of Mississippi, 1998.

O'Pray, Michael. *Avant-garde Film: Forms, Themes and Passions*. London: Wallflower Press, 2003.

O'Toole, Laurence. *Pornocopia: Porn, Sex, Technology and Desire*. London: Serpent's Tail, 1999.

Osgerby, Bill. *Playboys in Paradise*. Oxford: Berg, 2001.

Ouellette, Laurie. "Inventing the Cosmo Girl." *Media, Culture and Society* 21, no. 3 (May 1999): 359–383.

Packard, Vance. *The Naked Society*. New York: David McKay Company, 1964.

———. *The Sexual Wilderness*. New York: David McKay, 1968.

Payne, Jack B. "The Changing Right to Read: American Society, the Courts, and the Problem of Literary 'Decency.'" MA thesis, University of Wyoming, 1951.

Petersen, James R. *The Century of Sex: Playboy's History of the Sexual Revolution, 1900–1999*. New York: Grove Press, 1999.

Petigny, Alan. "Illegitimacy, Postwar Psychology, and the Reperiodization of the Sexual Revolution." *Journal of Social History* 38, no. 1 (2004): 63–79.

Poland, Jefferson F., and Valerie Alison. *The Records of the Sexual Freedom League*. New York: The Olympia Press, 1971.

Poland, Jefferson, and Sam Sloan, eds. *Sex Marchers*. Los Angeles: Elysium Press, 1968.

Poole, Wakefield. *Dirty Poole: The Autobiography of a Gay Porn Pioneer.* Los Angeles: Alyson Books, 2000.

Potts, Annie. *The Science/Fiction of Sex: Feminist Deconstruction and the Vocabularies of Heterosex.* New York: Routledge, 2002.

President's Commission on Obscenity and Pornography. *Report of the Commission on Obscenity and Pornography.* Washington, DC: U.S. Government Printing Office, 1970.

Pronger, Brian. *The Arena of Masculinity: Sports, Homosexuality, and the Meaning of Sex.* New York: St. Martin's Press, 1990.

Qvist, Per Olov, and Tytti Soila. "*Eva—Den Utstötta; Swedish and Underage.*" In *The Cinema of Scandinavia,* edited by Tytti Soila, 151–158. London: Wallflower Press, 2005.

Radner, Hilary, and Moya Luckett, eds. *Swinging Single: Representing Sexuality in the 1960s.* Minneapolis: University of Minnesota Press, 1999.

Rainer, Peter, ed. *Love and Hisses: The National Society of Film Critics Sound off on the Hottest Movie Controversies.* San Francisco: Mercury House, 1992.

Randall, Richard S. *Censorship of the Movies: The Social and Political Control of a Mass Medium.* Madison: University of Wisconsin Press, 1968.

Reich, Wilhelm. *The Mass Psychology of Fascism: Third Edition.* Translated by Vincent Carfango. New York: Farrar, Strauss, and Giroux, 1971.

———. *The Sexual Revolution: Toward a Self-Governing Character Structure.* New York: Farrar, Strauss and Giroux, 1951.

Reimold, Daniel. *Sex and the University: Celebrity, Controversy, and a Student Journalism Revolution.* New Brunswick, NJ: Rutgers University Press, 2010.

Reiss, Ira L. *Premarital Sexual Standards in America.* Glencoe, IL: Free Press, 1960.

Rembar, Charles. *The End of Obscenity: The Trials of Lady Chatterley, Tropic of Cancer, and Fanny Hill by the Lawyer Who Defended Them.* New York: Harper and Row, 1968.

Reumann, Miriam G. *American Sexual Character: Sex, Gender, and National Identity in the Kinsey Reports.* Berkeley: University of California Press, 2005.

Rich, B. Ruby. *Chick Flicks: Theories and Memories of the Women's Film Movement.* Durham, NC: Duke University Press, 1998.

Robins, Louise S. *Censorship and the American Library: The American Library Association's Response to Threats to Intellectual Freedom, 1939–1969.* Westport, CT: Greenwood Press, 1996.

Rosen, Philip, ed. *Narrative, Apparatus, Ideology: A Film Theory Reader.* New York: Columbia University Press, 1986.

Rosenberg, Jerry M. *The Death of Privacy.* New York: Random House, 1969.

Ross, Andrew. *No Respect: Intellectuals and Popular Culture.* New York: Routledge, 1989.

Roszak, Theodore. *The Making of the Counter Culture.* Berkeley: University of California Press, 1995.

Rotolo, Suze. *A Freewheelin' Time.* New York: Broadway Books, 2008.

Rotsler, William. *Contemporary Erotic Cinema.* New York: Ballantine Books, 1973.

Sandler, Kevin S. *The Naked Truth: Why Hollywood Doesn't Make X-Rated Movies.* New Brunswick, NJ: Rutgers University Press, 2007.

Sarris, Andrew. "A View from New York." *Sight and Sound* 38 (autumn 1969): 202–203, 219.

Schaefer, Eric. *"Bold! Daring! Shocking! True!": A History of Exploitation Films, 1919–1959.* Durham, NC: Duke University Press, 1999.

———. "Gauging a Revolution: 16mm Film and the Rise of the Pornographic Feature." *Cinema Journal* 41, no. 3 (spring 2002): 3–26.

———. "Pandering to the 'Goon Trade': Framing the Sexploitation Audience through Advertising." In *Sleaze Artists: Cinema at the Margins of Taste, Style, and Politics*, edited by Jeffrey Sconce, 19–46. Durham, NC: Duke University Press, 2007.

———. "Plain Brown Wrapper: Adult Films for the Home Market, 1930–1969." In *Looking Past the Screen: Case Studies in American Film History and Method*, edited by Jon Lewis and Eric Smoodin, 201–226. Durham, NC: Duke University Press, 2007.

Schaefer, Eric, and Eithne Johnson. "Quarantined! A Case Study of Boston's Combat Zone." In *Hop on Pop: The Politics and Pleasures of Popular Culture*, edited by Henry Jenkins, Tara McPherson, and Jane Shattuc, 430–453. Durham, NC: Duke University Press, 2002.

Schatz, Thomas. *Hollywood Genres: Formulas, Filmmaking and the Studio System.* New York: Random House, 1981.

Schindler, Gordon, ed. *A Report on Denmark's Legalized Pornography.* Torrance, CA: Banner Books, 1969.

Schneemann, Carolee. *Imaging Her Erotics: Essays, Interviews, Projects.* Cambridge, MA: MIT Press, 2002.

Schulman, Bruce. *The Seventies: The Great Shift in American Culture, Society, and Politics.* New York: De Capo Press, 2002.

Schur, Edwin M. "Social Science and the Sexual Revolution." In *The Family and the Sexual Revolution*, edited by Edwin M. Schur, 3–16. Bloomington: Indiana University Press, 1964.

Scoglio, Stefano. *Transforming Privacy: The Transpersonal Philosophy of Rights.* Westport, CT: Praeger, 1998.

Sconce, Jeffrey. "'Trashing' the Academy: Taste, Excess and an Emerging Politics of Cinematic Style." *Screen* 36, no. 4 (winter 1995): 371–393.

———. "XXX: Love and Kisses from Charlie." In *Swinging Single: Representing Sexuality in the 1960s*, edited by Hilary Radner and Moya Luckett, 207–226. Minneapolis: University of Minnesota Press, 1999.

See, Carolyn. *Blue Money: Pornography and the Pornographers. An Intimate Look at the Two Billion Dollar Fantasy Industry.* New York: David McKay Company, 1974.

Segal, Lynne. *Straight Sex: Rethinking the Politics of Pleasure.* Berkeley: University of California Press, 1994.

Segal, Lynne, and Mary McIntosh, eds. *Sex Exposed: Sexuality the Pornography Debate.* New Brunswick, NJ: Rutgers University Press, 1993.

Senelick, Laurence. "Private Parts in Public Places." In *Inventing Times Square: Commerce and Culture at the Crossroads of the World*, edited by William R. Taylor, 329–353. Baltimore: Johns Hopkins University Press, 1991.

Sherfey, Mary Jane. "A Theory of Female Sexuality." In *Sexual Revolution*, edited by Jeffrey Escoffier, 91–99. New York: Thunder's Mouth Press, 2003.

Shumach, Murray. *The Face on the Cutting Room Floor: The Story of Movie and Television Censorship*. New York: William Morrow, 1964.

Siebenand, Paul Alcuin. "The Beginnings of Gay Cinema in Los Angeles: The Industry and the Audience." PhD diss., University of Southern California, 1975.

Slade, Joseph W. *Pornography in America: A Reference Handbook*. Santa Barbara, CA: ABC-CLIO, 2000.

Sloan, Don. "The Dual Therapy Approach to the Treatment of Sexual Dysfunction." In *Gynecology and Obstetrics Volume 6*, edited by John J. Sciarra, 1–17. Philadelphia: Harper and Row, 1983.

Smigel, Edwin O., and Rita Seiden. "The Decline and Fall of the Double Standard." In *Annals of the American Academy of Political and Social Science* 376 (March 1968): 6–17.

Smith, Jacob. "Filling the Embarrassment of Silence: Erotic Performance on Recorded 'Blue Discs.'" *Film Quarterly* 58, no. 2 (winter 2004–05): 26–35.

———. *Spoken Word: Postwar American Phonograph Cultures*. Berkeley: University of California Press, 2011.

Smith, Jeff. *The Sounds of Commerce: Marketing Popular Film Music*. New York: Columbia University Press, 1998.

Smith, Tom W. "The Polls – A Report, The Sexual Revolution?" *Public Opinion Quarterly* 54, no. 3 (autumn 1990): 415–435.

Soila, Tytti, Astrid Söderbergh Widding, and Gunnar Iversen, eds. *Nordic National Cinemas*. New York: Routledge, 1998.

Sontag, Susan. *Styles of Radical Will*. New York: Viking, [1969] 1994.

Sorokin, Pitirim A. *The American Sex Revolution*. Boston: Portor Sargent, 1956.

Staiger, Janet. *Perverse Spectators: The Practice of Film Reception*. New York: NYU Press, 2000.

Starr, Paul. *The Creation of the Media: Political Origins of Modern Communications*. New York: Basic Books, 2004.

Steel, John M. "Comments: Freedom to Hear. A Political Justification of the First Amendment." *Washington Law Review* 46 (1971): 323–334.

Steinem, Gloria. *Outrageous Acts and Everyday Rebellions*. 2nd ed. New York: Owl Books, [1983] 1995.

Stevenson, Jack. "Dead Famous: The Life and Movies of Erotic Cinema's Most Exploited Figure." In *Fleshpot: Cinema's Sexual Myth Makers & Taboo Breakers*, edited by Jack Stevenson, 177–189. Manchester, England: Critical Vision, 2000.

———. "From the Bedroom to the Bijou: A Secret History of American Gay Sex Cinema." *Film Quarterly* 51, no. 1 (autumn 1997): 24–31.

Strub, Whitney. "Perversion for Profit: The Politics of Obscenity and Pornography in the Postwar United States." PhD diss., University of California, Los Angeles, 2006.

Suárez, Juan. *Bike Boys, Drag Queens and Superstars: Avant-garde, Mass Culture, and Gay Identities in the 1960s Underground Cinema.* Bloomington: Indiana University Press, 1996.

Sundholm, Charles A. "The Pornographic Arcade: Ethnographic Notes on Moral in Immoral Places." *Urban Life and Culture* 2, no. 1 (1973): 85–104.

Tarshis, Jerome. "Eros and the Muses." *Evergreen Review* no. 88 (April 1971): 18+.

Taylor, Lawrence S. *Decision in Denmark: The Legalizing of Pornography*, 2 vols. San Diego, CA: Academy Press, 1970.

Technical Report of the Commission on Obscenity and Pornography. 9 vols. Washington, DC: U.S. Government Printing Office, 1971.

Telotte, J. P. "Beyond All Reason: The Nature of the Cult." In *The Cult Film Experience: Beyond All Reason*, edited by J. P. Telotte, 5–17. Austin: University of Texas Press, 1991.

Thomas, Geoffrey L. "The Listener's Right to Hear in Broadcasting." *Stanford Law Review* 22, no. 4 (April 1970): 863–902.

Thomison, Dennis. *A History of the American Library Association, 1876–1972.* Chicago: American Library Association, 1978.

Thomson, David. *Last Tango in Paris.* London: British Film Institute Publishing, 1998.

Toffler, Alvin. *Future Shock.* New York: Bantam, 1970.

Toro, Amy. "Standing up for Listeners' Rights: A History of Public Participation at the Federal Communications Commission." PhD diss., University of California, Berkeley, 2000.

Trippett, Frank. "What's Happening to Sexual Privacy?" *Look*, October 20, 1970, 50.

Turan, Kenneth, and Stephen F. Zito. *Sinema: American Pornographic Films and the People Who Make Them.* New York: Praeger, 1974.

Tyler, Parker. *Sex, Psyche, Etcetera in the Film.* New York: Horizon Press, 1969.

U.S. Senate. Committee on Commerce, Subcommittee on Communications. *Federal Communications Commission Policy Matters and Television Programming*, 91st Cong., 1st sess. Washington, DC, 1969.

Vale, V., and Andrea Juno. *Re/Search: Incredibly Strange Music.* Vol. 2. San Francisco: Re/Search Publications, 1994.

Vogel, Amos. *Film as a Subversive Art.* New York: Random House, 1974.

Wagner, Dana R. "The First Amendment and the Right to Hear: *Urofsky v. Allen.*" *Yale Law Journal* 108, no. 3 (December 1998): 669–67.

Wasser, Frederick. *Veni, Vidi, Video: The Hollywood Empire and the VCR.* Austin: University of Texas Press, 2001.

Watson, Steven. *Factory Made: Warhol and the Sixties.* New York: Pantheon, 2003.

Waugh, Thomas. *Hard to Imagine: Gay Male Eroticism in Photography and Film from Their Beginnings to Stonewall.* New York: Columbia University Press, 1996.

———. "Homosociality in the Classical American Stag Film: Off-Screen,

On-Screen." In *Porn Studies*, edited by Linda Williams, 127–141. Durham, NC: Duke University Press, 2004.

———. *Out/Lines: Underground Gay Graphics from before Stonewall*. Vancouver: Arsenal Pulp Press, 2002.

Weintraub, Jeff. "The Theory and Politics of the Public/Private Distinction." In *Public and Private in Thought and Practice*, edited by Jeff Weintraub and Krishan Kumar, 1–42. Chicago: University of Chicago Press, 1997.

Werth, Barry. *The Scarlet Professor, Newton Arvin: A Literary Life Shattered by Scandal*. New York: Anchor Books, 2001.

Wheeler, Leigh Ann. *Against Obscenity: Reform and the Politics of Womanhood in America, 1873–1935*. Baltimore: Johns Hopkins University Press, 2004.

White, Edmund. *States of Desire: Travels in Gay America*. New York: Plume, 1980.

Wilinsky, Barbara. *Sure Seaters: The Emergence of Art House Cinema*. Minneapolis: University of Minnesota Press, 2001.

Williams, Linda. "Cinema and the Sex Act." *Cineaste* 27 (winter 2001): 20–25.

———. *Hard Core: Power, Pleasure and the "Frenzy of the Visible."* Exp. ed. Berkeley: University of California Press, 1999.

———. "Of Kisses and Ellipses: The Long Adolescence of American Movies." *Critical Inquiry* 32, no. 2 (winter 2006): 288–340.

———. "Porn Studies: Proliferating Pornographies On/Scene: An Introduction." In *Porn Studies*, edited by Linda Williams, 1–23. Durham, NC: Duke University Press, 2004.

———. "A Provoking Agent: The Pornography and Performance Art of Annie Sprinkle." *Social Text* no. 37 (winter, 1993): 117–133

———. *Screening Sex*. Durham, NC: Duke University Press, 2008.

———. "'White Slavery" versus the Thenography of 'Sexworkers': Women in Stag Films at the Kinsey Archive." *Moving Image* 5, no. 2 (fall 2005): 106–139.

Williams, Linda Ruth. *The Erotic Thriller in Contemporary Cinema*. Bloomington: Indiana University Press, 2005.

Williams, Raymond. *The Sociology of Culture*. New York: Schocken Books, 1982.

Williamson, Bruce. "Porno Chic." In *Flesh and Blood: The National Society of Film Critics on Sex, Violence and Censorship*, edited by Peter Keough, 10–27. San Francisco: Mercury House, 1995.

Winston, Brian. *Claiming the Real: The Griersonian Documentary and Its Legitimations*. London: British Film Institute, 1995.

Wittern-Keller, Laura. *Freedom of the Screen: Legal Challenges to State Film Censorship, 1915–1981*. Lexington: University Press of Kentucky, 2008.

Wojcik, Pamela Robertson. "The Girl and the Phonograph; Or the Vamp and the Machine Revisited." In *Soundtrack Available: Essays on Film and Popular Music*, edited by Pamela Robertson Wojcik and Arthur Knight, 433–454. Durham, NC: Duke University Press, 2001.

Wolf, Reva. *Andy Warhol, Poetry and Gossip in the 1960s*. Chicago: University of Chicago Press, 1997.

Wolpe, Joseph. *The Practice of Behavior Therapy*. New York: Pergamon, 1973.

Wolpe, Joseph, and Arnold A. Lazarus. *Behavior Therapy Technique: A Guide to the Treatment of Neuroses*. New York: Pergamon Press, 1966.

Wyatt, Justin. "The Stigma of X: Adult Cinema and the Institution of the MPAA Rating System." In *Controlling Hollywood: Censorship and Regulation in the Studio Era*, edited by Matthew Bernstein, 238–263. New Brunswick, NJ: Rutgers University Press, 1999.

Yewker, Anthony. *Acid Party*. N.p.: Bell House Classics, 1969.

Yingling, Thomas. "How the Eye Is Caste: Robert Mapplethorpe and the Limits of Controversy." *Discourse* 12, no. 2 (spring/summer 1989): 3–28.

Youngblood, Gene. *Expanded Cinema*. New York: E. P. Dutton, 1970.

Zurcher, Louis Jr., and R. George Kirkpatrick. *Citizens for Decency: Antipornography Crusades as Status Defense*. Austin: University of Texas Press, 1976.

Contributors

JOSEPH LAM DUONG is a PhD candidate in U.S. history at the University of California, Berkeley. He is completing a dissertation on the history of the hardcore pornographic film industry from 1957 to the present.

JEFFREY ESCOFFIER writes on the history of sexuality and gay history. His most recent book is *Bigger than Life: The History of Gay Porn Cinema from Beefcake to Hardcore*. He is the author of *American Homo: Community and Perversity*, and edited *Sexual Revolution*, a compilation of the most important writing on sex published in the 1960s and 1970s. He is working on *Rethinking the Sexual Revolution* and has written for the *New York Times Book Review*, the *Nation*, and the *Journal of Homosexuality*.

KEVIN M. FLANAGAN is a PhD candidate in the Critical and Cultural Studies Program at the University of Pittsburgh. He is the editor of *Ken Russell: Re-Viewing England's Last Mannerist*. His essays and reviews have been published in *Framework*, *Media Fields Journal*, the *Journal of British Cinema and Television*, and *Film & History*.

ELENA GORFINKEL is assistant professor of art history and film studies at the University of Wisconsin, Milwaukee. She is editor, with John David Rhodes, of *Taking Place: Location and the Moving Image*, and her writing has appeared in *Framework*, *Camera Obscura*, *Discourse*, *Cineaste*, *World Picture*, *LOLA*, and a number of edited collections. She is writing a book about sexploitation cinema of the 1960s.

RAYMOND J. HABERSKI JR. is professor of history at Marian University. He is the author of numerous books, including *It's Only a Movie: Films and Critics in American Culture*, *Freedom to Offend: How New York Remade Movie Culture*, *The Miracle Case: Film Censorship and the Supreme Court* (with Laura Wittern-Keller), and *God and War: American Civil Religion Since 1945*.

JOAN HAWKINS is an associate professor in the Department of Communication and Culture, Indiana University, Bloomington. She is the author of *Cutting Edge:*

Art Horror and the Horrific Avant-Garde and has written numerous articles on art cinema, the avant-garde of the 1960s, and alternative film cultures.

KEVIN HEFFERNAN teaches in the Division of Film and Media Arts in the Meadows School at Southern Methodist University. He has written books, articles, and documentary films on American film exhibition and distribution, horror movies, gender and sexuality in film and video, underground and exploitation cinema, and East Asian film. He is currently writing two books, tentatively titled *A Wind from the East: Currents in Popular East Asian Film after 1997*, and *From Beavis and Butt Head to the Teabaggers: Dumb White Guy Culture and Politics in America*.

EITHNE JOHNSON publishes essays on media, culture, and gender that have appeared in journals including *Camera Obscura, Jump Cut*, the *Journal of Film and Video*, and *The Velvet Light Trap*, as well as edited collections such as *Media, Culture, and the Religious Right, Collecting Visible Evidence*, and *Swinging Single: Representing Sexuality in the 1960s*. She has taught at Babson, Emerson, and Wellesley Colleges.

ARTHUR KNIGHT teaches Film, American Studies, and English at the College of William & Mary. He has published *Disintegrating the Musical: Black Performance and American Musical Film* and, coedited with Pamela Robertson Wojcik, *Soundtrack Available: Essays on Film and Popular Music*. He is currently at work on a book, tentatively titled *Black Star: A Cultural History of African American Fame*.

ELANA LEVINE is associate professor in the Department of Journalism, Advertising, and Media Studies at the University of Wisconsin, Milwaukee. She is the author of *Wallowing in Sex: The New Sexual Culture of 1970s American Television*, coeditor (with Lisa Parks) of *Undead TV: Essays on Buffy the Vampire Slayer*, and coauthor (with Michael Z. Newman) of *Legitimating Television: Media Convergence and Cultural Status*.

CHRISTIE MILLIKEN is an associate professor in the Department of Communication, Popular Culture and Film at Brock University, Ontario, and the author of *Generation Sex: Reconfiguring Sexual Citizenship in Educational Film and Video* (forthcoming). Her essays have been included in *Spectator, Velvet Light Trap*, and the *Journal of Lesbian Studies*, as well as anthologies including *Sugar, Spice, and Everything Nice: Cinemas of Girlhood* and *American Cinema of the 1960s*.

ERIC SCHAEFER is associate professor in the Department of Visual and Media Arts at Emerson College. His essays have appeared in such journals as *Cinema Journal, Film History*, and the *Moving Image* and a number of anthologies. He is the author of *"Bold! Daring! Shocking! True!": A History of Exploitation Films, 1919–1959* and is completing *Massacre of Pleasure: A History of Sexploitation Films, 1960–1979*.

JEFFREY SCONCE is associate professor in the Screen Cultures program at Northwestern University. He is the author of *Haunted Media: Electronic Presence from Telegraphy to Television* and the editor of *Sleaze Artists: Cinema at the Margins of Taste, Style, and Politics*.

JACOB SMITH is associate professor in the Radio-Television-Film Department at Northwestern University. In addition to writing the books *Vocal Tracks: Performance and Sound Media, Spoken Word: Postwar American Phonograph Cultures*, and *The Thrill Makers: Celebrity, Masculinity and Stunt Performance*, he has published articles on media history, sound, and performance.

LEIGH ANN WHEELER is professor of history at Binghamton University. She is coeditor of the *Journal of Women's History*, women's history editor for the *Oxford Reference Encyclopedia in American History*, and author of two books: *Against Obscenity: Reform and the Politics of Womanhood in America, 1873–1935* and *How Sex Became a Civil Liberty*.

LINDA WILLIAMS teaches in the Film and Media Department at University of California, Berkeley, where she is also in rhetoric. She is the author of *Hard Core: Power, Pleasure and the "Frenzy of the Visible," Playing the Race Card: Melodramas of Black and White from Uncle Tom to O.J. Simpson*, and *Screening Sex*. A new book on *The Wire* is forthcoming from Duke University Press.

Index

CPSIA information can be obtained
at www.ICGtesting.com
Printed in the USA
FFOW02n1448150314
4236FF

9 780822 356547